Culture, Contention and Identity in Seventeenth-Century Ireland

Antonius Bruodinus' *Anatomical Examination* of Thomas Carve's *Apologetic Handbook*

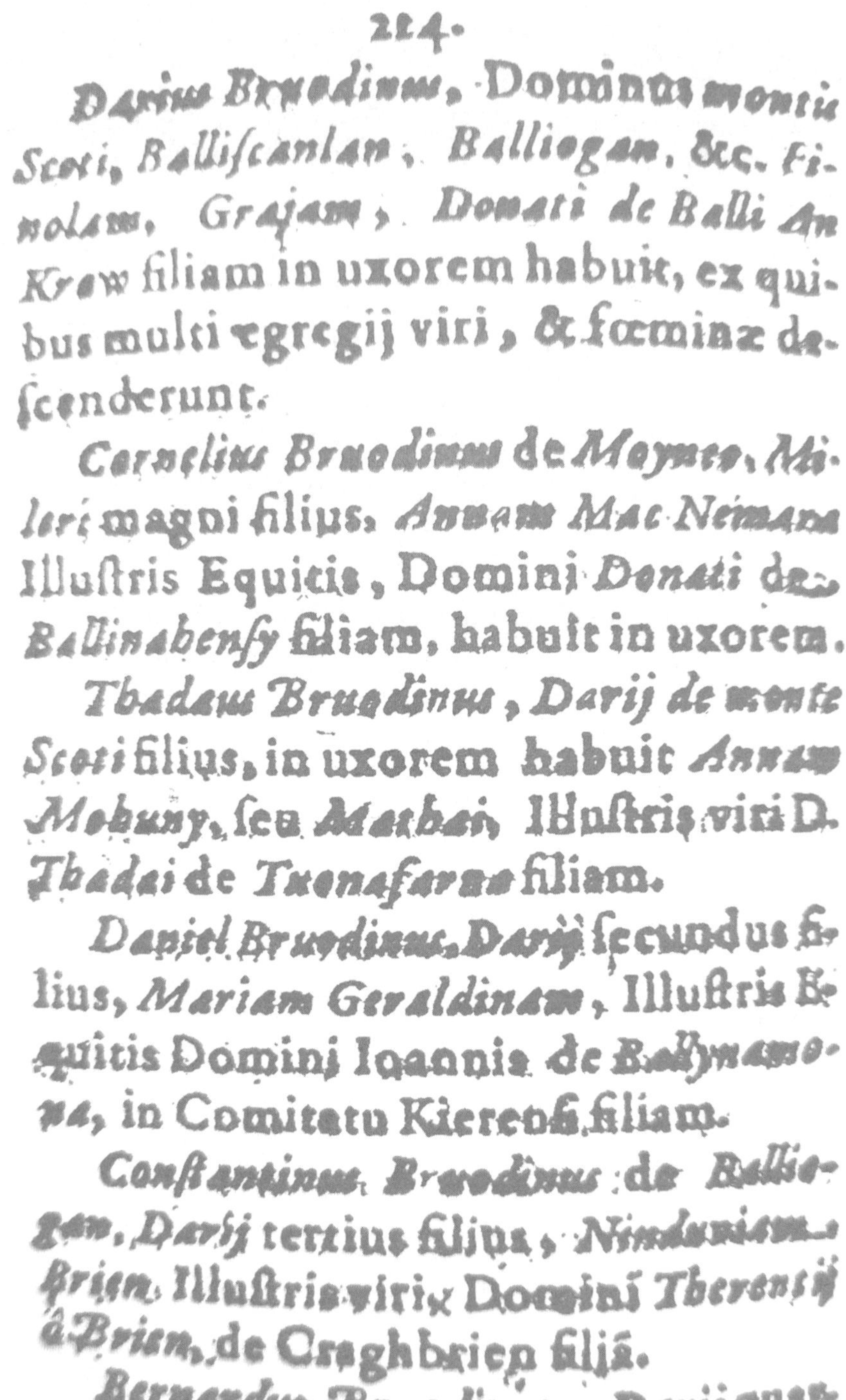
224.

Darius Bruodinus, Dominus montis *Scoti*, *Balliscanlan*, *Balliogan*, &c. *Finolam*, *Grajam*, *Donati de Balli An Krew* filiam in uxorem habuit, ex quibus multi egregij viri, & fœminæ descenderunt.

Cornelius Bruodinus de *Moyneo*, *Mileri* magni filius, *Annam Mac Nemara* Illustris Equitis, Domini *Donati* de *Ballinabensy* filiam, habuit in uxorem.

Thadaeus Bruodinus, *Darij de monte Scoti* filius, in uxorem habuit *Annam Mohuny*, seu *Mathon*, Illustris viri D. *Thadaei* de *Tuonafarna* filiam.

Daniel Bruodinus, *Darij* secundus filius, *Mariam Geraldinam*, Illustris Equitis Domini Ioannis de *Ballymanona*, in Comitatu Kierensi filiam.

Constantinus Bruodinus de *Balliogan*, *Darij* tertius filius, *Nimdamiam Brien*, Illustris viri Domini *Therentij* à *Brien*, de Craghbrien filiã.

Bernardus Bruodinus, *Darij* quar-

Image of page 124 of *Anatomicum Examen*, listing the branches of the Clann Bhruaideadha, beginning with Darius Bruodinus, father of poet Tadhg mac Dáire Mhic Bhruaideadha, who held extensive estates in Thomond.

Culture, Contention and Identity in Seventeenth-Century Ireland

Antonius Bruodinus' *Anatomical Examination* of Thomas Carve's *Apologetic Handbook*

Edited by Giacomo Fedeli, Luke McInerney and Brian Ó Dálaigh

CORK UNIVERSITY PRESS

First published in 2022 by
Cork University Press
Boole Library
University College Cork
Cork T12 ND89
Ireland

Library of Congress Control Number: 2022932557
Distribution in the USA Longleaf Services, Chapel Hill, NC, USA.

British Library Cataloguing in Publication Data
A CIP catalogue record for this book is available the British Library.

ISBN 9781782055075

Printed by Hussar Books in Poland

Design and typesetting by Alison Burns at Studio 10 Design, Cork

Cover image: Group of Irish Franciscans by Emanuele da Como, 1672, Aula Maxima, St Isidore's College, Rome. Picture courtesy Mícheál Ó Cléirigh Institute, UCD.

www.corkuniversitypress.com

Contents

Acknowledgements

This work is the culmination of over six years of collaborative effort. During this time, we have incurred debts of gratitude to numerous people. As with any project that is the sum of many efforts, this work has been greatly enhanced by the assistance of others.

First and foremost, it would be remiss if we did not mention that this book would not have been possible without the generous financial assistance of the following patrons: Declan Barron, Peter Beirne, Martin Breen, Brian C. Broderick, Clare Curtin, Gerry Kennedy, Oliver Moylan, Colmán Ó Clabaigh OSB, Liam Ó Dochartaigh, Pádraig Ó Riain, Dagmar Ó Riain-Raedel and Aileen Wynne. We also acknowledge the significant donations by Clara Hoyne of the Clare Roots Society, John O'Brien of the Shannon Archaeological and Historical Society and Liam Irwin on behalf of the Thomond Archaeological and Historical Society. We were struck by the readiness of people to support this project and help bring back, as it were, the memory of the participants to an important controversy concerning identity that exercised the Irish diaspora on the continent in the seventeenth century, and that has until now not been accorded its proper place in Irish historiography.

The authors express their gratitude to Prof. Pádraig Ó Riain (UCC), Dr John McCafferty (UCD), Liam Irwin (MIC), Dr Jason Harris (UCC), Prof. Damian McManus (TCD), Mícheál Mac Craith OFM, Dr Aoibheann Nic Dhonnchadha (DIAS), Dr Deirdre Nic Mhathúna (DCU), Dr Emma Nic Cárthaigh (UCC) and John Minahane for their helpful advice during the preparation of the introduction and the translated text. We thank Martin Breen for his photographic illustrations. The support and encouragement of the Mícheál Ó Cléirigh Institute, UCD, is gratefully acknowledged together with the assistance provided by Cork University Press in navigating the publication process. The judicious comments that we received from the Press' anonymous reviewers saved us from a number of oversights and errors. Needless to say, any remaining mistakes, failures or omissions are entirely our own.

List of Abbreviations

AFM	*Annála Ríoghachta Éireann: Annals of the Kingdom of Ireland, by the Four Masters, from the Earliest Period to the Year 1616*
DIB	*Dictionary of Irish Biography*
Éigse	*Éigse: A Journal of Irish Studies*
Eolas	*Eolas: The Journal of the American Society of Irish Medieval Studies*
JRSAI	*Journal of the Royal Society of Antiquaries of Ireland*
NMAJ	*North Munster Antiquarian Journal*
NLI	National Library of Ireland
ODNB	*Oxford Dictionary of National Biography*
PHA	Petworth House Archives, West Sussex, United Kingdom
TCD	Trinity College Dublin
TOC	*The Other Clare: Journal of the Shannon Archaeological and Historical Society*
RIA	Royal Irish Academy

Brollach

Go luath i mí na Nollag 2008, thug grúpa mac léinn ó Choláiste na hOllscoile, Corcaigh, faoi stiúir an Ollaimh Damian Bracken, cuairt ar Choláiste San Iosadóir sa Róimh. Iarradh orm seoda ealaíne na háite a thaispeáint dóibh. Agus muid ar tí dul isteach san Aula, mheabhraigh mé dóibh an dá inscríbhinn os cionn an dorais, ceann acu i Laidin, an ceann eile i nGaeilge. Sliocht ó Shalm 110 is ea an nath Laidine *initium sapientiae timor Domini* – tús na heagna eagla Dé. Déanta na fírinne, níor thuig mé tábhacht iomlán an tsleachta seo ag an am. Nuair a creachadh an Róimh sa bhliain 1527, scriosadh go leor foirgintí - an ollscoil san áireamh. Ní raibh mórán ratha ar na hiarrachtaí a rinneadh chun í a athbhunú go dtí gur tháinig an Pápa Alastar VII i réim sa bhliain 1655. Luigh sé isteach ar obair na hatógála le fonn agus le fuinneamh. Thóg sé an Aula agus an leabharlann agus rinne séipéal San Ivo, séipéal na hollscoile, a choisreacan go sollúnta 17 Samhain, 1659 agus d'oscail sé an ollscoil an lá dár gcionn. Bhí *La Sapienza* le gairm ar an institiúid nua feasta agus eisíodh bonn speisialta chun an ócáid a chomóradh agus an mana seo a leanas greanta air, *omnis sapientia a Deo* – ó Dhia gach uile eagna. Ina theannta sin, cuireadh leac marmair os cionn na príomhiontrála ar ar breacadh an inscríbhinn *initium sapientiae timor Domini*. Seo é an comhthéacs cuí don inscríbhinn os cionn dhoras an Aula i San Iosadóir. Bhí Proinsiasaigh na hÉireann ag iarraidh a fhógairt go neamhbhalbh go raibh institiúid ghradamach léinn á reáchtáil acu féin, fondúireacht nár leasc léi dul in iomaíocht (dá chairdiúla féin í an iomaíocht), le hollscoil na Róimhe. Ba é an Pápa Urbanus VIII a dheachtaigh na rialacha do leabharlann San Iosadóir agus is teist ar an gcairdeas idir Alastar VII agus Lúcás Wadding, bunaitheoir an Choláiste, gur bhronn an Pápa cóip shínithe dá fhilíocht luath ar an mbráthair bocht.

B'shin cúlra na hinscríbhinne Laidine. Cheap mé nach raibh sa rann Gaeilge ach saoraistriúchán ealaíonta ar an Laidin, ach bhí an Dr. Emma Nic Cárthaigh i dteannta na mac léinn Corcaíoch. Dúirt sí gur aithin sí an rann toisc gur bhain sé le dán a bhí díreach curtha in eagar aici, *Mór a-tá ar theagasg flatha, speculum principis* a chum Tadhg mac Dáire Mhic Bhruaideadha do Dhonnchadh Ó Briain, ceathrú hiarla Thuamhan, a chuaigh i mbun na hiarlachta sa bhliain 1581.

Ach má ba shnasta an réiteach ar fhadhb amháin é fianaise Emma, d'ardaigh sé ceisteanna eile fós. Cé a thug dán ón séú haois déag go dtí an Róimh beagnach céad bliain ina dhiaidh sin? Cad a thug ar na Proinsiasaigh leas a bhaint as dán a cumadh in ómós do thaoiseach a thacaigh le coróin Shasana agus leis an eaglais státbhunaithe? Bhí sé seo ní ba chigiltí fós, toisc gur bhain an Brianach leas as mainistir na mbráithre in Inis mar theach cúirte agus go raibh sé ar intinn aige earraíocht a bhaint as séipéal na mainistreach chun seirbhísí de chuid na heaglaise leasaithe a cheiliúradh inti. Mar bharr ar an iomlán, adhlacadh Donnchadh Ó Briain in ardeaglais Eaglais na hÉireann i Luimneach, seachas i mainistir Phroinsiasach na hInse, ionad adhlactha Bhrianaigh Thuamhan le cian d'aimsir.

B'ábhar machnaimh dom na ceisteanna sin go léir. Réiteach amháin, ná go bhfuil fáil ar dhán Thaidhg i Leabhar Uí Chonchúir Dhoinn, lámhscríbhinn a cumadh san Ísiltír Spáinneach don Chaptaen Somhairle Mac Domhnaill, pátrún liteartha a adhlacadh i gcoláiste na bProinsiasach Éireannach i Lováin. I ngeall ar na teagmhálacha seasta idir coláiste San Antaine agus coláiste San Iosadóir, níorbh iontas ar bith é dá mbeadh earraí liteartha á mbabhtáil chomh maith leis an bpearsanra bheith ag malartú. Agus i ndeireadh na dála, is féidir a shamhlú go raibh roinnt de na bráithre ar a laghad, sách leathanaigeanta chun tús áite a thabhairt don dea-fhilíocht ar aighnis reiligiúnda.

Dá réasúnta iad na féidearthachtaí sin, caithfidh mé a rá nach raibh mé céad faoin gcéad sásta leo. Ach de bharr thaighde Lúcáis Mhic an Airchinnigh, tá réiteach eile ag teacht chun cinn. Rugadh Antóin Mac Bruaideadha, garnia leis an bhfile aitheanta thuasluaite, c. 1618. D'fhreastail sé ar scoil cháiliúil na bProinsiasach i gCuinche sula ndeachaigh sé chun na Róimhe sa bhliain 1643 chun staidéar a dhéanamh don tsagartóireacht, seacht mbliana á gcaitheamh aige i gColáiste San Iosadóir. Nuair a tháinig deireadh lena thréimhse staidéir sa Róimh, bhí fonn air dul go Prág, áit a raibh fear gaoil leis, Bonabhentura Mac Bruaideadha, ina bhall de chomhluadar Choláiste Ghiniúint Mhuire gan Smál, coláiste a bunaíodh sa bhliain 1629. Cé go ndúirt Wadding gur bhreá an mac léinn é Mac Bruaideadha, níorbh áil leis go gceapfaí ina léachtóir sa choláiste Éireannach é. Bhain Mac Bruaideadha Prág amach sa bhliain 1650, ach roimh dheireadh na

bliana dár gcionn d'aistrigh sé go proibhinse Boihéamach na bProinsiasach. Bhí Coláiste na nÉireannach ag cur thar maoil ag an am agus tharlódh gurbh é seo thar aon ní eile a thug ar Mhac Bruaideadha aistriú. Chaith sé cúig bliana déag i measc na mBohéamach sular fhill sé ar Choláiste Ghiniúint Mhuire gan Smál sa bhliain 1675, cúig bliana sula bhfuair sé bás den phlá sa bhliain 1680.

Níl aon amhras ach gur chruthaigh sé go maith sa tréimhse sin. Ceapadh ina mhaor staidéir é sa scoil nua fealsúnachta a bunaíodh in Olomouc agus bhí sé le maíomh aige gurbh eisean a thionscain an Scótachas sna críocha Boihéamacha. Toghadh ina dheifneadóir ar an bproibhinse é sa bhlain 1659. Bhí sé ina chaomhnóir ar an mainistir in Olomouc (1662-3), i bpríomhmhainistir an phroibhinse i bPrág (1668 -70) agus i Neuhaus (1672-4). Sheas sé an fód go daingean in aghaidh na bProinsiasach Gearmánach a bhí ag iarraidh Proinsiasaigh na Bohéime a shlogadh isteach i bproibhinse na hOstaire. Bhí sé ina iarrthóir do phost an phroibhinsil sa bhliain 1674-5, ach nuair a cuireadh stocaireacht ina leith, díbríodh as an bproibhinse é.

D'ainneoin na gcúraimí seo go léir, ba tháirgiúil an t-údar é: téacsleabhar diagachta á fhoilsiú aige sa bhliain 1663, an chéad saothar ar dhiagacht Scotus a foilsíodh sa Bhoihéim. Foilsíodh an dara himleabhar sa bhliain 1664, ach ar an drochuair, tháinig an saothar seo salach ar Innéacs na Leabhar Coiscthe. D'fhoilsigh sé saothar eile fós ar dhiagacht Scotus i bPrág sa bhliain 1676.

Ach is é an t-aighneas idir é féin agus an sagart deoise Tomás Carve/Carew is mó a thabhaigh clú agus droch-chlú féin, déanta na fírinne, d'Antóin Mac Bruaideadha. Bhí Carve ina shéiplíneach ag saighdiúirí an Choirnéil Uáitéir de Buitléir a throid ar son an Impire le linn Chogadh na dTríocha Bliain. Bhí an Buitléarach ar dhuine de na comhchealgairí a dhúnmharaigh Wallenstein sa bhliain 1634, nuair a bhí eagla ar an Impire go raibh uisce faoi thalamh á bheartú ag an nGinearál ina choinne. Íocadh an Coirnéal go maith as an ról a d'imir sé san fheallbheart agus nuair a bhásaigh sé Lá Nollag na bliana 1634, d'fhág sé suim fhial airgid ag Coláiste Ghiniúint Mhuire gan Smál agus is i séipéal an Choláiste a adhlacadh é. Tharlódh gurbh olc leis an séiplíneach nár fágadh dada aige féin in uacht an Bhuitléaraigh agus nach raibh aon dea-mhéin aige i leith na bProinsiasach dá bharr sin. Scríobh Carve cuntas spéisiúil i Laidin ar an tréimhse a chaith sé ina shéiplíneach míleata sa bhliain 1639, agus sa bhliain 1651,

d'fhoilsigh sé saothar ar nósanna na nGael, *Lyra seu Anacephalaeosis Hibernica*. Bhain Carve le haicme na Sean-Ghall agus léirigh sé sa saothar seo dearcadh mórchúiseach saobhchlaonta na Sean-Ghall ar na Gaeil. Ina theannta sin, ní raibh meas dá laghad aige ar chóras oidhreachta na dteaghlach liteartha, gné nár chothaigh feabhas ealaíonta i gcúrsaí litríochta, dar leis, ach a mhalairt ar fad. Rud amháin an córas ar fad a dhamnú, ach níorbh fhada gur ídigh Carve a chuid gangaide ar aon teaghlach ar leith, muintir Mhic Bhruaideadha agus ar aon eiseamláir amháin, Tadhg mac Dáire Mhic Bhruaideadha, seanuncail Antóin. Ba leor seo chun an lasair a chur sa bharrach. D'fhreagair Antóin a chéile comhraic in ollsaothar tathagach a bhfuil breis agus míle leathanach ann agus a foilsíodh i bPrág sa bhliain 1669, *Propugnaculum Catholicae Veritatis*. Cé go ndíríonn an leabhar seo go sainiúil ar mhairtírigh na hÉireann, tá caibidil ar leith ann ina dtugann an bráthair bocht aghaidh a chraois ar Carve, *de Carve seu Carrani erroribus ac imposturis*. Ní hamháin gur cheartaigh sé botúin eolais a chéile comhraic, ach rinne sé mugadh magadh faoina chumas nó éagumas Laidine chomh maith. Ina theannta sin, chuir sé ina leith nár bhain sé le haicme na Sean-Ghall chor ar bith ach gur Corránach a bhí ann ó cheart. Níor leis an gCorránach ab fhaillí é agus d'fhill sé ar an gcomhrac le *Enchiridion Apologeticum* (Nuremberg, 1670). Spreag sé seo freagra ón mbráthair bocht, *Anatomicum Examen* (1671), a foilsíodh faoin ainm cleite *Cornelius O'Molony*, rud nár chuir dallamullóg ar éinne, arae b'shin sloinne a mháthar. Rinne Carve ionsaí amháin eile, *Responsio Veridica ad illotum libellum cui nomen Anatomicum Examen* (Sulzbach, 1672), an t-urchar deireanach a caitheadh san aighneas. Dealraíonn sé gur bhásaigh Carve go luath ina dhiaidh sin, agus breis agus ceithre scór bliain slánaithe aige.

Is é an *Anatomicum Examen* atá curtha in eagar agus aistrithe ag Giacomo Fedeli. Cé nárbh aon údar maíte ag ceachtar den bheirt sagart ar chaith siad de dhua ag sciolladh agus feannadh a chéile, fós féin, caithfear a admháil gur spreag an t-aighneas Mac Bruaideadha chun faisnéis luachmhar a sholáthar ar chóras na bairdne i gcoitinne agus ar shaol a sheanuncail go háirithe, ní áirím an meas a bhí air i measc lucht a chomhaimsire. Is i ngeall ar an eolas tábhachtach seo a chur ar fáil agus ar an iliomad nótaí mínithe a sholáthar, atáimid faoi mhórchomaoin ag Brian Ó Dálaigh. Díol spéise gur éirigh le hAntóin Mac Bruaideadha teistiméireachtaí faoi shéala a fháil ó na bráithre

bochta i bPrág, i Lováin agus sa Róimh féin, a dhearbhaigh an stádas ard a bhí ag teaghlach fileata Mhic Bhruaideadha in Éirinn. Díol suntais freisin gurbh é Proinsias Ó Maolmhuaidh ina cháilíocht mar *praeses* nó uachtarán Choláiste San Iosadóir, is túisce a shínigh an teistiméireacht ón Róimh: *testamur ... Bruodinianam familiam honoratam, aestimatam, et ab hospitalitate, doctrina, ac moribus fuisse merito semper laudatam*. Ach chomh maith lena sheasamh in ord na bProinsiasach, ní raibh aon easpa léinn air ach an oiread, idir léann na Gaeilge agus léann na Laidine. Cúig bliana tar éis dó an teistiméireacht a scríobh, d'fhoilsigh sé saothar creidimh i nGaeilge sa Róimh *Lucerna Fidelium/Lóchrann na gCreidmheach* agus an bhliain ina dhiaidh sin *Grammatica Latino-Hibernica* ina bhfuil cur síos chomh maith ar phrosóid na Gaeilge. Chum Ó Maolmhuaidh filíocht idir Ghaeilge agus Laidin agus bhain Mac Bruaideadha leas as rainn Laidine dá chuid san *Anatomicum* chun tacú le teaghlach liteartha Mhic Bhruaideadha.

Díol spéise gur foilsíodh an *Anatomicum* sa bhliain 1671, bliain sular mhaisigh Emanuele da Como an Aula i San Iosdóir. Má bhí Proinsias Ó Maolmhuaidh ag soláthar véarsaí do Antóin Mac Bruaideadha, dealraíonn sé go ndearna bráthair bocht Phrág comaoin a chineáltais ar bhráthair bocht na Róimhe agus rann a chum a sheanuncail a sheoladh chuige. Thug sé le fios san *Anatomicum* go raibh dánta agus scríbhinní Thaidhg ina sheilbh aige: *nobis qui Domini Thadaei Bruodini scripta & poëmata prae manibus habemus*. Ní bheadh aon deacracht aige leas a bhaint as dán a cumadh do Dhonnchadh Ó Briain. Fiú má thug Iarla Thuamhan cúl le cine de réir gach dealraimh, bhí léamh eile ar an scéal ag Antóin. Má b'eiriceach ó bhéal é, ba Chaitliceach ina chroí istigh é, *ore haeretico, sed corde Catholico Viro*. Mar fhianaise air sin, luaigh sé cás an tsagairt Phroinsiasaigh Diarmuid Mac Bruaideadha, a céasadh i gcaisleán Luimnigh i ngeall ar an gcreideamh Caitliceach sa bhliain 1603. D'éirigh le hIarla Thuamhan tathant ar an mbreitheamh nach raibh sa phríosúnach ach gealt gan dochar. Ligeadh a shaoirse leis agus thosaigh sé ag seanmóireacht arís ar fud na Mumhan, aibíd an oird á caitheamh go poiblí aige. Níor chuir na húdaráis isteach ná amach air toisc gur thuig siad go rímhaith go raibh sé faoi choimirce Dhonnchadha Uí Bhriain.

Ach scríbhinní Antóin Mhic Bhruaideadha a scrúdú go mion, tuigimid cén fáth nár leasc le Proinsiasaigh San Iosadóir gaisneas a

bhaint as dán a cumadh do cheathrú hIarla Thuamhan. Agus mar bharr ar an iomlán, d'fheil an rann go cruinn beacht don mhana a bhí tofa ag na Proinsiasaigh don Aula: *Initium sapientiae timor Domini*. Tá sé le feiceáil ansin os cionn an dorais i gcónaí, teachtaireacht ghlé shíochánta nach bhféadfadh creidmheach Críostaí ar bith a shéanadh, ach finné balbh os íseal ar bhriatharchath binbeach a d'ídigh fuinneamh bheirt shagart Éireannacha i gceartlár na Boihéime trí chéad go leith bliain ó shin:

Ná tréig choidhche ceachtar dhíbh,
Searc is omhan a náird rí;
Tús gach fíoreagna a sé sin,
Sír eagla Dé air na daoinibh.

Mícheál Mac Craith OFM,
Dún Mhuire,
Cill Iníon Léinín,
Co. Bhaile Átha Cliath

Introduction[1]

Ut tua terra vacat prorsus Bruodine veneno, sic tua felle carent biblia, melle scatent.

[Just as your homeland is truly without poison, Bruodinus, so are your books without bile, but full of honey]

[Froinsias Ó Maolmhuaidh, St Isidore's College, Rome][2]

In the 1670s two Irish Catholic clerics clashed bitterly over their views regarding Ireland's history and Gaelic heritage. The clerics were the Franciscan Antonius Bruodinus[3] and the secular priest Thomas Carve (alias Carew or Carran).[4] Both had been living in exile in Europe for many decades. These clerics held opposing views about Ireland's past. Their viewpoints were rooted in their different identities, belonging as each did to the nation's two principal ethnic communities, the Gaelic-Irish and Old-English. The dispute, which was characterised by much personal animosity, was aired in a number of extraordinary Latin publications. These publications stand as testimony to the divisions within Irish society and to the preoccupation of exiles not only with contemporary politics, but also with contentious questions relating to Ireland's past. Their concerns echoed the type of debates that were occurring in Ireland regarding identity, legitimacy and authority. The controversy, which forms the main focus of this book, occurred at a time when the two contending groups, Gaelic-Irish and Old-English,

1. The authors wish thank Prof. Pádraig Ó Riain, Dr John McCafferty and Liam Irwin for their helpful comments.

2. This quote is contained in the unpaginated *Epistola* section at the beginning of: Antonius Bruodinus, *Propugnaculum Catholicae Veritatis libris X constructum, in duasque partes divisum. Pars prima historica in quinque libros* (Prague, 1669).

3. Sometimes known as Anthony MacBrody or Anthony Bruodin in English, he is called here by the Latin form of his name. His surname has been anglicised variously as MacBrody, MacBrodin, Bruodin, etc., from the Irish nominative form, Mac Bruaideadha, and from the Irish diminutive form, Mac Bruaidín. See Rev. Patrick Woulfe, *Sloinnte Gaedheal is Gall: Irish names and surnames* (Dublin, 1923, repr. Baltimore, 1969), p. 324.

4. He was also known as Carew (or Carrue) but Bruodinus labels him as Carran(e). For the sake of consistency, he is referred to as Carve here, except in translations where Bruodinus labels him as Carran(e).

found themselves increasingly trying to seek common cause against the New English Protestant élite which had recently assumed power in Ireland.

This contention provides historians with a window through which to view the world of seventeenth-century Irish intellectuals living in exile. What is presented in the following pages is a translation of one of the most important but seldom used works by Antonius Bruodinus. This first complete English translation of one of his works shows that copious detail about Irish matters may be gathered from his Latin writings. These cast light on the world of classical Gaelic scholarship prior to its decline in the seventeenth century and reveal the types of networks cultivated by Irish clerics on the continent, networks which crossed Europe from Ireland to Louvain, Prague and Rome, traversing different linguistic, cultural and ethnic boundaries.

A commemorative volume in honour of the great Irish Franciscan Fr Luke Wadding, published in 1957, featured an essay by Thomas Wall on the life, activity and writings of Antonius Bruodinus.[5] In his characteristically authoritative style, Wall quotes extensively from the Latin texts of Bruodinus and his protagonist Carve. Although he was among the first to recognise Bruodinus' works as useful in highlighting the 'native professional writers' whose plight, in his view, had become 'a pitiful one' by the seventeenth century,[6] Wall did not translate these Latin quotations.

Modern historians have dealt rashly with Bruodinus, being either too quick to point to his shortcomings, to dismiss him, to gloss over his extensive writings in virtual silence, or quote selectively from his oeuvre. Little of his output has been properly evaluated, despite its obvious potential for cultural, social and historical research.[7] Benignus Millett was one of the few Franciscan historians to voice support for the neglected author and to recognise the true value

5. See Thomas Wall, 'Bards and Bruodins', in *Father Luke Wadding: Commemorative volume*, ed. Franciscan Fathers (Dún Mhuire, Killiney, 1957), pp. 438–62.
6. Ibid., p. 439.
7. A recent exception being Luke McInerney, 'A "most vainglorious man": The writings of Antonius Bruodin', *Archivium Hibernicum*, vol. 70, 2017, pp. 202–83. Others who have explored Bruodinus' life include Benignus Millett, *The Irish Franciscans, 1651–1665* (*Analecta Gregoriana*, 129) (Rome, Pontificia Universitas Gregoriana, 1964), pp. 245–8; and Jan Pařez and Hedvika Kuchařová, *The Irish Franciscans in Prague: 1629–1786* (Prague, 2015), pp. 76–85. Details about Bruodinus' life are also found in Kevin McGrath, 'The Bruodins in Bohemia', *Irish Ecclesiastical Record*, vol. 77, 1952, pp. 333–43.

of his writings.[8] Whereas another Franciscan scholar, Fr Brendan Jennings, claimed that Bruodinus missed an opportunity to become a 'first class propagandist' of the Irish Catholic martyrs.[9] Given the importance and rich potential of Bruodinus' reflections on issues such as the status, training and responsibilities of the bardic poets, a comprehensive assessment of his writings, complete with English translation and explanatory commentary, is necessary.

The purpose of publishing a translation of one of Bruodinus' lesser-known works, *Anatomicum Examen Enchiridii Apologetici* (Prague, 1671), is to reveal the worldview of a highly educated Gaelic-Irish cleric. Bruodinus is important because his early education embodied both classical Gaelic and Latin learning and because he left an impressive corpus of scholarly writing. These show that he maintained an interest in the traditional genealogies of the O'Briens and other leading Gaelic families, and was well versed in Irish history, poetry and antiquities. Writing in Prague with all the pangs and disadvantages of an exile whose family lost considerable property during the Commonwealth period, Bruodinus' scholarly achievements are noteworthy. When he had access to documentary sources or first-hand accounts, his commentary on Irish matters in general, and people and places of his native Thomond in particular, is accurate.

The contention between Carve and Bruodinus was as much a clash of views as culture. Both were informed by their different world views, with Carve claiming to be the product of Old-English culture, taking a condescending view of the Gaelic learned classes generally, and the poets in particular. For his part, Bruodinus belonged to a Gaelic learned family and he was familiar with the literary culture of Gaelic Ireland and acutely conscious of his family's position within it. The tension that animated their divergent views was the chief reason behind the acrimony that had developed between these Irish clerics who represented, at that time, two irreconcilable interpretations of Irish culture and history.

It is timely to re-assesses the contribution Bruodinus made to the topical debates that were troubling the Irish community on the continent in the seventeenth century. While his writings have attracted

8. Patrick J. Corish and Benignus Millett (eds), *The Irish Martyrs* (Dublin, 2005), pp. 198–9.
9. Fr Brendan Jennings, 'The Irish Franciscans in Prague', *Studies*, vol. 28, 1939, pp. 210–22, at p. 220.

criticism from modern historians, he was no less controversial in his day. Thanks to Fr Thomas Carve's criticisms of Bruodinus, the two men's commentaries contain rare historical information on issues and details about people and landholding in Thomond which would not otherwise have survived. This book, therefore, seeks to retrieve from obscurity an especially interesting text and demonstrate its value in understanding not just Ireland's Latin literature, but also the history and heritage of the Gaelic learned classes among whom Bruodinus' own family belonged.

THE CONTENTION

The origin of the contention that arose between Bruodinus and Carve can be traced to the publication of Thomas Carve's views about the Gaelic-Irish in his works *Itinerarium R.D. Thomae Carve Tipperariensis* ... (Mainz, 1639–46)[10] and *Lyra seu Anacephalaeosis Hibernica* ... (Vienna, 1651).[11] Extremely critical of the manners and customs of the Irish and their history, *Lyra* draws heavily from older works including that of the anti-Irish late twelfth-century Cambro-Norman chronicler Giraldus Cambrensis. In his 1,099-page tome *Propugnaculum Catholicae Veritatis* (Prague, 1669),[12] Bruodinus took serious issue with Carve's representation of the people and history of Ireland. This was not the first time that Carve had been censured for his writings on Irish history and culture and it would appear that opposition to his writings had developed among the Irish Franciscans in Prague. In 1640 two Irish Franciscans wrote to Carve expressing objections to the way he portrayed the Irish of Connacht and Ulster. [13] Bruodin's criticism of Carve nearly two decades after this initial salvo would have had broad support within his own community.

10. Thomas Carve, *Itinerarium R.D. Thomae Carve Tipperariensis ... cum historia facti Butleri, Gordon, Lesly & Aliorum* (Mainz, 1639–41, pts. I–II; Speyer, 1648), III pts., new edn, 1 vol., 1640–1).
11. Thomas Carve, *Lyra seu Anacephalaeosis Hibernica, in qua de exordio, seu origine, nomine, moribus ritibusque Gentis Hibernicae succinte tractatur, cui quoque accessere Annales ejusdem Hiberniae nec non rerum gestarum per Europam 1148–1650* (Viennae, 1651; 2nd edn, Sulzbach, 1666). The first part of the title translates: 'The Lyre, or the Recapitulation of Ireland'.
12. Antonius Bruodinus, *Propugnaculum Catholicae Veritatis libris X constructum, in duasque partes divisum. Pars prima historica in quinque libros* (Prague, 1669). The first part of the title translates: 'The Bulwark of Catholic Truth'.
13. Micheál Mac Craith and David Worthington, 'Aspects of the Literary Activity of the Irish Franciscans in Prague, 1620–1786', in Thomas O'Connor and Mary Ann Lyons (eds), *Irish Migrants in Europe after Kinsale* (Dublin, 2003), pp. 118–34, at pp. 125–7.

Traditionally, the dispute was thought to have begun with Bruodin taking umbrage with Carve's writings. However, another issue also caused tension between the two men. This stemmed from a bequest made by Colonel Walter Butler of Ballinakill, near Roscrea in County Tipperary, to the Irish Franciscans of Prague. Butler, like other successful Irish military men of rank in Bohemia, was a supporter of the Irish Franciscan community in Prague and his enthusiasm translated into material support. Butler not only gifted the community horses, carriages and furniture, but he stayed in regular communication with them, instructing that his mortal remains be interred in their church. The Irish Franciscans, benefitting from the raised profile of the Irish who served in the imperial forces and other generous patrons, served as an important focal point for the Irish émigré community and were, in turn, patronised by a number of important Czech nobles and had the support of Emperor Ferdinand III who in 1654 took the Irish College under his own protection and became its patron. When Colonel Walter Butler died on Christmas Day in 1634, his will bequeathed 30,000 florins to the Irish Franciscans in Prague and to Peter Wadding, the Irish Jesuit chancellor of the University of Prague.[14] Butler had acquired large sums of money and possessed two castles and extensive estates, and he possibly saw it as his role as both an Irish émigré and member of the nobility to provide material support to the Irish Franciscans.[15] His generous bequest was added to by his widow, Countess Anna Marie von Dohna, who gave 16,000 florins to the Franciscans between 1658 and 1666.[16] The significant financial assistance to the Irish Franciscans and their popularity among the Irish of central Europe was bound to cause tensions with other Irish foundations and clergy who lacked such support.

In the 1620s and 1630s Carve served as chaplain and secretary to Butler's regiment in the imperial forces during the Thirty Years War. It is clear from his writings that he had a personal relationship with Butler and regarded him as his patron. Given that Carve's *Itinerarium*

---

14. Pařez and Kuchařová, *The Irish Franciscans Prague*, p. 8. On Butler's bequest also see T. Corcoran, 'A Man of Action: Action for Irish Catholic education three centuries ago. II: Walter Butler of Friedberg', *Irish Monthly*, vol. 63, no. 742, 1935, pp. 243–53, at p. 252.

15. David Worthington, *Scots in Habsburg Service, 1618–1648* (Leiden and Boston, 2004), pp. 173, 300.

16. Mary Ann Lyons, 'The Role of St Anthony's College, Louvain in Establishing the Irish Franciscan College Network, 1607–60', in Edel Bhreathnach, Joseph MacMahon OFM and John McCafferty (eds), *The Irish Franciscans 1534–1990* (Dublin, 2009), pp. 27–44, at p. 38.

was written during his service in Butler's regiment and contains excerpts about Butler's life, Carve may have felt entitled to, or perhaps should have received, a portion of Butler's bequest. Disputes concerning bequests were often protracted and hard-fought and the matter undoubtedly added extra animus to the dispute between Carve and Bruodinus. By the 1650s when Bruodinus had moved to Prague, the community of Irish friars was growing quickly, both as a result of donations from members of the Irish émigré community, and the support rendered by the emperor. These facts would have made any dispute over Butler's bequest bitter, and one suspects that Carve, having lost his main patron in Butler and being aware of the prosperity of the Irish Franciscans, may have felt resentment towards them.

Whatever the cause of the disagreement, it quickly descended into a debate about the status of Bruodinus' family, the Clann Bhruaideadha (MacBrodys), and the role of the Gaelic learned classes (*An t-Aos Dána*).[17] Carve, who claimed to be of Anglo-Norman ancestry, was hostile to the Gaelic-Irish and their scholarship. In a chapter titled *De Carve, seu Carrani, erroribus et imposturis* in his *Propugnaculum Catholicae Veritatis …* (Prague, 1669),[18] Bruodinus presented an acrid critique of Carve's writings, which deemed his opinions to be slanderous and ill-informed. Bruodinus took issue with Carve's argument that the Gaelic-Irish were civilised through contact with the English. Bruodinus was angered by Carve's repetition of words ascribed to St Bernard of Clairvaux about the Irish people's lack of civility. He also took issue with Carve's criticism of Archbishop Giovanni Battista Rinuccini, papal nuncio to the Irish Confederates (1645–9) and his stance of non-accommodation with the Protestant lord lieutenant of Ireland, James Butler, duke of Ormond. It is clear from his writings that Carve's sympathies lay squarely with Ormond; his links to him can be traced through feudal and kinship ties with the Butlers in Tipperary, the county of his birth.[19]

17. The Gaelic learned classes referred to here are the professional literary families that specialised in history, poetry, law, genealogy, medicine and music. Some of these families were especially active in the late medieval Church, naturally on account of their literacy, but also because some of them had ancient origins that can be traced to erenaghs (*airchinnigh*) and coarbs (*comharbaí*) of the pre-twelfth-century Irish church.

18. Bruodinus, *Propugnaculum*, pp. 802–20.

19. On the life of Thomas Carve see M.P. Kerney, *Itinerarium Thomæ Carve, Tipperariensis … cum historia facti Butleri, Gordon, Lesly et aliorum* (London, 1859), pp. iii–x. A bibliography of his works is found at pp. xi–xii.

In 1670 the energetic Carve, then around eighty years of age, published a rebuke to Bruodinus' criticisms titled *Enchiridion Apologeticum contra sordidorum mendaciorum faraginem R. P. Antonii Bruodini* (Nuremberg).[20] It was thought that no copy of Carve's book survived but one has recently come to light in the Bavarian State Library.[21] Much of its argument can be interpreted by studying Bruodinus' reply in *Anatomicum*, published a year later. This book is so named because it dissects Carve's arguments chapter by chapter in the form of an anatomical, or bodily, examination. From this point both men entered into a bitter dispute, fuelled by personal acrimony and articulated in a torrent of derogatory Latin, replete with biting puns and vitriolic quips. Bruodinus' *Anatomicum* is a somewhat unusual work, on the one hand being an attempt to refute Carve's arguments in lengthy and stylistic rebuttals, and on the other hand presenting historical and genealogical information about the Clann Bhruaideadha in an attempt to prove their nobility and status. What emerges is a vindication of Bruodinus' Gaelic-Irish culture and his own family's role in it, written at some remove from the people and events that adorn its pages.

Perhaps in a bid to provide the work with a veneer of impartiality, Bruodinus wrote *Anatomicum* under the pseudonym Cornelius O'Molony. This was not a very convincing pseudonym given that Bruodinus' mother was an O'Molony (Mairéad Ní Mhaoldhomhnaigh)[22] and Carve had no doubt that the work was by Bruodinus. *Anatomicum* contains intimate details about the Clann Bhruaideadha, such as their genealogical connections and landed possessions, to which only a family member could have had access. The arguments made by Bruodinus to refute Carve's claims show just how sensitive the Gaelic-Irish were regarding their origins. The level of detail presented by Bruodinus, including listing families with whom the Clann Bhruaideadha contracted marriage, shows his preoccupation with proving the family's high social status. But the main aim of *Anatomicum* was to refute the assertions made by Carve in his previous works, notably his aspersions on Gaelic culture. The spectacle of two

20. Thomas Carve, *Enchiridion Apologeticum contra sordidorum mendaciorum faraginem R.P. Antonii Bruodini* (1670). The first part of the title translates: 'An Apologetic Handbook against the Indiscriminate Sordid Mendacities of the Rev. Fr. Antonius Bruodin'.

21. *Bayerische Staatsbibliothek* (Bavarian State Library).

22. Bruodinus, *Propugnaculum*, p. 961.

ageing clerics hurling abuse at one another continued into the early 1670s when Carve responded with a final publication titled *Responsio veridica ad illotum libellum* in 1672.[23] This contained new arguments and information about Carve's own family. The feud only ended upon the death of the aged Carve shortly after the publication of this work.

Of all Bruodinus' writings, it is *Anatomicum* which presents the most interesting and accurate information about matters that are no longer found elsewhere. In it, he delves into detail about the status and role of the Gaelic learned classes such as the poets, chroniclers, physicians and lawyers, and does so with particular reference to Thomond. But his commentary is more than simply a recounting of facts regarding his own country. In *Anatomicum* the reader is taken into a world replete with references to clergy, soldiers and merchants of the Irish diaspora on the continent, and digressions on matters as diverse as his own red hair and clean-shaven face! Readers are informed about the author's teaching duties, his travels to Rome, and the generosity of the Czech nobility toward the Irish Franciscans. Bruodinus provides impressive genealogical detail about the Clann Bhruaideadha, but also interesting anecdotes about his illustrious great-uncle, bardic poet Tadhg mac Dáire Mhic Bhruaideadha.

In his writings, Bruodinus castigates Carve, dubbing him a 'miserable old man' and lambasts him for his slanderous 'evil speaking'. Bruodinus also passes comment on an engraving of Carve which was printed in his second edition of *Lyra*, stating that the engraver had embellished his hair and beard, but he could not fashion Carve a brain: such was the vitriol that animated the contention. Bruodinus also took issue with Carve's proficiency in Latin, citing passages from his writings that were marred by grammatical errors. In *Anatomicum* Bruodinus criticises Carve for his use of pseudo-Latin suited only to a 'student of elementary grammar'. It is apparent from Carve's writings that he was not as accomplished as Bruodinus in Latin, his style exhibiting awkwardness and a forced fluency. In re-publishing Carve's *Itinerarium* in 1859 its editor, Michael Kerney, found fault with Carve's Latin, calling it 'medieval' rather than 'renaissance' in style.[24]

The contention between Carve and Bruodinus touched on many topics including the life of the archbishop of Cashel, Miler Magrath

23. Thomas Carve, *Responsio veridica ad illotum libellum, cui nomen Anatomicum Examen P. Antonii Bruodini* (Sulzbach, 1672).

24. Kerney, *Itinerarium Thomæ Carve*, p. iv.

(*c.* 1523–1622).[25] Their exchange of words on the subject is particularly important in terms of historiography. Magrath was a controversial figure for Irish Catholics on account of his opportunistic conversion to the Anglican Church. Much of his career was fraught with division and his every activity courted controversy for the English authorities, who were suspicious of his Catholic contacts. Carve, in attacking the Franciscans, used Magrath as an example of their imprudence and cast aspersions on him. Bruodinus zealously defended Magrath, refusing to condemn him despite his conversion to Protestantism, after having initially being ordained a Franciscan.

Bruodinus argued that Magrath converted under duress in England when returning to Ireland from Rome.[26] He cited the fact that Magrath had a large family and all of them, including his wife, remained Catholic, and emphasised that at the end of his life, Miler reconverted to Catholicism. While some of these claims cannot be substantiated, it is notable that Bruodinus' apologetical account of the archbishop's life is one of the earliest on record. What Bruodinus wrote about Magrath's early education in Spain is credible, although difficult now to establish. His other points about Magrath appear to be vindicated elsewhere, including his imprisonment and conversion under duress in London.[27]

We are fortunate that Bruodinus had first-hand experience both as a cleric and as a member of a learned family. As such, he was a recipient of ecclesiastical education and privy to matters such as the duties of bardic poets and their methods of training. This fact alone makes Bruodinus a reliable commentator who transcended the boundaries between the classical Gaelic scholarship of the bardic schools and the Latin learning of the Church. Having left Ireland for religious studies abroad just prior to the Cromwellian conquest, he witnessed the last vestiges of professional hereditary scholarship. The Clann Bhruaideadha traditionally provided poets, chroniclers and genealogists to the O'Briens of Thomond. One of their earliest known members was Seán Buidhe Mac Bruaideadha who composed a poem for Mathghamhain Maonmhaighe Ó Briain (d. 1369), which reminded his patron about the rights and respect owing to the *ollamh*,

---

25. See Patrick J. Ryan, *Archbishop Miler McGrath: The enigma of Cashel* (Lisheen, 2014).
26. Ibid., pp. 35–6.
27. Ibid., pp. 21, 35–7. On his activities and incarceration in London see L. Ó Mearáin, 'The Apostacy of Miler McGrath', *Clogher Record*, vol. 2, no. 2, 1958, pp. 244–56.

or master poet.[28] The Clann Bhruaideadha made a major contribution to the production of the *Annals of the Four Masters*, and the Franciscan brother Mícheál Ó Cléirigh visited them at Kilkee in the parish of Ruan, County Clare, in 1636,[29] seeking their approval of that monumental work.[30]

It is perhaps this aspect of *Anatomicum* that is of most interest to modern historians. Bruodinus describes the various branches of the Clann Bhruaideadha, the books they produced, and how they were kept. In the absence of such material surviving in Ireland, Bruodinus' account is a valuable historical source.

THE IRISH FRANCISCANS IN PRAGUE

The Irish Catholic religious communities on the continent became increasingly aware of their precarious position as the seventeenth century wore on. Many had left Ireland following the final defeat of Irish forces by the Cromwellians in 1652. Colleges had been established in a number of European countries earlier in the century following enforcement of the Elizabethan religious settlement. These seminary colleges took on an added importance as places of refuge in the 1650s. The most important were Louvain in the Spanish Netherlands, Paris and Douai in France, as well as Salamanca in Spain and St Isidore's in Rome.[31] The college at Prague was established in 1629 during the tumultuous period of the Thirty Years War by Emperor Ferdinand II. The emperor wished to have Catholicism re-introduced to the Habsburg territories of Bohemia following Protestant rule and saw

28. L. McKenna, SJ, 'Poem to Ó Briain', *The Irish Monthly*, vol. 49, 1921, pp. 112–17, at p. 112. Also see Láimhbheartach Mac Cionnaith (ed.), 'Dlighidh Ollamh Urraim Ríogh', in *Dioghluim Dána* (Dublin, 1938), pp. 252–6.

29. This placename has been confused with Kilkeedy in north Clare. The townland of Kilkee is situated in the modern parish of Ruan (old parish of Dysert) and was held jointly by Conor and John MacBrody in 1618. In *Anatomicum*, Bruodinus makes this clear in his spelling of the placename as 'Kilky'. See PHA Ms 16 B.E [Great Office, 5 September 1618 – Inchiquin]. Also see Pádraig Ó Riain, Diarmuid Ó Murchadha and Kevin Murray, *Historical Dictionary of Gaelic Placenames / Foclóir Stairiúil Áitainmneacha na Gaeilge*, Fascicle 3 / Fascúl 3 (London, 2008), p. 139.

30. Paul Walsh, *Gleanings from Irish Manuscripts* (Dublin, 1933), p. 78.

31. On the Irish missionary activities in and beyond Europe in the seventeenth century, including lists of Irish Franciscans in Rome and elsewhere, see Matteo Binasco, 'Establishing Mission Networks in the Early Modern Catholic Church: Ireland, Rome and the West Indies, 1600–1669', unpublished PhD thesis, NUI Galway, 2013. Also see Matteo Binasco and Vera Orschel, 'Prosopography of Irish Students Admitted to the Irish College, Rome, 1628–1798 [with index]', *Archivium Hibernicum*, vol. 66, 2013, pp. 16–62.

the Irish Franciscans as a convenient vehicle by which this could be achieved.[32]

The setting up of the Prague college alleviated the crowded conditions at Louvain and in time it would become the largest Irish college on the continent, housing up to fifty Irish friars.[33] Many of the friars had familial links to the professional learned families who had been so prominent in late medieval Gaelic Ireland. Colleges that were affiliated with the Franciscans were particularly attractive to clergy from Gaelic regions, because of the on-going Franciscan ministry in those areas.[34] Partly on account of Bruodinus' writings and the influence of men such as Patrick Fleming, Philip O'Reilly and Bernardine Clancy, the Irish College in Prague was elevated in status, not just as a place of refuge, but also as a seat of learning, for Irish Franciscans. The college gained a Europe-wide reputation as a centre of Scotist theology, and some former members of the Gaelic learned classes found employment as lectors there, including several from Bruodinus' own family, the Clann Bhruaideadha.

In the second half of the seventeenth century extensive networks of Irish clerics, as well as merchants and military men, grew up in Prague and other cities under Catholic control. These networks helped sustain an interest in Irish affairs and encouraged a well-informed intellectual tradition. An important part of this was hagiographical research designed to strengthen Ireland's Catholic tradition as a bulwark against Protestantism. The most important effort in this respect came from the Franciscans in the form of John Colgan's monumental *Acta Sanctorum veteris et maioris Scotiae, seu Hiberniae Sanctorum insulae* (Louvain, 1645). Also, in this *milieu* a number of other important works were produced on the continent by Irish clerics such as Luke Wadding's *Duns Scotus* (1639), and his monumental work on Franciscan history, *Annales Minorum* (1625–54).[35]

32. On the Irish College in Prague and the Irish Franciscan community in Bohemia, see Helga Hammerstein (ed.), *Migrating Scholars: Lines of contact between Ireland and Bohemia* (Dublin, 1998).
33. Lyons, 'The Role of St Anthony's College', pp. 35–41.
34. On the spread of the Franciscans in Gaelic areas during the later medieval period see Colmán Ó Clabaigh, *The Friars in Ireland, 1224–1540* (Dublin, 2012), pp. 62–5.
35. Canice Mooney, 'The writings of Father Luke Wadding, O.F.M', *Franciscan Studies*, vol. 18, nos. 3 & 4, 1958, pp. 225-39. There are a number of published works completed on the continent by Irish clerics. These include Peter Lombard's *De regno Hiberniae sanctorum insula commentarius* (Louvain, 1632), Patrick Duffy's *Mercurius sive Nuntius Occidentalis* (Louvain, 1642), as well as Patrick Fleming's *Collectanea sacra: seu S. Columbani Hiberni abbatis* (Louvain, 1667) which was printed posthumously by Fr O'Sheeran. Fleming was the first guardian of the Irish College in Prague and was killed outside the city in 1631 by a group of Hussite peasants, his funeral oration appearing in Bruodinus' *Propugnaculum*. See Patrick O'Neill, 'Ireland and Germany: A survey of literary and cultural relations before 1700, Part II', *Studies: An Irish quarterly review*, vol. 71, no. 282, 1982, pp. 152–65, at p. 160; and Bruodinus, *Propugnaculum*, p. 752.

The Irish Franciscans in Prague were notable for the books they produced. Fr Maurice Conry, who lectured in Prague, authored, under the pseudonym Maurice Morison, *Threnodia Hiberno-Catholica* (Innsbruck, 1659), a book that described the Cromwellian persecution of Irish Catholics. Such books, with their focus on the persecution of the Catholics in Ireland, were undoubtedly used by Bruodinus as exemplars for his own work *Propugnaculum*.[36] Bruodinus wrote and published four substantial theological works between 1663 and 1676, including his two-volume work *Oecodomia Minoriticae Scholae Salomonis* (Prague, 1663–4). Works by other authors survive in manuscript form such as Fr Philip O'Reilly's Irish translation of *Introduction à la vie devote* (Lyon, 1609) by Francis de Sales, or the theological tract *De profundissimo incarnationis mysterio* (1653) by Fr Anthony O'Connor, who served as guardian of the Irish College in Prague. It has been suggested that at least twenty significant works were published by the Irish Franciscans in Prague, excluding unpublished lectures and other material.[37]

The writings of Bruodinus offer a window into the world of Gaelic scholarship which to date has not been fully utilised by historians. While there exists contemporary writings on the training and role of the Gaelic learned classes, notably the hostile views promulgated by Richard Stanihurst, Edmund Campion, Sir John Davies and Fynes Moryson which received criticism in Seathrún Céitinn's *Foras Feasa ar Éirinn*,[38] the by-product of Bruodinus' and Carve's exchanges is the level of new detail they provide on these matters.[39] This new information that arises from their writings can help historians to

36. Bruodinus' writings on the killing of Irish religious at the hands of Cromwellian troops have been used by historians, although no systematic study of his claims has yet appeared. In many cases Bruodinus is the only authority on these killings. The most detailed survey of Bruodinus' claims is found in Millett, *Irish Franciscans*, pp. 248–89. Others have drawn from Bruodinus' work to identify instances of suppression against Catholic clergy and to document Cromwellian military activities. See, for example, James Frost, *The History and Topography of County Clare* (Dublin, 1893), pp. 46–7, 53, 69, 97, 118–19; and see Myles O'Reilly et al., *Lives of the Irish Martyrs and Confessors: Also, a very full and complete history of the penal laws* (New York, 1881).
37. See R.J. Kelly, 'The Irish Franciscans in Prague (1629-1786): Their literary labours', *JRSAI*, vol. 12, no. 2, 1922, pp. 169–74.
38. See Geoffrey Keating, *Foras Feasa ar Éirinn: The history of Ireland*, D. Comyn and P.S. Dinneen (eds), 4 vols (London, 1902–14).
39. See John Barry and Hiram Morgan, *Great Deeds in Ireland: Richard Stanihurst's De Rebus in Hibernia Gestis* (Cork, 2013); Edmund Campion, *A Historie of Ireland, Written in the Yeare 1571* (Dublin: reprint, 1809); and Henry Morley (ed.), *Ireland under Elizabeth and James the First Described by Edmund Spenser, by Sir John Davies Attorney-General for Ireland under James the First, and by Fynes Moryson, Secretary to the Lord Mountjoy, Lord Deputy* (London, 1890).

better understand the issues of identity and culture among Irish clerics living in exile in the aftermath of the Cromwellian period. The views of the Gaelic-Irish and Old-English are brought into sharp relief here, including matters of cultural achievement, identity and status in the tumultuous seventeenth century.

ANTONIUS BRUODINUS: LIFE AND WORK

Antonius Bruodinus was born in County Clare, formerly known as Thomond. His family were well known as a learned family of the classical Gaelic tradition, acting as chroniclers and master poets to the O'Brien kings (later earls) of Thomond.[40] They had a bardic school and held the position of historians to the O'Briens from medieval times, placing them in the front rank of the Gaelic literary classes. His relative, Maoilín Óg Mac Bruaideadha, *ollamh seanchais* (historical lore), defended in poetry the raid by Aodh Ruadh Ó Domhnaill and his forces into Thomond in 1599.[41] In the 1590s, Maoilín Óg contributed to William Daniel's (Uilliam Ó Domhnuill) Protestant-led project of translating the New Testament into Irish.[42] In the following century Bruodinus' great-uncle, Tadhg mac Dáire Mhic Bhruaideadha, initiated the famous literary exchange with the northern poets known as *Iomarbhágh na bhFileadh* (Contention of the Poets), sometime around 1616.[43] Bruodinus' family, therefore, was heavily involved in some of the most notable literary events of the period in addition to their production of high register classical bardic poetry for aristocratic patrons.

We are fortunate that details of Bruodinus' early life have come down to us. Antonius Bruodinus was born at Ballyogan, north of Ennis in County Clare, in about 1618.[44] His Irish name, Antóin Mac

40. The Clann Bhruaideadha are recorded in a mid-seventeenth-century list of learned families who are described as *ollamhuin seanchais*. See James Carney, 'De Scriptoribus Hibernicis', *Celtica*, vol. 1, 1946, pp. 86–110, at p. 91.
41. *AFM*, vol. VI, pp. 2103–5.
42. Brian Ó Cuív, 'The Irish Language in the Early Modern Period', in T.W. Moody, F.X. Martin and F.J. Byrne (eds), *A New History of Ireland: Early modern Ireland 1534–1691*, vol. 3 (Oxford, 2009 reprint), pp. 509–45, at p. 512.
43. See Pádraig A. Breatnach, 'Litir Ó Thadhg Mac Bruaideadha', *Éigse*, vol. 28, 1994–5), pp. 97–9. Also see Lambert McKenna, *Iomarbhágh na bhFileadh: The contention of the bards*, 2 vols (London, 1918).
44. He states that Ballyogan was the place where his parents were domiciled. Bruodinus, *Propugnaculum*, p. 961. His parents' estate at Ballyogan prior to the Cromwellian confiscations of the 1650s is recorded in R.C. Simington (ed.), *Books of Survey and Distribution ... County of Clare*, vol. 4 (Dublin, 1967), p. 121.

Bruaideadha, indicated that he belonged to the learned family of the Clann Bhruaideadha.[45] His father was Maoilín Mac Bruaideadha[46] who died in 1668 aged eighty-one, and his mother was Mairéad Ní Mhaoldhomhnaigh,[47] whose anglicised maiden name, O'Molony, was used by Bruodinus as a *nom de plume* in *Anatomicum*.[48]

We may assume that on account of his knowledge of Gaelic culture, genealogy and history, Bruodinus probably received part of his education in a bardic school operated by his family. We know from other sources that bardic schools were still operating in Thomond and surrounding areas well into the seventeenth century.[49] His writings show a deep familiarity not only with Gaelic culture and language, but also with the professional activities of his family. Among his writings Bruodinus relates a number of anecdotes about his early life. In one of his narratives, he recalls a scene that he witnessed as a young man in about 1632 at Moynoe in east Clare. The reader is rewarded by this digression as he narrates an event that hints at local custom and folk superstition. The event occurred on 1 May which is the festival of Bealtaine and marked the beginning of summer. The festival was associated with rituals performed to protect cattle, crops and people:

> *Rem referam, quam ipse oculis meis vidi, dum enim circa annum 14. meae aetatis, D. Florentii Bruodini D.ni de Moyneo, mei patrui, in domo fuissem; & nobilium nostrarum partium juvenum more, 1 Maii in aurora (illa die specialiter in lacte & butyro sagae solent nocere, seque transformare) cum primogenito praefati Domini (postea Franciscanus fuit, Bonaventura Bruodinus dictus, sed brevi absoluto studio consummatus Compluti in Hispania non sine sanctitatis fama anno 1643. explevit tempora multa*[50]*) assumptis canibus venaticis sagam (sic apud nos illa die*

45. On the Clann Bhruaideadha of Thomond see Luke McInerney, 'Lettermoylan of Clann Bhruaideadha: A résumé of their landholding, topography and history', *NMAJ*, vol. 52, 2012, pp. 81–113.

46. Maolin was recorded in the Protestant Depositions of 1641 as living in Kilraghtis and was present at the siege of Ballyallia castle on the side of Confederate Irish forces. See 'Deposition of Andrew Chaplin', 12/5/1643, *1641 Depositions*, TCD Ms 829, fol. 97v. Another deposition refers to his residence as Ballyogan: 'Deposition of Anthony Heatcote', 16/3/1647, *1641 Depositions*, TCD Ms 829, fols 75v; while another gives his address as the parish of Inchicronan: 'Deposition of Beatrice Hepditch', 23/5/1643, *1641 Depositions*, TCD Ms 829, fol. 73r.

47. Bruodinus, *Propugnaculum*, p. 961.

48. Cornelius O'Molony, *Anatomicum Examen Enchiridii Apologettici* (Prague, 1671).

49. T.F. O'Rahilly, 'A Poem by Piaras Feiritéar', *Ériu*, vol. 13, 1942, pp. 113–18. There is a reference in this poem, which dates from *c.* 1640, to Finavarra in north Clare, a place associated with the Uí Dhálaigh and their bardic school.

50. This appears to be an allusion to *Sapientiae* 4.13 (The Book of Wisdom): *consummatus in brevi explevit tempora multa*, which has been used to refer to those who die young but achieved much in their comparatively short lives.

lepus vocatur) investigarem, illis in locis, in quibus vaccae pascebantur; ecce repente a famulis videtur lepus unius vaccae ubera sugens, qui audito clamore, fugae se commisit; insequuntur canes, alias optimi, sed non assequuntur, antequam ad vicinum se retraxisset pagum (urgebat enim illum multitudo canum, qua illi omnis alia via aufugiendi praecludebatur) ubi videns periculum, intravit quondam domunculam per fenestrellam, ex qua tam cito se extricare non poterat, quin ab uno ex canibus in clunibus morderetur taliter, quod pars pellis simul cum cauda, in canis ore remaneret; superveniunt famuli, & canum circa domunculam latratus considerantes, pellisque leporinae particulam videntes, vi aperiunt ostium: ubi sordidam unam solam deprehenderunt vetulam natione Scotam quam vel invitam examinarunt; vulneratamque non leviter (prout nobis dixerunt) retro deprehenderunt, & ad veritatem de sua in leporem transformatione dicendam compulerunt.[51]

[I shall relate a thing that I saw myself with my own eyes, when I was about 14 years old and I was staying in the house of my paternal uncle Florence Bruodin [Flann MacBrody], Master of Moynoe. Following the custom of the young nobles of our parts, on the first of May at daybreak (it is especially on that day that hags [*cailleacha*] are wont to do harm with milk and butter and to transform themselves), having taken the hounds with us, I was with the firstborn of the aforesaid Master (he was later a Franciscan, called Bonaventure Bruodin, but he died soon after achieving great results on quick completion of his studies in Alcalá de Henares in Spain, not without a reputation of holiness, in the year 1643) tracking the hag (this is how the hare is called among us on that day) in those places where cows were grazing. Suddenly – behold! – there was seen by the servants a hare sucking the udder of a cow, and when it heard the clamour, it started fleeing: the dogs, in general very good, followed it but could not catch up with it before it withdrew to a neighbouring village (for the multitude of dogs was pressing it hard and shutting to it every other way of escaping) where, seeing the danger, it entered a small house through a little window, out of which it was not able to extricate itself quickly enough so as to be bitten on the buttocks by one of the dogs in such a way that a bit of skin together with the tail remained in the

51. Antonius Bruodinus, *Corolla Oecodomiae Minoriticae Scholae Salomonis Doctoris Subtilis* (Prague, 1664), pp. 73–4. Bonaventure mentioned here was not the same individual who held the chair of philosophy and theology in Prague in the 1660s. See Alice Stopford Green, *The Making of Ireland and its Undoing* (London, 1908), p. 455.

dog's mouth. Thereupon the servants arrived, and, considering the barks of dogs around the small house and seeing the little bit of hare skin, they forced the door. There they discovered a dirty little old woman alone, an Irish native,[52] whom they examined, though against her will; and they discovered that she was badly wounded (according to what they told us) behind, and they forced her to say the truth about her transformation into a hare].

Bruodinus also tells us about his early education. According to a passage in *Propugnaculum*, he received rudimentary training in grammar under Denis O'Nelan, a close relative and parish priest of Kilraghtis.[53] The O'Nelans, or Uí Nialláin in Irish, were a notable medical kindred whose family members served as hereditary physicians to the O'Briens of Thomond.[54] A branch of the family held the towerhouses of Ballyallia and Ballycarroll in Templemaley parish, not far from Bruodinus' family in Kilraghtis.[55] After having studied the basics of grammar in his local parish at a young age, he went on to further his studies at the Franciscan friary of Quin.[56]

52. *Natione Scotam* is taken here to denote a native of Ireland. Usually, Bruodinus employs the term *Hiberni* to denote Irish people, but there is no reason to think that the term employed here meant anything other than a native Irish person.

53. Bruodinus, *Propugnaculum*, p. 709. About his early education Bruodinus writes: *Pater Nelanus meus proximus consanguineus, sub cujus disciplina grammaticae rudimentis in puerili aetate studui* (Father Nelan, my closest kinsman, under whose teaching I studied the rudiments of grammar in my childest age).

54. On this family see Luke McInerney, 'The O'Neylons of Dysert and Austria', *TOC*, vol. 42, 2018, pp. 25–32. On the exploits of one of the leading branches of the family during the seventeenth century see Luke McInerney, '"Goeth over onely to obtaine breeding": William O'Neylon's certificate of passage to Spain, 1652', *NMAJ*, vol. 58, 2018, pp. 95–110.

55. See Brian Ó Dálaigh, 'Doctors Donnell and James Neylon and the O'Briens of Thomond 1530–1599', *TOC*, vol. 15, 1991, pp. 15–19. Also see *AFM*, vol. VI, p. 2141. On their towerhouses see R.W. Twigge, 'Edward White's Description of Thomond in 1574', *NMAJ*, vol. 1, no. 2, 1910, pp. 75–85, at p. 79.

56. Quin friary was constructed in 1402 by the MacNamaras, lords of Clann Chuiléin, as a mausoleum for the main branch of the family. Quin friary was a substantial construction founded on the ruins of the late-thirteenth-century Anglo-Noman castle, and its size and presence is more congruent with the political standing and aspirations of its MacNamara patrons than the austerity of the friars. The friary received a papal grant in 1433, which was issued to '*M[a]con Macnamara, nobleman, duke of Clandcullyan*'. Bruodinus' description of the friary and its scholarly affairs is the only one that has come down to us. See *AFM*, vol. IV, p. 775. On the MacNamaras of Clann Chuiléin see N.C. MacNamara, *The Story of an Irish Sept: The origin and history of the MacNamaras* (London, 1896). Also see Luke McInerney, 'The West Clann Chuiléin Lordship in 1586: Evidence from a forgotten inquisition', *NMAJ*, vol. 48, 2008, pp. 33–62; and Ó Clabaigh, *The Friars*, p. 66. On the papal grant see J.A. Twemlow (ed.), 'Lateran Regesta 319: 1431–1433', *Calendar of Papal Registers Relating to Great Britain and Ireland: Volume 8, 1427–1447* (London, 1909), p. 457. The Franciscan Donatus Mooney visited the friary in *c.* 1615 but he makes no mention of the Franciscan *studium*. See Brendan Jennings, 'Brussels MS. 3947: Donatus Moneyus, De Provincia Hiberniae S. Francisci', *Analecta Hibernica*, vol. 6, 1934, pp. 12–138, at pp. 59–60.

He provides detail on the Franciscan lectors at Quin and asserts that over eight hundred students attended the friary school, and he was counted among them:

> *Eugenius [O'Cahane] noster superiorum jussu publicas aperuit in Conventu Oppidi de Quenhi, in Tuomonia, scholas (quas ipse simul cum Reverendo Patre Thaddaeo o Brien ejusdem Ordinis Lectore, viro pio ac docto, moderabatur). Confluit ex variis Hiberniae provinciis ad dictas scholas tanta juvenum multitudo, quod anno Domini 1644. ultra 800 numeraverint studiosos (inter quos ego ipse, cum aliis octodecim Bruodinis fui). Dissipatis bellorum injuria ac Catholicorum (proh pudor!) dissensionibus praedictis scholis, Pater Eugenius in Guardianum Conventus de Inish (regiis o Brieni Principis sumptibus magnifice fabricati) fuit assumptus.*[57]
>
> [Our Eugene O'Cahane, by direction of his superiors, opened public schools in the Convent of Quin in Thomond (which he presided over together with Rev. Father Thaddeus O'Brien, lector of the same order, a pious and skilled man). Such a great multitude of youths came together to the said schools from various provinces of Ireland, that in the year of the Lord 1644 there were more than 800 students (among whom was I and eighteen other Bruodins). When, through the evil chance of wars, and (alas!) the dissensions of the Catholics, these schools were dispersed, Father Eugene was made Guardian of the Convent of Ennis (which had been magnificently founded thanks to the royal generosity of Prince O'Brien)].

While Bruodinus' reference to the number of students is an exaggeration designed to impress a foreign audience, it is significant to note that Quin was considered an important place of learning and operated freely until the Cromwellian conquest put an end to the school.[58] Later in his writings on the Irish martyrs for which he is probably best known, Bruodinus notes that his lector, Eugenius O'Cahane, was

57. Bruodinus, *Propugnaculum*, p. 712.

58. One of the earliest references to Quin friary being re-used following its suppression is a complaint by the Protestant bishop of Killaloe, John Rider, when he wrote in 1622 that the friary was resorted to on occasion by many of the population and the friars. Rev. Philip Dwyer, *The Diocese of Killaloe, from the Reformation to the Close of the Eighteenth Century* (Dublin, 1878), p. 142.

killed by Cromwellian troops.[59] In a separate incident which seems to have been based on a first-hand account, he notes that two Franciscan brothers of Quin friary, Jeremias de Nerihiny (MacInerheny) and Daniel MacClancy, were killed by Cromwellian soldiers in 1651 when the friary was attacked.[60]

It is significant that learned families like the Clann Bhruaideadha were attracted to the Franciscans and the ideology of Tridentine Catholicism.[61] There is little evidence to suggest that members of the Clann Bhruaideadha were involved in the medieval Church prior to the reformation (despite holding Church lands), or that they contributed to the ranks of the Franciscans on the scale that they did in the seventeenth and eighteenth centuries.[62] However, a striking number of them entered the Franciscan order and served at Ennis friary during the latter period.[63] The principal reason for this was the introduction of English law, language and administration in Thomond which made the Clann Bhruaideadha's traditional occupations redundant and compelled them to seek support and employment elsewhere, such as in religious orders like the Franciscans. The fact that Ennis friary contained the burial tomb of the Clann Bhruaideadha, which reputedly was built in marble next to the O'Brien funerary monument, suggests that the family had important connections with Ennis friary.[64] These connections were encouraged by the links they cultivated with their O'Brien patrons over generations.

Tridentine Catholicism, as propounded in the Irish colleges on the continent, attracted the talents of men from the professional learned families whose traditional specialisations were perfected in the bardic schools.[65] In the absence of secular aristocratic patronage by the seventeenth century, male members of learned families turned to religious orders like the Franciscans as an outlet for intellectual

59. Bruodinus, *Propugnaculum*, pp. 711–12.
60. Ibid., pp. 716–17.
61. On the Gaelic learned families and counter-reformation Catholicism see Samantha Meigs, *The Reformations in Ireland: Tradition and confessionalism, 1400–1690* (New York, 1997), pp. 77–89.
62. Luke McInerney, *Clerical and Learned Lineages of Medieval Co. Clare: A survey of the fifteenth-century papal registers* (Dublin, 2014), pp. 154–61.
63. On the life of one such Franciscan, Dermot McBruodin (Diarmuid Mac Bruaideadha), see Luke McInerney, 'Two Seventeenth-Century Franciscans from Thomond: Dermot McBruodin (d. 1617) 'the mad friar' and Antonius Bruodin (*c.* 1618–80)', *Studia Hibernica*, vol. 47, 2021, pp. 21–61.
64. Bruodinus, *Propugnaculum*, p. 968.
65. On the training offered in the bardic schools see Brian Ó Cuív, 'The Linguistic Training of the Medieval Irish Poet', *Celtica*, vol. 10, 1973, pp. 114–40.

expression and for attainment of higher learning.[66] At least six members of Bruodinus' family became Franciscan friars in the seventeenth century, and a number of others were active in religious life in the eighteenth century.[67] Like other young men from learned families, Bruodinus joined the Franciscans in his early twenties and he received his tonsure by 1642.[68] One of the recollections about his early adult life in Ireland involves a miracle that occurred to a woman named Maria MacGorman, whom he describes as of 'ancient nobility' (*antiquae nobilitatis*).[69] This woman, from a well-known family of west Clare, was cured of sciatica and kidney pains after frequenting the holy well of St Michael at Kilmihil. As a young friar in September 1642, Bruodinus witnessed the miraculous healing of a cripple at the well, which he relates at length in *Propugnaculum*.[70]

Bruodinus left Ireland in 1643[71] and initially studied under the direction of Luke Wadding at St Isidore's College in Rome. He was ordained a priest in 1646,[72] he concluded his thesis at St Isidore's in March 1648, and in August his cousin, Bonaventure, also concluded his thesis there.[73] The following year Bruodinus requested to

66. Bernadette Cunningham, *The Annals of the Four Masters: Irish history, kingship and society in the early seventeenth century* (Dublin, 2010), pp. 282–6. On the amalgam of native learning and the Franciscans see Edel Bhreathnach, 'The Mendicant Orders and Vernacular Irish Learning in the Late Medieval Period', *Irish Historical Studies*, vol. 37, no. 147, 2011, pp. 357–75.

67. Those contemporaneous with Bruodinus include Nicholas (*fl.* 1659–63) and Bonaventure (d. 1670), the former of whom appears in a list of clergy and laity of Killaloe diocese in 1663. See Cuthbert McGrath, 'Materials for a History of Clann Bhruaideadha', *Éigse*, vol. 4, no. 1, 1943, pp. 48–66, at p. 50; Benignus Millett, 'Calendar of Volume 13 of the *Fondo di Vienna* in Propaganda Archive: Part 2, ff. 201–401', *Collectanea Hibernica*, vol. 25, 1983, pp. 30–62, at p. 31. On those Franciscan Bruodins at Ennis friary see Patrick Conlan, *Franciscan Ennis* (Athlone, 1984), pp. 64–5. Examples include Francis Bruodin (1666–9), Bonaventure Bruodin (1669–72), Francis Bruodin (1672–5), Francis Bruodin (1680–1), Francis or Thaddeus Bruodin (1683–4), Thaddeus Bruodin (1684–5), Francis Bruodin (1685–7), Thaddeus Bruodin (1687–9), Florence Bruodin (1702–5) and Simon Brodin (d. 1792). While some of these names are repeat references, it is striking how many friars at Ennis were of the Clann Bhruaideadha. A number of the family also appear in Rev. Wiliam P. Burke, *Irish Priests in the Penal Times (1660–1760)* (Waterford, 1914), pp. 400–6, 408–9.

68. Bruodinus, *Propugnaculum*, p. 964.

69. Ibid., p. 961.

70. Ibid., pp. 964–5.

71. Ibid., p. 964. The date of 1643 contradicts Bruodinus' earlier statement that he was a student at Quin friary in 1644. The former date may be a typological error for 1634. See Bruodinus, *Propugnaculum*, p. 712.

72. Hugh Fenning, 'Irishmen Ordained at Rome, 1572–1697', *Archivium Hibernicum*, vol. 59, 2005, pp. 1–36, at p. 19. Bruodinus was ordained on 31 March 1646. His relative, Bonaventure Bruodin, was ordained on 29 September 1646, also in Rome. Ibid., p. 20.

73. Brendan Jennings, 'Theses Defended at St Isidore's College, Rome, 1631–1649', *Collectanea Hibernica*, vol. 2, 1959, pp. 95–104, at p. 104.

move to Germany[74] and, having been granted permission, arrived in Habsburg-controlled Prague in 1650 where he lectured in theology.[75] His time in Rome brought him into contact with leading members of the Irish Catholic diaspora, such as the Franciscan author Francis O'Molloy (Froinsias Ó Maolmhuaidh, *c.* 1606–77), whose approbation appears in *Anatomicum* and who had been a resident of St Isidore's since 1642.[76]

According to his own account, Bruodinus' ecclesiastical career in Bohemia was busy with travel both within the Franciscan province in Bohemia, and elsewhere. He tells us that he managed schools of philosophy for fifteen years and his involvement in the business of his order required travel to Rome to attend general assemblies of the Franciscans. At one assembly convened in 1667 he helped adjudicate on an important theology thesis by one of his students at the Vatican.[77]

Upon arriving in the Bohemian province of the Franciscans in 1650, Bruodinus appears to have been a controversial but imposing figure. The exact reasons behind his move from Rome to Bohemia are not clear but according to Cuthbert McGrath he was exiled by Fr Luke Wadding.[78] By Bruodinus' own account his cousin, Bonaventure Bruodin, held the chair of theology in Prague, which could have been a factor in his relocation.[79] Other friars from Thomond were already living at the Irish Franciscan College in Prague, such as Bernardine Clancy who moved there from Louvain in 1646. Bruodinus was clearly well-connected to leading Irish religious and military exiles in the Habsburg imperial lands.

Anatomicum gives some insight into Bruodinus' own intellectual formation. It is clear, not only from his attempt to emulate an embellished classical Latin style, but from frequent references to ancient authors whom he would find quoted in learned sources, that he was well read and proficient in Latin.[80] This was no doubt thanks to his further education in Rome. During his residency there, Bruodinus would have been exposed to instruction in higher philosophy and

74. Brendan Jennings, 'Miscellaneous Documents II 1625–1640', *Archivium Hibernicum*, vol. 14, 1949, pp. 1–49, at p. 8.
75. McGrath, 'Materials', p. 49.
76. Jennings, 'Miscellaneous Documents II', p. 6.
77. O'Molony, *Anatomicum*, pp. 197–8.
78. McGrath, 'Materials', p. 49.
79. O'Molony, *Anatomicum*, p. 125.
80. On Bruodinus' Latin, see the translator's introduction.

theology and his superior command of Latin must have been augmented by his studies there, for he writes in a developed and ornate fashion. His erudite use of rhetorical tropes and metaphorical devices are further evidence of a sophisticated and nurtured Latin.

Bruodinus' references to biblical themes and quotations from scripture, such as the Psalms, Acts of the Apostles and the Book of Daniel, are unsurprising given his theological formation. His knowledge of popular Latin grammars like William Lily's *Grammar of Latin in English* (1540–3), and his quotation from English writers, suggests fluency in English. He was familiar with the works of foreign authors who wrote (often critically) about Irish matters, and he cites the Venerable Bede,[81] Giraldus Cambrensis,[82] the Scottish historian George Buchanan[83] and Old-Englishman Richard Stanihurst, among others.[84]

His digressions on Irish toponymy and his rendering of Gaelic-Irish names and placenames[85] suggests a command of Irish due no doubt to familiarity with, if not a study of, classical literary Irish. In one example, he explains the origin of the name County Clare, identifying it as an Irish placename denoting a wooden board bridge (*Clár*), rather than a name recalling the Anglo-Norman De Clare family of the thirteenth century, as has since been proposed by some authors:[86]

> *Locus ille non a cognomine Comitis Clarensis dicitur Clare, sed ab assere pontis loco quondam supra fluvium Forgium extenso: asser enim Hibernice Clare dicitur.*[87]

> [That place is not called Clare after the earl of Clare; it comes, rather, from the board which once spanned the river Fergus; the Irish word for board is 'Clare'].[88]

81. Bruodinus, *Propugnaculum*, p. 806.
82. Ibid., pp. 779–83.
83. Ibid., pp. 854–67.
84. Ibid., pp. 788–9.
85. Examples include: 'Cluon Tarbh', 'Chill Michil', 'Teach Eoin' and 'Ceann Coradh' for placenames, and the use of genealogical terms such as 'Siol mBrion' and 'Siol Aodha' which appear in Bruodinus, *Propugnaculum*, pp. 922, 926, 962, 981, 1080–1. Other Irish terms appear thoroughout the work, including *cláirseach* and *gallogloch*.
86. For example, see Samuel Lewis, *A Topographical Dictionary of Ireland*, 2 vols (London, 1837), p. 479. Also, on the placename *Clár* (plank bridge) see Pádraig Ó Riain, Diarmuid Ó Murchadha and Kevin Murray, *Historical Dictionary of Gaelic Placenames / Foclóir Stairiúil Áitainmneacha na Gaeilge*, Fascicle 5 / Fascúl 5 (London, 2013), p. 63.
87. Bruodinus, *Propugnaculum*, p. 958.
88. Chris O'Mahony and Brian Ó Dálaigh, 'A Seventeenth-Century Description of Co. Clare', *Dal gCais*, vol. 9, 1988, pp. 27–38, at p. 28. The word 'Irish' is used here instead of 'Gaelic' in the printed translation.

Bruodinus also had access to modern books, both religious and secular. In *Anatomicum* he refers to Francis Lanovius' *Chronicon Generale Ordinis Minorum* (Paris, 1635) and Luke Wadding's *Scriptores Ordinis Minorum* (Rome, 1650), while his chapter on the reformation in *Propugnaculum* demonstrates considerable understanding of the progress of the reformation in England, Scotland and Ireland. This chapter contains commentary on the newly established Protestant 'sects' such as the Quakers, Independents and Brownists.[89] Bruodinus provides interesting miscellanea in this chapter, such as his story about Fr John O'Hehir, a native of Thomond, whom along with other Irish Catholics had gone to New England in America and witnessed the preaching of Anne Hutchinson, a religious reformer who became prominent in the so-called Antinomian Controversy. Bruodinus' story confirms that not only was there a community of Irish Catholics settled in New England at this early period, but that some had connections with County Clare.[90]

He also refers to Thomas Good, English academic and clergyman, and appears to have been familiar with the writings of John Coppinger, an Irish cleric from Cork. In another example, Bruodinus mentions that he had in his hands a manuscript of the Tipperary priest and historian Seathrún Céitinn (Geoffrey Keating) which he calls *manuscripta Hibernica historia Doctoris Ketten*.[91] This was Céitinn's popular work which is more commonly titled in Irish *Foras Feasa ar Éirinn* (Foundation of Knowledge on Ireland).[92] Bruodinus' reference to it indicates that he not only read popular works in Irish but that he was using copies of such works in Prague as reference material. Even his incursion into the field of Czech etymology suggests more than a casual acquaintance with the language of his host country.[93] His writings contain evidence of the intellectual interests of Irish Franciscan scholars and graduates from the Irish colleges on the continent. From this perspective, his writings serve as a way to understand the mental world of a Gaelic-Irish Franciscan imbued in ecclesiastical, Latin and Gaelic scholarship.

89. Bruodinus, *Propugnaculum*, pp. 588–618.
90. Ibid., pp. 611–12.
91. On all references to Céitinn see ibid., pp. 770, 807, 909, 912, 924, 936, 950, 1086.
92. On this important text and its role in shaping a distinctive Irish Catholic identity see Bernadette Cunningham, '*Foras Feasa Ar Éirinn* and the Historical Origins of Irish Catholic Identity', *New Hibernia Review / Iris Éireannach Nua*, vol. 5, no. 4, winter 2001, pp. 144–7.
93. Pařez and Kuchařová, *Irish Franciscans Prague*, p. 82.

Bruodinus' scholarly achievements among others, combined with his considerable personal abilities, ensured that he rose quickly in the Franciscan communities where he lived. His election as guardian of the Franciscan friaries of Olomouc (1663), Our Lady of the Snows in Prague (1668) and Jindřichův Hradec (1672) stand testimony to his administrative ability.[94] He appears to have been a noted teacher and his students included Fr Bernard Sannig who became a professor of theology, vicar general of the Franciscan order, and one of the most important Czech theologians of the baroque period.

Some of Bruodinus' administrative activities in Prague can be recounted from his writings. By his own admission he contributed to the material well-being of the Franciscans in Prague, and while serving three years as guardian of Our Lady of the Snows he helped secure its financial stability. As proof of his prudent financial management, he includes in *Anatomicum* an inventory, witnessed on 23 November 1670, which details the condition of the convent and lists its repairs and the gifts from benefactors. Among the repairs undertaken was the erection of buildings and a chapel, a large crypt, an infirmary, a pharmacy, a granary and the equipping of a school, all undertaken at Bruodinus' instigation.

Some historians have criticised Bruodinus, portraying him as responsible for sowing discord among the friars of the Bohemian province, being unruly and even antagonistic, while suggesting that his works were not accurate and cannot be relied upon.[95] Such views persist, with one recent author dismissively describing Bruodinus as a 'maverick'.[96] These comments have been made in the absence of a considered and detailed assessment of his writings. On closer examination, it is clear that he was a scholarly figure and a capable administrator who left an impressive array of theological, philosophical and historical works.

What sets him apart from his contemporaries is the energy he devoted to publishing his books, many of which contain miscellanea

94. Ibid., pp. 76–9.

95. In fact, the historical record indicates that it was his cousin, Bonaventure, who was regarded as 'always ... a disturbing element'. See Benignus Millett, 'Calendar of Volume 3 (1672–5) of the "Scritture riferite nei congressi, Irlanda", in Propaganda Archives: Part I, ff. 1–200', *Collectanea Hibernica*, vols 18/19, 1976/7, pp. 40–71, at p. 43.

96. Kevin Whelan, *Religion, Landscape and Settlement in Ireland: From Patrick to present* (Dublin, 2018), p. 110, n.19.

about Ireland not found in comparable works. His success rested on securing aristocratic patronage to finance his publications, and it is notable that the Šternberk family, to whom he dedicated *Anatomicum*, financed his principal work, *Propugnaculum Catholicae Veritatis*.[97] The Šternberks, like other Bohemian nobles, had cultivated close relations with the Irish Franciscans. The Irish friars served as tutors to the sons of Czech nobles and in return some of these renowned Czech families sought burial in the Irish Franciscan church and bequeathed donations to the Irish community.[98] We can assume that Bruodinus had developed links to the Šternberks and it is understood that the Irish in Prague harboured sympathy towards the Czechs whose plight in the German-speaking Habsburg Empire reflected their own subjection by the English.

Bruodinus was an influential figure among the Franciscans and Irish exiles in the imperial lands of central Europe. He was by specialisation a Scotist theologian and he supplemented his lectures with prolific writing. As perhaps was fitting, his first publication was a book devoted to Scotist theology. It was printed in two volumes during the years 1663 and 1664.[99] During 1667 and 1668 he completed his *magnum opus*, titled *Propugnaculum Catholicae Veritatis* (Prague, 1669), which must have been of unique, if not peculiar interest to his Czech students, in that it relates many particulars about Ireland. For example, in *Propugnaculum* he includes a detailed description of the counties of Ireland and a chapter titled *De Brieni Regis Interitu* (Destruction of the O'Brien Kingdom), parts of which drew on his family's chronicles.[100] He mentions a curious story which also appears earlier in Seathrún Céitinn's *Foras Feasa ar Éirinn* about the claim that Donnchadh, son of Brian Bóroimhe, was the progenitor of the 'Pueraigh', 'Planchedigh' and 'Jusdasaigh' families (that is, Power, Plunkett and Eustace).[101] According to Céitinn, this doubtful claim is only substantiated in a single poem composed by Maoilín Óg

97. For example his principal work, *Propugnaculum Catholicae Veritatis* (1669), was dedicated to Venceslao, Joanni and Ignatio (Jan and Ignác Václav), counts of Šternberk, who financed the cost of printing. See Bruodinus, *Propugnaculum*, preface.

98. Pařez and Kuchařová, *Irish Franciscans Prague*, pp. 20–1.

99. Antonius Bruodinus, *Oecodomia Minoriticae Scholae Salomonis Doctoris Subtilis quadraginta quinque columnis sustenata* (Prague, 1663); Antonius Bruodinus, *Oecodomia Minoriticae Scholae Salomonis Doctoris Subtilis* (Prague, 1664).

100. Bruodinus, *Propugnaculum*, pp. 924–37. On the description of the counties see pp. 952–1068.

101. Ibid., pp. 930, 1079. Also see Keating, *Foras Feasa* (vol. III), p. 293.

Mac Bruaideadha, a kinsman of Bruodinus and the likely source for Bruodinus' comments.[102]

Propugnaculum was an impressive undertaking, one that was envisaged to have consisted of ten books, but only five were eventually completed. It serves as an almanac on the history of heresy, culminating in lengthy descriptions of the killing and martyrdom of Irish Catholics by English forces. His catalogue of Irish martyrs under Henry VIII, Edward VI, Elizabeth I and James I contains notices of around two hundred martyrs. It seems likely that in listing these he was attempting a similar work to David Rothe's *Analecta* (1617–19).[103] Bruodinus made use of writers such as Luke Wadding and the notable Jesuit historiographer Philippe Alegambe. His list of Irish martyrs in part relied on a manuscript compiled by Matthew Magrath, the vicar-general of Killaloe, which was brought to the Irish Franciscans of Prague in 1660 by Daniel Conry (Domhnall Ó Maolchonaire), a native of Thomond.[104] It would appear that he also based his list on personal connections who had first-hand accounts of persecutions of clergy and indiscriminate killings by the Cromwellian forces.

In writing *Propugnaculum* Bruodinus marshalled a long list of sources. His reference to Maurice Conry's *Threnodia Hiberno-Catholica*, shows that wherever available he consulted written material rather than solely relying on oral reports and stories. Conry's *Threnodia* was part of a genre of printed pamphlets and books that were circulating on the continent in order to make Catholics aware of the suffering and persecution of their co-religionists in Ireland. Bruodinus had at his disposal other material such as a *vita* of the martyr John Kearney, written by Joseph Sall OFM and Canon Geoffrey Sall.[105] He also drew from a copy of a rare pamphlet, *Sanguinea Eremus Martyrum Hiberniae Ord. Eremit S.P. Augustinii*, which was printed by an Augustinian, James O'Mahony, in 1655, possibly in Brussels.[106] This is seldom found among the works of other writers of the seventeenth century.

102. On this see Meidhbhín Ní Úrdail, 'A Poem on the Adventures Abroad and Death of Donnchadh Son of Brian Bóraimhe', *Zeitschrift für celtische Philologie*, vol. 59, 2012, pp. 169–99.
103. Edited and republished by Patrick F. Moran, *The Analecta of David Rothe, Bishop of Ossory* (Dublin, 1884).
104. Frost, *History*, p. 553. Also see Corish and Millett (eds), *Irish Martyrs*, p. 199. Conry belonged to the well-known learned family of Ó Maolchonaire, who kept a school of chronicling at Ardkyle near Bunratty, in County Clare.
105. O'Molony, *Anatomicum*, p. 258.
106. F.X. Martin, 'Sanguinea Eremus Martyrum Hiberniae Ord. Eremit S.P. Augustini (1655)', *Archivium Hibernicum*, vol. 15, 1950, pp. 74–91, at p. 77.

Propugnaculum provides an important account of the Confederate and Cromwellian wars in Ireland, during which Bruodinus' family suffered considerably. We should take many of Bruodinus' references to priests and religious killed in Thomond as originating from first-hand statements by Thomond exiles, several of whom resided in Prague and Vienna.[107] Members of his own family feature, such as Dermit Bruodin of Moynoe who, along with six others, died when the house they occupied near Scariff was burned by Cromwellian forces.[108] Bruodinus' writings were not only focused on these matters; in 1669 he made an interesting contribution to the field of Franciscan hagiography by publishing a work about the life of the Spanish Franciscan Pedro de Alcántara, titled *Synopsis vitae, virtutum et miraculorum S. Petri de Alcantara*.[109] This relatively modest work of forty-eight pages was published in 1669, the same year as *Propugnaculum*.

In 1676 Bruodinus produced a theological work titled *Armamentarium Theologicum ad mentem Doctoris Subtilis, in quatuor deambulacra distinctum, officinis auctum repositoriis secretis accumulatum & sectionibus divisum* (Prague).[110] In the preface, Bruodinus claimed that he was responsible for introducing Scotist philosophy and theology to Bohemia.[111] We know from this work that Bruodinus was well placed to be regarded as a leading figure in Scotist theology, having lectured on the subject and subsequently written two books.[112] Bruodinus' claims about his role in introducing Scotist theology to Bohemia might be overstated but certainly his students, among whom was the esteemed Franciscan theologian Bernard Sannig, became some of the finest contemporary proponents of Scotist theology.[113]

107. O'Molony, *Anatomicum*, pp. 35–8, 125. His cousin Bonaventure Bruodin taught philosophy and theology for twelve years at the archbishop's seminary in Prague, and from 1651 to 1654 he lectured theology at the friary of Our Lady of Snows in Prague. See Millett, *Irish Franciscans*, p. 152 and G. Cleary, *Father Luke Wadding and St Isidore's College, Rome: Biographical and historical notes and documents* (Rome, 1925), pp. 153–6.

108. Bruodinus, *Propugnaculum*, p. 717.

109. Antonius Bruodinus, *Synopsis vitae, virtutum, et miraculorum S. Petri de Alcantara (A synopsis of the life, virtues and miracles of St Pedro de Alcántara)* (Prague). Pedro de Alcantara (1499–1562) was a Spanish Franciscan who was proclaimed a saint in 1669 and was noted for his austerity and poverty and his preaching to the poor.

110. The translation of the first part reads: 'A Theological Arsenal for the Mind of a Subtle Doctor'.

111. Pařez and Kuchařová, *Irish Franciscans Prague*, p. 85.

112. See Antonius Bruodinus, *Oecodomia Minoriticae Scholae Salomonis Doctoris Subtilis quadraginta quinque columnis sustenata* (Prague, 1663), and Antonius Bruodinus, *Oecodomia Minoriticae Scholae Salomonis Doctoris Subtilis* (Prague, 1664).

113. O'Molony, *Anatomicum*, pp. 197–8.

What may have been regarded as Bruodinus' last work was published under the title *Descriptio Regni Hiberniae Sanctorum insulae, et de prima origine miseriarum & motuum in Anglia, Scotia et Hibernia, regnante Carolo Primo Rege* (Rome, 1721).[114] The authorship of the work has yet to be verified, but it is thought to be largely based on a text by Bruodinus, which he may have prepared for publication before his death. It contains a chapter on martyred Catholic clerics which drew heavily on events in County Clare.[115] This work was edited by the son of Phelim O'Neill who himself was an *émigré*, so it is not clear if it represented a separate or unfinished work left by Bruodinus. In the *approbatio* to the work, Bruodinus is erroneously referred to as 'Antonius Prondinus'. In what perhaps was an exercise in nostalgia and with a nod to its editor's own lineage, the book contains the funerary epitaph engraved on the tomb of Hugh (d. 1609), baron of Dungannon, eldest son of Aodh Mór Ó Neill (d. 1616), at San Pietro church in Montorio, Rome.[116]

Bruodinus died on 7 May 1680 during an outbreak of plague in Prague in which a number of Irish friars succumbed, including a fellow friar from Thomond, Joannes Clancy.[117] The exact cause of Bruodinus' death was recorded as *phthisis*, indicating that he died from tuberculosis, and it is thought that he was buried in an unmarked grave in the city.[118]

114. Translation reads: 'A Description of the Kingdom of Ireland, Island of Saints, and about the first source of miseries and troubles in England, Scotland and Ireland during the reign of King Charles the first'.
115. Antonius Bruodinus, *Descriptio Regni Hiberniae Sanctorum insulae, et de prima origine miseriarum & motuum in Anglia, Scotia et Hibernia, regnante Carolo Primo Rege* (Rome, 1721), pp. 101, 103–4. In particular he mentions three clerics: 'Daniel de Clanchy' (i.e. Clancy); 'Dionysius de Nelan' (i.e. Donough Neylan) of Kilraghtis parish who hid at the house of 'Laurentii de Neherenny' (i.e. Laurence MacInerheny) but was captured and executed at Inchicronan; and cleric 'Taddeaus de Carighy' (i.e. Teige Carrigy).
116. Ibid., pp. 107–8.
117. Benignus Millett, 'Some Lists of Irish Franciscans in Prague, 1656-1791', *Collectanea Hibernica*, vols 36–7, 1994–5, pp. 59–84, at p. 63.
118. I wish to thank Martin Breen of Ruan, County Clare, for his advice on this point, which was communicated to him in 2014 by Jan Pařez, curator of the manuscript collection of the Strahov Library, Prague.

THOMAS CARVE (ALIAS CAREW OR CARRANE)

The other protagonist of the contention was the secular priest and ostensibly Old-Englishman, Fr Thomas Carve. A well-travelled and insightful observer of some of the most important events during the Thirty Years War, Carve was born in 1590 in south Tipperary. Of his early life, some facts are known, thanks mainly to his own writing.[119] He spent his early life at Mobarnan in the parish of Magorban which, he informs us, is situated one Germanic mile east of Cashel.[120] This is confirmed on the title page of his work *Lyra*, which refers to him as *Thomas Carve de Mobernan, Tipperariensis*. We are fortunate that his work *Enchiridion* contains a note about his early life of which otherwise few specific details are known:

> *Reverendum Dominum Patrem Thomam Carve Sacerdotem & Pronotarium Apostolicum nobili stemmate & parentibus ex legitimo thoro a praenobili & strenuo Domino Malachia Carve de Mobernan & Domina Johanna nata Buttlerin de Cnocraphon binis conjugibus in Tipperariensi Comitatu in Hibernia ortum, natum, & honestum educatum esse.*[121]

> [Rev. Master Father Thomas Carve, a priest and apostolic protonotary with a noble ancestry and with parents who contracted legitimate marriage, originated, was born and was educated as an honest man in County Tipperary in Ireland by the two spouses, Master Malachia Carve of Mobarnan, a very noble and energetic man, and Lady Johanna, born Butler of Knockgraffon].

Carve's ties to the Butlers of Knockgraffon, south of Cashel, derived from his mother's lineage. He was close to the Butlers and several of his publications were dedicated to James Butler, marquis (and first duke) of Ormond (d. 1688). It was to people in these circles that Carve was linked. He was aware of notable persons connected to the house of Ormond, such as the celebrated doctor and poet Dermot O'Meara, who composed a eulogy on the death of Thomas Butler, earl of

119. On an informative overview of the life and activities of Thomas Carve see Kerney, *Itinerarium Thomæ Carve*, pp. iii–x. A bibliography of his works is found at pp. xi–xii.
120. Equivalent to about 7.4 kilometres.
121. Carve, *Enchiridion*, pp. 135–6.

Ormond, in 1615. Carve was acquainted with the eulogy, noting that it appeared in a short but excellent book called *Ormonius*.[122]

Born in Mobarnan in the plain of Fethard, Carve probably received his education locally. Bruodinus, in his invective against him, reveals interesting details about Carve's early life and background in Tipperary. Carve's paternal family were well established in Mobarnan and his nephew, Conald O'Carran, was a local schoolmaster. Carve informs us that his nephew, by right of postliminy, received proprietorship of an estate formerly held by the family.[123] Carve, in seeking to refute Bruodinus' claims that Conald was but a plebeian pedagogue who taught simple Latin to 'stupid and ignorant' students, maintained that Conald's ancestors were 'governors' and they were recorded as such in official documents. Conald kept a school where he taught rhetoric and poetry; he was capable of teaching the latter in both Irish and English.

In writing about his nephew, Carve says that the Franciscans and other notable persons requested that Conald become a schoolmaster because the friars were not permitted to teach openly. Under the patronage of the duke of Ormond, Conald was permitted to teach humanities, motivated by an honest and pious motive to ensure that the Catholic youth were not corrupted by attending non-Catholic schools.[124] Mobarnan, the family's patrimony, appears in the Civil Survey of 1654–6 as the property of 'Teige Carran' who may have been a brother to Carve. In the 1665–6 Hearth Money Rolls, Mobarnan was recorded as held by 'Connell Carne', who was almost certainly Carve's schoolmaster-nephew, and possibly Teige's son.[125] If Conald did indeed receive his estate by right of postliminy, it would square with the fact that he was in possession of it after the 1662 *Act of Settlement*, as Mobarnan was restored to 'Teige Carrue alias O Carron' in 1663, following its earlier forfeiture.[126]

122. Carve, *Lyra seu Anacephalaeosis*, p. 355. Also see Keith Sidwell and David Edwards (eds), *The Tipperary Hero: Dermot O'Meara's Ormonius (1615)* (Turnhout, 2011). The epic poem *Ormonius* consists of nearly 4,000 hexameters on the military career of the tenth earl of Ormond, Thomas Butler.
123. Carve, *Responsio*, p. 138.
124. Ibid., p. 143.
125. Thomas Laffan, *Tipperary Families: Being the hearth money records for 1665–6–7* (Dublin, 1911), p. 11 [Mobearbane *recte* Mobarnan].
126. Geraldine Tallon (ed.), *Court of Claims: Submissions and evidence, 1663* (Dublin, 2006).

Thomas Carve knew and spoke Irish and his writings display knowledge of the logic that governs the translation of Irish names into English. Carve divulges this in *Lyra* when discussing the Irish annals, noting that he had read Irish manuscripts which he regarded as authoritative and reliable.[127] Moreover, Carve remarks that he had read Irish history 'most trustworthily reported in written form in Irish manuscripts ... in the very ancient gymnasium of Burgess whose prefect was at that time Doctor Roger Craheus'.[128] This statement by Carve is a rare reference to the bardic school run by the Clann Chraith (MacGraths) at Burgess in south Tipperary which, if we take Carve at his word, was convened by Ruadhrí Mac Craith in the early seventeenth century.[129] From this it can be concluded that Carve was not necessarily hostile to Gaelic scholarship *per se*. His negative comments were made in direct response to criticisms from Bruodinus, suggesting that he had a circumscribed interest in this form of scholarship – especially the panegyric poetry of the bardic poets. What is clear from his writings is that he regarded Latin learning and literature as superior to Gaelic learning.

Arguments over Carve's ancestry inflamed the contention with Bruodinus which had become characterised by barbed comments and semantic quips. In *Enchiridion*, Carve wrote that he was of Anglo-Norman lineage, tracing his ancestry back to Thomas Carve (or Carew), an Anglo-Norman lord whose estate in Desmond was inherited by an ancestor of the Fitzgerald family before the year 1467.[130] In an earlier work he stated that the family name was 'incorrectly called Carran in Irish idiom' (*abusive Hibernico idiomate Carran appellantur*), and that illustrious members of the family dwelt at Mobarnan.[131] Bruodinus, however, dismissed all such claims, instead providing Carve with an alternative progenitor, Tomás Ó Corráin (from *corrán*, denoting a sickle in Irish) who, Bruodinus asserted, 'sacrilegiously cut off the

127. Carve, *Lyra seu Anacephalaeosis*, p. 2.
128. Ibid. *Craheus* is a Latinisation of Mac Craith (MacGrath).
129. On the bardic school run by the Clann Chraith in south Tipperary see Luke McInerney and Caroline Smiddy, 'The Clann Chraith Bardic School of Burgess, South Tipperary', in Luke McInerney and Katharine Simms (eds), *Gaelic Ireland (c. 600–c. 1700), Lordship, Saints and Learning: Essays for the Irish Chiefs' and Clans' Prize in History* (Dublin: Wordwell Books, 2021), pp. 153–73.
130. Carve, *Enchiridion*, p. 85. Also see the same claim, made decades earlier, in Carve, *Lyra seu Anacephalaeosis Hibernica*, pp. 45–6.
131. Ibid., p. 47.

arm of the most saintly Bishop Lachtín'. Carve's family, according to Bruodinus, infamously attained the dubious honour of having the cognomen Ó Corráin (descendant of a sickle-man), owing to the malicious action of their ancestor.

This pretext was invented by Bruodinus in order to foist upon Carve a lowly occupation appropriate to someone of plebeian Gaelic, rather than Anglo-Norman, origin. Bruodinus first made this claim in *Propugnaculum*[132] and thereafter he refers to Carve as 'Carran'. In that work he declares the arm of Lachtín was enclosed in a silver case and preserved in the church of Kilnamona in Thomond before it was stolen by a sacristan and brought to County Kerry, where it was venerated at Lislaughtin, near Tarbert, until the reformation.[133] The claim about the violent amputation of Lachtín's arm has no historical basis and nothing about the saint's life refers to this violent act. However, Bruodinus appears to be correct in associating the saint's relics with Kilnamona church. Nineteenth-century Ordnance Survey maps mark a place nearby called Autkeenlaughteen (*Áit Chinn Lachtín*, 'head place of Lachtín') which would suggest a place or shrine where a reliquary once stood.[134]

Bruodinus' doubt about Carve's ancestry had some basis in fact. Carve's father was Malachy which is from the Gaelic-Irish name Maolsheachlain, a name rarely encountered among the descendants of Anglo-Normans in Munster. A 'Melaghlen Roe O'Carren' appears as the late owner of lands in 'Ballenwillen alias Miltown in the Crosse' in 1591, a place located nine kilometres south of Carve's birthplace of Mobarnan.[135] This could have been the father of Carve, who went by the Gaelic appellation 'roe' (*rua*, red). Mobarnan was the family's hereditary estate and it first appears in a grant from 1518 documenting that it was transferred to 'Cornelius son of Thatheus Karrayn' by John O'Hadyan.[136] We might take it that Cornelius (Conchobhar) and Thatheus (Tadhg) were Carve's direct forebears, living two or three generations before him. Six years later other members of the family were transacting land agreements to the north around Foulkstown.

132. Bruodinus, *Propugnaculum*, p. 985.
133. Ibid.
134. On Lachtín's life and his twelfth-century arm-shaped reliquary (*Lámh Laichtín*) which was associated with the church of Donaghmore in County Cork, see Pádraig Ó Riain, *A Dictionary of Irish Saints* (Dublin, 2011), pp. 387–8.
135. Edmund Curtis, *Calendar of Ormond Deeds, 1584–1603*, vol. 6 (Dublin, 1970), p. 46.
136. Edmund Curtis, *Calendar of Ormond Deeds, 1509–47*, vol. 4 (Dublin, 1937), p. 53.

Nothing about these names or grants suggests Anglo-Norman ancestry which Carve claimed for his family.

The fact that the Fiant Rolls record a pardon issued to Donald O'Carrane of 'Mobernayne' in 1586 indicates that the family were indeed called Ó Corráin.[137] Other sources confirm this. A request lodged in the Court of Claims for 1663 for the restitution of Mobarnan notes that it was forfeited by 'Teige Carrue alias O Carron'.[138] This was Teige Carran who occupied an estate at Mobarnan and its 433 plantation acres in 1640. It was in his possession, according to the Civil Survey of 1654–6, by virtue of 'descent from his ancestors' and he also possessed a small castle.[139] As further proof, we read that a 'Conor Carve' (alias 'Carew') of Mobarnan was counted among the personnel of the general assemblies of the Confederate Catholics during the 1640s. He was one of the minor landholders who were members of the Confederation and whose estate at Mobarnan amounted to some 479 acres, and it is reasonable to think that he shared close family ties with both Teige and Thomas Carve.[140] Conor's membership of the Confederation is perhaps surprising on account of the fact that Thomas Carve cultivated links with, and dedicated books to, the Ormond Butlers who were staunch royalists.

All these references serve as strong proof that the name Carew (or Carrue) was adopted as a synonym of the original Gaelic-Irish surname Ó Corráin and that they were well established at Mobarnan. The family were prominent in the locality and also further south around Clonmel, where they are attested in records from the mid-fourteenth century as 'betaghs' (*biataigh*, or food-renderers).[141] Conversely, Ballycarron, situated southwest of Cashel, is not derived

137. See K.W. Nicholls (ed.), *The Irish Fiants of the Tudor Sovereigns: during the reigns of Henry VIII, Edward VI, Philip and Mary, and Elizabeth I* (Dublin, 1994) [no. 4935]. The same fiant also records 'Peirs Butler, of Knockgraffon, gent.', who was likely a relation of Thomas Carve's mother.

138. Tallon (ed.), *Court of Claims* (Dublin, 2006).

139. T. Corcoran, 'The Civil Survey of Tipperary, 1654–1655', *Studies: An Irish quarterly review*, vol. 23, no. 90, 1934, pp. 323–9, at p. 328. Corcoran held the view that Thomas Carve was of this O'Corran or Carew branch of Mobarnan. It is believed that the castle of Mobarnan was incorporated into Mobarnane House, an eighteenth-century Georgian house, which still stands.

140. John Cregan,'The Confederate Catholics of Ireland: The Personnel of the Confederation, 1642–1649', *Irish Historical Studies*, vol. 29, no. 116, 1995, pp. 490–512, at p. 503.

141. Edmund Curtis, *Calendar of Ormond Deeds, 1172–1350*, vol. 1 (Dublin, 1932), p. 275. Betaghs were vassals or tenants who rendered food dues to an overlord and were typically of middle or low social rank and of Gaelic background. Other references to Carrans in the 1659 'census' and in the hearth money rolls of *c.* 1665 contain anglicised Gaelic-Irish forenames such as Connor and Donogh. The surnames Carren (8) and Carrane (34) were popular in Middlethird barony in 1659. See Pender (ed.), *Census*, p. 309.

from *Baile Uí Chorráin* but from *Béal Átha Cáirthinn* (ford of the Rowan tree), and attests the name is unconnected with Uí Chorráin hereditary lands.

In Carve's final work, *Responsio veridica ad illotum libellum cui nomen Anatomicum Examen* (1672), he offered extraordinary 'evidence' about his family's nobility. He claimed that his brother Ross was knighted and married Anne Hyde, sister to earl Hyde, the chancellor of England, and that a daughter of the earl married the duke of York, brother to the king of Germany, and later King James II.[142] In fact this claim was not new and first appeared in his work *Lyra seu Anacephalaeosis Hibernica* where he claimed that Ross Carve, who was knighted, was of Mobarnan where Carve himself was born, and that another 'gilded' member of the family, Robert Carve, was of Imokilly.[143] Carve's claim in *Responsio* was somewhat misleading as the earl Hyde (that is, Edward Hyde, earl of Clarendon) was a nephew to Ann Hyde's father Nicolas (*c.* 1572–1631), who himself was not the chancellor of England but rather the chief justice. Nevertheless, these claimed illustrious connections are presented in a matter-of-fact way that is not altogether convincing, considering the status and property of the family at Mobarnan.[144]

142. Carve, *Responsio*, pp. 138–9.

143. Carve, *Lyra seu Anacephalaeosis Hibernica*, p. 47. Carve wrote the following in respect of his claimed connections: *Praeter hos alia est antiquae nobilitatis domus nimirum Domini Carue Imakellanse, qui a Thomas Carue (de quo paulo ante tractavimus) suam protrahit parentelam, ex qua etiam aliae non ignobiles familiae excreverunt, quae abusive Hibernico idiomate Carran appellantur. Ex his orti sunt Robertus Carve de Imakelly, & Roseus Carve de Mobernan equites aurati* ['In addition to these, there is another house of ancient nobility, namely that of Master Carve of Imokilly, who is genealogically related to Thomas Carve (about whom we spoke a few paragraphs above). From this house, other families of no insignificant nobility also descended, which are incorrectly called "Carran" in Irish idiom. From these families were born the gilded knights Robert Carve of Imokilly and Ross Carve of Mobernane'].

144. There is a Latin memorial stone in Westminster Abbey erected to Dame Anne Carey which translates: 'Anne, daughter of Nicholas Hyde Kt., chief justice of England, wife of Ross Carey (who, deserving most highly of his country on the expedition to Rhé, and being adorned with the title of knight banneret, yet further adorned that title), is buried here. Once Britain was restored to Charles, once Charles was restored to Britain, Anne joyfully yielded up her soul on 23 August in her 50th year and year of salvation 1660'. There is a record of a knighthood conferred on 'Rosse Carey' in Ireland on 26 October 1629. However, whether there was an actual connection to Carve and Sir Ross Carey seems doubtful. See W.A. Shaw, *The Knights of England: A complete record from the earliest time to the present day of the knights of all the orders of chivalry in England, Scotland, and Ireland ...*, vol. 2 (London, 1906), p. 196. Sir Ross Carey appears in a petition to King Charles I in 1632 which mentions his role in the expeditions to Cadiz, Rhé and Rochelle. He died in 1641 and was buried at St Andrew's in Holborn, London, where the parish register calls him an Irish gentleman. See John Bruce (ed.), *Calendar of State Papers, Domestic Series, of the Reign of Charles I*, vol. 5 (London, 1862), p. 472. On his burial and the mixed usage of 'Carey' and 'Carew' by Sir Ross's wife, see Joseph Lemuel Chester (ed.), *The Marriage, Baptismal, and Burial Registers of the Collegiate Church or Abbey of St Peter* (London, 1876), p. 152.

Upon ordination Carve ministered in the diocese of Leighlin within the archdiocese of Cashel where, it was alleged by Bruodinus, he unlawfully left his parish for Germany. Whatever the reason for his departure, and Bruodinus insinuated that he left under suspicious circumstances, it seems that when he left, he adopted the surname Carve, something for which Bruodinus admonishes him, stating that no member of his family, including his schoolmaster nephew, ever called themselves anything but O'Carran. Carve appears to have been related to another priest from Cashel called Fr James O'Carran who converted to Protestantism and was the subject of derision by Bruodinus.[145] In submitting further evidence that Carve's family were really O'Carrans and of Gaelic-Irish rather than Old-English stock, Bruodinus dubbed Fr James O'Carran a 'Puritan heretic', and wryly noted that instead of taking an English girl as his 'maid and bed partner', he took only an Irish one. The point of Bruodinus' derision was to show that Carve himself was an imposter who had assumed an Old-English background when in fact he and his ancestors were Gaelic-Irish.

Carve was well travelled and his departure from Ireland in 1630 when he wrote *Itinerarium* was not his first journey abroad. He seems to have first gone abroad in 1624 when he was appointed chaplain to Colonel Walter Butler of Ballinakill.[146] He visited Prague around this time, as can be evinced from his description of Wallenstein's palace in the city, which he saw.[147] Carve's appointment as chaplain enabled him to gain access to elevated circles among the Irish in the Habsburg forces and from his own account in *Itinerarium* he was well-connected. His patrons, Colonel Walter Butler along with Walter Devereux, who Carve was later to serve as chaplain, were implicated in the notorious

145. Fr James O'Carran has not been positively traced but he was probably the James Carey who was noted as a convert to Protestantism from Catholicism. Rev. Carey ministered in the diocese of Meath and Dublin. He was rector of Stackallan, County Meath in 1637 and commonwealth minister of St. Bride's in 1656, 'on account of his ability to preach the Word in English and Irish', and on account of his usefulness in converting the 'ignorant natives' he was ordered to preach 'in St Bride's every Lord's Day and occassionally repair to Trim at a salary of £60'. See J.B. Leslie, *Clergy of Dublin & Glendalough: Biographical succession lists* (Belfast, 2001), p. 462.

146. The dating in the original is 1634 but it appears to be a typographical error and ought to read 1624. See Kerney, *Itinerarium Thomæ Carve*, pp. iv–v.

147. David Worthington, 'Toward a Bibliography of the Irish in central Europe, 1618–48', *Archivium Hibericum*, vol. 56, 2002, pp. 206–27, at p. 214.

assassination of Albrecht von Wallenstein in February 1634.[148] This act immediately made the Irish an influential if not controversial element in the Habsburg forces. It can be surmised that his connection to Colonel Butler was procured through his mother's family, the Butlers of Knockgraffon, and his links to the earl of Ormond, insofar as they were invoked, were through distant kinship. Carve served four years with Colonel Walter Butler's regiment in Austria before returning to Ireland. He set out again for the continent in 1630 to serve once more with Colonel Butler, showing that he had a great attachment to the man. On the death of the colonel on Christmas Day 1634, Carve's ties to his long-standing patron were evident when he personally officiated at Butler's funeral mass.

On the death of Butler, Carve transferred his services to Walter Devereux. In 1640, he was appointed chaplain to the English, Scotch and Irish forces in Austria. He held that position until 1643 when he was made a vicar-choral of the cathedral of St Stephen in Vienna. From this time Carve appears to have settled permanently in Vienna where he continued to publish. Bruodinus' comment in *Anatomicum* that Carve was involved in the arrangements for his niece's marriage to a comber in the city suggests that he may have had family living in Vienna.

Carve's first work, *Itinerarium,* was written based on his eye-witness experience of the Thirty Years Wars.[149] Described as a terse and dramatically phrased work, it was nonetheless a considerable achievement and provides a rich description of people and events. In *Itinerarium,* Carve included rare details and happenings such as the dialogue between the Swedish king, Gustavus Adolphus, and Colonel Walter Butler at the siege and capture of Frankfurt-on-Oder in 1631.[150] On these grounds alone *Itinerarium* stands as a work of insight and observation, not only about the happenings of the Catholic imperial forces, but also of military life through the eyes of an Irish cleric.

148. On Walter Butler's involvement see Mary M. Macken, 'Wallenstein and Butler: 1634–1934', *Studies: An Irish quarterly review*, vol. 23, no. 92, 1934, pp. 593–610. Also see Dagmar Ó Riain-Raedel, 'The Man from Roscrea: Famous or infamous?', in Peter Harbison and Valerie A. Hall (eds), *A Carnival of Learning: Essays to honour George Cunningham and his 50 conferences on medieval Ireland in the Cistercian abbey of Mount St Joseph, Roscrea, 1987–2012* (Roscrea, 2012), pp. 163–72.
149. On the Irish contribution to the war see John Hennig, 'Irish Soldiers in the Thirty Years War', *JRSAI*, vol. 82, no. 1, 1952, pp. 28–36.
150. T. Corcoran, 'A Man of Action: Action for Irish Catholic education three centuries ago. I: Walter Butler of Roscrea', *Irish Monthly*, vol. 63, no. 741, 1935, pp. 181–90, at p. 184.

Carve narrates his travels and those of the regiment to which he was attached through Germany, Bohemia and Poland. He was not the first Irish cleric to write about his service during the Thirty Years War; the Jesuit Henry Fitzsimon produced two works about his life as a priest and confessor in the imperial forces in 1621.[151] Nevertheless, Carve's descriptions are adroit, proving his aptitude for perceptive commentary.

His fondness for his patrons, the Butlers, is evident in the preface and dedication of *Itinerarium*. In no uncertain terms he explains his *raison d'être* for writing the work and its focus on the military exploits of Colonel Walter Butler: 'I was also myself very much touched by the domestic funeral of my esteemed Butler … having been always treated by him as a brother, having always respected him as a father.'[152] The first part of *Itinerarium* was published in 1639 and dedicated to James Butler, earl of Ormond, and in vivid detail Carve recounts the toil which he endured in writing it: 'not in the quiet chamber of study has it been composed, but beneath the tents of war, where my busy pen found no peace from the ominous clangour of the hoarse trumpet and the loud roll of the battle-drum'.[153] His attachment to the Butlers of Ormond is again evident at the end of the second edition of *Itinerarium* (1641) where he includes a chapter titled '*Series Butlerianae Prosapiae*'.[154] In this account of the Butler lineage, he enumerates different branches of the family, including the Knockgraffon branch from which he claimed maternal descent.[155]

The work contains a number of fascinating and valuable accounts, not least its report on the assassination of Wallenstein by Colonel Walter Butler. For this reason *Itinerarium* has been a work of considerable interest for historians of seventeenth-century Germany.[156] Its 1854 re-publication included an engraving of Carve which originally

151. Worthington, 'Towards a Bibliography', pp. 210–11.
152. Translated in Francis Prendergast, 'An Authentic Account of the Death of Wallenstein: With a vindication of the motives of Colonel Walter Butler', *Transactions of the Kilkenny Archaeological Society*, vol. 2, no. 1, 1852, pp. 9–32, at p. 27.
153. Kerney, *Itinerarium Thomæ Carve*, pp. vi–vii.
154. Thomas Carve, *Itinerarii R.D. Thomae Carve Tipperariensis, Sacellani Maioris Anglorum, Scotorum, & Hybernorum in exercitu Caesareo militantium pars II. cui sub finem accedunt vindiciae In Momos authoris item paucula quaedam de Butleriana prosapia* (Kutz, 1641), pp. 363–70. In the reference to the Knockgraffon Butlers, Carve writes that they were related to 'Thomas Butler the lame', who was an illustrious member of the family.
155. Ibid., p. 365.
156. Leopold von Ranke, *Geschichte Wallensteins* (Leipzig, 1870).

featured in his other work, *Lyra seu Anacephalaeosis Hibernica* (1651).[157] This is the only known image of Carve, who was around sixty years old at the time of its composition, and was a point of derision for Bruodinus, who commented on Carve's long beard. *Itinerarium* contains interesting miscellanea, including an account of Carve's visit to London, while on his journey to Gravesend en route for Hamburg in 1630. He explains that he finally reached Germany via an intrepid journey from Gdansk where he was received by the Dominicans, to Wrocław where he continued his travels, sometimes in disguise as a trader, through Silesia and into Bohemia, and finally to the area near Stuttgart where he learned of Colonel Walter Butler's death.[158]

In his account Carve recalls London and its monuments in almost eulogistic terms, describing St Paul's Cathedral and Westminster Abbey. Carve visited Westminster Abbey and its tombs and epitaphs of kings, as well as its 'inner choir' where the royal coronation throne was situated. He tells us that above the throne hung the famous stone (*tabula*) of Scone with its now vanished inscription (*cum hac epigraphe*), which Carve copied. Carve describes the stone of Scone and records its inscription thus: *ni fallat fatum, Scoti quocunque locatum, etc.*[159] Other writers of the period noted that the stone was adorned with such an inscription,[160] but the official stone now housed in Edinburgh Castle does not bear any inscription. Amongst his descriptions in *Itinerarium*, Carve writes about his visit to a Jewish synagogue in the town of Friedberg in Hessen in 1639. His remarks show that the visit was a curiosity for him and his companions and that he imagined the type of Jewish rituals performed there.[161]

It is thought that Carve died in 1672 shortly after publishing his *Responsio*. A search of the Viennese archives has not revealed his burial place or any register recording his death.[162] However, the fact that he served as the vicar-choral of the cathedral of St Stephen in

157. Kerney, *Itinerarium Thomæ Carve*, pp. i, viii–ix.
158. Carve, *Itinerarium*, pp. 44–59.
159. Ibid., p. 38. The inscription given by Carve constitutes only half of that given by others. The full inscription reads in English, 'that the Scots should reign, wheresoever that chair should be'. See William Howell, *Medulla historiae Anglicanae: Being a comprehensive history of the lives and reigns of the monarchs of England* (London, 1679) p. 187.
160. See, for example, Howell, *Medulla historiae Anglicanae* (1679).
161. Carve, *Itinerarium*, pp. 310–16.
162. A search of the death records for the parishes of the city of Vienna (St Stephan and St Michael) for the period 1672–84 do not reveal any record of Carve's burial, while the death records of the third parish, the Schottenpfarre, are missing for this period.

Vienna from 1643 suggests that he was buried in the extensive crypt of the cathedral church. Unlike Bruodinus who died of plague which swept through Prague in 1680, it is not possible to know the cause of Carve's death. His long life had witnessed much travel in Ireland, England and throughout Germany and central Europe, and he was present at, or in the vicinity of, many historical events of the age. In death he shared the same fate as his antagonist Bruodinus, in that both lie in unmarked graves in foreign cities.

WRITINGS ON GAELIC IRELAND

Bruodinus presents us with detailed and contemporary information on the Gaelic learned classes. Owing to his digressive style, Bruodinus' narrative is punctuated with anecdotes on the role and status of different learned families in order to construct a wider argument about their achievements, high standing and links to nobility. He uses this style to refute Carve's critical comments and to educate a foreign audience unfamiliar with Gaelic culture regarding the importance of this class of *literati* in Ireland. In addition to concentrating on the learned classes as a prominent group, he specifically focuses on the professional activities of his own family, the Clann Bhruaideadha. In *Anatomicum* Bruodinus presents much detail on Gaelic practices that were either still extant or had been in living memory prior to his departure from Ireland.

Aside from learning the rudiments of Latin grammar from his clerical relative, Fr Denis O'Nelan of Kilraghtis, Bruodinus may also through his family have been tutored in classical Irish at a bardic school prior to his novitiate at the Franciscan friary of Quin. Bruodinus' writings suggest that he was familiar with poetic compositions in Irish, and his comments on the episode known to history as the 'Contention of the Poets' (*Iomarbhágh na bhFileadh*) suggests that he had command of, or at least familiarity with, the literary language of the bardic classes (*béarla na bhFileadh*, dialect of the poets).[163] His detailed rendering of the O'Brien genealogy in *Propugnaculum* also suggests that he had copies of his family's genealogical manuscripts to hand in Prague.[164]

163. Bruodinus, *Propugnaculum*, p. 851. On *Béarla na bhFileadh* see John O'Donovan, *A Grammar of the Irish Language* (Dublin, 1845), p. lxxii.
164. Bruodinus, *Propugnaculum*, pp. 1077–86.

No bardic poetry is attributed to Bruodinus, nor did he write any works in Irish that have survived.[165] However, others from his circle were active in classical Gaelic scholarship. Fellow Franciscan Froinsias Ó Maolmhuaidh (Francis O'Molloy) published in Latin a grammatical tract on Irish poetry in 1677 containing several of his own poems, suggesting that he was educated in the bardic schools.[166] Two manuscripts written in Irish by Franciscans Fr Antóin Ó Conchubhair and Fr Antóin Ó hAille, while living in Prague, attest that the type of scholarship pursued there included Gaelic learning.[167]

Bruodinus and Ó Maolmhuaidh were acquainted from the time when Bruodinus was in Rome (*c.* 1643–50). Bruodinus marshalled the verses of Ó Maolmhuaidh to support his claims regarding the Clann Bhruaideadha. In *Anatomicum,* he appended the following elegiac couplets from Ó Maolmhuaidh as a sort of approbation for the work:

Inter Tuomonides priscis fulsere Bruodini,
moribus & vita, nobilitate sati.
Si genus & proavos horum Carrane notasses,
horreres celsos vellere dente viros.
Consule vel vivos, chronicos vel consule regni:
istos heroas aequiparasse leges.[168]

[Among the old inhabitants of Thomond, the MacBrodys,
sprung of nobility, shone bright in their customs and way of life.
Had you noted their noble stock and forefathers, Carran,
You would shudder to pull down by tooth these eminent men.
Consult the living, or consult the chronicles of the Kingdom:
you will read that those MacBrodys were equal to heroes].

Ó Maolmhuaidh also wrote a testimony regarding the authenticity of Bruodinus' writing about the Clann Bhruaideadha at the back of *Anatomicum*; this was similar in style to the testimony he gave earlier

165. Bruodinus did, however, compose poetry in Latin, examples of which survive in print. See his lengthly dedicatory poem to the Šternberk family in the unpaginated 'Dedicatoria' section of *Propugnaculum*.
166. Examples of Froinsias Ó Maolmhuaidh's poems composed in Irish appear in his scholastic work on Irish poetry, *Grammatica Latino-Hibernica nunc compendiata* (Rome, 1677). See Tomás Ó Flannghaile (ed.), *De Prosodia Hibernica* (Dublin, 1908), pp. 109–14.
167. Ríona Nic Congáil, Máirín Nic Eoin and Meidhbhín Ní Úrdail et al., *Litríocht na Gaeilge ar fud an Domhain Imleabhar I: Cruthú, caomhnú agus athbheochan* (Baile Átha Cliath, 2016), pp. 125–6.
168. O'Molony, *Anatomicum*, p. 136.

in *Propugnaculum*, which included a couplet.[169] It helped vindicate the claims of Bruodinus' family, the Clann Bhruaideadha, which formed a core component of Bruodinus' wider argument regarding the status and role of the bardic class. Bruodinus was of the same mould as Ó Maolmhuaidh, a cleric who combined both Gaelic scholarship and the Latin learning of the Church. This approbation for Bruodinus' work, as well as those of other Irish Franciscans at Prague, such as Francis Burke, Francis O'Kennedy and Andrew MacVeigh,[170] is reminiscent of the approbations which Micheál Ó Cléirigh received from fellow Gaelic *literati* in the 1630s. Bruodinus' kinsman Conchobhar Mac Bruaideadha of Kilkee and Lettermoylan in County Clare, and Flann Mac Aodhagáin of Ballymacegan, County Tipperary, both gave their imprimatur to Ó Cléirigh's *Annála Ríoghachta Éireann* in 1636.[171]

What makes Bruodinus intriguing from a scholastic point of view is his family's former role as chronicler-poets to the O'Briens of Thomond and his enduring reverence for those bonds of service. In this sense his mentality, as much as we may ascertain, reflected elements of an official *file* or poet, albeit in changed circumstances, tinged by experience of living in exile and defending the cultural achievements of the Gaelic-Irish. Bruodinus' scholarly connections and Latin writings enabled him to reach a wider audience beyond simply Irish *émigrés* and fellow Irish religious communities in Europe. Thus, his references to people and places in Ireland are sometimes described in exaggerated terms, in a bid to impress a foreign audience and to compensate for the depressed state of affairs that obtained in his homeland.

The divergent viewpoints of Carve and Bruodinus reveal the kernel of the disagreement regarding the Gaelic learned classes. Carve took the view that the Irish poets were not true poets and could not be regarded as learned, and that their mode of learning and hereditary transmission of office made them credulous, if not untruthful, in their poetry and writings. Carve's criticism extended to the Gaelic learned

169. Ibid., pp. 267–70; and see under 'censrae approbatorum' in the unpaginated *Epistola* section at the beginning of Bruodinus, *Propugnaculum*.

170. Millett, *Irish Franciscans*, pp. 488. MacVeigh authored a text on St Patrick's Purgatory in 1652 titled *Tractatulus de Purgatorio S. Patricii Hiberniae Apostoli*.

171. Walsh, *Gleanings*, p. 78. Also see Cunningham, *The Annals of the Four Masters*, pp. 278–98; and John O'Donovan (ed. and trans.), *Annála Rioghachta Éireann: Annals of the kingdom of Ireland by the Four Masters, from the earliest period to the year 1616*, vol. 1 (Dublin 1848–51; repr. Dublin, 1856; repr. Dublin, 1990), p. lxix.

classes in general and with their system of training in particular. His most hostile comments, however, were reserved for the poets, who he regarded as dishonest.

In his attack on Bruodinus, Carve presented a cynical argument about the efficacy of the hereditary principle that operated among the Gaelic professional orders. According to Carve, the sinews of learning and the integrity of professional writers were not to be found within the hereditary principle, which itself militated against novelty and worth. Rather, a system that permitted hereditary transmission of learning and the rewards given to those who cultivated that type of learning, such as the bardic poets, ensured that the sort of writing produced would be neither original nor truthful, but exhibit a degree of venality:

> *Nec tam facile parentes veracitatem et virtutem transmittunt in filios, quam bona; et ubi non est alienae et pauperi virtuti locus, veritas patitur.*[172]
>
> [Neither do parents transmit truthfulness and virtue to their children as easily as they transmit their possessions; and where there is no place for the virtue of the poor and [of] the stranger, truth suffers]

This was a strong, principled argument, and Bruodinus sought to refute it by emphasising the virtue of hereditary learning and defending the profession of poetry. He likened this argument to the respect accorded to learning, such as professional poetry in Gaelic Ireland, and how it was nurtured among certain families over generations.

Bruodinus chose to cite the works of classical authors, such as Cicero's *Pro Archia* and Ovid's *Fasti*, in defending the ancient profession of poetry.[173] He likens the respect accorded to poets in the classical world to the respect and the esteem enjoyed by the bardic poets in Ireland. Bruodinus goes to some length in explaining the diligence of the hereditary chroniclers as the record keepers in Gaelic lordships. When writing about the historical role of the poets and chroniclers, he acknowledges that as a 'Bruodin' he felt compelled and honour-bound to recount his family's ancient

172. Carve, *Responsio*, pp. 19–20.
173. On his use of classical authors see the translator's introduction.

profession. Moreover, he included a genealogy of his family's O'Brien patrons, which prominently appears at the end of *Propugnaculum*:

> *Chronologi & poetae in summa semper fuerunt in Hibernia veneratione, poetarum fictionibus & persuasionibus multa commissa sunt a proceribus Regni priscis temporibus mala, ob quae non immerito eos expellere voluit Rex Dermitius, Fergusii filius. De chronologorum conditionibus & obligationibus, jam supra circa initium huius libri c.4. egi. Inter alia, quae posteris memoriae tradiderunt antiquarii, maxime genealogia nobilium familiarum proceribus Hibernis summe semper placuit. Porro ipsi chronologi tam exacte arbores illas chronologicas & ramos omnes ab illa descendentes notabant, ut in Hibernia vix sit hodie notabilis familia, quae ex libris chronologorum suam deducere non posset genealogiam, usque ad ipsum Adamum; quod ut videas gratiose Lector (cum mei muneris nec hujus loci sit, arbores omnes genealogicas describere) pro fine hujus libri hic subjungam veram genealogiam regiae ò Brienorum familiae Principis, nimirum Tuomoniae Comitis moderni. Nec mihi Hiberni alii rationabiliter vitio vertent, si omissis aliarum familiarum genealogiis ò Brienorum genealogiam subjungam: Bruodinus namque sum, sic mirum non est, si familiae hujus illustrissimae, cujus antecessores mei semper fuerunt chronologi, recordabor, omissis pro nunc aliis.*[174]

> [Chroniclers and poets have always been held in the highest respect in Ireland. Many evils were committed in olden times by the leading men of the kingdom due to the inventions and persuasions of poets, because of which King Dermot, son of Fergus, not undeservedly wanted to ban them. The subject of the situations and obligations of chroniclers, I have already treated above, towards the beginning of Chapter 4 of this book. Among other things that antiquarians have transmitted to the memory of following generations is the genealogy of noble families which is, above all, always highly appreciated by the Irish leading men. Moreover, chroniclers themselves so precisely represented those chronological trees and all the branches descending from it, that there is hardly any distinguished family today in Ireland that could not trace its genealogy from the books of the chroniclers back to Adam himself. So that you

174. Bruodinus, *Propugnaculum*, pp. 1075–6.

may see this, dear reader (as it is my role, but not here the place, to describe all genealogical trees), I will annex here as a conclusion to this book the true genealogy of the chief of the kingly O'Brien family, namely today's earl of Thomond: nor will other Irishmen reasonably reckon it as a fault on my part if I omit the genealogies of other families and annex the genealogy of the O'Briens: for I am a Bruodin, so it is not surprising if I will give my thoughts to this most illustrious family, whose chroniclers my predecessors have always been, omitting the others for now].

In writing about the learned classes Bruodinus pays particular attention to the elevated social position of the bardic poets. His preoccupation with their status was a direct response to Carve's criticisms that the bards were deceitful 'plate-lickers' whose panegyric poetry was composed for the highest bidder, devoid of any sentiment of affection. Such comments had resonance with earlier English commentators to whom Gaelic Ireland presented a strange and at times perplexing culture, such as we find in the writings of the seventeenth-century soldier and publicist Thomas Gainsford.[175]

Bruodinus' arguments on this point were nuanced and made a careful distinction between the higher-status poets and the lower-status bards. Bruodinus tells us that the poets were distinguished by different grades, each reflecting their status and learning, and that his own family 'was only a noble one, from which always a single man was brought forth as the head of the family, or the senior (generally called Mac Bruodin)', who was entrusted to keep a historical chronicle of the realm and was responsible for recording the genealogies and deeds of the O'Briens.[176] Bruodinus' description is interesting in that it draws from recollections about his family which are rightly referred to as 'chroniclers' who maintained genealogies and produced literary texts for the O'Briens. He also wrote that the head of the family was denoted 'MacBruodin' (in Irish, *Mac Bruaideadha*), and it was he, in this designation and with sufficient learning, who was conferred with the role of master chronicler-poet (*ollamh*).

---

175. See Luke McInerney, 'A Description of Ireland: AD 1618', *TOC*, vol. 36, 2012, pp. 33–7.
176. O'Molony, *Anatomicum*, pp. 40–1. This follows the tract on the Gaelic learned classes by Dubhaltach Mac Fhirbhisigh that the Clann Bhruaideadha were, by profession, *seanchaidhe* (historians) rather than *filí* (poets). See James Carney, 'De Scriptoribus Hibernicis', *Celtica*, vol. 1, 1946, pp. 86–110, at p. 91.

We know that other learned families in the later medieval period functioned in a similar manner. In these examples, the *ollamh* of the family was the recognised 'head' and he held the position on account of his learning. His eligibility for the role was not pre-ordained but rested on both hereditary right and the attainment of sufficient competency in respect of his professional learning. Bruodinus illuminates this subject in *Propugnaculum*, whereby seniority and learning were important qualifiers for attaining an official role such as that of *ollamh*:

> *Non omnes qui ex familia erant, sed unus tantum vel alter ex senioribus, & in facultate maxime doctis, judicis v.g. munus, vel historici exercere poterant.*[177]
>
> [Not all members of the family could exercise the function of, for example, judge or historian, but only one or two of the elders and most learned in the field].[178]

Bruodinus makes clear that an *ollamh* of a learned family was acknowledged as its 'head' or 'senior' and was distinguished from other kinsmen who held familial lands or were recognised heads of family branches by virtue of hereditary right. Being an *ollamh* did not necessarily imply hereditary land rights as the estate of the *ollamh* was usually provided for by a rent-free grant of separate land by his patron. In addition, several 'heads' or 'seniors' of the family existed at the same time and these designations denote important individuals who held hereditary lands but not necessarily the *ollamhnacht*.

A survey of Clann Bhruaideadha source material reveals that several leading kinsmen were acknowledged family heads. It appears that Bruodinus understood 'head of the family, or the senior', to mean an individual who was both the head of a family branch and had attained status by virtue of his learning. Bruodinus uses the latter distinction for Flann of Moynoe and Maoilín Óg Mac Bruaideadha, distinguished men whose learning was recognised and who were

177. Bruodinus, *Propugnaculum*, p. 787.

178. These comments echo those made by the Irish antiquarian Dubhaltach Mac Fhirbhisigh about the transmission of learning and the holding of the position of *ollamhnacht*, or the official position of a master professor of learning. See Nollaig Ó Muraíle (ed.), *Leabhar Mór na nGenealach: The great book of Irish genealogies, compiled (1645–66) by Dubhaltach Mac Fhirbhisigh*, 5 vols (Dublin, 2003–4), pp. 184–5.

accorded high status. This view is supported in other sources. The main branch of the family who were situated at Lettermoylan on Slievecallan held the *ollamhnacht seanchais* in the late sixteenth century. The annals note that Giolla Brighde Mac Bruaideadha succeeded his kinsman Maoilín as *ollamh seanchais* in Thomond in 1582 upon the latter's death.[179] Maoilín Óg succeeded as *ollamh* around 1588,[180] and on his death in 1602 it appears that his son Conchobhar inherited the designation *Mac Bruaideadha* – evidenced by the fact that he signed a land deed in 1606 as 'Connor Brodyn otherwise McBrodye'.[181] Around the same time Tadhg mac Dáire Mhic Bhruaideadha and Conchobhar Mac Bruaideadha tutored the German settler Matthew de Renzy in classical Irish, and subsequent contact with de Renzy suggests that Conchobhar was regarded as the hereditary head of the family,[182] while Tadhg mac Dáire, holding the *ollamhnacht* following the death of its previous holder Maoilín Óg in 1602, was *ollamh* to O'Brien of Thomond.[183]

While nowhere is it explicitly recorded that Tadhg mac Dáire, who was Bruodinus' great-uncle and the subject of much of his writings, had the official title *ollamh flatha* (professor to a prince), the fact that he held rent-free land at Knockanalban points to his fulfilling that role. Tadhg mac Dáire's estate at Knockanalban to the south of Slievecallan was rent-free a year or so after his death in 1626, and while it appears to have been his *fearann ollamhnachta* (professional lands), the relationship he came to cultivate with his patron, Donough O'Brien, seems less rooted in traditional designations and more about

179. *AFM*, vol. V, p. 1791.

180. Maoilín Óg's claim to the *ollamhnacht* of Thomond may be traced to 1588, around the time when he is credited with writing a pedigree for Clann an Oirchinnigh (MacInerhenys). See RIA Ms 23/H/22, p. 11. A set of annals compiled by him were begun in 1588 indicating that he was fulfilling the role of official *seanchaidhe* from this time. See Bernadette Cunningham, 'The Historical Annals of Maoilín Óg Mac Bruaideadha, 1588–1603', *TOC*, vol. 13, 1989, pp. 21–4.

181. See PHA Ms C/13/34a [23 September 1606] printed in Luke McInerney, 'Documents from the Thomond Papers at Petworth House Archive', *Archivium Hibernicum*, vol. 64, 2011, pp. 7–55, at pp. 40–2.

182. A poem composed by Maoilín Óg Mac Bruaideadha for his son in *c*. 1600 shows the poet dissuading his son Conchobhar to enter a bardic school and pursue Gaelic learning on account of the lack of reward and patronage for professional poets. See Pádraig Ó Macháin, 'Maoilín Óg Mac Bruaideadha and the Decline of Patronage', *Celtica*, vol. 32, 2020, pp. 217–35.

183. Brian Mac Cuarta, 'Conchubhar Mac Bruaideadha and Sir Matthew de Renzy (1577–1634)', *Éigse*, vol. 27, 1993, pp. 122–6. It seems from the correspondence that de Renzy was at the bardic school of the Clann Bhruaideadha in *c*. 1606.

personal links.[184] It would therefore appear that Tadhg mac Dáire's standing was akin to that of an *ex officio* adviser to the earl. This role had its origins in a personal relationship that stretched back to the earl's youth when Tadhg mac Dáire acted as his guardian and tutor.

On the relationship between the learned classes and their patrons, Bruodinus was careful to point out that the nobility of the two groups meant that they developed mutually beneficial ties. In *Anatomicum* he treats the reader to information which otherwise would have been lost. Bruodinus describes a system of private tutoring between the Clann Bhruaideadha and the O'Briens. He claims that the Clann Bhruaideadha helped foster and educate Donough O'Brien, fourth earl of Thomond. This claim is an important one and goes to the heart of Bruodinus' argument about the indispensable role of the learned classes. Specifically, Bruodinus states that Donough O'Brien was fostered by Conor MacClancy and his wife Finola MacBrody and that Tadhg mac Dáire was responsible for tutoring him for fourteen years in different parts of Ireland. Bruodinus goes on to claim that Donough travelled to the court of Elizabeth I, accompanied by his tutor, whereupon under the influence of the earl of Ormond he converted to Protestantism.[185] Bruodinus' statement that the young earl travelled to England and was resident there is corroborated by reports in the State Papers which mention that Donough was resident in England in 1577.[186]

Bruodinus' claims help explain the personal connection between Tadhg mac Dáire and the earl, which was to continue until 1624 when Tadhg mac Dáire composed an elegy for the earl upon his death.[187] The fosterage claim is significant because it confirms that the Meic Fhlannchadha (MacClancy) tutors and custodians of the brehon laws were involved in fostering the young earl.[188] This can also be evidenced from the historical record. In 1570 Conor MacClancy held

184. Martin Breen, 'The 1626 Rental of Thomond Property', *NMAJ*, vol. 54, 2014, pp. 1–25, at pp. 24–5 (original shelfmark at PHA is Ms C/27A/39).
185. O'Molony, *Anatomicum*, pp. 112–13.
186. H.C. Hamilton (ed.), *Calendar of State Papers Ireland: Elizabeth I, 1574–85* (London, 1867), p. 113. Also see J.S. Brewer and W. Bullen (eds), *Calendar of the Carew Manuscripts Preserved in the Archiepiscopal Library at Lambeth 1575–1588* (London, 1868), p. 115.
187. Brian Ó Cuív, 'An Elegy on Donnchadh Ó Briain, Fourth Earl of the Thomond', *Celtica*, vol. 16, 1984, pp. 87–105.
188. On the Meic Fhlannchadha and their fosterage of other families see Luke McInerney, 'A Meic Fhlannchadha Fosterage Document, *c.* 1580', *NMAJ*, vol. 51, 2011, pp. 61–70.

the towerhouse of Inche near Ennis.[189] Members of the family held the traditional position of *ollamh féineachais* (professor of law) and they remained important followers of the earl in later times.[190]

Bruodinus provides us with further evidence concerning the standing of the learned classes. In one example he singles out the chroniclers who were specialists in *seanchas* and *genelach* (genealogy) and were appointed as official historian-chroniclers to Gaelic lords. The cultivation and recording of the genealogies of leading families was not undertaken for antiquarian reasons but had a crucial role in charting proprietorship and other rights to lands and tribute. In a society where kinship with the ruling dynasty determined landholding, status and wealth, the keeping of genealogical records by a cadre of professional historians was an important function. Bruodinus explains:

> *Denique notandum est, quo in honore inter Hiberniae Principes semper fuere chronologi illi, qui diligenter, sincere, & veridice acta regum & praecipuarum familiarum, earumque genealogias, observabant. Nam praeterquam quod ipsi antiquissimae erant nobilitatis, ex eodem ordinarie stipite originem trahentes, ex quo ii quorum erant chronologi descenderunt (Bruodini v. g. qui o Brienorum semper fuere chronologi originem trahunt non solum ab Eibero Mileri primogenito, sed etiam a Cassio, a quo ò Brieni descenderunt; Bruodiga namque a quo Bruodini dicuntur, filius fuit Deaghi, filii Aenae capitosi, filii Cassi, ex cujus primogenito Bloid dicto descendunt ò Brieni, ut inferius fusius ostendam) sed & exemptione plus quam Ecclesiastica gaudebant. A principibus enim annuam recipiebant pensionem. In publicis sessionibus, non infimas post principes sedes occupabant. Tam pacis quam belli tempore a contributionibus militumque quartiriis exempti erant. His aliisque privilegiis gaudebant eo fine, ut diligenter suo insisterent muneri postpositoque omni respectu nitidam describerent veritatem.*[191]

189. See 'Connoghor Maglanchy' who held the towerhouse of 'Enenshy' in 1574. See Twigge, 'Description of Thomond in 1574', p. 84.

190. One of the earl's principal followers was Boetius Clancy (Baothghalach Mac Fhlannchadha). He was granted immunities in 1585 as part of the composition agreement. See A. Martin Freeman (ed.), *The Compossicion Booke of Conought* (Dublin, 1936), p. 29. Also see *AFM*, vol. VI, p. 2051. On the Meic Fhlannchadha of Thomond see Luke McInerney, 'The Síol Fhlannchadha of Tradraighe, Co. Clare: Brehon lawyers of the Gaelic tradition', *Eolas*, vol. 9, 2016, pp. 19–54.

191. Bruodinus, *Propugnaculum*, p. 771.

> [Finally, it should be noted in what honour those chroniclers, who diligently, sincerely and truthfully kept the deeds of kings and of the most important families, and the genealogies of the latter, have always been held among the princes of Ireland. For they themselves were from very ancient nobility, drawing their origin from the same root as those for whom they were chroniclers (the Bruodins, for example, who were always the chroniclers of the O'Briens, draw their origin not only from Eber, first-born of Milesius, but also from Cas,[192] from whom the O'Briens are descended; for Bruodiga, after whom the Bruodins are called, he was the son of Deagh, son of 'Aena capitosus' [i.e. Aengus Ceann Nathrach][193] son of Cas, from whose first-born, who was called Bloid, the O'Briens are descended, as I shall demonstrate more at length below). Aside from this fact, they also enjoyed greater exemption than that of the Church, for they received a yearly pension from the princes. In public sessions, they occupied seats that were not the lowest, behind the leading men. In times of peace as well as in times of war, they were exempted from contributions and quartering of soldiers. They enjoyed these and other privileges to this purpose, so that they might devote themselves carefully to their duty and, disregarding all other respects, describe the clear truth].

Anatomicum contains numerous anecdotes about Gaelic culture. In one passage Bruodinus quotes Carve regarding a tradition that existed in the eleventh century whereby Gaelic lords had the right to have intercourse with a just-married virgin before her husband performed the marital act. By the seventeenth century, Carve tells us, the custom had been modified and in parts of Leinster a just-married virgin was required to pay a 'fine' to her overlord to buy her chastity back.[194] Carve refers to this custom as *Kystonady*. Bruodinus reacted

192. It has been suggested that Clann Bhruaideadha disregarded their early links to one of the chiefly Corcomroe lineages and instead re-imagined a genealogical connection to the Dál Cais. See Diarmuid Ó Murchadha, 'The Origins of Clann Bhruaideadha', *Éigse*, vol. 31, 1999, pp. 121–30.

193. The early medieval lineage grouping known as the *Cineal Fearmaic* claimed descent from Aengus Ceann Nathrach. The genealogies name him as an ancestor of the Uí Dheaghaidh and a brother of Caisín and Bloid, two individuals recognised as the respective ancestors of the Meic Conmara and Uí Bhriain.

194. A similar story is repeated by the English traveller John Dunton in his 1698 tour of Ireland. According to Dunton, the custom still prevailed on the estates of the earl of Cavan, where the custom was sometimes stipulated in land leases. See John Dunton, *Teague Land, or a Merry Ramble to the Wild Irish*, ed. Edward MacLysaght (Dublin, 1982), p. 46.

vehemently against what he saw as Carve's 'pretences', writing that such tales 'worsened the bad cause of the enemies of the kingdom of Ireland'. The precise meaning of *Kystonady* is unclear, but it could be a garbled form of the Irish *cíos tóna duibhe* (black-buttocks tax). There is no way of knowing the veracity of Carve's statement, but it is interesting that a Gaelic version of *Jus Primae Noctis* (law of the first night) appears to have survived into the early modern period. Early examples of this law can be found in old Irish texts. In a story from the twelfth century 'Book of Leinster' (*Lebor na Núachongbála*) the king of Ulster, Conchobhar mac Nessa, had the right of the first night over the marriages of his subjects, which in Irish was called *coll cétingen*.[195]

In *Anatomicum* Bruodinus mentions a great many people and places. It is apparent from a number of references that he was in touch with networks of Irish religious and military men on the continent. In one such instance he corrects Carve's mistake of conflating the name of Lieutenant Tadhg O'Higgin with Tadhg O'Hassey, whom Bruodinus identified as a man of Thomond known to him personally. Bruodinus remained in contact with such individuals, and it is notable that quite a few bore Thomond surnames like MacClancy, MacGrath and O'Molony, showing that he cultivated a network of fellow countrymen on the continent.

Intimate and forthright information is given about Fr Bernardine Clancy, a fellow Thomond man, whom Bruodinus mentions as closely related to the Inchiquin O'Briens. He narrates the details of Clancy's life, including his admission to St Anthony's Irish College in Louvain, and his later appointment as guardian of the Irish College in Prague. He goes on to mention the service Clancy rendered as a lecturer at the archiepiscopal seminary in Prague which was situated opposite the Irish Franciscan College. Bruodinus uses another Thomond man whom we may assume to have been a close acquaintance, Maurice O'Loughlin, to pen an invective poem against Carve. O'Loughlin was a scholar of law at the Charles-Ferdinard University in Prague, whose poem must have been procured by Bruodinus in much the same way as other satirising poems about Carve which appear in *Anatomicum*. The poem was used by Bruodinus for both stylistic and literary effect.

He also turns his attention to the dwelling places of the Gaelic-Irish, including those of his own family in Thomond. In Carve's

195. R.I. Best and Osborn Bergin, *Lebor na hUidre: Book of the Dun Cow* (Dublin, 1929), p. 317.

earlier work, *Enchiridion,* he criticised the residence of Bruodinus' family at Ballyogan in a rather sarcastic tone.[196] For us, Carve's criticism is fortuitous in that it provides detail on the settlement of a literary family of the classical Gaelic tradition seldom encountered in contemporary texts. In describing the dwelling places of the Clann Bhruaideadha at Ballyogan, Bruodinus quotes Carve as saying that the Clann Bhruaideadha had 'stalls' (that is, bothies) in the ridges of mountains where they dwelt with their cattle and that their other residences were 'small cabins, built with light material out of crossbeams', that were covered with 'straw and smeared with cow dung on the inside'.[197]

Elements of Carve's description of Ballyogan are consistent with other seventeenth-century accounts of low-status Gaelic domestic buildings, including one by Fynes Moryson which mentions 'cabins made of the boughs of trees and covered with turf'[198] and the later seventeenth-century description of the summer habitation of Brian O'Flaherty in Iar-Connacht.[199] It is unlikely that Carve was referring to habitations at Ballyogan associated with the Clann Bhruaideadha's professional activities. Rather, he appears to have been passing comment on the temporary abodes erected in upland areas for seasonal transhumance where the family's cattle would have sheltered and been looked after by herdsmen.

Carve's description of Ballyogan predictably drew the ire of Bruodinus. In response, Bruodinus launched a concerted attack on Carve. He casts doubt on Carve as an eyewitness in Thomond, alleging that Carve invented his descriptions and thus was not to be believed. Bruodinus asserted that Carve's description of the 'dwelling-place of so many honourable men' was absurd and that he deliberately overlooked the building materials of lime, pitch and argil which most of the inhabitants in Thomond used.[200] Bruodinus assured his readers that the dwelling places of the nobles of Thomond were honourable and fit for their standing.

196. Carve, *Enchiridion*, pp. 98–9.
197. O'Molony, *Anatomicum*, pp. 154–5.
198. Moryson cited in Katharine Simms, 'Guesting and Feasting in Gaelic Ireland', *JRSAI*, vol. 108, 1978, pp. 67–100, at p. 81.
199. Dunton, *Teague Land*, p. 25.
200. O'Molony, *Anatomicum*, pp. 155–6.

From this exchange, a clearer picture emerges of the housing of the Gaelic-Irish. Building materials such as lime, pitch and argil (potter's clay) were plentiful in Thomond. The single most important contribution in Bruodinus' writings, however, is not the effort he expends in detailing the material culture of Thomond, but rather the level of detail he devotes to explaining the role of the Gaelic learned classes. His central theme is transparent in that it is the defence of Gaelic culture and the defence of the professional poets and historians, who in Bruodinus' view embodied the virtues of Gaelic civilisation. In doing this, his defence is more akin to a vindication of his own family as he cloaks his argument about the Clann Bhruiadeadha in a wider defence of Gaelic literary culture.

VINDICATION OF CLANN BHRUAIDEADHA

The core argument of Bruodinus which runs through *Anatomicum* is the defence of his own family, the Clann Bhruaideadha. His defence rests on several pillars. First, because they were members of the Gaelic learned classes, they were noble and enjoyed privileges. Second, because of this membership they were endowed with lands, some of which were rent-free by virtue of their professional calling. Third, Bruodinus' great-uncle, Tadhg mac Dáire Mhic Bhruaideadha, was a *literatus* – a man of distinction – who achieved fame for his poetry and literary works. Bruodinus' preoccupation with refuting Carve's criticisms has left a rich store of historical information that would not otherwise have survived.

One of the main pillars of Bruodinus' argument about Clann Bhruaideadha concerned their role as a learned family. In Gaelic Ireland, the learned families – poets, historians, chroniclers, genealogists, lawyers, physicians, harpists and master craftsmen – were organised into hereditary kindreds that transmitted learning in professional schools. Entry to their professions was strictly regulated, the most learned members of which enjoyed an exalted status and were wealthy. The highest office was the *ollamhnacht*, or the official position of a master-professor of learning, to which were attached emoluments and rent-free lands among other privileges.

The cultivation of a vernacular literary tradition characterised the activity of the Gaelic learned classes. This tradition, which stretched back to the early medieval period and had links to the *scriptoria* of the native monasteries, conferred prestige on members of the class.[201] The scholarship of the learned classes was an amalgam of Christian Latin teaching and native lore (*seanchas*), some of which had ancient origins. Arguably, elements of the vernacular tradition dated back to the pre-Christian druids and their system of learning (*draoidheacht*) but underwent significant revision in the early medieval monasteries.[202] Together these formed a coherent body of scholarship which dominated the intellectual ethos of the learned classes in the medieval period.[203] In Bruodinus' time the learned classes and their Gaelic patrons were much reduced. According to Thomas O'Sullevane, in his biography of the life of the Marquis of Clanricarde, the bardic schools were 'preserv'd in Ireland upon the same footing, till the beginning of the troubles in 1641'.[204] After this disturbed period the bardic schools were discontinued and the patronage that learned families received, including their privileged tenurial conditions, also ended.

Bruodinus' anecdotes about the Clann Bhruaideadha first appear in *Propugnaculum* as a retort to Carve's pejorative writings about Gaelic culture. In his writings, Bruodinus notes that his family kept a library at Moynoe in east County Clare. Bruodinus' description of the library is interesting, and is derived from his own eyewitness testimony:

---

201. For a general summary of these developments see Robin Flower, *The Irish Tradition* (Oxford, 1947); and Proinsias Mac Cana, 'The Rise of the Later School of *Filidheacht*', *Ériu*, vol. 25, 1974, pp. 126–46. On a more recent view see Elva Johnston, *Literacy and Identiy in Early Medieval Ireland* (Woodbridge, 2013).
202. See Kim McCone, *Pagan Past and Christian Present in Early Irish Literature* (Maynooth, 1990). Also see John Minahane, *The Christian Druids: On the filid or philosopher-poets of Ireland* (Dublin, 2008).
203. On the different types of narrative and the intellectual framework that underpinned the body of learning in the medieval period, see Proinsias Mac Cana, *The Learned Tales of Medieval Ireland* (Dublin, 1980). On the repertoire of a bardic poet and the types of tales, stories and poems which an accomplished poet was expected to know, see ibid., pp. 8, 41–9.
204. Thomas O'Sullevane, *Dissertation, Memoirs of the Right Honourable The Marquis of Clanricarde, Lord Deputy General of Ireland, containing Several Original Papers and Letters of King Charles II, Queen Mother, the Duke of York, the Duke of Lorrain, the Marquis of Ormond, Archbishop of Tuam, Lord Viscount Taaffe, &c. relating to the Treaty between the Duke of Lorrain and the Irish Commissioners, from February 1650, to August 1653* (London, 1722), p. cxxxii.

Vidi insuper ego non semel in bibliotheca minimae meae familiae Senioris (vulgo mac Bruodin) nobilis viri D. Florentii mac Bruodin, Domini de Moyneo, antiquissimas Regni Hiberniae historias, ante tot saecula a Bruodinis in membrana mundissime exaratas, & duobus tomis (quorum unus Rufus & alter Ruber dicitur) contentas. In Rufo omnia facta regum & principum familiarum (praesertim vero earum quae ex Eibero primogenito Milerii Hispani primique ex illa stirpe Regis Hiberniae descenderunt) continebantur. In Rubro vero libro, inter alia arbores genealogicae non solum regiae ò Brienorum familiae, sed & praecipuarum omnium Hibenicarum familiarum artificiose collocatae videntur.[205]

[Moreover, I myself have seen not just once in the library of the Senior (called Mac Bruodin) of my very humble family, the noble man Master Florence Mac Bruodin [Flann MacBrody], Master of Moynoe, the most ancient histories of the Kingdom of Ireland, set down on parchment by the Bruodins very neatly so many centuries ago, and contained within two volumes (of which one is called *Rufus* [Reddish] and the other *Ruber* [Red]). In *Rufus* were contained all the deeds of the families of kings and princes (but especially of those that have descended from Eber [i.e. Éibhear Fionn], the firstborn son of Milesius the Spaniard [i.e. Mil Espáine], and of the first King of Ireland from that branch). In the book *Ruber*, however, there can be seen, skilfully put together, among other things, genealogical trees, not only of the royal family of the O'Briens, but also of all the principal Irish families].

This is one of only a handful of contemporary descriptions existing about a library or place of scholarship belonging to a learned family from Thomond.[206] Bruodinus claims that manuscripts were compiled

205. Bruodinus, *Propugnaculum*, p. 770.

206. In County Clare there exists a handful of references to libraries and bardic schools. There is a reference to the library and books of the Uí Mhaoilchonaire of Ardkyle; two references to the cultivation of poetry and music at the Uí Dhálaigh school at Finavarra; and a number of references to the law school of the Uí Dhuibhdhábhoireann of Cahermacnaughten. Few of these references, however, refer to the actual books or their contents, in the same manner as Bruodinus does. See Robin Flower, *Catalogue of Irish Manuscripts in the British Museum*, vol. 2 (London, 1926), p. 66–7; Eoghan Ó Neachtain, 'Tochmarc Fhearbhlaide', *Ériu*, vol. 4, 1908, pp. 47–67, at p. 51; John O'Donovan (ed.), *The Tribes of Ireland: A satire by Aenghus O'Daly; with poetical translation by the late James Clarence Mangan; together with an historical account of the family of O'Daly; and an introduction to the history of satire in Ireland* (Dublin, 1852), pp. 82–3; and Kathleen Mulchrone and Elizabeth FitzPatrick (eds), *Catalogue of the Irish Manuscripts in the Royal Irish Academy*, fasc. 27 (Dublin, 1943), no 1236, pp. 3421–4.

by the Clann Bhruaideadha centuries before his time, implying that the family's literary credentials stretched back to the medieval period. The earliest reference to a learned member of the family dates from the mid-fourteenth century, which shows that they were composing bardic poetry for the O'Briens.[207] The fourteenth century is when a number of the hereditary learned families of Thomond are first recorded in the annals. Little else is known about the professional activities of the Clann Bhruaideadha in the medieval period, until members of the family appear in the annals in 1563.[208]

Bruodinus' description brings into focus the professional activities of the family; that is, chronicler-poets whose role brought together the study of history with the official role of writing and notarising land deeds and composing formal poetry.[209] It is likely that the description of Flann Mac Bruaideadha and his *bibliotheca* pertained to the place at Moynoe where Mícheál Ó Cléirigh visited in 1636 and saw the eleventh-century religious text *Saltair Chaimín*. At that time the text was in the custody of the sons of Mac Bruaideadha, Bernard and Flann, who, according to Ó Cléirigh, lived on '*Tearmann Caimín*, like their ancestors before them'.[210] It was usual for learned families to have ancient texts which they copied, and around this time another learned family of Thomond, the Clann Chruitín, appear to have possessed a copy of the Psalter of Cashel which one of their members, a certain 'Æd O Cruitin' (Aodh Ó Cruitín), shared with the Dublin antiquary James Ware.[211]

207. See the poem in Mac Cionnaith (ed.), *Dioghluim Dána*, pp, 252–6, and its translation in L. McKenna, 'Poem to O Briain', *The Irish Monthly*, vol. 49, 1921, pp. 112–17.

208. *AFM*, vol. V, p. 1597. A genealogy printed in O'Hart traces further generations back to the early fifteenth century, but the exemplar used by O'Hart is not known. It appears to be taken from Richard Cronnelly, *Irish Family History: Being an historical and genealogical account of the Gaedhals, from the earliest period to the present time* (Dublin, 1865) and unattributed by Hart. See John O'Hart, *Irish Pedigrees or, the Origin and Stem of the Irish Nation*, vol. 1 (Dublin, 1892, 2 vols), pp. 104–5.

209. On the notarisation of deeds by the Clann Bhruaideadha and other learned families in the seventeenth century, see Luke McInerney, 'Six Deeds from Early Seventeenth-Century Thomond', *Eolas*, vol. 10, 2017, pp. 33–76.

210. Nollaig Ó Muraíle (ed.), *Mícheál Ó Cléirigh, His Associates and St Anthony's College, Louvain* (Dublin, 2008), p. 110.

211. See TCD, Ms 6404, folio 146 [James Ware's commonplace book]. The transcription appears to read 'w^{h} Æd O Cruitin in Thomond', indicating that the name was Aodh, a forename found among the Clann Chruitín. On the family see Luke McInerney, 'The Origins of Clann Chruitín: Chronicler-poets of the learned Gaelic tradition', *TOC*, vol. 38, 2014, pp. 19–30. I thank Dr Mark Empey for locating this reference and Prof. Pádraig Ó Riain for his assistance with the transcription.

In *Anatomicum* Bruodinus goes to great lengths to prove his family's nobility and standing in response to Carve's jibes. Being noble was important to Bruodinus as he saw in it proof of his family's credibility and it was inextricably linked to their holding of professional office. According to him, in the time 'when the Irish of old reigned' they did not assign the 'office of chronicler to [just anyone] but to trustworthy noble men, who had the means to sustain their social ranks'.[212] In support of his argument he stated that he could identify nineteen 'noble Bruodins', many of whom were *praeclaros nobiles* (outstanding noblemen)[213] and who enjoyed estates in Thomond before being deprived of them by the Cromwellians.[214] In enumerating the different branches of the Clann Bhruaideadha, Bruodinus tell us that the noble status of the family was acquired on the basis of being a professional learned family and their lands were held from 'leading men of the country'.[215] This reflects the fact that learned families were allocated land, often mensal land, that constituted the personal estate of a Gaelic lord, in exchange for their professional services. Bruodinus' passages about the poets tend to reflect what the Ulster poet Eochaidh Ó hEoghusa articulated a few decades before Bruodinus' time. That is, a master poet, or an *ollamh*, expected an estate allotted to him in perpetuity, rent-free and close to his overlord.[216]

In his second pillar of defence about his family, Bruodinus explained that the Clann Bhruaideadha held lands in different parts of Thomond. He devotes a whole section in *Anatomicum* identifying the heads of landholding family-branches in the seventeenth century. According to him the Clann Bhruaideadha possessed lands in the following places: Moynoe and Coolcusaun in Moynoe parish; Aughrim, Ballyminoge and Toburkulan (now Callahy) in Tomgraney parish – these townlands and parishes are in east Clare; Ballyogan in Kilraghtis parish; Drumbonniv, Cloonawillin and Knocknamucky in

212. O'Molony, *Anatomicum*, p. 40.
213. Ibid., p. 41.
214. Ibid., p. 44.
215. Ibid., pp. 43–4.
216. James Carney, *The Irish Bardic Poet* (Dublin, 1967, reprint 1985), pp. 24–5.

Inchicronan parish; Kilkee in Ruan parish[217] – these townlands and parishes are in central Clare; Shanavogh, Coor and Knockanalban in Kilmurry-Ibrickan parish; Ballyduff in Inagh parish; and Lettermoylan on Slievecallan[218] – these townlands and parishes are in west Clare.

The veracity of these claims is, for the most part, corroborated by the historical record.[219] This suggests that Bruodinus is a more reliable source of information than has hitherto been acknowledged by historians. In detailing the landholding of the Clann Bhruaideadha he pays special attention to the Moynoe branch of the family with whom he shared a close affinity. He refers to the head of that branch as 'Master Florence Bruodin [Flann MacBrody], commonly called Mac Bruodin, who was twice captain of County Clare, otherwise called sheriff'. We read in the *Stuart Warrants* that 'Flan McBruodine' served as high constable of Tulla barony in 1634.[220] This was Flann Mac Bruaideadha who appears in land records from 1617 to the 1630s, confirming that he held the lands that Bruodinus attributed to him.[221]

217. This has been confused by writers, including Edmund Hogan, as Kilkeedy in County Clare on the basis of Conchobhar Mac Bruaideadha's approbation of Mícheál Ó Cléirigh's *Annála Ríoghachta Éireann* in 1636. Conchobhar noted his residence as '*Chill Chaoide 7 ó Leitir Mhaoláin i ccontae an Chláir*'. *Cill Chaoide* should, in actuality, read *Cill Chaoidhe* (i.e. Kilkee). This is confirmed in the 1618 Great Office inquisition for Inchiquin barony where Connor MacBrody and Shane MacBrodin were recorded jointly holding 'Kilky'. In the 1641 *Books of Survey and Distribution* a 'Conor mc Moyllin' MacBrody was recorded holding 'Kilkie alis Lissinrahahick' followed by John MacBrodyn of 'Kilkie alias Lissnecreuy'. None appear at Kilkeedy. See Edmund Hogan, *Onomasticon Goedelicum* (Dublin, 1910), p. 179; and Walsh, *Gleanings*, p. 78. Also see PHA Ms 16 B.E [Great Office, 5 September 1618 – Inchiquin]; and Simington (ed.), *Books of Survey and Distribution*, pp. 553–4. A recent work that repeats the error in identification is Frank Brew, *The Parish of Kilkeedy: A local history* (Tubber, 1998), pp. 81–4.

218. See the various denominations listed under their Latinised equivalents in O'Molony, *Anatomicum*, pp. 41–3, 123–35.

219. Related sources include the 1618 Great Office inquisitions for Inchiquin and Tulla at PHA Ms 16 B.E [Great Office, 5 September 1618 – Inchiquin]; and Ms B. 16 B [Great Office, 20 March 1621 – Tulla]. Also see the 1615 survey of Ibrickan in Luke McInerney, 'The Earl of Thomond's 1615 Survey of Ibrickan, Co. Clare', *NMAJ*, vol. 53, 2013, pp. 173–91 (original shelfmark at PHA is Ms C/27/A/60); Martin Breen, 'The 1626 Rental of Thomond Property', *NMAJ*, vol. 54, 2014, pp. 1–25 (original shelfmark at PHA is Ms C/27A/39); Séamus Pender (ed.), *A Census of Ireland, c. 1659: With supplementary material from the poll money ordinances (1660–1)* (Dublin, 1939); and John Ainsworth (ed.), *The Inchiquin Manuscripts* (Dublin, 1961).

220. Mark Empey, *Early Stuart Irish Warrants, 1623–1639: The Falkland and Wentworth administrations* (Dublin, 2015), p. 115.

221. PHA Ms 16 B.E [Great Office, 5 September 1618 – Inchiquin]. In 1617, 'fflan Mc Broodyn', 'Charles alias Callogh Mc Broodyn', 'Donogh O Cormochan' and 'David Mac Cormochan' surrendered their leases to the Church land of Moynoe. See National Library of Ireland, Ms 1777, p. 7: *Typescript copy of a survey of lands in the diocese of Killaloe made for Bishop Worth* (1661), transcribed by J.B. Leslie, NLI (1936).

Not only does Bruodinus relate information about the various branches of the Clann Bhruaideadha, he also notes their links to other learned families. For instance, he tells us that Gabriel Donleavy of the Meic Dhuinnshléibhe, hereditary physicians of Ulster, was an *Excellentissimus Medicinae Doctor in Comitatu Tyrconellensi* (excellent medical doctor in County Tyrconnell), and he took Maria Bruodin as his wife.[222] Bruodinus mentions the marriage links between his family and the learned families who served the O'Donnells of Ulster such as the O'Clerys and MacWards. Bruodinus states that Fergal Ward was O'Donnell's *Archipoeta, & Historicus* (arch-poet and historian), and he married Maria Bruodin, the sister of the bardic poet Tadhg mac Dáire Mhic Bhruaideadha. Fergal Ward can be identified as Fearghal Óg Mac an Bháird (*c.* 1550–*c.* 1618), a celebrated bardic poet noted for his poem *Trí Coróna i gCairt Shéamais*, on James I's ascension to the throne in 1603.[223] This exposition of the Clann Bhruaideadha's matrimonial links is quite unusual and stems from two things. Firstly, documenting marriages with prominent families was purposely intended to refute Carve's denigration of Bruodinus' family. It also positioned Bruodinus as a well-informed historian, setting out exact relationships between people and places and which, in turn, lends credibility to his statements.

The third pillar of Bruodinus' argument, and one that he takes up with vigour in *Anatomicum*, is his defence of his great-uncle, bardic poet Tadhg mac Dáire Mhic Bhruaideadha. Through his writings Bruodinus offers new material on the life of Tadhg mac Dáire. He describes him as a *praefectus* (prefect) at the court of the earl of Thomond.[224] It is difficult to now verify, but prefect can denote a chief officer or a magistrate in one of the earl's baronial courts. In responding to criticisms made by Carve, Bruodinus confirms that Tadhg mac Dáire held an official position at one of the earl of Thomond's manor courts, stating that he was appointed sheriff of Clare three times and served as seneschal of Ibrickan.

Carve neither confirms nor denies this claim in his subsequent work. Tadhg mac Dáire's most famous poem, *Mór a-tá ar Theagasg*

222. O'Molony, *Anatomicum*, p. 135.
223. Osborn Bergin (ed.), *Irish Bardic Poetry* (Dublin, 1970), pp. 37–48.
224. Bruodinus, *Propugnaculum*, p. 851; and O'Molony, *Anatomicum*, p. 107.

Flatha (Great responsibility, the teaching of a prince), combines elements of the Irish literary tradition and eulogistic motif poetry, proffering advice in the manner of a court official.[225] Bruodinus' remarks indicate that Tadhg was regarded as a *literatus*, learned not only in Irish but also in Greek, Latin and English.[226] His staunch defence of Tadhg is exemplified by the following passage that refers to the poet's involvement in the literary exchange known as the 'Contention of the Poets' which commenced in 1617: [227]

> *Momoniensium partes scriptis & verbis tuebatur patruus meus magnus bonae memoriae, Dominus Thaddaus mac Bruodin, seu de Bruodin, Darii filius, Dominus de Monte Scoti.*[228]
>
> [The cause of the people of Munster was defended through the writings and words of my great-uncle of good memory, Master Thaddeus Mac Bruodin [MacBrody], or the Bruodin, son of Darius, (and) Master of Knockanalban].

Bruodinus appears well informed about the literary controversy that arose between his great-uncle and the northern poets. Bruodinus stated that the exchange had occurred fifty years prior to his writing. The charge by some historians that Bruodinus is reticent in providing dates is unfounded when it comes to matters involving his family, about which he goes to some length to provide a wealth of detail.

The impression formed from Bruodinus' writings is that Tadhg's achievements were considerable. He stresses that Tadhg was well versed and erudite, the product of native schools of *filidheacht* and *seanchas*. He says that Tadhg's writings and poems were in his hands and he refers to what he terms 'humorous Irish-Latin rhymes', in which Tadhg figuratively divided Ireland between himself and the family of John de Burgo, and he uses this as evidence that Tadhg was competent in Latin.[229] What is interesting about this reference is that

225. Theophilus O'Flanagan, 'Advice to a Prince, by Thaddy Mac Brody' and 'Institutio principis, carmen Hibernicum, auctore Thaddeo, filio Darii, filio Brodaei', *Transactions of the Gaelic Society*, vol. 1, 1808, pp. 1–54, 1–36, 229–31.
226. O'Molony, *Anatomicum*, p. 107.
227. On the date of the initiation of the 'Contention of the Poets', see Breatnach, 'Litir', p. 99.
228. Bruodinus, *Propugnaculum*, p. 851.
229. O'Molony, *Anatomicum*, p. 116.

a poem written by Tadhg and titled *Rannam le Chéile, a Chlann Uilliam Inis Banbha*[230] is dedicated to the de Burgo (Burke) family. Tadhg writes from 'stream-wasted' and 'rough-fielded *Leitir Maoláin*' on Slievecallan when addressing his patrons.[231] Along with Bruodinus' inclusion of a genealogy of the O'Briens as an appendix to *Propugnaculum*, his reference to Tadhg's poem in his hands suggests that Bruodinus had either a *duanaire* (poem-book) or copies of poems dedicated to the O'Briens, as well as genealogies, with him in Prague.

In a final defence of Tadhg, Bruodinus endeavoured to set the record straight and reminded Carve that Knockanalban, which was held by Tadhg, was not only free from the dues owed to the O'Briens, but also those claimed by the Church. Bruodinus, whom we may regard as credibly informed about such matters, wrote that Knockanalban was not Church land and that following the death of Tadhg, it was inherited by his son James in the manner of private property.[232] This comment was in response to Carve's claim that the Clann Bhruaideadha did not own their land but leased it from the Church. Although largely incorrect in his charge, Carve, living in Vienna and many decades after the event he was describing, was still well informed. Carve's comment was partly true as it was Lettermoylan on Slievecallan that was ecclesiastical land.[233] In 1614 Lettermoylan was claimed by the Protestant bishop of Killaloe as property of the Church against its occupant, 'Teig McBroodie gent', who held it along with his 'houses and mancons'.[234] Bruodinus corrected Carve by pointing out that Knockanalban was never Church land; rather it was the homestead of his great-uncle, Tadhg mac Dáire Mhic Bhruaideadha.[235] In correcting Carve, Bruodinus remained silent about the status of Lettermoylan.

230. Bruodinus must have been in error here as the poem *Rannam le Chéile, a Chlann Uilliam* is dedicated to the sons of Richard Sasanach de Burgo, second earl of Clannricard (d. 1582), namely John and Uileag de Burgo. See Gearóid Mac Eoin, 'Crosántacht Íorónta, a Chúlra agus a hÚdar', in Máirtín Ó Briain (ed.), Pádraig Ó Héalaí (ed.), *Téada Dúchais: Aistí in omós don Ollamh Breandán Ó Madagáin* (Gaillimh, 2002), pp. 111–19. The poem is printed and translated in Lambert McKenna SJ, 'A Partition of Ireland', *The Irish Monthly* [Historical Poems], vol. 57, January–June, 1929, pp. 330–3; Lambert McKenna SJ, 'A Partition of Ireland', *The Irish Monthly* [Historical Poems], vol. 57, July–December 1929, pp. 368–72.

231. McKenna SJ, 'A Partition of Ireland', p. 368. *Leitir Maoláin* is anglicised as Lettermoylan and was a placename located on Slievecallan. In 1614 Lettermoylan was held by Tadhg mac Dáire. See NLI Ms 45,686/1 [*c.* 1614]; and Ainsworth, *Inchiquin*, p. 432 (no. 1318).

232. O'Molony, *Anatomicum*, p. 109.

233. Simington (ed.), *Books of Survey and Distribution*, p. 533.

234. See NLI Ms 45,686/1 [*c.* 1614]; and Ainsworth, *Inchiquin*, p. 432 (no. 1318).

235. See Breen, '1626 Rental', pp. 24–5.

Much of Bruodinus' commentary about the lands of the Clann Bhruaideadha can be verified by other historical sources. In a survey of the earl of Thomond's Ibrickan estate in 1615, Knockanalban was held by 'Teig McBroady' who 'holdeth for which he payeth noe rent'.[236] Knockanalban was still held, rent-free, by his widow in 1626.[237] This is proof enough that Tadhg died soon after composing an elegy on the death of Donough O'Brien, fourth earl of Thomond, in 1624.[238] It also disproves the story collected by the eighteenth-century Irish scholar Theophilius O'Flanagan, of Tadhg being hurled ingloriously to his death from the precipice of Doonogan by a Cromwellian soldier.[239]

Carve railed against Bruodinus' claim in *Anatomicum* that Tadhg mac Dáire Mhic Bhruaideadha served as the personal tutor to Donough O'Brien, fourth earl of Thomond (d. 1624).[240] But Carve's criticism also struck at the status of the Clann Bhruaideadha as poets to the O'Briens. He points out the lowly situation of Tadhg whom he describes as *familiae caput* (head of the family) and compares him to a country rustic in a broadside that was calculated to create lasting enmity with Bruodinus:

> *Objeceram tibi quod vane & impudenter toties jactares te esse ex sanguine Principum ô Brienorum, regum Hiberniae, Scythiae, & Aegypti, cum majores tui ad mensam serviverint ô Briennis, inconditum carmen ad fides ibidem canere debuerint, ac vibrissare; & illi ex tua gente habuerint interdum obstetrices & nutrices, ut ipse fateris pag.112 examinis, ubi dicis Donatum ô Brien annos septem fuisse nutritum, lactatum, & ablactatum apud Finolam Bruodinam & suum maritum Cornelium Clanchii: et ego hisce meis oculis viderim Thadaeum Bruodinum filium Darii, familiae caput (psoricum profecto), sine equo, sine famulo, sine carro aut curru (nisi quod obvio cisio aliquo rustico interdum vehebatur, cum rustico lubebat), sine veste quae decem valeret florenos, iter facientem; quod de ô Briennis cogitare nefas esset.*[241]

236. See McInerney, '1615 Survey', p. 188.
237. See Breen, '1626 Rental', pp. 24–5.
238. Ó Cuív, 'Elegy', pp. 91–103.
239. See O'Flanagan, 'Advice to a Prince', p. 27.
240. O'Molony, *Anatomicum*, pp. 112–13.
241. Carve, *Responsio*, pp. 124–5.

[I had thrown in your face your false and shameful claim, which you were so tirelessly repeating over and over again, that you are of the bloodline of the O'Brien princes, kings of Ireland, Scythia and Egypt. Whereas your ancestors were servants at the table of the O'Briens and they were forced on the spot to sing an improvised song to the sound of a lute and to shake their voices. Whereas your kin sometimes had midwives and nurses, as you admit on page 112 of the relevant text, where you say that Donatus O'Brien was for seven years nursed, suckled and weaned at the house of Finola Bruodin and her husband Conor MacClancy. Whereas I have seen with these very eyes of mine Thaddeus Bruodin [Tadhg mac Dáire], son of Dáire, head of the family (and a scabious beggar indeed) travelling somewhere without horse, servant, wagon or a carriage (except that from time to time he was given a lift on some buggy[242] by a peasant he met on the way when the peasant was happy to do so) and even without a shirt worth ten florins; something which even to think about with regard to the O'Briens would be an aberration].

Carve paints a powerful image of the ageing bardic poet being reduced to a lowly station, casting doubt on the poet's status as a member of the *literati*. Carve claimed to have met Tadhg at the residence of James Butler, second baron Dunboyne (d. 1624), where he examined the poet on his knowledge of other languages but was disappointed only to have received a reply in Irish. Carve went on to mention that the poet travelled by foot and wore Gaelic dress rather than English attire. Bruodinus rejected these criticisms levelled by Carve and questioned his integrity.

Recent research of the Thomond papers at Petworth House, Sussex, reveals an altogether different picture which throws serious doubt on Carve's charges. Evidence shows that poet Tadhg possessed substantial estates in Ibrickan, making him one of the largest landholders in that barony.[243] In 1615, he held seven quarters of land including Doonogan (probably Doonogan castle as well).[244] According

242. Alternatively, a 'two-wheeled cart'.
243. McInerney, 'vainglorious', pp. 220–1.
244. McInerney, '1615 Survey', p. 186. Also see RIA Ms R.R. 14, B-18, ff 498–530, *Ordnance Survey Ireland: Co. Clare extracts*, vol. II, pp. 510–11 ['Extract of a letter from Mr E. Curry to George Smith Esq., College Green, Dublin, dated at Limerick 8 July 1835'].

to modern measurements Tadhg's lands amounted to over 6,000 acres, just over half of the Clann Bhruaideadha lands in Ibrickan. This included the 900-acre estate at Knockanalban which was rent-free and held by Tadhg in his right as an *ollamh*-poet. By all accounts, Tadhg was an important personage and landholder, much of which can almost certainly be attributed to the link that he cultivated with the earl of Thomond.[245] It is likely that these extensive estates were granted under favourable lease to the Clann Bhruaideadha by their Uí Bhriain patrons but precisely when, and under what conditions, is not known. Favourable marriage alliances may have also played their part; Tadhg married into the powerful Clann Mhathghamhna (MacMahons) of Corkavaskin, and it was probably on this basis that he was involved in land transactions with that family in the early seventeenth century.[246] This confirmation about the landholding of Tadhg mac Dáire Mhic Bhruaideadha adds weight to Bruodinus' claims about his family and their status in Thomond. It shows that Bruodinus can be relied upon for matters regarding his early life and family background, as well as for matters touching people and places in Thomond. It is therefore only proper for us to regard him as a perceptive and trustworthy witness, not least a distinctive voice from seventeenth-century Thomond.

CONCLUSION

The contention ended with the death of Thomas Carve sometime after 1672 following the publication of his *Responsio* – or reply – to *Anatomicum*. While such a vigorous and often unseemly spat between the two men did neither of them any favours, it does allow historians to salvage facts that otherwise would have been lost. When viewing the contention, we must remain cognisant of the cultural *milieu* in which each man operated. Carve was attached to Old-English culture and had depended on the Butlers for his livelihood. His views on Gaelic Ireland were influenced by his background and a general

245. On a newly-discovered reference to his landholding in Kilfarboy parish that appears in a catalogue of legal deeds possessed by Barnaby, sixth earl of Thomond in 1640, see Luke McInerney, 'A 1640 Register of the Thomond Papers at Petworth House', *Archivium Hibernicum*, vol. 74, 2021, pp. 27–134, at p. 115.
246. Ainsworth, *Inchiquin*, pp. 303–4 (no. 964).

disdain for the Gaelic learned classes, most especially the poets. His own Gaelic-Irish origins are downplayed and instead he claims that his lineage was connected to the Anglo-Norman Carews. Bruodinus, for his part, straddled the worlds of Gaelic Ireland, which included the classical tradition of Gaelic scholarship, and the Latin learning of the Church. Writing in exile in Prague, he cultivated a large network of fellow countrymen and by any measure produced an impressive array of writings.

The contention between Bruodinus and Carve bore unexpected fruit. From among the longwinded and contested picture of Gaelic culture emerge new fragments of detail and historical insight. For Bruodinus, it was incumbent on him to defend the status of the Clann Bhruaideadha due to the family's loss of property and influence making them vulnerable to criticism by detractors like Carve. The 'mutual vituperation', as one scholar coined it,[247] was fundamentally a clash of different worldviews. In attacking the poets and Bruodinus' claims about the Clann Bhruaideadha, Carve forced Bruodinus to clarify his arguments. Much of what followed is found in *Anatomicum* and it provides a new window on the Gaelic learned classes. For this alone modern readers have much to thank Bruodinus for, not least his spirited defence of the Gaelic learned classes to which he felt honour-bound through ties of kinship, solidarity and ancestry.

247. Wall, 'Bards and Bruodins', p. 445.

Translator's Note

LANGUAGE AND STYLE

In his letter 'To the Reader', serving as an introduction to the whole of *Anatomicum*, Cornelius O'Molony – alias Antonius Bruodinus – anticipates his three main lines of criticism against Carve's pamphlet. Firstly, the irregular way in which *Enchiridion* was published and distributed, furtively and without the necessary permissions; secondly, the content of the pamphlet itself, regarded as calumnious and slanderous for the Catholics of Ireland; and finally, Carve's use of Latin, which allegedly made *Enchiridion* 'almost full of as many grammatical mistakes as there are lines'. Although this final point may seem the most negligible of the three, Bruodinus reiterates it throughout *Anatomicum* as much as he does the other two, if not more. To his biting criticism of Carve's use of Latin, he often pairs some disapproving comments about the style of his opponent's writings, including the choice of specific terms and turns of phrase. All this is not simply an accessory to the argumentative strategy of *Anatomicum*, but rather a fundamental part of it.

At the core of Bruodinus' debate with Carve stands the issue of credibility. That is, why should the readers trust Bruodinus' writings, rather than the writings of his opponent? In *Anatomicum*, Bruodinus generally takes pains to develop logical arguments in order to refute specific statements about the history of Ireland (and, less often, about theology or philosophy) in Carve's *Enchiridion*. While forming the pivotal plank of his defence against Carve, this is not always a viable or sufficient strategy. Accordingly, Bruodinus ultimately resorts to the so-called 'principle of authority', a tactic of disputation which Christian writers had been employing in their arguments since the Middle Ages. This age-old strategy denoted that authority and status were the main determinants of trustworthiness in a debate. In the period when Carve and Bruodinus were writing, proficiency in Latin was a hallmark of a man's degree of erudition, and also of his ability to participate in the chief debates and controversies of the day. Proficiency in Latin, especially in ecclesiastical affairs, also reflected the author's social and ecclesiastical status. By repetitive criticism of his

opponent's faulty and stylistically defective Latin, Bruodinus casts Carve as a man of inferior learning and standing, thus debasing his credibility and competence.

While Bruodinus certainly goes too far when he brands Carve's Latin as a basic and corrupted form that only a child may speak (*puerilis Latinismus*) and he calls him a student of elementary grammar (*grammatista*), the Latin of *Anatomicum* is remarkably more sophisticated than the language of *Enchiridion*. Hypotaxis tends to be favoured over parataxis, with some paragraphs consciously deploying a flamboyant style complete with rhetorical tropes. Consider, for instance, the very first sentence of the dedicatory letter, and thus of *Anatomicum* itself. It contains eleven verbs (including the implicit *est*, in the relative clause about the title of Carve's work), with five subordinate clauses (which become ten, if attributive participles are counted) and a single main verb (*prodiit*). Although the subject of the subordinate clause with which the sentence begins is the same as that of this main verb, the nominative (*inimicus ... et tenebrio quidam Thomas Carranus*) does not occur until quite late, after the main predicate, so as to increase the suspense created by the opening reference to an impelling threat. Stylistically, this *hyperbaton* is enriched by the use of metaphorical imagery of light and darkness, which is picked up again through a *polyptoton* by the subject itself. After this, another and longer *hyperbaton* immediately follows, separating the subject from the verb in the first relative clause (*qui ... moliebatur*), through the in-between insertion of several other subordinate clauses.

Such a complex syntax could not possibly be reflected in the English translation, lest clarity be compromised. Readers who study or have studied Latin know that turning a single long sentence with several subordinate clauses into a series of shorter and simpler main clauses is a necessary trade-off when translating many classical authors, most notably Cicero. Arguably, what Bruodinus aims to reproduce in his work, albeit with fluctuating results, is precisely the complexity of 'Ciceronian Latin', understood as a particularly ornate use of the literary language rather than the imitation of any specific Latin author. Cicero had been canonised as a model of perfection of prose composition already in classical antiquity. However, it was particularly in later epochs, when Latin was felt to be departing or to have departed from its original standards, that his figure

was referred to as a symbol for the exemplary use of ornate Latin – especially in late antiquity, when several grammarians attempted to crystallise the rules of a language which was going through substantial transformations, and during the Renaissance, when the humanist scholars gave birth to Neo-Latin in direct opposition to the corrupted grammar, syntax and lexicon of Medieval Latin. In fact, Bruodinus explicitly uses the expression *Ciceroniana eloquentia* as an ironical rebuke against Carve's Latin, implying that *Enchiridion* (and the other works written by his opponent) failed to keep up with the standards of grammatical correctness and stylistic virtuosity which characterised Neo-Latin imitations of Cicero's prose. Bruodinus' choice of Priscian, a famous late-antique Latin grammarian, as a figure with whom he sarcastically commiserates when quoting from Carve has to be interpreted in the same way; for in Priscian's *Institutes of Grammar*, a monumental textbook in eighteen volumes, Cicero often features as a key author to be imitated by whoever intends to achieve perfect fluency in complex Latin. This is not to say that *Anatomicum* is faultless from a grammatical point of view (see below). However, Bruodinus' manner of writing is by all means closer to 'Ciceronian' standards than Carve's, whose use of language he classifies under the label of *Latinismus* (that is, tentatively reconstructed Latin, and therefore pseudo-Latin) as opposed to *Latinitas* (that is, true Latin, in line with the tradition of ancient Roman writings).

Although the use of a sophisticated language and style is the result of a deliberate choice by Bruodinus in formulating his argument, from time to time the prose of *Anatomicum* may sound pretentious and redundant to modern readers. While aiming at striking a fair balance between a literal translation and a reader-friendly one, the English text of the present edition attempts to reflect the pompousness of Bruodinus' Latin. Accordingly, whereas some of the longest sentences have been split into shorter clauses for greater lucidity in English, features such as the author's favouring of hypotaxis and his abundant use of superlatives have oftentimes not been altered in the translation. In such cases where difficult turns of phrase may result in obscure points being made by Bruodinus, endnotes have been provided to assist in the understanding of those passages. Square brackets have sometimes been employed in the translation, in order to elaborate on details or include words implied in the text.

TYPOS AND MISTAKES

Although Bruodinus' proficiency in Latin occasionally enables him to summon some 'Ciceronian virtuosities', the language of *Anatomicum* is a form of artificial Latin produced in the early-modern era and purposely wrought more sophisticated than that of other contemporary works. As a result, when reading through *Anatomicum* in Latin, it is not uncommon to encounter words, or entire turns of phrase, which are not in accordance with what a Latin grammar book would teach. Examples include morphological imprecisions and cases of erroneous use of moods, conjunctions, pronouns and pronominal adjectives. A few mistakes in the sequence of tenses are also present.

Genuine typos are not always easily distinguishable from actual mistakes made by Bruodinus. In preparation of the present edition, two different copies of *Anatomicum* have been consulted and collated, both of which are available in digitalised form through the British Library (London) and the Bayerische Staatsbibliothek (Munich). Mistakes occurring only in one of the two copies have been regarded as being typos, and have been emended from the text of the present edition. The two lists of typographical *corrigenda* provided at the end of those copies, which only partially overlap with one another, are not reported in the present edition, but have been implemented by directly correcting the text where and how indicated by Bruodinus himself. We have also allowed some margin of error to the author and typographer of *Anatomicum*, as explicitly asked for by the former at the end of one of the *corrigenda* (the scrupulous reader shall easily correct further mistakes). Accordingly, all spelling mistakes occurring inconsistently throughout the text have been corrected in the present edition without further indication. The remaining linguistic errors, which are to be found in the Latin printed in the present edition, fall under either of the following categories:

A) *Errata* by Bruodinus himself which do not affect the translation of the text. These are taken to be the result of Bruodinus' artificial command of Latin and are neither emended nor highlighted to the reader in our edition.

B) *Errata* affecting the translation of the text which could be typos or genuine authorial mistakes. These have been emended in the present edition by using chevrons (< >) in the Latin text, while substantial emendations are accompanied by an endnote. From time to time, readers with knowledge of textual criticism may dissent with our readings and prefer alternative emendations or exegetical solutions.

Readers should also be aware that our translation tries to render the grammatical and syntactical mistakes characterising many of the quotations from Carve's *Enchiridion* to be found in *Anatomicum*. These have not been emended in the present edition. Bruodinus often remarks on his opponent's misuse of Latin by means of caustic comments on sentences which he reports, though not all of the mistakes he criticises are genuinely Carve's. In fact, in line with the practice of his times, Bruodinus' quotations are generally paraphrases or re-elaborations of Carve's original passages, rather than *verbatim* extracts from the source. Some of the mistakes to be found in these misquotations are the result of abridgement, or they have been deliberately added by Bruodinus to overemphasise and criticise Carve's inferior command of Latin grammar. In the present edition, we have chosen to add an endnote only to those misquotations where a mistake is falsely attributed to Carve, though the reader should know in advance that word-to-word excerpts from *Enchiridion* are rarely found in *Anatomicum.*

LEARNED QUOTATIONS AND REFERENCES

(Mis)quotations from Carve's writings, which are generally the starting point of Bruodinus' refutation of his opponent's points, are not the only kind of citations to be found in *Anatomicum*. Some sources are quoted in support of a statement made by the author, or to disprove Carve. Other citations are merely ancillary to the main text. These include short Latin poems by contemporary individuals, mostly Bruodinus' fellow Irish clerics and acquaintances, which often consist of satiric pieces about Carve. Likewise accessory to the logical refutation of *Enchiridion* are the wide-ranging references to cultural

aspects of Greek and Roman antiquity, including short extracts from ancient poets, as well as the numerous mentions of figures of the classical world. These are given as tacit evidence of O'Molony's (that is, Bruodinus') erudition. These elements drawn from the Greco-Roman antiquity do not substitute, but rather complement, the religious and specifically Christian ingredients naturally embodied in a work written by a Franciscan to refute the writings of another cleric. Theological arguments, concerns about ecclesiastical customs and hierarchy, as well as quotations from and references to the Bible constitute the substratum, as it were, of Bruodinus' interests and works.

One may be tempted to compare this juxtaposition of classical with clerical elements to a tendency characteristic of the writings of some early Fathers of the Church (St Augustine, in particular, who is often mentioned by Bruodinus and whose synthesis of pagan and Christian literature genuinely promoted Catholicism in the Greco-Roman world). Yet, the religious ingredients of *Anatomicum* generally have the flavour of being simple displays of erudition aimed at enhancing Bruodinus' standing as a cleric in comparison to Carve. When reading *Anatomicum*, one could certainly choose to focus only on the details provided by Bruodinus about the history and culture of seventeenth-century Ireland, and to give little or no importance to the language and style of the work, to the quotations from classical as well as post-classical sources, to the cultural and literary references and allusions to the pagan as well as to the early-Christian world, or to the attention the author attributes to doctrinal issues. Doing so, however, would risk losing sight of the *raison d'être* of *Anatomicum* itself: that is, the controversy between Bruodinus and Carve, which involved displays of superior erudition and stylistic delivery in rebutting one's opponent.

Whether Bruodinus' display of erudition actually proves anything about his direct knowledge of the relevant sources is an altogether different matter. There exist a number of other early-modern writings that Bruodinus could have consulted, which might have served as sources for quotations from more ancient texts. The format of some of these writings, such as collections of adages from classical and Christian authors, was particularly useful to this purpose. It is worth noting that several mistakes and imprecisions characterising some

learned references in *Anatomicum* can also be found in contemporary texts which Bruodinus could access. Endnote 395 of the present edition discusses the details of a particularly revealing case: in quoting from a passage from Cicero's speech *Pro Archia*, Bruodinus mistakenly attributes to Cicero some words which later scholars had written about that passage. Given that the same mistake is attested in early-modern writings which antedate *Anatomicum*, one must conclude that Bruodinus is passing off a quotation from one of these writings as a quotation from Cicero's speech itself. In other words, Bruodinus probably had only an indirect knowledge of several of the ancient sources he mentions, especially Greco-Roman, but also biblical and early Christian ones. Long quotes, such as that from Cicero's *Pro Archia*, more likely come from early-modern works uncredited by him, rather than from copies of the original sources. For shorter quotes from particularly famous sources, such as the Gospels, citation from memory was another option available to a man as learned as Bruodinus – though one cannot exclude the possibility that many of these come from primary or secondary texts too. In general, it is worth bearing in mind that writers of his time did not entertain modern standards of academic referencing.

EDITORIAL CHOICES

Whereas the Latin titles of ancient works mentioned by Bruodinus have been rendered in the English translation of the present volume by using the Latin or English form most commonly found in modern scholarship, we have kept the titles of early-modern works in the original Latin form attested in *Anatomicum*. An exception has been made with regard to *Anatomicum Examen* and *Enchiridion Apologeticum*, but only in the frontispiece of the translation. Both Bruodinus' and Carve's works are often referred to in *Anatomicum* by means of abridged Latin titles, which have been kept un-translated throughout.

A choice had to be made also with regard to the translation of toponyms as well as modern personal names and surnames. These presented a particular challenge, because of Bruodinus' inconsistent Latinisation of them in the text. For toponyms, we have used a translation

that reflects the official modern anglicised forms and, where forms differ or are obscure, we have followed those given in the Ordnance Survey maps. In a small number of cases, where a modern name does not exist or has fallen out of general use, toponyms are spelt according to their seventeenth-century anglicised form. In general, the most common anglicised forms have also been used for the rendering of modern personal names and surnames, including Gaelic-Irish ones, which are Latinised by Bruodinus (for example, *O Brieni, de Burgo, Macnamarii, Mathaei, Clanchii, Gormani, Gradii, Molloni* have become, respectively, O'Briens, Burkes, MacNamaras, MacMahons, Clancys, MacGormans, O'Gradys and O'Molonys). An exception has been made with respect to those Gaelic-Irish names and surnames which are associated with bardic poets and other members of the learned class in order to distinguish them from others (for example, *Thaddaeus Bruodinus,* i.e. Tadhg mac Dáire Mhic Bhruaideadha, the famous bardic poet and great-uncle to Bruodinus; *Ferallus Wardaeus,* that is Fearghal Óg Mac an Bháird, a celebrated bardic poet of the early seventeenth century). The rendering of their names and surnames into standard modern Irish seemed more appropriate than anglicising their names.

Another notable exception has been made with regard to the two protagonists (and antagonists) of the work: *Bruodinus* and *Carranus.* The former surname has been kept as Bruodinus when referring to the *alter ego* of O'Molony, the author of *Anatomicum,* whereas it has been anglicised as MacBrody when referring to the members of his family. The usage of MacBrody conforms to the general anglicisation of Gaelic-Irish surnames in the text, while also being more faithful to its original form Mac Bruaideadha, than the anglicised forms Brody or Bruodin. The surname *Carranus* has been rendered in English as Carran when referring to Bruodinus' opponent in the main body of the text. This form has been felt by the editors to be more 'neutral' than the English surnames Carve or Carew, and it has therefore been chosen to reflect Bruodinus' point about the falseness of his opponent's claim of having English ancestry. The anglicised form Carve, under which Thomas Carve's works were published, has been used in the endnotes, where Bruodinus' voice is no longer heard.

When transcribing the Latin text from the digitalised editions indi-

cated above, some adaptations were made so as to improve its readability, which could not always be guaranteed by seventeenth-century typographical instruments. Abbreviations have been spelled out in the transcription, with the exception of personal titles. Inconsistent usage of the grapheme *v* in the place of *u*, and *j* in the place of *i*, has been standardised. Paragraph numbers have been restored, when missing. Punctuation, italics as well as upper- and lower-case letters, which were employed unsystematically by the typographer, have been normalised in our transcription and translation. The inconsistent usage of italics for quotations in the editions consulted posed a particularly complex problem, because – as previously noted – Bruodinus does not cite *verbatim* from his sources, nor does he always mention the source itself. Therefore, when transcribing the text, one cannot always be sure about the exact starting and closing point of a quotation or, in some cases, whether the text given in italics actually is a quotation. Instead of italics, we have resorted to using inverted commas in the present edition, though the reader should constantly bear in mind that some statements apparently reported by Bruodinus, and given in italics in the editions consulted, may not be quotations at all.

Text and Translation

ANATOMICUM
EXAMEN
Enchiridii Apologetici,
seu
famosi cujusdam libelli a
Thoma Carve (verius Carrano)
sacerdote Hiberno furtive
publicati,
quo
Carrani imposturae & calumniae
religiose refutantur,
authore
R.P.F. Cornelio ò Mollony,
Tuomoniensi Hiberno, Ordinis Min:
Strictioris Observantiae, S.S. Theologiae Lectore,

Permissu Superiorum.

Pragae,
Typis Universitatis Carolo-Ferdinandeae,
in Collegio Societatis Iesu ad S.
Clementem, anno 1671.

ANATOMICAL
EXAMINATION[1]
of *Apologetic Handbook*,[2]
or
of a certain infamous pamphlet[3]
published furtively by
Thomas Carve (Carran, actually),
an Irish priest,
by which
Carran's impostures and calumnies
are scrupulously refuted
by
Reverend Fr Friar Cornelius O'Molony,
an Irishman from Thomond, of the Order of the Friars Minor,
of Strict Observance, Lector of Holy and Sacred Theology.

Printed by permission of his Superiors.

Prague,
Charles-Ferdinand University,
College of the Society of Jesus in St Clement's,
1671.

ILLUSTRISSIMIS
DOMINIS DOMINIS,
D. WENCESLAO
ADALBERTO,
D. JOANNI
NORBERTO,
&
D. IGNATIO
CAROLO,
S.R.I. Comitibus de Sternberg,
Dominis in Grünberg, Wrschowitz,
Kanitz, Dürnholtz, Bechin, Gischin, Setz,
Plana, Kumberg, Aulowitz, Horasciowitz,
Sedlitz, Zaluschan, Skotzitz, Pacziwo,
Horisedl, Budin, Libochowitz, Krupna, & c.

Sac: Caes: Regiaeque Maiest: Camerariis
actualibus, Conventuum Fratrum Min: Discalceatorum,
Bechinensium, Horasdiovincensium & Krupensium Fundatoribus
munificentissimis,
Dominis Maecenatibus ac Patronis suis gratiosissimis.

TO THE MOST ILLUSTRIOUS
LORDS
WENCESLAS
ADALBERT,
JOHANN
NORBERT,
and
IGNATIUS
KAROL,
Counts Sternberg of the Holy Roman Empire,[4]
Lords in Zelená Hora, Vršovice,
Dolní Kounice, Drnholec, Bechyně, Jičin, Setz,
Planá, Kumburk, Úlovice, Horaždovice,
Sedlice, Zalužany, Skočice, Pačejov,
Hořesedly, Budyně nad Ohří, Libochovice, Krupka, etc.[5]

Official Chamberlains of the Holy Emperor
and Royal Majesty, and most generous founders
of the Convents of the Discalced Friars Minor
of Bechyně, Horaždovice and Krupka,[6]
His most gracious Lords, Maecenases and Patrons.

Nihil veritus stelliferae & gentilitiae lucis Vestrae, robore illustrissimi Domini Domini Patroni & Maecenates mei gratiosissimi, prodiit non tam in lucem quam e tenebricosa & male sana lue sua veridicae inimicus lucis & tenebrio quidam Thomas Carranus, qui opus a Reverendo Patre Antonio Bruodino, cujus titulus *Propugnaculum Catholicae Veritatis*, sub auspiciis Vestris, Sacri Romani Imperii Comites illustrissimi, paucis ab hinc annis in lucem editum honorique Vestro dicatum, figmentis & imposturis suis non tam obnubilare, quam totam in Hibernia seraphicam religionem, publicatione cujusdam libelli sui in haeretica civitate editi, mendis & erroribus depravati, nec ulla approbatione firmati, diffamare moliebatur; quod cum minime ferre debuerit licet rationabili ex causa patienter hucusque tulerit praenominati *Propugnaculi Catholicae Veritatis* author, saltem ego, brevi hac mea *Anatomia*, ne totum connivere videamur Zoilo, eundem exenterare coactus eram, ut sic & clarius lux veritatis fulgeat & firmiori fulcro *Propugnaculum Catholicae Veritatis* solidetur. Quia vero nihil tam firmum ac stabile est quod in suos quandoque non labatur recessus, nisi firmiori sustentatum auxilio roboretur, converti & ego *Anatomiam* hanc meam ad gentilitii scuti Vestri, Comites illustrissimi, firmissimum firmamentum, ut in hoc velut fixo & immobili polo *Anatomia* mea in perpetuas etiam clarescat aeternitates. Quam dum Vestro illustrissimi Domini Domini Comites gloriosissimo subscribo nomini, spero quod a clarissimo familiae Vestrae jubare novum nunc acceptura sit favoris & lucis incrementum, & inter gentilitias stellas Vestras, nullo unquam in secundo motu motas, benevolam inventura patrocinii sui sedem; ad quam tanquam munificentissimum & tutissimum asylum eam depono perpetuum gratitudinis pignus & argumentum. Ita sperat

illustrissimarum
dominationum
Vestrarum
obligatissimus cliens
Cornelius Mollony, Ordin:
Min: S. Francisci, SS. Theologiae Lector

O most illustrious masters, patrons and most gracious Maecenases[7] of mine, a certain Thomas Carran, an enemy of the light of truth and a trickster who enjoys darkness, has made his appearance, feeling no awe at all for the force of your nobility, which shines as brightly as a star. Rather than coming to light, this man came out of the shadowy and unhealthy filth which characterises him, and plotted to dim through falsehoods and deceits the work entitled *Propugnaculum Catholicae Veritatis*[8] by Rev. Fr Antonius Bruodinus, which saw the light of publication a few years ago under the favours of yourselves, the most illustrious counts of the Holy Roman Empire. Even more than this, Carran plotted to defame the whole seraphic religion in Ireland through the edition of a certain slanderous pamphlet of his, published in a heretical town,[9] corrupted by mistakes and errors, and not supported by any approbation. The author of the above-mentioned *Propugnaculum Catholicae Veritatis* must have hardly tolerated this; and yet, so far, he has been bearing this with patience, for a good reason. Nonetheless, lest we appear to be fully conniving accomplices to the misdeeds of a Zoilus,[10] as far as I am concerned I felt compelled to disembowel that very same author in this brief work of mine, *Anatomia*,[11] so that the light of truth can shine more brightly, and *Propugnaculum Catholicae Veritatis* can be supported more strongly in this way. Nothing, in fact, is so firm and stable that it may not one day fall down onto itself, if it is not held by a firmer stand. Therefore, I too have turned this work of mine, *Anatomia*, to the strong support of your noble shield, most illustrious counts. In this way, my *Anatomia* may even shine bright forever, as if it were fixed amongst the eternal stars of heaven. While I dedicate this work of mine to your glorious names, most illustrious earls, I hope that it is now destined to receive a new addition of favour and light from the bright splendour of your family, and to find a benevolent abode under the patronage of your noble stars, who have always been the prime mover of all.[12] Into this abode I place it just as if into a very generous and safe place of refuge, as an eternal token and proof of gratitude. So hopes

the most obliged client[13]
of your most illustrious
lordships,
Cornelius O'Molony
of the Order of the Friars Minor of Saint Francis,
Lector of Holy and Sacred Theology

Infamatorius *Apologiae* libellus, quo ab auctore suo non tantum particulares personae, sed tota seraphica religio impudenter traducitur, stylum quo configeretur merebatur acerbiorem. Praestat id solide & nervose *Anatomicum* hoc *Examen* mihi a venerabili consistorio ad censurandum commissum, ita ex fundamento famam suorum vindicans, ut post *Apologiae* Carranianae anatomiam, praeter calumnias & imposturas, nihil in ea residuum esse demonstret. Cum ergo tam ea quae sunt fidei, quam bonorum morum tueatur & defendat, lucem videat (si ita ad quos de jure spectat judicabitur) ut falsitatem ad meritas tenebras depellat.

In Collegio S. Clementis,
9. Iulii, anno 1671.

Matthias Tanner, e Soc. Iesu, SS. Theol. Doctor, & in Universitate Pragensi, ejusdem Professor Ordin: & Facultatis Philosophicae p. t. Decanus.

That slanderous pamphlet of defence, *Apologia*, in which not only specific individuals, but the entire seraphic religion is shamelessly exposed to public ridicule by its author, deserved a sharper pen by which it could be pricked. This *Anatomicum Examen*, which has been entrusted to me for censorship by the venerable consistory, fulfils this function firmly and vigorously; for it vindicates the reputation of its own subjects to such a degree that, after the dissection of Carran's *Apologia*, it demonstrates that there is nothing left in it but slanders and deceits. Therefore, since it protects and defends what characterises faith as much as the good customs, may this book see the light (if so, it will be judged by those who are entitled by right to do this), to drive falsehood into the darkness it deserves.

St Clement's College,[14]
9 July, 1671

Matthias Tanner,[15] from the Society of Jesus, Doctor of Holy and Sacred Theology, and Ordinary Professor of the same subject in the University of Prague, and temporary Dean of the Faculty of Philosophy.

Facultas R. Adm: Patris Vicarii Provincialis.

Frater Petrus Geanor, Ord. Min. Strict. Observ. provinciae Hiberniae Vicarius Provincialis dilecto in Christo R. Patri Fratri Cornelio ò Mollonii, nostrae Provinciae Sacrae Theol: Lectori, salutem. Cum, ut intelleximus, reverentia vestra zelo honoris patriae & religionis nostrae seraphicae ac multorum bonorum virorum famae tuendae mota *Anatomiam* scripserit famosi libelli Thomae ò Carran, qua solide Carrani imposturas & calumnias refutas, harum tenore tibi facultatem concedimus ut, servatis servandis, dicta *Anatomia* a deputatis ad id lecta & approbata typis mandetur, in cujus rei fidem has literas manu nostra subscriptas consuetoque officii sigillo munitas, dedi Dublinii in Hibernia 24. Martii, anno 1671.

Imprimatur.

Ex Cancellaria Archi-Episcopali Pragensi 10. Iulii, anno 1671.
Thomas Pessina a Czechorod, Officialis

Authorisation of the Most Reverend Father Provincial Vicar.

Friar Peter Geanor,[16] of the Order of the Friars Minor, of Strict Observance, Provincial Vicar of the province of Ireland, sends his greetings to Rev. Fr Friar Cornelius O'Molony, dear in Christ, Lector of Holy Theology of our province. It is our understanding that your reverence, moved by zeal for the honour of your homeland, as well as for the defence of our seraphic religion and of the renown of many good men, has written *Anatomia*, a dissection of Thomas O'Carran's slanderous pamphlet, by means of which you firmly refute Carran's calumnies and deceits. Therefore, by the tenor of this letter we give you the authorisation that, having observed what is required, the above-mentioned *Anatomia*, having been read and approved by the people deputed to do this, may be put into print. As a confirmation of this, I provided this letter, signed by our hands and equipped with the customary seal of office, in Dublin, Ireland, on 24 March 1671.

Let it be printed.

From the Archbishop's Chancellor's Office of Prague, 10 July, 1671.
Thomas Pessina[17] from Czechorod, Official

AD LECTOREM

1. Benevole lector, in manus meas nuper incidit famosus quidam libellulus, cujus titulus est, *Enchiridion Apologeticum contra sordidorum mendaciorum faraginem R. P. Antonii Bruodini & c.* anno 1670. (in qua nescio latebra) a R. D. Thoma Carve (ò Carran verius) sacerdote Hiberno, sine typographi & loci impressionis mentione & sine omni omino approbatione Ordinarii editus.

2. Primo aspectu credebam quod opusculum titulo corresponderet, & consequenter quod Dominus Carranus apologetice propugnaret ea quae in lepidis suis *Annalibus* scripserat & a R. P. Bruodino lib. 5. c. 6. sui *Propugnaculi* emendata sunt, refutando ratione vel authoritate fide dignorum Bruodini argumenta & inductiones contra ipsum.

3. At demum, excurrendo per Carrani libellulum & ea quae scribit conferendo cum R. P. Bruodini scriptis loco jam supra citato, deprehendi clare, non sine mea admiratione, Domini Carve (ut se vocat) libellum non apologiam, sed apologum esse, innumeris prope modum manifestis mendaciis, convitiis enormibus, imposturis patentibus, scommatibus pudendis ad rem non facientibus, & (quod execrabilius est) blasphemiis in gloriosos ac fortes heroes, qui pro defensione Catholicae fidei, sedis apostolicae authoritatis, serenissimi regis Angliae praerogativorum, ac patriae libertatis, a rebellibus regicidis parlamentariis haereticis crudeliter necati sunt.

4. Insuper mirabar qua fronte Dominus Carranus, qui se Catholicum & sacerdotem esse dicit, spretis tot Summorum Pontificum gravissimis censuris latis contra eos non solum qui famosos libellos, verum etiam qui ullos libros in lucem dant sine Ordinariorum facultate vel alterius habentis facultatem, ausus est in Catholica Viennensi civitate opusculum tam infame (tot grammaticalibus erroribus, quot fere lineis scatens) scribere & in haeretica una civitate (dicitur quod

TO THE READER

1. Benevolent reader, a certain infamous short book has recently fallen into my hands, whose title is *Enchiridion Apologeticum contra sordidorum mendaciorum faraginem R. P. Antonii Bruodini* etc.,[18] by Rev. Master Thomas Carve[19] (O'Carran, actually), an Irish priest, which was produced in the year 1670 in some hidden recess I do not even know, with no mention of the publisher or the place of publication, and certainly without all the required authorisations from an ordinary.[20]

2. At first sight, I thought that the small book corresponded to its title, and consequently that Master Carran, refuting Bruodinus' arguments and inferences against him through rational reasoning or by the authority of trustworthy witnesses, apologetically defended those things that he had written in his frivolous *Annales*[21] and that had been amended by Rev. Fr Bruodinus in Book V, Chapter 6 of his *Propugnaculum*.

3. But in the end, skimming through Carran's small book and comparing what he writes with what was written by Rev. Fr Bruodinus in the passage mentioned above, I clearly realised, not without astonishment, that the short book of Master Carve (as he calls himself) is not an *apologia*, but an apologue, with many semi-disguised lies, immoderate insults, plain deceits, shameful taunts, that have nothing to do with the topic. Also (which is more appalling), he included slanders against men of glorious and brave deeds, who were cruelly killed by the regicidal heretical parliamentarian rebels because they defended the Catholic faith, the see of the apostolic authority, the privileges of the most serene king of England, and their homeland's freedom.

4. Moreover, I was surprised by the impudence with which Master Carran, who claims to be a Catholic and a priest, scorned the instances of robust censorship by so many supreme pontiffs, that are carried out against those who bring to light not only slanderous pamphlets but also any book without the authorisation of the ordinaries or someone else who holds the faculty. He dared to write such a defamatory short work (almost full of as many grammatical mistakes as there are lines) in the Catholic city of Vienna. He put it in print in a certain heretical

Norenbergae), non sine Catholicae religionis singulari detrimento, praelo dare; ac tandem hinc inde Viennae & alibi (ubi R. P. Bruodini opera prae manibus multorum sunt) furtive spargere, quasi illi liceret impune contra leges in tam gravi materia peccare, sicut licuit fingere se ex Anglica Dominorum Carve esse familia, cum nobis omnibus Momoniensibus Hibernis certo constet illum esse ex prosapia Thomae ô Carran, qui ante multa saecula sanctissimo Episcopo Lactino impie amputavit brachium. Sed quid non tentaret bonus senex Carranus, qui fol. 380. suorum *Annalium*, anno 1650. Viennae Austriae typis Matthaei Cosmeri impressorum, agendo de tragedia mortis Caroli Primi, Angliae Regis (qui in hora mortis publice protestatus est se non in papistica, sed in reformata religione sibi a Rege Iacobo suo parente relicta vixisse & velle mori) pro formali haeretico his verbis ausus est orare:

> "Verum ad te, o Carole, mea convertitur oratio: quemadmodum nunc diem illum exspectas, quo omnium retributor ad extremum judicium venturus, cuique secundum merita poenas praemiave dabit, ita nunc eundem omnium misericordiarum & scientiarum Deum precor ut anima tua una cum aliis piis animabus in omnium requie Deo vivat", & c.

5. His cum admiratione impunitis excessibus ponderatis, R. P. Bruodinum accessi quidque ad Carrani *Apologiam* respondere vellet sciscitatus sum. Pater Bruodinus respondit famosum libellum, foetore tot mendaciorum & calumniarum putredine emunctis naribus abigendum a tali Pantolabo, quali Carranus esse dignoscitur, immature editum, non mereri ut ipse, omissis gravissimis suis domesticis curis & scholasticis occupationibus, pretiosum terat tempus in illius confutatione.

city (Nuremberg, so they say), not without causing singular harm to the Catholic religion. And finally, he dared to spread it furtively in all corners of Vienna and elsewhere (where the works of Rev. Fr Bruodinus are in the hands of many people), as if he was permitted to break with impunity the laws in such a serious matter, just as he was permitted to pretend to be of the English family of the Lords Carve. However, it is no doubt evident to all of us Irish people of Munster that he is from the family of Thomas O'Carran, who sacrilegiously cut off the arm of the most saintly Bishop Lachtín[22] many centuries ago. But what deplorable tricks would you not have expected from good old Carran, who on page 380 of his *Annales* printed in the year 1650 in Vienna, Austria, at the printing house of Matthaeus Cosmerus,[23] when dealing with the tragic death of King Charles I of England (who at the point of his death publicly declared that he lived and wished to die not in the pope's religion, but in that reformed one which was passed to him by his father King James), dared to pray for an official heretic with these words:

> "Actually, my discourse turns to you, Charles: just as you are now expecting that day on which the Requiter of everything, who is destined to come for the last judgement, will distribute to each man punishments or rewards according to what is deserved, so I now pray to the same God of all mercies and knowledge that your soul, together with other pious souls, may live in God, who is peace from all troubles",[24] etc.

5. After reflecting on these excesses that had surprisingly received no punishment, I approached Rev. Fr Bruodinus and asked what he wanted to say to reply to Carran's *Apologia*. Fr Bruodinus answered that the infamous pamphlet, prematurely published by such a Pantolabus as Carran is distinctively known to be,[25] had to be kept at a distance by people of civil discernment because of the stench of so many lies and the rot of its calumnies; such work – he said – did not merit that he neglected his very important private affairs and teaching duties to spend his precious time in refuting it.

6. "For", he said, "this pamphlet by Carran, that cannot be considered

6. "Nam", inquit, "Carranianus iste libellus, qui re ipsa nihil aestimatur, si a me refutaretur, crederetur aliquid esse, cum nihil sit." Deinde, "Carranus genuinus istius libelli parens, desperata causa quam apologetice defendere debebat, in arenam innumeris scommatibus, convitiis & calumniis armatus tanquam alter Goliath descendit; quibus armis non solum me honestamque meam familiam (quae illum non laesit) invadit, verum etiam in universam Hibernicam nationem totumque statum religiosum, praesertim vero seraphicae religionis alumnos & sanctissimae memoriae heroes, tam saeculares quam regulares, qui in odium fidei Catholicae a rebellibus regicidis Anglis trucidati sunt, invehitur. His," inquit Bruodinus, "ego armis pugnare non didici, quare Domino Carrano in hoc passu cedo, ne si illi juxta stultitiam suam responderem, similis ei efficerer."

7. Ego religiosa simul ac generosa hac Patris Bruodini (cui variis sum devinctus titulis) resolutione percepta, non scribendi pruritu aut conviciandi libidine, sed zelo & amore Catholicae meae patriae studioque defendendae innocentiae tantorum virorum quorum famam impie conatur Carranus in suo libellulo maculare, in arenam adversus falcarium hunc Philisteum (*Carran* Hibernice, Latine *falx* dicitur) descendere decrevi; & ne externi (qui R. P. Bruodini opera non legerunt & in rebus Hibernicis veraciter informati non sunt) decipiantur, credendo vera esse quae Carranus in famoso suo libello insulse cominniscitur, novum hunc illius foetum seu informem embrionem anatomice exenterare proposui, ut hac arte aperto ulcere foetor tot calumniarum ac mendaciorum, quibus libellus iste Carrani ubique scatet, curiosos veritatis indagatores procul pellat ab ulteriori illius lectione & usu.

8. Tuum quod est, benevole lector, certaminis nostri indifferentem ut agas arbitrum & patronum oro, utque attendas qualiter falcarius hic Goliath, meus antagonista Carranus, nudae veritatis praesentia supinus in terram dejicietur.

of any value by virtue of its subject, would be thought to be of some importance if I engaged with a refutation of it, whereas it is not of any." Then he added: "Because of the hopelessness of the cause that he had to defend by means of an *apologia*, Carran, the authentic father of that libel, enters the arena like another Goliath, armed with innumerable taunts, insults and calumnies. With these weapons not only does he assault me and my honourable family (who did him no harm), but he also attacks the entire Irish nation, and the entire state of the clergy, especially the pupils of the seraphic religion, and the men of great deeds of truly holy memory, secular and ecclesiastical alike, who were slaughtered by the English regicidal rebels out of hatred of the Catholic faith." Finally, Bruodinus concluded: "I have not learned to fight with these weapons, and therefore I yield in to Master Carran in this matter, in order not to prove myself like him, if I replied to him on a par with his foolishness."

7. Having understood this explanation of Fr Bruodinus (to whom I am bound for various reasons),[26] which was pious and noble at the same time, I decided to enter the arena against this Philistine cut-throat (the word 'Carran', in Irish, translates as *falx*[27] in Latin).[28] I was not moved by the itch of fighting or the desire of insulting him, but by zeal and love for my Catholic homeland, and by my eagerness to defend the innocence of so many men, whose reputation Carran profanely tries to stain in his short slanderous pamphlet. And so, lest non-Irish people (who have not read the works by Rev. Fr Bruodinus and have not been given true information about Irish matters) be cheated by thinking that what Carran foolishly invented in his infamous libel is true, I resolved to disembowel anatomically this new foetus or unformed embryo of his. Once the ulcer is opened through this technique, I hope that the stench of so many defamations and lies, of which every page of Carran's slanderous pamphlet is full, will drive the careful seekers of truth far away from any further reading and use of that book.

8. As for you, benevolent reader, I ask you to act as an impartial judge and patron of our fight, and to direct your attention to how this cut-throat Goliath – my antagonist Carran – is thrown onto his back on the ground by the presence of bare truth.

Anatomia tituli & capitis primi *Apologiae* Carrani

1. Apologias varii magni nominis vitaeque sanctitatis viri ab exordio scripserunt Christianitatis, quibus fidem Catholicam Ecclesiae ritus ac consuetudines, statum religiosum, se, suaque scripta & asserta, adversus venenosas oppugnationes haereticorum & aliorum obtrectatorum solide & subtiliter propugnarunt. Horum e numero (ut centenos alios omittam) nominandi merito veniunt clarissima illa Ecclesiae lumina, Sanctitatis spectacula, Hieronymus, Augustinus, Bernardus, Thomas, & Bonaventura, qui calumnias & imposturas diversorum pie eruditeque refutarunt.

2. In cathalogo horum ut te non inscribam, Carrane, multa vetant. Nam (ut de cursu ante actae vitae tuae ob sacerdotis respectum nihil dicam) scripta tua ita sunt pietate, charitate, modestia, & eruditione destituta, ut multorum prudentum judicio censeantur a rabula quodam potius quam a Sacerdote dictata: praecipiti enim ac effraenato furore in quavis fere linea tui libelli P. Bruodinum scommatibus ita oneras, ut in hac maledicendi palestra neminem te ego exercitatiorem unquam legerim.

3. Materiam quam apologetice defendere quamque optime rationibus & authoritate fide dignorum munire deberes, Carrane, alto silentio ita transis (quod deploratae causae tuae certissimum est argumentum) ut non solum tua taciturnitate confirmes ea quae P. Bruodinus lib. 5. sui *Propugnaculi* contra errores tuorum (si Diis placet) *Annalium* scripserat, verum etiam immaturum hunc tuum novum foetum non *Apologiam* sed *Apologum* intitulari debere ostendas.

Dissection of the Title and Chapter I of Carran's *Apologia*

1. Since the beginning of Christianity, many different men who enjoyed great reputation and lived lives of sanctity wrote apologetic works.[29] Through these works, they firmly and accurately defended the Catholic faith as practised by the Church, as well as its customs, the state of the clergy, themselves and their own writings and assertions, against the poisonous attacks of the heretics and other detractors. Amongst these men, some names come to my mind which particularly deserve to be mentioned (to omit hundreds of others): Jerome,[30] Augustine,[31] Bernard,[32] Thomas[33] and Bonaventure,[34] all famous lights of the Church and miracles of sanctity, who achieved renown and who piously and learnedly refuted the slanders and lies of their opponents.

2. Many factors, Carran, forbid me from including your name in the list of these men. In fact (not to say anything, out of respect for your calling as a priest, regarding the course of the life you previously lived) your writings have been abandoned by piety, charity, modesty and erudition to such a degree that – in the opinion of many wise men – they are thought to have been composed by some rabble-rouser rather than by a priest. For it is with an inconsiderate and unrestrained fury that you load Fr Bruodinus with taunts in almost every line of your slanderous pamphlet, insomuch that I have never read the writings of anyone better trained than you in this gymnasium of evil-speaking.

3. With a deep silence, Carran (which is the strongest argument of your hopeless cause), you pass over the subject that you should have defended by means of an *apologia*, and that you should have greatly strengthened by means of logical arguments, as well as by the authority of trustworthy sources. You do this in such a way that not only through your reticence you confirm what Fr Bruodinus had written against the errors of your (gods[35] granting this)[36] *Annales* in Book V of his *Propugnaculum*, but you also show that this new premature foetus of yours should not be entitled *Apologia*, but rather *Apologus*.[37]

4. Apologia, Carrane, Latinis idem significat quod defensio, responsio, vel satisfactio adversario data. Tu vero infamoso tuo libellulo nihilominus facis quam defendere ea quae in lepidis tuis *Annalibus* male consuisti & a P. Bruodino loco jam supra citato refutata sunt; & consequenter *Apologia* titulum non meretur opus tuum.

5. Porro ne gratis hoc videar dicere, ut candidus lector percipiat quam inepte libellulo tuo *Apologia* titulus quadret, consequenter hic adducam ea quae R.P. Bruodinus refutavit lib. 5. cap. 6. sui *Propugnaculi*. Nempe haec:

In tuis *Annalibus* Viennae impressis, fol. 21. sic scribis: "Anno 644. Hiberni in tantam barbariem & ignorantiam lapsi sunt, ut nulla prorsus politia apud ipsos viguerit nec politas literas retinuerint", & c.

Item: "Anno 644. Egfridus Nortumbriae rex ferro ignique Hiberniam devastavit."

Item fol. 35. tuorum *Annalium*: "liberali benignitate & clementia Domini Carve, ò Mohuin circumvicina loca & praedia accepit."

Item ibidem: "Mauritius Geraldinus a Thoma Carve Desmoniam dono accepit."

Item fol. 54.: "Ex Anglica nobilitate sunt Butleri, Geraldini, de Burgofitzpatrick, Taffe, & Demsi", & c.

Item fol. 84.: "Burgones cum Hibernis amicitiam & connubia contraxere, paulatimque degenerando ab Anglica civilitate Hibernicis moribus se imbuerunt."

Item fol. 98.: "Inter omnes Armachanos Archi-Episcopos Sancti Malachiae fama praecurrit, qui primus in Hibernia sacerdotibus connubia interdixit."

Item fol. 116.: "Circa annum 1080 scelus apud Hibernos vigebat Catholicae religioni multum adversans, scilicet ut unicuique pro opibus plures uxores ducere liceret, magnatibus pro deliciis ac libidinosa

4. The Latin word for 'apologia', Carran, has the same meaning as the ones for a 'defence', a 'reply' or a 'plea' offered to an opponent. In your slanderous pamphlet, however, you do nothing less than defend those statements that you wickedly weaved together in your frivolous *Annales*, and which were refuted by Fr Bruodinus in the passage already mentioned above. Therefore, your work does not deserve the title *Apologia*.

5. But in order not to seem to be saying this gratuitously, I will here put forward those statements that Rev. Fr Bruodinus refuted in Book V, Chapter 6 of his *Propugnaculum*, so that the honest reader may perceive how improperly the title *Apologia* fits your libellous pamphlet. These are the following:

In your *Annales*, printed in Vienna, on page 21 you write as follows: "In the year 644, the Irish people fell into such a degree of barbarousness and ignorance that no civilised polity at all was thriving amongst them, and they had no civilised literature", etc.

Besides: "In the year 644, Ecgfrith, King of Northumbria,[38] ravaged Ireland by fire and sword."

Also, on page 35 of your *Annales*: "thanks to the generous kindness and liberality of Lord Carew, O'Mahony[39] received the territories and estates around the neighbourhood."

Besides, on the same page: "Maurice Fitzgerald received Desmond from Thomas Carew[40] as a gift."

Moreover, on page 54: "The families of the Butlers, Fitzgeralds, Burke-Fitzpatricks, Taffes and Dempseys[41] are of English nobility", etc.

Besides, on page 84: "The family of the Burkes contracted relations of friendship and marriage with the Irish and, departing from English civilisation little by little, they imbued themselves with Irish customs."[42]

Also, on page 98: "Amongst all the archbishops of Armagh, the fame of Saint Malachy[43] excelled, who was the first to prohibit marriage for priests in Ireland."

Moreover, on page 116:[44] "Around the year 1080, a wicked tradition that was severely against the Catholic religion existed amongst the

voluptate plebejorum uxores habere, ac loci domino virginem nuptam ante viri coitum cognoscere; quae priora duo religio Catholica sustulit, posterius autem longo tempore duravit, donec hortatu uxoris Milcholmi sublatum fuit, qui demum sancivit ut virgo nupta unum aureum pudicitiae redimendae causa domino fundi solveret, quod adhuc in his & quibusdam partibus Lageniae servatur vocaturque Hibernice *Kystonady*."

6. Quo tibi Carrane majori cura ac diligentia nitendum erat, ut haec tua figmenta, quae a P. Bruodino lib. 5. cap. 6. sui *Propugnaculi* refutata sunt, quam optime rationibus vel authoritatibus fide dignorum remunires & confirmares, eo minus nova hac tua prole praestas; & sic, cum malam causam adversariorum Regni Hiberniae, quam defendendam suscepisti, pessime scribendo in tuis *Annalibus* pejorem fecisti, eam plane modo ut desperatam & iniquam tua taciturnitate non solum deseris, verum etiam Bruodino in hoc puncto subscribis juxta vulgarem illam juristarum regulam in 6.: "qui tacet consentire videtur."

7. Apologiae ergo loco nova convitia, imposturas, fabulas, & mendacia palpabilia adducis, sic non *Apologia*, sed *Apologus*, id est fabula in qua brutalia monstra loquuntur, intitulabitur imposterum libellus iste tuus.

8. In tua ad lectorem praefaciuncula, Carrane, praeter scommata <&> grammaticales errores (tibi quoties scribis familiares) haec emendari debent: "Propterea petulans ille Bruodinus famam (absque praevia causa) meam levi calamo malitiose denigrare minime destitit", & c.

9. Carrane famam tuam R. P. Bruodinus ut potuit non laesit sine causa; sed te merito reprehendit, refutavit, & arguit ob ea quae praecipiti ac effrenato furore in praejudicium nationis ac catholicae patriae tuae

Irish, namely that each man was allowed to marry more than one woman according to his wealth, and that the aristocrats were allowed to take the wives of the commoners for their own luxuriousness and lustful desire. Also, that the local lord was allowed to have intercourse with a just-married virgin before the husband performed the sexual act.[45] The former two of these three customs were removed by the Catholic religion, whereas the last one persisted for a long time, until it was removed by the urging of the wife of Malcolm.[46] It was finally decreed that a just-married virgin had to pay one golden coin to the lord of the estate to buy her chastity back. This habit is still preserved in these and certain parts of Leinster and is called 'Kystonady'[47] in Irish."

6. The brighter you ought to have shone, Carran, by taking care and attentiveness to reinforce and strengthen, by means of logics and authoritative opinions of trustworthy sources, the above fabrications of yours (which were refuted by Fr Bruodinus in Book V, Chapter 6 of his *Propugnaculum*), the less you stand out in this new offspring of yours.[48] And so, with your most disgraceful writing you have added further disgrace to the already vile cause of the enemies of the kingdom of Ireland, that you took upon yourself to defend in your *Annales*. After doing this, you abandon it clearly as a hopeless and unjust one by keeping silent, and you even concur with Bruodinus on this point; for, according to the well-known common rule of the jurists in the sixth book:[49] "He who is silent appears to consent."

7. So, instead of an *apologia*, you throw out new insults, impostures, fables and palpable lies. Therefore, this libellous pamphlet of yours, in the future, will be entitled *Apologus*, that is a fable in which brutal monsters speak out, rather than *Apologia*.

8. Besides the taunts and grammatical mistakes that characterise your style every time you write something, Carran, these words also need to be corrected in your short and foolish preface to the reader: "Therefore that impudent Bruodinus has by no means desisted from wickedly denigrating my reputation (without a previous motive)", etc.

9. Rev. Fr Bruodinus did not harm your reputation without any motive, Carran, as he could have done. Instead, he rightly rebuked

insipienter scripsisti, vel ab alio cum dispendio tui marsupii scribi fecisti. Calumniatores & detractores, Carrane, (exemplo Christi, *Matthaei* 22. qui Judaeos ignaros, stultos & caecos vocat, & Pauli *Act.* 9 qui convalescebat & confundebat pertinaces Judaeos) juste possunt argui & confundi. Te in societate horum jam dudum professum esse demonstrant supra citata tua verba, & inferius alia tua scommata adducenda confirmabunt: non ergo verum est quod "sine praevia causa opus in te" (utor tuis puerilibus terminis & Latinismo) "contra conscientiam ordine literario perpetravit" Bruodinus.

10. In fine praefaciunculae subjungis: "Hic injuste maledicentia me affecit, ideo par pari referam". Pulchrum Carrane te propositum habere Christiani hominis & sacerdotis ostendis. "Noli", miserrime senex, "vinci a malo, sed vince in bono malum". Diligere inimicos & orare pro persequentibus & calumniantibus docuit nos Christus, monuit Evangelista Ioannes, & exemplo hortatus est Stephanus. Generosior te Carrane fuit regius Psaltes, *Psal.* 7. dum ait: "si reddidi retribuentibus mihi mala, decidam merito ab inimicis meis inanis", & c.

11. Mox in haec verba concludis Carrane epistolam tuam: "Precor insuper benevolum lectorem me a Zoilorum morsibus tueri minime gravetur." Quid Carrane, Zoilorum facile princeps, times confratres tuos? Canes a latratibus & morsibus quis cohibere potest? In te, ne dubites Carrane, non habent tui quod mordeant Zoili. Bono igitur sis animo & cum patientia *Apologi* tui nervalem anatomiam aspice, & vale.

and refuted you, and he argued against what your inconsiderate and unrestrained fury, whose aim was to damage your nation and Catholic homeland, led you to foolishly write – or to urge someone else to write at your own expense. Quite rightly, Carran, it is possible to prove slanderers and disparagers to be wrong and throw them into confusion (following the example of Christ, who calls the Jews ignorant, foolish and blind men in *Matthew* 22, and also Paul, who recovered from his own blindness and baffled the obstinate Jews in *Acts* 9). Your words, that have been quoted above, show that you have already confessed that you were in league with these men some time ago; and the other taunts of yours, which will have to be detailed below, will confirm this. Therefore, it is not true that Bruodinus "against good conscience produced a work of literary condition[50] against you without prior cause" (I use your childish terms and pseudo-Latin).

10. At the end of your short preface you add: "This person unfairly inflicted evil-speaking on me, and therefore my payback will be equal to his abuse." You demonstrate to have the good intention of a Christian man and priest, Carran! "Do not be overcome by evil, but overcome evil by goodness,"[51] you most miserable old man! Christ taught us to love our enemies and pray for those who persecute and slander us. Likewise, the Evangelist John instructed us, and Stephen,[52] with his own example, urged us to do this. The king who wrote the *Psalms* was more magnanimous than you, Carran, when he said in *Psalm* 7: "if I have rewarded with evil those who repaid evil to me, may I deservedly be struck down dead by the hand of my enemies."[53]

11. Soon afterwards, Carran, you conclude your letter with these words: "Moreover, I beg the reader not to feel annoyed by defending me from the bites of Zoiluses."[54] Why do you fear your own brothers, Carran, you who are unquestionably the first and foremost amongst the Zoiluses? Who could restrain dogs from barking and biting? Without a doubt, Carran, there is nothing in you that the Zoiluses you are talking about could possibly bite. Therefore, be in good spirit and patiently consider my dissection of the sinews of your *Apologus*, and farewell.[55]

Anatomia Capitis Primi *Apologiae* Carrani

1. Famosus tuus Carrane libellus non solum raris jam in praefatione & tituli anatomia assignatis gaudet privilegiis & praerogativis, verum etiam inter grammatistas tibi singularem deberi locum demonstrat: quo enim frequentius argumenta, themata, seu compositiones suas in melius mutant grammatistae, eo a ludimagistris praestantior illis locus assignatur. Tu vero scribendo apologum apologiae loco non solum mutasti in hoc libello argumentum tibi propositum, verum & stilum & Latinismum nunc in pejus, nunc in melius (prout furtum tibi succedit) vix non mutato folio varias. In hoc ergo capite cultiori aliqualiter stilo Carrane quam in praefaciuncula ingenii tui acumen ac malevoli animi inclinationes erga statum religiosum ostendis. Insuper animose conaris ostendere praeeminentiam sacerdotum saecularium supra regulares.

2. Quid hoc ad tuum propositum, seminator discordiarum Carrane, facit? De illa materia P. Bruodinus, quem apologetice refutare proposuisti, ne verbum quidem habet; ad quid itaque tam insipienter, relicto scopo a te praefixo, hanc tractas materiam, nisi ut regularem & saecularem clerum contra se invicem concitares? Frustra laboras miselle! Unio cleri utriusque status major est quam ut possit per tuas dissolvi nugas. Regulares enim venerantur & amant sacerdotes saeculares non tibi similes, sed sobrios, castos, pudicos, doctos, zelosos, & charitativos; reciproce etiam regularis vitae veros observatores honorat clerus saecularis. Sed videamus parum tuas in hac materia nugas.

"Religiosi" inquis, "gloriari solent fundatoribus suis, nimirum Augustino, Benedicto, & c., sacerdotesque saeculares de Iesu Christo, quia praecipuum ordinis sacerdotalis caput est. Nam omnes Romani Pontifices, Cardinales, Archi-Episcopi & Episcopi ex hoc ordine sunt."

Dissection of Chapter I of Carran's *Apologia*

1. Your infamous slanderous pamphlet, Carran, not only enjoys the rare privileges and prerogatives that I have already conferred upon it in the preface and dissection of the title, but it also shows that you deserve a special place[56] among the students of elementary grammar.[57] For the more often students of elementary grammar improve their arguments, topics or word arrangements, the closer their teachers place them to the front of the class. Indeed, you have altered the argument that you had committed yourself to in this short book, by writing an apologue instead of an *apologia*. Moreover, the quality of your style and pseudo-Latin is inconsistent, as it varies sometimes for the worse and sometimes for the better (depending on the outcome of your plagiarism), without even needing to spread your mistakes across different pages. So, Carran, in this chapter you show the pungency of your temper and the inclinations of your ill-disposed spirit against the clerical state, in a style which is rather more polished than the one you used in your short preface. Furthermore, you fervently try to show the pre-eminence of the secular priests over the regular ones.

2. How does this support your objective, Carran, you sower of discord? Fr Bruodinus, whom you intended to refute by means of your *apologia*, does not have even a single word on that subject. And thus, having abandoned the goal you had set yourself, for what purpose do you deal with this subject so foolishly, if not to stir the regular and secular clergy against each another? Your efforts are in vain, you miserable fellow! The union of the state of both clergies is too strong to be possibly dissolved through your trivia. The regular priests, in fact, revere and love the secular ones who are not like you, but are even-minded, pure, bashful, learned, zealous and charitable; and, in turn, the secular clergy respect the true observers of the regular life. But let us consider your trivia on this subject for a bit.

"The clerics" – you say – "are accustomed to boast about the founders of their orders, namely Augustine, Benedict, etc., while the secular priests boast about Jesus Christ because he is the first and foremost figure of the sacerdotal order. For all the Roman pontiffs, cardinals, archbishops and bishops are from this order."

3. Quid praedicas Domine Chronologe? An tibi persuades lectores tui famosi libelli tam pusilli esse judicii ut tibi contra omnem historicam fidem & ocularem experientiam scribenti credant? Pontifices Romani, Carrane, per aliquot saecula fuerunt ex statu religioso assumpti. Cardinales, Episcopi, & Archi-Episcopi per Europam centeni fuere & defacto sunt non solum ex eodem religioso statu assumpti, verum etiam qui nullo sacro ordine initiati sunt: non ergo verum est, Domine Carrane, quod Pontifices omnes Romani sacerdotes fuerunt saeculares, aut quod Cardinales omnes & Episcopi ex ordine sunt sacerdotali. Sed haec missa in gratiam tuae ignorantiae faciamus, ut ad ulteriora paradoxa tua exenteranda tempus nobis non deficiat.

4. Pergis consequenter Carrane, tua falce armatus, fol. 3., 4., & 5. tui famosi libelli, omnemque quaeris viam, qua regulares ferire possis; porro quia nulla justa occasio occurrit, praecipiti furore agitatus, fol. 5. per totum, omni convitiorum genere, maledica tua lingua religiosos in genere invadis, eorum bonam vitam & famam defoedare & minuere frustra conaris, quae ego, ne tibi similis videar, silentio praetereo: "nullius enim authoritatis esse potest sententia" (inquit Seneca) "ubi qui damnandus est" (Carranus) "damnat, & ubi male loquuntur, qui bene loqui nesciunt."

5. Ulterius progrederis in malo, Carrane, folio 7. circa finem, ubi prius male citatis paucis lineolis ex *Chron. Frat. Minor.* quae beatum dicunt illum qui patienter suffert injurias, insano non absimilis in haec exclamas verba: "O utinam aetate nostra tales existerent fratres, qui se ab obtrectationibus, contentionibus, vana gloria, verbisque otiosis absterrerent; meliorem tunc reportarent famam ac aestimationem", & c.

6. Quid audio infelix Carrane? Non dantur ergo, caeco tuo judicio, hac nostra aetate religiosi morum gravitate, vitae sanctitate, ac doctrinae

3. What are you preaching, Master Chronicler?[58] Do you really convince yourself that the readers of your infamous pamphlet have such little sense of judgement that they believe you, the one who writes against any historiographical credibility and eyewitness experience? Over several centuries, Carran, the Roman pontiffs were chosen out of the clerical state. Across Europe, there were – and, in actual fact, there are – hundreds upon hundreds of cardinals, bishops and archbishops, who were not only chosen out of the same clerical state, but not even initiated into any sacred order. Therefore, Master Carran, it is not true that all the Roman pontiffs were secular priests, or that all the cardinals and bishops are from the order of the priests. But, for the sake of your ignorance, let us stop bothering ourselves about these things, so that we do not run out of time to disembowel your further contradictions.

4. Consequently, armed with your sickle, you persist on pages 3, 4 and 5 of your libellous pamphlet, Carran, in seeking a way in which you could wound the regular clerics. Then, driven by an inconsiderate fury because no appropriate occasion occurs, by means of your slanderous tongue you attack the clerics in general using every type of insult throughout the entire page 5, and you uselessly try to defile and diminish their good life and reputation. I skip over such attempts in silence so as not to look like you: "a verdict" – Seneca[59] says – "can be of no authority, when he who condemns is someone who is to be condemned" (this is you, Carran!) "and when those who are incapable of speaking favourably, speak unfavourably."

5. You go further in wickedness, Carran, on page 7, towards the bottom. There, not unlike a madman and after having incorrectly quoted a few short lines from the *Chronicon Fratrum Minorum*[60] which call the one who endures wrongs with patience a blessed man, you exclaim with these words: "Would to heaven that such friars existed in our time, who would deter themselves from disparaging comments, from fights, from vainglory and from superfluous words; under these circumstances, they would achieve a better reputation and esteem", etc.

6. What do I hear, you miserable Carran? Are you saying that, according to your blind judgement, in this age of ours there are no

splendore illustres qui ab assignatis a te defectibus abstinerent? Si tu, Carrane, vel angelus vel propheta vel apostolus vel vir bonus vel doctus esses, merito moveremur religiosi iniqua tua censura. At cum eorum nihil sis, non nimium tua hac commovemur sententia.

7. Audi tantum, oro, cum patientia non me, sed prophetam Danielem cap. 13. tibi tuaeque farinae detractoribus pro Susanna & innocentibus Religiosis, quos injuste damnas, loquentem:

"Semen Chanaan" (id est famosissimi illius praedonis Thomae Carrani praedecessoris tui, qui sanctissimo Lactino dextrum amputavit brachium) "nunc venerunt peccata tua, quae operabaris prius judicans judicia injusta, innocentes" (religiosos) "opprimens, & dimittens noxios" & infra "recte mentitus es in caput tuum."

8. Porro ut ipse tanquam conterraneus paucis te alloquor candide fateor quod in te Carrane agnosco non solum protoplasti tui Thomae Carrani, verum etiam veterum & recentiorum haereticorum genium, quibus nihil familiarius est quam in religiosos viros maledicas armare linguas.

9. Nisi tu noctua esses Carrane Viennae Austriae (ut de aliis mundi partibus nihil dicam) ubi a tot continuis annis latitas & impune latras in regulares & Catholicos saeculares, plurimos quotidie videres religiosos qui ab obtrectationibus, contentionibus, vana gloria, invidia, gula, verbisque continue abstinent otiosis. Tuam ergo hanc Carrane censuram meram esse calumniam, nemo est qui ignorat; quare ulterioribus anatomia non indiget. Tantum haec amore tui subjungam. Timeo Carrane, nisi tibi fuga consulueris tempestive, quod Viennensis Catholicus populus, audita hac tua calumnia, adversus te consurget, teque mulctabit poena tali, quali in Babilonia, ob injuriam innocenti Susannae factam, Danielis 13. ab universo coetu castigati sunt illi senes. Nunc ad alia.

clerics honourable for their severity of customs, holiness of life, and excellence of erudition, who could refrain from the vices that you have attributed to them? If you, Carran, were an angel or a prophet or an apostle or a good man or a learned one, we clerics would be disturbed by your injurious criticism. But since you are none of these, we are not too shaken by your words.

7. With patience, I beg you, just lend an ear not to me, but to the prophet Daniel, who, in Chapter 13, talks to you and to disparagers of your ilk in favour of Susanna and the innocent clerics whom you unfairly condemn:[61]

"O seed of Canaan" (namely, of that most infamous robber, Thomas Carran, your predecessor, who cut off the right arm of the most holy Lachtín)[62] "now your sins have come out, which you committed before, judging unjust judgements, oppressing innocent people" (namely the clerics) "and letting guilty ones go", and – further down in the text – "well you lied against your own head."

8. Moreover, I frankly confess that when I, as a fellow countryman of yours, speak a few words to you, Carran, I recognise in you the spirit not only of your forefather, Thomas Carran, but also of the ancient and modern heretics, to whom nothing is more customary than to arm their slanderous tongues against devout men.

9. If you, Carran, were not a night-owl in Vienna, Austria (not to say anything about other parts of the world), where you lurk and bark[63] with impunity against the regular and secular Catholics for so many years continuously, you would see every day a great many clerics who ceaselessly refrain from disparaging comments, from fights, from vainglory, from envy, from gluttony and from superfluous words. Therefore, Carran, there is nobody who does not know that this criticism of yours is a bare calumny; and so, my dissection of it does not need further words. For your own sake, I will add only the following: I am worried, Carran, that if you will not take care of yourself by fleeing in a timely fashion, the Catholic people of Vienna, having heard this slander of yours, will rise up against you and will castigate you with a punishment such as the one which those old men in Babylon received from the crowd, because of the injustice they had committed against Susanna, as it is told in *Daniel* 13.[64] Now, let us turn to other issues.

10. Proficis in malo Carrane, nam fol. 8., 9., 10. & 11. continue pro tua consuetudine adversus religiosos in genere latras, adducisque aliquot Patrum loca & Scripturae textus ad propositum non facientes, quos ita ignoranter, ridicule, & inepte consuis & combinas cum puerili tua exhortatione, ut nullo meliori argumento inscitiam & ignorantiam tuam lectori famosi tui libelli demonstrare possis.

11. Qualis est Carrane connexio sequentium tuorum verborum quae fol. 9. habes cum textu Scripturae quem immediate ante citas. "Cum ergo" (inquis) "quilibet religiosus sciat se non esse immunem a passionibus & affectionibus pravis, non deberet proprio judicio fidere," & c. Et infra fol. 10. circa medium: "ejusmodi religiosi qui sunt vanae gloriae, voluptatibus, & superbiae nimis dediti non sunt absimiles utriculari<i> tibiae, quae tunc maxime stridet cum vento plena sit: ita volubilis eorum lingua tunc plurimum garrit cum vino permaduit."

12. Nondum Carrane finis est convitiorum, quibus religiosorum famam denigrare conaris? Cur in alienam messem falcem imponis tuam? Frustra laboras miserrime senex! Religiosorum communiter vita bona & fama ita illorum statui consolidata est, ut detractorum calumniis ab invicem separari non possit. Si tuae farinae homines Carrane essent religiosi, facile nobis persuaderes quod affectibus pravis & post merum garrulitati essent dediti: non sunt autem, mi Carrane. Tu enim scis ob quos affectus ex patria exulare debuisti; qualiterque post pocula (scribente expensis tui marsupii pro te fabulas aliquo grammatista) otiaris & latras, Viennenses testari possunt. Religiosi respective, Carrane, habent quotidiana sua exercitia in choro, ecclesia, scholis, cathedris, administratione Sacramentorum, visitatione infirmorum, pauperum, & benefactorum; quae incompatibilia sunt cum pravis affectibus & garrulitate post pocula.

10. You carry on in evilness, Carran, for on pages 8, 9, 10 and 11, according to your custom, you continuously bark against the clerics in general, and you adduce several passages from the Church Fathers and the Scriptures, which are irrelevant to your argument. You stitch these together and combine them with a childish exhortation of yours in such an ignorant, ridiculous and improper manner, that you could not show your lack of skill and knowledge to the reader of your infamous libel with any better argument.

11. What kind of connection is there, Carran, between the following words of yours, which you have on page 9, and the text of the Scripture, which you quote immediately before: "Therefore," – you say – "since any cleric knows that he is not free from perverse passions and purposes, he should not trust his own judgement", etc.? And below, around the middle of page 10: "clerics of such a kind who have an excessive inclination for vainglory, pleasures and arrogance are no different from the pipe of a bagpiper that produces the loudest sound when it is full of air: in the same manner, their loose tongues blather about the most when they are drenched with wine."

12. Carran, are you not yet done with insults, through which you try to blacken the reputation of the clerics? Why do you inflict your sickle upon somebody else's harvest? You, most miserable old man, are striving in vain! The clerics' communal life is so honest, and the reputation for their status is so strong, that it is impossible for these to be ripped apart from each other by the calumnies of detractors. If the clerics were people of your ilk, Carran, you would easily persuade us that they were given to perversities and to blathering on after drinking unmixed wine: but they are not, my dear Carran. For you know what led you to go into exile from your homeland; and the people of Vienna can attest to how you laze around and growl after your drinks, while one of your fellow students of elementary grammar, paid by you, writes fables on your behalf. On the other hand, Carran, the clerics have their daily activities in the choir, in the church, in schools, in their offices as bishops,[65] in the administration of the sacraments, in visiting ill people, poor people, and benefactors. These activities are incompatible with such perversities and with blathering on after drinking.

13. Calumnia itaque mera est Carrane, quae tu religiosis objicis. Cum *P.* Bruodino, qui fabulas *Annalium* tuorum solide refutavit, tibi res erat. Cur ergo illo in pace relicto religiosos alios, qui te non offenderunt, invadis? "Quibusdam canibus" (inquit Seneca) "sic innatum est, ut non pro feritate sed pro consuetudine latrent." Te Carrane caninam hanc malam habere consuetudinem non solum testantur qui te personaliter noverunt, verum etiam demonstrant haec quae in hoc tuo informi embrione contra innocentes regulares inepte publicasti. Prudentius profecto senex Carrane fecisses, si, priusquam toti religiosorum statui tam petulanter tanquam alter Goliath insultares, pauca illa quae contra te Pater Bruodinus scripserat refutares.

14. Nolo ulterius lectoris abuti patientia in referendis & confutandis aliis calumniis & convitiis, quibus petulanter fol. 12., 13. & 14. regularium vitam & mores taxas, malevolumque tuum erga statum regularem ostendis Carrane animum. Hoc unicum pro fine anatomiae cap. 1. tui *Apologi* in perpetuam tui nominis memoriam subjungam: me nimirum neminem unquam in maledicendi palestra te exercitatiorem vidisse aut legisse.

13. For this reason, Carran, what you throw at the clerics is nothing but a calumny. You had a controversy with Fr Bruodinus, who had firmly refuted the fables of your *Annales*. Why, then, do you leave him in peace and instead attack other clerics who did you no harm? "It is innate for certain dogs" – Seneca says – "to bark not because of their nature as beasts, but out of habit."[66] The fact that you have this deplorable canine habit, Carran, is not only attested by those who know you personally, but also shown by the foolish statements that you publicly made against innocent regular clerics in this shapeless embryo of yours. You would have certainly acted more prudently, old Carran, if, before insulting so disrespectfully the entire state of the clerics like another Goliath, you had refuted those few things written by Fr Bruodinus against you.

14. I do not want to abuse the reader's patience any further in reporting and refuting the other slanders and insults, through which you impudently reproach the life and customs of the regular clerics on pages 12, 13 and 14, and you show your malevolent attitude towards the state of the regular clergy, Carran. To conclude the dissection of Chapter I of your *Apologus,* I will append the following single statement in eternal memory of your name: that, without doubt, I have never seen or read anyone more trained than you in the gymnasium of evil-speaking.[67]

Anatomia capitis secundi *Apologiae* Carrani.

1. Nugas, Carrane, somnia & nenias furatus est ex diversis authoribus, & in unum adversus regulares imperite capite primo tui libelluli male consuit scriba tuus. Jam amoto amanuensi hoc secundo capite tu ipse, mutato stylo in pejus, pro calamo falcem (nobile familae tuae insigne) arripis, & in Bruodinum caeco modo palam irruis. Porro, ut ostendas te non solum grammatistam esse, sed etiam dialecticum, per demonstrationes promittis te velle convincere intentum. Ad rem ergo Carrane.

"Nunc" (inquis) "sine fuco demonstrare intendo absurda R. P. Bruodini commenta, unde pro mei propositi affirmatione ipsius verba hic inserere volui veluti habentur lib. 4. cap. 15. ita dicentis."

2. Animose, mi Carrane, in tua senectute non bona in arenam descendis contra Bruodinum, exercitatum alias in materia demonstrationum militem! Ingenioseque promittis te velle demonstrare Bruodiniana commenta. At timeo Carrane quod ex numero illorum sis quibus perquam familiare est multa se posse jactare, sed ubi ad rem ventum nihil praestant. Videamus autem illam Bruodini narrationem, quam fictam esse te demonstraturum promittis. Est, inquis, haec:

3. "Marcus Bruodinus, verus & legitimus haeres Domini de Moyneo, fidelia Caesari Leopoldo a multis jam annis praestitit militaria obsequia in Belgio, Hungaria ac Pomerania, & modo sub praetoriano Caesaris regimine, quod ab excellentissimo Principe Conzaga consilii bellici Praesidente ducitur, capitaneum agit peditum, milesque arte & manu expertissimus, cujus fortitudinem durante Hibernico bello saepe probarunt adversae partis propugnatores. Tandem praevalente

Dissection of Chapter II of Carran's *Apologia*

1. In the first chapter of your short libellous pamphlet, Carran, the scribe you had hired stole nonsense, dreams and trifling songs from different authors, and he wickedly stitched them together unskilfully into a single text against the regular clerics. Now, after discarding your scribe, in this second chapter you grab a sickle yourself instead of the pen (a noble deed, typical of your family)[68] and begin to write in a style that is worse, and you openly attack Bruodinus in a random way. Then, so as to show that you are not simply a student of elementary grammar but also one of dialectic logic, you promise that your intention is to prove your argument with zeal by means of demonstrations. So, let us move on to the point, Carran.

"Now" – you say – "with no trickery I intend to demonstrate Rev. Fr Bruodinus' contrivances to be absurd, from which, in confirmation of my purpose, I resolved to quote here his own words, just as they occur in Book 4, Chapter 15, where he states as follows."

2. My dear Carran, it is certainly in a bold manner that you, in your unenviable old age, enter the combat field against Bruodinus, a soldier who has done training in the art of demonstrations on other occasions! And you ingeniously announce beforehand to be resolved to demonstrate that Bruodinus' statements are fabrications. But I am afraid, Carran, that you might belong to the category of those people who are deeply accustomed to boast that they can do many things, but who actually excel in nothing, when it comes down to it. Yet, let us consider that account by Bruodinus, which you promise to demonstrate as fictitious. This is how you report it:

3. "Marcus MacBrody – the true and legitimate heir of the master of Moynoe[69] – fulfilled his duties many years ago in Belgium, Hungary and Pomerania as part of the military entourage that was loyal to Emperor Leopold.[70] Now, under the praetorian command of the emperor, that is led by the most excellent Prince Gonzaga[71] as president of the military council, he holds the office of captain of infantry. He proved himself to be a most expert soldier in the art of war and in combat, one whose strength the defenders of the opposite side often tasted during the war in Ireland. When eventually the

Calvinistica perfidia per regnum, Bruodinus aliorum Catholicorum exemplo arma deposuit, fidem ab adversariis oblatam & promissam acceptat, & amnistiae subscribit. Demum petit a victoribus (quibus in patria subesse periculosum fore prudenter credidit) facultatem navigandi extra natale solum in alias regiones. Haereticorum dux non solum hoc Bruodino, sed etiam vivere illum negavit posse, nisi a fide apostatando sectariorum subscriberet perfidiae. Apostolicae veritatis sectator Bruodinus respondit se millies potius velle mori, quam ab avita Catholica religione recedere. Tyrannus, hac fortis atletae resolutione offensus, subito in Bruodinum mortis sententiam tulit. Rapitur ergo a carnificibus pius & magnanimus heros, nulloque habito respectu amnistiae per totum regnum publicatae aut fidei ipsi Bruodino in particulari antequam arma deposuerat promissa, suspenditur anno 1652."

4. Tandem de victoria certus subjungis Carrane: "videat hic benevolus lector contradictiones Bruodini, Lectoris Jubilati, vel potius frustrati, in tam parva circa Capitanei Bruodini praeconium descriptione errantis, in eodem enormiter proferendo quod anno 1652. fuerit ab haereticis in Hibernia patibulo suspensus, & tamen anno 1667. & 1668. inservivit Leopoldo Imperatori hic Viennae, & consequenter secundum Patris Bruodini relationem iterum resurrexit. Unde risus quomodo hic fieri poterit sine cachinno? Nonne hoc sufficit tantum ad circumveniendam P. Bruodini imposturam?"

5. Salutare consilium est, Carrane, non canere triumphum ante victoriam. Promisisti nobis in initio hujus anatomiae, n. 1. demonstrationem, loco cujus manifestum adduxisti in medium commentum. Non scis, Carrane, quod prudentes quem semel in pernicioso mendacio deprehendunt semper in reliquis suspectum habent.

faithlessness of Calvinism was prevailing around the kingdom,[72] MacBrody, following the example of other Catholics, laid down his weapons and accepted the safe-conduct offered and promised by his enemies, and he subscribed to the amnesty. Eventually he asked the victors (under whom he prudently thought it would be dangerous to live in his homeland) for the authorisation to set sail to other territories outside his native land. The leader of the heretics denied MacBrody not only this but also the possibility to stay alive, unless he subscribed to the unfaithfulness of the members of that sect, by apostatising from his faith. MacBrody, a follower of apostolic truth, replied that he preferred to die a thousand times, rather than desist from his ancestral Catholic religion. Offended by this resolution of the strong champion of Christ,[73] the tyrant immediately proclaimed a sentence of death against MacBrody. The pious and bountiful man of great deeds was then taken away by the executioners, and hanged in the year 1652, without showing respect for the amnesty that had been declared around the entire kingdom, or for the safe-conduct that had been in fact promised to MacBrody after he had laid down his weapons."

4. Finally, Carran, sure of your victory you add: "may the benevolent reader here see the contradictions of Bruodinus, a *lector jubilatus* – or, rather, a deceiving *lector*[74] – who strays from the truth in such a short sketch about the commendation of Captain MacBrody. For in the same account it is said that he had been hanged from the gallows in Ireland by the heretics in the year 1652, and that nevertheless in the years 1667 and 1668 he served the Emperor Leopold here in Vienna; and therefore, according to Fr Bruodinus' report, he must have experienced a resurrection. From this, how will it be possible to laugh without derision? Is this alone not sufficient proof to circumvent Fr Bruodinus' deception?"

5. It is a healthy resolution, Carran, not to sing triumphantly before the victory. In the passage I quoted in paragraph 1 at the beginning of this part of my dissection, you promised us a demonstration; but instead you have introduced an evident contrivance in the middle of the passage.[75] You do not seem to know, Carran, that a person who is surprised once in the pernicious act of telling a lie is forever

Si Bruodini opera in Germania non extarent, impune hic tibi mentiri licuisset; sed cum multorum manibus, non solum Viennae, sed etiam per Austriam, Boëmiam, & Moraviam (ut de Italia, Imperio, Gallia, Belgio, & Polonia nihil dicam) quotidie terantur, miror equidem imprudentiam tuam, qui<d> tam temere scripseris, in quo tam cito mendacii posses coargui. Ecce, mi Carrane, P. Bruodini textum verbo ad verbum ex lib. 4. cap. 5. fol. 736. sui *Propugnaculi*, ad te convincendum adduco, ut indifferens Lector videat, quam impudenter imponis P. Bruodino, quod nunquam scripserat. Quae Bruodinus loco citato habet, haec sunt:

6. "Minima Bruodinorum tribus in Tuomonia, certantibus Martyrum more variis aliis per regnum pro fide athletis, debitum dedit Christo tributum in effusione injusta generosi sanguinis animosi militis militumque Catholicorum saepe experti ac probati tribuni, Domini Bernardi de Bruodin. Fuit Bernardus hic meus nepos praenobilis viri D. Dermitii Bruodini (vulgo *Nasaffagh* agnominati) multorum bonorum in baronia de Tully, in Tuomonia toparchae (alter hujus Dermitii, ex Domino Carolo Bruodino nepos, Marcus Bruodinus, verus & legitimus haeres Domini de Moyneo, fidelia Caesari Leopoldo a multis jam annis praestitit militaria obsequia in Belgio, Hungaria ac Pomerania, & modo sub praetoriano Caesaris regimine, quod ab excellentissimo Principe Conzaga consilii bellici Praesidente ducitur, capitaneum agit peditum), milesque arte & manu expertissimus," & c. Reliquam partem historiae martyrii Domini Bernardi Bruodini vide supra num. 3. a Carrano mala fide descriptam & attributam Domino Capitaneo Marco Bruodino.

regarded with suspicion by wary people in everything he says or does. If Bruodinus' works had not appeared in Germany it would have been possible for you to safely tell your lies here; but since those works are read daily until worn away by the hands of many men, not just in Vienna, but also throughout Austria, Bohemia and Moravia (to say nothing of Italy, the empire, France, Belgium and Poland), for my part, I marvel at your recklessness, and at what you wrote so thoughtlessly, in which you were able to show yourself guilty of falsehood so quickly. Look, my dear Carran, I put the text of Fr Bruodinus in front of you, word by word, from Book IV, Chapter 5, page 736 of his *Propugnaculum*,[76] in order to refute you, so that the impartial reader may see how brazenly you impute to Fr Bruodinus statements that he had never written. The words that actually appear in the passage mentioned are these:

6. "Through the unjust shedding of the noble blood of Master Bernard MacBrody – a brave soldier and a tribune of the Catholic army who was often enlisted and put to the test – the very small clan[77] of the MacBrodys in Thomond paid the tribute they owed to Christ. They did this while various other champions of Christ were fighting to defend the faith around the kingdom in the manner of martyrs. This Bernard of mine was the grandson of the very noble man Master Dermot MacBrody (commonly nicknamed Nasaffagh),[78] proprietor of many holdings in the barony of Tulla and governor in Thomond (the second nephew of this Dermot, the one born from Master Charles MacBrody, Marcus MacBrody – the true and legitimate heir of the master of Moynoe – fulfilled his duties many years ago in Belgium, Hungary and Pomerania as part of the military entourage which was loyal to Emperor Leopold. Now, under the praetorian command of the emperor, that is led by the most excellent Prince Gonzaga as president of the military council, he holds the office of captain of infantry). He proved himself to be a most expert soldier in the art of war and in combat", etc. See the remaining part of the history of the martyrdom of Master Bernard MacBrody, which Carran has in bad faith described and attributed to Master Captain Marcus MacBrody, in the passage I have quoted in paragraph 3 above.

7. Prudens quivis jam considerare poterit quo calumniandi pruritu Carranus locum hunc P. Bruodini detruncavit. Bruodinus, ut vides, scribit historiam martyrii Bernardi Bruodini, & in parentesi tantum obiter facit memoriam Domini Capitanei Marci Bruodini; Carranus autem, ut calumniandi sibi sterneret viam, omissis studio tot lineis in initio historiae & paragraphi principio ab hac parentesis clausula "Marcus Bruodinus" incipit, & tanquam si non clauderetur parentesis post haec verba, "Capitaneum agit peditum", consequenter pergit, ut sic, si Diis placet, miser grammatista demonstrare possit Bruodinum sibi contradicere & consequenter falsum scripsisse.

8. Carrane mi, ubi jam frons, ubi pudor, ubi sacerdotalis tua modestia? An putas te apud exteros ullam habiturum amplius unquam fidem circa alia, quae de ignotis ipsis Hibernicis rebus in famoso tuo scribis libellulo, postquam ad oculum vident ex Bruodini libro te jam de crimine falsarii & impostoris fuisse convictum? Pater Bruodinus scribit Bernardum in Hibernia fuisse anno 1652. martyrio affectum, & Dominum Capitaneum Marcum Bruodinum anno 1668. fuisse Viennae Capitaneum; ubi hic Carrane contradictio? Ubi causa ridendi aut cachinandi? Ridere Carrane solent mente capti, cum nihil quod recte respondere possint illis occurrit. Cave obsecro inveterate senex ne dum Bruodinum ridere vis te ipsum plane ridiculum praebeas.

9. In principio cap. 2. tui *Apologi*, Carrane, non ridere, sed demonstrare te intendere Bruodini commenta promisisti: nec ego diffido quin ita <s>it. At mi Carrane, aliud est intendere, & aliud facere. Tu ut video (persuasus ab eo qui 3. *Reg*. 22. dicebat "ero spiritus mendax in ore omnium prophetarum") intendis demonstrare verum esse falsum, &

7. Any judicious reader may have already been able to observe how the desire to give false information led Carran to truncate this passage from the original text by Fr Bruodinus. Bruodinus, as you see, writes the story of the martyrdom of Bernard MacBrody; and only in parenthesis does he incidentally make mention of Master Captain Marcus MacBrody.[79] In order to pave the way to his bringing of false accusations in his own favour, Carran intentionally omitted a certain number of lines at the beginning of the history, and started the paragraph from the end of the parenthesis with the words "Marcus MacBrody". He then continued just as if the parenthesis had not been closed after the words "he holds the office of captain of infantry", in order for him, a wretched student of elementary grammar, to be able (if it pleases the gods) to demonstrate that Bruodinus contradicts himself and therefore wrote a falsehood.

8. My dear Carran, where is your decency now, where is your sense of shame, where is your priestly discretion? Or do you really think that you will enjoy any trust ever again among people of a different country with regard to the other things that you write in your infamous pamphlet about facts unknown even to Irish readers, now that those foreigners have distinctly seen from the book of Bruodinus that you have already been proven guilty of the fault of being a forger and a deceiver? Fr Bruodinus writes that Bernard suffered martyrdom in Ireland in the year 1652, and that Master Captain Marcus MacBrody was captain in Vienna in the year 1668: where is the contradiction here, Carran? Where is the reason to laugh or deride? Laughing, Carran, is what demented people usually do, when nothing they may say as a proper reply occurs to them. Old man – you of ingrained habits – please beware not to make yourself look utterly ridiculous, while trying to ridicule Bruodinus!

9. At the beginning of Chapter 2 of your *Apologus*, Carran, you promised that you did not intend to ridicule, but to expose Bruodinus' deceits: and I have no reason not to trust this. But, my dear Carran, having an intention is one thing, and doing something is another. As far as I see (convinced as I am by the one who said "I will be the mendacious spirit in the mouth of all the prophets", in Book III of *Kings*, Chapter 22)[80] you intend to demonstrate that truth is false, and

lucem tenebras. At frustra caece laboras! Nos enim, tui famosi libelli lectores, magis sumus oculati, quam ut te caecum ducem sequamur aut tuis imposturis credamus.

10. Pro affirmatione tui ad demonstrandum propositi verba Bruodini adducis. Vidimus illa Carrane supra num. 3. a te autem mala fide corrupta & truncata; sed ubi quaeso latitat demonstratio, quam ex illis deducere nobis promisisti? Non praevidisti forte quod Lectores, antequam fictis & ad risum excitantibus tuis accusationibus crederent, alteram aurem P. Bruodino accommodarent, & sic aspicerent in ipsius libro num res ita se haberet ut tu fingis? Caecitatem & fatuitatem tuam, Carrane, in hoc passu tetigit sequens qui composuit distichon:

> "Cernis quo tandem te caeca insania duxit?
> Non praevidisti? Non, quia caecus eras."

11. Frustra Carrane rogas fol. 18. lectorem ut contradictiones aspiciat Bruodini: tibi namque lectores non sunt similes, ut possint videre quod in rerum natura non est. Ex Lilliana tua grammatica ad summulas, si placet, Carrane saltes, & videbis illum solum sibi contradicere qui affirmat quod antea negavit, vel e contra. At Bruodinus in sua narratione penitus nihil negavit, sed duo tantum affirmavit: nempe Bernardum in Hibernia fuisse in causa fidei suspensum anno 1652. & Capitaneum Marcum fuisse Viennae in servitio Caesaris anno 1668. Quomodo ergo vis ut contradictiones illius videantur a lectore? Urgebo te fortius.

12. Vel tibi idem est, Carrane, Bernardum fuisse suspensum & Marcum Viennae fuisse Capitaneum, vel non est? Si idem, nulla duo tibi erunt diversa, quod est paradoxum; si non est (ut affirmare, velle nolle, teneris), qua fronte ausus es imponere P. Bruodino quod sibi contradicat, aut quod de Domino Marco scribat ea quae non scripsit de illo, sed de solo Bernardo?

light is darkness. But your efforts are in vain, you blind man! In fact, we readers of your infamous pamphlet are gifted with such good eyes as not to follow you, a blind leader, or believe your deceptions.

10. In confirmation of your intention to give a demonstration, you put forward Bruodinus' words. Yet, Carran, we have seen in paragraph 3 above that they have been corrupted and omitted by you in bad faith; but where – I ask you – is the demonstration hiding itself, that you had promised us to draw out from those words? Did you not perhaps foresee that the readers, before believing the ridiculous accusations invented by you, could lend their other ear to Fr Bruodinus and thus check, by consulting his own book, if the reality of the facts was like you depicted it? It is to your blindness and foolishness in this matter, Carran, that the person who composed the following couplet was referring:

> "Do you see where your blind folly has led you at last?
> Did you not foresee this? No, because you were blind."

11. In vain, Carran, you ask the reader on page 18 to look at Bruodinus' contradictions; the readers, in fact, are not like you, such that they could see what is not in existence. If you please, Carran, jump from your copy of Lily's *Grammar*[81] to the textbooks of dialectic logic, and you will see that the only person who contradicts himself is the one who affirms what he previously denied, or *vice versa*. On the contrary, Bruodinus did not deny anything throughout his whole account, but he simply stated two things: namely, that Bernard had been hanged in Ireland in a lawsuit on issues of faith in the year 1652, and that Marcus had been a captain in Vienna at the service of the emperor in the year 1668. So, how do you want his contradictions to be evident to the reader? I am going to press you further in this matter.

12. In your view, Carran, is the fact that Bernard had been hanged the same as the fact that Marcus had been captain, or is it not? If it is the same, you will not end up having two different facts – namely, you have no paradox. If it is not the same (as you are bound to say, whether you want to or not), with what impudence did you dare to accuse Fr Bruodinus of contradicting himself, or writing about Master Marcus what he did not write about him, but only about Bernard?

13. Quid? Non te Carrane tam manifesti mendacii pudet? Quis jam non facile intelligit nihil te in P. Bruodini libro quod jure reprehenderes invenire potuisse, cum ut aliquid habeas in quo illum reprehendas, tam manifesta illi commenta affigis tua quae in mentem illi nunquam venerunt? Ubi illa est victoria, quam tibi in initio hujus capitis promisisti? Ecce quomodo in foveam quam fecisti incidisti! Victoria tua Carrane a quodam ex genere poëtarum hoc versu videtur fuisse tacta:

> "Vicisti, ac tandem tua te victoria perdit;
> Infelix ille est, quem sua damna docent."

14. Nondum est finis mendaciorum ac calumniarum tuarum Carrane? Pergis eodem itinere eademque fronte qua cepisti, & adducis non refutationem eorum quae contra te P. Bruodinus scripserat (de his alto silentio tacet) sed nova commenta ad rem non facientia.

"Addemus" (inquis fol. 19) "adhuc majora de futilibus ipsius" (id est, Bruodini) "falsisque relationibus." Adde, Carrane, sed cum cautela, ne incidas in poenas temere litigantium.

"Non obstante" (subdis) "quod dicat Capitaneum Bruodinum legitimum Dominii de Moyneo esse haeredem, attamen ego majori certitudine veritatisque evidentia contrarium plane affirmo, scilicet quod tota familia Bruodinorum nullum unquam dominium habuerit nec defacto habeat in Regno Hiberniae vel Comitatu <Tuomondiae>. Res est certa: multo minus Capitaneus Bruodinus de Moyneo," & c.

15. Perdifficile est Carrane assuetum calumniis & mendaciis ingenium tuum ad dignum Christiano pectore candorem ac veritatis amorem traducere! Quid tibi nocuit Dominus Capitaneus Bruodinus illis annis quibus Viennae Capitaneum egit? quid tota Bruodinorum honorata familia, in quam rabidi ad instar canis injuste latras, contra te fecit, ob quod tam inique illam diffamas & contemnis? P. Bruodinus solus tuorum *Annalium* fabulas & deliria emendavit, non vero Capitaneus

13. What? You do not feel ashamed of such a blatant lie, Carran? By this time, who is there who does not easily understand that you could not find anything in Fr Bruodinus' book that you could justly criticise, when you ascribe to him contrivances so evident, that never came to his mind, as if you had something for which you could blame him? Where is that victory that you had announced in advance at the beginning of this chapter? Here is how you fell into the pit you dug yourself! It seems that your victory, Carran, was hinted at in the first of these lines by a man who is ranked amongst the poets:[82]

> "You won, and eventually your victory ruined you;
> miserable is he who learns through his own injuries."

14. Are you not done with your falsehoods and calumnies yet, Carran? You go on along the same path and the same impudence with which you began. You do not put forward a refutation of those statements that Fr Bruodinus had written against you (he says nothing about these, keeping a deep silence), but new deceits that have nothing to do with the matter.

On page 19 you state: "We are going to add even more important points about his" (that is, Bruodinus') "futile and false accounts". Do add them, Carran, but do it with caution, lest you incur in the penalties set for those who litigate recklessly.

"Although" – you add – "Bruodinus says that Captain MacBrody was the legitimate heir of the master of Moynoe, nevertheless with greater certainty and unvarnished truth I assert the complete opposite, namely that the entire family of the MacBrodys never held any possessions, and does not actually have any, in the kingdom of Ireland or in the county of Tuomondia.[83] That fact is certain: much less was held by Captain MacBrody of Moynoe", etc.

15. It is extremely difficult, Carran, to turn your own natural inclination, which is accustomed to calumnies and falsehoods, into purity worthy of a Christian heart, and into love for the truth! What harm did Captain MacBrody do to you in those years in which he served as a captain in Vienna?[84] What did the entire family of the MacBrodys, at whom you unjustly bark like an enraged dog, do against you, that makes you unfairly defame and disparage them in this way? The only one who reprimanded the fables and mad statements of your *Annales*

Bruodinus aut tota simul Bruodiniana familia: ad quid igitur, Carrane, innocentes tuis opprimis calumniis & adversario tuo parcis?

16. Nisi (ut antea dixi) prudentum esset consuetudo, illi quem semel in pernicioso mendacio deprehendunt amplius facile non credere, & quod jam supra n. 2. & 3. & 6. in flagranti mendacio Carrane sis deprehensus, moverentur merito, turbarenturque justo dolore Tuomonienses pleraeque omnes nobiles familae (Bruodinis vel affinitate, vel consanguinitate, vel alio aliquo honorifico titulo conjunctae) hac tua impostura. At cum palam jam sis de mendacio n. 6. convictus, non debemus amplius mirari tuam in malo perseverantiam & in calumniis texendis constantiam.

17. Ego Carrane in Tuomonia, non "Tuomondiae" (ut tu inepte scribis) natus sum, ex nobili familia per patriam notissima, Bruodinisque conjunctissima; sic audacter cum Propheta Daniele c. 13. dicerem, nisi sacerdotii tui & religiosae meae vitae respectum haberem, quod tu in tua de Bruodiniana familia calumnia "mentiaris in caput tuum". Nam ex Bruodinis multi egregii nobiles diversa bona haereditario jure in Tuomonia possederunt semper, usque ad annum 1650. quo occupato jam toto fere Regno Hiberniae Tuomonia nostra cessit in praedam rebellibus Crumwellistis. P. Bruodinus de sua familia satis humiliter Carrane scripsit "minima" (inquit supra n. 6) "Bruodinorum tribus in Tuomonia," & c. Quomodo potuisset modestius loqui Carrane?

18. Inter Hibernos Carrane (more omnium per Europam nationum) sunt nobiles, nobiliores, nobilissimi: divites, ditiores, ditissimi. Bruodinus non negavit, sed palam confessus est suam familiam esse tantum nobilem, ex qua semper unus fuit familiae caput seu senior (vulgo *mac Bruodin* dictus) cujus erat priscis regnantibus Hibernis inter alios regni chronologos historiam regni scribere, genealogias, et

was Fr Bruodinus, definitely not Captain MacBrody, or the whole MacBrody family. Why, then, do you trouble innocent people with your slanders and spare your real enemy, Carran?

16. Wary people have the habit to stop easily believing a person whom they caught in the pernicious act of telling a lie even just once (as I said before); and you, Carran, have already been caught in the very act of lying in paragraph nos. 2, 3 and 6 above. Were it not for this, this deceit of yours would understandably shake and disturb most, if not all, of the noble families of Thomond with the distress that any righteous man would feel (families which are bound to the MacBrodys by affinity or kindred or by some other honorific title). But since you have clearly proven yourself guilty of lying in paragraph 6, we should no longer be surprised by your perseverance in evil or your constancy in weaving lies.

17. I was born in Thomond,[85] Carran, and not in "Tuomondia" (as you improperly write), from a noble family very well-known throughout my homeland, and closely bound to the MacBrodys. Thus, if I did not have any respect for your priesthood and for my religious life, I would dare say, together with the prophet Daniel in Chapter 13, that "you tell a lie against your own head"[86] by slandering the MacBrody family. For many distinguished nobles of the MacBrodys always owned diverse possessions in Thomond in right of inheritance, until the year 1650, in which our Thomond fell into the hands of Cromwell's rebels at a time when almost all of the kingdom of Ireland had already been occupied. Fr Bruodinus was quite humble in writing about his family, Carran: "the very small clan" – he says, as you can read in paragraph 6 above – "of the MacBrodys in Thomond", etc. How could he have said more modest words, Carran?

18. Among the Irish, Carran (as by custom of every nation across Europe), there are noble people, nobler people and the noblest people: the rich, the richer and the richest. Bruodinus did not deny, but actually openly confessed that his family was only a noble one, from which always a single man was brought forth as the head of the family, or the senior (generally called MacBrody). Back in the time when the old Irish reigned, it was up to him to write, among other chroniclers of the realm, the history of the kingdom, and to keep note

facta notabilia principum ô Brien & aliarum certarum magnatum familiarum observare. Hoc munus chronologi non dabatur Carrane a principibus quondam Hibernorum, nisi viris nobilibus, fide dignis, qui media habebant sustentandi gradus suos, ut P. Bruodinus ostendit lib. 5. cap. 2. sui *Propugnaculi.*

19. Ex Bruodinis Carrane (crepa prae invidia si vis) nominabo tibi diversos praeclaros nobiles, qui usque ad annum 1650. subditos multos & diversa commoda habuerunt bona in Tuomonia, ut testimonio non solum meo, sed & omnium qui in Tuomonia hodie vivunt & aliorum fide dignorum (ut videre est in fine & principio hujus libelli) calculo probabo, ut sic tua calumnia cedat in perpetuam laudem & honorem Bruodinorum inter externos & tuam confusionem & ignominiam inter domesticos & extraneos. Jam ad rem.

In Baronia de Tully in Tuomonia, Carrane, Dominus Florentius Bruodinus, vulgo *mac Bruodin* dictus, qui binis vicibus Comitatus de Clare fuit Capitaneus, vulgo *Schirriff,* fuit Dominus in Superiori Moyneo, Kulkosan, & Achrem.

Carolus Bruodinus, Dominus in Bealanegh, in inferiori Moyneo & Bally Mennogh; hujus filius est Capitaneus Bruodinus, de quo tu tam male scribis.

Caherus Bruodinus, Dominus in Sannobogh.

Daniel Bruodinus, Dominus in Toburkulan.

Bernardus Bruodinus, Dominus de Rosnahally.

Myllerus Bruodinus (Patris Antony parens) Dominus in Balliogan, Drumbanuff, Kluon an Wullin, & Knocknamuchky.

Ioannes Bruodinus, Dominus in Bally an Tonny.

Donatus Bruodinus, in Ballyscanlan.

In Baronia Insularum, Dominus Gilbertus Bruodinus fuit Dominus in Boly, Duff, & in parte Montis Callani.

Cornelius Bruodinus, Dominus in Rossin.

Daniel Bruodinus, Dominus Montis Callani.

In Baronia de Insequen, Dominus Milerus (juvenis dictus) Dominus in Superiori Kilky.

Dominus Boëtius Bruodinus, Dominus in Rachalan.

of the genealogies, and the remarkable deeds of the O'Brien lords and those of certain other families of magnates.[87] Those who were rulers of the Irish people back then, Carran, did not assign this office of chronicler to just anyone but to trustworthy noble men, who had the means to sustain their social ranks, as Fr Bruodinus shows in Book V, Chapter 2 of his *Propugnaculum*.[88]

19. From the MacBrodys, Carran (grumble with envy, if you wish!), I will give you the names of various outstanding noblemen who, until the year 1650, had many people under their control and diverse possessions held by privilege in Thomond. I will prove this not only by my own testimony, but also by the reckoning of everyone who lives in Thomond today and of other trustworthy people (as you can see at the end as well as the beginning of this short book). In this way, may your slander turn into perpetual praise and honour for the MacBrodys among foreigners, and into shame and disgrace for you amongst both natives and foreigners. Now to the point:

In the barony of Tulla in Thomond, Carran, Master Flann MacBrody, commonly called MacBrody, who was twice the captain of County Clare, generally called the sheriff, was the master of upper Moynoe, Coolcusaun[89] and Aughrim.[90]

Charles MacBrody,[91] master of Bealanegh, in lower Moynoe and Ballyminoge;[92] his son is Captain MacBrody, of whom you so improperly write.

Caher MacBrody, master of Shanavogh.[93]

Donall MacBrody, master of Tobercoolan.[94]

Bernard MacBrody, master of Rosnahally.[95]

Maolin MacBrody[96] (father of Fr Anthony), master of Ballyogan, Drumbonniv, Cloonawillin and Knocknamucky.[97]

John MacBrody, master in Ballyantonny.[98]

Donough MacBrody, in Ballyscanlan.[99]

In the barony of the Islands, Master Giolla Brighde MacBrody[100] was the master in Boolyduff[101] and on one side of Slievecallan.[102]

Conor MacBrody, master in Rossin.[103]

Donall MacBrody, master of Slievecallan.[104]

In the Barony of Inchiquin, Master Maolin (called the younger)[105] was master of Upper Kilkee.[106]

Master Boetius MacBrody,[107] master in Rathcahaun.[108]

Dominus Gilbertus Bruodinus, Ioannis filius, Dominus in inferiori Kilky.

In Baronia de Ibrickan, Dominus Iacobus Bruodinus (Thadaei filius) Dominus Montis Scoti.

Dominus Bernardus Bruodinus, Dominus de Kurr.

Praeter hos jam nominatos Carrane in Tuomonia nostra multi erant alii Bruodini Nobiles, qui (more multorum per Hiberniam nobilium) bona habuerunt conducta ab uno vel altero ex proceribus patriae; quique vixerunt tam honorate sua industria & oeconomisandi peritia, ac alii nobiles qui propria habuerunt bona.

20. An mihi & aliis dignissimis viris (qui suo testimonio confirmant veritatem quam scribo) vel invido & passionato Carrano, qui Tuomoniam vix unquam vidit, sit in hac parte credendum, maturo lectoris relinquo judicio.

Jam consideremus quomodo, Carrane, probas vera esse ea quae de Bruodiniana familia inverecunde scribis! Non teste, non signo, non apice; "probo" (inquis fol. 19.) "quia nullum unquam dominium habuerunt, res est certa," &c.

21. Nobis Carrane, qui Tuomonienses sumus nati, certissimum est quod tu calumniaris in hac parte; nam a me jam num. 19. nominati Bruodini in Tuomonia nobiles erant, qui diversa & pulchra habuerunt bona. Si tu autem vis ut tibi potius quam nobis lectores credant, oportet ut evidenti saltem aliquo signo probes illius te spiritus testimonio niti qui nec falli nec fallere potest: quod cum facere nequeas, non tibi persuadeas Carrane lectores adeo tibi devinctos ut arbitrio tuo fidem suam committant.

22. "Adduco", inquis "evidens hoc argumentum, quia, si Capitaneus Bruodinus habuisset dominium aliquod in Tuomondia, certe non maneret in Bohemia." Quid rogo cogitas senex Carrane? Argumento enim tuo acumine digno, id est quod nec in modo est nec figura, conaris colorare calumnias tuas, miselle! Nonne serenissimus noster Carolus Rex fuit Magnae Britanniae & Hiberniae, durante potentia

Master Giolla Brighde MacBrody, son of John, was master in Lower Kilkee.[109]

In the Barony of Ibrickan, Master James MacBrody (son of Tadhg) was master of Knockanalban.[110]

Master Bernard MacBrody, master of Coor.[111]

Beside these people just mentioned, Carran, there were many other noble MacBrodys in our Thomond who (in the manner of many nobles throughout Ireland) had possessions on lease from one or another of the leading men of the country; and by their industry and managing skill, they lived as honourably as the other nobles who had possessions of their own.

20. As to whether in this matter one should believe me and other most worthy men (who confirm by their testimony the truth that I write) or the envious and passionate Carran, who has hardly ever seen Thomond, I leave it to the reader's mature judgement.

Let us now examine, Carran, how you prove that the things you shamelessly write about the MacBrody family are true! Not with a witness, not with a sign, not with a document: "I prove" – you say on page 19 – "that they have never had any property, the fact is certain", etc.

21. To us, Carran, who were born men of Thomond, it is absolutely certain that you are calumniating on this point; for the MacBrodys I have just named in paragraph 19 were members of the nobility in Thomond, who had various and beautiful possessions. But if you want the readers to believe you rather than us, you need to prove by at least one evident sign that you are relying on the testimony of that spirit which can neither be deceived nor deceive. Since you cannot do this, Carran, do not convince yourself that the readers are so bound to you as to lend their trust to your judgement.

22. "I put forward" – you say – "this clear argument, namely that, if Captain MacBrody[112] had had any lordship in Tuomondia,[113] he would certainly not be lingering in Bohemia." What are you imagining, I ask you, Carran, you old man? For with an argument worthy of your shrewdness, that is to say, not an argument in any manner or shape, you are attempting to give a colouring to your calumnies, you wretch! Was not our most serene Charles still king of Great Britain and Ireland

rebellium parlamentariorum & suo in Belgio & Gallia longo exilio?

Hodie etiam, proh dolor!, centeni sunt ex primaria nobilitate Regni Hiberniae qui habuerunt amplissima dominia in Hibernia, antequam fuissent a Cromwellistis debellati, & injuste privati bonis omnibus, (quod tu, quamvis alias effrons, negare non audebis) & tamen debent haerere hinc inde, in Hispania, Germania, Gallia, Anglia, & Belgio, vel in ipsa patria misere vivere dolenterque aspicere haereticos Anglos in iniqua possessione suorum dominiorum. An ergo inde infertur quod non sint legitimi domini bonorum illorum?

Dominus Carolus Bruodinus, Capitanei Marci Parens, habuit satis commodum bonum (ut dixi n. 19) in quo honorati nobilis more honeste se ac suos sustentabat. Hoc illi rapuerunt Krumwellistae; mirum ergo non est, si illius filius & haeres, Dominus Capitaneus Bruodinus, maneat in Bohemia, expectans fortunam suam, quamvis a parte rei legitimus & verus sit paternorum bonorum in Hibernia haeres.

23. Nolo amplius in hoc passu haerere, tantum moneo te Carrane ut patienter legas sequentes versus, quos tibi dedicavit eximius SS. Theologiae Doctor & simul abbas, Joannes de Burgo, Annae Bruodinae dignissimus filius:

"Caece quid opprobriis oneras petulanter Hibernos?
    Impia qui profert solvit in or<e> deos.
Ecquid habes, referas, obscuri in stirpe Brodina?
    Nocte vides modicum noctua; luce nihil:
proscindis multos, nescis requiescere, Mome.
    Nosti quos debes scindere? Scinde tuos."

while the power was held by the parliamentarian rebels and he was spending his long exile in Belgium and France?

Nowadays – alas! – there are hundreds of high-ranking Irish nobles who used to have very large estates in Ireland before they were defeated by Cromwell's forces and unjustly deprived of all their possessions (facts that you will not dare deny, though you are shameless in other matters); and notwithstanding this, they are forced to bide time in all sorts of places such as Spain, Germany, France, England and Belgium, or else live wretchedly in their own country and lamentably see the English heretics enjoy the unjust possession of their estates. So how can one draw the conclusion that these Irish nobles are not the rightful masters of their possessions?

Master Charles MacBrody, father of Captain Marcus, held possessions suitable enough (as I said in paragraph 19), in which he provided sustenance for himself and his family in an honourable way, as it is customary for a respectable nobleman. The Cromwellians robbed him of these. It is, therefore, no surprise if his son and heir, Master Captain MacBrody, lingers in Bohemia, waiting for his fortune, despite that he is, objectively, the legitimate and true heir of his father's possessions in Ireland.

23. I do not want to labour this point any further. I only admonish you, Carran, to patiently read the following lines, that were dedicated to you by the abbot as well as distinguished doctor of holy and sacred theology, John Burke, worthiest son of Anna MacBrody:[114]

> "Blind man, why do you wantonly burden the Irish people with insults?
>
> He who utters blasphemous words demolishes religion in his mouth.[115]
>
> Tell us, do you know of anything shadowy in the family of the MacBrodys?
>
> The owl has a decent eyesight at night, but sees nothing in the daylight:
>
> You revile many people, Momus,[116] and you are unable to rest.
>
> Do you know which people you should revile? Revile your own."

24. Jam malevolentiae tuae ulteriorem successum videamus Carrane; eo enim impietatis es progressus, quod haereticorum vestigia sequens martyribus pro Christo occisis invideas Coelum.

P. Bruodinus lib. 4. cap. 15. fol. 699. sui Propugnaculi scripsit synopsem vitae sanctae memoriae Patris Francisci Matthaei, quem anno 1642. rebelles parlamentarii haeretici Corcagiae in Hibernia crudeli mortis genere aetatis suae anno 65. martyrisarunt.

25. Tu, mi Carrane, rebellium haereticorum facinus ut defendas, dignissimum Patrem Franciscum martyrii gloria privare infelici successu conaris. Unde fol. 20. tui libelli promittis te demonstraturum "Patrem Bruodinum," in sua narratione, loco supra citato, "fabulam inassuetam scripsisse", & ut te ad demonstrandum intentum disponas mala fide synopsem vitae sanctae memoriae Patris Matthaei describis. Tandem, solita convitiorum arma resumens, subdis:

"Enorme hic R.P. Bruodinus commentus est mendacium; quantumvis illemet tempore hujus executionis fuerit in Hibernia, & tamen in re tanti momenti veritatisque asseveratione non scit nomen Commendantis civitatis Corcagiensis, qui tum fuerat, neque etiam ego (qui sum annorum aetate 79.) numquam audivi de tali genere martyrii illic contingente, neque Doctor Donnellanus, nec P. Edmundus Kennedi, nec P. Terentius Ofluing, qui paulo post Catholico cum exercitu fuit in Momonia; nec sacerdotes qui pone 42 morabantur in Hibernia, neque milites etiam qui hic sunt & tunc militiam istic exercuerunt; & tamen Pater Bruodinus, sine ullo in re fundamento, talem anilem fabulam imprimere audebat (haud sine magno sui ordinis offendiculo) alias aliquos viros fide dignos pro sua credendi facilitate nominasset," & c. Tandem P. Bruodinum pro conclusione demonstrationis, "insulsum", "infamem", "petulcum", & hujusmodi aliis tibi ordinariis scommatibus vocas.

24. Now, Carran, let us see how your malevolence proceeds even further. For you have reached such a level of impiety, that you follow the foot-tracks of the heretics and look askance at the place in heaven gained by the martyrs who were killed for their defence of Christ.
In Book IV, Chapter 15, page 699 of his *Propugnaculum*,[117] Fr Bruodinus wrote a synopsis of the life of Fr Francis O'Mahony, of holy memory, who in the year 1642 was martyred at the age of 64 by the heretical parliamentarian rebels in Cork, Ireland, by a cruel kind of death.[118]

25. In order to defend the villainy of the heretical rebels, my dear Carran, you try to strip Fr Francis, a man full of dignity, of the glory of martyrdom, but with an unfortunate outcome. Starting with this intention, on page 20 of your slanderous pamphlet you promise that you will demonstrate that Fr Bruodinus, in his narration in the passage mentioned above, "wrote an uncommon fable". So as to settle your endeavour to this demonstration, you outline the synopsis of Fr O'Mahony's life of holy memory in bad faith. At the end, taking up again the usual weapons of your insults, you add, below it:

"Here, Rev. Fr Bruodinus concocted a huge falsehood. Although he was in Ireland himself at the time of this execution, nevertheless in a situation of such importance and in the assertion of truth, he does not know the name of the commander of the city of Cork, who held the office at that time. Actually I, who am 78 years old, have never heard of such kind of martyrdom taking place there,[119] nor did Doctor Donnellan,[120] nor Fr Edmund Kennedy, and neither did Fr Terence O'Flynn[121] who was in Munster with the Catholic army shortly after. And nor did the 42 priests who remained in Ireland back then, and neither did even the soldiers who are here, and who were stationed in that place at that time. And yet, Fr Bruodinus (not without cause of offence to his order) dared put in print a tale of such nature, with no grounds in the fact itself, one that an old woman might narrate – had he given the names of some men worthy of trust elsewhere, to make it easier to believe his words", etc. At last, as a conclusion of your demonstration, Carran, you call Fr Bruodinus "silly", "infamous", "barefaced", and award him other offensive epithets of this kind, as you are accustomed to do.

26. Carrane quid cogitas? Honesti viri munus est stare promissis. Jam supra fol. 20. tui *Apologi* animose promisisti te demonstraturum P. Bruodinum, agendo de glorioso agone fortissimi athletae P. Francisci Matthaei, "fabulam inconsuetam absque veritatis cohaerentia" (verba sunt tua) scripsisse. Si probabili saltem syllogismo probares quod demonstrandum suscepisti, esset aliquid; at cum nullum penitus formas argumentum, non possum aliter te excusare, quam dicendo quod dux illorum sis qui multa promittunt & nihil praestant.

"Demonstro" (inquis) "quod promisi, quia ego non audivi de tali genere martyrii illic contingente, nec P. Donnellanus, nec P. Kennedy," ergo baculus est in angulo.

27. Dignissimi illi duo viri, Domine Magistelle, una tecum Viennae Austriae occupati non ut tu nescio quibus in rebus, sed in scholis & aliis suis negotiis erant, quando in haeretica Corcagiensi civitate in Momonia Franciscus noster passus est; & P. Fluin in Conatia sua sollicitus forte tunc erat de eventu belli Conacensium contra rebelles parlamentarios, non vero de rebellium Corcagensium in Momonia tyrannide. Sic non est mirum si in tanta rerum tunc Hibernicarum confusione de passione hujus vel illius Patris non audiverunt honorati illi a te nominati Patres. Ubi sunt Carrane 42 illi sacerdotes, quos in testes tacitis nominibus adducis? Duo soli praeter te Viennae sunt saeculares Hiberni sacerdotes quos supra n. 25. nominasti; reliqui 42 in spatio forte sunt imaginario, sed haec ut parum ad rem facientia transeamus.

Tantum te interrogo Carrane (sed veritatem fatere): utrum tu unquam audivisti, antequam legisti librum P. Bruodini, quod medietas illorum de quorum martyrio P. Bruodinus scripsit fuisset nata, aut in hac vel illa Religione professa? Respondebis dubio procul (si vir probus es) quod non. Valetne igitur haec consequentia: "Ego

26. What are you thinking, Carran? Keeping his promises is what an honest man should do. Already above, on page 20 of your *Apologus*, you promised that you would demonstrate that Fr Bruodinus, in discussing the glorious contest of Fr Francis O'Mahony – a very strong champion of Christ – wrote "an uncommon fable without consistency with truth" (these words are yours). If, by means of a credible syllogism, you demonstrated at least what you had taken upon yourself as the object to be proven, your words would have some value; but since the argument you shape is completely empty, I cannot excuse you in any other way than by saying that you are the leader of those who make many promises but fulfil none.

You state: "I demonstrate what I promised, since I have not heard about any martyrdom of that kind taking place there, neither did Fr Donnellan, and neither did Fr Kennedy" – *ergo baculus est in angulo*.[122]

27. Master Carran, what an insignificant teacher you are! When our Francis suffered his passion in the heretical city of Cork in Munster, those two most worthy men, who are together with you in Vienna in Austria, were not busy – like you – in goodness knows what occupations. Rather, they were busy in schools and at their own affairs. Also, maybe Fr O'Flynn, in his province of Connacht, was full of anxiety about the outcome of the war of the Connacht men against the parliamentarian rebels, but certainly not about the tyranny of the rebels of Cork in Munster. So, it is no surprise if, in this great confusion of events in Ireland at that time, those honourable fathers mentioned by you did not hear about the passion suffered by this or that priest. Where are those 42 priests whom you cite as witnesses, without giving us their names, Carran? Apart from you, there are only two Irish secular priests in Vienna, whom you have mentioned above, in the quotation in my paragraph 25: perhaps, the remaining 42 inhabit an imaginary place. But let us skip these points as matters that have little to do with the topic itself.

I ask you only this, Carran (but do confess the truth!): before reading Fr Bruodinus' book, had you ever heard about the birth of even half of those people, whose martyrdom Fr Bruodinus wrote about, or whether they professed this or that religion? Undoubtedly (if you are an honest man) you will answer that you had not. So, is the following consequential argument valid: 'I did not hear that those

non audivi illos fuisse natos aut professos: ergo non fuerunt nati, aut professi"? Compatior tibi, Carrane.

28. Subsistis adhuc Carrane. "Bruodinus" (inquis) "nescit nomen Commendantis Corcagiensis: ergo Patris Francisci Matthaei martyrii historia est fabula." Concedo in tui Carrane gratiam consequentiam esse dignam tuo acumine. Scriptor *Actuum Apostolorum*, Carrane, nescivit nomina illorum qui Stephanum lapidarunt. Barronius ignoravit nomina centenorum tyrannorum, sub quibus passi sunt multi martyres de quibus egit in suo *Martyrologio*, quod *Romanum* dicitur; valetne igitur Carrane haec illatio: "Ergo fabulae sunt, quae scriptura de Stephano & Barronius de aliis martyribus testantur"? Si Catholicus es, dices quod non; & si vir bonus, amplius non dubitabis de martyrio Patris Matthaei, qui bis fuit Provincialis & bis Generalis Visitator Hiberniae, & pro defensione sui ordinis contra diversos tuae Carrane farinae calumniatores nobile opus sub nomine Edmundi Ursulani edidit.

29. Seriem vitae & martyrii nostri P. Matthaei anno 1644. in Generali Ordinis Capitulo Tolleti celebrato notarunt Carrane in suo Archivio Patres ordinis nostri, juxta informationem ad Capitulum ab Hibernis Patribus missam; illius etiam honorificam facit mentionem, non solum author *Threnodiae Hibernorum*, cap. 5. fol. 62., sed etiam nominatissimus ille scriptor & ordinis chronologus, Lucas Waddingus, in suo de scriptoribus ordinis nobili opere, Romae anno 1650. impresso, his verbis:

"Franciscus Matthaei Hibernus, Corcagiensis, in Sacra Theologia & jure canonico eruditus, Guardianus collegii Lovan. Fratrum Hibernorum, Definitor & Minister Prov. Hiberniae, pro qua post tot persecutionum aerumnas restituenda impigre laboravit, cum audiret quosdam insulsas insanasque propositiones regularibus Regni Hiberniae adscripsisse, & tanquam ab eis prolatas & protelatas

people were born, or that they professed a faith: accordingly, they were not born, or they did not profess a faith'? I feel pity for you, Carran.

28. You still insist on your position, Carran. "Bruodinus" – you say – "does not know the name of the commander of Cork: therefore the history of the martyrdom of Fr Francis O'Mahony is a fable." In your favour, Carran, I concede that this logical conclusion is worthy of your discernment. The writer of the *Acts of the Apostles*, Carran, did not know the names of those who stoned Stephen.[123] Baronio ignored the names of the hundreds of tyrants under whom many martyrs suffered their passions, which he described in his martyrology, which is called *Martyrologium Romanum*.[124] So, is the following logical conclusion valid: 'accordingly, what the Scriptures attest with regard to Stephen and what Baronio attests with regard to other martyrs are fables'? If you are Catholic, your answer will be no; and if you are an honest man, you will not have any further doubts about the martyrdom of Fr O'Mahony, who was Provincial Father twice, and General Visitor[125] of Ireland twice, and who published, under the name of Edmundus Ursulanus,[126] a celebrated work in defence of his order against slanderers of your kind, Carran.

29. Immediately after the report[127] sent to the chapter by the Irish fathers, Carran, the fathers of our order recorded in their archive the course of the life and martyrdom of our Fr O'Mahony at the celebrated general chapter of the order in Toledo, which was held in the year 1644. Also, a respectful mention is made not only by the author of *Threnodia Hibernorum*,[128] in Chapter V, page 62, but even by that very renowned writer and chronicler of our order, Luke Wadding,[129] in his honourable work about the writers of the order, which was printed in Rome in the year 1650.[130] Here is the passage:

"Francis O'Mahony, Irish, of Cork, a learned man in holy theology and canonical law, was guardian of the College of the Irish friars of Louvain,[131] *Definitor*[132] and minister of the province of Ireland, for whose restoration after the troubles of so many persecutions he actively exerted himself. Certain men had ascribed to the regular clerics of the kingdom of Ireland some absurd and foolish statements, which they reported to the Faculty of Theology and the archbishop

Theologicae Facultati & Archi Episcopo Parisiensi exhibuisse censurandas, celeriterque ab his latum fuisse judicium; ut a tanta calumnia innocuos liberaret, in illorum defensionem librum edidit sub nomine Edmundi Ursulani, ita praenotatum: *Examen juridicum censurae facultatis Theologiae Parisiensis & ejusdem civitatis Archi-Episcopi latae, circa quasdam propositiones regularibus Regni Hiberniae falso impositas, in quo per exceptiones juris & facti mala accusatoris & testium fides propositionum impostura & praepropera censurae divulgatio ostenditur.* Scripsit etiam *Tractatum de Stigmatibus Sacti Francisci,* alterum *Pro defensione privilegiorum eidem Sancto Francisco & religioni ejus concessorum*. Extant apud suos consodales Corcagiae M.SS.

Brevem Historiam Provinciae Hiberniae, quam habeo M.S. pariter scripsit.

Occisus" —NB.— "est crudeliter vario tormentorum genere in urbe Corcagiensi ab haereticis Puritanis, qui Parlamenti Anglicani partes sequebantur, ob suspicionem quod persuaserit tradi Catholicis civitatem. Mira constantia & invicta martyris patientia cruciatus pertulit bis, demum suspensus anno millesimo sexcentesimo quadragesimo secundo."

Quid Carrane, an Waddingus tibi videtur fide dignus? Si sic, repone quaeso falcem tuam in vaginam suam & noli amplius incredulus esse, sed fidelis, virosque bonos tot scommatibus desine onerare; alias invenies multos, qui te insanum ac sycophantam esse, ut timeo, dicent.

30. Ulterius te rogo Carrane ut promissione tot demonstrationum lectores non decipias, antequam primo scias quid sit terminus. In quovis fere paragrapho tui libelli minaris nescio quae P. Bruodino, sed frustra: ille enim probe scit in te nihil esse praeter scommata quod timere deberet. Et quid, obsecro, formidabile in te Carrane esset?

of Paris to be censured, as if those words had been really pronounced and repeated over and over again by the Irish clerics. A trial was promptly arranged in Paris. Having heard about all this, and in order to acquit innocent men of such a great calumny, he published a book in their defence, under the name of Edmundus Ursulanus, that was entitled as follows:[133] *Juridical examination of the censorship of the Faculty of Theology of Paris and of the Archbishop of the same city, that has been imposed about certain statements forcefully and falsely attributed to the regular clerics of the kingdom of Ireland, in which it is shown that the statements are impostures and that censorship has been promulgated hastily, through exceptions of the right and the accuser's and witnesses' bad faith regarding the fact.* He also wrote a *Treatise on Saint Francis' Stigmata*, and a second one *In defence of the privileges conceded to the same Saint Francis and to his religion*. The manuscripts are extant and kept by the brothers of his confraternity in Cork.

Likewise, he wrote a *Brief History of the Province of Ireland*, whose manuscript I possess.

He was killed" – N.B.[134] – "in a cruel manner, subjected to diverse means of torture, in the city of Cork by the heretical Puritans who were followers of the factions of the Anglican parliament. The reason was that they suspected him of having persuaded the city to surrender to the Catholics. With extraordinary constancy and the invincible patience of a martyr he endured torture twice, and was eventually hanged in the year one thousand, six hundred and forty-two."

So what, Carran? Does Wadding seem trustworthy to you? If so (I beg you), put your sickle back into its scabbard, and doubt no longer, but believe,[135] and stop burdening righteous men with so many taunts. On other occasions you will find many people who, as I fear, will say that you are a fool and a slanderer.

30. I further ask you this, Carran: do not deceive the readers with a promise of so many demonstrations, before knowing where you are going to end up. In almost every paragraph of your pamphlet you threaten Fr Bruodinus with menaces I can hardly understand, but you do it in vain: for he is well aware that there is nothing about you that he should fear, aside from taunts. And what could possibly be frightful in you, Carran, for Heaven's sake? You barely went beyond

Limites *Lillianae Grammaticae* vix superasti. Recentiorum Latinos libros difficulter intelligis: totum ergo fulcrum quo niteris, vel convitia sunt, vel pagellae aliquot, hinc inde ex diversis scriptoribus mala fide transcriptae. Audi ergo Carrane quid uni tui furfuris homuncioni, Evangelista Ioannes, *Apocal.* cap. 3. v. 17 loquitur his verbis: "dicis, quod dives sum & locupletatus & nullius egeo: & nescis, quia tu es miser & miserabilis & pauper & caecus & rudis." Si de te aliter Carrane sentis, non bene te nosti, nec est quod sculptori, qui nuper in secunda impressione *Annalium* tuorum eximia specie effigiem tuam efformavit, credas; nam te decepit: comam, barbam, & prothonotariam reverendam, ut vocant, seu vestem, eleganter tibi exornavit; cerebrum autem tibi formare non poterat.

Stomachari me fortasse dices Carrane? Ita est, sed tu me coëgisti, qui nullum optimis saecularibus ac religiosissimis viris maledicendi finem facis: ignosce Carrane quod tam sincere tecum agam; amicus enim tuus sum, & conterraneus: sic recordare, sacro testante textu, quod "meliora sunt vulnera amantis quam fraudulenta oscula odientis". Jam ad alia.

31. Credebam, Carrane, quod solis vivis & non divis, solis religiosis & non archi-episcopis, praesulibus, saecularibus & sacerdotibus martyrii gloriam invideres. At tu, furiosi hominis ad instar, pergis sicut incoepisti & sic, cum Bruodinum quem hostem vocas ferire non possis, vibrata circumquaque tua falce aërem tu insanus verberas nulliusque parcis honori.

In archidioecesi Casselensi in Momonia natus cum sis & ad Sacerdotium promotus, Carrane, putabam quod Archi-Episcopo Hurlaeo, perillustris ac antiquissimae nobilitatis in illa patria viro, non invideres martyrii lauream, quam gloriose pro Christo certando sibi comparavit.

the limits of Lily's *Grammar*. You have difficulties in understanding the Latin books of recent authors. Thus, the entire support against which you prop yourself consists of insults or a few trivial pages which you have transcribed haphazardly from different authors in bad faith. Come on, Carran, lend an ear to what John the Evangelist says to an insignificant little scrap of a man like you, in Chapter III, line 17 of the *Apocalypse*, with these words: "you say 'I am wealthy, I have become rich and I am in need of nothing'; and you do not know that you are wretched and pitiful, poor and blind and uncultivated".[136] If you have a different perception of yourself, Carran, you do not know yourself well, and you have no reason to believe the engraver who, not so long ago, in the second edition of your *Annales*, produced a portrait that gave you the appearance of an eminent man. For he deceived you: he elegantly embellished your hair, your beard and your '*prothonotaria reverenda*',[137] as they call it, or clothing. However, he could not fashion you a brain.[138]

Perhaps, Carran, you will say that I am being bad-tempered? It is so, but I was compelled by you, the one who does not put an end to evil-speaking against excellent secular priests and profoundly religious clerics. Forgive, Carran, the fact that I speak so frankly with you. Indeed, I am your friend, and fellow-countryman. So remember that, as the testimony of the holy Scripture says, "the wounds from one who loves you are better than the deceitful kisses from one who hates you".[139] Now let us turn to different matters.

31. I believed, Carran, that you were looking askance at the glory of the martyrdom of living men only, and not at that of people who have departed from our terrestrial world; at that of clerics only, and not at that of archbishops, prelates, secular priests and ordained ones. But you, in the manner of a madman, continue in the same way as you started. As you are unable to hurt Bruodinus, whom you call an enemy, you, like a madman, strike the air with the swinging of your sickle all around, and show no mercy for anybody's honour.

Since you were born and promoted to the priesthood in the archdiocese of Cashel, Carran, I thought that you hold no grudge for the glory of the martyrdom of Archbishop Hurley,[140] a man of very illustrious and ancient nobility in that native place of his: a glory that he procured for himself by honourably fighting in defence of Christ.

Non ille, Carrane, sanctae memoriae archipraesul Casseliensi sedi praefuit quando tu, ob causam nobis notam, salutem in fuga posuisti; adquid igitur illum persequeris? Sed jam tuum pro tortoribus haereticis patrocinium & argumenta, quibus Hurlaeum e numero martyrum eliminare conaris, videamus.

32. Describis primo (more tuo) truncate & mala fide, ex lib. 3. c. 20. *Propug*. P. Bruodini illustrissimi Archipraesulis Hurlaei fol. 29. tui famosi libelli vitam; tandem subdis:

"Ego natus sum" (dolendum profecto) "anno 1590. & domus patris mei uno tantum milliari germanico distat Casselia, & nunquam hac de re audivi quidquam," & c.

Nihil ergo credendum est, Carrane, nisi quod tu audivisti vel vidisti? illustrissimi Hurlaei crudelem martyrii tragediam dolenter inspexerunt plurimi boni Catholici, & audiverunt & legerunt milleni probi viri, in quorum manibus teritur hodie illud nobile opus magnae memoriae admodum reverendi Domini Thomae Goud, Angli, quod intitulatur *Theatrum Catholicae & Protestanticae Religionis*, Duaci anno 1620. impressum, cujus verba mox subjungam interim.

33. Dic sodes Carrane, an eo usque furor iste tuus te praecipitem egit, ut tibi persuadeas ea sola nos debere credere de quibus tu audivisti? Si obturatis auribus fuisses natus Carrane (sicut modo dura cervice & incircumciso corde resistis veritati) quid nobis esset agendum? Deberemusne aliquid credere quod tu non audivisti? Scio te senem esse, ut dicis, sed te senior est malus spiritus, qui mendaciorum est parens, prout tu illorum es propagator & fautor. Dicis te non audivisse de martyrio illustrissimi Hurlaei, credo bene te non audivisse de illius passione, ob multas quas tunc in Hibernia habuisti occupationes alias; et si illarum non recordaris, interroga neptem tuam, quam pectenario Viennae in uxorem ante paucos annos dedisti, & dicet tibi. Porro ut

It was not that arch-prelate of holy memory who held the chair of Cashel, Carran, when you hoped to save yourself by fleeing because of the reason we know. For what purpose, then, do you persecute him? But now let us have a look at the protection you guarantee to heretic torturers, and at the arguments by which you try to eliminate Hurley from the category of the martyrs.

32. At first, on page 29 of your infamous pamphlet, you transcribe the life of the most illustrious arch-prelate Hurley from Book III, Chapter XX of Fr Bruodinus' *Propugnaculum*, mutilating the quotation (as it is customary for you to do) and writing in bad faith; and at the end, below the text, you add:

"I was born" (something to be sorry about, indeed) "in the year 1590 and my father's home is just one Germanic mile distant from Cashel,[141] and I never heard anything about this fact", etc.

Do you mean that nothing is to be believed, Carran, except what you have heard or seen? A great number of good Catholics looked at[142] the tragedy of the cruel martyrdom of the most illustrious Hurley, along with thousands and thousands of honest men who heard and read about it. With their hands, in our times, these men wear away the pages of the famous masterpiece written by an Englishman of great memory, Adm. Rev. Master Thomas Good,[143] that is entitled *Theatrum Catholicae et Protestanticae Religionis*,[144] which was published in Douai in the year 1620, and whose words I will soon append below.

33. If you please, Carran, tell me: has this madness of yours led you headfirst to the point that you convince yourself that we should believe only those things about which you have heard? If your ears were plugged from birth (just as you now resist the truth with a rigid neck and irreligious heart), what should we do, Carran? Should we not believe something that you have not heard? I know you are old, as you say, but older than you is the evil spirit which is the father of all lies, just as you are a propagator and favourer of them. You say that you have never heard about the martyrdom of the most illustrious Hurley. I bet that you did not hear about his passion because of the many other occupations you had in Ireland at that time! And if you do not remember them, ask your niece whom you gave in marriage to a comber[145] in Vienna a few years ago, and she will tell you. From

inexcusabilis imposterum sit ignorantia tua de martyrio illustrissimi Hurlaei. Hic ut promisi subjungo vitae illius synopsem, prout lib. 11. cap. 3. fol. 574. *Theatri* verbo ad verbum Anglice habetur. Placebit haud dubie Carrane tibi lingua illa, qua raro antecessores tui Carrani sed semper Domini de Carve (in quorum familiam te intrusisti) loquebantur. Jam ad rem:

34. "Derby ò Hurley, Archbishopp of Cashall, Doctor of both lawes and professor of that facultie in the universitie of Rheames in France, under Cardinall Guise, Archibishopp of The same. Was taken in Ireland, and cast into a Darck Dungeon in the Castle of Dublin: and being fore vexed with this ugly prison and pensive restrainct, was more vexed and tormented by an usuall and exquisitt torment of bootes full of boylling oile and talloe; into which he was compelled to putt his legges, already wearied with heavie bolts, and to stand by a great fire, with which his flesh was consumed unto the bare bonas; all which he endured with great patience and constancy. And atterwardes, when by that torment he could not be wonne, nor by feare and alluring promisses of uncertaine and deceitfull promotion could nott be inveigled to relent or to faint in the profession of the Catholique religion, or to embrace the protestant negative religion, was upon fridaice morning in the dawning, strangled with à vith, in the moneth of May 1584 and so suffred a blessed martirdome and enioieth a blessed crowne."

35. Lepide senex Carrane, cum ex Hiberno te in Anglum ex Carrano nimirum in Carve transformasti (ut sic mentiendo major tibi fides ab ignaris adhiberetur), non dubito quin intelliges quae hic ex *Theatro Catholicae & Protestanticae Religionis* scribo; & si non, consule dignissimos illos Patres quos supra n. 25. nominasti, & dicent tibi quod vita gloriosi martyris Hurlaei a P. Bruodino scripta re ipsa verbo quasi ad verbum conveniat cum iis quae ex Patre Guod jam descripta sunt Anglice.

Ecce, Carrane, unius Angli (sed melioris ecclesiastici quam tu es) de Hurlaei glorioso agone, affatu & in ferventis olei & saevo

this time on, may your ignorance about the martyrdom of the most illustrious Hurley be inexcusable in the future. As I promised, I add, below here, the synopsis of his life, word by word, just as it appears in English in Book XI, Chapter III, page 574 of *Theatrum*. That language, Carran, which was rarely spoken by your Carran predecessors,[146] but always by the Masters de Carve (into whose family you intruded), will undoubtedly please you.[147] Now, to the point:

34. "Dermot O'Hurley, Archbishop of Cashel, doctor of both laws, and professor of that faculty in the university of Reims in France, under Cardinal Guise, archbishop of the same city.[148] He was taken in Ireland, and cast into a dark dungeon in the castle of Dublin: and having being previously vexed with this ugly prison and pensive restraint, he was more vexed and tormented by an unusual and exquisite torture of boots full of boiling oil and tallow; into which he was compelled to put his legs, already wearied with heavy bolts, and to stand by a great fire, with which his flesh was consumed until the bare bones; all of which he endured with great patience and constancy. And afterwards, when by that torment he could not be won, nor by fear and alluring promises of uncertain and deceitful promotion could he be inveigled to relent or to faint in the profession of the Catholic religion, or to embrace the negative Protestant religion, he was on Friday morning in the dawning strangled with a vith,[149] in the month of May 1584, and so he suffered a blessed martyrdom and enjoyed a blessed crown."

35. You whimsical old man, Carran, you transformed yourself from an Irishman into an Englishman, namely from a 'Carran' into a 'Carve' (in order to attract greater credibility before the people unaware of the truth by deceiving them in this way). For this reason, I have no doubts that you will understand my quotation from *Theatrum Catholicae et Protestanticae Religionis*. If not, consult those most worthy Fathers whom you mentioned above in the passage I have reported in paragraph 25. They will tell you that Fr Bruodinus' written version of the life of the glorious martyr Hurley fundamentally coincides, almost word for word, with the report that I have just quoted from Fr Good in English.

Here, Carran, is the testimony about Hurley's glorious struggle, speech and cruel bath in boiling oil, provided by the only Englishman

balneo testimonium! Quid Bruodinus de haereticorum Anglorum tyrannide Carrane scripsit, quod ab hoc Anglo in hac Hurlaei vita non affirmatur? Nihilne Deum vindicem Carrane times, quando fortes heroës, qui pro ejus amore sanguinem fuderunt, tot scommatibus & injuriis afficis? Scimus protoplastum tuum, Thomam Carranum, sanctissimo Episcopo Lactino multis saeculis antequam ullus Carve Hibernicum calcasset solum amputasse sua falce brachium: tu vero, illo tuo antecessore iniquior, pro viribus laboras ut in gratiam haereticorum tot fortissimos athletas vita aeterna & martyrii gloria spolies! Hoc ex tuo <c>um percepisset libello perillustris ac eximius ille SS. Theologiae Doctor Carolus ô Molloy, justo zelo motus, sequentes versus tibi Roma misit & dedicavit:

"Falx insigne tuo est prothoposto nomine Thomas,
 nomen, & agnomen prodiit inde tibi.
Falce tuum divos genus olim sustulit orbi,
 Lactino scidit gens tua Carve manum.
Nec Coelo nec jota solo, Carrane, remittis,
 in tua lingua deos invehit inque deas.

36. Nondum Carrane finis est persecutionum tuarum in martyres, aut calumniarum quibus viros bonos oneras! Credidi te jam de tam manifestis mendaciis & patentibus imposturis toties convictum ad mentem rediturum! Sed nihil minus cogitas, nam pergis eadem via qua coepisti, adducisque nova accusationis capita.

"Et" (inquis fol. 30.) "quemadmodum meus adhuc compescere nequit calamus a Bruodini mendaciorum reprehensione, simul etiam cum ejusdem confutatione," & c. Lingua tua Carrane calamus est scribae mendaciter scribentis, sic cessare non potest a calumniis quibus innocentes opprimis. Toties jam in *Anatomia* hujus capitis

who reported it (but a better cleric than you are)! What did Bruodinus write about the tyranny of the English heretics that is not attested in this biography of Hurley by this Englishman, Carran? Do you not fear the punishment of God at all, Carran, when you inflict so many taunts and insults upon the strong men of great deeds who shed their blood for His sake? We know that the founding-man of your ancestry, Thomas Carran, cut off the arm of the most saintly Bishop Lachtín with his sickle, many centuries before any Carve put his feet onto the soil of Ireland. You, who are more wicked than that predecessor of yours, are certainly striving as hard as you can, in favour of the heretics, to deprive of eternal life and of the glory of martyrdom so many and strong champions of Christ! Having realised this from your libel, the famous Charles O'Molloy,[150] a very illustrious and eminent doctor of holy and sacred theology, was moved by a righteous zeal and sent to you from Rome the following lines, which he dedicated to you:

> "Since your first name is 'Thomas', 'Sickle' is a remarkable
>
> surname, and a nickname sprung up from it for you.
>
> With a sickle your race once deprived the world of the divine,[151]
>
> one of your family, the Carves, severed the arm of Lachtín.
>
> You, Carran, do not allow one iota of rest for yourself, in heaven or on earth:[152]
>
> your tongue inveighs against gods and goddesses alike."[153]

36. Are you not done yet with your persecutions against martyrs, or with the slanders with which you burden honest men, Carran? I thought that you had come to your senses by now, as you have been so often convicted of such manifest lies and evident deceits! On the contrary, your mind is by no means less active; in fact, you continue on the same path on which you started and you put forward new accusations.

On page 30, you state: "And so far my pen has not been able to restrain from criticising Bruodinus' lies, just as it has also refuted him at the same time", etc. Your tongue, Carran, is the pen of a clerk who writes falsehoods. Therefore, it cannot cease from tormenting innocent men by slandering. You have already been convicted of

& praecedentium de mendacio es convictus; adhuc tamen nequis compescere linguam. Quid jam habes contra Bruodinum?

"Pseudolus" (inquis) "Bruodinus de uxore Domini Ioannis de Burgo, quam in Gratiam Chrahy vocat, & tamen de ipso neque de ipsa penitus quicquam scivit, donec P. Clanchy, ejusdemque Ordinis, mihi literulam misit interrogatoriam (quam mihi tradidit Dominus Leutinantius Thadaeus o Higen, qui hic moratur) secundum hunc tenorem," & c. O Carraniana Latinitas!

37. Miranda res est, Carrane, quod tu audes Viennae, ubi Bruodiniana opera in multorum manibus habentur, tam palpabiliter veritatis semitas transilire! Bruodinus, Carrane (ut videre est lib. 3. cap. 20. fol. 487. ipsius *Propugnaculi*) uxorem gloriosi martyris Ioannis de Burgo non Gratiam Chrahy <ut> tu fingis, sed Gratianam vocat Geraldinam, credens illam fuisse ex illustrissima illa Geraldinorum familia. Viennae etiam in diebus tuis Carrane nullus fuit Leutinantius Higgin cognomine, sed bene Dominus Leutinantius Thadaeus ô Hassie Tuomonensis, Patri Bruodino variis titulis charus, ibi fuit & defacto est. Hic tibi forte literulas illas (quas R.P. Chlanchy non scripsit, aut misit) dedit; & si scripsisset R. Pater Chlanchy illas, quam grande hoc esset Carrane peccatum? Te ergo (qui, ut alter G<o>rgias, nihil ignorare videri vis) non possumus interrogare de hac vel illa materia sine peccato? Scripsit tibi illam Carrane schedulam non P. Chlanchy, non Bruodinus (qui tunc impressam habuit vitam invicti animi martyris Ioannis de Burgo), sed alius tibi ignotus, qui dubitavit de veritate illorum punctorum in schedula positorum. Et quid hoc mali est? Monuit nos (verum est) sapiens, ut nobis a tuae farinae hominibus caveamus. "Non" (inquit *Ecclesiasticus* cap. 8.) "litiges cum homine linguato, nec communices homini indocto," id est Carrano.

38. Jam capio Carrane cur effrenata errandi libidine Patri Bruodino inter alia imponis quod vocet uxorem Ioannis de Burgo Gratiam

falsity so many times in the dissection of this chapter and in that of the previous ones;[154] and yet, you still cannot hold your tongue. What have you got to say now against Bruodinus?

You state: "Bruodinus, a liar *par excellence*,[155] about the wife of John Burke,[156] he calls her Grace Magrath,[157] even if he knew absolutely nothing about him or her, insomuch that Fr Clancy,[158] also of the same order, sent me a short letter asking questions (which was delivered to me by the master lieutenant Tadhg O'Higgins, who is staying in this place) in line with this tenor,"[159] etc. How typical of your Latin, Carran!

37. It is an astonishing fact, Carran, that you dare to stray so patently from the path of truth in Vienna, where many men have Bruodinus' works in their hands. As it is possible to see in Book III, Chapter XX, page 487 of *Propugnaculum* itself, Carran, Bruodinus does not call the wife of the glorious martyr John Burke Grace Magrath, as you contrive, but Grace Fitzgerald,[160] since he believes she belonged to that most illustrious family, the Geraldines. Also, there was no lieutenant with the surname Higgins in Vienna while you were there, Carran, but actually in that city there was – and still is, in fact – a master lieutenant Tadhg O'Hassett,[161] from Thomond, who is dear to Fr Bruodinus for various reasons. Maybe it was this man who gave you that short letter, which Rev. Fr Clancy did not write or send. And even if Rev. Fr Clancy had written it, how big a sin would this be, Carran? So, do we commit a sin if we address questions about this or that subject to you (who, like another Gorgias,[162] want to give the impression of all-knowing)? That short note, Carran, was not written to you by Fr Clancy, not by Bruodinus (who, at that time, was having his biography about the invincible soul of the martyr John Burke printed),[163] but by another person unknown to you, who had doubts about the veracity of those points indicated in the short note. And what is wrong with this? The Sage[164] warned us – and this is true – to be wary of men of your ilk. "Do not dispute with a man who possesses a quarrelsome tongue" (says *Ecclesiasticus* in Chapter VIII), "and restrain from having anything to do with an ignorant man," that is with you Carran..

38. Now I understand, Carran, why your unrestrained lust for mistakes led you to falsely attribute to Fr Bruodinus, amongst other

Chrachy, ut nimirum ansam reassumend<o> solita convitiorum arma capere possis, quibus Franciscanam religionem ferire valeas.

"Unde" (inquis) "amicus lector perpendere quaeso dignetur hujus P. Bruodini garrulitatem" (non dignabitur Carrane, quia totus est occupatus in lectione impudentissimorum tuorum mendaciorum) "quomodo hac in causa dolose mecum egerit, & quam perverse scripserit ingratissimus fraticellus omnia de illa, quamvis ea pone sui mariti martyrium" (Priscanum, Carrane, injuste martyrisas semper) "sic viro orbata suo spacio 6 annorum manserit vidua, posteaquam nupsit Terentio Cracheo, a quo nunquam denominari voluit, sed proprio nomine, ex eo quod maritus apostatae Franciscani filius fuerit, nimirum Mileri Crachei Archi-Episcopi Casseliensis," & c.

Jam evomuisti Carrane extrema mala quae poteras contra Franciscanos; & quod amplius non miramur, narratiunculam illam tuam sine palpabili mendacio inique excogitato finire non poteras. Nulla in Hibernia Carrane unquam foemina (solis Anglis exceptis) a marito fuit nominata: nam proprio cognomine, vel a parentibus, semper foeminae nostrae appellantur, ut omnes qui in mundo sunt Hiberni, te pseudo-Hiberno excepto, testabuntur: non ergo verum est quod nobilissima illa Domina Gratiana non dicebatur Crachia post secundas nuptias quia maritus apostatae Franciscani (ut tu impertinenter blateras) fuit filius; sed potius, quia patriae antiqua consuetudo hactenus semper fuit, ut a maritis foeminae non vocentur, sed potius proprio parentum cognomine.

39. Ad reliquam odiosae tuae narrationis partem ut respondeam, fateor, Domine detractor, Millerum illum fuisse apostatam & pseudo-archi-episcopum Casseliensem, qui multos habuit filios & filias qui in potentes, praeclaros & catholicissimos evaserunt dominos. Sed quid hoc ad propositum tuum Carrane fuit narrare? Promisisti te

things, that he calls John Burke's wife Grace Magrath! You surely do that in order to be able to take up your usual weapons of insults, brandishing which, once again, you feel strong enough to strike the Franciscan order.

You state: "On the basis of this, I beseech the friendly reader to deign to examine Fr Bruodinus' blathering," (yet, he will not do so, Carran, because he is extremely busy with the reading of your most insolent lies) "and to consider in what manner that most unpleasant and insignificant friar[165] behaves deceitfully with me in this discussion, and how wicked he was in writing all those falsities about that woman. He did this in spite of the fact that she had been, back previously, deprived of her man in the martyrdom of her husband" (like every time, Carran, how unjustly you martyrise Priscian!)[166] "and she remained a widow for a period of 6 years, after which she married Terence Magrath.[167] From him she never wanted to take the surname, but rather kept her own, precisely because the husband was the son of a Franciscan apostate, namely of Miler Magrath,[168] archbishop of Cashel," etc.

You had already vomited against the Franciscans the vilest evilness you could, Carran. And yet, you could not finish that short and insignificant exposition of yours without depending on an evident lie, that you have unfairly devised – which no longer surprises us. No woman in Ireland, Carran, ever took the surname from her husband (with the only exception of English ones). In fact, our women are always called by their own surname, or, in other words, with the one they receive from their fathers, as all the Irish people on earth will be able to testify (with the exception of you, a pseudo-Irishman). Therefore, it is not true that after her second marriage the most noble Lady Grace was not called Magrath because her husband was the son of a Franciscan apostate (as you impudently blather). Instead, it was because, so far, the old custom of our homeland has always been that women are not called after their husbands, but rather after the surname of their fathers.

39. In response to the remaining part of your offensive account – you master detractor – I admit that the Miler whom you mention was an apostate and pseudo-archbishop of Cashel, who had many sons and daughters who ended up being powerful, very illustrious and

Apologetice confutare velle ea quae in tuis *Annalibus* P. Bruodinus emendavit; cur, si vir honestus es, in alienam messem falcem tuam imponis & propriam negligis? Promissa primo observa, & postea quodvis scribe.

40. Judas, Carrane, Christi fuit discipulus; adhuc tamen apostatavit. Petrus, Apostolorum princeps, terrore correptus Christum ter negavit. Marcellinus Papa, Diocletiani persecutione perterritus, deorum simulacris thus adhibuit. Si fortes hae Ecclesiae columnae (ut de centenis aliis nihil dicam) ceciderunt & apostatarunt a fide, cur miraremur Patris Chrachy casum? Legas tu Carrane librum 1. 2. & 3. *Propugnaculi* Patris Bruodini & deprehendes aliquot duodenas sacerdotum saecularium qui post & ante Calvinum & Carolstadium a fide apostatarunt & filios procrearunt. Sicut raro Carrane invenitur triticum sine zizania & lolio, sic vix ulla unquam fuit congregatio tam sancta, in qua aliqui non essent mali. Mirandum ergo non est, si in Franciscana familia, quae ad trecenta millia animarum in suo continet gremio, inventi sunt & defacto inveniantur aliqui apostatae & a fide recedentes.

41. Millerus ille, cujus tu Carrane mentionem in odium Franciscanae religionis facis, religiosus fuit primo doctus, zelosus & pius; quare superiorum jussu in Hiberniam ex Hispania (ubi studia absolvit) tyrannisante Elisabetha remeare volens, captus & pro religioso cognitus fuit in Anglia, ubi exquisitissimis tormentis ejus in fide constantia probata fuit, quae omnia constantissime pertulit. Tandem abscissis jam auribus, naso in duas partes scisso, intrusisque vi sub unguibus manuum & peduum aciculis, fragilitate humana victus, cessit cruciatibus & a fide recessit. Elisabetha hoc intelligens, illum pingui illo beneficio archi-episcopatus Casseliensis remuneravit; in cujus administratione ita potentiam suam per 34 annos extendit, ut per totum Hiberniae Regnum timeretur a multis. Genuit ex antiquae

true Catholic masters. But what was the point in narrating this for your purpose, Carran? You promised that you wanted to refute, by means of your *Apologia*, those comments that Fr Bruodinus made in correcting the errors of your *Annales*. If you are an honest man, why do you inflict your sickle upon somebody else's harvest and neglect your own? First keep your promises, and then write whatever you want.

40. Judas was a disciple of Christ, Carran; and yet, he apostatised. Taken by fear, Peter, the first of the apostles, denied Christ three times. Pope Marcellinus,[169] terrified by Diocletian's persecution,[170] offered incense to the statues of the pagan gods. If even these strong columns of the Church fell and apostatised from the faith (not to say anything about the hundreds of others), why should we be surprised of Fr Magrath's lapse? Read, Carran, Book I, II and III of Fr Bruodinus' *Propugnaculum*, and you will find out about several dozens of secular priests who, before and after Calvin and Karlstadt,[171] apostatised from the faith and procreated children. Just as it is rare to find wheat without darnel and tares, in the same way there was hardly ever a congregation so saintly not to include any member who sinned. We should not be surprised, then, if some apostates and abandoners of their faith were (and actually are) to be found in the Franciscan family, which contains three hundred thousand souls in its womb.

41. First of all, Carran, that Miler, whom you mention out of hatred against the Franciscan order, was a learned, zealous and devout cleric. It was for this reason that he had the desire to obey his superiors' orders and go back to Ireland from Spain (where he had completed his studies) under the tyrannical reign of Elizabeth. He was arrested and went through a trial for being a cleric in England, where his constancy in his faith was put to the test by means of tortures that had been very carefully chosen, all of which he endured with great fortitude. At last, after his ears had been already cut off, after his nose had been divided into two parts and after small pins had been thrust under the nails of his hands and feet, he was won by human frailty: he surrendered to the tortures and abandoned his faith.[172] Appreciating this, Elizabeth rewarded him with that rich benefice, the arch-bishopric of Cashel. And in the 34 years of his administration of it he increased his power so much that many people were afraid of him throughout the entire

nobilitatis foemina (in hoc ignobilis, quod apostatae quantumvis potenti nupserit) multos filios & filias, quos a Catholica semper uxore (seu si mavis concubina) in fide Catholica educari voluit.

42. Suis filiis (quos ad magnos honores Elisabetha Regina promovit) plurima & maxima dominia in Momonia, Legenia & Ultonia procuravit. Filias primariae authoritatis Catholicis viris matrimonio collocavit. Tandem aetatis suae anno 80. ad cor rediens renunciavit titulari suo archi-episcopatui, sicut & omnibus aliis publicis functionibus; bona sua omnia filiis cessit; ac tandem opera R. P. Iacobi Nelani, Tymologensis tunc guardiani, ejurata haeresi (quam ore tantum profitebatur) ad fidem conversus est Catholicam.

43. Praefuit tunc seraphicae religioni provinciae Hiberniae dignissimus Pater & jam Christi martyr Franciscus Matthaei (quem tu Carrane inter alios martyres inique persequeris), qui visa poenitentia ac verae contritionis indiciis fratris Mileri illum ab haeresi & apostatia absolvit sacraque religionis veste induit. Jam Catholicus & Franciscanus existens vixit Milerus 18 mensibus, durante quo tempore jejuniis, disciplinis, vigiliis, meditationibus & orationibus ita se exercuit, ut omnibus fratribus & Catholicis saecularibus (qui ad illum videndum frequenter confluebant) praeluceret sanctitatis exemplo, ansamque praeberet omnibus miserentis Dei (qui nullum despicit & quantumvis peccantibus veniam peccatorum largitur) laudes extollendi. Tandem P. Chrachius plenus dierum ac fiducia in Christi meritis piissime obdormivit in Domino.

44. Putativa Chrachi uxor (quae pro ejus conversione diu multumque laboravit) statim ac maritus absolutus fuit ad pedes A.R. P. Provincialis Francisci Matthaei volavit, praeviaque sacramentali delictorum confessione absolutionem ab illo obtinuit; demum habitu Tertii

kingdom of Ireland. From a woman of ancient nobility (admittedly not so noble in this, that is in marrying an apostate, albeit a powerful one) he procreated many sons and daughters, whom he wanted to be educated in the Catholic faith by his wife (or, if you prefer, concubine), who was always a Catholic.

42. He managed to obtain many extensive possessions in Munster, Leinster and Ulster for his sons (whom Queen Elizabeth promoted to important offices). He gave his daughters in marriage to Catholic men of first rank of authority. At last, redeeming himself at the age of 79, he renounced his title of arch-bishop as well as every other public office. He ceded all his goods to his children, and eventually he converted to the Catholic faith after abjuring the heretic one (which he professed only in words) thanks to Rev. Fr James O'Nelan,[173] the guardian of Timoleague[174] at that time.

43. In that period, the person who presided over the seraphic religion of the province of Ireland was Francis O'Mahony (whom you, Carran, unjustly persecute amongst the other martyrs), a truly worthy Father and now a martyr of Christ. This man, having seen Friar Miler's penitence as well as pieces of evidence of his true contrition, absolved him of heresy and apostasy, and clothed him with the sacred vest of religion. Miler, who was by this time a Catholic and a Franciscan, lived for eighteen months more, during which time he was so assiduous in observing fasts, ascetic discipline, vigils, meditation and prayer, that he outshone all the friars and secular Catholics (who frequently went to see him in multitudes) in exemplary sanctity, and he offered everybody the opportunity to sing hosannas to merciful God (who despises nobody and dispenses pardon to sinners, regardless of the degree of their sins). At last Fr Magrath, at the end of his life and with faithfulness in Christ's favours, fell asleep in the Lord in a very pious way.

44. As soon as her husband was absolved, Magrath's putative wife (who had taken long and great pains to favour his conversion) threw herself at the feet of Adm. Rev. Provincial Father Francis O'Mahony and she obtained the absolution from him upon sacramental confession of her wrongdoings. Finally, once she put on the clothes

Ordinis S. Francisci (quem humiliter petiit) induta omnibus vitae suae diebus in rigidissimis poenitentiae exercitiis se maceravit.

Filii autem & filiae, ne a Catholicis objiceretur illis quod essent spurii, Romam ad Summum tunc Catholicae Ecclesiae Pontificem per interpositam personam recurrerunt; qui visa illorum innocentia, quam summis precibus rogarunt, apostolicam benedictionem illis una cum legitimatione paterne largitus est.

Haec omnia ita contigisse non solum testatur archivium provinciae Hiberniae & Thomas Lodgus Anglus agendo de papistarum induratione, sed & tu Carrane optime scivisti adhuc in patria. Ad quid igitur modo nobis Franciscanis objicis Mileri lapsum & de illius resipiscentia taces?

45. Ecce Carrane quam candide veritatem refero tecumque ago! Fac tu jam similiter & sine fuco fatearis: an non tibi probe notus fuit sacerdos ille, qui in Comitatu Tipperariensi non procul ab arce perillustris Domini Therentii Chrachei parochum aliquot annis egit, ac tandem nosti quare exulare debuit sine ullis honestis testimonialibus? Respondebis dubio procul, si vir bonus es, quod sic. Jam ergo rogo te illum efficaciter moneas ut exemplo Fratris Milleri Chrachei poenitentiam agat & resipiscat, si cum poenitente Millero in Coelis coronari praetendit. Nunc ad alia.

46. Credebam Carrane te amicum esse Comitis Ormoniae, potentissimae Butleriarorum familiae Principis: sed ex his quae in fine cap. 2. tui Apologi fol. 33. falso scribis de glorioso martyre Ioanne de Burgo demonstras contrarium, cum ministris illius tribuis captivitatem martyris his verbis: "Accusatus apud pro regem" (Joannes scilicet) "confestimque proscriptus est Dublinii, dein Richardus Schea, aulae Ormoniae praefectus, nimirum Thomae Comitis, qui tum oculo-

of the Third Order of Saint Francis (which she humbly asked for),[175] she mortified her flesh with hard exercises of penitence for all the remaining days of her life.

As for Miler's sons and daughters, they resorted to the high pontiff of the Catholic Church of that time through a third party, so that the Catholics could not hold against them that they were of illegitimate birth. Having discerned their innocence, the pope gave his fatherly consent to what they were asking with great prayers, and bestowed upon them the apostolic benediction together with his legitimisation.

That all these things happened in this way is not only attested by the archive of the province of Ireland and by the Englishman Thomas Lodge[176] in his discussion about the hardening of the papists, but it was also very well known to yourself, Carran, at the time when you were in your homeland. For what purpose, then, do you hold Miler's lapses against us Franciscans now, and you say nothing about his repentance?

45. Look at how sincere I am in telling the truth and conversing with you, Carran! Behave in a similar manner now, and frankly confess: were you honestly not familiar with that priest who, for several years, was in charge of a parish in County Tipperary, not far from the castle of the most illustrious master Terence Magrath? Also, do you know the reason why he had to go into exile without any creditable testimonial letter?[177] Undoubtedly, if you are an honest man, your answer will be yes. So now I ask you to effectively admonish him to do penance and show repentance, following the example of Friar Miler Magrath, if he demands to receive his crown in heaven with Miler the penitent. Now let us turn to a different issue.

46. I thought, Carran, that you were a friend of the earl of Ormond, a lord of the very powerful family of the Butlers. But from what you falsely write about the glorious martyr John Burke on page 33 at the end of Chapter II of your *Apologus*, you show the opposite, when you attribute the imprisonment of the martyr to that man's ministers, with these words: "He" (that is, John) "was accused in front of the viceroy and he was immediately outlawed in Dublin. Then [he was abandoned by two men:][178] Richard Shee,[179] the prefect of the court of the earl of Ormond, namely earl Thomas, nicknamed 'Black', who

rum visu carens, cognomento nigri, & Robertus Route, ejusdemque Thomae a secretis. Hi ambo intelligentiam habuerunt de adesse" (o grammatista!) "Ioannis in civitate eum deprehendi mandarunt & istinc Limericium miserunt. Haec est veritas, & non adulatoria Bruodini commenta", & c.

47. Nullum ego Carrane hic vel levissimum video argumentum, quo lector moveretur a<d> tibi (toties jam in mendacio deprehenso) potius in hac narratione credendum quam R. P. Bruodino, nisi forte authoritatem tuam omnium nobis argumentorum instar esse velis; quod Deus avertat. P. Bruodinus martyris de Burgo vitam descriptam a reverendissimo Domino Matthaeo Chracheo, Laonensis diocesis vicario generali & martyris confessario, prae manibus pro teste habet: tu vero nullum tuae assertionis producis confirmatorem; quare ergo tibi potius quam P. Bruodino, religioso tam honorato, credere deberemus?

48. P. Bruodinus per 15 continuos annos publice & privatim philosophiae ac theologiae scholas cum applausu rexit. Repetitis vicibus Romae in comitiis generalibus Ordinis theologicis Germaniae thesibus Augustissimo Romanorum Imperatori Leopoldo dedicatis plausibiliter praefuit. In variis ac honorificis officiis sui Ordinis fuit probatus & semper inventus majoribus muniis dignior. Tu vero, Carrane, semper fuisti & es (ut omnes qui te noverunt dicunt) homo rudis & ignarus, ad convitia & scommata a natura pronus, qui nulla publica aut privata munia unquam habuisti praeter militarem sacellaniam & unius parochiae in comitatu Tipperanensi penes arcem Domini Therentii Chrachei per paucos annos administrationem. Quare ergo in re dubia non deberemus P. Bruodino potius quam tibi credere?

49. Nollem Carrane ut dicas convitium esse quod de te scribo; non: nam tunc convitium est (ut de Sartorio tuo collega quondam ait Bechanus) quando quis ex odio personae conjicit in aliquem verba odiosa sine sufficienti causa aut fundamento: quo pacto tu P. Bruodinum

was already blind at that time;[180] and Robert Rothe,[181] the secretary of the Thomas mentioned above. Both these men knew about John was being in town,"[182] (what a mistake, worthy of a student of elementary grammar!) "they gave the order to arrest him and they sent him to Limerick from there. This is the truth, and not the lies which Bruodinus invented in order to flatter", etc.

47. Here, Carran, I see no argument, or a very weak one, that could possibly lead the reader to believe you (you, who have been already caught in the act of lying so many times) rather than Rev. Fr Bruodinus in this report – unless you demand that we give your authority the same value as all logical arguments ought to have: God forbid it! Fr Bruodinus has at hand the written testimony of the very reverend Master Matthew Magrath,[183] vicar general of the diocese of Killaloe, about the life of the martyr Burke. Conversely, you adduce no witness confirming what you say. For this reason, then, why should we trust you rather than Fr Bruodinus, who is such a respectable cleric?

48. Fr Bruodinus managed schools of philosophy and theology for fifteen uninterrupted years with success, both in the public and in the private sectors. At the general assemblies of the order in Rome, he frequently supervised theses of theology written in Germany, which were dedicated to the most august emperor of the Romans, Leopold. He was put to the test in various and honourable duties of his order and he was found worthier of more important offices each time. Conversely, Carran, you are and have always been (as all the people who know you say) an ignorant and inexperienced man, inclined by nature to insults and taunts; this is you, who never held any office, public or private, outside the military chaplaincy and the administration for a few years of a single parish in County Tipperary under the control of master Terence Magrath's castle. Accordingly, then, should we not trust Fr Bruodinus rather than you in this uncertain matter?

49. I would not like you to say that what I am writing about you is an insult: it is not. For as Becanus[184] once said about your colleague Sartorius[185], it is an insult whenever someone throws words full of acrimony at somebody out of hatred for that person, without sufficient motive or reason. It is in this manner that you call Fr Bruodinus (and

(& alios dignissimos viros) vocas "calumniatorem", "stultum", "bardum", "garrulum", "nebulonem", "fratricellum", "mendacem", & c. At convitium non est, quando quis aliquid jocosum aut asperum conjicit in alterum non ex odio personae sed ex merito causae de qua agitur; quo pact ego te voco rudem, quia re vera te talem esse, ostendunt tua scripta. Mendacem, quia in flagranti mendacio toties jam es deprehensus; & sic de aliis tibi charitative objectis defectibus discurrendum est: suscipe ergo grato animo quae tibi charitative dico, & ad sequentia sine cholera obduratas aures tuas applica.

other excellent men) "a slanderer", "a fool", "a bard", "a blatherer", "a sluggard", "an insignificant friar", "a liar", etc. But it is not an insult when somebody throws at someone else some witty or biting comments not out of hatred for that person, but because that person deserved them with regard to a matter under discussion. It is in this manner that I call you ignorant, because your writings show that you are truly such; and a liar, because you have been already caught red-handed in the act of lying so many times; and one should apply this discourse to the other defects which I have thrown out to you in the loving way of a Christian.[186] Therefore, accept with agreeable mind what I am charitably telling you, and lend with no anger your hardened ears to what I will tell you next.

Anatomia Capitis tertii *Apologiae* Carrani

1. Caput hoc tuum Carrane, omni cerebro destitutum, *de falsis martyribus in R. P. Bruodini libro insertis* intitulatur. Bene est. Male tibi successit hactenus tua cum martyribus pugna; nec felicior, ut spero, erit eventus novae persecutionis tuae, quam in hoc capite contra martyres impie moves. Pugnat pro gloria martyrum suorum Carrane Christus, contra quem solitis convitiorum & mendaciorum armis quibus pugnas non praevalebis: durum enim est tibi contra stimulum calcitrare. Praelude jam pugnae Carrane.

"Pater Bruodinus" (inquis cap. 3. fol. 35.) "perduelles monachos, sacerdotes & episcopos qui militari modo in hostem pugnarunt vocat martyres" (& paulo post, fol. 36.) "Audacter inter suos martyres enumerat Archi-Episcopum Tuomensem, & simili modo (Lector erratus) sentit de Clocherensi Episcopo," & c.

2. Justo, fateor, dolore moverer si alicujus fidei vir illustrissimum Quaeleum, Tuomensem Archi-Episcopum, delicias & decus patriae meae, tanquam perduellem e numero excluderet martyrum. At cum a te Carrane, qui bene loqui nescis, excludatur, non multum moveor: sed videamus, si placet Carrane, quod te argumentum in tam absurdum errorem ita praecipitem dedit, ut auderes dignissimos praesules a rebellibus Crumwellistisis supplicio affectos perduelles & falsos vocare martyres.

3. "Quia" (inquis) "hi episcopi exercitum in suum hostem adduxere pugnavereque animose, donec ab inimico expugnati fuerunt & jure belli interempti, & tales non sunt veri martyres. Est sententia omnium theologorum." Grammatistarum forte Carrane.

Noctua in luce media caecutiens es Carrane, non vero aquila; ad quid igitur relicta tua Lilliana *Grammatica* (cujus adhuc rudimenta ignoras) ad theologiam volare frustra conaris? Quid theologi sentiunt

Dissection of Chapter III of Carran's *Apologia*

1. This chapter of yours, Carran, which shows no sign of a brain,[187] is entitled "On the false martyrs that have been reckoned in Rev. Fr Bruodinus' book". Good. So far, your fight against the martyrs has not turned out well for you; and, as I hope, the outcome of your new persecution, which you impiously undertake against the martyrs, will not be more successful. Christ fights in defence of his martyrs' glory, Carran: you will not prevail against Him with your weapons of insults and lies, with which you are accustomed to fight. In fact, it is hard for you to kick against the goad.[188] Get ready for the battle now, Carran! In Chapter III, on page 35 you state: "Fr Bruodinus gives the appellation of martyrs to rebellious monks, priests and bishops who directly engaged in combat against their enemy in the manner of soldiers." Also, shorty after, on page 36: "He dares enumerate among his martyrs the archbishop of Tuam[189] and (the reader mistakenly)[190] supposes that a similar conclusion applies to the bishop of Clogher,"[191] etc.

2. I confess that I would be disturbed by rightful indignation if a man of any faith excluded from a catalogue of martyrs, just like a public enemy, the most illustrious O'Queely, archbishop of Tuam, the delight and glory of my homeland. But since he is excluded by you, Carran, who are unable to speak well of anybody, I am not much disturbed. Yet, if you please, Carran, let us see what argument exposed you so heedlessly to such an absurd mistake, that you dared give the appellation of enemies and false martyrs to truly worthy prelates who suffered torture by Cromwell's rebels.

3. You say: "Since these bishops led an army against their enemy and engaged in the battle with fervour until they were defeated by the opponent and were killed according to the right of war, and such are not true martyrs.[192] It is the opinion of all the theologians."[193] Perhaps it is the opinion of the students of elementary grammar, Carran!

You are a night-owl who cannot see properly in daylight hours, Carran, and certainly not an eagle-eye.[194] Why, then, do you try to take flight towards theology in vain, after abandoning your copy of Lily's *Grammar* (whose rudiments you still have to learn)? The theologians'

de martyribus nobis qui theologi sumus notum est; non tibi, cui ne de nomine quidem centesima theologorum pars nota est. Legisti forte aliquot folia in Tolleto vel Laymanno, quae non intellexisti; adhuc tamen, tanquam si omnes legisses Theologos, audacter scribis deliria tua: "sententiam esse omnium theologorum." Sed haec missa faciamus.

4. Carrane, praesules illi a te diffamati pugnando non fuerunt occisi; nam Malachias, Tuomensis Archi-Episcopus, nulla unquam a quo in Pontificem consecratus fuit arma portavit (ut omnibus Hibernis qui illum viderunt notum est), fuit tantum excellentissimo Domino Generali Taffe a supremo Catholicorum consilio non ut pugnaret, sed ut sua praesentia & authoritate neocollectum Catholicorum exercitum, ad discordias & dissentiones pronum, in debita Domino Generali obedientia foveret, eisque sicut & Domino Generali in spiritualibus assisteret. Sic inermis ut erat captus est a victoriosis rebellibus regicidis & cognitus. Tandem non obstante fide sibi data in odium Catholicae religionis in partes sectus fuit.

Clocherensis Episcopus (verum est) exercitum in rebelles parlamentarios (ut tu loqueris Carrane) duxit. At in pugna non fuit occisus, sed captus & sequenti primo die contra datam illi fidem suspensus. Vitam & honores rebelles haeretici parlamentarii illi promiserunt, si a fide apostatare vellet, noluit autem & sic in despectum tuum Carrane vitam cum martyribus consecutus est aeternam. Lege *Threnodiam Hiberno-Catholicam*, Oeniponti anno 1659. impressam, & noli o amplius Thoma esse incredulus, sed fidelis.

Frustra te rogo Carrane, nam in malo proposito ita es induratus, quod non videam remedium quo animus tuus, calumniarum & mendaciorum callo obductus, ad rectam veritatis semitam traduci possit: pergis itaque sicut incepisti.

opinion about the martyrs is known to us who are theologians, not to you, who are acquainted with just one per cent of the theologians, not even by name. You probably read some pages in Toledo or Laymann,[195] which you did not understand. Nevertheless, just as if you had read all works by every theologian, you still dare write your delirious statements, affirming that "it is the opinion of all the theologians". But let us stop bothering ourselves about these things.

4. The prelates whom you have defamed, Carran, were not killed while they were fighting. In fact Malachy [O'Queely], the archbishop of Tuam, never bore any weapons ever since he was consecrated bishop (as it is known to all the Irishmen who saw him). He simply was on the side of the most illustrious Master General Taffe,[196] by decree of the supreme council of the Catholics, with a different purpose than fighting. By his presence and authority, his role was to promote the obedience that was owed to the master general within the army of the Catholics, which had been just recently gathered and which was prone to disagreements and dissensions. Also, his function was to give spiritual assistance to those soldiers as well as to the master general. Unarmed as he was, he was captured by the regicidal rebels after they won, and he was recognised. At last, in spite of what had been promised to him, he was cut into pieces out of hatred against the Catholic religion.[197]

The bishop of Clogher – it is true – led an army against the parliamentarian rebels (as you say, Carran). However, he was not killed in battle, but captured and hanged at dawn on the next day, against what had been guaranteed to him. The heretical parliamentarian rebels promised to spare his life and give him rewards, if he had wished to apostatise from his faith, but he refused; and thus, in spite of you, Carran, he obtained eternal life with the martyrs.[198] Read *Threnodia Hiberno-Catholica,*[199] published in Innsbruck in the year 1659, and no longer doubt, but believe, O Thomas![200]

My prayer for you is in vain, Carran; for you have become so firm in your evil intention, that I see no remedy by which your soul could be brought back to the right path of truth, now that it has been led astray by the callousness of your lies and calumnies. Accordingly, you continue like you began.

5. "Pari" (inquis) "modo, dico de quibusdam fratribus Franciscanis belli Hibernici tempore, qui aperte tanquam perduelles se gessere non solum contra supremum Catholicorum consilium, sed etiam Coronam Angliae, non sunt martyres, si propter perduellionem sunt occisi; est communis sententia omnium theologorum praeter P. Bruodinum, qui suo infrunito capite sentit inconsulte contrarium."

Pater Bruodinus, tuis jam contumeliis & injuriis assuetus, ridet Carrane tuas calumnias. Quo in loco, libro, vel folio, Bruodinus Carrane docet quod occisus propter perduellionem fit martyr? Nomina, si audes Carrane, unum Franciscanum, qui ob perduellionem in Hibernia occisus est. Miserrime senex, nullumne calumniandi aliquando finem facies? Nisi ob tua malefacta indignus esses honore, tuam venerarer merito senectutem; quare oro lectores, ut non cogitent me tuam senectutem vituperare: nam senes amo, malos vero vetulos odio prosequor.

Falsorum martyrum Carrane loco tu (qui continue veritatem martyrisas) odiosam adducis narrationem dissensionum & tricarum quondam in Hibernia inter Nuntium Apostolicum & sibi adhaerentes praesules, nobiles & religiosos ex una parte, & haereticum Proregem Hiberniae & alios haereticos & Catholicos ipsi faventes ex altera parte ortarum: quam ex parte fictam historiam dudum verbo ad verbum furatus es, ex quodam (elegantis alias stili) Romae prohibito libello sub titulo *Vindiciarum Catholicorum Hiberniae,* Parisiis anno 1650. publicato, authore (sic ficte se nominat) Philopatro Ireneo. Tu in tuis (si diis placet) *Annalibus Hiberniae* Carrane, Sulzbaci anno 1666. reimpressis, ut veterem tuam *ollaepadridam* (sic *Annales* tuos merito Bruodinus baptisavit) anagyri condires, odiosam illam & partialem Philopatri narrationem fol. 334. tacito ejus nomine inseruisti; porro cum jam calumniandi melior tibi non occurrit materia reimprimis eandem historiam, ut sic Franciscanis infamiae notam in tua imaginatione adurere possis.

5. You say: "In the same way, about certain Franciscan friars at the time of the war in Ireland, who openly behaved just like rebels not only against the supreme council of the Catholics but also against the crown of England, I affirm: they are not martyrs, if they were killed because they rebelled. This is the universal opinion of all theologians apart from Fr Bruodinus, who inconsiderately thinks the opposite with his foolish mind."[201]

Fr Bruodinus, who is by now used to your invectives and insults, laughs at your slanders. In which passage, book or page, Carran, does Bruodinus say that a man killed as a rebel becomes a martyr? Give me the name – if you dare, Carran! – of a single Franciscan who was killed because he rebelled in Ireland. Will you not bring your slanders to an end at some point, you most wretched old man? If you were not unworthy of honour because of your wrongdoing, I would show some respect for your old age, which would deserve it. For this reason, I beg the readers not to think that I am disparaging your old age; for I love old people, but I direct my hatred at little wicked old men.

Instead of false martyrs, Carran, you (who keep on martyring the truth) adduce a despiteful account of the worthless discords which once arose in Ireland between two factions. On the one hand, the apostolic nuncio[202] and the prelates, noblemen and clerics who adhered to him; on the other, the heretical viceroy of Ireland[203] and the other heretics and Catholics who endorsed him. From this latter side you have recently stolen a fictitious history, word by word, from a certain pamphlet under the title *Vindiciae Catholicorum Hiberniae*,[204] published in Paris in the year 1650 by an author who gave himself the pseudonym Philopatrus Ireneus[205] – a book which is prohibited in Rome (in spite of its elegant style). In your (gods granting this) *Annales Hiberniae*, which were reprinted in Sulzbach in the year 1666, Carran, you have inserted that despiteful and partisan account by Philopatrus on page 334, without mentioning his name, in order to season your old *olla podrida*[206] (Bruodinus deservedly baptised your *Annales* with this name) with anagyris.[207] Again, now that no better pretext occurs to you for your calumnies, you reprint the same history, so as to be able to brand the Franciscans with a note of infamy[208] in your imagination.

6. Cum Deum, Carrane, non videaris timere vindicem, mirum est quod illustrissimum D. Nuncium Apostolicum non verearis Viennensem; qui si sciret te tam infamiter in *Annalibus* tuis, vel si mavis *ollaepadrida*, & in hoc tuo libello post Alexandri VII. decretum de fautoribus Hibernici quondam legati scripsisse, dubio procul justam non praetermitteret animadversionem. Romae Carrane dudum Alexandro Septimo regnante lis illa illustrissimi Domini Archi-Episcopi Firmani Legati quondam Extraordinarii in Hibernia Summi Pontificis Innocentii X. & suorum adhaerentium, cum acatholico Prorege Hiberniae Ormonio & Catholicis ac haereticis multis sibi associatis, fuit decisa: lege ergo, si vis, bullam Alexandri, & doctior, si possibile est, eris; eam aspice.

ALEXANDER PP. VII

Venerabiles Fratres salutem & apostolicam benedictionem. Sedes Apostolica pia mater recurrentibus ad eam post excessus cum humilitate filiis propitiam se exhibere consuevit & benignam. Cum itaque bonae memoriae Ioannes Baptista dum viveret Archiepiscopus Firmanus, tunc temporis Apostolicae Sedis in Regno Hiberniae Nuntius Extraordinarius, cum delegatis archiepiscoporum & episcoporum Regni praedicti varias ob causas multos tam ecclesiasticos & regulares quam saeculares excommunicaverint, & aliquot civitates ecclesiastico subjecerint interdicto, sicut autem accepimus plures ex personis, ut praedicitur, excommunicatis sibi absolutionis beneficium ab excommunicatione hujusmodi, a qua fuerat alias ad f<e>l. re<c>. Innocentium Papam praedecessorem nostrum appellatum, & ab eo appellatio hujusmodi tanquam frivola rejecta auctoritate nostra concedi, interdictumque praedictum ubi adhuc viget & servatur amoveri summopere desiderent, nos earumdem personarum animarum saluti pro paterna nostra charitate quantum cum Domino possumus consulere volentes, ipsarumque singulas a quibusvis excommunicationis suspensionis &

6. Although you do not seem to be afraid of God the Avenger, Carran, it is surprising that you feel no reverence or fear for the most illustrious master apostolic nuncio of Vienna.[209] Undoubtedly, he would not neglect to inflict a just punishment if he knew that you wrote things so defamatory in your *Annales*, or – if you prefer – *olla podrida*, and in this libel of yours, after Alexander VII's decree about the supporters of the former legate of Ireland. Not long ago, Carran, a final decision was made in Rome under the pontificate of Alexander VII with regard to the famous dispute between these two factions. On the one hand, the archbishop of Fermo, a most illustrious prelate and former legate extraordinary of the supreme pontiff in Ireland, and the people who adhered to him; on the other, the non-Catholic viceroy of Ireland, Ormond, and the great number of Catholics and heretics who had united with him.[210] If you want, then, read Alexander's bull, and you will learn more than you know now, if possible. Have a look at it.

ALEXANDER PP.[211] VII[212]

Greetings and apostolic blessing to you, venerable brothers. The apostolic see, a pious mother, has always been accustomed to show herself benevolent and well-disposed to the sons who return to her with humility after they abandoned her. Therefore:
While he was still alive, Giovanni Battista of blessed memory, archbishop of Fermo, nuncio extraordinary of the apostolic see in the kingdom of Ireland at that time, together with the delegates of the archbishops and bishops of the aforementioned kingdom, excommunicated for various reasons as many clerics and regular priests as secular ones, and he bestowed the ecclesiastical interdict upon several cities. Nevertheless, it has been brought to my attention that most of the people, who, as it is said above, were excommunicated, greatly wished to be conceded the favour of absolution from an excommunication of this kind through my authority. Against this excommunication an appeal had been made on another occasion to my predecessor, Pope Innocent of happy memory, but such appeal had been rejected as frivolous. Also, those people expressed the deep desire to see the aforementioned interdict repealed in those towns where it is valid and still in force. According to my paternal charity,[213] I want to look after the salvation of the souls of these same people as much as I can with the help of God. Therefore, since I am favourably disposed towards

interdicti, aliisque ecclesiasticis sententiis, censuris & poenis a jure vel ab homine quavis occasione vel causa latis, si quibus quomodolibet innodatae existunt praeterquam ratione praemissorum absolventes & absolutas fore censentes supplicationibus earum nomine nobis super hoc humiliter porrectis inclinati, fraternitatibus vestris & vestrum cuilibet quoscumque ex praedictis etiam quacumque ecclesiastica dignitate & praeminentia praeditis ut praedicitur excommunicatis, qui hoc a vobis seu vestrum aliquo humiliter petierint imposita singulis aliqua arbitrio vestro poenitentia salutari ab excommunicationis hujusmodi sententia aliisque censuris contra eos per dictum Ioannem Baptistam Archiepiscopum & dictos delegatos vel eorum subdelegatos fulminatis auctoritate nostra apostolica in forma Ecclesiae consueta, defunctos autem per modum suffragii absolvendi, & ab illis locis in quibus adhuc viget interdictum, si eorum nomine id a vobis humiliter postulatum fuerit, interdictum praedictum amovendi, nec non cum illis ecclesiasticis saecularibus & regularibus, qui ob contemptum seu violationem excommunicationis aliarumque censurarum praedictarum ac interdicti hujusmodi irregularitatis notam sive maculam contraxerunt super eadem irregularitate dispensandi, eosque ad quaevis alia rehabilitandi plenam & amplam facultatem auctoritate praedicta, tenore praesentium concedimus & impertimur, non obstantibus praemissis ac apostolicis & in universalibus, provincialibusque & synodalibus conciliis editis generalibus vel specialibus constitutionibus & ordinationibus caeterisque contrariis quibuscumque. Datum Romae apud Sanctam Mariam Majorem, sub Annulo Piscatoris, die XXVII. Augusti M. DC. LV. Pontificatus nostri anno primo.

G. GUALTERIUS

their supplications about this, which have been humbly offered to me by name, I do not simply absolve them but I also decree that full absolution shall be given to each of them from any kind of excommunication, suspension and interdict and from any other ecclesiastical decision, censorship and punishment that have been promulgated by right or by man on any occasion or for any reason, if they exist for anyone, in any way in which they may have been imposed. By the tenor of the present dispositions, despite the general or special apostolic regulations, edicts and any other decrees affirming the opposite, that have been announced in the past and ratified at universal, provincial and synodical councils, by means of the aforementioned authority, I grant and concede to your fraternities and to anyone of you the full and wide faculty to do as follows:

Through the imposition of some beneficial penance of your choice to individual people, bestow absolution on each and every person, who shall present a humble request for it to you or to one of your deputies, out of the aforementioned people who have received the excommunication outlined above, including those who enjoy any form of ecclesiastical rank and prominence. Those who shall request the absolution shall be acquitted of such excommunication, judgement and other censures that were struck against them by our apostolic authority in the customary form of the Church through the aforementioned Archbishop Giovanni Battista and the aforesaid delegates or their sub-delegates. By way of suffrage the absolution shall concern the souls of dead people as well.[214] Also, I give you the power to repeal the aforementioned interdict from those places where it is still in force, if you will be officially asked to do so in their name with humility. Moreover, those secular and regular clerics, who received a note or *macula* because of their indifference to, or violation of, the excommunication, the other censures mentioned above, and the interdict of such irregularity, shall be accorded by you my dispensation from the same irregularity and my rehabilitation to whatever role they held previously.

This letter was handed over in Rome, in the Basilica of Saint Mary Major, with the impress of the Piscatory Ring,[215] on 27 August 1655, in the first year of my Pontificate.

G. Gualterio[216]

Huic Indulto affixum erat Sigillum ex cera rubra, & superscriptum "Venerabilibus Fratribus Rapotensi, Laghliniensi, Clonfertensi, & Corcagiensi Episcopis, & eorum cuilibet", ut absolverent excommunicatos aliisque censuris innodatos per Nuncium Apostolicum in Regno Hiberniae.

7. Pater Bruodinus lib. 4. cap. 14. de origine illarum miseriarum veridice & acute scripsit: tuum vero quod erat Carrane ex omnibus pagellis quos ex Philopatro furatus es, ne unum quidem nominare potuisti Franciscanum, qui supplicio fuisset affectus ob rebellionem, nam suo regi fideles semper extiterunt Franciscani & Dominicani Clerusque totus Hibernicus: omnes itaque illi a te nominati vel defacto vivunt vel naturali morte extincti sunt. Ad quid ergo bonos Patres hic producis? Videatur index martyrum, de quibus Bruodinus in suo libro egit, & alius martyrum Hiberniae magis copiosus index a R.P. Iosepho Saulo Casseliensi Hiberno conscriptus, & nullius ex nominatis a te post Philopatrum Patribus nomen ibi invenietur. Si Patres illi *Carrane* peccarunt, Archi-Episcopus Firmanus Innocentii X. legatus a latere (cui nimis forte zelose adhaeserunt) erravit; erravit etiam Sacra Congregatio, & Christi vicarius Alexander VII, qui praefatorum Patrum zelum & erga sedem apostolicam reverentiam approbavit & laudavit, nunciique sententiam excommunicationis contra suos in Hibernia adversarios validam fuisse declaravit.

8. Persecutor martyrum Carrane, ecce continue pro viribus jam laborasti a fol. 20. tui libelli, usque ad fol. 75. ut possis athletas pro Christos occisos laurea martyrii privare. At invanum te sudasse abunde jam percipis: unde cum apostolico piscatore dicere possis "Ecce laborantes tota die nihil cepimus". Ne tamen omnino gratis sit labor tuus, R. Adm. & eximius SS. Theologiae Parisiensis Doctor, Joannes o Mollony, Decanus Casseliensis, praemii loco sequentes versus tibi praesentandos Lutetia misit:

A seal of red wax had been impressed onto this indult,[217] and the following words written above it: "To the venerable brothers, the Bishops of Raphoe, Leighlin, Clonfert and Cork, and to any of them without distinction", so that they might absolve those who had been excommunicated and upon whom other forms of censure had been imposed through the apostolic nuncio in the kingdom of Ireland.

7. Fr Bruodinus wrote a truthful and insightful account of the origin of those misfortunes in Book IV, Chapter 14 [of his *Propugnaculum*]. As for yours, instead, which derives from the insignificant pages which you have plagiarised from Philopatrus, you could not name even a single Franciscan who underwent torture because he had rebelled. In fact, the Franciscans always remained loyal to their king, and so did the Dominicans and the entire Irish clergy. Accordingly, all those named by you are actually either still alive, or they died a natural death. What is your purpose, then, in citing those good fathers on this occasion? I invite anyone to consult the index of the martyrs about whom Bruodinus spoke in his book, as well as another richer index of the martyrs in Ireland, written by the Irish Rev. Fr Joseph Saul of Cashel:[218] the name of none of the fathers whom you, following Philopatrus, mentioned will be found there. If those fathers sinned, Carran, the mistake was on the part of the archbishop of Fermo, Innocent X's legate a *latere*[219] (to whom, maybe, they adhered too zealously). The mistake was also on the part of the Holy Congregation and of the Vicar of Christ, Alexander VII, who approved and praised the zeal of the fathers mentioned above and their reverence towards the apostolic see, and who declared that the nuncio's sentence of excommunication against his enemies in Ireland was valid.

8. Behold, Carran, you persecutor of martyrs! You have already been striving as hard as you could, incessantly from page 20 all the way to page 75, to be able to deprive of the glory of martyrdom the champions killed for their defence of Christ. But now you understand abundantly that you sweated in vain; therefore you may say, together with the apostolic fisherman: "Look, we toiled all day but caught nothing."[220] Nevertheless, in order for your toil not to be completely without recompense, Adm. Rev. John O'Molony, distinguished doctor of holy and sacred theology of Paris and Dean of Cashel,[221] sent from Paris the following lines as a reward to be handed to you:

"Carve tuos laceras, mordes holocaustaque regni
    nec famam innocuis subdola lingua sinis;
nunc tua te produnt Carranum, Carve, nefanda:
    dum crocitas, nullum corve latere potes.
Quid nisi martyribus majores ipse secutus
    invideas Coelum Momus, ut ante solum?"

"Carve, you torture and bite your own people, and with your deceitful tongue

you permit the kingdom to be sacrificed,[222] but not fame to be accorded to the innocent.

Now, Carve, your abominations reveal you as a Carran:

while you croak loudly, you crow,[223] you cannot conceal it at all!

Why should one be surprised that you, a Momus,[224] envy the martyrs for their heavenly life,

just as you envied them for their earthly life before their death, following the manner of your ancestors?"

Anatomia Capitis sexti *Apologiae* Carrani

1. In anatomia hujus capitis diu nobis morandum non erit: abhorret enim animus a contemplatione capitis fronte, cute & cerebro carentis. Per totum hoc sextum sicut & subsequens septimum tuum caput monstrose Carrane ita fulminas & evomis scommata in Bruodinum ejusque honoratam familiam, ut nihil aliud quam furiosi hominis speciem nobis exhibeas, qui cum hostem ferire non valet vibrata circumquaque falce aërem ut insanus secat.

2. "Ostendimus" (inquis fol. 75.) "hactenus impudentia P. Bruodini mendacia." Noli Carrane agere judicem simul & actorem tuae litis; interroga potius lectores, & dicent te hactenus ostendisse magna ignorantiae & imprudentiae tuae specimina. Toties jam prostratus & convictus de mendaciis, imposturis & male fide adhuc canis triumphum ante victoriam? Progredere in malo & produc si quid habes.

"Nunc" (subdis) "in relatione Regni Hiberniae ipsum plane convincere intendo." Credo bene te hoc intendere: at, Carrane mi, expertum & oculatum habes antagonistam, a quo toties jam es profligatus; sic nisi aliis uteris armis quam hactenus usus es, legionesque in campo melius disposueris quam hucusque fecisti, de tua actum erit victoria. Evagina jam Carrane falcem prothoplasti tui Thomae *Carrani* (qui S. Lactino brachium amputavit) insigne<m> & in arenam animose descende.

3. "Sic" (inquis Carrane fol. 75.) ille habet lib. 4. cap. 7. ipsum diploma Adriani IV. Pontificis Romani esse subreptitium & falsum. Christianus videat lector qualem sedi apostolicae infert injuriam," & c.

Dissection of Chapter VI of Carran's *Apologia*

1. We will not have to linger too long over the dissection of this chapter; for our soul shrinks back from the attentive consideration of a chapter which is without sense of shame, without a decent skin and without a brain. Throughout this sixth chapter of yours, just as in the seventh one which follows, you cast your bolts of lightning and you vomit your taunts against Bruodinus and his honoured family. You do this in such a monstrous way, Carran, that you show us nothing other than the view of a man out of his mind, who cuts the air by brandishing a sickle all around because he is unable to strike his enemy, just as a madman would do.

2. On page 75, you state: "So far, we have exposed the shameless lies of Fr Bruodinus." Carran, do not take up the roles both of the judge and the prosecutor in a trial which you have also prepared yourself. Rather, ask your readers, and they will tell you that what you have exposed is strong evidence of your ignorance and shamelessness. Are you still singing triumphantly before victory, after you have already been thrown to the ground and convicted of lies, impostures and bad faith so many times? Go even further in your wicked purpose, and cite your evidence if you have any.

"Now" (you add) "I intend to refute [Bruodinus] himself in the report concerning the kingdom of Ireland, incontestably." I am sure that you have this intention; but, my dear Carran, you have an expert and scrupulous antagonist, who has already defeated you so many times. Therefore, if the weapons you will use are not different from those you have used so far, and if you will not arrange your legions in the battlefield better than you have done so far, we will be speaking about a victory over you. Now, Carran, unsheathe your sickle, that distinctive weapon of your ancestor, Thomas Carran (who cut off the arm of Saint Lachtín), and enter the arena with courage!

3. On page 75, Carran, you state: "So, in Book IV, Chapter 7 he [that is, Bruodinus] reports that the actual bull of Adrian IV,[225] the Roman pontiff, is surreptitious and false. May any Christian reader notice what an insult he throws at the apostolic see",[226] etc.

Toties nos lectores, Carrane, fatigas gratis: nam cum jam experti sumus te semper mala fide hactenus processisse citando P. Bruodinum, debemus illum ad manum continue habere, & in fonte videre num aquam tu vel lutum inde hauris. Liber 4. Bruodini (cum tua bona venia Carrane) non habet nisi 16 capita, & in nullo horum mentio habetur "diplomatis Adriani". Repone caece ocularia & videbis quod lib. 5. cap. 17. fol. 947. Bruodinus de illa agit controversia; ubi solide refutavit Sanderum & Lombardum a te (tanquam si ex numero essent prophetarum, quibus contradicere nefas foret) citatos fol. 76.

Bruodinus, Carrane, subditus est & subjectus pedibus S. Romanae Ecclesiae, stabilisque majorum suorum more in fide Catholica; sic nisi evidenti aliquo novo argumento confirmabis Sanderi Angli authoritatem, Christianus lector in tui gratiam non videbit injuriam quam Bruodinus sedi apostolicae infert, quia nullam illi intulit.

4. Plurimas emanasse ab origine Christianitatis subreptitias bullas, Carrane qui negat, omnem veridicis historicis fidem ut neget necesse est. Bruodinus in illa bulla quae Adriani IV. nomine circumfertur invenit rationabilia motiva, ob quae merito dixit bullam fuisse subreptitiam: bulla enim subreptitia dicitur illa vel quae datur praevia ficta & mala informatione, vel quae Pontifice nihil penitus sciente expracticatur. At utroque modo bulla illa Adriani peccare videtur, ut bene probat Bruodinus lib. 5. cap. 17. fol. 947. et ut ex sequentibus clare ostendetur.

In Adriani diplomate, Carrane, quod apud te folio 32. neo-impressionis tuorum (si diis placet) *Annalium* habetur, haec ponitur clausula:

"Sane Hiberniam & omnes insulas, quibus sol justitiae Christus illuxit & <quae> documenta fidei Christianae c<e>perant, ad B. Petri & sacrosantae Romanae Ecclesiae patrimonium non dubium est pertinere," & c.

So often you wear us readers out for nothing, Carran! From our experience with you so far, we already know that your quotations from Fr Bruodinus' work have always been reported in bad faith. Therefore, we have to constantly keep his text at hand and consult it to see if you are drawing water or mud from your source. Bruodinus' Book IV (I beg your kind pardon, Carran) does not have but sixteen chapters, and none of these contains any mention of the "bull of Adrian". Put on your spectacles again, you blind man, and you will see that Bruodinus deals with that controversy in Book V, Chapter 17, page 947. There, he firmly refuted Sander[227] and Lombard,[228] who had been quoted by you on page 76 (just as if they belonged to the category of the prophets, whom it would be sacrilegious to contradict).

Bruodinus is a subject who has thrown himself at the feet of the holy Roman Church, Carran, and he is steady in following the custom of his ancestors in the Catholic faith. Thus, if you will not strengthen the authority of Sander the Englishman through the evidence of some new argument, a Christian reader will not agree with you in recognising the insult allegedly thrown at the apostolic see by Bruodinus, since he threw none at it.

4. Whoever denies that a great many surreptitious bulls were promulgated since the origin of Christianity, Carran, must be necessarily denying truthful historians every reliability. In that bull which circulates under the name of Adrian IV, Bruodinus found reasonable motives on the basis of which he rightly stated that the bull was a surreptitious one. In fact, if a bull is produced upon fictitious and bad information or is ratified by a pontiff who does not have a full and deep knowledge of its content, that bull is called surreptitious. In either case, however, that bull of Adrian seems to be a fraud, as Bruodinus convincingly proves in Book V, Chapter 17, page 947, and as the following evidence clearly shows.

In the bull of Adrian which you, Carran, report on page 32 of the new edition of your (gods granting this) *Annales*, this sentence occurs:

"Indeed there is no doubt that Ireland and all the islands upon which Christ, the sun of Justice, arose and which obtained proofs of the Christian faith belong to the patrimony of the beatified Peter and of the holy and sacred Roman Church",[229] etc.

Si tu Carrane credis hanc clausulam esse veram, magna est profecto fides tua. Anglia, Scotia, Candia, Cor<s>ica, Cyprus, Sardinia, Majorica, Dania & Hibernia sunt insulae, quibus sol justitiae Christus illuxit, quae suos semper antiquitus Catholicos habuerunt reges qui in temporalibus nullam agnoverunt supra se potestatem. Quod non fecissent, si recognoscerent regna sua ad Ecclesiae patrimonium pertinere; ergo vera non est clausula illa, quae maris insulas ad Papam pertinere dicit.

5. Adrianus Papa, Carrane, fuit mortuus anno 1159. (ut omnes fatentur historici) & Angli primo in succursum Dermitii ô Morphei Lageniae Principis venerunt in Hiberniam anno 1166. septem nimirum annis post Adriani mortem. Et ipse Rex Henricus II. primo venit anno 1172. tredecim nimirum annis (error est calculi ubi loco supra citato Bruodinus habet "viginti duobus annis") post Adriani mortem. Quomodo jam absque contradictione posset esse Carrane verum quod Sanderus tuus (in cujus authoritate tute fundas) dicit, nimirum quod "postquam Henricus II. nonnulla insulae loca armis acquisita tenebat clerus Hibernicus simul cum proceribus suppliciter rogarunt Adrianum IV. ut totis Hiberniae Dominium Henrico II. concedere vellet"? Adrianus in cineres fuit redactus antequam Henricus II. pedem terrae habuit in Hibernia (ut, velle nolle, fateri teneris): quomodo ergo Carrane poterant Hiberni supplicare illi? Compatior tibi.

6. Alexandro III. summo Pontifice sedente Angli primo in Hiberniam appullerunt; huic si Henricus II. una cum clero & populo Hibernico supplicuisset, ut "pro restringendo vitiorum decursu, pro dilatandis Ecclesiae terminis, pro corrigendis moribus, pro Christianae religionis augmento" (verba sunt bullae & ficta concessionis motiva) dominium insulae, cujus nonnulla tunc loca armis suorum acquisita jam habebat, concedere vellet, esset aliquid (quamvis nihil obtineret ab Alexandro,

Fig. 1. Portrait of Fr Thomas Carve. This engraving featured in the second edition of Carve's work *Lyra sive Anacephalaeosis Hibernica* (Sulzbach, 1666). Carve was around sixty years old at the time of its composition and it portrays him in a sacerdotal cassock. (Photo: Luke McInerney)

Fig. 2. Kilraghtis church, Barefield, was where in the mid-1630s Bruodinus received his early instruction in Latin and grammar from the parish priest, Donnchadh Ó Nialláin, who was a kinsman. (Photo: Martin Breen)

Fig. 3. Quin Friary, founded by the McNamaras, lords of Clann Chuiléin, in the early fifteenth century, was the largest Franciscan foundation in County Clare and it was here in the early 1640s that Antonius Bruodinus began his noviciate. (Photo: Luke McInerney)

Fig. 4. Inscription above the entrance to St Isidore's College, Rome, quoting Tadhg mac Dáire Mhic Bhruaideadha's quatrain:

> Ná tréig choidhche ceachtar dhíbh: [Never forsake either of them]:
> Searc is omhan a náird rí, [Love and fear of the high king],
> Tús gach fíoreagna a sé sin, [That is the beginning of all true wisdom],
> Sír eagla Dé air na daoinibh [People's constant fear of God].

(Photo: Mícheál Mac Craith)

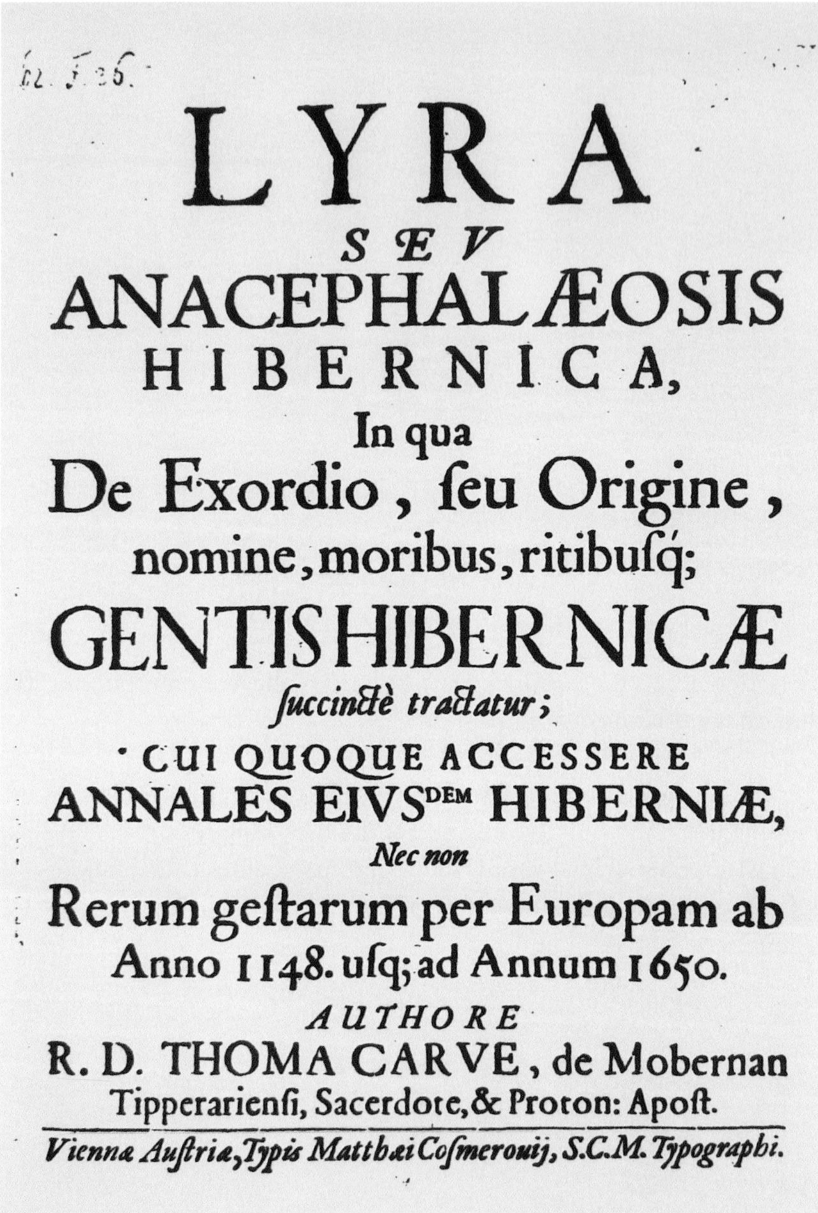

LYRA
SEV
ANACEPHALÆOSIS
HIBERNICA,
In qua
De Exordio, ſeu Origine,
nomine, moribus, ritibuſq;
GENTIS HIBERNICÆ
ſuccinctè tractatur;
CUI QUOQUE ACCESSERE
ANNALES EIVSDEM HIBERNIÆ,
Nec non
Rerum geſtarum per Europam ab
Anno 1148. uſq; ad Annum 1650.
AUTHORE
R. D. THOMA CARVE, de Mobernan
Tipperarienſi, Sacerdote, & Proton: Apoſt.
Viennæ Auſtriæ, Typis Matthæi Coſmerouij, S.C.M. Typographi.

Fig. 5. Title page of *Lyra Seu Anacephalaeosis Hibernica*, which was authored by Thomas Carve (alias Carew) of Mobarnan, Tipperary, in 1651 (revised in 1666).

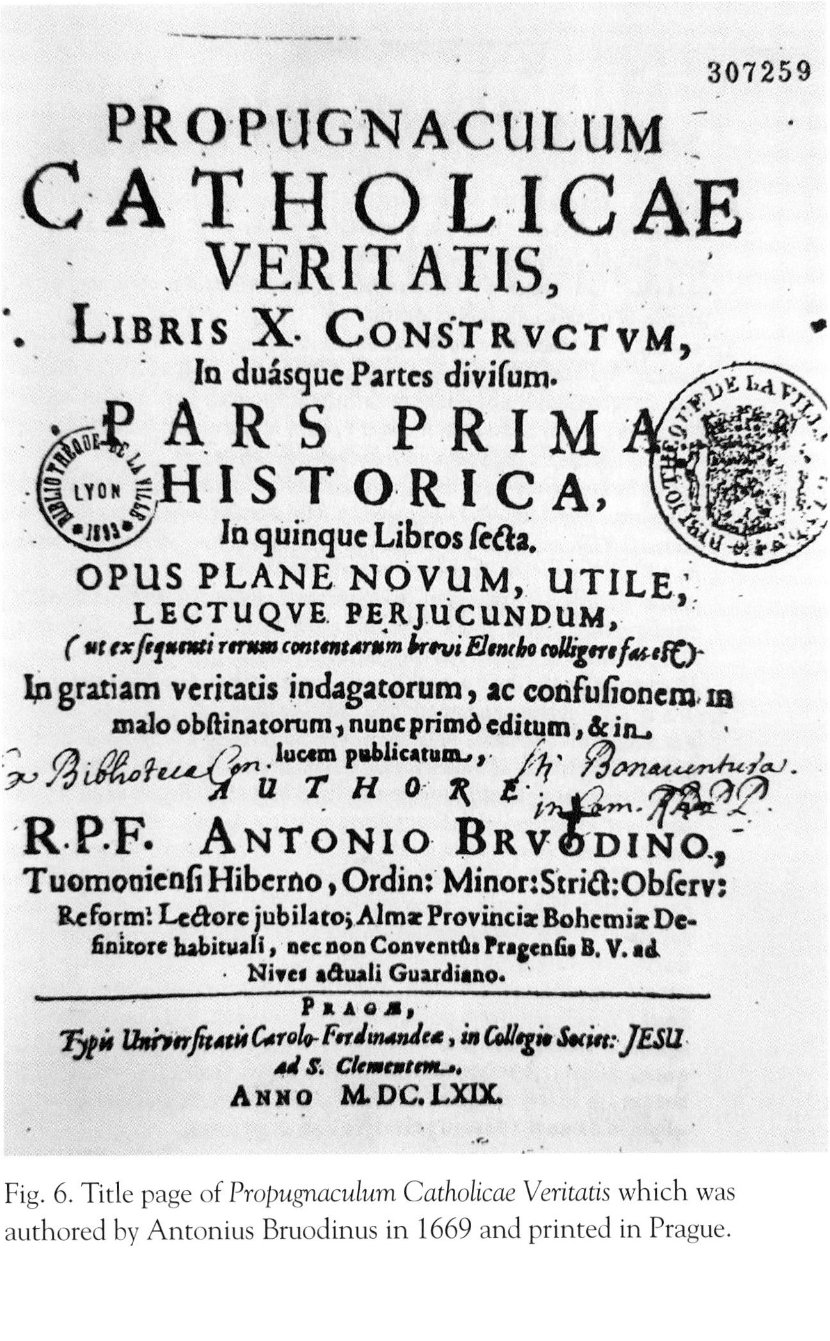

307259

PROPUGNACULUM
CATHOLICAE
VERITATIS,
LIBRIS X. CONSTRVCTVM,
In duásque Partes divisum.
PARS PRIMA
HISTORICA,
In quinque Libros secta.
OPUS PLANE NOVUM, UTILE,
LECTUQVE PERJUCUNDUM,
(ut ex sequenti rerum contentarum brevi Elencho colligere fas est)
In gratiam veritatis indagatorum, ac confusionem in malo obstinatorum, nunc primò editum, & in lucem publicatum,
AUTHORE
R.P.F. ANTONIO BRVODINO,
Tuomoniensi Hiberno, Ordin: Minor: Strict: Observ: Reform: Lectore jubilato; Almæ Provinciæ Bohemiæ Definitore habituali, nec non Conventûs Pragensis B. V. ad Nives actuali Guardiano.

PRAGÆ,
Typis Universitatis Carolo-Ferdinandeæ, in Collegio Societ: JESU ad S. Clementem.
ANNO M.DC.LXIX.

Ex Biblioteca Con. S[ti] Bonaventura in Cam. [illegible]

Fig. 6. Title page of *Propugnaculum Catholicae Veritatis* which was authored by Antonius Bruodinus in 1669 and printed in Prague.

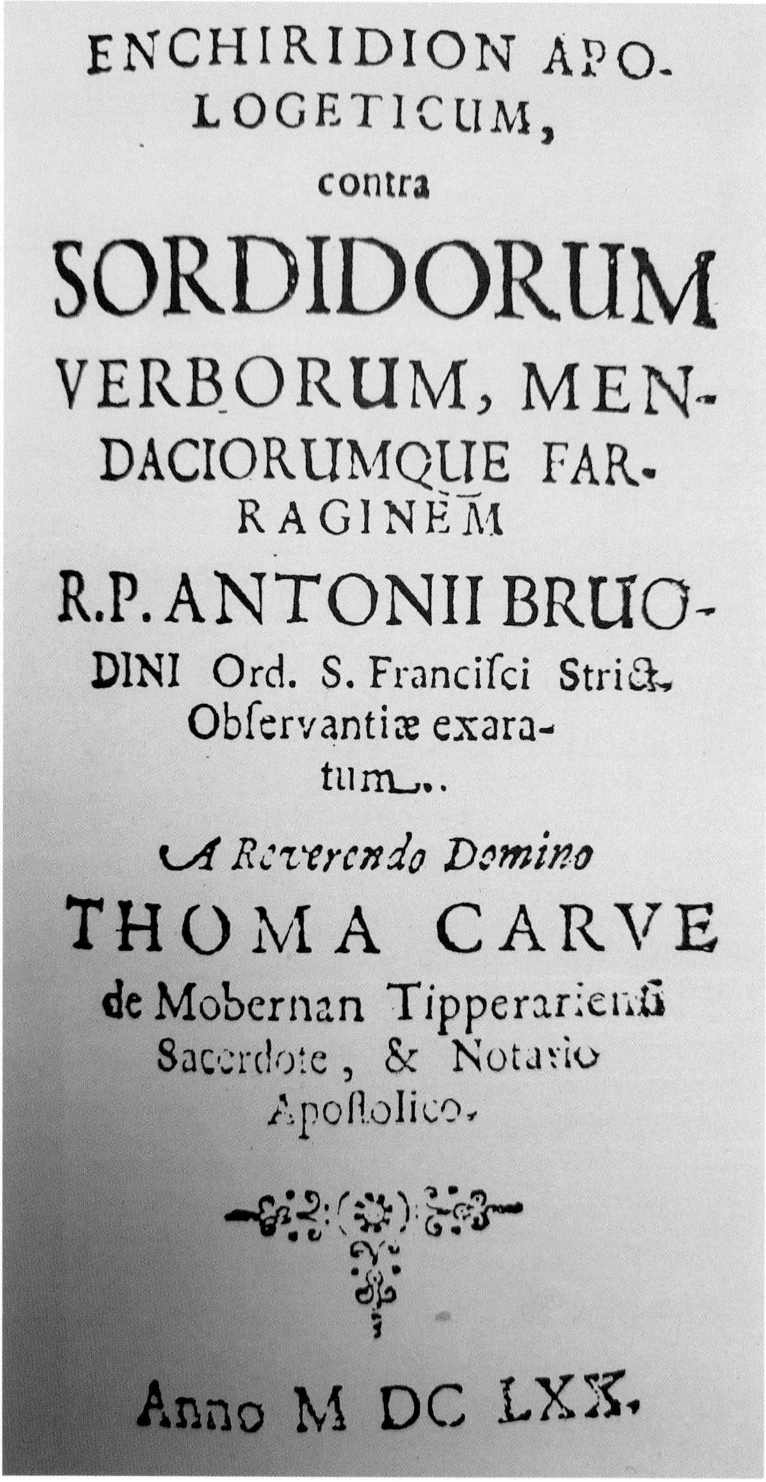
ENCHIRIDION APO-
LOGETICUM,
contra
SORDIDORUM
VERBORUM, MEN-
DACIORUMQUE FAR-
RAGINEM
R.P. ANTONII BRUO-
DINI Ord. S. Franciſci Strict.
Obſervantiæ exara-
tum...
A Reverendo Domino
THOMA CARVE
de Mobernan Tipperarienſi
Sacerdote, & Notario
Apoſtolico.

Anno M DC LXX.

Fig. 7. Title page of *Enchiridion Apologeticum contra sordidorum mendaciorumque faraginem R. P. Antonii Bruodini* which was authored by Thomas Carve in 1670 and printed in Nuremberg.

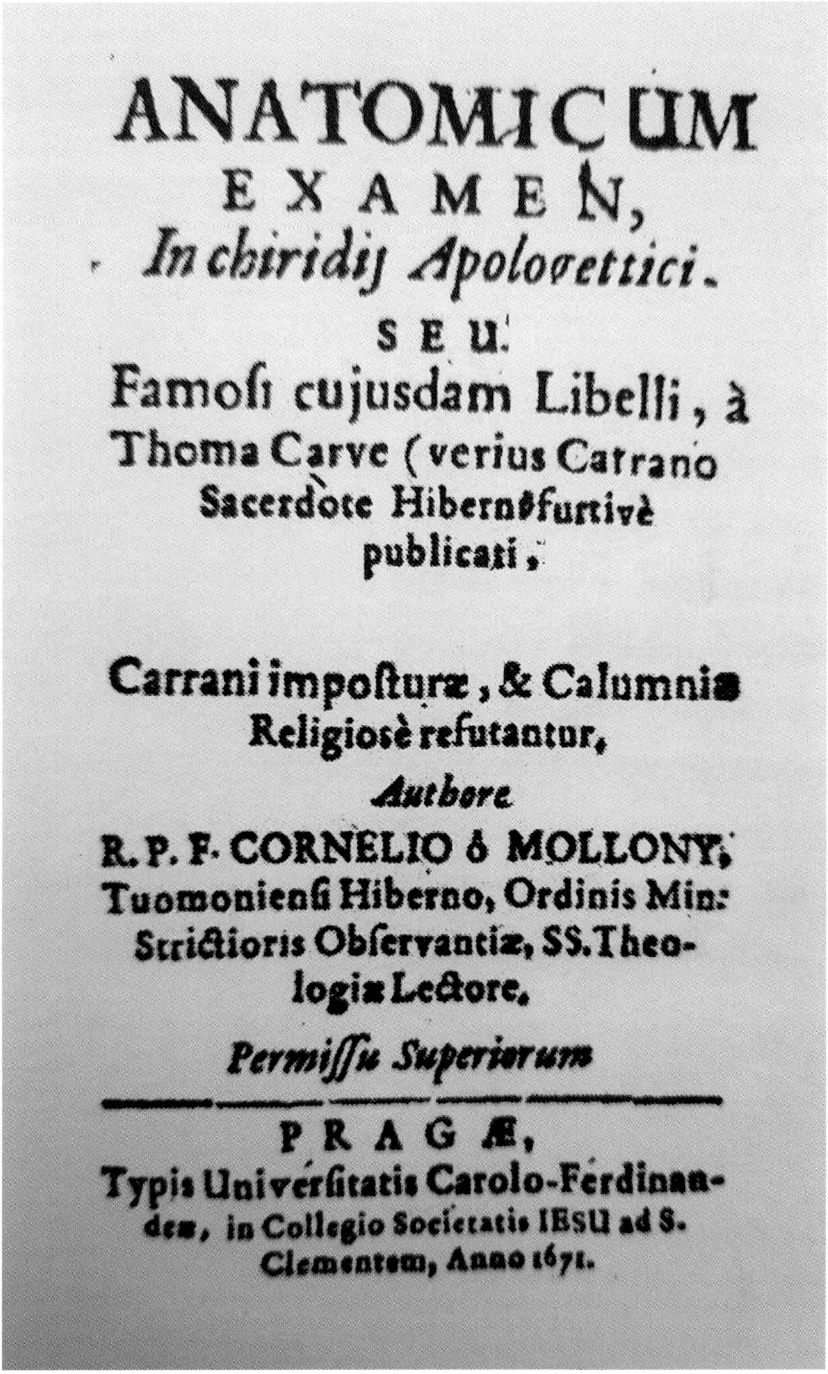

ANATOMICUM
EXAMEN,
In chiridij Apologettici.
SEU:
Famosi cujusdam Libelli, à
Thoma Carve (verius Carrano
Sacerdote Hiberno furtivè
publicati,

Carrani imposturæ, & Calumniæ
Religiosè refutantur,
Authore
R.P.F. CORNELIO ó MOLLONY,
Tuomoniensi Hiberno, Ordinis Min:
Strictioris Observantiæ, SS.Theo-
logiæ Lectore,
Permissu Superiorum

PRAGÆ,
Typis Universitatis Carolo-Ferdinan-
deæ, in Collegio Societatis IESU ad S.
Clementem, Anno 1671.

Fig. 8. Title page of *Anatomicum Examen* which was authored by Antonius Bruodinus under the pseudonym, Cornel O Mollony, in 1671 and printed in Prague.

Fig. 9. St Isidore's College, Rome, founded by Franciscan Luke Wadding in 1625. Antonius Bruodinus was resident here in the mid-1640s.

Fig. 10. The entrance to the church of Our Lady of the Snows is located off Jungmann Square, Prague. Antonius Bruodinus served as guardian of the church in 1668–70. (Photo: Martin Breen)

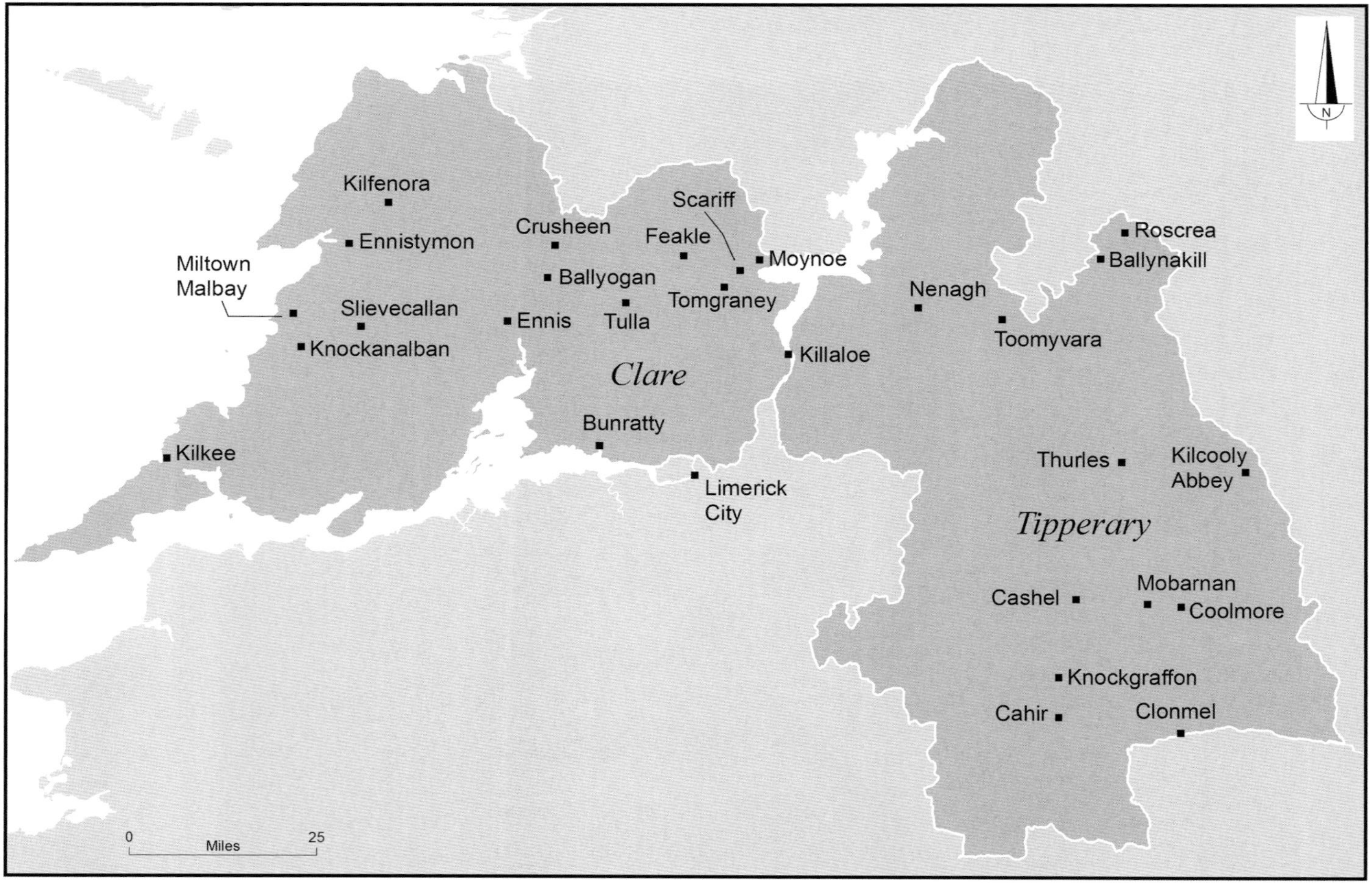

Fig. 11. Map of key places in the counties of Clare and Tipperary mentioned in the text.

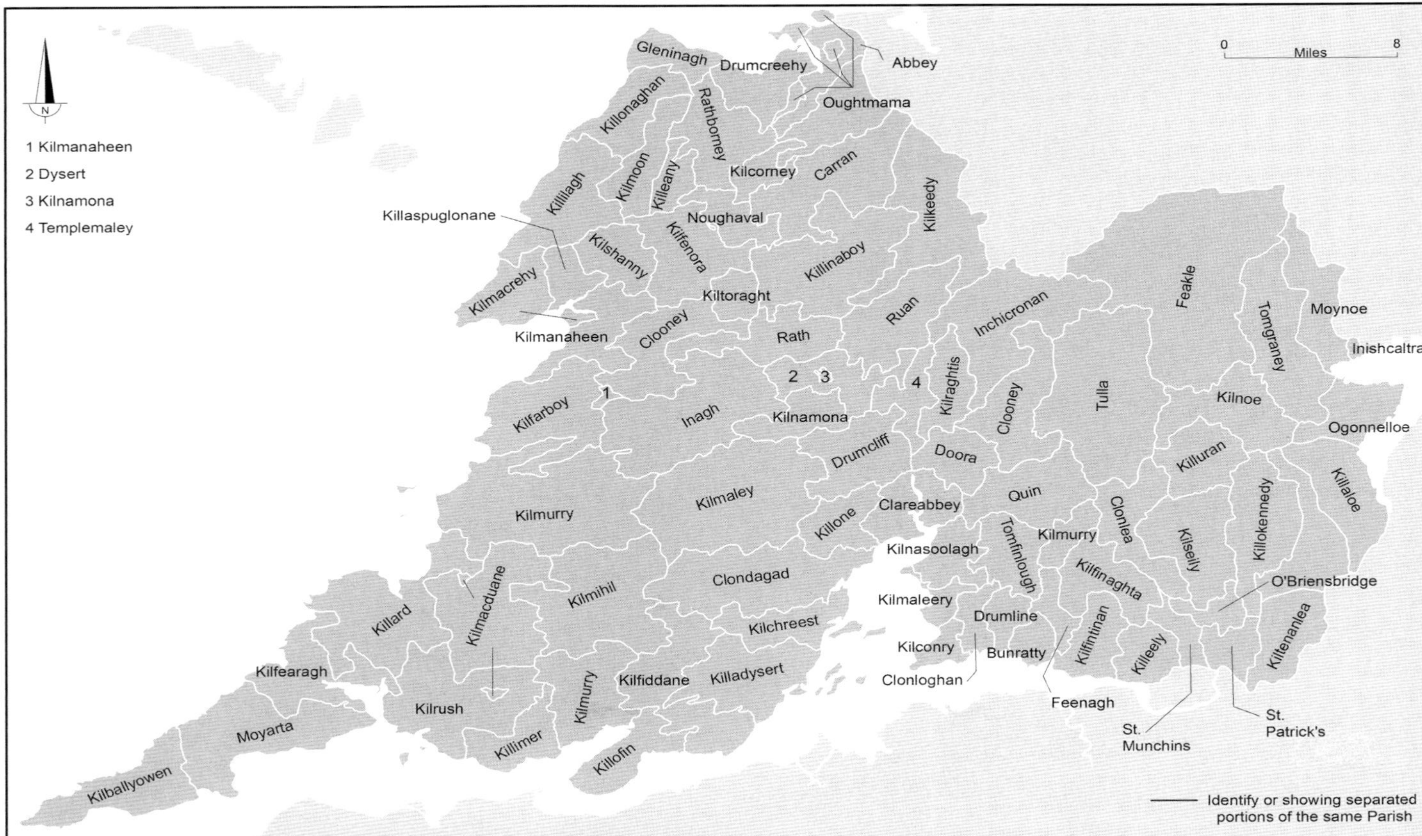

Fig. 12. Map of civil parishes of county Clare.

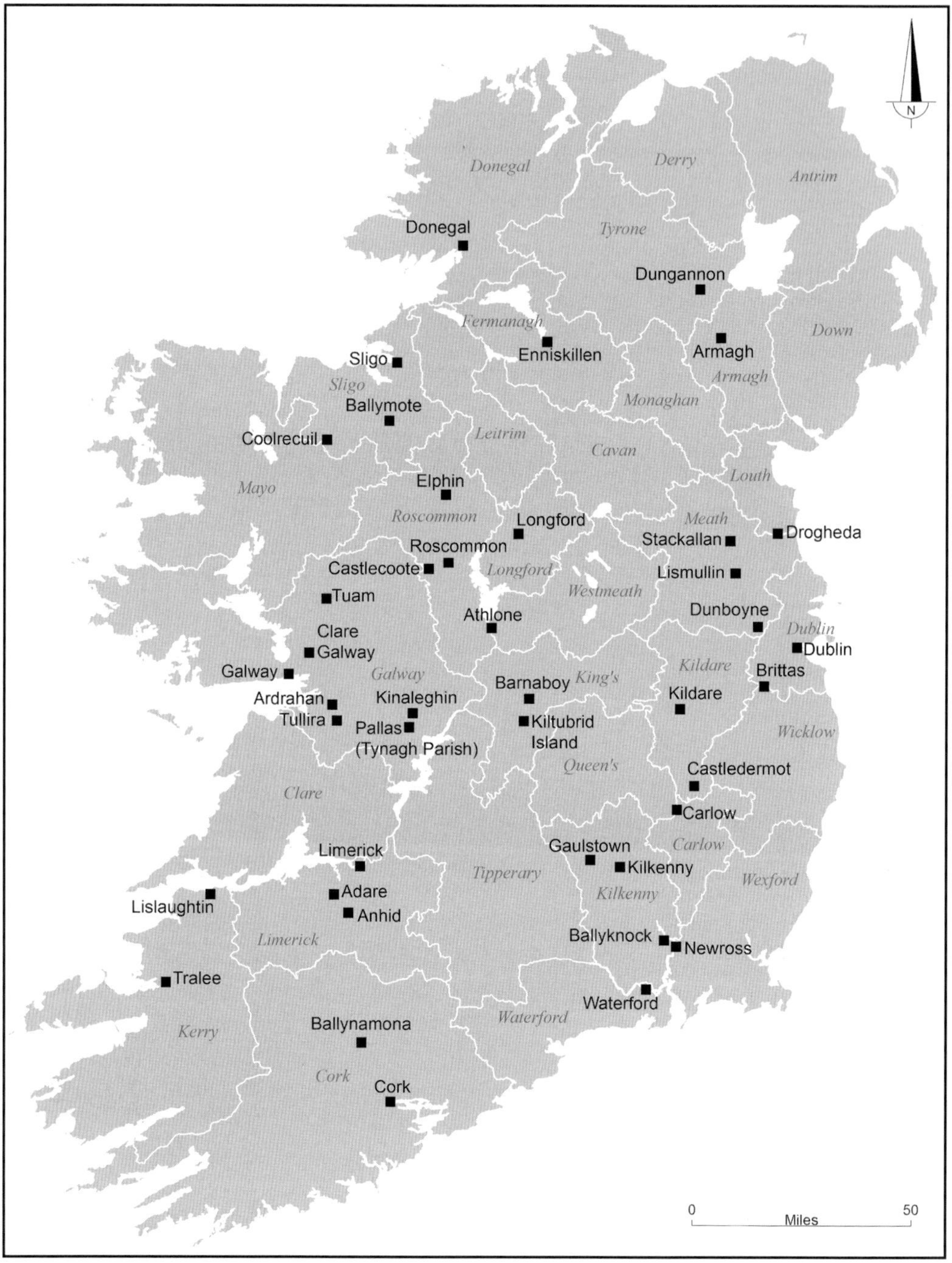

Fig. 13. Map of key towns and places in Ireland mentioned in the text.

If you, Carran, believe this sentence to be sound, your faith is certainly great. England, Scotland, Crete, Corsica,[230] Cyprus, Sardinia, Majorca, Denmark and Ireland are islands upon which Christ, the sun of Justice, arose, but which always had, from ancient times, their own Catholic kings, who did not recognise any political sovereignty over them in their temporal affairs. They would not have done so, if they had acknowledged that their kingdoms belonged to the patrimony of the Church. Therefore that sentence, which affirms that the sea islands belong to the pope, is not genuine.

5. Pope Adrian, Carran, died in the year 1159 (as all the historians attest) and the English came to Ireland in support of Dermot MacMurrough,[231] the ruler of Leinster, for the first time in the year 1166,[232] namely seven years after Adrian's death. Even King Henry II[233] himself came for the first time in the year 1172, namely thirteen years after Adrian's death (there is a calculation mistake where, in the passage mentioned above, Bruodinus says "twenty-two years"). Now, Carran, how could your Sander (whose authority is the very grounds of your argument) be telling the truth without contradiction, when he states that "the Irish clergy, together with the noblemen, imploringly asked Adrian IV to be willing to grant the domain of the entire Ireland to Henry II, after Henry II was holding several places of the island which he had conquered by fighting"? Adrian had been already burnt to ashes before Henry II set foot in Ireland (as you are bound to acknowledge, whether you want to or not): how could the Irish people have possibly begged him then, Carran? I feel compassion for you.

6. The English landed in Ireland for the first time under the pontificate of Pope Alexander III. It would make some sense if Henry II, together with the clergy and people of Ireland, had implored this pope to be willing to grant him the domain of the island (several places of which he was already holding at that time, having conquered them with his men in arms) "to promote the restraint of the spread of vices, the extension of the boundaries of the Church, the correction of customs, the growth of the Christian religion" (these are the words of the bull and the devised motives of the concession) – although he would not have obtained anything from Alexander, who had had the chance to

qui probe expertus fuit in persecutione ac homicidio S. Thomae Archi-Ep. Henricum fuisse, iniquarum legum in praejudicium ecclesiaricarum immunitatum conditorem). At quod supplicaverunt Adriano in cineres dudum antea redacto, crede tu Carrane si vis, ego autem non. Festino ad alias tuas nugas Carrane emendandas.

7. "Praeterea" (inquis fol. 77) "Bruodinus lib. 5 c. 4. reprehendit Cambrensem circa gentis Hiberniae hospitalitatem." Merito pseudo-Hiberne reprehendit illum, quia reprehensibilis erat dum ait quod "gens nostra inhospita sit".

"Non" (inquis Carrane) "bene Bruodinus intelligit Cambrensem. Sic Cambrensis intelligendus est, nimirum quod non fuerint tunc in Hibernia diversoria ad peregrinos accipiendos, & sic est vera Cambrensis assertio", & c.

O praeclarum Cambrensis interpretem! Nesciebam sane te tam feliciter intimos Cambrensis cordis sensus penetrasse. Hoc unicum acumini tuo Carrane deesse video, quod nullo Cambrensis testimonio tam subtilem tuam interpretationem confirmas. Unde tibi Carrane constat quod hospitia in Hibernia non erant antiquitus? Tu tunc non vixisti, ex regni chronicis pro tua subtili interpretatione ne verbum quidem adducere vales. Quis ergo tibi credet? Nemo.

8. Non placet tibi Carrane fol. 75. refutatio tui magistri Domini Cambrensis ab eximio Doctore Linceo facta? Non: quia opera lucis principi tenebrarum nunquam placent. Ad alia.

Nimio credo zelo, ut soles Carrane, in transversum actus fol. 79. blateras nescio quid de vice Comite de Cahir, Adriano IV. & Lombardo, quae a nullo intelligi bene possunt. Consuas rogo parum melius illos tuos centones, si vis ut ab ullo intelligantur. Interim ad alia festinabo. Fol. 80. fere per totum mera scommata explodis gratis in P. Bruodinum, lorica patientiae contra te munitum; quae ne similis tibi esse dicar silentio praetereo. Unde ad alia emendanda recurram.

perfectly know, by the experience of the persecution and murder of the Archbishop St Thomas,[234] that Henry had established unjust laws to the detriment of the immunities of the Church. But if you want, Carran, do believe that it was Adrian who was petitioned sometime after he had been burnt to ashes; as far as I am concerned, I do not. I quickly turn to the correction of other nonsensical statements of yours, Carran.

7. On page 77 you say: "Moreover, in Book V, Chapter 4 Bruodinus refutes Cambrensis[235] about the hospitality of the people of Ireland." He justly refuted that source, you pseudo-Irishman, because he deserved to be refuted in that passage where he states that "our people are inhospitable".

O most illustrious interpreter of Cambrensis! I was completely unaware that you had so successfully penetrated the innermost feelings of Cambrensis' heart. I see that your acumen falls short of this single detail only, Carran, namely that you do not support such an astute interpretation of yours with any testimony by Cambrensis himself. What tells you that there were no inns in Ireland in ancient times, Carran? You did not live at that time and you are unable to cite even a single word from the chronicles of the kingdom in support of your shrewd interpretation. Who will believe you then, Carran? Nobody.

8. Do you not like, Carran, the refutation of your teacher, Master Cambrensis, which was put forward by Lynch,[236] a distinguished doctor,[237] on page 75? No, because a prince of darkness never likes the works of light. Now, let us turn to different issues.

Led astray, I think, by an excess of zeal (as is usual for you, Carran), on page 79 you foolishly say goodness knows what, about the Viscount of Cahir,[238] Adrian IV, and Lombard – some nonsense which cannot be properly understood by anybody. I invite you to weave together your centos[239] a bit better, if you want them to be understood by anyone. Meanwhile I shall quickly turn to other issues.

Throughout nearly the entire page 80 you unreasonably throw bare taunts at Fr Bruodinus, who is, however, protected by the armour of patience against you; but I pass over these in silence, lest I be said to be like you. From this point, I quickly return to amend your other mistakes.

9. Timeo supra modum, Carrane, quod turbati cerebri te esse tenebrionem homines dicent, quando fol. 81. legent ea scommata quae sine ratione evomis in Patrem Bruodinum. Quale est, Carrane, Bruodini delictum, ob quod tanquam furiosus ursus in illum saevis? Potiora convitia omitto; haec tantum pauca enucleabo.

"Bruodinus" (inquis) "sic dicit lib 5. c. 3.: 'itaque existimo vitam S. Malachiae a S. Bernardo non fuisse scriptam.'" Quid per hoc Bruodinus peccavit, Carrane? "Quia," inquis fol. 84. "Bruodinus authorem hunc, nempe S. Bernardum, qui in suo Ordine servatur tot centenis annis & ab Ecclesia approbatus repellere nititur." Compatior Prisciano.

10. Haecne Carrane tonitrui tui causa est? Bruodinus, tua bona venia, Doctorem Mellifluum, quam ab Infantia ut Patronum se coluisse fol. 779. sui *Propugnaculi* dicit, non oppugnavit aut refutavit; sed motivis valde evidentibus ductus, duo asseruit: nimirum, vel quod S. Bernardus vitam illam S. Malachiae non scripsit; vel, si scripsit, quod ex mala informatione quam a malevolis habuit ea exaravit, quae veritati non sunt consona. Si tu refutares motiva quae Bruodinum induxerunt ad scribendum quae scripsit, esset aliquid; sed cum praeter scommata & convitia nihil in favorem causae quam assumpsisti aut in praejudicium Bruodini adducis, in cathalogo illorum imposterum numeraberis advocatorum qui nec proprias aut clientum suorum causas sciunt propugnare.

11. Adverto, ex iis quae furiose scribis fol. 85. tui libelli, quod tibi non placet distichon hoc, honori tuo quondam a pie defuncto Domino Canonico Magranna, dum te jactares quod tibi tuoque libro Hibernia esset obligata, dedicatum & per modum viatici a Patre Bruodino tibi nuper missum:

> "Multa tibi libroque tuo mea patria debet.
> Debet & huic flammas & tibi Carve rotas."

9. My greatest fear, Carran, is that people will say that you are a swindler with a disturbed brain, when they will read on page 81 those taunts which you vomit against Fr Bruodinus without reason. What kind of crime did Bruodinus perpetrate, for which you violently rage at him like a furious bear, Carran? I will examine only the following few taunts, and say nothing of some more disgraceful ones. You say:

"In Book V, Chapter 3, Bruodinus states as follows: 'therefore I reckon that the life of St Malachy was not written by St Bernard'."[240] Why do you claim that Bruodinus committed a sin by means of this statement, Carran?[241] "Because" – you say on page 84 – "Bruodinus takes pains to repulse this author, namely St Bernard, who is venerated in his own order for so many hundreds of years and who he received the favour of the Church."[242] I feel pity for Priscian.

10. Is this why you thunder against Bruodinus, Carran? I beg your kind pardon, but Bruodinus did not attack or refute the Mellifluous Doctor,[243] whom on page 779 of his *Propugnaculum* he says he venerated as a patron since his early childhood. Instead, motivated by very strong and clear evidence, he affirmed two things, namely that St Bernard[244] did not write that life of St Malachy; or, if he wrote it, he derived and reported[245] those details which are not in agreement with the truth from the misinformation he received from malevolent sources. If you refuted the reasons that led Bruodinus to write what he wrote, you would make your point. However, the arguments you put forward to support the case you took on, or to prove your preliminary judgement in Bruodinus' trial, are nothing but taunts and insults. So, in the future, you shall be included in the category of lawyers who do not know how to defend their own or their clients' cases.[246]

11. From the words you write on page 85 of your libellous pamphlet in the manner of a madman, I notice that you do not like the couplet quoted below. It was once dedicated to your honour by Master Magranna,[247] a pious canonical priest now dead, in response to your claims about Ireland's debt to you and your book. It was recently sent to you by Fr Bruodinus by way of payment.[248]

"My homeland has a huge debt to you and your book.
The book is owed flames; and you, Carve, are owed wheels of torture."[249]

Placeat tibi Carrane vel displiceat: non potuit Pater Bruodinus sine onere restitutionis tua retinere. Sic, quando supposuit prudenter te fugi<t>um ex Austria, viatici loco tibi quod tuum erat misit; nec in hoc illum peccasse sapientibus persuadebis.

12. Fol. 86. inter tot alia convitia in haec tanquam insanus exclamas verba: "O Bruodine! O infamis barde!" & c. Clama, Carrane, ne cesses; caute tamen, ne prudentes habeant ansam te stultum aut sycophantam esse judicandi. Bardus, Carrane, Latinis nunc stultum nunc philosophum significat. Si in secundo sensu P. Bruodinum "bardum" vocas, contra tuam consuetudinem non erras: nam Bruodinum philosophum esse & theologum per varias Europae provincias notum est. Si autem in primo sensu Bruodinum "bardum" vocas, jam judicatus es & hac Evangelistae sententia condemnatus: "qui dixerit fratri suo 'fatue', reus erit gehenna ignis."

13. At forte Hibernice loqueris, Carrane? Si sic, in tuum damnum scribis; Hibernis enim "barde" idem significat quod detractor, seu homo mordacis & efferenatae linguae, in quo sensu omnes qui te noverunt dicunt te ita esse in arte diffamandi doctum, quod merito posses bardorum omnium agere ludimagistrum. Etsi hujus veritatis alii deessent testes, famosus hic tuus quem refuto libellus (in quo rabulae ad instar tam vivos quam mortuos, maledicta tua lingua laceras) abunde probaret. Ad sequentia jam attende.

14. Praecipiti ac effraenato furore, Carrane, fol. 86. 7. & 8. inveheris in bonae memoriae dignissimum virum Dominum Thadaeum Bruodinum, ante 50 circiter annos jam mortuum, cujus honorifica memoria per omnes Hiberniae provincias hodiernam usque in diem perseverat, ob singularem quam in antiquitatibus Regni habuit & post

Whether you like it or not, Carran, Fr Bruodinus could not keep what was owed to you without the burden of repayment. So, when he supposed that you had prudently escaped from Austria, he sent you this payment which was due to you instead of money. And you will not persuade any person with good sense that he acted wrongly in this.

12. Amongst so many other insults, like a madman on page 86 you exclaim in these words:[250] "O Bruodinus! O abominable bard!", etc. Shout aloud, Carran, do not stop; but do it with caution, lest sensible people have the opportunity to judge you a fool or a slanderer. For Latin speakers, Carran, the word *bardus* sometimes means 'fool', sometimes 'philosopher'.[251] If you are calling Fr Bruodinus a "bard" in the latter sense of the word, Carran, you are not wrong, in contrast to your usual practice. For all around various provinces of Europe it is known that Bruodinus is a philosopher and theologian. If, instead, you are calling Bruodinus a "bard" in the former sense of the word, an Evangelist[252] already judged and condemned you when he stated: "he who shall say 'you fool!' to his brother shall deserve to be condemned to the fire of Gehenna".[253]

13. But maybe you are speaking in Irish, Carran? If so, you are writing to your own detriment. For Irish people, in fact, addressing anyone by the Latin word *bardus* is the same as calling him a detractor, or a man with a stinging and unrestrained tongue; in which sense, all those who know you say that you are so skilled in the art of slandering that you could deservedly act as teacher for "bards". Even if there were no other witnesses to this truth, this infamous slanderous pamphlet of yours, which I am refuting, would abundantly prove it; for in it you, like a rabble-rouser, torture with your abusive tongue the living as well as the dead. Now, direct your attention to what follows.

14. On pages 86, 87 and 88, Carran, with an inconsiderate and unrestrained raging you inveigh against Master Tadhg MacBrody,[254] a most worthy man of good memory. He has been dead for around 50 years now,[255] but the honourable memory of him persists all around in every province of Ireland until today, because of the extraordinary fame which he enjoyed in the ancient period of the kingdom and

se reliquit notitiam & in arte Poëtica excellentiam. Quid tibi, Mome, mali fecit vir ille honoratus (cujus memoria in benedictione est) ob quod illum "squalidum bardum", "vilem hominem", "ignobilis ac obscurae familiae caput," & c. vocas? Sicne decet sacerdotem detrahere famae & honestati viri jam mortui? "De mortuis", Carrane, "non nisi bene", suadet proberbium "esse loquendum"; at quia tu malus es, nec de vivis nec mortuis bene loqui scis.

15. Pater Bruodinus lib. 5. cap. 9. fol. 851. agendo de prima divisione Regni Hiberniae a Millerianis Principibus facta rem omnibus nobis veris Hibernis notissimam scripsit, de historica altercatione orta ante annos 50 inter chronologos procerum, qui ex Eibero (Millerii Hispani primogenito primoque ex Millerianis Hiberniae Rege) originem trahunt, & alios qui ex Erevono, Eiberi fratre ac in regno sucessore, descendunt; additque Pater Bruodinus quod Eiberianorum seu, quod idem est, Momoniensium causam progugnabat "Thadaeus Bruodinus, Dominus de Monte Scoti, Tuomoniae Comitis Aulae Praefectus, vir in Graecis, Latinis, Anglicis & Hibernicis literis doctus," & c.

16. Tu Carrane omissa causa quam apologetice defendere promisisti (in odium haud dubie P. Bruodini, quem directe aggredi timuisti) innocentem virum Dominum Thadaeum Bruodinum in pace requiescentem instar rapacis lupi invadis: primoque illum paternis privas bonis; secundo officio praefecturae; tertio donis linguarum a Deo sibi datarum; quarto vero fama & nobilitate.

17. "Falsissimum est" (inquis fol. 86.) "quod Thadaeus fuerit Dominus Montis Scoti, quia Episcopus Killaloensis" (Laonensis Carrane) "est verus dominus istius villae, & ipse Thadaeus annuum censum dare tenebatur." Carrane, rogo te, si Episcopo Laonensi vis aliquid donare, dona quod tuum est; latronis, non sacerdotis munus est uni rapere & alteri dare. Pater Bruodinus (cujus duo consequenter patrueles,

which he left after him, and because of his excellence in the art of poetry. What harm did that honourable man (whose memory is in benediction)[256] do to you, Momus, because of which you call him "a filthy bard", "a worthless man", "the head of an ignoble and obscure family", etc.? Is it seemly for a priest to discredit in this manner the reputation and the honour of a man who is now dead? The proverb recommends that "nothing but good is to be said about the dead". Since you are a bad person, however, you are unable to speak well either of the living or of the dead.

15. In Book V, Chapter 9, page 851, dealing with the first division of the kingdom of Ireland undertaken by the Milesian princes, Fr Bruodinus reported something that is well known to all of us true Irish. He wrote about the dispute that arose fifty years before between the chroniclers of the nobility, who ascribe the ultimate descent to Eber (the first-born of Milesius the Spaniard and first of the Milesians to become king of Ireland), and others who derive it from Eremon, Eber's brother and successor in the kingdom.[257] Also, Fr Bruodinus added that the cause of the people of Munster, or Eber's subjects (which is the same), was defended by "Tadhg MacBrody, master of Knockanalban,[258] prefect of the court of the earl of Thomond,[259] a man learned in Greek, Latin, English and Irish letters", etc.

16. Laying aside the case you promised to defend by means of an apologia (doubtlessly out of hatred against Fr Bruodinus, whom you are afraid to attack directly), you, Carran, like a rapacious wolf assail Master Tadhg MacBrody, an innocent man who rests in peace. Firstly you deprive him of his father's possessions; secondly, of his office as prefect; thirdly, of the linguistic gifts which God gave him; fourthly, and most importantly, of his reputation and nobility.

17. On page 86, you state: "It is absolutely false that Tadhg was master of Knockanalban, because the true master of this settlement is the bishop of Killaloe" (the Latin name of the town is *Laon*, Carran)[260] "and Tadhg actually had an obligation to pay a tribute every year." Carran, I beg you, if you want to give something to the bishop of Killaloe, give him what is yours. Stealing from one person and giving to another is the work of a bandit, not a priest. Fr Bruodinus (whose

Malachias ô Mallonii & Joannes ô Mollonii, per 46 annos Laonenses erant Episcopi) melius deberet scire quae bona spectant ad suam familiam & Laonensem Episcopum quam tu, Carrane, qui in Laonensi Diocesi (laudetur Deus) nec natus nec educatus aut ordinatus fuisti. Unde tibi Carrane co<n>stat quod Dominus Thadaeus Bruodinus annuum cens<u>m Episcopo dare tenebatur? An forte fuisti aliquando scriba redituum Laonensis Episcopi? non: ne sis etiam amplius rogo te tam mendax & protervus ac hactenus te esse experti sumus, "quia os quod mentitur occidit animam." Mons Scoti Carrane in Baronia est de Ibrickan, in qua nec abbas nec episcopus ullus pedem terrae unquam habuit. Dominum Thadaeum Bruodinum ac post illius obitum Dominum Jacobum, Thadaei filium, Montis Scoti fuisse dominum nobis Tuomoniensibus notum est; tu itaque fave viris bonis bona quae illis auferre non vales. Jam ad secundum.

18. "Praeterea" (inquis Carrane fol. 88.) "quod Thadaeus ille erat Aulae Praefectus comitis Tuamundiae" (Tuomoniae ignare) "quod minime verum est, quia ille comes fuit haereticus, cujus famulatus" (vae Prisciano) "erant Angli, Aulaeque Praefectus tunc fuit unus Waterfordensis," & c.

Recordare Carrane veteris illius proverbii, "oportet mendacem memorem esse." Famulatus omnes comitis erant (sic loqueris) Angli; quomodo Carrane hoc erit verum, si Aulae Praefectus fuit Waterfordensis? Waterfordenses Carrane omnes sunt Hiberni: sicut Pragenses sunt Bohemi & Viennenses Austriaci, sed in famulatu comitis primus nempe Aulae Praefectus, secundum te, fuit Waterfordensis; ergo in famulatu comitis fuit Hibernus, & consequenter falsum est quod "famulatus omnes" (utor tuo Latinismo) "erant Angli." Ecce Carrane quomodo tua te falce jugulo ac ore convinco! Quam ridiculum est hoc Carrane argumentum, quo Dominum Thadaeum Bruodinum excludere ab obsequiis sui Principis (quem ob infantia instruxit & educavit) conaris. "Comes Tuomondiae," inquis, "fuit Haereticus,

two cousins Malachy O'Molony[261] and John O'Molony[262] were bishops of Killaloe for forty-six years, one succeeding the other) should know which goods pertain to his family and to the bishop of Killaloe better than you, who were neither born nor educated or ordained in the diocese of Killaloe (may God be extolled for this!). What tells you that Master Tadhg MacBrody had an obligation to pay a yearly tribute to the bishop, Carran? Were you ever the secretary of the revenues of the bishop of Killaloe, perhaps? No. I ask you to be no longer as untruthful and as shameless as our experience so far has revealed you are, "since a mouth that lies kills the soul".[263] Knockanalban, Carran, is in the barony of Ibrickan, in which neither an abbot nor any bishop ever held a foot of land. It is known to us people of Thomond that Master Tadhg MacBrody and, after his death, Master James, the son of Tadhg, ruled over Knockanalban.[264] For the sake of good men, then, say nothing of the properties which you do not have the power to take away from them. Now, let us turn to a second point.

18. On page 88, Carran, you say: "Moreover, as for the claim that Tadhg was the prefect of the court of the earl of Tuomondy," (the correct name is Thomond, you ignorant man) "which is not true at all, since that earl was a heretic whose entourage were entirely formed by Englishmen" (woe to Priscian!)[265] "and the prefect of the court at that time was a man from Waterford", etc.

Remember that old proverb, Carran: "it is necessary for a liar to have a good memory."[266] The earl's entourage "were" (this is how you phrase it) all English: how will this be true, Carran, if the prefect of the court was a man from Waterford? All the people of Waterford are Irish, Carran, just as the people of Prague are Bohemian and the people of Vienna are Austrian. According to you, however, the first-rank position of prefect of the court in the earl's entourage was held by a man from Waterford: then there was an Irishman in the earl's entourage, and consequently it is false that "all the entourage were English" (I use your own pseudo-Latin). Look, Carran, this is how I cut your throat with your own sickle and refute you with your own words! How ridiculous is this argument, Carran, by which you try to exclude Master Tadhg MacBrody from the retinue of his lord, the very lord whom he brought up and educated since his early childhood. "The earl of Thomondy" – you say[267] – "was a heretic, and therefore

ergo famulatus erant Angli." Dux Saxoniae, Carrane, haereticus est, & tamen in famulatu suo habet non solum Saxones, sed & Croatas & Bohemos, Dux Ormoniae (cujus tu natus es subditus) est haereticus hodie, & tamen habet in famulatu suo tres Hibernos pro uno Anglo.

19. Domestica similitudine te convincam Carrane. Patruelis tuus, Pater Jacobus ô Carrane, sacerdos qui aliquot annis parochum egit in Archi-Diocesi Casseliensi, illius quam tu deseruisti parochiae ante 9 annos, cum summo scadalo Catholici populi & cleri ejurata Catholica fide factus est puritanus haereticus &, ut scis, pseudo-abbas & praedicautius, seu Minister Monasterii de Arvicampo, vulgo *Kicuol*, in tua patria olim a Principe Donaldo ô Brien Cisterciensibus Monachis fundati. Hic vero pro famula ac thalami consorte non Anglam sed puram accepit putam Hibernam; quare ergo non obstante haeresi Hibernus Comes ô Brien non haberet in suo famulatu Hibernos? Donatus ô Brien, Carrane, excellentissimae suae familiae quondam Princeps, ex Catholicissimis parentibus fuit natus, Catholico ritu baptizatus, ac tandem delicate lactatus, nutritus per annos 7 in domo viri illustris, Domini Cornelii Clanchi, Domini de Inse, & Finolae Bruodinae ejus uxoris. Crescente aetate Principis pueri, parentis jussu, Dominus Thadaeus Bruodinus Finolae frater curam illius accepit illumque sub sua disciplina in diversis Hiberniae locis, in quibus studuit, per annos 14 habuit; tandem mortuo Catholico suo parente, juvenis comes 21. circiter tunc agens annum in Angliam cum suo praefecto Bruodino navigavit; ubi persuasione Thomae Butleri, Ormoniae tunc potentissimi Comitis, (ut reginae favores sibi conciliaret) a fide defecit Catholica. Post duos tandem annos in Hiberniam comes una cum Thadaeo Bruodino, Catholico suo praefecto, venit; ubi Thadaeus ex illustrissima Mohuniorum familia uxorem duxit. Demum excellentissimo Domino Comite (qui postea Praeses fuit Momoniae) auxiliante trinus vicibus

his entourage were formed by Englishmen." The duke of Saxony, Carran, is a heretic, and yet he has not only Saxons but also Croats and Bohemians in his entourage; nowadays, the duke of Ormond (under whose dominion you were born) is a heretic, and yet he has a ratio of three Irishmen to one Englishman in his entourage.

19. I will refute you with a parallel concerning your own family, Carran.[268] Your paternal cousin, Fr James O'Carran,[269] a priest who was in charge of a parish in the archbishopric of Cashel – that parish which you abandoned nine years ago – abjured the Catholic faith, with great scandal for the Catholic people and clergy. He became a Puritan heretic and, as you know, a pseudo-abbot and *praedicautius*, namely the minister of the monastery of *Arvicampus*,[270] commonly called Kilcooly,[271] which was founded long ago in your homeland by the sovereign, Domhnall Mór Ó Briain,[272] for the Cistercian monks. This cousin of yours, however, did not take an English girl as his maid and bed partner, but one who was entirely Irish. Why, then, should it not have been possible for earl O'Brien, an Irishman, to have Irish people in his entourage in spite of the heresy? Donough O'Brien,[273] Carran, who was a prince of his most eminent family in the past, was born from true Catholic parents, was baptised under the Catholic rite and was delicately breast-fed at length, nurtured for seven years in the house of that illustrious man, Master Conor MacClancy,[274] who was master of Ennis, and Finola MacBrody, his wife. Over the course of the boy prince's years, Master Tadhg MacBrody, the brother of Finola, received the care of him by order of his father, and kept him for fourteen years under his tutorage at diverse places in Ireland, where he studied. When at last his own Catholic parent died, the young earl, at about the age of twenty years, sailed for England with his guardian MacBrody; whereupon, through the persuasion of Thomas Butler,[275] at that time the powerful earl of Ormond, he forsook the Catholic faith (in order to commend himself to the queen's favours). Eventually, after two years, the earl, together with Tadhg MacBrody, his Catholic guardian, came back to Ireland; whereupon Tadhg took a wife from the most illustrious family of the MacMahons.[276] At last, with the help of the most eminent master earl (who later became president of Munster), he was three times the

fuit Capitaneus (vulgo, *Schirriff*) districtus seu Comitatus de Clare; & usque ad mortem Schinischalus Baroniae de Ibrickon: quae officia non nisi nobilibus doctis in Hibernia committuntur viris. Credis tu haec Carrane? si non: saltem crede quod tibi in persona Grafferii loquatur jucunde Beccanus.

> "Nulli tu veterum credis nullique tuorum,
> et tibi vis omnes credere? Nemo facit."

20. In duobus jam locis profligatus es Carrane; nescio quomodo subsistet tertium notae tuae calumniae fulcrum, quo sustentas ea quae de ignorantia Domini Bruodini ignoranter scripsisti.

"Revera" (inquis) "egomet toties quoties habui cum ipso colloquium in domo Domini Baronis Domboii, & tamen" (pulchra connexio) "ille nihil in istis linguis scivit. Et tamen non ego solus, verum etiam alii probarunt ipsum, & tamen solummodo in Hibernice assidue respondit. Semperque pedes ire solebat" (bonum est Carrane, quod non habuit podagram) & c.

Quis haec quae scribis, Carrane, non videat haud argumenta esse sed procacis linguae impudentissima mendacia? Tu domi inter tuos consodales notas nobis habuisti alias occupationes in patria incompatibiles cum officio examinatoris vitae & doctrinae tanti viri, quomodo igitur illum examinare poteras? Deinde si post tot annos, quibus Viennae & alibi extra patriam (ubi lingua Latina in flore est) fatigas te in libris, adhuc tam luride, pueriliter & inepte hoc tuum commentum Latine narras, ut nemo sit qui ex ejus lectione non deprehendat te hominem esse ignorantissimum; quomodo possumus conjecturare de sufficientia tua in Hibernia ad ullum examinandum? Cape tibi hoc.

captain (or, as it is more commonly termed, the sheriff) of the district, namely of County Clare,[277] and seneschal of the barony of Ibrickan until his death,[278] offices with which learned men are not entrusted in Ireland unless they are noble. Do you believe these things, Carran? If not, believe at least what Becanus[279] amiably tells Graser,[280] while he is in fact speaking to you:

> "You trust none of the old men and none of your own people,
> and yet you want everybody to trust you? Nobody does."

20. With regard to two of your claims,[281] Carran, you have already lost your argumentative battle; I do not know how the third pillar of your famous calumny could hold up. I am referring to your argument in support of what you ignorantly wrote about the ignorance of Master [Tadhg] MacBrody.

"In fact" you say "each and every time I had a conversation with him in the house of the lord baron of Dunboyne[282] and notwithstanding" (a beautiful logical conjunction!)[283] "he had no knowledge at all of these languages.[284] And yet, I was not the only one who put him to the test, but others did so too, and still he constantly replied only in Irish. Also, he always used to go around by foot"[285] (luckily he did not have the gout, Carran!), etc.

Who would not be able to see, Carran, that these things you write are not arguments at all, but the most shameless lies of an insolent tongue? In your native land, at home with your own fellows, you were busy with other occupations which are known to us and which are incompatible with the duty of being the examiner of the life and erudition of such a great man. So, how could you assess him? Secondly, I should say this: in spite of so many years you spent tiring yourself over books in Vienna and in other cities outside your homeland, places where the Latin language is in a flourishing condition, your use of Latin in this fabricated account of yours is still so ghastly, trivial and improper to a degree that there is nobody who, reading it, would not realise that you are an incredibly ignorant man. So, how can we assume that your language skills in Ireland were sufficiently developed to judge him? Take this rebuke – it is for you!

21. Carrane, sine mendacio rogo dic: quis tam procul te misit extra domum tuam Domboynam ad examinandum Dominum Bruodinum? Scisne quis tuae huic fictioni facile credet? Mendax aliquis ea tamen conditione ut illi pariter mentienti fidem adhibeas alia vice nobis, qui Domini Thadaei Bruodini scripta & poemata prae manibus habemus, praesertim jocosos illos rithmos Latino-Hibernicos quibus Hiberniam inter se & illustrissimi Domini Joannis de Burgo filios jucunde divisit (ex quibus abunde constat illum in lingua Latina fuisse fundatissimum, & consequenter te in iis quae de illo narras Aesopi esse discipulum, ne dicam mentitum).

Non erat tibi satis, Carrane, Dominum Thadaeum Bruodinum elinguem facere, nisi (in satisfactionem damni illi illati) etiam & vestimenta illi componeres fol. 89.: "nec unquam" (inquis) "vestibus Anglicanis indutus est, sed longis caligis, fusca clamide, more puti puri Hiberni usus; neque bardi meo tempore aliter incedere debuissent." O Latinitas!

22. Te sartorem fuisse, Carrane, antea non scivi, licet in arte scindendi veritatem te dudum superasse Viennenses sartores intellexeram; forte studio tu, Carrane, Domboynam tam procul extra tuam excurristi parochiam, ut pro raritate aspicere posses "purum putum" (ut loqueris) "Hibernum" vestitum Hibernico more. Poteras, crede mihi, domi manere & magis prope in Comitatu Tiperariensi centenos aspicere alios puros putos Hibernos nobiles ex Butleris, ô Brienis, Carovallis, Kenediis, de Burgo, Geraldinis & c. qui consuetis tunc per Hiberniam vestibus induebantur: Hibernus ergo cum erat purus putus Thadaeus Bruodinus, cur non pariter vestiretur? Carrane mi, Bruodinus tibi similis non erat; sic se ex Hiberno in Anglum (prout lepide tu te ex Carrano in Carve) transformare merito noluit. Cujus

21. Tell me, Carran – with no lies, I beg you: who sent you to Dunboyne, so far away from your home, to examine Master MacBrody? Do you know who would easily believe this fiction of yours? Somebody who is used to lying, but on the following condition: that, when he lies, you give him the same trust he gives you, unlike you do when it comes to you trusting us, who have Master Tadhg MacBrody's writings and poems in our hands. In particular, I am referring to those humorous Irish-Latin rhymes, in which he delightfully divided Ireland between himself and the sons of the most illustrious Lord John Burke.[286] From these poems, it is abundantly proved that he was most thoroughly instructed in the Latin language,[287] and therefore that you are a disciple of Aesop,[288] not to openly say that you told a lie, in what you wrote about him.

It would not be enough for you, Carran, to deprive Master Tadhg MacBrody of his linguistic skills, unless you put together even a collection of clothes for him on page 89 (as a form of apology for the damage you have caused him). You say: "and he never wore English clothes, but he used long sandals and a dark cloak, in the customary manner of a pure Irish boy; but in my time bards should not have been supposed to walk around dressed in a different way."[289] What a use of Latin!

22. Before you wrote this, Carran, I did not know that you had worked as a mender of clothes, although I had already understood a little while ago that you had outdone the tailors of Vienna in the technique of cutting up the truth. Perhaps it was your zeal, Carran, that led you to quickly go to Dunboyne, so far away from your parish that you could see "a pure Irish boy" (as you say) dressed according to the Irish custom and gaze upon him as a rarity. Believe me, you could have stayed in your hometown and seen, in a closer place in County Tipperary, hundreds of other pure Irish boys, high-born from the families of the Butlers, the O'Briens, the O'Carrolls, the O'Kennedys, the Burkes, the Fitzgeralds, etc., who were wearing clothes that were common across Ireland at that time. So why should Tadhg MacBrody have not dressed in the same way, when he was a pure Irish boy? MacBrody was not like you, my dear Carran; therefore, he justly had no desire to transform himself from an Irishman into an Englishman (just like you, who smartly switched yourself from Carran to Carve).

formae, figurae, vel materiae erant tunc nobilium Hibernorum vestes nec mihi nec tibi constare potest, quia non eodem ubique modo incedebant: hoc saltem certo conjecturare possumus, quod vir tam potens, prudens & in officiis constitutus, prout Bruodinus fuit, non aliter incessit publice extra suam patriam quam deceret honoratum virum.

23. "Nec" (inquis) "Bardi meo tempore aliter incedere debuissent." Quid per Ciceronianam hanc tuam eloquentiam Carrane intelligis? An tempore tuo in Hibernia certa aliqua fuit congregatio Bardorum, quibus ex constitutionibus forte Regni aliter non licebat incedere quam cum "longis caligis, fusca clamide, petasoque" (verba sunt tua) "loco cudonis"? Si fuit, sub quo Carrane titulo Dominus Bruodinus in illam fuit susceptus congregationem? Non sub titulo philosophi, quia nec Graece nec Latine, ut tu vis, scivit; non sub titulo stulti, quia ob timorem Gehennae non audebis illum sic vocare; non denique sub titulo detractoris (hos tres sensus habet bardus) quia tu, qui detractorum es Momus, ex innato tuo in Bruodinos odio illum in tuam suscipi congregationem non permitteres. Compatior tibi, Carrane, tuaque figmenta rideo.

24. Jam pro coronide omnium convitiorum in Dominum Bruodinum explos<orum> subdis: "Et quod Thadaeus Darii filius Bruodinorum caput extiterit, ex hoc bene apparet obscura familiae ignobilitas, quae tantum psoricum habuit caput." Item fol. 94. repetis & conformas his verbis: "Familia Bruodina plane inter regni nobiles locum non habet, quia bardi sunt", & c.

Gratias tibi quod agant, Carrane, non habent Tuomonienses nobiles familae Bruodinis millies, ut antea dixi & mox ostendam fusius, mutua affinitate & consanguinitate conjunctissimae; nec benevolas tibi falsa

It is impossible both for me and for you to have firm knowledge of the shape, figure or material of the clothes of the Irish noblemen of that time, because the clothes they used to wear when walking around were different from place to place. Yet, we can make at least the following guess beyond all doubt: that a man so skilful, sensible and dedicated to his duties, as MacBrody was, would not have walked around publicly outside his country dressed differently from what would have been appropriate to a honourable man.

23. "And at my own time" – you say – "bards should not have been supposed to walk around dressed in a different manner." What are you claiming to know so well through this Ciceronian eloquence of yours?[290] Was there any specific guild of bards in Ireland in your time, who were not allowed, maybe by a set of laws of the kingdom, to walk around dressed in a different way than wearing "long sandals, a dark cloak and a hat instead of a helmet" (these are your own words)?[291] If there was any such guild, Carran, under what title was Master MacBrody admitted into it? Not under the title of being a philosopher, since, as you claim, he knew neither Greek nor Latin; not under the title of being a fool, since your terror for the Gehenna will not make you dare call him so; finally (for the Latin word *bardus* has these three meanings),[292] not under the title of being a detractor, since you, who are the Momus of all detractors, would not allow that he be admitted into your guild, because of your innate hatred for the MacBrodys. I feel pity for you, Carran, and laugh at your fabrications.

24. Now, instead of drawing a *coronis* to put an end to all the insults you have thrown out against Bruodinus,[293] you add: "and the fact that the head of the MacBrodys was Tadhg, the son of Darius, clearly demonstrates the obscure ignoble status of a family with such a scabious head." Likewise, you repeat the same view on page 94, only reformulating it in these words: "The family of the MacBrodys clearly has no place amongst the noblemen of the kingdom, since they are bards", etc.

The noble families of Thomond have no thanks to offer you, Carran, since, as I said before and as I will show presently in more detail, these families have established strong ties of mutual affinity and kindred with the MacBrodys a thousand times. Nor will strangers

narranti praebebunt extranei aures, postquam te toties de mendaciis & imposturis a me convictum esse in hoc opusculo intelligent.

Interrogatus Carrane sapiens quidam, "quid prodest homini quod mentiatur?" "Prodest," inquit, "quia non creditur postea ipsi, dum veritatem narrat." Si verum esset Carrane quod tu hic de Bruodinis comminisceris, adhuc tamen nemo tibi crederet, quia toties es de mendacio convictus. Obscurane Carrane dici debet Bruodiniana familia, ex qua semper fuit excellentissimae ô Brienorum familiae sive qua Regum Hiberniae sive qua Principum Momoniae & Tuomoniae Chronologus? Obscurane & ignobilis est familia Bruodinorum, quae in Tuomonia usque ad Crumuvellis tyrannidem tot egregios numeravit viros qui bona, subditos & sequaces habuerunt multos, ut dixi supra in *Anatomia* c.2. n.17 ?

An obscura tibi Bruodiniana dici debet familia, tot nominatissimis familiis affinitate conjuncta? Non in tui Carrane gratiam sed veritatis scribendae causa nominabo ex multis paucos nobiles viros & foeminas, in Comitatu Clarensi (vulgo Tuomonia), Galviensi, Sligoensi, Tipperarensi, Limiricensi, Corcagiensi & Tyrconnellensi affinitate & sanguine Bruodinis junctos, ut indifferens lector videat quam false tu de familia quae te non laesit loqueris.

25. Nullus in Hibernia est comitatus in quo non sunt illustrissimae, perillustres & respective nobiles civiles & rusticae familiae. Nulla etiam est in Hibernia tam illustrissima familia ex qua praeter principem non sunt multi puri simplices nobiles & nobilissae; sic ex ô Brienis, verbi gratia, praeter Comitem Tuomoniae, Comitem de Insequen, Vice Comitem de Clare multi erant ante tempora Crumuvellis & defacto sunt equites & simplices nobiles. Ex Butleris, praeter Ducem & alios Comites, vice Comites & Barones, centeni sunt puri nobiles, &

lend benevolent ears to you, who report false stories, after they realise that I have already proven you guilty of lies and forgeries so many times in this short book of mine.

A certain wise man was once asked, Carran: "What does a person gain from telling a lie?" He replied: "He gains the advantage of not being believed even when he is telling the truth." Even if the fabrications that you have contrived in this chapter of yours about the MacBrodys were true, Carran, nobody would believe you at this point, since you have already been proven guilty of lying so many times. Should the family of the MacBrodys, which always provided a chronicler to the most excellent family of the O'Briens, or, if you like, to the family of the kings of Ireland, or to the princes of Munster and Thomond, be called obscure? Is the family of the MacBrodys obscure and ignoble, a family that, until the tyranny of Cromwell, counted amongst it in Thomond so many eminent men who had numerous possessions, subjects, and followers, as I pointed out above in the 'Dissection of Chapter II', paragraph 17?

According to you, the family of the MacBrodys, which has ties of affinity with so many well-known families, should be called obscure? Not with a view to doing you a favour, Carran, but to writing the truth, I will name a few of the many male and female members of the nobility in County Clare (commonly called Thomond), County Galway, County Sligo, County Tipperary, County Limerick, County Cork and County Donegal, who had ties of affinity and blood with the MacBrodys, so that the impartial reader shall see how falsely you speak about a family which did you no harm.

25. There is no county in Ireland in which the families based in the countryside as well as those based in the town enjoy all the same degree of aristocracy: instead, there are in turn most illustrious, very illustrious, and noble families. Also, there is no family in Ireland enjoying such an eminent place amongst the most illustrious aristocracy, that it does not include many male and female members belonging to the rank of the pure and yet modest nobility, in addition to the individual who holds the highest rank. So, for example, amongst the O'Briens there were many knights and members of modest nobility before Cromwell's time – and, in actual fact, there are still many of them now – besides the earl of Thomond, the earl of

denique ex familia de Burgo, praeter Marchionem Clanrichardiae & alios Comites, vice Comites, Barones & Equites Auratos, plurimi sunt nobiles & nobilissae, qui mutuo inter se & cum aliis nobilibus familiis affinitate conjunguntur.

Amplissimae unius familiae princeps, v. g. Dux Ormoniae, Butlerianorum princeps, nullam pa[t]itur jacturam in reputatione per hoc, quod simplex nobilis, ex quacumque regni familia, Butlerianam duceret uxorem, vel e contra si Butlerus aliquis Bruodinianam, v. g. vel Nelonam duceret uxorem, & c. Haec pro informatione extranei lectoris.

26. Jam ad propositum nominabo certas illustrissimas, illustres ac respective nobiles familias Bruodinis conjunctas affinitate & sanguine, ut sic mundus videat tuam procacitatem, qua motus familiam tam honoratam, quae te non laesit, diffamas: et si invenietur unus Hibernus in Tuomonia versatus, qui salva conscientia dicere audebit me vera non referre, contentus sum ut dicar opprobium esse hominum & abjectio plebis. Jam ut ad rem veniam, solos illos nominabo quos ipse vidi, eorumque parentes & avos; nam ultra veritatem indagare esset multiplicare labores sine causa & fine.

27. Milerus Bruodinus, vulgo Magnus dictus, Dominus de Moyneo, in uxorem habuit Margaritam de Grady, illustris Domini Joannis Grady, Aurati Equitis de Creny & Tarumun, filiam, ex qua tot egregios filios & filias genuit.

Darius Bruodinus, Dominus Montis Scoti, Balliscanlan, Balliogan & c. Finolam Grajam Donati de Balli An Krow filiam in uxorem habuit, ex quibus multi egregii viri & foeminae descenderunt.

Cornelius Bruodinus de Moyneo, Mileri Magni filius, Annam

Inchiquin and the Viscount Clare; amongst the Butlers, besides the duke and the other counts, viscounts and barons, there are hundreds of pure noblemen; and, to conclude, there are a great many noblemen and noblewomen of the Burke family who are inter-related with one another and with other noble families by affinity, besides the marquis of Clanricard and other counts, viscounts, barons and gilded knights.

The individual who holds the highest rank of nobility in a single very large family, for instance the earl of Ormond, who holds this rank amongst the Butlers, suffers no loss of reputation by the fact that a simple nobleman, whatever family of the kingdom he came from, would marry a woman of the Butler family, or, vice versa, if any man of the Butler family would marry a woman of the MacBrody family, or for example the O'Nelan family, etc. I am saying these things to provide some explanation to the reader, who may be a foreigner.[294]

26. Now, to address the topic, I will name certain families of different degrees of aristocracy, some most illustrious ones, some very illustrious ones and, in turn, some noble ones, who established ties of affinity and blood with the MacBrodys. In this way your shamelessness, which leads you to defame a family that is so honourable and did no harm to you, shall be visible to the entire world. And if a single Irishman will be found, who has lived in Thomond and who will dare state, without compromising his conscience, that I am not reporting true information, I am happy to be called the disgrace of humankind and the refuse of the rabble. Now, to go straight to the point, I will name only those whom I saw with my own eyes, and their parents and grandparents; for investigating beyond the reality I have seen would mean multiplying my efforts without reason and purpose.

27. Maolin MacBrody, commonly called 'the great',[295] master of Moynoe, married Margaret O'Grady, daughter of the illustrious Master John O'Grady, the gilded knight of Creny and Tarumun,[296] who gave birth to so many eminent sons and daughters.

Daire MacBrody,[297] master of Knockanalban,[298] Ballyscanlan, Ballyogan,[299] etc, married Finola MacGrath, daughter of Donough of Ballyankrow,[300] from the two of whom descended many exceptional men and women.

Conor MacBrody of Moynoe,[301] son of Maolin 'the great',

Mac Nemara, illustris equitis Domini Donati de Ballinahensy filiam, habuit in uxorem.

Thadaeus Bruodinus, Darii de Monte Scoti filius, in uxorem habuit Annam Mohuny, seu Mathaei, illustris viri D. Thadaei de Tuonafarna filiam.

Daniel Bruodinus, Darii secundus filius, Mariam Geraldinam, illustris equitis Domini Ioannis de Ballynamona in Comitatu Kierensi filiam.

Constantinus Bruodinus de Balliogan, Darii tertius filius, Ninduviam Brien illustris viri, Domini Therentii ô Brien, de Craghbrien filiam.

Bernardus Bruodinus, Darii quartus filius & Dominus montis Callani & Balli Antonna, in uxorem accepit Catharinam Maguivir, ex illustrissima familia in Comitatu Fermanaghensi in Ultonia natam.

Florentius Bruodinus, vulgo *Mac Bruodin*, Cornelii de Moyneo filius, Onoram de Mara, illustris viri Domini Thadaei Mac Nemara de Fiechel & Cecilia Saghnasii filiam.

Bernardus Bruodinus, Florentii frater, Slaniam de Mara, illustris viri Domini Joannis Mac Nemara filiam (horum primogenitus R.P. Bonaventura Bruodinus, in Archi Episcopali Pragensi seminario multis annis theologicam cum applausu rexit cathedram).

Jacobus Bruodinus, Thadaei de Monte Scoti filius, Mariam Gormanam, Thomae Gormani de Drumelihy filiam.

Daniel Bruodinus, Jacobi frater, Elionoram Fitz Patrick praenobilis Domini Thadaei Fitz Patrickae filiam.

Milerus Bruodinus, Constantini filius & Dominus de Balliogan (antagonistae tui Carrane dignissimus parens), in uxorem habuit, ex qua 27 filios & filias accepit, Margaritam de Mollonii, Gellatii ô Molloni, Domini de Ballikrom & Sabinae de Mara, illustris D. Donati de BallinaHense filiam.

Hujus Margaritae patrueles duo, illustrissimi Domini Malachias ô Mollonii & Joannis ô Mollonii, per 46 circiter annos Laonensis sedis consequenter erant Episcopi.

married Anna MacNamara, the daughter of Master Donough of Ballynahinch,[302] the illustrious knight.

Tadhg MacBrody,[303] son of Daire of Knockanalban, married Anna MacMahon, or Matthews, daughter of the illustrious man Master Tadhg[304] of Tuonafarna.[305]

Donall MacBrody,[306] second son of Daire, married Maria Fitzgerald, daughter of the illustrious knight Master John of Ballynamona[307] in County Kerry.

Constantin MacBrody of Ballyogan,[308] third son of Daire, married Ineenduv[309] O'Brien, daughter of Master Turlough O'Brien of Craghbrien,[310] an illustrious man.

Bernard MacBrody, fourth son of Daire, and master of Slievecallan and Ballyantonna, took as a wife Catharine Maguire born of the most illustrious family of County Fermanagh in Ulster.

Flann MacBrody, commonly called the MacBrody, son of Conor of Moynoe, married Onora MacNamara, daughter of Master Tadhg MacNamara of Feakle,[311] an illustrious man, and Cecilia O'Shaughnessy.

Bernard MacBrody, brother of Flann, married Slaine MacNamara, daughter of the illustrious man Master John MacNamara (the first-born of these two, Rev. Fr Bonaventure MacBrody,[312] held the chair of theology at the archbishop of Prague's seminary for many years, receiving praise).

James MacBrody, son of Tadhg of Knockanalban, married Maria MacGorman, daughter of Thomas MacGorman of Drumellihy.[313]

Donall MacBrody,[314] brother of James, married Eleanor Fitzpatrick, daughter of Master Tadhg Fitzpatrick, a great nobleman.[315]

Maolin MacBrody[316] (the truly worthy father of your antagonist, Carran), son of Constantin[317] and master of Ballyogan,[318] took as a wife, from whom he had 27 sons and daughters, Margaret O'Molony, the daughter of Gellatius O'Molony, master of Ballycroum,[319] and Sadhbh MacNamara, daughter of the illustrious Master Donough of Ballynahinch.[320]

This Margaret's two cousins, the most illustrious Masters Malachy O'Molony and John O'Molony, were later bishops of the see of Killaloe for around 46 years.[321]

Donatus Bruodinus, Mileri frater, Dominus de Knacknamucky, Margaritam de Mara, Cormachi de Balli Moylinae filiam.

Cutbertus Bruodinus de Fernan, Mileri tertius frater, Phinolam de Gripha in uxorem accepit.

Gilbertus Bruodinus, Mileri junior frater, in uxorem habuit Onoram de Burgo, illustris equitis Domini Edmundi de Ballyan Kurnin in Comitatu Limericensi filiam et sororem nominatissimi equitis Domini Joannis de Burgo, Edmundi primogeniti.

Carolus Bruodinus Dominus de Bealanegh Onoram Minogh Joannis de Burgo, Domini de Pallis in Comitatu Galviensi neptem.

Joannes Bruodinus de Kilky Mariam Nelanam, Jacobi de Balli Nielan filiam.

Gilbertus Bruodinus de Boly Duff Mariam Hein, illustris viri Domini Florentii ô Hein de Keilovieragh filiam.

Constantinus Bruodinus, juvenis dictus, Milerii de Balliogan filius, Onoram Saghnassii, illustris viri Domini Danielis Saghnassii in Comitatu Galviensi & Elionorae Gradii filiam.

Cornelius Bruodinus, Florentii de Moyneo filius, Onoram Mohunii, praenobilis D. Matthaei Mochunii & Slanae de marra filiam.

Lucas Bruodinus, Cornelii frater, Elionoram Kusag, praenobilis Domini Geraldi de Lismolin in Midia filiam.

Jacobus Bruodinus de Kilgki, Joannis filius, Mariam Clanchi, praenobilis viri Domini Cornelii Clanchi filiam.

Milerus, juvenis dictus, Cornelii Bruodini de Kilky filius, Phinolam Brien, Domini Matthaei ô Brien de Drommile & Elionorae Sunigani filiam.

Taceo brevitatis gratia plurimos alios nobiles Bruodinos qui ex Clancheis, Girmanis, Nelanis, Gradiis, de Mara, Ghrahis, Gilriegh, Fitz Patrick, & c. uxores habuerunt. Si Bruodini tam viles essent, ac tu Carrane sine fronte fingis, non acciperent uxores ex familiis tam praeclaris potiori ex parte per totam Hiberniam notis.

Donough MacBrody, brother of Maolin, master of Knocknamucky, married Margaret MacNamara, daughter of Cormac of Ballymoylin.[322]

Cuthbert MacBrody of Fernan,[323] third brother of Maolin, took as a wife Finola O'Griffey.[324]

Giolla Brighde MacBrody, younger brother of Maolin, married Onora Burke, daughter of the illustrious knight Master Edmund of Ballyankurnin in County Limerick, and sister of Master John Burke, a knight who achieved great renown, first-born of Edmund.

Charles MacBrody,[325] master of Bealanegh, married Onora Minogue, the granddaughter of John Burke, master of Pallas in County Galway.[326]

John MacBrody Kilkee[327] married Maria O'Nelan, daughter of James of Ballyneillan.[328]

Giolla Brighde MacBrody[329] of Boolyduff married Maria O'Hynes, daughter of an illustrious man, Master Flann O'Hynes of Killovyeragh.[330]

Constantin MacBrody, called 'the younger', son of Maolin of Ballyogan, married Onora O'Shaughnessy, daughter of Master Donall O'Shaughnessy in County Galway, an illustrious man, and Eleanor O'Grady.[331]

Conor MacBrody, the son of Flann of Moynoe,[332] married Onora MacMahon, daughter of Master Mahon MacMahon, a great nobleman, and Slaine MacNamara.

Lucas MacBrody,[333] brother of Conor, married Eleanor Cusack, the daughter of Master Gerald of Lismullin in Meath,[334] a great nobleman.

James MacBrody of Kilkee,[335] son of John, married Maria MacClancy, daughter of Master Conor MacClancy, a great nobleman.

Maolin, called 'the younger', son of Conor MacBrody of Kilkee, married Finola O'Brien, daughter of Master Mahon O'Brien of Drommile[336] and Eleanor Sunigan.[337]

I omit, for the sake of brevity, a great many other noblemen of the MacBrody family, who took wives from the families of the MacClancys, MacGormans, O'Nelans, MacNamaras, MacGraths, Gallerys, Fitzpatricks, etc. If the MacBrodys were as base-born as you shamelessly portray them, Carran, they would not take wives from families of such a great prestige, most of which are known throughout the whole of Ireland.

28. Jam nominabo paucos ex multis praeclaros illustres viros ex diversis per Hiberniam familiis, qui reciproce ex Bruodinorum familia uxores habuerunt. Et primo in Tuomonia:

Praenobilis vir Dominus Cornelius Mac Mohony, seu Matthaei, Dominus de Tuonafarna, accepit in uxorem Brigittam Bruodinam, Darii de Monte Scoti filiam, ex qua natus fuit gloriosus Christi martyr Joannes Matthai Societatis Jesu, cujus vitam scripsit Alegambe & Bruodinus l. 3. sui *Propugnaculi*, cap. 20.

Ioannes Mohuny de Tuonafarna in uxorem habuit D. Annam Bruodinam, Thadai Bruodini Domini Montis Scoti filiam.

Cornelius Clanchy Dominus de Inse Phinolam Bruodinam, Thadaei de Monte Scoti sororem, in uxorem habuit.

Perillustris Dominus Rolandus De la Heud, potentissimus quondam Auratus Eques in Tuomonia horum filiam Annam (Hibernice *Una*) Clanchy in uxorem duxit, ex qua 6 filios & duas filias accepit.

Oliverus Dela Haid horum primogenitus in uxorem duxit Annam Conoram, illustrissimi Domini ô Conori Kiery filiam.

Ioannes secundogenitus Margaritam Winckfeld perillustris equitis Domini Eduardi Winckfeld & Onorae Brien natae Baronissae de Insiquen filiam.

Iunior filius Gerardus DelaHaid duxit illustris Domini ô Mary in Comitatu Tipperaniensi filiam.

Margarita Dela Haid, Rolandi primogenita, maritum accepit illustrissimum Dominum Thadaeum, Baronem Mac Namara Riegh.

Catharina Dela Haid, Margaritae soror, nupsit illustri equiti Domino Thomae de Burgo, Ioannis de Burgo de Tulleire primogenito.

Rogerius Mac Nemara de Bonnaneu in uxorem accepit Margaritam Bruodinam, Constantini de Balliogan filiam, quae praeclaros genuit filios & filias matrimonio respective conjunctos cum Mac Mohunis, ô Brienis, Hoganis, Mollonis & Hurleis.

Daniel Mac Nemara de Cahir Ballymorana Nabliam Bruodinam, Constantini de Balliogam filiam, in uxorem duxit.

Moriathus Clanchy de Ballynaklohy Mariam Bruodinam, Cornelii de Moyneo filiam.

28. Now I shall name a few out of many celebrated illustrious great men from various families across Ireland, who in turn had wives from the family of the MacBrodys. I start with those in Thomond:

Master Conor MacMahon or Matthews, a great nobleman, master of Tuonafarna, took as a wife Bridget MacBrody, the daughter of Daire of Knockanalban; from her a glorious martyr of Christ was born, John MacMahon of the Society of Jesus, whose life was written down by Alegambe[338] and by MacBrody in Chapter XX of his *Propugnaculum*.[339]

John MacMahon of Tuonafarna married Mistress Anna MacBrody, daughter of Tadhg MacBrody, master of Knockanalban.

Conor MacClancy, master of Inch[340] married Finola MacBrody, the sister of Tadhg of Knockanalban.

Master Roland Delahoyde, a great nobleman and once a most powerful gilded knight in Thomond, married their daughter Anna (in Irish Úna) MacClancy,[341] from whom he had six sons and two daughters.[342]

Oliver Delahoyde,[343] their first-born son, married Anna O'Conor, daughter of the most illustrious Master O'Conor of Kerry.

John, the second-born, married Margaret Wingfield, daughter of Master Edward Wingfield, a knight of great nobility, and Onora O'Brien,[344] who was born baroness of Inchiquin.

Gerard Delahoyde, the younger son [of Roland Delahoyde and Anna MacClancy], married the daughter of the illustrious Master O'Meara[345] of Tipperary.

Margaret Delahoyde, first-born daughter of Roland, married the most illustrious Master Tadhg, Baron MacNamara Reagh.[346]

Catherine Delahoyde, the sister of Margaret, married the illustrious knight Master Thomas Burke, first-born of John Burke of Tullira.[347]

Roger MacNamara of Bunnahow[348] married Margaret MacBrody, daughter of Constantin of Ballyogan, who gave birth to sons and daughters of great renown, who, in turn, established relationships of marriage with the MacMahons, O'Briens, Hogans, O'Molonys and Hurleys.

Donall MacNamara of Cahir Ballymorana[349] married Anabla MacBrody, daughter of Constantin of Ballyogan.

Murtough MacClancy[350] of Ballynacloghy[351] married Maria MacBrody, daughter of Conor of Moynoe.

29. Thomas de Burgo de Polmore Annam Bruodinam, Gilberti filiam, ex qua natus est Abbas de Burgo.

Iacobus Grady de Crossin Mariam Bruodinam, Constantini de Ballyogam filiam.

Cornelius ô Dea de Brentire in uxorem accepit Annam Bruodinam, Thadaei de Monte Scoti filiam.

Iacobus Mac Nerinhy de Lagh Bally Ninduviam Bruodinam, Mileri de Balliogan filiam.

Dermitius ô Brien de Mogona & Drommile Margaritam Bruodinam, Mileri de Balliogam secundo genitam.

Dionitius Gormanus de Geran Phinolam Bruodinam, Margaritae sororem, duxit.

Donaldus Gormanus de Dromelihy Mariam Bruodinam, Thadaei de Monte Scoti filiam, duxit.

Thadaus Mohony de Tuonafarna Elionoram Bruodinam, Cornelii de Kilky filiam.

Cornelius Cruttin de Ballybeg Elionoram Bruodinam, Cutberti de Fernan filiam, in uxorem accepit.

Matthaeus o Brien de Bealnafirvarnin Eleonoram Bruodinam, Domini Bernardi de Monte Callani filiam, duxit.

Extra Tuomoniam in Conatia aliquos nominabo.

30. Ioannes de Burgo de Barnaboy in Comitatu Galviensi & Baronatu de Knalehin in uxorem accepit Onoram Bruodinam, Mileri magni de Moyneo filiam, ex qua plurimi nominatissimi & potentes viri & foeminae nobiles in Comitatu Galviensi descendunt.

Thadaeus ô Higgin de Kulracheil Comitatus de Sligo toties Capitaneus (vulgo *Schirriff*) & Pacis Justiciarius, in uxorem habuit Phinolam Bruodinam, Constantini de Balliogan filiam. Horum filius Paulus in uxorem accepit Caeciliam Iordanam, perillustris Domini mac Iordan filiam. Filia vero primogenita, Maria Higgin dicta, nupsit nobilissimo viro Domino Therentio Mag Donoghu. Iunior autem filia, Mithilda dicta, nupsit perillustri Domino Ioanni de Hara, potenti quondam in illa patria dynastae.

29. Thomas Burke of Polmore married Anna MacBrody, daughter of Giolla Brighde, who gave birth to the Abbot Burke.[352]

James O'Grady of Crusheen[353] married Maria MacBrody, daughter of Constantin of Ballyogan.

Conor O'Dea of Brentire[354] married Anna MacBrody, daughter of Tadhg of Knockanalban.

James MacInerney[355] of Laghbally[356] married Ineenduv MacBrody, daughter of Maolin of Ballyogan.

Dermot O'Brien of Magowna and Drommile[357] married Margaret MacBrody, second-born of Maolin of Ballyogan.

Dionysus MacGorman of Geran[358] married Finola MacBrody, sister of Margaret.

Donall MacGorman of Dromellihy[359] married Maria MacBrody, daughter of Tadhg of Knockanalban.

Tadhg MacMahon of Tuonafarna married Eleanor MacBrody, daughter of Conor of Kilkee.

Conor MacCruttin of Ballybeg[360] married Eleanor MacBrody, daughter of Cuthbert of Fernan.

Mahon O'Brien of Bealnafirvarnin[361] married Elenora MacBrody, daughter of Bernard of Slievecallan.[362]

I will name some outside of Thomond. In Connacht:

30. John Burke of Barnaboy[363] in County Galway and baron of Kinaleghin[364] married Onora MacBrody, daughter of Maolin 'the great' of Moynoe,[365] from whom a great number of renowned and potent nobles, men and women, descend in County Galway.

Tadhg O'Higgin[366] of Coolrecuill, who was captain (commonly termed sheriff) and lord justice general of the peace so many times in County Sligo, married Finola MacBrody, daughter of Constantin of Ballyogan. Their son Paul married Cecilia MacJordan, daughter of Master MacJordan, a great nobleman. Indeed, their first-born daughter, named Maria O'Higgin, married Master Turlough MacDonagh, a great nobleman, whereas their younger daughter, named Matilda, married Master John O'Hara,[367] a very illustrious nobleman, formerly a powerful ruler in that country.

In Momonia:

Donatus ô Hogan de Ballynamona in Ormonia in uxorem habuit Helenam Bruodinam, Cornelii de Moyneo filiam, quae multos genuit filios & filias cum ô Kenediis, ô Brienis & aliis praeclarissimis familiis in illo tractu matrimonio ligatos.

Jacobus Bary de Balty Naknock in Comitatu Corcagiensi Phinolam Bruodinam, Gilberti filiam, in uxorem habuit.

Horum filiam in uxorem accepit praenobilis Dominus Iacobus Rocheus, in praefato Comitatu potens quondam eques.

In Ultonia:

Ferallus Wardaeus in Comitatu Tyrconellensi nominatissimus quondam vir Principisque ô Donel archipoeta & historicus Mariam Bruodinam, Darii filiam, in uxorem habuit.

Daniel Clery, jam nominati Principis ô Donel consiliarius & chronologus, Margaritam Bruodinam, Mariae sororem. Ab his duabus foeminis plurimi praeclari viri saeculares & ecclesiastici in Ultonia originem traxerunt.

Gabriel Donlevi (vulgo Ultanus dictus), excellentissimus medicinae doctor in Comitatu Tyrconellensi, accepit in uxorem Dominam Mariam Bruodinam, Chuttberti de Fernan filiam.

Si voluissem nominare omnes praeclaras familias Bruodinis mediantibus filiis, filiabus, ac nepotibus jam nominatorum dominorum sanguine junctas, citius mihi charta quam scribendi materia deficeret. Haec quae notavi abunde sufficiunt ad Bruodinianae familiae honestatem ostendendam & ad tuas Carrane calumnias refutandas, & si his non contentatur, sequentes versus tibi a tuo populari reverendo admodum Patre Francisco ô Molloy, SS. Theologiae Lectore Emerito ejusdemque facultatis in Romano S. Isidori Collegio Professore Primario, missos accipe & tace.

"Inter Tuomonides priscis fulsere Bruodini,
moribus & vita, nobilitate sati.
Si genus & proavos horum Carrane notasses,
horreres celsos vellere dente viros.
Consule vel vivos, chronicos vel consule regni:
istos heroas aequiparasse leges."

In Munster:

Donough O'Hogan of Ballynamona in Ormond[368] married Helen MacBrody, daughter of Conor of Moynoe, who gave birth to many sons and daughters who were bound in marriage with the O'Kenedys, O'Briens, and other most illustrious families in that region.

James Barry of Ballynaknock[369] in County Cork married Finola MacBrody, daughter of Giolla Brighde.

Master James Roche, a great nobleman who was once a powerful knight in the aforementioned county, married their daughter.

In Ulster:

In County Tyrconnell Fergal Ward,[370] who was once Lord O'Donnell's arch-poet and historian, a great and notable man, married Maria MacBrody, daughter of Daire.

Donall O'Cleary,[371] counsellor and chronicler of the aforementioned Lord O'Donnell, married Margaret MacBrody, Maria's sister. From these two women very many distinguished men in Ulster, both of the world and of the Church, were born.

Gabriel Donlevy[372] (commonly named 'the Ulsterman'), an excellent medical doctor in County Tyrconnell, married Maria MacBrody, the daughter of Cuthbert of Fernan.

Had I wished to name all of the most renowned families which now have relationships of blood with the MacBrodys through the sons, daughters and grandchildren of the masters whom I have already mentioned, I would have sooner run out of paper than of subject matter to write on. These names, which I have indicated, are sufficient to show the honourable lineage of the MacBrody family and to refute your slanders, Carran; and if they do not satisfy, then receive these following verses sent to you by your fellow countryman, Adm. Rev. Fr Francis O'Molloy,[373] emeritus lector in holy and sacred theology and *Professor Primarius* of the same faculty at St Isidore's College in Rome, and be silent.

"Among the old inhabitants of Thomond, the MacBrodys,
sprung of nobility, shone bright in their customs and way of life.
Had you noted their noble stock and forefathers, Carran,
you would shudder to pull down by tooth these eminent men.
Consult the living, or consult the chronicles of the Kingdom:
you will read that those MacBrodys were equal to heroes."

31. Frustra te rogo, Carrane, ut sileas aut ut solita tibi convitiorum arma deponas; progrederis enim sicut incepisti, sine fronte f. 90. "Bruodini" (inquis Carrane) "comentitia fabula est, quae in nullo authore legitur, quod tempore Finacti Regis nives in Hibernia in vinum resoluta sunt."

Credo, Carrane, quod a te aut ab aliis tuae farinae ignavis hominibus in nullo authore historia illa fuit lecta; R.P. Bruodinus vero (sicut & nos omnes, qui genuinas Regni Hiberniae chronicas legimus) non semel legit in diversis authoribus illam historiam. Omnium loco tibi Carrane, si vir bonus es, sufficiat authoritas eximii SS. Theologiae Doctoris antiquitatumque Hibernicarum sagacissimi indagatoris Domini Syardi Ketten, qui lib. 2. *Historiae Hiberniae* agendo de Hiberniae regibus refert ut verissimam Historiam illam de resolutione nivium Finacti Regis tempore in vinum, sicut & quod Dermitius Morphei, Lageniae quondam Princeps, praeter Evam filiam filium habuerit Arthurum nomine. Tu Carrane Kettengum, qui Hibernice suam scripsit historiam, legere non didicisti, sic tuam excusatam habeo imprudentiam & ignorantiam. Unicum hoc a te scire vellem: an tu putas, Carrane, incredibile esse quod in Hibernia nives in vinum sint resolutae? Si sic, ad sequentia rogo te obturatas tuas applica aures, & mirabiliora ex authenticis Historicis desumpta audies.

32. Anno salutis 1550. Martii 22. in diversis carentiae locis siliginem & triticum pluit Deus ex coelis.

Anno 1598. die 25. Iunii medio milliari Glogovia in Silesia pluit Deus in copia panes desuper pistos.

Anno 1307. die 30. Iulii pluvia magnorum lapidum Constantinopolis multis abbreviavit vitam.

Anno 1572. a die sexta Ianuarii usque ad octavam inclusive Thoreni (vulgo *Thoren*) in Prussia sanguineus fluvius apparuit.

Anno 1416. die 22. Februarii sanguineae nives per Bohemiam ceciderunt, quae in puram postea resolutae sunt aquam.

31. In vain I ask you, Carran, to keep silent or to lay down your usual weapons of insults; for, on page 90, you continue in the same way as you started, without any sense of shame. You say, Carran: "The story of the snows of Ireland dissolving into wine in the time of King Fionnachta[374] is a fictitious fable by Bruodinus, which one cannot read in any other author."[375]

I believe you, Carran, when you say that you or other lazy people of your kind did not read that story in any other author; however, Rev. Fr Bruodinus (just like all of us, too, who read the authentic chronicles of the kingdom of Ireland) read that story more than once in various authors. If you are a good man, Carran, may the authority of the distinguished doctor of holy and sacred theology and very sagacious investigator of the Irish antiquities, Master Geoffrey Keating,[376] be enough for you in place of all others. In the second book of his work on the history of Ireland,[377] while treating the subject of the kings of Ireland, he reports as absolutely true the famous story concerning the dissolution of the snows into wine in the time of King Fionnachta,[378] just as he does with the fact that Dermot MacMurrough, once ruler of Leinster, had a son called Art besides his daughter Aoife.[379] You, Carran, never learned how to read Keating, who wrote his history in Irish, so I regard your lack of judgement and your ignorance as excusable. I would like to know just this single thing from you: do you consider unbelievable, Carran, that the snows dissolved into wine in Ireland? If so, please lend your plugged ears to the following, and you shall hear yet more extraordinary facts picked out from authentic historians.

32. In the year of salvation 1550, on 22 March, God rained wheat, both fine and whole, down from the skies in various places of famine.

In the year 1598, on 25 June, a half-mile from Głogów[380] in Silesia, God rained down loaves of flatbread from above.

In the year 1307, on 30 July, a rain of big stones in Constantinople cut the life of many people short.

In the year 1572, from 6 to 8 January inclusive, a river of blood could be seen in Thorenum[381] (commonly called Thoren) in Prussia.

In the year 1416, on 22 February, snows made of blood fell all around Bohemia, which then dissolved into pure water.

Anno 1586. die 26. Martii Gitczinii in Bohemia pluit Deus sanguinem, tertio postea anno ignis vorax totam in favillam redegit civitatem.

Anno 1551. die 8. Maii Erfurti & Lipsiae impetuosus sanguinis imber cecidit.

Anno 1532. die 27. Octobris Ulisoponae, & anno 1572. die 30. Decembris Constantinopoli, sanguinea pluvia cecidit.

His portentis Carrane si tu credis, quae a verissimis tot referuntur scriptoribus, quare pariter non credis Doctori Ketten & aliis qui post illum ex chronicis Hiberniae scribunt sub Finacto Rege nives fuisse resolutas in vinum? Si his non credis, crede saltem Carrane quod milleni sunt viri praeclarissimi qui de veritate illarum historiarum non dubitant, quique nunquam somniarunt tale portentum, quale tu es, Viennae Austriae in angulo latere aut intra oceani maris simul fuisse natum. Jam ad alia.

33. Blateras Carrane varia, quae a doctis non intelliguntur, fol. 92. de illustrissima familia de Burgo, quam innato tuo erga illam odio sed inani exitu conaris supprimere. Tandem in R. P. Bruodinum convitia explodis varia, eo quod uni ex excellentissima Butlerianorum familia majorem dederit titulum (vocando nimirum ipsum Vice Comitem de Cahir, cum tamen non sit ut tu fingis nisi Baro) quam a rege accepit. Vitulos Carrane Bruodinus non habuit, quos Butleris daret: sic sine invidia permittas tu ut illis bona fide det titulos, quos sunt bene meriti.

Satis jam Carrane pugnasti, repone igitur falcem tuam in vaginam, & cum abunde senueris, post tot maledicta nil restat, nisi ut impiae illius Jobi coniugis consilium adimpleas suadentis: "Benedic Domino, & morere"."Non," inquis Carrane, fol. 94 "quia volo ulterius me vindicare"; animose ergo falcem stringe. "Bruodinus" (inquis) "sic habet lib. 5. c. 24. in quo se dicit esse ex sanguine ô Brienorum, & sic

In the year 1586, on 26 March, God rained blood upon Jičín[382] in Bohemia, and in the third year after this event a devouring fire reduced the entire town to ashes.

In the year 1551, on 8 May, a heavy rain of blood fell upon Erfurt and Leipzig.[383]

A rain of blood also fell upon Lisbon in the year 1532, on 27 October, and upon Constantinople in the year 1572, on 30 December.

If you believe these prodigies, which are reported by so many writers of great truthfulness, Carran, why do you not believe in the same way Doctor Keating and other authors after him, who report from the Chronicles of Ireland that the snows dissolved into wine under the reign of King Fionnachta? If you do not believe them, Carran, do believe at least the fact that there are thousands of men of great renown who have no doubts about the truth of those stories, and who, at the same time, never dreamed that such a portent as you are could hide in a corner of Vienna in Austria or could be born on this side of the ocean. Now, let us turn to other issues.

33. On page 92, Carran, you blather on about various things, which not even learned men are able to understand, about the most illustrious family of the Burkes, whose status you try to lower, albeit with vain results, out of your innate hatred against them. In the end you throw various insults at Rev. Fr Bruodinus because he gave a member of the most excellent family of the Butlers a higher title than the one he received from the king (specifically, because he called that man a Viscount of Cahir,[384] although he is – according to how you depict him – no more than a baron). Bruodinus has no calves to give to the Butlers, Carran:[385] so, hold no grudge and allow him to attribute to members of that family, in good faith, titles that have been well deserved.

You have already done enough fighting, Carran. So, put your sickle back into its scabbard; and now that you have become very old, after throwing so many insults the only thing left for you to do is to fulfil the advice which the famous wife of Job impiously gave her husband, attempting to persuade him: "Bless the Lord, and die."[386]

On page 94, Carran, you state: "I am not moved by desire for further revenge."[387] But then you feverishly brandish your sickle: "Bruodinus" – you say – "reports this in Book V, Chapter 24, where

superbire conatur inter Bohemos, ut existimarent eum esse ex sanguine augusto regum & principum," & c.

34. Nisi jam toties in tot perniciosissimis mendaciis & imposturis librorum fuisses Carrane deprehensus, facile hic nos deciperes, credendo vera esse quae scribis; at quia suspectae fidei homo es, sic semper ad manum Bruodini librum habere debemus, ut videamus num ita se res habeat sicut tu scribis. Aspeximus jam Carrane diversi simul Bruodini caput 24. a te citatum, & contrarium plane quae tu scribis invenimus; nam fol. 1076. dicti capitis, haec habet: "Alii Hiberni mihi rationabiliter vitio non vertent, si omissis aliarum nobilium familiarum genealogiis ô Brienorum genealogiam subjungam: Bruodinus namque sum, sic mirum non est si familiae hujus illustrissimae," (NB. Carrane) "cujus antecessores mei semper fuerunt chronologi recordabor, omissis pro nunc aliis."

Ecce, Carrane, quomodo Bruodinus candide gloriatur se non ex sanguine esse Brienorum, sed potius ex sanguine chronologorum regiae ô Brienorum familiae, prout revera est: quo ergo folio vel linea se ex sanguine esse ô Brienorum dicit? Pudeat te! Lege genealogiam Principis ô Brien & Tuomoniae Comitis fol. 1077. a te jam citati capitis, & cum tua confusione videbis quod Bruodinus fol. 1081. dicat familiam suam descendisse a Diago Aengusii filio. Estne hoc Carrane dicere quod descendat ab ô Brienis? etsi diceret, non mentiretur more tuo: nam ipsius paterna avia, Ninduina nata ô Brien, filia fuit Domini Therentii ô Brien de Craghbrien. Et materna avia fuit Sabina de Mara, D. Donati de Ballinahensii filia; ecce Carrane, quomodo cum veritate poterat Pater Bruodinus dicere (quod tamen non dixit) quod ab ô Brienis & Mac Nemaris (quae sunt primae duae familiae in Tuomonia) originem trahat.

he claims to be of the blood of the O'Briens; accordingly, he tries to take pride amongst the Bohemians, so that they may regard him to be of imperial blood of kings and princes," etc.

34. Had you not already been caught so many times in the act of filling your work with so great a number of utterly baleful lies and misquotations from books, Carran, you would easily deceive us on this point, by making us take as true the things that you write. But since you are a man of dubious trustworthiness, we must always keep Bruodinus' original book at hand, to see whether it reports exactly the same things as you write. Individually and separately from one another, we readers have already checked Chapter 24 of Bruodinus' work, mentioned by you, Carran, and we found the exact opposite of what you write. In fact, page 1076 of the aforementioned chapter contains these words: "Reasonably, other Irishmen will not reckon it as a fault on my part if I will omit the genealogies of other families but annex the genealogy of the O'Briens; for I am a MacBrody, so it is not surprising if I will omit other families for now and give my thoughts to this specific family of great renown," (N.B., Carran!) "whose chroniclers my ancestors have always been."

Here is how Bruodinus guilelessly prides himself on being not of O'Brien blood, but rather of the blood of the chroniclers of the royal family of the O'Briens, Carran, just as it is indeed. Tell me: in which page or line does he say that he is of the blood of the O'Briens? Shame on you! Read the genealogy of the O'Brien sovereign and of the earl of Thomond on page 1077 of the chapter mentioned above by you, and you will see, to your bewilderment, that Bruodinus says on page 1081 that his family descended from Deaghadh, son of Aonghus.[388] Is this the same as saying that he descends from the O'Briens, Carran? Even if he said so, he would not be lying in the same way as you do. For his paternal grandmother, Ineenduv – born O'Brien – was the daughter of Master Turlough O'Brien of Craghbrien;[389] and his maternal grandmother was Sadhbh MacNamara, daughter of Master Donough of Ballynahinch. Here is how Fr Bruodinus could have claimed in truth to have taken his origin from the O'Briens and the MacNamaras, which are two families of first rank in Thomond, Carran – a claim which, however, he did not make.

35. Tu tamen adhuc Carrane sine fulcro subsistis. "Bruodini" (inquis fol. 94. circa finem) "Bardi sunt & non nobiles, qui virorum mulierumque laudes vel vituperia suis decantabant rhythmis."

Lege Carrane quae supra in *Anatomia* hujus cap. n. 29. dixi, & si veniam vis consequi tuae imposturae fateberis culpam tuam. Interim ego fateor quod per hanc tuae calumniae repetitionem doctior sim factus; nam antea quid per bardum velles non bene percipere poteram; Musae ergo, Carrane, & poëtae ex despectu, ut video, a te dicuntur bardi. Cur, quaeso, quod non intelligis tam temere taxas? Grammatista es tantum ultimi scamni; poëtas ergo altioris scholae professores cur spernis? Audi, Carrane, Ciceronem in oratione *pro Archia poëta* defendentem poëtas contra te: "Ennius" (inquit) "sanctos appellat poëtas, quod quasi aliquo deorum dono atque munere commendati nobis esse videantur. Proinde minus mirum, si non alium esse poëtam, quam virum bonum statuunt prudentiores," & c. Plato lib. 2. *de Rep.* poëtas "deorum filios & sapientiae patres ac duces" vocat. Hoc sciens Ovidius *Fast.* 6. ait:

"Est deus in nobis, agitante calescimus illo,
impetus hic sacrae semina mentis habet."

Magnus ille Carrane Israëlitarum imperator Moyses, statim ac mare rubrum transgressus est, divino numine afflatus excellentem se poëtam fuisse ostendit, dum assistentia sororis hexametro carmine suaviter cantans Deo suo gratias *Exodi* 15. egit. David, Judaeorum Rex, entheus erat Carrane poëta, nam vario genere carminis psalmos suos immortali Deo decantavit. Hieremias Propheta threnos partim Saphico metro partim trimetro suaviter cecinit & conscripsit. Isaias prophetias suas sacris condidit Carrane versibus. Sapientissimus regum Salomon in hortis Eugaddensibus *Canticum canticorum* in morem drammatis suavissime Hebraice cecinit. Et ne in re clara

35. Nonetheless, Carran, you still stand fixed in your position without support. Around the end of p. 94 you say: "The MacBrodys are not noble, but bards who used to sing men and women's praises and invectives with their rhymes."

Read, Carran, what I said above in paragraph 29 of this *Dissection* of your chapter, and you will need to confess your fault if you want to obtain forgiveness. Meanwhile, I confess that I have learned something new through the repetition of your false statement; for I could not properly understand what you previously meant by 'bard'.[390] So, Carran, you call the muses[391] and the poets 'bards', as I see, out of spite. Why are you so thoughtless in criticising things that you do not understand, I ask you? You are a student of elementary grammar who only deserves to be placed on the farthest bench.[392] So, why do you scorn poets who are professors in schools of higher rank? Listen to Cicero defending the poets against you, Carran, in his speech *Pro Archia Poeta*:[393] "Ennius"[394] (he says) "calls poets 'holy', because they seem to have been recommended to us almost by some form of gift and bestowal of the gods. Therefore, it appears less surprising if rather judicious people state that there is no difference between a poet and a good man",[395] etc. Plato, in Book II of the *Republic*, calls the poets "sons of the gods, fathers of wisdom and guides".[396] Ovid, who was aware of this, says the following in Book VI of the *Fasti*:[397]

> "There is a god inside us; we grow warm as he stirs us.
> This impulse possesses the seeds of a sacred mind."

The great Moses, the famous leader of the Israelites, as soon as he crossed the Red Sea was inspired by divine power and showed that he was an excellent poet, while he was thanking his God by singing a delightful song in hexameters together with his sister, as we read in Chapter 15 of *Exodus*.[398] David, king of the Jews, was a poet inspired by God, Carran; for he sang his psalms to the immortal God using a variety of poetic genres.[399] The prophet Jeremiah[400] delightfully sang and wrote down his *Lamentations* partly in Sapphic metre,[401] partly using the trimeter.[402] Isaiah composed his prophecies in holy verses, Carran. Solomon, the wisest of the kings, sang the *Canticle of Canticles* in a most pleasing tone in Hebrew in the gardens of Ein Gedi, using the poetic form of drama.[403] And lest I be long-winded in

prolixus sim, sanctissimi plerique omnes Ecclesiae veteris & novi testamenti prophetae, patres, doctores & professores poëtae erant laudatissimi, ex quibus (ut millenos alios taceam), Caelius noster Sedulius, natione Hibernus, qui inter patres merito nominatur, non solum nobile illud *Opus mirabilium*, seu *Paschale*, & ordine alphabetico piissimum *Hymnum ad Christum*, sed etiam jucundissima carmina in laudem Theodosii Iunioris composuit, anno Christi 430.

Prophanos poëtas omnes, tam viros illustres quam nobiles virgines & foeminas, qui nominare vellet citius tempus eum deficeret quam obligationi satisfaceret. Quid, Carrane, an hos omnes tam sacras quam prophanas Musas & poëtas "ignobiles, viles, & bardos" in tuo sensu esse vis? Si non, cur Hibernorum condemnas poëtas?

36. A mundi exordio, Carrane, in omnibus Orbis provinciis Musae & poëtae in veneratione semper erant summa; & ut hujus rei multa alia omittam exempla, non tibi Carrane sed doctis Historicis obvia, unum hoc referam: poëtae apud Gallos in tanta olim aestimatione fuerunt (teste Diodor. lib. 5. cap. 9.) quod, cum acie instructa strictis acinacibus hostem aggrederentur, interventu poëtarum ob reverentiam artis & Musarum tam ipsi quam hostes a continuatione pugnae quiescebant.

Inter primarios Hibernorum principes & magnates antiquitus tantus fuit Musarum poëtarumque respectus, ut non credam ullibi terrarum sapienties in majori fuisse reverentia quam poëtae in Hibernia; libertate enim gaudebant vix non plus quam ecclesiastica. Annuos a proceribus reditus accipiebant, illis in vita vel substantia nocere crimen fuit laesae majestatis. An haec, Carrane, privilegia ignobilibus personis per decursum tot saeculorum dari posse credis? Haec in gratiam poëtarum.

an argument which is already evident, the greatest part of all saintly prophets, fathers, doctors and professors of the Church of the old and new testament were highly-praised poets. Amongst these (not to mention thousands of others), our Caelius Sedulius, a man of Irish nationality who is deservedly named amongst the Fathers of the Church,[404] composed not only the famous and noble *Work of Marvels* or *Carmen Paschale,* as well as the *Hymn to Christ,* a poem of great devotion in alphabetical order,[405] but also very delightful songs in praise of Theodosius the Younger,[406] in 430 AD.

Whoever wanted to name all of the profane poets, whether they were illustrious men or noble virgins or women, would run out of time sooner than completing his commitment. What, Carran? Are you saying that all these muses and poets,[407] both the holy and the profane ones, are "ignoble, worthless and bards" in your view?[408] If not, why do you disapprove of the poets of the Irish people?

36. Ever since the origin of the universe, Carran, muses and poets have always been held in the highest respect in every territory of the world; and not to mention a number of other examples of this fact, Carran, which are obvious to the learned historians but not to you, I shall report only the following one. In the past, poets enjoyed such a high esteem amongst the Gauls (as attested by Diodorus in Book V, Chapter 9),[409] that while they were launching an assault against their enemies, with the army drawn up in order of battle and the sabres already in their hands, they used to desist from continuing the fight if the poets intervened, because of their reverence for the art and the muses, and so did the enemies.

In ancient times, amongst the first-rank chiefs and magnates of the Irish people, the respect for the muses and the poets was so great that I do not think that the wise men of any other land were held in a higher degree of esteem than poets in Ireland. In fact, the freedom they enjoyed was scarcely inferior to the kind reserved for the ecclesiastics. They used to receive yearly revenues from the noblemen, and it was a crime of lese-majesty[410] to do harm to their lives or properties. Do you believe, Carran, that these privileges could be granted to ignoble people in the course of so many centuries? I say these things in favour of the poets.

Ex Bruodinis, Carrane, quamvis multi erant praeclari poëtae, quorum opera tam pia quam prophana in summa aestimatione per omnes Hiberniae provincias hodie sunt, adhuc tamen eorum nullus unquam professione fuit poëta: nam, sicut antiquitus reges & principes Hibernorum ex certis & nobilibus respective familiis suos habuerunt judices controversiarum, medicos, musicos & poëtas, sic pro chronologis certae erant & determinatae familiae; inter quas merito numeratur Bruodiniana familia, ex qua regiae familiae ô Brienorum chronologi semper fuere: unde sicut theologus, quantumvis excellens poëta, adhuc non perdidit theologi nomen, ita nec Bruodini, quamvis ex illis aliqui erant excellentes poëtae, nobilium & chronologorum nomen & honorem amiserunt. Tu ergo, mi Carrane, caeco tuo more scommata in Bruodinos explosisti, si putas calumniando poëtas illos te tetigisse. Jam ad alia.

37. Ulterius Carrane recto tremite sicut incepisti titubas adducisque nova figmenta fol. 96. de expeditione illustrissimi Domini Generalis Feralli contra rebellem Crumwellistam Zankium, quae ad rem non faciunt; tuum officium erat (ut jam te toties monui) refutare ea quae contra tuam *Olleapatridam* Pater Bruodinus in suo scripsit *Propugnaculo*; ad quid ergo alto silentio de his taces, & impertinentia sine ratione & authoritate tractas? Generalis Ferallus ejusque in Hibernia potens & ampla quondam familia plus Bruodino bona fide erranti crederet, quam tibi (toties jam in flagranti mendacio deprehenso) veritatem asserenti: nam illi qui frequenter mentitur nemo credit, etiamsi subinde vera loquatur. Quae Pater Bruodinus de illa Carrane scripsit expeditione accepit non solum ex Hibernorum & Anglorum historiis de bello Hibernico scriptis; verum etiam a diversis Hibernis, qui dixerunt se tunc fuisse in exercitu Ormonii, omnia ut scripsit audivit.

There used to be a huge number of very famous poets of the family of the MacBrodys, Carran, whose religious as well as profane works are nowadays held in high esteem throughout all the provinces of Ireland; so far, however, none of them was ever a poet by profession. In fact, the kings and princes of the Irish people in antiquity chose their judges of contentions,[411] physicians, musicians and poets from specific families which were renowned for these professions respectively. In this very same way, there were specific and precise families occupying the position of chroniclers; and it is amongst these that the family of the MacBrodys, which always provided the royal family of the O'Briens with chroniclers, deserves to be included. Accordingly, just as a theologian, however great a poet he may be, never lost the appellation of theologian, in the same way the MacBrodys never lost the appellation and honour of being chroniclers and a renowned family either, although there were some of them who were excellent poets. Therefore, my dear Carran, you have been as blind as usual in spouting taunts against the MacBrodys, if you believe to have struck a blow against them by unjustly blaming the poets. Now, let us turn to other issues.

37. Rightly shaken even further, Carran, you keep faltering just as you started. On page 96, you put forward new fabrications about the expedition of the most illustrious Master General O'Farrell[412] against Sankey,[413] one of Cromwell's rebels, which have nothing to do with the purpose of your work. What you had to do (as I have already reminded you so many times) was refute the things that Fr Bruodinus wrote against your *olla podrida* in his *Propugnaculum*. Why, then, do you pass over them in deep silence, and deal with irrelevant matters, with no reason and no authority to do so? General O'Farrell and his family, which was once large and powerful in Ireland, would trust Bruodinus even if he were wrong in good faith, more than they would trust you even if you were telling the truth (given that you have been already caught in the act of lying so many times); for nobody believes a man who frequently lies, even if he then started telling the truth. What Fr Bruodinus reported about that expedition, Carran, comes from the works written by Irish and English historians about the war in Ireland. Also, he heard all that he wrote being confirmed by various Irishmen, who affirmed that they were in the army of Ormond at

Tu pro opposita tua assertione nec argumentum aut authoritatem adducis; quis itaque tibi vellet potius credere quam Patri Bruodino, quem adhuc de mendacio non convicisti?

38. Taedet te merito, Carrane, tam diu in refutatione *Propugnaculi* Patris Bruodini gratis laborasse; sic generose extollis te supra te & relicta inexpugnabilis P. Bruodini *Fortalitii* obsidione, ad *Theologiam* illius expugnandam sine alis volas in coelum.

"Deinde" (inquis fol. 97.) "Bruodinus in sua *Theologia* col. 8. assert. 4. de sua incipit gloriari barba compararreque Christi barbae. Sed quid habet theologia cum Bruodini barba ad agendum? Quia theologia versatur circa Deum rerumque divinarum contemplationem, & non circa barbam," & c.

Si Bruodini *Theologiae Summa* in Pragensibus non haberetur bibliothecis, facile nos Carrane hac tua impostura decipere poteras; at cum non solum Pragae, sed per omnes haereditari<a>s Caesaris provincias multorum manibus Summa illa quotidie teratur, qua fronte ausus es tam inverecunde imponere bono Patri Bruodino, quae numquam scripsit, dixit, aut somniavit? Toties jam in flagranti errore & impostura deprehensus & correctus, non te emendas? Miseret profecto me tui, quando considero quod in omnem te partem vertas ferae ad instar irretitae, ut operibus P. Bruodini palpabilia commenta affigere possis, quae illi in mentem nunquam venerunt, ut sic aliquid habeas in quo eum reprehendas.

Bruodinus loco a te Carrane citato nec verbum habet de barba aut capillis: nam in illa assertione tantum agit de opere 4. 5. & sextae diei creationis; de creatione vero, statura & pulchritudine (theologorum more) prothoparentum fol. 90. circa finem agit.

Demum conatur ostendere fol. 91. non solum Adamum fuisse rufum, sed etiam Christum. Porro ut lector percipiat illum "pro

that time. To support your opposite claims, you adduce neither an argument nor the authority of a source. Who, then, would prefer to trust you rather than Fr Bruodinus, whom you have been unable to prove to be a liar so far?

38. You are reasonably annoyed, Carran, by having taken pains to refute Fr Bruodinus' *Propugnaculum* for so long, but without reward. Consequently, you generously exalt yourself above your own stature and fly up in the sky without wings, so as to assault Fr Bruodinus' *Theologia*,[414] after abandoning the siege of his *Propugnaculum*, an inexpugnable fortress.[415]

On page 97 you say: "Then, in his *Theologia*, column 8, assertion 4,[416] Bruodinus starts boasting about his beard and comparing it to Christ's beard. But what does theology have to do with Bruodinus' beard? For theology deals with God and the discussion of divine matters, and not with a beard",[417] etc.

If the libraries of Prague did not hold copies of Bruodinus' *Summa Theologiae*,[418] Carran, you could have easily deceived us with this imposture of yours. However, since that *Summa* is worn away by the hands of many readers everyday, not only in Prague but across all the hereditary provinces of the emperor, with what impudence did you dare attribute so shamelessly to Fr Bruodinus things which he never wrote, said or dreamed? Do you not chastise yourself, even after having been caught in the act of making mistakes and lying, and having been corrected so many times already? Indeed, I feel pity for you, when I consider that you turn everywhere, resembling a wild animal ensnared in a net, in order to be able to attribute to Fr Bruodinus' works palpable fabrications which never came to his mind, so that you may have something about which you could refute him.

In the passage mentioned by you, Carran, Bruodinus does not say a single word about any beard or hair: in fact, in that assertion he only deals with the work of the fourth, fifth and sixth day of Creation. Around the end of page 90, however, he does speak about the creation, height and beauty of the first two parents of the human race (as theologians generally do).

Finally, on page 91, he tries to show that not only Adam, but also Christ had red hair. Then, in order for the reader to understand that

sua non agere" (ut in vulgari) "domo", fol. 92. concludit se non asserere Christum fuisse Rufum propter se, sed gratia potius veritatis indagandae. Nullibi suam comparat Christi barbae, nisi tu aliam habes alibi impressam *Theologiae Summam* Bruodini quam nos non habemus: quomodo igitur tu jam impostoris & calumniatoris evadere poteris praedicata non capio. Nulli Carrane facilius quantumvis mentienti homines credunt quam illi quem in mendacio nunquam deprehenderunt; te jam toties in flagranti depraehenderunt famosi tui libelli lectores mendacio: amplius itaque tibi nihil credunt.

Si Bruodinus caprae in morem, sicut tu, barbatus incederet, posset aliquis imaginari te vera scripsisse; at cum nullam prorsus alat barbam, quam singulis tribus septimanis novacula totaliter non deponit, quomodo possit de illa gloriari?

39. "Theologia" (inquis, Carrane) "versatur tantum circa Dei rerumque divinarum contemplationem, non circa barbam rubram aut nigram."

Vulgare dictum est, Carrane, "ne sutor ultra crepitam." Grammatista tantum es tu, infimi scamni; mirum igitur non est, si ignoras circa quae agit theologia objecta. Theologia, misercule grammatista, agit non solum de Deo, sed etiam de diabolo; non solum de virtutibus, sed & vitiis; non solum de anima, sed & de corpore ejusque delineamentis & ornamentis (inter quae capilli & barba reputari possunt) & c. Ecce, Neo-Theologe, objecta distincta a Deo, de quibus theologia pace tua hactenus egit.

Jam Carrane, cum theologica facultas tam infeliciter tibi successerit, ad nota solitaque tibi convitiorum arma confugis, quibus totam simul Bruodinorum honoratam familiam caeco more dilaniare de novo conaris.

"he is not blowing his own trumpet" (as the common saying goes),[419] on page 92 he concludes by saying that he is not stating that Christ was red-haired because he, the author, has red hair, but rather with a view to enquiring into the truth. Nowhere does he compare his beard to Christ's, unless you have a different edition of Bruodinus' *Summa Theologiae*, printed elsewhere, which we do not possess. At this point, then, I do not understand how you will be able to get rid of the signs that publicly label you as a deceiver and a slanderer. Nobody, Carran, is more easily trusted, regardless of how many lies they may tell, than a person who has never been caught in the act of lying. The readers of your infamous pamphlet have already caught you red-handed telling lies so many times: therefore, they no longer trust you to any extent.

If Bruodinus went around wearing a beard in the manner of a goat, as you do, someone could imagine that you wrote the truth; but since he absolutely does not let his beard grow, and he shaves it completely with a razor every three weeks, how could he boast about it?

39. "Theology" (you say, Carran) "deals only with God and the discussion of divine matters, not with a beard, whether it is red or black."

There is a common saying, Carran: "A cobbler should stick to his last."[420] You are only a student of elementary grammar, and one of the worst ones in the class. Accordingly, there is nothing to be surprised about, if you do not know on what subjects theology focuses. Theology, you pitiable and insignificant student of elementary grammar, deals not only with God, but also with the devil; not only with virtues, but also with vices; not only with the soul, but also with the body and its lineaments and additional features (amongst which hair and beard can be reckoned), etc. Look, you new theologian: these are subjects which are different from God, but which, with all due respect to you, theology has been considering to this day.

Now, Carran, given that your ability in theology led you to so unhappy a result, you seek shelter for yourself by resorting to the weapons of your insults, which are well-known and to which you are accustomed. Again, with these you try to assail the honoured family of the MacBrodys all at once, acting like a blind man.

40. "Bruodini" (inquis fol. 98 tui famosi libelli) "mandras nonnullas habere consueverunt in montium jugis suis vaccis & capris inhabitandas" (ditiores sic erant Christo qui non habuit ubi reclinaret caput suum) & infra, fol. 99. "in Balliogan sunt parva tuguriola, levi materia aedificata ex transtris, stramine contecta & introrsus bovino stercore illinita satis liquet, saltem meo tempore, quando fui in Tuamundia, sic apparuit Bruodinorum locus," & c.

Bone Deus, Carrane, eritne aliquando finis mendaciorum & calumniarum, quibus innocentes in pace requiescentes diffamas? Ex iis quae dixi n. 26. & 27. hujus capitis abunde lectoribus constabit haec quae sine fronte scribis non argumenta esse, sed procacis linguae impudentissimas fabulas, quae alio non stabiliuntur fulcro quam tua authoritate, quae inter viros probos nullius est fidei.

Non ita pridem theologum infelici successu egisti; jam Carrane mechanicum more tuae prosapiae agis, transtraque e navibus furaris, ut ope tuae falcis Bruodinis mandras construas, quas relicta calce, bitumine & argilla, quibus Tuomonia plerisque in locis abundat, bovinis excrementis obducis.

Nisi tu Carrane scarabeus potius esses, non haberes in ore tam faetidum pulmentum & non fingeres quod in tua Catholica patria honestorum virorum habitatio tam absurdo lineretur excremento. Mi Carrane, non Tuomoniensis sed Transsinnanus es tu verna; quid ergo in Tuomonia nostra habuisti quod ageres, in qua vix subsistere integrum tibi fuisset? Quare mihi Carrane facile persvadeo te nunquam fuisse ausum illam patriam visitare, & consequenter haec quae hic comminisceris, reclamante tua conscientia, in odium P. Bruodini te finxisse. Nam Bruodini nostri, more aliorum patriae multorum nobilium, honoratas semper habuerunt aedes multas, quae primarii proceres, nobiles, praelati, & ecclesiastici non solum Tuomoniae, sed etiam vicinorum comitatuum & provinciarum frequenter visitarunt & intrarunt. Lege quae de tuae farinae scriptoribus Bruodinus habet lib. 5. cap. 1. fol. 764. sui *Propugnaculi*, & videbis quod omnia quae scribit

40. On page 98 of your infamous pamphlet, you say: "The MacBrodys were accustomed to have some animal shelters on the ridges of the mountains to be inhabited by their cattle and flocks" (they were thus richer than Christ, who did not have a place to lay his head);[421] and below, on page 99: "in Ballyogan there are small huts, built with light material out of crossbeams, quite clearly covered with straw and smeared with cow dung on the inside; the area of the MacBrodys had this appearance at least in my time, when I was in Tuomondy",[422] etc.

Good God, Carran, will there ever be an end to the lies and calumnies with which you defame the innocent while they rest in peace? From what I said in paragraphs 26 and 27 of this chapter, it will be abundantly evident to the readers that the things which you shamelessly pen are not arguments, but the most impudent tales of an insolent tongue that rest on no other basis than your own authority, which finds no credence amongst righteous men.

Not so long ago, you played the theologian, with unhappy results. Now, Carran, you play the builder after the manner of your family, and you steal crossbeams from ships so that with the aid of your sickle you can construct stalls for the MacBrodys, which you, leaving behind the lime, pitch, and argil[423] in which Thomond is rich in most of its places, smear with cattle excrement instead.

If you were not rather a dung-beetle,[424] Carran, you would not hold such a disgusting kind of food in your mouth, and you would not invent that, in your Catholic country, the dwelling-place of honest men is so absurdly plastered with cow dung. My dear Carran, you are not from Thomond, but a foreigner born across the Shannon. So, what did you have to do in our Thomond, where the bare act of staying would have been a novelty for you? For this reason, Carran, I easily persuade myself that you never dared to visit that country and, consequently, those things which you invent in your work, in spite of the claims of your conscience, you contrived in hostility towards Fr Bruodinus. For our MacBrodys, in the manner of many other noblemen of the country, always owned honourable buildings which the foremost chiefs, nobles, prelates and ecclesiastics, not only of Thomond, but also of neighbouring counties and provinces, would frequently visit and enter. Read what Bruodinus has to say about writers of your kind in Book V, Chapter 1, page 764 of his

tibi perbelle quadrabunt. Interim videamus quid ulterius ululas.

41. "Bruodinus" (inquis Carrane fol. 100.) "non sine menda ponit ex mera adulatione inter Momoniae primores Gall de Burgo, qui non habet pedem in Momonia, sed in Lagenia exstat ipsius Patrimonium," & c. A quingentis jam annis in Momonia illustrissima, Carrane, potensque familia de Burgo, inter primarias semper provinciae familias nominata fuit; quomodo ergo peccavit Bruodinus scribendo quod Gall de Burgo sit inter Nobiles Momoniae familias numerandus? "Non ibi", inquis, "sed in Lagenia habet bona."

Quis Carrane non habet in Momonia bona? Bruodinus nullum nominat, tantum dixit inter primarias Momoniae familias Gall de Burgo nominari. Familiam, caece, non vero individuum, hoc & illud Bruodinus dixit esse Momoniensem. Deinde Carrane tu more tuo argumentaris pessime inferendo Gall de Burgo non esse Momoniensem familiam, quia Comes Gall non in Momonia sed in Lagenia habet bona. Pessime inquam, nam Austriaci, Belgae, Lusenburgenses, Hiberni, Scoti & Galli sunt diversi nobiles, qui in sola Bohemia, Moravia, vel Silesia bona habent, per hoc tamen non desinunt esse Austriaci vel Hiberni, multo minus eorum familia desinit esse Austriaca vel Hibernica. Quare ergo per hoc quod unus ex Momoniensi familia de Burgo bona haberet in sola Lagenia, eo ipso desineret esse Momoniensis? Pro tua misera capacitate satis de hac re dixi. Jam ad alia.

Progrederis consequenter Carrane, in malo proposito veritatisque semitas tua falce secas fol. 100. circa finem. "Bruodinus", inquis, "suo barditu lib. 5. cap. 20. suis non destitit mendaciis, nam inter nobiles Comitatus Caterloghensis o Brien, Tuomoniae Comitem & Caterloghiae Toparcam, ponit."

Propugnaculum, and you will realise that everything he writes will fit you very neatly.[425] Meanwhile, let us see what further nonsense you howl.

41. On page 100, Carran, you say: "Out of bare adulation, Bruodinus mistakenly includes amongst the men of first rank of Munster the Gall Burke family,[426] which does not possess a foot of land in Munster; but its patrimony is in Leinster",[427] etc. In Munster, Carran, the very illustrious and powerful family of the Burkes has always been named amongst the first-rank families of the province for five hundred years now. How, then, did Bruodinus make a mistake when writing that the Gall Burkes are to be enumerated amongst the noble families of Munster? You say: "the family does not hold possessions there, but in Leinster."

With regard to whom, Carran, are you claiming that he had no possessions in Munster? Bruodinus makes no mention of any specific person. He only said that the Gall Burkes are named amongst the first-rank families of Munster. Bruodinus stated that the family is from Munster, and not any specific member of it: just this thing and this thing only, you blind man! Next, Carran, you put forward a very poor argument, inferring that the Gall Burkes are not a family of Munster because Count Gall[428] does not own possessions in Munster, but in Leinster. I say your argument is very poor for this reason: there are various Austrian, Belgian, Luxembourger, Irish, Scottish and French noblemen who own possessions only in Bohemia, Moravia or Silesia; nevertheless, they do not cease to be Austrian or Irish for this reason, and even less so their family does not cease to be Austrian or Irish. Why, then, should a single member of the Burke family, which is from Munster, have ceased to be from Munster just because he owned possessions only in Leinster? I have said enough about this matter, in proportion to your poor comprehension skills. Now, let us turn to other points.

Afterwards, you go further in your mischievous intention, Carran; and with your sickle you dig a furrow in the path of truth, thus obstructing it, around the end of page 100. You say: "with his bard-song, Bruodinus did not desist from his lies in Book V, Chapter 20; for he places an O'Brien, the earl of Thomond and governor of Carlow, amongst the noblemen of County Carlow."

42. Tu Carrane probas Tuomoniae Comitem non esse Caterloghiae Toparcham non ratione aut fide dignorum autoritate, sed convitiis & scommmatibus, quae ne tibi similis esse videar silentio praetereo: scommata enim illius qui bene loqui nescit a prudentioribus spernuntur. Te autem talem esse me tacente probant opera tua; unde merito dicta tua spernuntur a sapientibus. Adduc ergo pro te testem unum fide dignum vel rationem convincentem, si tu vis ut credamus tibi. Interim scias Jacobum Angliae Regem donasse excellentissimo Domino Donato ô Brien, Tuomoniae Comiti & Momoniae quondam Praesidi, Caterloghiam cum vicina toparchia, ex qua Comites Tuomoniae annuos census hactenus semper receperunt; quare itaque non posset cum veritate Bruodinus inter nobiles familias Comitatus Caterloghensis nominare ô Brien (ex qua tot fuerunt Reges Hiberniae & Laghmogiae Principes) & dicere quod Comes Tuomoniae sit Caterloghiae Toparca? Subdis, Carrane, fol. 101.: "fallax Bruodinus Dominum Bagnellum suo minime inter nobiles inseruit libro," & c.

43. Dic sodes, Carrane: an non te pudet canitiem prolixae tuae barbae tot manifestis imposturis & fallaciis coinquinare? In cathalogo nobilium familiarum regni fol. 1096. sub lit. B. primam in ordine familiam Bruodinus nominat Bagnalf. Pudeat te quod toties consequenter in tua senectute non bona mentiaris. Pater Bruodinus, Carrane, nullam omisit nobilem familiam Regni Hiberniae, cujus non faceret mentionem! Aliquae tamen ipsius diligentiam praeterierunt; inter quas mihi occurrit familia de Bahii, nobilis in Conatia medica familia, ex qua olim regnantibus antiquis Hibernis prothomedici multorum in Ultonia principum fuerunt. Hujus familiae Bruodinis alias amicissimae non fuit P. Bruodinus memor alias quam meretur in cathalogo nobilium sedem acciperet. Jam ad alia.

Sicut caput hoc incepisti Carran, sic illud concludis. "Non obstante" inquis fol. 101. "quod ille Bruodinus minime famam denigrare ô

42. Your argument that the earl of Thomond is not the governor of Carlow, Carran, is not based on a rational reasoning or the authority of trustworthy testimonies, but on insults and taunts which I pass over in silence, lest I seem to be akin to you; for the taunts of that person who is unable to speak well are spurned by wiser people. Even if I keep silent, however, your works show that you are this kind of person; accordingly, what you say is deservingly spurned by wise people. Come on, cite in your favour a single witness who may deserve our trust, or a convincing argument, if you want us to believe you. Meanwhile, be aware that James, king of England, donated to the most excellent Master Donough O'Brien, earl of Thomond and former president of Munster, Carlow and the governorate of the region nearby, from which, so far, the earls of Thomond have always received yearly revenues. How, then, could Bruodinus not be telling the truth by naming the O'Briens (a family which produced so many kings of Ireland and princes of Leath Mogha)[429] amongst the noble families of County Carlow, and by saying that the earl of Thomond is the governor of Carlow? On page 101 you add, Carran: "the deceitful Bruodinus did not even include Master Bagnall[430] amongst the noblemen in his book," etc.

43. Please, Carran, tell me: do you not feel ashamed to contaminate the hoariness of your long beard with so many patent impostures and deceits? In his catalogue of the noble families of the kingdom, on page 1096, under the letter B, the first family mentioned by Bruodinus in alphabetical order is Bagnall. Shame on you for telling so many lies, one after another, in your "not-good"[431] old age! There is not a single noble family of the kingdom of Ireland, Carran, which Bruodinus did not mention and omitted from his catalogue! Some, however, escaped his diligence; and amongst these, the family of MacVeigh[432] comes to my mind, a noble family of physicians in Connacht, members of which the ancient rulers of Ireland once kept as *protomedici*[433] of many princes in Ulster. Fr Bruodinus forgot about this family, which was once very close to the MacBrodys and which should have been given the place it deserves in his catalogue of the noble ones. Now, let us turn to other matters.

You conclude this chapter, Carran, in the same manner as you opened it. On page 101, you say: "Despite the fact that Bruodinus is

Ferollorum familiae non vereatur; nam ô Feralli in omnibus chronicis & historiis quae de nobilibus Hiberniae tractant inscripti sunt." Bene est, mi grammatista: nonne & P. Bruodinus de Ferallis eorumque quondam potenti familia lib. 5. cap. 22. fol. 1027. & sequentibus honorifice uti debuit loquitur? Quid igitur contra illos peccavit, ob quod tu illum tot scommatibus fol 102. oneras? "Mendaciloquus" (inquis Carrane) "Bruodinus dicit, quod eorum comitatus tantum se extendat ad 12. milliaria Hibernica." Carrane, non Patris Bruodini, sed typographi error est iste, qui pro 24. mendose 12. posuit. Si tu christiane multos alios typographicos errores operum P. Bruodini emendares, rem illi faceres gratam; cum autem hoc non velis, cur maledicta tua lingua innocentem pungis? Deinde si studio Pater Bruodinus errasset circa dimensionem Comitatus Longfordensis, quomodo per hoc Carrane famam Ferallorum denigrasset? A quo tyrannice Crumwellus anno 1650. & sequentibus Hiberniam occupavit bonisque omnibus regni proceres & nobiles fere omnes privavit, Feralli non habuerunt decimam partem bonorum quae haereditario jure ad illos spectabant, per hoc tamen eorum fama laesa non est: cur pariter laederetur per hoc, quod scriptor aliquis diceret patriam illorum ad 12. tantum milliaria se extendere? Festino ad alia.

Non potui hactenus intelligere causam ob quam tanquam insanus per sex jam exenterata famosi tui libelli Carrane capita in deos & deas, vivos & mortuos, sine respectu saevisti. Jam vero in conclusione hujus sexti capitis causam his ostendis verbis: "et ex eo," inquis, "quod Bruodinus scripta mea vocet '*ollopadridam*', ideo hic suas refuto nugas."

44. Audivi non raro quod insani ad mentem subinde redeant per bona fercula; at quod aliquis sibi alias bene praesens more tuo, Carrane, praecipiti ageretur furore ob nobilissimi unius ferculi

not afraid of defaming the reputation of the family of the O'Farrells not at all; for the O'Farrells were named in all the chronicles and histories which deal with the noblemen of Ireland."[434] Well, my dear student of elementary grammar: is it not true that Fr Bruodinus also speaks about the O'Farrells and their once powerful family, showing the respect which is due to them, in Book V, Chapter 22, page 1027? What wrong did he do to them, then, in response to which you overload him with so many taunts on page 102? "Mendacious Bruodinus" – you say, Carran – "states that their county extends over only twelve Irish miles." This is not Fr Bruodinus' mistake, Carran, but the typographer's, who erroneously typed 12 instead of 24. If you emended many other typos in Fr Bruodinus' works with the kindness of a Christian, you would do him a favour; but since this is not what you want, why do you sting an innocent man with your ill-speaking tongue? Moreover, if Fr Bruodinus had intentionally reported a wrong detail about the dimension of County Longford, how would this have been a denigration of the O'Farrells' reputation? Ever since Cromwell tyrannically occupied Ireland from the year 1650 onwards, and deprived the kingdom's leading men and noblemen of all their possessions, the O'Farrells did not hold a tenth of the estates to which they were entitled by hereditary right. Nevertheless, their reputation was not damaged because of this. Likewise, why should it have been damaged because of any writer's statement that their home territory extended only for 12 miles? I quickly turn to other points.

So far, Carran, I have been unable to understand the reason why, like a madman, you disrespectfully vented your rage against gods and goddesses, and against the living and the dead, throughout six pages of your infamous pamphlet, which I have already disembowelled. But now, in the conclusion of this Chapter VI of yours, you show the reason with these words: "and it is because Bruodinus calls my writings an *olla podrida*" – you say – "that I hereby refute his nonsensical statements."

44. I often heard of madmen who regained their mind by eating good food. Before you, however, I never heard of anyone who, being otherwise in control of his mind, was moved by an inconsiderate madness as you are, Carran, because of the mention of a single dish of a very famous food. Therefore, I feel pity for you, poor little old man.

mentionem, ante te nunquam audivi. Compatior ergo tibi, misercule senex: Bruodinum autem ex eo quod *Annales* (si diis placet) tuos "*Ollopadridam*" compellaverit damnare non possum nisi in hoc, quod non assignaverit diversitatem utriusque *ollopadridae,* tuae nimirum & Hispanicae, quae talis est.

Ollopadrida enim Hispanica ex diversis exquisitis cibis, palato & stomacho gratis, componitur; tua vero, Carrane, Hibernica *ollopadrida* meris fabulis, imposturis & nugis ad rem non facientibus plena est. Unde popularis quidam tuus sequenti disticho ingredientia tuae descripsit *ollae padridae* sicut & ingenii singulares dotes:

> "Ira, furor, menda, dolus, inclementia, Carve,
> *ollae padridae* sunt munimenta tuae."

Nonetheless, I cannot condemn Bruodinus for having mocked your (gods granting this) *Annales* by calling them an *olla podrida*, except for the fact that he did not remark on the difference between the two *olla podridas*, namely yours and the Spanish one, which I outline below.

Indeed, the Spanish *olla podrida* is a variegated mix of excellent kinds of food, which give delight to the palate as well as the gullet. Instead, Carran, your Irish *olla podrida* is full of bare fables, lies and nonsensical statements that have nothing to do with its topic. Accordingly, a certain fellow-countryman of yours described the ingredients of your *olla podrida* as well as the peculiar qualities of your mind, in the following couplet:

> "Wrath, madness, blemish, deceit, un-mercifulness, Carve,
> are the defence weapons of your *olla podrida*."

Anatomia capitis 7. *Apologiae* Carrani

In exenteratione hujus tui Carrane capitis non diu me detinebo; nam praeter enormia scommata & innumera convitia quibus R. P. Bruodinum oneras, fabulasque quibus Hiberniae & Hibernorum famam, gloriam & aestimationem minuere conaris, nihil invenio cerebri in hoc tuo cranio anatomia dignum; nisi vellem puerilem tuum Latinismum repraehendere & errores grammaticales, quibus caput hoc per omnes fere lineas ubique scatet, emendare, & sic pretiosum gratis terere tempus. Porro utcumque est, ne debita careat sectione, omissis scommatibus Carrano authore dignis, breviter elucidabo defectus & infirmitates hujus tui cranii, ac tandem vale tibi dicam.

Titulus Carrane tui hujus cranii, potius quam capitis, sic incipit: "de R. P. Bruodini injusta contra authorem obtrectatione." De titulis non est sicut non de gustibus tecum, Carrane, vini potabilis disputandum. Insuper tibi authoris convitiorum, mendaciorum, & calumniarum hujus tui capitis dignitatem & praeeminentiam cordicitus faveo. Caeterum quae subjungis breviter anatomizare modice & medice conabor.

1. Mirum in modum Carrane apprehendis R. P. Bruodini verba lib. 5. cap. 6. fol. 803 sui *Propugnaculi*, ubi dicit "te ob causam sibi & tibi notam fuisse ex Hibernia expulsum." "Is" (inquis Carrane fol. 104. tui famosi libelli) "non tanquam frugi homo mecum incepit, sed potius velut infrunitus Franciscanus absque discretione," & c.

Non incepit tecum, bone vir, sed incepit cum pseudohistoricis tuis magistris, qui patriam illius diffamarunt; tandem te charitative redarguit tuasque calumnias solide refutavit. Quod dicat te ex Hibernia fuisse ob causam sibi notam expeditum, quid per hoc, Carrane, peccavit? Causam non retulit, nec ego cui probe nota est

Dissection of Chapter VII of Carran's *Apologia*

I will not spend much time in the disembowelment of this chapter of yours, Carran. For besides huge taunts and innumerable insults, with which you burden Rev. Fr Bruodinus, as well as fables, with which you try to diminish the fame, glory and value of Ireland and the Irish people, I find no trace of a brain in this skull of yours,[435] which would be worth anatomising – unless I wished to waste precious time by carping at your boyish pseudo-Latin and correcting the grammatical mistakes of which this chapter is everywhere full, almost throughout every line. But be that as it may, lest this chapter remain without the dissection which is owed to it, passing over the taunts which befit its author, Carran, I will briefly expose the defects and weak parts[436] of this skull of yours, and I will finally say farewell to you.

The title of this skull, rather than chapter, of yours bears the following opening words, Carran: "about the unjust disparaging by Rev. Fr Bruodinus against the author." There should be no dispute in matters of titles, Carran, just as there should be no dispute with you in matters of taste of drinkable wine.[437] Above all, for your own sake and from the bottom of my heart, I have decided not to say anything about the excellence and pre-eminence of the author of the insults, lies and slanders characterising this chapter of yours. As for the rest, with the prudence of a surgeon,[438] I will try to briefly anatomise what you subjoin below your title.

1. You, Carran, give a weird interpretation to Rev. Fr Bruodinus' words in Book V, Chapter 6, page 803 of his *Propugnaculum*, where he says that you "were expelled from Ireland because of the reason which he and you know". On page 104 of your infamous pamphlet, Carran, you state: "This man begins his chapter by speaking about me not as an honest man would do, but rather as a silly Franciscan with no discernment", etc.

He did not begin with you, good man, but he began with the pseudo-historians you had as teachers, who defamed his homeland. At the end, he rebuked you in the loving way of a Christian, and he refuted your calumnies with strong arguments. As for the fact that he says that you were expelled from Ireland because of the reason which he and you know, what wrong did he do, Carran, by means of this

referam. Ad quid ergo promptissima tua ad maledicendum lingua non solum P. Bruodinum, sed seraphicam religionem mendaciter laceras?

"Sicut" (inquis fol. 105.) "ipsum hactenus in suis mendaciorum relationibus refutavi, ita etiam nunc abunde ipsum confundam." Papae, non scis Carrane quod jactantia describitur "inanis & stultae creaturae de se praedicatio"? Toties jam prostratus & convictus, tuas victorias mixte praedicas? Succedat tibi imposterum certamen sicut hactenus, & eris victus melius quam fuisti.

"Terra sancta" (id est Hibernia) "me", inquis, "non patitur, quamvis apostatas Franciscanos, qui defacto & longe ante suas habent & habuerunt concubinas, patiatur."

Bonorum nisi esset Carrane virorum non solum benefacere, sed mala a malis patienter audire & tolerare, commoveres merito viros bonos ad te urgendum, ut ea quae mendac<i> ore de Franciscanis comminisceris probanda vel ad palinodiam cantandam. P. Bruodinus non dixit quod te Hibernia pati noluit, sed tantum in genere Carrane dixit Hiberniam terram sanctam esse, quae non patitur sacerdotes nisi sint sine macula: tu vero, quasi tibi conscius esses, putas te illis verbis fuisse tactum. Etsi ita esset, cur non in Bruodini solius caput retorques sua dicta, omissis innocentibus Franciscanis qui te non offenderunt? At tu Carrane discipulus fuisti noti istius impostoris, Matthaei Roch Dioecesis Leghlinensis, in Lagenia quondam Vicarii Generalis (a quo dicis te accepisse dimissoriales, quando ex patria exulare debuisti), sic mirum non est si persequeris Franciscanos, quos ille excommunicatus & publice postea degradatus nebulo (ut inferius dicam) per annos 30. scriptis & sermonibus inique persecutus fuit.

statement? He did not report the reason, and neither will I, to whom it is well known.[439] Why, then, do you torture not only Fr Bruodinus, but even the seraphic religion by telling lies with your tongue, which is always ready for ill-speaking?

On page 105, you state: "Just as I have refuted him so far in the false information he reports, in the same way I will now also throw him into great disconcertment." Good heavens, Carran, do you not know that bragging is described as "the action of praising oneself done by a worthless and stupid creature"?[440] After having already been defeated and overcome so many times, are you still confusedly proclaiming your victories? May it happen in the future that you partake in battle as you have been doing so far! For you will achieve a greater defeat the next time, than the one you previously accomplished.

You say: "The holy land" (that is, Ireland) "does not tolerate me, although it tolerates the apostate Franciscans, who have and had their own mistresses, now as well as long ago."

It is customary for good men, Carran, not only to do good actions, but also to patiently hear evil-speaking from wicked people, and bear to it. Were it not so, these good men would be justly disturbed by your words and would urge you to prove the truthfulness of what you are fabricating with your mendacious mouth about the Franciscans, or to sing a palinode.[441] Fr Bruodinus did not say that Ireland was not willing to tolerate you; instead, Carran, while speaking only in general, he said that Ireland is a holy land, that does not tolerate priests if they are not without blemish. You, however, as if you were aware of your own condition, regarded yourself to have been touched by those words. Even if it were so, why do you not throw Bruodinus' accusations back in his face alone, without involving innocent Franciscans who did not offend you? But you, Carran, were a pupil of nothing less than Matthew Roche,[442] the famous impostor of the diocese of Leighlin,[443] who once was general vicar in Leinster (from whom you say you received a letter of discharge[444] when you had to live in exile from your homeland). Accordingly, there is nothing to be surprised about, if you persecute the Franciscans, who were unjustly persecuted for 30 years by means of writings and speeches by that good-for-nothing, who was excommunicated and then publicly demoted (as I will say below).

Unicum quem a 100 annis potuisti Carrane invenire Franciscanum apostatam, Milerum Chrachium, nominasti cap. 2. hujus tui famosi libelli (ut videre est supra in *Anatomia cap. 2.* n. 40), ubi tamen de ejus resipiscentia maliciose tacuisti. Cur hic pariter, Carrane, non nominas alios illos quos apostatas & concubinarios vocas, si aliquos nosti?

2. Mi Carrane, nec Dominicani nec Franciscani nec Augustiniani tui unquam aut degradati Rochi in Hibernia fuerunt condiscipuli, consodales aut studiosi; quare per annos plus minus 24 illos (praesertim Franciscanos) degradatus & ob sua nota scelera patibulo publice postea affixus ille tuus Matthaeus Roch pro viribus in Hibernia (pro ut tu in Germania) persecutus est; excogites itaque alia aliqua delicta, quibus mentiaris Franciscanos esse reos, omissa apostasia & concubinatu quibus Dei gratia in Hibernia nunquam fuerunt notati.

Si ego Carrane exraneus essem, in rebus tamen Hibernicis versatus, ut modo sum, dicerem coram Deo & mundo quod in tota Christianitate, inter Haereticos, Indos aut Turcas, religiosi non sunt aut a 100 annis fuerunt, qui pro Christi nomine sanctaeque Matris Ecclesiae conservatione & exaltatione plura supportarunt incommoda, aut majores fecerunt fructus, quam Hibernorum religiosi omnes indifferenter, a quo haeresis in Anglia praevaluit. Ut hic mihi non esset difficile ostendere, nisi Europae constaret, qualiter in mediis persecutionum fluctibus nullo labilis hujus vitae habito respectu, pro salute gregis Dominici constantes, vigilantes & patientes, inventi sunt semper. Jam ad alias tuas imposturas.

3. Frustra laboras Carrane fol. 105., 106. & 107. praemissis tot scommatibus, instruendo Patrem Bruodinum circa observantiam suae regulae. "Sus" (ut in adagio est) "Minervam." Bruodini, Carrane, doctrina conjuncta cum religiosa vita & compositis moribus notior per Europam est quam ut tuis imposturis & convitiis possit obnubilari;

In 100 years of history, Carran, the only Franciscan apostate you could find, Miler Magrath, was mentioned by you in Chapter II of this infamous pamphlet of yours (as one can see above, in my 'Dissection of Chapter II', paragraph 40), where, however, you wickedly said nothing about his repentance. Why do you not do the same here, Carran, and name those other Franciscans whom you call apostates and whom you say had mistresses, if you know some?

2. My dear Carran, neither the Dominicans nor the Franciscans nor the Augustinians in Ireland were ever companions, fellows or attached to you or to Roche, who was downgraded. Accordingly, for more or less 24 years, that Matthew Roche of yours, who was degraded and would later be publicly hanged at the gibbet because of his famous misdeeds, dedicated all of his strengths to persecuting those orders (especially the Franciscans) – just as you are doing in Germany. Therefore, give up the accusation of apostasy and concubinage, of which – thanks be to God – the Franciscans were never branded in Ireland, and instead invent some other crimes, of which you could falsely declare them to be guilty.

If I were a foreigner, but nonetheless with some expertise in the customs and affairs of Ireland, as I am at the moment, Carran, I would declare before God and the world that in the entire Christendom, amongst the heretics, the Indians or the Turks, there are or have been for 100 years no clerics who, in defence of Christ's name and for the preservation and elevation of holy Mother Church, endured more troublesome situations or obtained greater results than all the clerics of the Irish people, with no distinctions, ever since the heresy took hold in England. As I could easily show, if it were not already evident to the whole of Europe, Irish clerics were always found to be determined, vigilant and firm in defending the safety of Dominic's flock, in the middle of whatever surge of persecutions, without any regard for this perishable life. Now, let us turn to other lies of yours.

3. On pages 105, 106 and 107, Carran, after introducing so many taunts, you strive in vain, instructing Fr Bruodinus about the observance of his own rule: "A pig teaching Minerva"[445] (as the proverb goes). Across Europe, the fame of Bruodinus' erudition, associated with religious life and suitable habits, is greater than the extent to which

doce tu ergo, si ludimagistrum (more honesti tui patruelis, Connaldi o Carran) vis agere, tuae farinae discipulos, ignaros nimirum & stupidos, relicto Patre Bruodino, qui per annos 16 theologicas & philosophicas cum applausu rexit cathedras.

Fol. 108. 109. & 110., nimio forte mero obrutus, talia evomis in Patrem Bruodinum scommata, ut majora non possis nisi demens esses aut ab inferis missus ad claros viros accusandos. Bone vir, non catholici scriptoris sed sycophantae haeretici est conviciis & scommatibus, omissis rationibus, causam suam propugnare. Quae in defensionem patriae contra imposturas *Lyrae* tuae (vel, si mavis, *Delirii*) scripserat Bruodinus refutare promisisti in principio tui famosi libelli; quare, si vir bonus es, non observas promissa, omissis scommatibus ad rem non facientibus?

"Iam" (inquis Carrane fol. 111.) "defendam omni ratione adhuc indubitate verba meae *Lyrae* vera esse, nimirum quod anno" (644. in tuo habes *Ollopadrida*) "Hiberni in tantam barbariem & ignorantiam lapsi sunt, ut nulla prorsus politia apud ipsos viguerit."

Promissis tuis Carrane nemo amplius, postquam toties lectores decepisti, credet. Adduc itaque, si quod habes, novum fulcrum, quo dicta tua contra Venerabilis Bedae lib. 3. *Historiae gentis Anglorum* cap. 27. (cujus authoritate Bruodinus lib. 5. cap. 6. fol. 806. te prostravit) testimonium consolidare vales.

4. "Adduco" (inquis fol. 112.) "ex assertione ipsiusmet Bruodini lib. 5. cap. 14. sic habet: 'Et tunc turbatis rebus per regnum a Danis Universitates illae eversae sunt & studiosi dissipati'."

Si argumentum est ad hominem, Carrane, ubi est consequentia? Est haec; inquis: "ubi non sunt Universitates, quomodo in tali regno

it could possibly be obscured by your slanders and insults. So, if you want to play the role of a school-master (in the manner of your honest cousin Conald O'Carran),[446] teach students of your ilk, namely stupid and ignorant ones, leaving Fr Bruodinus alone, who successfully held chairs of theology and philosophy for 16 years.

Overflowing with too much wine, strong and unmixed with water, on pages 108, 109 and 110 you spew out against Fr Bruodinus such terrible taunts, that you would not be able to devise bigger ones, unless you were out of your mind or you had been sent from hell with the purpose of blaming honourable men. It does not befit a Catholic writer – good man! – but a heretical slanderer, to fight for his cause with insults and taunts, and neglect rational arguments. At the beginning of your infamous pamphlet you promised to refute what Bruodinus had written in defence of his homeland against the impostures of your *Lyra* (or, if you prefer, *Delirium*);[447] if you are a good man, why do you not keep your promises, giving up the taunts that have nothing to do with the topic?

On page 111, Carran, you say:[448] "Now, in every way, I am going to defend my claim that the words of my *Lyra* are undoubtedly true, namely that in the year [1644]" (this is the year which you mistakenly indicate in your *olla podrida*, but the correct one is 644)[449] "the Irish fell into such a severe degree of barbarousness and ignorance that their state was in complete disarray."[450]

Nobody will believe your promises any longer, Carran, after you have deceived the readers so many times. Therefore, put forward a new support, if you have any, by which you can strengthen what you say against the testimony of Bede the Venerable in Book III, Chapter 27 of his *Historia gentis Anglorum*[451] (on whose authority Bruodinus relied when definitely defeating you in Book V, Chapter 6, page 806).

4. On page 112, you say: "I cite from a statement of Bruodinus himself; in Book V, Chapter 14 he says: 'and then, after the situation became confused across the kingdom, those universities[452] were subverted by the Danes,[453] and scholars were dispersed.'"

If you use an argument *ad hominem*,[454] Carran, where is its consequence? It is the following. You say: "How can a fine liberal education flourish in such a kingdom, where there are no universities?

politae literae vigere possunt? & consequenter ex Bruodini dictis Hiberni tunc erant barbari, & Bruodinus sibi contradicit."

"Spectatum admissi risum teneatis amici?"

Carrane mi, argumento tali logico digno qualis tu es, in quo nec antecedens est aut consequens, ridicule conaris Bedam & Bruodinum refutare tuaque figmenta confirmare. O he Carrane, dic amabo: num, praevalentibus tot annis per Moraviam aliasque haereditarias Caesaris provincias Suecis, Silesitae & Moravi in barbariem & ignorantiam lapsi sunt? Respondes (si non amore veritatis, saltem timore procerum & incolarum illarum nobilium provinciarum) quod non; & tamen Carrane per decursum tot annorum nulla fuit in illis duabus provinciis Universitas aut Academia Catholica, quae non fuisset eversa & cujus studiosi non fuissent dissipati; non sequitur itaque (nisi in tua forte Carrane dialectica) ex hoc antecedenti Universitates per bella eversae sunt & studiosi dissipati, ergo Hiberni tunc fuerunt barbari. Baculus in angulo.

Jam centum Carrane & plures anni fluxere, a quo in Anglia, Hibernia & Scotia Universitates omnes Catholicae eversae & studiosi Catholicae doctrinae dissipati sunt; hoc tamen non effecit ut Catholici utriusque regni in barbariem sint lapsi aut ignorantiam. Imo Carrane per Europam notum est quod hoc jam elapso saeculo, quo haeretici dominantur in illis regionibus, viri tot praeclari, saeculares & diversorum ordinum religiosi, moribus, vita & doctrina excellentes fuerunt & defacto sunt, ut vix plures fuerint florentibus Catholicis Universitatibus in illis regnis.

Quomodo ergo Carrane ex Bruodini verbis tu probare te posse putas tua figmenta, nimirum "quod anno 644. in tantam barbariem & ignorantiam lapsi sunt Hiberni, ut nulla prorsus politia apud ipsos viguerit"? Nisi Hibernia proh fat<a> fuisset ab haereticis oppressa,

And consequently, according to what Bruodinus says, the Irish at that time were barbarians, and Bruodinus contradicts himself."

> "If you were allowed to see this, my friends, could you restrain from laughing?"[455]

My dear Carran, with an argument worthy of such a logician as you are, in which there is neither an antecedent nor a consequence, you try to refute Bede and Bruodinus, and to strengthen your fabrications. Ho there! Carran, please, tell me: in so many years during which the Swedes have been exercising their power across Moravia and the other hereditary provinces of the emperor, have the people of Silesia and Moravia fallen into barbarousness and ignorance perhaps?[456] Your answer shall be no (if not for the sake of truth, at least for fear of the leading men and the inhabitants of those noble provinces). Nonetheless, Carran, in the course of so many years there was not a single Catholic university or academy in those two provinces, that was not subverted and whose scholars were not dispersed. Accordingly – unless one follows your dialectic, Carran – the fact that universities were subverted because of the wars and the scholars were dispersed, and that therefore the Irish were barbarians at that time, are not consequences of this logical antecedent. *Baculus est in angulo.*

One hundred years and more have already passed, Carran, from when all Catholic universities were subverted and scholars of Catholic doctrine were dispersed in England, Ireland and Scotland. This, however, did not entail that the Catholics of either kingdom fell into barbarousness or ignorance. As a matter of fact, Carran, it is commonly known across Europe that in this century, which is already passing away, during which the heretics have been dominating over those regions, the number of distinguished secular priests and clerics of different orders, who excelled in customs, lifestyle and learning, was – and, indeed, still is – so high, that there were hardly more in those kingdoms at the time when the Catholic universities were flourishing.

So, Carran, how do you think you can use Bruodinus' words to demonstrate your fabrications, namely that "in the year 644 the Irish fell into such a severe degree of barbarousness and ignorance that their state was in complete disarray"? If Ireland had not been under

Carrane, quantumvis <Amasis> & tenebrio, adhuc tuo sanguine forte debuisses abluere sordes & scelera, quibus inique illam diffamas & conspurcas.

5. Pergis consequenter, Carrane, ut afflictam patriam tuam magis affligere & diffamare valeres; & laboras fol. 112. & 113. ut authoritate Lombardi & nescio cujus Speeder haeretici probare possis defacto Hibernos esse barbaros. At mi Carrane, una hyrundo non facit ver: fateor enim te Hibernum esse & quidem barbarum, per hoc tamen concedere non possum ob authoritatem illorum duorum, qui fabulas more tuo narrant, Hibernicam gentem, quam illi duo denigrare conantur, incivilem esse. Lombardus fundat se in bulla Adriani IV., per quam ignoranter putat dominium Regni Hiberni Henrico II. fuisse traditum, ob causas & motiva in subreptitia illa bulla assignata. Bruodinus ostendit motiva illa fuisse ficta & falsa, & consequenter Lombardi authoritas & fundamentum supra labilem arenam positum nihil probat: nam Adrianus IV. non dedit nec dare potuit dominium regni alieni (in quo fides Catholica & ritus Romanae Ecclesiae tam bene illius temporibus ac in Gallia vel Anglia viguit) Henrico secundo.

Adde quod Henricus II. nunquam de occupanda Hibernia cogitavit antequam in succursum adulteri Lageniae Principis permisit Geraldinos, Stephenson & alios in Hiberniam navigare. Sed Adrianus IV. fuit mortuus 6 adminimum annis antequam succursus venit; imo, antequam Dermitius ô Morphei, Lageniae Princeps, Deforgillam Breffiniae Principis uxorem rapuit, <h>aut succursum petiit ab Henrico II. Ergo Adrianus IV. Carrane non dedit Henrico II. Dominium Regni Hiberniae sub ullis conditionibus, & consequenter bulla quae Adriani IV. nomine circumfertur subreptitia est & ficta.

Hoc argumento (inter alia) prostravit Bruodinus loco a te ante citato Sanderum, Lombardum, & omnes alios quantumvis alias

the oppression of the heretics (alas the Fates!), perhaps you, Carran, a true Amasis and a trickster,[457] should still be washing off with your blood the filthy and evil crimes with which you unjustly defame and pollute that nation.

5. You proceed accordingly, Carran, so as to put yourself in the condition of further afflicting your homeland, which is already afflicted, and defaming it; and on pages 112 and 113 you take pains to be able to prove, with the authority of Lombard and of a certain Speeder,[458] a heretic I have never heard about, that the Irish people are actually barbarians. But, my dear Carran, one swallow does not make a spring,[459] in fact, I admit that you are Irish and, indeed, a barbarian, but nevertheless, by doing so, I cannot concede, on the ground of the authority of those two men who narrate fables after your fashion, that the Irish nation, which those two try to defame, is uncivilised. Lombard grounds his arguments in the bull of Adrian IV, on the basis of which he mistakenly believes that the dominium over the kingdom of Ireland had been handed to Henry II for the motives and reasons indicated in that surreptitious bull. Bruodinus shows that those reasons were fictitious and false, and therefore Lombard's authority and argumentative basis, which is grounded in shifting sands, proves nothing. For Adrian IV did not assign, nor could he assign, to Henry II the dominion over a foreign kingdom (in which the Catholic faith and the rite of the Roman Church was so strong and alive in his time, in France as well as in England).

Add to this that Henry II never thought about occupying Ireland sooner than when he allowed the Fitzgeralds, the Stephensons[460] and others to sail to Ireland to offer assistance to the adulterous prince of Leinster. But Adrian IV had been dead for at least 6 years by the time the assistance arrived[461] – actually,[462] he did not ask for Henry II's help before Dermot MacMurrough, prince of Leinster, kidnapped Derbfhorgaill,[463] the wife of the prince of Bréifne.[464] Therefore, Carran, under no conditions did Adrian IV give Henry II the dominion over the kingdom of Ireland; accordingly, the bull that circulates under the name of Adrian IV is surreptitious and a forgery.[465]

With this proof (among other evidence) Bruodinus, in the passage you cited above, won the argumentative battle against Sander, Lombard and all other historians who, albeit very eminent as far

praeclaros historicos qui scripserunt "Henricum II., postquam diversa Hiberniae loca jam occupasset, accepisse ab Adriano dominium Regni Hiberniae." Si tu, Carrane, tua falce vales Bruodini argumentum secare & enervare, tuas praedicabimus militares vires; interim rogo te, si nos Hibernos vis probare esse barbaros, utaris aliis mediis quam ex supposititia Adriani Bulla hactenus assumpsisti, alias tuos latratus nullus curabit aut imposturis credet. Sed haec missa faciamus, ut tuas ulterius impertinentias enucleare possimus.

< >Jam Carrane fol. 114 in medium adducis mensale illud & vulgare SS. Trinitatis doctoris Augustini (explosis prius more tuo, tot convitiis in Bruodinum) distichon:

"Quisquis amat dictis absentum rodere vitam
hanc mensam vetitam noverit esse sibi."

Cur, detractorum facile princeps Carrane, porrigis adversario arma quibus te, renitente tua falce, ferire possit? Accipias te rogo parum per nasum, & depraehendes neminem hodie esse aut inter Catholicos sacerdotes ab uno saeculo fuisse in arte detrahendi, calumniandi & diffamandi te doctiorem & consequenter minus dignum Augustinia mensa. Emenda igitur te primo, & postea alium doce: nam

"Turpe est doctori cum culpa redarguit ipsum."

Eodem, Carrane, fol. puerili tua connectione & stylo haec subdis: "nam est certum quod Pater Bruodinus ex mera ambitione in me in suo *Hiberniae Comitatus* libro inseruit ad meam tamen imitationem: nam" (qualis Carrane connectio?) "eorum quae vera scripsit, sane nihil habet praeter meae historiae spicilegium, & tamen ingratus est sicut cuculus, quia nullus Franciscanus ante me invenit" (esne tu, Carrane, Franciscanus?) "istum de Hibernia exarandi" ("errandi"

as the rest is concerned, wrote that "Henry II, after he had already occupied various territories of Ireland, received from Adrian the dominium over the kingdom of Ireland."[466] If you, Carran, are strong enough to cut and enervate Bruodinus' arguments with your sickle, we shall proclaim your military skills; until then, if you want to prove that we Irish people are barbarians, please use means other than those to which you have resorted so far on the basis of Adrian's spurious bull; otherwise, nobody will care about your barking, or believe your fabrications. But let us stop bothering ourselves about these things, so that we can fully examine your irrelevant statements even further.

Now,[467] Carran, in the middle of page 114 (after hooting so many taunts against Bruodinus, in your usual manner) you cite that common saying of Augustine, doctor of the holy and sacred Trinity, a couplet which he had inscribed on his dining table:[468]

> "Whoever loves gnawing at the life of absent people
> be aware that this dining table is forbidden to him."

Why, Carran, do you, who are unquestionably the first and foremost of disparagers, offer your opponent the weapons with which he could strike you, while your sickle hesitates? Do not be oversensitive,[469] I beg you, and you will understand that there is nobody today, or there has been nobody amongst the Catholic priests for a century, who is or was more learned than you in the art of disparaging, slandering and defaming, and who is or was therefore less worthy[470] of Augustine's dining table. So, correct your own mistakes first, and then be a teacher to someone else; for

> "it is shameful for a learned man when he is to be blamed for a mistake."[471]

In the same page, Carran, with your childish logic and style, you add these remarks:[472] "it is in fact certain that Fr Bruodinus inserted out of sheer ambition towards me in his book entitled *Hiberniae Comitatus*,[473] though aiming at my imitation: for" (what kind of connection is this, Carran?) "of those things which he wrote in truth, by all means he has nothing besides a harvest of sparse elements of my history,[474] and nevertheless he is unpleasant like a cuckoo, because no Franciscan before me" (are you a Franciscan, Carran?) "has found such a way

debeas dicere) "modum, & ex mera ambitione Bruodinus secutus est meam formam," & c.

6. Qui bene intelligit hanc tuam grammaticalem Carrane ignorantiam spiritum ut habeat deorum necesse est, qualem me non habere fateor; exenterabo tamen verba tua in quantum profunditatem sermonis tui intelligo, ne sine debita nota pereant. "Ex mera," inquis Carrane, "ambitione in me" & c.

Ambitio, mi homo, "inordinatus est appetitus laudis & honoris." Tu nec gloria, laude, aut honore adhuc coronatus es: imo qui intima cordis tui arcana penetrarunt palam afferunt, si diceres te praesbyterum esse rudem & a bonarum artium & scientiarum studio a natura alienum, quod more tibi consueto, non errares; non tibi igitur persuadeas quod R.P. Bruodinus aut suae conditionis religiosus ullus honoratus & doctus invideat tibi miserias tuas aut illas ambit. Dormi igitur secure, nam praeter Thrasonicam jactantiam in te, crede mihi, nihil est quod admirari aut appeti posset.

"In suo" (inquis Carrane) "*Comitatus Hiberniae* libro ad meam tamen imitationem." Carrane, nullum scripsit Bruodinus de comitatibus Hiberniae librum, sed de illis comitatibus egit lib. 5. sui *Propugnaculi*, quo (ne Hibernorum res gestae oblitterarentur aut eorum facta interciderint) veridicam regni historiam, incipiendo a prima colonia quae post diluvium illam occupavit, usque ad nostra tempora scripsit; quam historiam ante ipsum in lucem nullus Latine unquam veridice dedit. Quid jam, Carrane, ad tuam imitationem in hac sua narratione inseruit? Non respondes sed, tanquam si esses caecus, sine consideratione ad superiora tua verba subdis: "nam eorum quae vera scripsit, sane nihil habet praeter meae historiae spicilegium."

7. Carrane, non historam, sed fabularium ex Spensero, Hanmero, Camdeno, Morisono, Davisono, Campione, Barklio, Spendero,

of making a report" ('making a mistake', you should say)[475] "about Ireland; and out of sheer ambition Bruodinus followed my model", etc.

6. Undoubtedly, Carran, whoever is able to understand properly what you say in this ungrammatical fashion of yours must be gifted with a divine inspiration of a kind which I confess I do not possess. I will disembowel your words anyway, as far as I understand the gist of your discourse, lest they be left without the censorial mark they deserve. You say, Carran: "out of sheer ambition towards me", etc.

Ambition, my fellow, is "a confused appetite for praise and honour."[476] You have been crowned neither with glory, nor with praise or honour so far. Indeed, those who penetrated the innermost secrets of your heart publicly assert that you would not be wrong if you said that you are an unskilled presbyter, who is alien to the cultivation of the good arts and sciences in a manner which is typical of you. Therefore, do not persuade yourself that Rev. Fr Bruodinus, or any honoured and learned cleric of his condition, envies you for your miseries, or feels ambition for them. So, sleep without preoccupations; for, trust me, there is nothing in you which he could admire or desire, apart from Thrasonical[477] vainglory.

You say, Carran: "in his book entitled *Hiberniae Comitatus*, though aiming at my imitation." Bruodinus did not write any book entitled *Hiberniae Comitatus*, Carran, but he dealt with those *comitatus* [that is, counties] in Book V of his *Propugnaculum*, in which (lest the deeds of the Irish people be forgotten or their achievements falsified) he wrote down the true history of the kingdom, starting from the first colony which was founded in that territory after the flood, until our own times; and nobody before him ever shed light on this history, speaking the truth and writing in Latin. Now, Carran, what did he insert in this report of his, with the purpose of imitating you? You do not answer, but, as if you were blind, you inconsiderately add these words to your previous ones: "for of those things which he wrote in truth, by all means he has nothing besides a harvest of sparse elements of my history."

7. Paid by you, Carran, the writer of your *olla podrida* – or, as you call it, *Lyra Hibernica* – did not come up with a history, but with a

Lindano & hujusmodi aliis putridi spiritus pseudo-historicis Calvinistis expensis tui marsupii extraxit & male in unum consuit scriptor tuae *Ollopadridae*, seu ut tu loqueris *Lyrae Hibernicae*.

Historiam, Carrane, (quae vitae est memoria, & veritatis nuntia) qui scribit debet vir esse bonus, prudens, ac propositi tenax (ut aeviternum Austriacae domus ornamentum Carolus V. teste Surio in ejus vita ait, dum Sleidani haeretici historiam reprobasset). In te autem nemo non notat qualitates illas in gradu esse remisso; noli ergo gloriari de historia, quam nondum publicasti.

Nec etiam oro dicas quod R. Pater Bruodinus spicilegium historiae tuae collegit; in tuo agro, mi vir, non seminasti bonum semen, sic in illo frumentariae spicae non creverunt, & consequenter, postquam tua falce resecasti messem malorum fructuum tuorum, qui a tergo tibi se inclinarunt non spicas, sed tribulos, urticas, zizania & spinas invenerunt. Quare vacuis manibus domim reversi sunt; tandem messem tuam non incongrue illorum unus, ex stirpe poetarum, sequenti disticho descripsit:

> "Quod metis est lolium; sevisti pessima: quidni?
> Cui multum bibere est vivere & esse nimis."

Ulterius Carrane usque ad fol. 116. nihil habes notatu dignum, praeter lepidum Latinismum, scommata & plurima mendacia quae ridentur abomnibus doctis. Demum, fol. 116, subdis: "Itaque aequus consideret lector, quid non Bruodini improba fecerit lingua? Cujus verborum vulnera in me satis expertus sum. Imo etiam in suo gloriatur libro" (o Carraniana connexio & eloquentia!) "se ligasse me reste," & c.

8. Liget te Carrane quispiam alius, non P. Bruodinus aut alius ipsi similis. Lectorem toties jam decepisti tuis imposturis, sic non

collection of fables that he took from Spenser,[478] Hanmer,[479] Camden,[480] Moryson,[481] Davies,[482] Campion,[483] Barclay,[484] Spender,[485] Lindanus[486] and other similar Calvinist pseudo-historians of rotten spirit, and which he stitched together into a single work.

Whoever writes a history, Carran, which consists in narrating the memories of a life and reporting the truth, ought to be an honest man, wise and tenacious in his intentions (as Charles V, the eternal ornament of the Austrian household, said, according to what Surius[487] attested in the biography of him, when he was condemning the history written by the heretic Sleidanus[488]). However, nobody fails to notice that you are very poor in those qualities; therefore, do not boast about a history which you never published.

Also, please do not say that Rev. Fr Bruodinus put together a harvest of sparse elements of your history.[489] In your field you did not sow a good seed, my fellow; and so, wheat stalks did not grow in it. Therefore, after you reaped the crop of your bad fruits with your sickle, the harvesters who bent down behind your back did not find heads of wheat, but leaves of tackweed,[490] nettle, darnel and tares. Thus, they went back home empty-handed. At last, a member of a family of poets described your harvest not unsuitably in the following couplet:

> "What you reap is ryegrass. You sowed seeds of terrible quality: what did you expect differently?
>
> Even existing is a huge result for a person for whom drinking a lot is the same as living."[491]

Further down, Carran, until page 116, you report nothing worthy of being noted, besides an elegant use of pseudo-Latin, some taunts, and a great number of lies, which are laughed at by all learned readers. Finally, on page 116, you add: "Therefore, the impartial reader should consider this: what did Bruodinus' wicked tongue not dare to fabricate? But I have sufficiently experienced the wounds of his words against me. Indeed, in his book he even brags of having tied me up with a rope" (what a logical sequence and eloquence typical of you, Carran!), etc.

8. May someone else tie you up, Carran, not Fr Bruodinus or any other man similar to him. Since you have already deceived the

dignabitur amplius tua considerare figmenta. Quo libro, Carrane, capite vel folio Pater Bruodinus dicit quod te reste ligaverit? Libro forte nullo, folio fracto, capite raso? Legi & relegi omnia Bruodini opera philosophica, theologica & historica, & non inveni in omnibus umbram illorum quae tu sine verecundia, Carrane, adducis verborum. Et si alius in Bruodini operibus verba illa invenerit, caecus sum ego & fide indignus. At quid itaque voluntarie mentiris & calumniaris? Aut Aesopianam aliam folio 117. de impatientia unius in Gallia Franciscani fabulam in medium adducis? Sed quid inaniter te interrogo, aut cum homine disputo potentiore ad calumniandum quam disserendum?

Laboras frustra, mi grammatista Carrane, fol. 18. ut ex Theologis, quos nunquam legisti, ostenderes R. Patrem Bruodinum obligari ad restitutionem tuae famae quam non Bruodini scriptis sed tuis demeritis laesam agnoscit mundus.

9. Tandem cum furore & vecordia fol. 119. in haec prorumpis verba: "Jam" (inquis Carrane) "ostendam quomodo Bruodinus suum generalem commissarium callide deceperit, ipsum fraudulenter informando de suo libro, cui serio commissarius credidit, mimine tamen sciens enormia libri mendacia & crassissimos errores; tamen eundem temere sine ulteriori inquisitione approbavit."

Intemperiis quibusdam agitatum te, Carrane, vel certe a bile in praecipitem maniam datum fuisse multi credunt, dum tam insolenti ne dicam impudenti ore ausus es reverendissimum Patrem Joannem à Molino, sacri sui ordinis per Germaniam superiorem regnaque adjacentia generalem commissarium & augustissimae Romanae imperatricis regnantis conscientiae moderatorem, temeritate arguere. Dignissimum illum, Carrane, Patrem non solum in Caesarea aula, sed etiam per omnia Hispaniarum regna ob religiosae vitae probitatem,

reader with your impostures so many times, he will not deem your fabrications worthy of further consideration. In which book, chapter or page, Carran, does Fr Bruodinus say that he tied you up with a rope? Perhaps in no book, in a broken page, or in a torn chapter? I read and read over again all of Bruodinus' works of philosophy, theology and history, and in them I found no trace of those words which you, Carran, shamelessly cite. And if another reader shall find those words in Bruodinus' works, this would imply that I am blind and unworthy of being trusted. But why, then, do you deliberately tell lies and make false accusations? Or why, in the middle of page 117, do you put forward another fable comparable to Aesop's, about a certain Franciscan's inability to endure suffering? But why am I unavailingly asking questions of you, or why am I arguing with a man who is more capable of slandering someone than discussing a topic?

In vain, my dear student of elementary grammar, on page 118 you take pains to demonstrate that, according to theologians you never read, Rev. Fr Bruodinus is under the obligation of restoring your reputation. However, Carran, the world acknowledges your reputation as damaged not by Bruodinus' writings, but by your own demerits.

9. At last, with rage and madness, on page 119 you burst out in these words: "Now" (you say, Carran) "I will show how Bruodinus cunningly deceived his general commissioner,[492] giving him false information about his book, information which the commissioner earnestly believed, knowing nothing of the huge lies and gross mistakes of the book. In spite of these, he rashly gave his approval to it, without enquiring any further."

Many readers, Carran, believe that you were troubled by some form of folly, or surely led to violent madness by anger, while you dared to pronounce inconsiderate accusations against Johannes à Molino;[493] for you talked so arrogantly, not to say impudently, against a most respectable father, general commissioner of his holy order across Upper Germany and the neighbouring kingdoms,[494] and spiritual director of her majesty, the reigning Roman empress.[495] Without fear of punishment, Carran, do you dare to insult with such a serious abuse, with no reason, that most worthy father, who was beloved, relished and well-accepted by princes and other noblemen, by the commoners as well as by the clerics? He was so admired on

morum gravitatem, doctrinae excellentiam, familiae antiquitatem, & in rebus agendis prudentiam saepe probatam, principibus & aliis proceribus, populo & clero charum, gratum & acceptum, audes tu impune convicio tam insigni sine causa injuriare? Patrem, inquam Carrane, illum, quem unicum e multis praeclarissimis ac doctissimis seraphicae religionis subjectis sibi propositis magnus ille sanctae memoriae Hispaniarum monarcha Philippus in directorem conscientiae ac spiritualem consolatorem Caesareae tunc sponsae, Margaritae, Hispaniarum serenissimae infantis, elegit, audes tu tam temere arguere & repraehendere?

Cum superos Carrane non videris timere, mirum <non> est te cogitasse quod impune tibi < > succederet tantum virum in tali constitutum Viennae authoritate sine causa laedere. Sed supposuisti prudenter, Carrane, quod reverendissimi Patris à Molino sicut & aliorum bonorum virorum non solum sit bene facere, sed mala patienter audire; & dubio procul etiam intellexisti dignissimum illum Patrem non parum participare de natura & humore patientissimi Atheniensium philosophi Socratis, qui cum impetuose ab improbo quodam (Carranianae farinae) conviciatore calce percuteretur, monereturque ut nebulonem repercuteret, "Quid?" respondit Socrates, "si me asinus calce petivisset, num etiam illum calce repercutere deberem?" Has ob rationes te fuisse ausum in tantum latrare virum, Carrane, mihi facile persuadeo.

Sed videamus quod te argumentum, Carrane, in tam insolentem errorem praecipitem dedit. "Iam" (inquis fol. 119.) "ostendam quomodo Bruodinus suum generalem commissarium callide deceperit, ipsum fraudulenter informando de suo libro, cui serio commissarium credidit," & c.

Non semel, Carrane, te monui quod lectores tuis promissis amplius non moventur, & merito; nam toties jam tuis promissionibus eos decepisti, sic tibi amplius nihil credunt. Quare non ostendis Carrane juxta promissa, quomodo P. Bruodinus reverendissimum suum

account of the honesty of his pious life, the severity of his customs, the excellence of his erudition, the antiquity of his family and his wisdom in fulfilling his duties. This wisdom was often put to the test not only in the emperor's court, but also across all kingdoms of the Spanish Empire.[496] Do you dare, Carran, to accuse and blame with such a lack of consideration that Father – I say – whom Philip, king of Spain,[497] chose, the only man out of the most learned subjects of the seraphic religion who were offered as candidates to him, as spiritual director and comforter of the soul of Margaret, the most serene daughter of Spain, who was the emperor's wife at that time?

Since you seem to have no fear of those above you, Carran, it is not surprising that you thought that you could get away safely with damaging without a reason a man so important, who was appointed to hold such a position of authority in Vienna.[498] You showed some good sense though, Carran, in supposing that it is customary for Fr à Molino, a most respectable man, just as it is for other good men, not only to do good, but also to listen to insults with tolerance. There is no doubt that you even understood that he, a famous and truly worthy father, shares much of his natural disposition and temper with the philosopher Socrates,[499] the most unyielding of the Athenians. While he was being violently kicked by a certain dishonest reviler (one of your ilk, Carran) and he was being urged to kick the wretch back, Socrates replied: "Why? Suppose that a donkey kicked me: should I retaliate with a kick myself?"[500] I easily persuade myself, Carran, that it is on these grounds that you dared to growl against such a great man.[501]

But let us see which argument, Carran, led you to inconsiderately make such an arrogant mistake. "Now" (you say on page 119) "I will show how Bruodinus cunningly deceived his general commissioner, giving him false information about his book, information which the commissioner earnestly believed", etc.

I have warned you more than once, Carran, that the readers are no longer persuaded by your promises, and for a good reason; for you have already deceived them with your pledges, and therefore they no longer believe you at all. If you can, Carran, why do you not show what you have just promised, namely how Fr Bruodinus deceived his general commissioner, a most reverend man? Or, if you

generalem commissarium decepit, si scis? Vel si non scis, quomodo te non pudet scribere quod jam ostendes modum quo illum decepit? Tu, ut video Carrane, ignavorum hominum more, plus habes verborum quam operae; lingua namque es potens, sed manu debilis; bellator es ore, sed in re ignavum pecus: uno verbo, ut vetus ait adagium, "tibi", mi Carrane, "verba sunt sine penu & pecunia."

"Callide" inquis "& fraudolenter decepit commissarium, ipsum informando de suo libro." Si tu, Carrane, fuisses aliquando reverendissimi Patris commissarii secretarius (prout est R. P. Clemens Schram) vel intimus aliquis amicus, facile nobis persuaderes quod tibi literas subditorum & secreta suorum Patrum negotia communicasset. At dignissimo illi Patri tua vita cum vix sis verbum locutus, quis non judicabit te os habere supra modum garrulum & mendax, dum promittis te ostensurum modum quo Bruodinus suum decepit superiorem, & nihil praestas?

"Commissarius," inquis, "serio credidit, minime sciens enormia libri mendacia, & tamen eundem temere sine ulteriori inquisitione approbavit."

Tu mi Carrane pro viribus in hoc tuo famoso libello laborasti gratis ut P. Bruodini operum errores ostendere posses; sed malo tuo, nam oleum simul & operam (ut patet clare ex refutatione omnium tuarum calumniarum per decursum hujus opusculi) perdidisti. Nisi tu, Carrane, in arte scribendi, puer esses, & quod haereticorum more libellos expensis tui marsupii a quodam ignorante grammatista ("similes habent labra lactucas") sub tuo nomine scriptos acatholicos, sine omni approbatione doctorum & ordinariorum facultate, imprimi semper curasses, non ignorares commissarii generalis & aliorum similium superiorum consuetudinem & obligationem; sciresque distinguere inter librorum censores, seu approbatores, & superiores, qui non solent ("disce puer virtutem ex me verumque laborem") libros

cannot, how do you not feel ashamed for writing that now you will show how he deceived him? As I see it, Carran, you have more words than results to show, just like all lazy men. In fact, you are strong with your tongue, but weak with your hand. You are a fighter with your mouth, but in practice you are a cowardly sheep. In a nutshell, as the ancient proverb says, my dear Carran, "you have words with neither provisions nor money."[502]

"[Bruodinus]" – you say – "deceived the commissioner by cunningly cheating him when he gave him information about his book." If you had even been the secretary of the most respectable father commissioner (a position currently held by Rev. Fr Clemens Schram[503]) or a close friend of his, Carran, you would easily persuade us that he shared with you the letters of his subordinates, as well as the secret affairs of the fathers under his jurisdiction.

But since you have hardly exchanged a single word with that truly reverend father in your entire life, who will not conclude that you have the excessively prattling mouth of a liar, while you promise that you will show how Bruodinus deceived his superior, and then you do not keep your promise at all?

You say: "the commissioner earnestly believed [Bruodinus' words], knowing nothing of the huge lies of the book. In spite of these, he rashly gave his approval to it, without enquiring any further."

Without recompense, my dear Carran, in this infamous pamphlet of yours you strove as hard as you could to find a way to point at mistakes in Fr Bruodinus' works. It was unfortunate for you though, for you wasted oil and effort at the same time[504] (as is clearly shown by the refutation of all of your false accusations in the course of this short book). If your skills in the art of writing were not those of a child, and if you had ever taken care not to publish pamphlets which are not in line with the Catholic religion and which some ignorant student of elementary grammar, paid by you ("like lips, like lettuce"),[505] wrote under your name in the manner of the heretics, without all necessary approval from the experts and permission from the ordinaries, you would not be unaware of the custom and duty of the general commissioner and of other superiors with a similar role. Also, you would know how to distinguish between the censors of books and the superiors. The former give their approval for books,

approbare; sed supposita doctorum virorum censura & ordinarii licentia facultatem dant libros imprimendi. Solitum hunc stylum adamussim servavit reverendissimus Pater commissarius generalis quando P. Bruodino facultatem dedit publicandi suos labores, ut tu, nisi caecus esses, ex hac P. Bruodino a reverendissimo P. commissario data facultate, quam in initio libri ipsius impressam videmus, colligere sine labore poteras:

> "Fr. Joannes à Molino Navarrete, & c. P. F. Antonio Bruodino & c. Nolentes te indefessi laboris tui debito praemio carere, concedimus vigore praesentium facultatem & licentiam ut opus a te conscriptum & intitulatum *Propugnaculum Catholicae veritatis, Pars prima in 5. libros partita,* juxta constitutiones apostolicas & nostri seraphici ordinis statuta revisum ac approbatum, servatis servandis, imprimatur & ad usum fidelium typis publicis evulgetur. In cujus fidem praesentes manu nostra subscriptas dedimus Ebersdorfii 7. Septembris, anno 1668."

Quid, mi Carrane, si sanae mentis sis homo, in hac reverendissimi Patris commissarii generalis facultate Bruodino data repraehesione dignum invenire poteras? An non igitur te pudeat quod effrenata conviciandi libidine in tantum virum, nulla data causa, tam injuriose inveheris? Sed haec missa faciamus.

10. Jam fol. 120. Carrane sacerdotalis decoris immemor solito agitatus vertiginis spiritu falce tua alios praeclaros viros de Deo, patria & Caesare bene meritos ferire conaris; Patrem demum Bruodinum "bardum," "Sphingem," "insulsum," "versutum", "nequitiarum architectum" & c. tanquam si a te mens & prudentia longe abessent,

while the latter generally do not have the duty to give their approval ("Boy, learn virtue from me, and true work"),[506] but rather to authorise publication, after the learned experts have exercised their censorship and the ordinary has provided permission. The most respectable father general commissioner accurately complied with this customary *modus operandi,* when he gave Fr Bruodinus the authorisation to publish his works, as you could have concluded without any effort, were you not blind, from this authorisation given to Fr Bruodinus by the most respectable father commissioner, which we see printed at the beginning of the book itself:

> "Friar Johannes à Molino of Navarre, etc. sends his greetings to his brother Fr Antonius Bruodinus, etc. Since we do not want you to be without the reward you deserve for your industrious work, by the power we hold we grant the authorisation and permission to print and divulge through public publication the work written by you and entitled *Propugnaculum Catholicae Veritatis,* first part, divided into five books, having observed what is required, so that any of the faithful may make use of the volume. Our decision comes after we revised the work according to the apostolic constitutions and the statutes of our seraphic order, and we approved it. To attest to the trustworthiness of the work, we attach the present document signed below by our own hand in Ebersdorf[507] on 7 September 1668."

If you are a man in control of his own mind, Carran, what could you find in this authorisation given to Bruodinus by the most respectable father general commissioner, that could possibly deserve criticism? Or, indeed, do you not feel ashamed for having assailed so great a man in such an offensive way, without reason and driven by an unrestrained desire to insult? But let us stop bothering ourselves about these things.

10. Now, Carran, forgetful of a priest's decency, on page 120 you try to hit with your sickle, which you whirl around driven by dizziness as usual, other illustrious men who deserved honour for their actions in favour of God, their homeland, and the emperor. Eventually, with anger, you call Fr Bruodinus "a bard", "a sphinx", "a fool", "a cheater",

iracunde vocas. Quae quia convitia sunt, contemptum non anatomiam merentur. Tantum videamus tuas de doctissimis Pragensibus Professoribus censuras. "Ceteri vero," inquis Carrane, "approbatores simili modo erant delusi, alias famosum scandalosumque librum non approbassent," & c.

Carrane mi, non parva injuria inuris tantos tamque doctissimos viros qui P. Bruodini opera approbarunt, dum garrula & effrenata tua lingua audes scribere illos approbasse famosum & scandalosum librum quem non legerunt.

Admodum R. Pater Maximilianus Reiohenberger e Societate Jesu sacrosanctae theologiae doctor ejusdemque facultatis in Universitate Carolo Ferdinandea senior & decanus religiosus vita & doctrina clarus, ideoque omnibus per totum regnum charus, caeco tuo Carrane judicio librum famosum, quem non legit, approbavit? Cui est credibile quod affirmas?

Admodum R. Dominum Wenceslaus Samuel Hattas, prothonotarius apostolicus, Archi Episcopalis seminarii dignissimus tunc rector, vir fundamentaliter doctus, qui jam duos concionum tomos non sine legentium magna utilitate in lucem dedit, te Carrane teste famam suam maculavit approbando scandalosum quem non legit librum? Quis credet?

R.P. Guilielmus Antonius Brauzeck, Ordinis Min. Strict. Observantiae SS. theologiae Lector Jubilatus, qui postquam Pragae in Regio Nivensi Conventu, & in Archi-Episcopali seminario per tot continuos annos theologiam ac respective philosophiam professus fuisset, ac integrum philosophiae cursum (concurrente suo collega, R. P. Ernesto Schaff, sacrosanctae theologiae Generali Lectore ac modo actuali almae suae provinciae Bohemiae Diffinitore dignissimo,

"an architect of wicked plans", etc., as if your intellectual faculties and good sense were far away from you. But since these are insults, they deserve contempt, not dissection. Let us only consider your severe criticism of the professors of Prague, men of great learning. You say, Carran: "In truth, the rest of those in charge of giving their approval [to works submitted for publication] were deceived in a similar way, otherwise they would not have given their approval to [Bruodinus'] infamous and sinful book", etc.

My dear Carran, with your prattling and unrestrained tongue you dare to write that those professors gave their approval to an infamous and sinful book without ever reading it. By stating this, the offence with which you are charging men so important and of such great learning, who gave their approval to Fr Bruodinus' works, is not a trivial one.

According to your blind judgement, Carran, the Adm. Rev. Maximiliam Reichenberger,[508] member of the Society of Jesus, doctor of holy and sacred theology and senior cleric and dean of the same faculty at the Charles-Ferdinand University, a man who is famous for his erudition and, for this reason, esteemed by everyone throughout the whole kingdom, gave his approval to an infamous book without reading it? Whom can your words sound credible to?

According to your testimony, Carran, the Adm. Rev. Master Vaclav Samuel Hatass,[509] a protonotary apostolic who was the rector of the archiepiscopal seminary at that time, a position he truly deserved, a man of deep erudition, who has already produced two volumes of orations, which are very useful for the readers, stained his own reputation by giving his approval to a sinful book without reading it? Who will believe this?

The Rev. Fr Wilhelm Anton Brauczek,[510] of the Order of the Friars Minor of Strict Observance, *Lector Jubilatus* of holy and sacred theology,[511] taught theology as well as philosophy for so many continuous years in Prague in the Royal Convent of the Snows[512] as well as in the archiepiscopal seminary, and he wrote and published a complete course book of philosophy in laconic style (together with his colleague, Rev. Fr Ernst Schaff,[513] general lector of holy and sacred theology and, recently, acting *definitor* of Bohemia, his bountiful province, a role he truly deserved, whom you, Carran, shamelessly

quem tu inverecunde Carrane cum aliis carpis) laconice in lucem edidisset. Romam anno 1664. una cum suo olim Professore, reverendo P. Bruodino, petiit ibique infra octavam Pentecostes in Ecclesia Aracaelitana, praesentibus universis Generalis Ordinis capituli vocalibus, eminentissimo Principe Cardinali Columna (qui Caesaris vices sustinuit) & 50 praelatis, theologicas theses, praesidente sibi Patre Bruodino, augustissimo Romanorum Imperatori Leopoldo dedicatas, cum tanto applausu ita defendit, quod non solum sibi & patriae suae Bohemiae in facie Ordinis honorem fecerit, verum etiam eminentissimum Principem Columnam illo suo actu moverit ad scribendum Caesari, Principi de Ausberg, supremo Cancellario Regni Bohemiae, Comiti de Nostitz, & aliquibus aliis ex primis suae Majestatis ministris, in recommendationem P. Brauzek ejusque praesidis Patris Bruodini. Pater hic, cumulo tot meritorum ornatus, te Carrane teste approbavit scandalosum librum quem non legit? Nulli persuadebis <per> hanc tuam imposturam.

R.P. Bernardus Sannig, ejusdem ordinis & provinciae, postquam aliquot annis in Archi Episcopali Pragensi seminario philosophiam & in generali Pragensi studio ad Nives Theologiam cum laude professus fuisset, Romam anno 1667. una cum R. Patre Bruodino, suo olim professore, vocatus ad Comitia Generalia Ordinis inter media universam *Theologiam Scholasticam* Augustissimo Romanorum Imperatori Leopoldo dedicatam in Aede Aracaelitana, praesente serenissimo Principe Cardinali Landgravio Hassie & multis praelatis Romanisque doctissimis professoribus, tam ingeniose defendit (ut in suis ad Caesarem literis testatur serenissimus Princeps), quod patriae, sibi ac suo professori R. P. Bruodino nomen comparaverit inextinguibile. Hic, Carrane, te teste famosum approbavit librum,

slander as you do others). Afterwards, in the year 1664, Fr Brauczek went to Rome together with Rev. Fr Bruodinus, who had once been his professor; and there, in the period of the Octave of Pentecost[514] in the church of the Altar of Heaven,[515] he defended his theological theses, supervised by Fr Bruodinus and dedicated to His Great Majesty Leopold, Emperor of the Romans.[516] He did so in the presence of all vocals of the General Chapter, the most eminent Prince Cardinal Colonna[517] (who acted in the emperor's stead), and fifty prelates; and his success was praised so greatly that not only did he bring honour to himself and his homeland, Bohemia, before the order, but he even inspired the most eminent Prince Colonna to do what he famously did, namely to write recommendation letters for Fr Brauczek and his supervisor, Fr Bruodinus, to the emperor, the prince of Habsburg,[518] to the count of Nostitz,[519] the supreme chancellor of the kingdom of Bohemia, and to some other prime ministers of His Majesty. According to your testimony, Carran, this father, who achieved distinction through the accumulation of so many merits, gave his approval to a sinful book without reading it? With this imposture of yours, you will persuade nobody.

Rev. Fr Bernard Sannig,[520] of the same order and province, taught for several years philosophy at the archiepiscopal seminary of Prague, and theology at the general school of Prague associated with the Church of the Snows, receiving commendation. Afterwards, in the year 1667, he was called to the general meetings of the order in Rome together with Rev. Fr Bruodinus, who had once been his professor. During those meetings, in the presence of the most serene Prince Cardinal Landgrave of Hesse[521] and many prelates and Roman professors of great erudition in the church of the Altar of Heaven, he defended his *Theologia Scholastica*, dedicated to His Great Majesty Leopold, emperor of the Romans; and his arguments during the defence were so clever (as attested by the most serene prince in his letters to the emperor), that he procured immortal renown for himself, his homeland, and his professor, Rev. Fr Bruodinus. According to your testimony, Carran, was this the person who gave his approval to a book, without reading it? Nobody will believe this. With these most worthy fathers whom I have just mentioned, Carran, you behave in a milder and gentler way than you do with Fr Bernardine Clancy,[522]

quem non legit? Hoc nullus credet. Cum his quos jam nominavi dignissimis Patribus mitius & modestius Carrane agis, quam cum reverendo, religiosissimo ac doctissimo Patre Bernardino Clanchy, in quem fol. 121. falcem tuam stringis & effrenatae linguae tuae aculeum dirigis.

11. "Non obstante" (inquis fol. jam citato) "quod unum ex his Bruodini libri approbatoribus, nimirum Reverendum Bernardinum Clachy mirum in modum reprehendo, quia is dolose egit hac in causa; ille enim contra doctorum virorum inhibitionem" (cur non nominas Carrane doctos illos viros, qui R.P. Clanchy monuerunt? Eorum unus vocatur, ut credo, Nullus & alter Nemo) "Bruodini librum approbavit, ut omnes scirent ambos esse ejusdem farinae & ineptitudinis, quia ergo manifeste in oculis omnium constat R. P. Clanchy commenta Bruodini rata habuisse, & sic iniqui approbatione libri peccasse, idcirco eadem poena refutationis in hoc libello contentae, una cum Bruodino perenne torqueatur," & c.

Finem, ut video Carrane, calumniandi & conviciandi innocentes & optimos quosquos viros primo facies, quando infausta mors sua falce, tua renitente sica, lineam illaudabilis vitae tuae secabit. Patrem Bruodinum paulo ante, fol. 120. "insulsum guardianum, versutam & nequam Sphingem in pelle humana palliatam" vocasti; mox vero R. P. Bernardinum Clachy, singulare nostrae patriae Tuomoniae ornamentum, eo quod approbavit Patris Bruodini opera, "dolosum mendaciorum approbatorem, ejusdemque cum P. Bruodino farinae & ineptitudinis hominem" esse dicis.

Non majorem ingrate, Carrane, meo judicio, inuris R. P. Clanchy (a quo multa bona accepisti) tuis calumniis injuram, quam Patri Bruodino contra tuum intentum facis honorem, affirmando quod ejusdem sit cum R. P. Clanchy farinae. Porro ut hoc percipias, necesse est ut seposita ad partem falce tua (Carran id est quod falx), qua prothoplasta tuus, Thomas Carranus, S. Lactino brachium impie secuit & tu triticum simul cum lolio metis, ad sequentia obturatas tuas applices aures.

a truly respectable, deeply religious and extremely learned man, against whom you brandish your sickle and direct the sting of your unrestrained tongue on page 121.

11. On the page I have just mentioned, you state: "Although I blame in particular one of these people who gave their approval to Bruodinus' book, namely Rev. Bernardine Clancy, because he behaved in a fraudulent manner in this matter. For he gave his approval to Bruodinus' book against the restriction set by learned men" (why, Carran, do you not name those learned men who warned Rev. Fr Clancy? One of them, I think, is named 'None' and the other one 'Nobody') "with the result that everybody realised that both are men of the same kind and silliness; for it is crystal clear in everybody's eyes that Rev. Fr Clancy confirmed Bruodinus' fabrications and thus committed a fault by approving an unfair volume. Therefore, may he be forever tortured together with Bruodinus by the same punishment of the refutation contained in this pamphlet,"[523] etc.

As I see, Carran, you will put an end to your slanders and insults against each and every innocent man of the best kind only when inauspicious death will cut the thread of your un-praiseworthy life with her sickle, in spite of your opposition with your dagger. Shortly before, on page 120, you called Fr Bruodinus "a foolish guardian, a cheating and dishonest sphinx clothed in human skin"; and now, immediately after, you say that Rev. Fr Bernardine Clancy, a unique ornament of our homeland Thomond,[524] is "a fraudulent approver of lies, a man of the same kind and silliness as Fr Bruodinus", because he gave his approval to Fr Bruodinus' works.

In my opinion, Carran, the mark of dishonour with which you, through your false accusations, ungratefully brand Rev. Fr Clancy (from whom you received many gifts) is not greater than the honour which you unintentionally bestow upon Fr Bruodinus, by stating that he is a man of the same kind as Rev. Fr Clancy. In order for you to understand this in turn, it is necessary that you lend your plugged ears to the following description, having put aside your sickle ('Carran' means 'sickle'), with which the founding-man of your ancestry, Thomas Carran, impiously cut off the arm of Saint Lachtín, and with which you are cropping wheat together with ryegrass.[525]

R. P. Bernardinus Clanchy, Tuomoniae in Hibernia ex perillustribus antiquissimaeque familiae parentibus, Domino nimirum Constantino Clanchy, multorum dominiorum in comitatu de Clare Toparcha, & Onora Brien (Comitis ó Brien de Insequen proxima consanguinea) natus, Ordinem Seraphicum (postpositis omnibus quae mundus dare poterat) anno salutis 1632. ingressus ac professione emissa, Lovanium anno 1635. venit. Inde, absolutis in Hibernorum S. Antonii Collegio philosophicis & theologicis studiis, moderatorum jussu Viennam Austriae anno 1641. appulit, ibique & Graecii per annos sex almae provinciae Austriae seraphicos alumnos non tam in philosophicis & theologicis quam in moribus & vita religiosa verbo & exemplo instruxit. Tandem anno 1646. a reverendissimo Patre Commissario Generali Commissarius visitator Collegii Pragensis Patrum Hibernorum institutus, Pragam venit; ubi, eo renitente, communi bonorum omnium Patrum voto & postulatione, in Guardianum anno sequenti 1647. electus & confirmatus est. Quod munus ita laudabiliter gessit, ut (non obstantibus quorundam oppositionibus, quibus Deus illius constantiam & patientiam probare voluit) non fuerat inventus qui doctrinam, domesticam disciplinam, aut religiosam illius vitam merito carpere posset.

Finito suo triennali Guardianatus officio, eminentissimus magnae memoriae Princeps Cardinalis ab Harrach, Pragensis Archi Episcopus (qui Reverendum Patrem Clanchy in summa semper veneratione habuit) petiit & a Revendissimo Patre Generali obtinuit, ut Pater Clanchy Primariam celeberrimi sui seminarii Pragensis theologicam cathedram regendam susciperet. Rexit illam cathedram Reverendus Pater Clanchy per 9. continuos annos cum tanta laude & satisfactione omnium, ut ejus inculpabili vita & conversatione religiosa moverit Patres suos anno 1661. ad denuo illum e scholis distrahendum & ad Collegii regimen resumendum.

Praefuit suis Patribus secunda vice in officio guardianatus per triennium cum tanta laude, pace & charitate, ut non posset magis. Absoluto triennio ad seminarii theologicas scholas regendas rediit;

Rev. Fr Bernardine Clancy was born in Thomond, in Ireland, from parents of a very illustrious and ancient family, namely Master Constantine MacClancy, governor of many domains in County Clare, and Onora O'Brien (the closest blood relative to earl O'Brien of Inchiquin). After joining the seraphic order (having disregarded every comfort which the world could offer him) and making his profession of faith in the year 1632, he moved to Louvain in the year 1635. From that city, once he completed his philosophical and theological studies at the Irish College of Saint Anthony,[526] he came to Vienna, Austria, in 1641 by order of his directors, and there as well as in Graz[527] for six years he educated pupils of the bountiful province of Austria not simply in philosophical and theological studies, but above all in manners and religious life through preaching and by his own example. Eventually, in the year 1646 he was made visiting commissioner of the College of the Irish Friars of Prague by the most reverend father general commissioner, and he came to Prague, where he was elected and confirmed as guardian in the following year, 1647, by unanimous vote and request from all the esteemed fathers of his community, despite his hesitation. He fulfilled this duty so praiseworthily, that nobody was ever found who could justifiably criticise his erudition, private discipline or religious life (notwithstanding the cases of opposition by certain men, with which God wished to put his perseverance and endurance to the test).

At the end of his three-year office as guardian, the most eminent prince of great memory, Cardinal von Harrach,[528] archbishop of Prague (who always held Rev. Fr Clancy in high respect) asked and obtained from the rev. father general that Fr Clancy take up the post of rector of the chief chair of theology of his much renowned seminary in Prague. The Rev. Fr Clancy was in charge of that chair for nine uninterrupted years with such praise and such degree of satisfaction by everyone that, through his un-blameable life and his religious behaviour, he persuaded his fellow fathers in 1661 to move him away from his teaching commitments again, and to give him the governorship of the college once more.

He presided over his fellow fathers for the second time in his office as guardian for a period of three years, receiving so much praise and acting in such conditions of peace and love that it would have been

quo in munere, cum studiosorum maximo fructu ac procerum, praelatorum & religiosorum totius Regni Bohemiae satisfactione & aedificatione, se infatigabiliter occupavit usque ad Annum 1669. quo secunda vice a Reverendissimo Patre Generali fuit institutus Commissarius Visitator Collegii. Tandem, illa cum laude finita commissione, ad scholas rediit seminaristicas, in quibus hodiernam usque in diem publice profitetur.

Majora illius encomia, merita & praedicata, quia adhuc vivit, subticeo, ne videar illi velle adulari. Haec vero quae scripsi vera esse, centenis qui in Belgio, Bohemia, & Austria vivunt notissima ita sunt, ut opus non habeam publicae hujus veritatis in individuo testes nominare. Sicut nec assignare illustrissimas & antiquissimas Hibernicas familias R.P. Clanchy sanguine & affinitate conjunctas; inter quas eminent, ò Brien, de Burgo, Geraldiny, Mohuny, seu Matthaei, de Mara, Kenedy, Loghlen, Fitz Patrick, ô Conori, & c.

Hujus ergo, Carrane, Patris farinae & ineptitudinis Bruodin<um> esse dicis? Aggratulor profecto Bruodino, quod mundissimae R. P. Clanchy, SS. Theologiae Lectoris Emeriti & Jubilati sit farinae religiosus, non vero tui furfuris, alias totus in fermento jaceret. Tibi etiam doctissime calumniator compatior, quia ira & livore obcaecatus adversarium quem denigrare pro viribus cogitasti te nesciente laudas. Debuisses primo, Carrane, probare Patris Bruodini librum scandalosum & famosum esse, antequam tantos viros qui illum approbarunt tam temere redargueres. At ut video homo es desperatus, qui nec Deum vindicem times aut hominem (alias famosum tuum libellum sine omni approbatione & ordinarii facultate in haeretica furtive imprimi non faceres civitate), & sic latras in obvios quoslibet

impossible to achieve more. At the end of the three years, he went back to presiding over the seminary's teaching of theology, a duty which he fulfilled with the greatest success for the students as well as with the satisfaction and edification of the noblemen, the prelates and the clerics of the entire kingdom of Bohemia. He dedicated himself tirelessly to this work until the year 1669, when he was made visiting commissioner of the college for the second time by the most reverend father general. At last, once he completed his mandate as commissioner receiving praise, he went back to the seminary schools, in which he has been publicly teaching until the present day.

Since he is still alive, I omit the greater commendations, merits and celebrations he has received, lest I seem to intend to fawn over him. Indeed, these things, which I reported as true facts, are so well-known to hundreds of people who live in Belgium, Bohemia and Austria, that there is no need for me to name individual witnesses to this public truth; nor, for the same reason, is it necessary to acknowledge the very illustrious and ancient Irish families that are bound to Rev. Fr Clancy by ties of kindred and affinity, amongst whom stand out the O'Briens, Fitzgeralds, MacMahons or Matthews, MacNamaras, O'Loughlins, Fitzpatricks, O'Connors, etc.

So, Carran, are you saying that Bruodinus is a man of the same kind and ineptitude as this father? By all means, I congratulate Bruodinus, on the fact that he is regarded as a cleric made of the very fine stuff of Rev. Fr Clancy, a *lector emeritus* and *jubilatus* of holy and sacred theology, and not as a scrap of a man of your ilk – otherwise, he would lie dead, completely overwhelmed by anger! Moreover, I feel compassion for you, most learned slanderer, because, blinded by wrath and envy, you do not realise that you are actually praising the opponent you thought you were defaming with all your strengths. Firstly, Carran, you should have proven that Fr Bruodinus' book is infamous and sinful, before rebuking so heedlessly men of such high standing, who gave their approval to it. But, as I see, you are a desperate human being, who is afraid of neither human revenge nor even God's (otherwise, you would not clandestinely make your infamous pamphlet available for publication in an heretic city without all necessary approval and without a permission from an ordinary); and thus, you bark against whoever comes in your way

indifferenter, sine consideratione an rei sint vel innocentes. Haec considerans ex tuis scriptis, nobilis ac ingenuus Dominus Maurus ô Loghen, Tuomoniensis Hibernus, in Pragensi Carolo Ferdinandeae juris utriusque studiosus, sequenti elogio, pro complemento hujus tui capitis tuas descripsit qualitates ac librorum tuorum argumenta.

> "Carve senex, latrare diu permitteris ultra,
> plus tamen haud fas est. Te lapidare licet.
> Quis furor aut rabies Fratres lacerare minores
> impulit, o cleri re viperina lues?
> Insatiate senex, quam te mens laeva fefellit,
> non parcis pecudi, non hominique faves.
> Nec satis est pecudes, bubulas volucresque vorare,
> pergis & humanum, Carve, vorare genus.
> Sic canis & lupus es. Quid & hoc? Monstrosa chymera,
> ore canis latras, ore lupique voras.
> Hinc & in ore tibi est livor, cor felle est abundans,
> omnia quae scribis toxica semper olent.
> Nulla tibi pietas, tibi nulla scientia rerum,
> nullaque te virtus, nullaque dona beant.
> Nullus amicitiae modus est, tibi nullus Achates,
> nullus amor patriae, nullus amorque Dei.
> Nullus in arte nitor, stylus est insulsus & errans,
> historia est fabulis tota referta tua."

14. Pro fine, tuum hoc Carrane caput coronas, sicut illud incepisti, explosione nimirum conviciorum & scommatum in reverendum patrem Bruodinum. "Bruodinus", inquis fol. 122, "a natura proclivis est ad mendacia perpetranda. Verus insuper Irus; nam, quando factus

with no distinction, without considering whether they are guilty or innocent. Examining this attitude of yours, which emerges from your writings, the noble and high-born Master Maurice O'Loughlin,[529] an Irishman from Thomond, a scholar in the field of both laws at the Charles-Ferdinand University of Prague,[530] described your features and the arguments of your books in the following poem of praise, as a complement to this chapter of yours:

"Carve, you old man, the time you have been allowed for barking over and over again is long.
It is not permitted by the gods, however, to give you more; now we are granted the right to stone you!
What madness or rage pushed you to torture the Friars Minor,
you pestilence of the clergy, you who spread evil like a viper?
Old man, you who could not satiate yourself, a victim of your own foolish mind,
you spare no sheep, you show favour for no man.
It is not enough for you to devour flocks, beef and birds:
you proceed with devouring even the human kind, Carve!
Thus, you are a dog and a wolf. Why do I also say this? You, monstrous chimera,[531]
you bark with the mouth of a dog, and you eat with the mouth of a wolf.
Hence, you have envy even in your mouth, your heart is full to overflowing with bile,
everything you write always stinks of poison.
You have no piety; you have no knowledge of things,
no virtue and no gifts to make you a blessed man.
You have no bond of friendship, no Achates,[532]
no love for your homeland, no love for God.
There is no splendour in your art, your style is insipid and full of mistakes,
your history is filled full with fables."

14. As a conclusion to this chapter of yours, Carran, you add the same *coronis* you drew at its beginning, namely you burst into taunts and insults against Rev. Fr Bruodinus. On page 122, you state: "Bruodinus is inclined to telling lies by nature. Indeed he is a true Iros;[533] for when

est Guardianus, quam primum se esse Croesum existimavit. & forsan vanissimus Thraso animo revolvit se futurum Patrem Provincialem saltem inter Bohemos," & c.

Humanum, Carrane, esse cadere, diabolicum vero perseverare, communi Sanctorum Patrum eloquio docemur: tu, mi homo, non solum toties hactenus per decursum famosi hujus (quem anatomiso) libelli cecidisti, veritatis & modestiae limites transgrediendo; verum etiam sine fine consequenter pergis & perseveras in aggregando mendaciorum, calumniarum & convitiorum cumulo, quo Bruodinum una cum aliis bonis opprimere valeres. Sed frustra: nam scommata tua sicut & fabulas prudentes spernunt, Bruodinus vero ridet. "Quam primum", inquis, Carrane, "& animo revolvit se futurum Provincialem," & c.

Quis tibi Carrane tribuit spiritum Deorum, quo secreta cordis P. Bruodini tam subtiliter penetrare poteras? Si ex operibus agnoscitur humilium & bonorum virorum ab ambitiosis & falsis Prophetis differentia, triurbs Pragensis testari potest R. P. Bruodinum durante suo triennali Guardianatus officio se semper exhibuisse humilem, mitem, affabilem, & mansuetum Franciscanum; ob quas qualitates benefactorum affectum (assistentia aliorum religiosissimorum Patrum & Fratrum, qui sub ipso erant) ita sibi reconciliavit, quod solutis debitis 700 florenorum, quibus locus erat aggravatus quando officum suscepit, sustentatisque semper sexaginta sex religiosis Conventum finito suo officio ad aliquot millia florenorum in meliori reliquerit statu quam invenit.

15. Scio quod tu Carrane haec non credes; ego tamen in tui mortificationem breviter hic assignabo aliqua ex multis quibus Deus benedixit Regio Pragensi Conventui ad Nives sub Guardianatu R. P. Bruodini; quae omnia accepi ex authentica & originali informatione status Conventus ad Nives facta & subscripta, 23. Novembris, anno 1670.

he became guardian, he immediately regarded himself as a Croesus;[534] and perhaps he, a most vainglorious Thrason,[535] repeated to himself over and over again that he would become provincial father, at least amongst the Bohemians", etc.

A common saying of the holy fathers, Carran, teaches us that to fall into sin is human, but to persist is devilish.[536] You, my fellow human, have not simply fallen into sin so many times so far in the course of this infamous pamphlet (which I am dissecting), by going beyond the limits of truth and moderation; but indeed you also go on endlessly committing the same sins, and you persist in putting together a pile of lies, calumnies and insults, with which you hope to be able to overwhelm Bruodinus together with other good men. Your hope is in vain, though; for your taunts as well as fables are scorned by wise men, and indeed laughed at by Bruodinus. You say, Carran: "immediately, he also repeated to himself over and over again that he would become provincial father," etc.

Who bestowed upon you the inspiration of the gods, Carran, which enabled you to penetrate so subtly the secrets of Bruodinus' heart? If the extent to which humble and good men differ from pretentious and false prophets is measured on the basis of their actions, the threefold city of Prague[537] can attest to the fact that Rev. Fr Bruodinus always showed himself to be a humble, gentle, affable and kind Franciscan during his three-year period of office as guardian. Thanks to these qualities he gained the affection of benefactors for himself (with the help of other very pious brothers and fathers who were his subordinates), insomuch that, at the end of his office, he left the convent with a positive balance of several thousand florins, in a better condition than he had found it, having paid the debts of 700 florins by which the place was burdened when he took office, and having always provided sustenance to sixty-six clerics.

15. I know, Carran, that you will not believe what I am about to describe. Nevertheless, for your mortification, I will hereby briefly mention some of the many gifts which God gave as a benediction to the Royal Convent of the Snows in Prague under Rev. Fr Bruodinus' guardianship. The source I relied on for all these details is the authentic and original informative account on the condition of the Convent of the Snows, which was compiled and signed on 23 November 1670

a reverendis Patribus discretis Conventus, P. Ludovico Kauka, Definitore Actuali, Ernesto Schaff, SS. Theologiae Lectore Generali & Diffinitore Actuali, P. Archangelo Mascul, Provinciae Secretario & Vicario Conventus, & P. Bernard Sannig, Generali SS. Theologiae Professore, ac tandem Nissam Silesiorum ad Capitularem Congregationem missa.

Primo thesaurus ecclesiasticus in ornatibus, casulis, albis, mappis, velis calicum, superpelliciis, substratoriis, antipendiis, baltheis, cortinis (vulgo spalier) baldachinis, tabernaculis, cyboriis, candelabris, palliolis, pluvialibus, lampadibus (inter quas eminet una pretio 500 florenorum ab excellentissimo Domino Humberto S.R.I. Comite Zcernin oblata), numismatibus, monilibus, armillis, catenis, anulis, lapidibus orientalibus, margaritis, crucifixis, crucibus, reliquiariis, imaginibus, vesticulis pretiosis pro statua D. Virginis, coronis & floribus pulcheriimis pro 2000 florenorum auctus est.

II. Sacellum S. Antonii fuit renovatum, & in eo pulchrum confessionale novum affabre sculptum erectum est una cum novis pulchris scamnis.

III. Duae magnae novae fenestrae, fracto ecclesiae muro, una in sacello S. Antonii & altera penes sacellum Bohemicum positae sunt.

IV. Duae novae portae factae sunt in ecclesia pro commoditate populi, una in sacello Bohemico, altera vero in antiqua ecclesia.

V. Nova magna crypta tot corporum capax in sacello S. Antonii erecta est.

VI. Spaciosum portae cubiculum & supra illud pulchra cella, reliquis in dormitorio cubiculis correspondens, a fundamentis fabricatum est.

VII. Diruto funditus antiquo dormitorio positisque in utraque illius extremitate magnis novis duabus fenestris, novum reaedificatum est lucidum et commodum dormitorium 12 cellarum, una cum 24 fenestris incipiendo a Bibliotheca usque ad loca communia inclusive, non sine magno conventus commodo & ornamento.

VIII. Ambitus, seu claustrum inferius, pulchris imaginibus S. Patris Francisci vitam ex una parte, & S. Antonii de Padua ex altera parte repraesentantibus per totum ornatus est.

by the reverend fathers of the convent's *discretorium*,[538] Fr Ludwig Kauka,[539] *acting definitor*, Ernst Schaff, general reader of holy and sacred theology and *acting definitor*, Fr Archangel Mascul,[540] secretary of the province and vicar of the convent, and Fr Bernard Sannig, general professor of holy and sacred theology, and which was finally sent to Nysa in Silesia, to the capitular congregation.

1) For the price of 2,000 florins, the church's treasure was increased by adding ornaments, chasubles, albs, towels, chalice veils, surplices, altar clothes, altar frontals, cinctures, *cortinae* (generally called *spalier*), canopies, tabernacles, *ciboria*, candelabras, short ceremonial cloaks, long ceremonial cloaks, lamps (amongst which one, costing 500 florins and donated by the most excellent Master Humprecht Czernin,[541] count of the Holy Roman Empire, is particularly noteworthy), medals, necklaces, bracelets, chains, rings, oriental stones, pearls, crucifixes, crosses, reliquaries, icons, expensive miniature garments for the statue of the Lady Virgin, crowns and very beautiful flowers.

2) The chapel of St Anthony was restored, and a beautiful new confessional was built inside it, skilfully chiselled, along with new beautiful benches.

3) Two new windows of big size were made by breaking through the wall of the church, one in the chapel of St Anthony and another for the use of the chapel of Bohemia.

4) Two new doors were made in the church for the people's convenience, one in the chapel of Bohemia, another one in the old church itself.

5) A new crypt of big size, which can hold so many corpses, was built in the chapel of St Anthony.

6) A spacious room above the gateway and above it a beautiful cell were built, corresponding to the other bedrooms in the dormitory.

7) After the demolition of the old dormitory to its foundations, a new dormitory was built up, bright and comfortable with twelve cells, and two new windows of large size were placed at both extremities. Twenty-four windows were also added, starting from the library to the common spaces included. These works embellished the architecture of the convent and made it very commodious.

8) The walkway, namely the lower cloister, was adorned throughout with beautiful icons, representing the life of St Fr Francis on some walls and that of St Anthony of Padua on others.

IX. Bibliotheca est aucta libris pro multis centenis florenis.

X. In medio antiquae ecclesiae sacellum sacri montis Calvariae sicut et sepulchrum B. Virginis, in illa forma qua in terra sancta extant et venerantur, a fundamentis usque ad tectum inclusive fabricata sunt. Et sub utroque sacello nova crypta centenorum corporum capax exstructa est.

XI. Pulchra nova apoteca sub titulo S. Antonii non sine magnis expensis exstructa est.

XII. Novum vivarium positum est in horto, sicut et novus aquae ductus per hortum tractus est.

XIII. Infirmaria antiqua alio commodiori loco translata, nova schola rebus omnibus necessariis bene provisa illius loco posita est.

XIV. Debita liquidissima ex parte jam accepta & in toto certo accipienda (quae anno 1670. sub Patris Bruodini officio inciderunt) mille 800 florenorum successori suo reliquit Bruodinus; solvenda vere non nisi ad 700 florenos ad summum.

Alia minora sub Reverendo Patre Bruodino, non sine magnis expensis (ut sunt granarium<, >tectum ecclesiae & conventus potiori ex parte renovatum, emptio & dejectio tot domorum in fundo, platearum fundi & horti accommodatio, ambitus ligneus ab ecclesiae porta usque ad novam portam antiquae ecclesiae ductus, locorum communium a fundamentis fabrica<tio>, & c.) exstructa transeo: haec vero retuli, ut tu Carrane videas una cum aliis invidis qualiter benedixit Deus Conventui ad Nives sub R. P. Bruodini Guardianatu, qualiterque ipse in spiritu humilitatis, charitatis & pacis assistentia suorum Patrum & Fratrum movit Benefactores ad benefaciendum paupereulis Fratribus ad Nives.

16. Tibi ergo, Carrane, quis nisi fatuus crederet, quod Reverendus Pater Bruodinus, statim ac factus est Guardianus, existimaverit se Croesum esse, aut ambiverit miserias & afflictiones quae inter Franciscanos Provincialatus dignitatem comitantur?

9) The library was stocked with additional books for the price of many hundreds of florins.

10) In the middle of the old church a chapel of the Holy Mount Calvary as well as a sepulchre of the Blessed Virgin were built, fully replicating, from foundation to ceiling inclusive, those which are extant and venerated in the Holy Land. Also, under both chapels a new crypt was built, which can hold hundreds of corpses.

11) Not without great expense, a new apothecary store of some beauty, dedicated to St Anthony, was built.[542]

12) In the garden, a new vivarium[543] was placed and a new aqueduct was laid out.

13) The old infirmary was moved to a different and more suitable location; in its place, a new school was accommodated, which was properly provided with all necessary equipment.

14) Bruodinus left to his successor a credit of 1,800 florins owed [to the convent] in liquid cash (a total which was reached under Fr Bruodinus' office in the year 1670). Part of this money was received already [under his office], and the rest of it was to be received in full. Conversely, the money owed [by the convent] was only 700 florins maximum.

I pass over other minor buildings constructed under Rev. Fr Bruodinus, not without great expense (such as a granary, the renovation of quite a large part of the church and convent's roof,[544] the purchase and demolition of so many houses on the estate, the repair of the paved areas of the estate and of the garden, the laying-out of a wooden walkway from the church door to the new door of the old church, the construction of common premises from the foundations, etc.). But indeed I have reported these undertakings so that you, Carran, may realise, together with the other envious readers, what benediction God bestowed upon the Convent of the Snows under Rev. Fr Bruodinus' office as guardian, and how Bruodinus himself, in his spirit of humility, Christian love and peace, inspired benefactors to support the poor and humble Friars of the Snows, with the help of his fellow fathers and brothers.

16. So, Carran, who – if not a fool – would believe that Rev. Fr Bruodinus, as soon as he became guardian, regarded himself as a Croesus, or longed for the miseries and afflictions which come with the office of provincial father amongst the Franciscans?

Fuit, Carrane, Pater Bruodinus ante Pragensem Guardianatum anno 1663. Olomucensis Conventus ad S. Bernardinum Guardianus, fuit suae provinciae Diffinitor; & quod majus est, jam ab octo annis Lector est Jubilatus (quae dignitas inter nos Franciscanos major est officio Custodis & Diffinitoris) tamen nunquam visus est per hoc superbire; quare ergo ob Pragensis Guardianatus ad Nives officium tumescere & superbire deberet? Crede mihi, Carrane, quod P. Bruodinus libentius est Arnoviensis residentiae inter paucos Fratres Praeses, prout jam est, quam esset Provincialis Bohemiae.

17. Ultima, Carrane, clausula hujus tui cranei est haec: "Quid mendaciloquus fraticellus habet ad agendum cum rebus Hibernicis? Nam PP. Societatis Jesu, Dominicani, Augustiniani, Carmelitae & Cistercienses se nunquam immiscuere in Hiberniae relationibus, quamvis hi majorem experientiam habeant in auriculari, quam Bruodinus in toto capite. Sed is potius tractare deberet de mendacimonio suo quam de impertinentibus rebus" & c.

Nisi scirem me in vanum laboraturum, rogarem te, Carrane, ut tandem aliquando a conviciis & scommatibus abstineres; sed induratum est cor tuum in malo animusque conviciorum habitu totus est informatus, si ut incepisti constanter perseveras. "Patres" (inquis Carrane) "Societatis, Dominicani, & c. nunquam se immiscuere in Hiberniae relationibus, quamvis plus habeant in auriculari quam Bruodinus in toto capite."

Non omnia, Carrane, possumus omnes. De excellentia doctrinae praedictorum Reverendorum Patrum sicut nullus dubitat, sic nemo est qui non miratur tuam (qui inferioris scamni vix es grammatista) Carrane temeritatem, qua praesumis judicium ferre in materia doctrinae, quam non intelligis. Bruodinus, cum tua bona venia Carrane, in variis occasionibus publicis et privatis sufficientiam

Before he took office as guardian in Prague, Carran, Fr Bruodinus was guardian of the convent of St Bernardin in Olomouc in 1663;[545] he was *definitor* of his province; and – which is even a more important position – he has been *lector jubilatus* already for eight years (a position which is higher in rank than the office of *custos*[546] and *definitor* amongst us Franciscans). Nonetheless, he never seemed to get haughty because of this honour. Why, then, should he have got insolent and haughty because of his office as guardian of the Convent of the Snows in Prague? Trust me on this, Carran: Fr Bruodinus would be more eager to be the superintendent of the Lodging of Hostinné amongst a few brothers,[547] as he already is, than be the provincial of Bohemia.

17. The final conclusion of this skull of yours, Carran, is the following: "What does [Bruodinus], a mendacious insignificant friar, have to do with Irish affairs? In fact, fathers belonging to the congregations of the Society of Jesus, of the Dominicans, of the Augustinians, of the Carmelites and of the Cistercians never meddled in the writing of reports about Ireland, although they retain more knowledge in their little finger, than Bruodinus does in his entire head.[548] Instead, he should have dealt with his hoard of lies, rather than with issues that do not pertain to the topic", etc.

If I did not know that my efforts would be in vain, Carran, I would ask you to abstain from insults and taunts once and for all; but your heart must have stiffened in its evilness and your soul must have been entirely shaped by your habit of telling lies, if you continue steadfastly as you started. You say, Carran: "fathers belonging to the congregations of the Society of Jesus, of the Dominicans, etc. never meddled in the writing of reports about Ireland, although they retain more knowledge in their little finger, than Bruodinus does in his entire head."

Not all of us, Carran, are capable of everything. Just as nobody has doubts about the excellence of the erudition of the reverend fathers mentioned above, in the same way there is none who does not marvel at the foolhardiness which characterises you, Carran, who are a student of elementary grammar of the lowest rank. With this foolhardiness you impertinently dare to put forward your judgements in matters of learning which you do not even understand. I beg your indulgent pardon, Carran, but Bruodinus showed sufficiency of

doctrinae suae ostendit; quare ergo non posset, ut fecit, patriae suae historiam scribere eamque contra tuos aliorumque tui furfuris pseudo-historicorum latratus, calumnias & imposturas tueri? Belgarum, Indiarum, Bohemiae, Lusitaneae, Moraviae & c. inter multos praeclaros historicos Patres Societatis sine invidia historias scripserunt; quare pariter non liceret Rev. P. Bruodino (cujus antecessores regum Hiberniae antiquitus chronologi erant) patriae suae historiam publicare, pseudo-historicorumque errores & figmenta reprehendere & emendare? Tibi, ut video Carrane, fraterna non placet Bruodini correctio, quod notae tuae fatuitatis indicium est (nam sapientissimo teste Salomone, *Proverb*. 10. "qui odit increpationem insipiens est") & sic non libenter habes, quod materiam illam tetigit in qua te emendare & reprehendere potuit. De hoc satis. Jam ad finem festino.

learning on various private and public occasions. Why, then, could he have not written a history of his homeland and defended it against the barking, slanders and lies of yourself and of other pseudo-historians of your insignificant ilk, as he did? Amongst many historians of great renown, the fathers of the society wrote histories of Belgium, the Indies, Bohemia, Portugal, Moravia, etc. without ill-will. Why should Rev. Fr Bruodinus (whose ancestors were the chroniclers of the kings of Ireland in antiquity) not be equally allowed to publish a history of his homeland, and refute and correct the mistakes and fabrications of pseudo-historians? As I see, Carran, Bruodinus' brotherly work of amendment does not please you —which is a sign of your well-known foolishness (for, as attested by Solomon, the wisest of men, at *Proverb* 10, "he who dislikes criticism is a fool"). Thus you hold a grudge, because he hit on that subject in which he could correct and refute you. Enough about this: I now hasten to the end of my dissection.

Anatomia Capitis 8. & 9. *Apologiae* Carraneae

1. Data opera haec duo in unum colligavi, Carrane, capita, quia in illis nihil invenio cerebri anatomia dignum, praeter scommata, quibus tanquam si ebrius esses in P. Bruodinum ejusque honoratam familiam (quae tibi non nocuit) latras, & testimonialium quarundam literarum copiam, quibus te ipsum, miserrime senex, diffamas. Quis te, bone vir, accusavit de crimine pessimo, aut diffamavit? Nullus. Adquid ergo te per fictas testimoniales literas purgas? Non audivisti forte tritum illud juristarum axioma, "excusatio non petita accusatio est manifesta"? Nec Bruodinus nec alius ullus Franciscanus in vita aut fama tibi nocuit; quare igitur intempestive te excusas?

2. "Bruodinus", inquis, "scripsit me fuisse ex Hibernia expulsum ob causam sibi et mihi notam." Quid hoc, Carrane, mali est? Milleni honoratissimi viri saeculares & ecclesiastici, a quo inter Anglos haeresis praevaluit, ex Hibernia expulsi sunt, ob causam mihi probe notam; per hoc illi nullam passi sunt aut patiuntur infamiam. Cur pariter tu deberes incurrere infamiam per hoc, quod Bruodinus dicat te fuisse ex patria expulsum ob causam sibi et tibi notam? Sed etiam videamus quo modo tuam defendis innocentiam. "Defendo" inquis fol. 115. "literis testimonialibus Reverendissimi Dn. Matthiae Rochi, civitatis Catherlaghensis & dioecesis Leghlinensis Vicarii Apostolici": bene est, Carrane, sed ad insipientiam tibi. Tu, mi Carrane, natus & educatus es in comitatu Typperariensi & archi-dioecesi Cassellensi, in Momonia; authoritateque Casseliensi Archi Praesulis, seu ejus Vicarii (ob penuriam pastorum & doctorum virorum, qui in abundantissima Catholica vinea in Hibernia tunc laborarent) ad sacerdotium & animarum curam in illa tua patria promotus. Extra illam archi-dioecesim nec parochum aut pastorem, Carrane, in Hibernia unquam egisti, ut volens nolens fateri debes nobis Momoniensibus, qui scimus

Dissection of Chapters VIII and IX of Carran's *Apologia*

1. After a careful examination, Carran, I linked these two chapters into a single one, because I see no trace of a brain in them which may be worth dissecting. They contain only taunts which you bark against Fr Bruodinus and his honourable family (which did no harm to you), as if you were drunk, as well as a great number of various testimonial letters, with which you defame yourself, you most wretched old man. Who accused you, good man, of a crime of the worst kind, or defamed you? Nobody. To what purpose, then, do you justify yourself through false testimonial letters? Perhaps you never heard about that principle often used by jurists, "an excuse that has not been sought is clear self-incrimination"? Neither Bruodinus nor any other Franciscan did any harm to your life or reputation; why, then, do you inappropriately excuse yourself?

2. You say: "Bruodinus wrote that I was expelled from Ireland for a reason known to him and myself."[549] What is wrong with this statement, Carran? Ever since the heresy prevailed amongst the English people, thousands of truly honourable men, secular and ecclesiastic alike, were expelled from Ireland, for a reason I know very well; but they did not suffer any dishonour because of this, nor do they suffer it now. Likewise, why should you have incurred dishonour because of the fact that Bruodinus says that you were expelled from your homeland for a reason known to him and to you? But even so, let us see in what manner you defend your innocence. On page 115, you say: "I defend it by means of the testimonial letter of Master Matthew Roche, most reverend apostolic vicar of the town of Carlow and of the diocese of Leighlin."[550] This is a good thing, Carran, but it is foolish for you.[551] You, my dear Carran, were born and educated in County Tipperary and in the archdiocese of Cashel, in Munster; and you were appointed to the priesthood and to the care of souls in that homeland of yours by the authority of the archbishop of Cashel, or his vicar (because of the scarcity of shepherds and learned men who were willing to toil in the very rich Catholic vineyard of Ireland at that time). Outside that archdiocese, Carran, you never held the office of priest or shepherd, as you must confess – whether you want to or not – to us born in Munster, who are aware of the motive of your

tuae extra patriam peregrinationis occasiones; cur ergo honestorum sacerdotum more, a tuo Archi Episcopo vel ejus Vicario Generali in tua extra Hiberniam peregrinatione testimoniales anteactae tuae vitae & morum sicut & dimissoriales non accepisti?

3. Sub Archi Episcopo Caseliensi septem sunt Suffraganei Episcopi, ex quibus aliqui vel eorum Generales Vicarii scire poterant quomodo tu te gessisti paucis illis annis quibus parochum egisti: si saltem ad unum aliquem ex his Episcopis Casseliensi tuo ordinario Archi-Episcopo subjectis recurrisses pro dimissorialibus literis, antequam extra natale solum navigasses, esset aliquid; at quod, relicto tuo Archi-Episcopo ejusque Vicario Generali, postpositisque omnibus Suffraganeis Episcopis illis subjectis, ad Archidioecesem Dublinensem in Lagenia, ubi notus non fuisti, Carrane, recurristi pro testimonialibus, mirantur prudentiores & rident qui te noverunt.

Sed dissimulemus in inusitato hoc tuo facto & recursu; tantum te interrogo, Carrane: cum in provinciam Lageniae & Archi-Episcopatum Dublinensem recurrendum tibi erat, ut anteactae tuae vitae testimoniales literas mendicare posses ab iis qui te non noverunt, cur non ab ipso Dublinensi Archipraesule, vel ab aliquo ex illustrissimis & honoratissimis quatuor aliis Suffraganeis Episcopis, aut eorum Generalibus Vicariis qui sub ipso sunt, dimissoriales ex Hibernia & testimoniales laudibus vitae tuae non mendicasti, relicto Matthaeo Roch, rebelli Lechlinensi Vicario Apostolico, viro scelerato & excommunicato qui per 35 annos, assistentia haeretici saecularis Brachii, elusit Sedis Apostolicae mandata & sui Dublinensis Archi-Episcopi jussa & censuras in illum toties fulminata sprevit?

Jam scio Carrane cur, spreto Dublinensi Archi-Episcopo aliisque quatuor Suffraganeis Episcopis illis una cum Leghlinensi Episcopatu subjectis, ad Matthaeum Rochum denominatum Leghlinensis Dioecesis Vicarium Apostolicum recurristi; scio, inquam, quia similia

travel abroad. Why then, when travelling outside of Ireland, did you not receive testimonial letters as well as letters of discharge from your archbishop or his general vicar, as honest priests generally do, which would tell about the life you used to live and your customs?

3. The archbishop of Cashel has seven suffragan bishops below him, some of whom, or their general vicars, could be aware of how you behaved during those few years in which you were in charge of your parish. You would have a point if you had at least turned to one of these bishops, who are the subordinates of the bishop of Cashel, your ordinary, asking for a letter of discharge before setting sail outside of your homeland. Instead, Carran, after abandoning your archbishop and his general vicar, and disregarding all suffragan bishops who are subordinates to them, you turned to the archdiocese of Dublin in Leinster, where you were a stranger, asking for a testimonial letter. This is a cause of surprise for people who are quite judicious, and of laughter for those who in fact know you.

But let us pretend that you never made this uncustomary decision and never turned to the man you turned to. I only ask you this, Carran: when you had to turn to the province of Leinster and the archbishopric of Dublin in order to be able to solicit a testimonial letter about the life you had previously lived from people who did not know you, why did you not beseech the archbishop of Dublin himself, or any of the four other suffragan bishops or their general vicars, who are all truly illustrious and venerable subordinates of him, to provide you with a letter of discharge from Ireland and a testimonial letter which would praise your life? Instead, you turned to Matthew Roche, the rebellious apostolic vicar of Leighlin, an excommunicated wicked man who, with the help of the secular heretic Brachy,[552] spent thirty-five years cheating on the mandates of the apostolic see and the orders of his archbishop of Dublin, and who disregarded the censures which were so often issued against him.

I already know, Carran, why you scorned the archbishop of Dublin and those four other suffragan bishops who were subordinate to him together with the bishopric of Leighlin, and instead you turned to Matthew Roche, the designated apostolic vicar of the diocese of Leighlin. I know why, I say: because anything similar rejoices at the similar,[553] and because wicked men are normally given letters attesting

similibus gaudent & quia mali honestae vitae testimoniales non nisi a se pejoribus ordinarie accipiunt. Mattahei Rochi (vulgo Roch) scelera, mi Carrane, ita publice nota sunt, ut non credam ullum fuisse a 40 annis in toto Regno Hiberniae virum literatum, qui de illius facinoribus non audiverit; ob quae anno 1644. praevalentibus in Hibernia Catholicis, authoritate illustrissimi Domini Thomae Flemengi, nati Baronis de Slana, Dublinensi Archi Episcopi (ex Ordine S. Francisci assumpti) captus fuit, & Waterfordiam vi ductus, ut in praesentia 18 Archi Episcoporum & Episcoparum, tot procerum ac praelatorum Regni, accusatus, juridice convictus, ac tandem canonico ritu degradatus, & ad condignas patibuli poenas tollerandas saecularis judicis brachio traditus erat.

Haec ita contigisse per Angliam, Scotiam & Hiberniam magis est notum, quam ut egeat testibus in individuo.

Si tu, Carrane, haec quae anno 1644. circa Rocheum facta sunt non audisti dudum, solus debes esse peregrinus in rebus Hibernicis; & si adhuc dubitas, fide dignissimos illos Patres Donnelanum, Kenedy & Flen (quos c. 2. f. 27. tui famosi libelli in testes citas) interroga, & dicent tibi perduellem illum tuum Matthaeum Roch cursum malae actae vitae finivisse ut jam dixi. Ecce, Carrane, quomodo testimonio hominis infamis & fide indigni tu, non rogatus, conaris imprudenter tuam defendere innocentiam, quam nullus oppugnavit!

Domine Carrane, si tacuisses prudens esses; at loquela tua manifestum te fuisse degradati Rochi discipulum fecit; quare rogo ut tibi ipsi, non vero R. P. Bruodino (qui famam tuam non laesit) imputes si in reputatione & honore (more illorum sacerdotum & religiosorum qui sine superiorum facultate & recommendatione de regno in regnum transeunt) inter prudentes patieris detrimentum.

to their honest life only by men who are even more wicked than them. The misdeeds of Matthew *Rochus* (Roche, as he is generally named) are so well known to the wider public, my dear Carran, that I do not believe that there has been any educated man in the entire kingdom of Ireland in forty years who has not heard about his crimes. It is because of these crimes that, in the year 1644, when the Catholics were prevailing in Ireland, he was arrested on behalf of the authority of the most illustrious Master Thomas Fleming, born of the baron of Slane, archbishop of Dublin[554] (raised from the Order of St Francis); and he was conducted to Waterford by force, so that, in the presence of eighteen archbishops and bishops, such a great number of noblemen and prelates of the kingdom, he could be accused, sentenced through a trial, and finally downgraded, according to canonical custom, and consigned to the arm of a secular judge, so that he might suffer the wholly-deserved punishment of the gibbet.

That these events did happen in this way is so well-known across England, Scotland and Ireland, as not to require individual testimonies.

If in the past, Carran, you never heard about what happened to Roche in the year 1644, you must be the only one alien to Irish matters; and if you still have doubts, ask Fr Donnellan, Fr Kennedy and Fr O'Flynn, those famous fathers who certainly deserve to be trusted (whom you adduce as witnesses in Chapter 2, page 27 of your infamous pamphlet). They will tell you that the course of the wicked life of Matthew Roche, that public enemy and friend of yours, ended as I have just said. Behold, Carran! This is how you, without having been asked to do so, imprudently try to defend your innocence, which nobody attacked, by citing the testimony of an infamous and untrustworthy man!

Master Carran, you would have shown prudence if you had said nothing; but your words made it clear that you were a pupil of Roche, a downgraded priest. Therefore, I ask you to impute only to yourself, and indeed not to Rev. Fr Bruodinus (who did no harm to your reputation), if you suffer detriment in your fame and honour amongst wise men, in the manner of those priests and clerics who move from kingdom to kingdom without their superiors' permission and recommendation.

4. Possim ulterius testimonialium tuarum literarum fidem & veritatem efficacissimis rationibus enervare, si opus esset, sed nolo, quia tibi faveo illam talem qualem habes Viennae reputationem; porro ne dicas me extrema tentasse ut literas tuas fictas & falsas esse possim probare, duas clausulas veritati apperte repugnantes in tuis Rochianis testimonialibus posit<a>s tangam; & primo hanc, "Matthaeus Rochus", & c, "Reverendo Domino Thomae Carve Sacerdoti Hiberno", & c.

Mi Carrane, in Hibernia nec tu nec ullus ex tua prosapia (ex qua novi diversos honestos & Catholicos plebeos in Tuomonia, sicut & patruelem tuum, D. Conaldum ô Carran, ludimagistrum, sub quo in Comitatu Typperariensi trivialibus in scholis fui< >in Hibernia ante te<)> unquam se Carve vocavit; falsum igitur est quod Rochus te in suis literis "Carve" cognominaverit. Secunda clausula est haec: "eodem omnibus ad quos praesentes pervenerint sincere attestantes, praefatum Dominum Thomam Carve" (Carran verius) "a cura animarum, quam apud nos aliquandiu laudabiliter gessit, non ob ullum crimen amotum, aut aliqua ecclesiastica censura irretitum", & c.

Tu, Carrane, tua vita extra Archi-dioecesem Casseliensem in Hibernia animarum curam non habuisti, ut nobis Momoniensibus, qui probe scimus tui ex patria abitus causam, notissimum est: quomodo ergo cum veritate degradatus Rochus testari poterat quod tu sub illo laudabiliter animarum curam administrasti, aut te non fuisse amotum ex tua in Comitatu Tiperariensi & Archidioecesi Caselliensi Parochia, ob aliquod crimen? Cum tali scelerato rebelli homine correspondentiam habuit nullam tuus in Casseliensi Archidioecesi ordinarius; nec eo usque aures isti tuo Roche creverunt, ut posset tam procul pro certo audire te non fuisse a cura animarum amotum ob ullum crimen: quomodo igitur veritate testari poterat te sub ipso in

4. If it were necessary, I could further debase the trustworthiness and truthfulness of your testimonial letters with arguments of great efficacy, but I do not want to, because, for your own sake, I say nothing about the notorious reputation you truly have in Vienna. On the other hand, lest you say that I have attempted the vilest course of action, so that I may be able to prove that your letters are forgeries and false, I am going to speak about two sentences, clearly at odds with the truth, which occur in your testimonial letter from Roche. So, let me begin with this one: "Matthew Roche" etc. "writing to the Irish priest Rev. Master Thomas Carve", etc. [555]

In Ireland, my dear Carran, the name 'Carve' was never used by you or anyone of your family[556] (to which various honest and Catholic commoners belong, with whom I am acquainted, such as your paternal cousin, Master Conald O'Carran, the teacher under whom I was in grammar school[557] in County Tipperary in Ireland before you).[558] Therefore, it is false that Roche addressed you with the surname 'Carve' in his letter. The second sentence I want to discuss is the following: "to everybody who will receive it at hand, the present letter to the same [that is, Carve] sincerely attests to the fact that the aforementioned Master Thomas Carve" (Carran, actually) "was never removed from the care of souls because of unlawful conduct, or was never hindered from it by any form of ecclesiastic censorship, praiseworthily fulfilling the duty for some time in my parish," etc.

In the course of your life, Carran, you never took care of souls outside the archdiocese of Cashel in Ireland, as it is perfectly known to us, who are from Munster and are well aware of the reason why you left your homeland. How, then, could Roche, a downgraded cleric, truthfully attest to the fact that you administered the care of souls under his supervision, or that you had not been removed from your parish in County Tipperary and in the archdiocese of Cashel because of any unlawful conduct? The ordinary in the archdiocese of Cashel never exchanged letters with such a wicked and rebellious man; nor, at least until now, have ears grown so large for this despicable Roche of yours, that he could possibly hear as a true fact from so great a distance that you had not been removed from the care of souls because of any unlawful conduct. How, then, could he truthfully attest to the fact that you dealt with the care of souls in a praiseworthy manner

Lagenia laudabiliter curam animarum gessisse, teque etiam non fuisse amotum ex tua parochia, quam in Momonia sola habuisti, ob ullum crimen? Compatior tibi, & ut alia vice cautior fias in producendis testimonialibus literis amice rogo.

5. Honestae tuae Carrane conversationis in Germania & nativitatis in Hibernia in pace dormientes adducis testes, quorum testimoniales literae tuum, mi Thoma, olent puerilem Latinismum, quamobrem a multis dicuntur fictae & falsae: quod tamen ego affirmare nolo; nam tibi faveo illarum literarum effectum. Unicum tantum hoc addo, me Pragae fuisse quando nobilissimus Dominus vice Colonellus Jacobus Butlerus (qui solus ex omnibus qui tuis testimonialibus quas adducis literis subscripserunt vivit) in suo ex Anglia per Pragam Viennam versus anno 1670. transitu interrogatus fuit, in multorum praesentia nobilium & religiosorum, num tibi Carrane dederit nativitatis & nobilitatis anno 1657. testimoniales literas una cum pie defuncto reverendissimo Domino Abbate Butlero. Respondit publice in haec verba: "Pater Thomas ô Carran a me nullas unquam petiit testimoniales literas, & sic nullas illi dedi; si vero petiisset, non denegarem illi, quia nulli conterraneo denegare soleo quod mihi non posset praejudicare & illi posset prodesse."

Vice Colonellus Butlerus adhuc Viennae Carrane vivit, & quia nobilis est cavalerus non negabit quod in multorum praesentia dixit. Porro, quia ad propositum nostrum parum refert quomodo te gessisti hic vel ibi, transeant tuae testimoniales per me ut volueris, ut sic anatomiae famosi libelli sequenti paragrapho finem imponam.

6. Spretis, Carrane, fictis tuis testimonialibus ad rem non facientibus, unicum quod restat est ut nimirum examinem ultima tria famosi tuoi libelli folia; at ut verum fatear, ab eorum relectione & anatomia ita adhorret animus meus, ut non videam modum quo intellectum meum

under his supervision in Leinster, and also that you had not been removed from the only parish you administered in Munster because of any unlawful conduct? I feel pity for you, my friend, and I ask you to be more cautious in putting forward testimonial letters.

5. To attest to your honourable staying in Germany and your birth in Ireland, Carran, you adduce witnesses who now rest in peace, whose testimonial letters, my dear Thomas, reek of your childish pseudo-Latin; and because of this reason many people say they are forgeries and false – an assertion which, however, I do not want to make. In fact, for your own sake, I say nothing about what those letters achieve. I add only the following single piece of information. I was in Prague when Master Vice-Colonel James Butler,[559] a nobleman of great renown (the only one to be still alive of all the witnesses of yours who signed the testimonial letters you adduce), during his journey towards Vienna from England in the year 1670, travelled through Prague. There, in the presence of many noblemen and clerics, he was asked whether in the year 1657 he had given you, Carran, a letter attesting to your birth and nobility, together with Master Abbot Butler, a pious and truly reverend man now dead. This is how he answered in front of everyone else: "Fr Thomas O'Carran never asked me for any testimonial letter, and therefore I never gave him any; indeed, if he had asked, I would not have denied him one, since I am not accustomed to denying any fellow-countryman of mine anything which could not possibly jeopardise me and could actually be useful to him."

Vice-Colonel Butler still lives in Vienna, Carran, and since he is a noble cavalier he will not deny what he said in the presence of many witnesses. But since the way you behaved here or there is of little importance to our proposed subject, I shall accept your testimonial letters and let them be as you wished, so that I may thus put an end to the dissection of your infamous pamphlet with the following paragraph.[560]

6. Once I ignore your fictitious testimonial letters, which have nothing to do with the topic, Carran, the only thing left is for me to examine the last three pages of your infamous pamphlet. But, to confess the truth, my spirit shudders so much at reading them again and dissecting them, that I cannot see a way in which I could induce my

inducere possim ad ea quae latras examinanda. Et quis, bone Deus, cordati spiritus religiosus sine horrore relegere posset inaudita tot convicia & scommata, quae in Patrem Bruodinum ejusque honoratam familiam pro coronide infamis tui opusculi explodis? Mirantur plurimi, quod tandem aliquando ad cor non readeas, & a scommatibus abstineas; ego vero non miror, nam trito Sanctorum Patrum testimonio didici, illum qui male incipit & in malo diu perseverat raro bene finire. Tu, Carrane, explosione conviciorum & mendaciorum, opusculum tuum famosum incepisti calumniando & conviciando martyres, religiosos & viros pios in genere; in specie vero R. P. Bruodinum ejusque honoratam familiam: & in maligno hoc proposito perseverasti per totum libellum, usque ad folium 140. Quare ergo quis miraretur, quod ultima tria folia famosi tui libelli conspurcas meris figmentis, mendaciis, scommatibus & conviciis, & sic infelicem tuum partum condigna pro fine ornas conviciorum mendaciorumque corolla?

7. Si Domitiani & Vitelli temporibus Carrane vixisses, inter calumniatores confratres tuos, quos illi apertis auribus libenter audiebant, supremum consecutus fuisses honorem; si vero Antonini Pii aetate floreres, capitis poena, qua calumniatores potentissimus Princeps coercebat, dudum fuisses castigatus, ni ea quae de tot illustrissimis & reverendissimis viris sicut & de reverendo P. Bruodino ejusque honorata familia per totum famosum tuum libellum comminisceris probares. Caeterum quia non minus justi & pii Caesaris aetate Augustissimi nimirum Rom. Imp. Leopoldi Viennae vivis, spirans adhuc minarum & c<a>edes in optimos quosque viros & religiosos, cavendum tibi est Carrane, ne te condignis castigari procuret piiissimus Princeps poenis. Porro quod meum est animitus Carrane (pro fine hujus Anatomiae) opto ut qui ex persecutore Christianorum Paulum fecit annunciatorem Christi te ex Martyrum oppugnatore, patriae

mind to examining the words you bark. Good Lord, what religious man of judicious spirit would be capable of reading again, without shuddering, so many unprecedented insults and taunts, which you throw out at Fr Bruodinus and his honourable family as a final *coronis* of your infamous pamphlet? Most readers are surprised that you do not regain control of your mental faculties and do not abstain from taunts even now, at last, but I am not surprised at all; for from the common saying so often used by the holy fathers I learned that the man who starts out wickedly, and persists in behaving wickedly for a long time, rarely ends well.[561] By bursting into insults and lies, Carran, you started your infamous booklet with slanders and abuses against martyrs, clerics and pious men in general, but in particular against Rev. Fr Bruodinus and his honourable family; and you persisted in this wicked intention throughout the entire pamphlet, until page 140. Why, then, should anyone be surprised that you pollute the last three pages of your pamphlet with bare fabrications, lies, taunts and insults, and thus you embellish what you have miserably given birth to with a little *coronis* as a wholly-deserving end for your insults and lies?

7. If you had lived in the epoch of Domitian[562] and Vitellius,[563] Carran, you would have achieved the greatest honour amongst slanderers worthy of your brotherly company, to whom those emperors willingly used to listen with open ears. But if you had flourished in the age of Antoninus Pius,[564] you would have long been punished by the capital penalty with which that great and powerful emperor used to suppress slanderers, unless you had provided evidence to support the truthfulness of your fabrications throughout the whole of your infamous pamphlet with regard to so many men of great eminence and respect, as well as Rev. Fr Bruodinus and his honourable family. Still, you live in Vienna, in the epoch of a no less just and pious emperor, namely Leopold, the most august emperor of the Roman people. Accordingly, since you are still breathing out murderous threats against each and every excellent man and cleric,[565] you ought to be careful, Carran, that the emperor, a profoundly pious man, does not take care that you are punished with penalties you would wholly deserve. Yet, in conclusion to this dissection, Carran, as far as I am concerned, I heartily wish that the One[566] who turned Paul from a persecutor of Christians into an announcer of Christ may convert

diffamatore ac optimorum quorumlibet virorum calumniatore in pium contriti cordis poenitentem convertat, Amen.

Series nominum quorundam fratrum Ord. Min. Strict. Obs. Provinciae Hiberniae, quorum memoriam non facit R. P. Bruodinus in suo de martyribus Hiberniae catalogo.

Vita Mart. Joannis Kernei

1. Pater Joannes Karneus Casseliae in Hibernia anno 1619. nobilibus ac Catholicis parentibus, D. nimirum Joanne Karneo & Elisabetha nata Creagh (quae in ipsa Cathedrali Ecclesia D. Patritio sacra anno 1647. una cum centenis aliis Catholicis ab hereticis Anglis in odium fidei crudeliter necata est) natus; piissimorum parentum diligentia in primo aetatis flore ea pietatis, temperantiae, pudicitiae & modestiae nitidissima animo concepit semina, quae annorum progressu tam firmas copiosasque fixerunt radices, ut nulla tempestate evelli poterant.

2. Annum vix attigit aetatis septimum, cum missae sacrificio ita quotidie attentus assistebat, ut omnium aspicientium animos in admirationem traheret. Praeterea illius domus (invalescente tunc per Hiberniam persecutione) ordinarium fuit latibulum & domicilium religiosorum, praesertim vero Patrum Franciscanorum, quorum conversatione & consortio puerulus Kerneus ita delectabatur, ut ab eis sejungi vix pro somno capiendo posset.

3. Jam in primis Catholicae fidei fundamentis a Patribus instructus, coetaneos alios suos gratiosus pusio Catholice cathechizabat & instruebat. Ad triviales missus scholas, brevi annorum intervallo non solum scribere, legere & grammaticae ac syntaxeos rudimenta exacte didicit; verum etiam inter alia pietatis exercitia officium B. Virginis (quod parvum dicitur) una cum officiolo Immaculatae illius Conceptionis memoriae tradidit & quotidie una cum Rosario Lauretanisque Litaniis lachrymantibus non raro oculis recitabat. Sacrosanctum

you, from a fighter of martyrs, a defamer of his own homeland and a slanderer of any excellent man without distinction, into a pious penitent of contrite heart, Amen.

List of names of some friars of the Order of Strict Observance of Ireland, of whom Rev. Fr Bruodinus makes no mention in his catalogue dealing with the martyrs of Ireland.

Life of Martyr John Kearney

1. Fr John Kearney[567] was born in Cashel, in Ireland, in the year 1619, from noble and Catholic parents, namely Master John Kearney and Elizabeth born Creagh (who was cruelly killed, together with hundreds of other Catholics, by the English heretics in the year 1647 in no less holy a place than the cathedral church of the Divine Patrick).[568] The diligence of his deeply pious parents in the first blossoming of his age made fertile in his soul the seeds of piety, chastity and modesty which, in the course of the years, fixed so firm and numerous roots, that they could not possibly be eradicated by any storm.

2. He had hardly reached his seventh year of age, when he was already used to attend the sacrifice of the mass every day and with such a degree of eagerness that he would impress to admiration the minds of all spectators. Moreover, at a time when the persecution was growing stronger and stronger across Ireland, his house was the refuge and dwelling-place of clerics, and especially Franciscan fathers. Kearney, still a little boy, enjoyed their company and closeness so much, that only with difficulty could he be separated from them to make him get some sleep.

3. Since the fathers had already educated him in the first foundations of the Catholic faith, the little boy, full of grace, used to catechise and instruct other children of the same age as him. Having been sent to grammar schools, it took him very few years not only to learn with precision how to read and write, and the rudiments of grammar and syntax, but also to learn by heart, amongst other exercises of piety, the Office (which is called 'Little') of the Blessed Virgin, as well as the Tiny Office of Her Immaculate Conception; and he used to recite these every day, together with the rosary and the Litanies of Loreto,[569] not rarely

Eucharistiae Sacramentum, exploratis prius conscientiae nervis eisque per sacramentalem poenitentiam ablegatis, septimanatim adminimum frequentabat, condiscipulos ad Coelestes illas Epulas frequentandas verbo & exemplo inducebat taliter, ut ejus conversatione piisque exhortationibus pueri & adolescentes multi, omissis ludicris coetaneorum jocis, non tam in literarum studio, quam consuetis contemplativorum exercitiis quotidie magis atque magis proficerent.

3. Reparatae salutis 1634. aetatis 16. anno nondum superato, Karneus spretis mundi vanitatibus serio cogitavit de mutando in melius vitae statu; haerebat tamen dubius quam religionem ingredi deberet. Patrum Jesuitarum (sub quorum disciplina in paterna domo humanioribus literis studuit) vivendi norma illi non displicebat, & ut eorum Societati se adjungeret non solum ipsi Patres rara juvenis indole moti, sed pia illius mater pro viribus stimulabat. Parentis vero consilium fuit ut cum mundum deserere omnino proposuerat verorum Evangelicae paupertatis professorum, Fratrum nimirum Minorum Strictioris Observantiae Regulae Sanctis Francisci, vivendi modum assumeret; ut, sic proprietate rerum omnium mundanarum nudatus, nudum imitaretur Christum.

4. Karneus a Deo se ad Coelestem hanc potius quam illam vocari Societatem advertens, parentum bona cum venia, dignissimum Patrem Fratrem Josephum Everardum, Seraphici Ordinis per Hiberniam ministrum tunc provincialem, accessit eique animi arcana & vocationis ad sacrum Ordinem stimulum apperuit. Pater Everardus (cui ab incunabulis juvenis Karnei laudata indoles explorata erat) paterne supplicantis votis annuit & ut valedicto parentibus, patriae ac cognatis se intra paucos dies ad peregrinandum Kilkeniam (ubi nominatissima totius Lageniae probationis aedes Fratrum Minorum tunc erat) disponeret, monuit.

with his eyes in tears. He attended the holy and sacred sacrament of the Eucharist at least every week, only after examining the concerns of his conscience and loosening them through sacramental penance; and with his words and example he was so effective in convincing his school-mates to attend the celestial banquet that, by spending time with him and listening to his pious exhortations, many children and young adults neglected the playful games of people of their age and made greater and greater progress every day, not just in the study of literature, but even more in the exercises to which contemplative people are generally accustomed.

3. In the year of accomplished salvation 1634, when he had not turned 16 yet, Kearney seriously considered rejecting the vanities of the world and changing the condition of his life into a better one; still, the doubt remained of which religious order he should enter. He did not dislike the rule of living of the Jesuit fathers (under whose discipline he studied humanities in his paternal house); and not only the fathers themselves, who had been excited by the young man's rare disposition, but also his pious mother urged him, as much as she could, to join their Society. His father's advice, however, was that he, once he had decided to abandon the secular world for good, take up the lifestyle of those who truly professed evangelic poverty, namely the Friars Minor of Strict Observance of the Rule of St Francis; by doing so, he would be stripped of the possession of every secular item, and thus he would be imitating the naked Christ.

4. Kearney, feeling that God was calling him towards this celestial society rather than the other one, with his parents' great favour went to Fr Joseph Everard,[570] a truly worthy friar who was provincial minister of the seraphic order across Ireland at that time, and he disclosed to him the secrets of his soul and the stimulus of the vocation towards the holy order. Fr Everard (who had had the chance to examine the much-praised disposition of young Kearney since he was still in the cradle) gave his fatherly consent to the suppliant's vows and urged him to say farewell to his parents, his homeland and kinsmen, and prepare to travel to Kilkenny within a few days (where the most renowned convent of the Friars Minor of all Leinster was located at that time).

5. Karneus spiritu exultans, peractis debitis Patri Provinciali gratiis, domum laetus dum regrederetur in via casu forte ex condiscipulis unum prae multis charum Casseliensis urbis ditissimi patritii filium, Josephum Saulum dictum, obviam habuit; cui post varios sermones de mundi contemptu ultro citroque habitos mentem suam & ad religionem S. Francisci vocationem confidenter apperuit; & ut suo exemplo, spretis mundi vanitatibus, Christo se sub suavi pauperum Patriarchae Francisci jugo consecraret pro viribus hortabatur.

Saulus, salutaribus Karnei monitis divinaque inspiratione motus, in Paulum conversus, Caelestis gratiae subito sensit effectus, quare paucis postea diebus in vocatione confirmatus Karnei ductu ad Reverendi Patris Provincialis praesentiam venit probationisque habitum ab eo humiliter petiit. Pater Everardus Provincialis paterne utrumque juvenem amplectens Karnei diligentiam & curam de condiscipuli salute laudavit; Sauli vero desiderio & postulatis benigne annuit, unde datis utrisque literis, Kilkeniam ad novitiatum neo-candidatos simul misit.

6. Praefuit tunc Kilkenensi Conventu antiquissimae nobilitatis vitaeque contemplativae laudatissimus religiosus, Reverendus Pater Frater Dominicus Demsii, qui pauca interposita dierum mora egregios juvenes Franciscana simul induit veste. Karneus jam Seraphicum tyronem se sub disciplina tanti Patris esse advertens, Seraphicamque vitam sibi ducendam fore intelligens, ita toto illo probationis anno in orationibus assiduum, in humilitatis exercitiis paratum, inedia crebra in se durum & quotidiana flagellatione corporis inclementem se ostendit, ut omnibus connovitiis sicut & reliquis Fratribus liberiori aura utentibus praeluceret sanctitatis exemplo.

5. Kearney, rejoicing in the spirit, thanked the provincial father as he ought to. By chance, while he was happily returning home, on the road he bumped into one of the class-mates, who was dear to him even more than many others, named Joseph Sall, the son of the wealthiest patrician of the town of Cashel. To him, after an exchange of conversations of various kinds about despising the world, he resolutely revealed his intention and his vocation to the creed of St Francis; and putting forward his own case as an example, he urged him, as much as he could, to neglect the vanities of the world and to devote himself to Christ under the delightful yoke of the poor followers of Patriarch Francis.

Sall, moved by Kearney's admonitions of salvation and by divine inspiration, turned into Paul and immediately felt the effects of the celestial grace.[571] For this reason, a few days later he became stronger in his vocation. Led by Kearney, he appeared before the reverend provincial father and humbly asked him for the attire of probation. Provincial Fr Everard, fatherly embracing both young men, praised Kearney's diligence and care for the salvation of his school-companion; and indeed, he benevolently consented to Sall's wish and requests. On the basis of this, having provided both with letters of recommendation, he sent the new candidates together to the novitiate in Kilkenny.

6. At that time, the person in charge of the convent of Kilkenny was a religious man of very ancient nobility and of contemplative life who had received great praise, the Rev. Fr Dominic Dempsey.[572] This friar, after a short period of a few days, clothed the two excellent young men at once with the Franciscan habit. Under the teaching of such an exemplary father, Kearney soon perceived of himself as a seraphic novice, and understood that he would be required to live a seraphic life. Thus, during that entire year of probation he showed himself unremitting in prayers, ready in exercises of humility, harsh on himself through frequent fasting, and merciless in daily flagellation of his body, so that he would shine forth with his example of sanctity before all his fellow novices as well as the other friars who enjoyed a freer contact with the outside world.

7. Tyrocinio completo nondum sextus effluxit mensis, cum moderatorum jussu, socio Fratre Saulo, in Belgium Karneus ut navigaret omnia disposuerat, ut in celeberrimo Lovaniensi Fratrum Minorum Hibernorum Collegio philosophicis & theologicis studiis se applicaret. Acceptis obedientialibus, obedientiae filius Karneus se accinxit ad iter, conscensaque navi in Waterfordensi portu Oceani maris fluctibus se cum socio commisit. Prima die ventis velis faventibus, iter feliciter prosecuti sunt: sequenti vero die, orta horribili tempestate, agitantibus indomiti pelagi ingentibus fluctibus inordinate sibi succedentibus navem, de vita omnium navigantium jam actum esse a nautis conclamatum est. Trepidantibus cunctis, solus Karneus, spiritu Dei confortatus, non timere visus est; quare nautas & navigantes omnes egregius juvenis zelose hortatus est, ut plena fide ad Deum cui venti & mare obediunt ductu Stellae maris, Immaculatae nimirum Christi matris Mariae, recurrerent. Nautae omnes Puritanae perfidiae erant alumni, adhuc tamen aliud nullum videntes remedium, mortis terrore percussi, in genua Catholicorum ritu ac exemplo procumbunt, & invocante summa cum devotione Fratre Karneo misericordiarum Matrem Anglice, per decursum Lauretanearum Littaniarum, haeretici, non minus quam Catholici, Patrio sermone respondebant, *ora pro nobis.*

8. Vix fidelis Dei servus Karneus Litanias finivit, cum subito cessantibus ventis tranquilitas facta est in mari, non sine ingenti consolatione Catholicorum, Haereticorum vero stupore & admiratione. Aeternae vitae haeredes Catholici Coeli & Maris Imperatrici (cujus intercessione fauces evaserunt mortis) condignas post Deum egerunt gratias; Haeretici vero in malo indurati, tam patenti miraculo quamvis victi, adhuc tamen in pristina perseverarunt perfidia. Superatis Oceani periculis, Frater Karneus cum socio Bristoliam in Anglia appulit, ubi

7. Six months had not yet passed after he had completed his novitiate, when Kearney had already made all arrangements to set sail to Belgium with Friar Sall as his companion. There, following the commands of their moderators, he devoted himself to philosophical and theological studies in the much-renowned college of the Irish Friars Minor in Louvain. Once he received the letters of obedience, Kearney, a son of obedience, got ready for the journey, and having boarded a ship in the port of Waterford he entrusted himself to the ocean's waves together with his companion. On the first day, they proceeded with their journey in fortunate conditions, since the winds were favourable to the sails; the next day, however, a terrible storm rose up. As the huge waves of the fierce sea were confusedly tossing about the ship one after another, loud shouts of despair were cried out by the sailors, lamenting that the lives of all those on board were by now over.[573] While everybody was bustling about anxiously, only Kearney, strengthened by God's spirit, seemed not to be in fear; therefore, the excellent young man passionately urged the sailors as well as everyone on board to resort in full faith to God, to whom the winds and the sea obey, by following the leadership of the Star of the Sea, namely Mary, the Immaculate Mother of Christ. All the sailors had been brought up in the false faith of Puritanism. Yet, since they could not see any other remedy in that moment, shaken by fear for death they prostrated themselves on their knees in the custom and example of Catholics; and while Friar Kearney, with the highest degree of devotion, was invoking the Mother of Mercies in English, the heretics, in the course of the Litanies of Loreto, responded *ora pro nobis* in their native language, no less than the Catholics did.

8. God's faithful servant Kearney had barely finished the litanies, when the winds suddenly stilled and calmness spread over the sea, not without great consolation for the Catholics, and indeed surprise and astonishment for the heretics. The Catholics, heirs to eternal life, thanked God and, after him, the Empress of the sky and the sea (by whose intercession they escaped from the jaws of death), as they truly deserved; the heretics, however, who were hardened in their pursuit of evil, albeit won by such a clear miracle, still persevered in their previous faithlessness. Having overcome the dangers of the ocean, Friar Kearney together with his companion landed in England,

Saulus in gravem ac periculosum incidit morbum. Vocati ab hospite medici deprehenderunt infirmum maligna laborare febri, pro qua sedanda varia descripserunt pharmaca. Frater Karneus infirmum monuit socium ut Haereticorum medicamentis omissis ad Christum, in cujus manibus vitae & mortis essent claves, recurreret, firmiterque crederet Sacratissimae Virginis auxilio (quae salus est infirmorum) brevi se convaleturum: nec aliter contigit; nam Fratre Karneo ante infirmi lectum devote genuflectente & Litanias Lauretanas summa cum pietate respondente Saulo infirmo recitante, incepit subito valetudinarius melius habere ita quod sequenti die iter suum sanus per Angliam prosequi poterat.

9. Superato Haereticorum refugio Anglia, Karneus una cum socio Lovaniam attigit, ubi sex annorum spatio in Phylosophicis & Theologicis singularem fecit profectum; multo tamen majorem in studio orationis, meditationum, humilitatis, & obedientiae visus est fecisse: nam in choro die noctuque inter primos ingressu & ultimos in egressu semper fuerat. In exercitiis omnibus humilitatis singularis ejus promptitudo ab omnibus fuit notata. Neminem unquam voluntarie durante sui studii cursu visus est offendisse; etsi quando advertebat confratrem aliquem adverso animo in illum ferri, quiescere non poterat, antequam flexis in terra genibus illi fuisset deprecatus. Ob has & multas alias virtutes (in Lovanensis Collegii Archivio notatas), quibus omnibus Patribus & Fratribus praelucebat religiosi viri exemplo, superioribus & subditis omnibus Collegii ita fuit charus, gratus & acceptus, ut non posset magis.

10. Sacrae Theologiae candidatus & sacerdos jam existens, Pater Karneus zelo salutis animarum ardens in patriam remeandi facultatem a superioribus petiit & accepit circa finem anni 1642. Non diu acceptis dimissorialibus cunctatus est, cum se indomitis

in Bristol, where Sall fell into a serious and dangerous disease. The physicians, who had been called by the host, found out that the patient was struggling with an evil fever, which in order to sedate they prescribed various medicines. Friar Kearney advised his companion to lay the heretics' medicines aside and resort to Christ, in the hands of whom – he said – the keys of life and death are, and to firmly believe that he would shortly be recovering with the help of the Holy and Saintly Virgin (who is health for sick people).[574] And things did not go otherwise; for, while Friar Kearney, devoutly genuflecting before the invalid's bed, was reciting the Litanies of Loreto with Sall as a most pious respondent, the sick man immediately started feeling so much better, that he was able to continue his journey across England in good health on the next day.[575]

9. Having left England behind – a nest of heretics – Kearney reached Louvain together with his companion, where he made extraordinary progress in philosophical and theological studies in a period of six years. However, he seemed to have made an even greater progress in the study of prayer, meditations, humility and obedience; in fact he was in the choir night and day, always being amongst the first ones to go in and the last to go out. His peculiar promptitude in all exercises of humility was noticed by everyone. He never seemed to have offended anyone deliberately during the course of his study; even when he felt that some fellow friar was behaving badly against him because of an unfriendly spirit, he was unable to rest before he had prayed in his favour on his bended knees upon the ground. He was so dear, beloved and well-accepted by all of his superiors and subordinates, that it would not have been possible for him to be more so, thanks to these and many other virtues (noted down in the archive of the College of Louvain), which made him shine bright by his example of a religious man in front of all his fellow fathers and brothers.

10. Accepted as candidate for Holy Theology and being already a priest, Fr Kearney, who was burning with zeal for the salvation of souls, asked and obtained from his superiors the permission to go back to his homeland, around the end of the year 1642.[576] Once he received his letters of discharge, he did not allow a long period of time to pass before entrusting himself to the fierce waves of the

Oceani undis commiserat. In via autem ipsis marinis fluctibus magis feros & inexplicabiles deprehendit praedones, inclementes nimirum & rebelles parlamentares Haereticos Anglos, in quorum sanguinolentas manus mansuetus Pater (Deo ita permittente ut ejus in fide Constantia tanquam auri in fornace probaretur) insperate incidit. Capitur itaque a rebellibus parlamentariis, & primo Bristoliam ac tandem Londinium, ligatis post tergum latronis ad instar manibus, ducitur ad carceres; quorum aerumnas & foetores per aliquot septimanas summa cum patientia sustinuit.

11. Demum sedentibus pro tribunal rebellibus Calvinistis examinatur. Pater Karneus intrepide respondit se Catholicum & Franciscani Ordinis sacerdotem juxta ritum Sanctissimae Romanae Ecclesiae (extra quam nulla esset spes salutis) ordinatum esse. Hoc audito, iniquorum judicum jussu condemnatur ad torturas, nisi Papismo renunciare vellet. Trahitur mox a carnificibus ad ordinarium torturarum locum, cruciaturque frustra variis tormentorum generibus, praesertim eculeo, ac exustione extremitatum manuum pedumque digitorum; quo in cruciatu Karneus spiritu exultans carnificibus (continue eum interrogantibus an a Papismo recedere vellet) exprobrabat, quasi satis suo satisfacere non scirent officio. Rebelles videntes per torturas Christi Athletam non posse infici contagioso puritanorum morbo, alia via excogitarunt de modo illum superandi, inedia nimirum ac durissimis carcerum cruciatibus & miseriis: reduci ergo imperant innocentissimum Christi confessorem ad tenebricos carceres.

12. Ibat a conspectu consilii gaudens Karneus (quod pro Christi Ecclesiae professione dignus habitus sit contumelias pati) cum inhumanis ductoribus ad destinatum miseriarum locum, ubi manibus pedibusque ponderosis ferreis catenis ligatus per continuos tres menses in spelunca quadam subterranea viginti pedum altitudine

ocean. During the journey, however, he was detected by fiercer and more unmanageable bandits than the actual sea-waves, namely by unmerciful and rebellious parliamentarian heretics of England; and he, a meek father, unexpectedly fell into their bloody hands (with God allowing this so that his resistance in faith could be put to the test just like the resistance of gold is tested in a furnace). Thus, he was kidnapped by the parliamentarian rebels and brought to prison with his hands tied up behind his back like those of robbers, first in Bristol and eventually in London, where he endured the prison's miseries and stench for several weeks with great patience.

11. At last he was interrogated before a tribunal with Calvinist rebels sitting as judges. Without trembling, Fr Kearney responded that he was a Catholic, and that he had been ordained a priest of the Franciscan order according to the rite of the Most Holy Roman Church (outside of which – he said – there is no hope of salvation). Having heard this, the unfair judges ordered that he be condemned to be tortured, unless he wished to renounce acceptance of the pope's authority. He was soon dragged by the executioners to the usual place for torturing, and he was tormented in vain with various tortures, above all the spike[577] and the burning of the extremities of the hands and of the toes. But during this torment Kearney, rejoicing in the spirit, kept blaming his executioners (while they were continuously asking him whether he wished to retreat from his acceptance of the pope's authority), as if they did not know how to satisfactorily fulfil their duty. The rebels, seeing that the champion of Christ could not be corrupted by the contagious disease of the Puritan heretics through torturing, thought to overcome him in a different manner, namely by starvation and the prison's harshest pains and miseries. Thus, they ordered that the completely innocent confessor of Christ be led back to the gloomy prison.

12. Pleased with this decision (since – he said – enduring abuses in support of the profession of Christ's Church is a worthy habit), Kearney walked away from the council's sight accompanied by inhuman attendants, who led him to the place of miseries to which he had been sentenced. There, with his hands and feet tied up by heavy iron chains, he had to lie for three uninterrupted months in a sort of

profunda solo pane & aqua contentus delitescere debuit. Lictoris uxor, quae mutatis cum filia vicibus assignatam modici panis portionem pauperi Karneo consuetis horis porrigebat (filiae ut credibile est, vel si mavis Cacodaemonis persuasione mota), considerans incarcerati juvenis egregiam pulchramque corporis dispositionem, castissimo Patri obtulit libertatem & dotem non spernendam ea conditione, ut filiam in uxorem ducat. Karneus stolidae foeminae postulata ridens respondit se jam dudum castissimae desponsatum esse Virgini (castitatem intelligens), cujus thorum per novas sibi non liceret violare nuptias: tandem foeminae professionis suae seriem aperuit eamque hortatus est si a diris liberari vellet inferni vinculis & cruciatibus, Calvinistis in malo perseverantibus certo praeparatis, fidem una cum fili<a> & marito amplecteretur Catholicam; quo dicto mulier disparuit, nec Patrem amplius ausa est tentare.

13. Paucis postea diebus, rebelles haeretici, considerantes quod nec torturis aut crudelissimis carcerum afflictionibus Karneus induci poterat ut a fide recedere, citarunt illum denuo coram tribunali. Sistitur itaque constantissimus Christi confessor injusti loco judicii, & ad mortem quam summis expectabat votis condemnatur. Prolata iniqua sententia, Karneus prae gaudio exultans Sanctorum Ambrosii & Augustini Hymnum cum jubilo cantare incepit; a prosecutione vero Anglicae melodiae Colaphis & verberibus impeditur a Sathanae satellitibus, & ad carceres paulo humaniores quam antea, judicum jussu, trahitur, ut sequenti die una cum aliis ob latrocinia ad mortem condemnatis ultimo afficeretur supplicio. Placuit tamen Altissimo Karneum ad majora pro sui nominis gloria sufferenda conservare:

deep underground cave, which extended to a depth of twenty feet, settling for bread and water only. A prison guard's wife, who alternated with her daughter to hand out the decreed portion of simple bread to poor Kearney at regular times of the day, noticed the remarkable and good-looking elegance of the body of the young man even in his cell. Considering this, the woman (successfully persuaded, as one can easily believe, by her daughter or, if you prefer, by an evil demon) offered the most chaste father freedom, and a not-indifferent dowry on one condition: that he marry her daughter. Kearney, laughing at what the silly woman had asked, replied that he had been already promised in marriage to a most chaste Virgin some time before (since – he said – he could discern true chastity), and that it would have been unlawful for him to dishonour her bed by committing to a new wedding. Finally, he revealed the consequences of his profession of faith to the woman, and he urged her to embrace the Catholic faith together with her son and husband, if she wished to be set free from the dreadful chains and tortures of hell, which were certainly ready for the Calvinists, who would persevere with their evil belief. After these words, however, the woman disappeared, and did not dare to lead the father into temptation any more.[578]

13. A few days later, the heretical rebels, considering that Kearney could not be convinced to retreat from his faith even by tortures or the most cruel pains of the prison, summoned him again before the tribunal. Thus, Christ's firmest confessor was produced in court to be trialled unfairly and he was sentenced to death, which he had been hoping for in his greatest wishes. When the unjust verdict was uttered, Kearney, leaping up because of his happiness, started singing the Hymn of St Ambrose and St Augustine with joy. Satan's spies, however, hindered him from continuing singing the English melody by punching and cudgelling him. By order of the judges, he was dragged into a prison barely more suitable to a human being than the previous one, so that he could suffer the final punishment on the next day together with other convicts, who had been sentenced to death because of robberies. However, the Almighty decided to keep Kearney alive so that he may suffer greater pains according to the glory of his name. Therefore, that very same night he was secretly lowered from a window of the prison inside a basket with the careful help of a single

unde illa ipsa nocte, diligentia illustris unius Catholici Angli, furtive ex carcerum fenestra in sporta fuit dimissus, & ad ipsius aedes caute adductus. Exinde habita secura navigandi comoditate praefati nobilis viri expensis in Galliam navigavit.

14. Callesiae in Gallia non diu subst<et>it Dei ac proximorum amore ardens Karneus, cum spretis marinis ac pyratarum periculis & insidiis denuo se oceani maris clementiae commisit; qua experta, Wexfordiam in Hibernia feliciter attigit. Inde Casseliam Momoniae metropolem venit, ubi praevia superiorum benedictione non solum subtiles in docendo per biennium Philosophiam (quam moderatorum jussu tradere debuit) ingenii dotes, verum etiam in proponendo Dei verbo ardentem suum zelum junctum cum facunda eloquentia ita ostendit, ut vicinae Casseliae Civitates non parum superiores molestarent, summis precibus rogantes ut ad ipsos Karneus mitteretur.

15. Reiteratis Waterfordensium civium votis satisfacere volens Pater Provincialis eximium verbi Dei praeconem Karneum Waterfordiam misit, ubi summa cum Cleri ac populi satisfactione Magistri Novitiorum vices & ordinarii Concionatoris partes laudabiliter egit, usque ad annum 1649., quo Cromwellistae (dissentientibus Catholicorum exercitum ducibus) occupata tota fere Hibernia Catholicorum ritum ubique turbarunt, monasteria funditus everterunt, Ecclesias in profanum usum converterunt, Ecclesiasticos omnes tam saeculares quam regulares proscripserunt vel supplicio affecerunt, & Regni proceres ac nobiles bonis fere omnibus privarunt.

16. Luctuosum illum patriae statum (in quo, fugientibus ad partes ultramarinas plerisque Ecclesiasticis, expulsisque ex Regno ad diversas mundi plagas supra 100 millia Catholicorum, relictae in patria Christi oviculae in medio luporum sine pastoribus de vita periclitabantur) dolenter considerans, Karneus firmiter statuit nullatenus se velle subjugatos pauperes suos populares deserere, nisi cum morte.

noble English man of Catholic faith, and he was cautiously brought to that man's house. From there, once a safe occasion to travel by sea was arranged at the expense of the honourable man mentioned above, he set sail for France.

14. Burning with love for God and his neighbours, Kearney had not been staying in Calais in France for long, when he entrusted himself to the mercy of the ocean sea again, disregarding the dangers and traps of the waves and the pirates; and having made trial of it, he successfully landed in Wexford in Ireland. From that place, he reached Cashel, the capital of Munster. There, after receiving the benediction of his superiors, he exhibited not only the fine talents of his mind in teaching philosophy for a period of two years (a teaching which he had to deliver by order of his moderators), but also his fervent zeal, combined with fluent eloquence, in setting forth the word of God. He achieved so much success in displaying his talents, that this caused no little trouble to more important communities near Cashel, which asked with great prayers that Kearney be sent to them.

15. The provincial father, wishing to satisfy the repeated requests of the citizens of Waterford, sent Kearney, the extraordinary herald of the word of God, to Waterford, where he commendably held the office of master of novices and acted as official preacher giving great satisfaction to the clergy and the population, until the year 1649. In that year, Cromwell's supporters occupied almost the entirety of Ireland (while the commanders of the armies of the Catholics were in dissention amongst themselves). They threw the observance of the Catholic rite into disarray everywhere, they destroyed monasteries to their foundations, they turned churches over to secular usage, they proscribed all clerics, secular as well as regular, or tormented them with torture, and they deprived the rulers and noblemen of the kingdom of almost all their possessions.

16. Kearney looked at that mournful condition of his homeland with grief (a situation of danger for the lives of God's little sheep, who had been abandoned in their homeland without shepherds, surrounded by wolves, while most clerics were fleeing to lands beyond the sea and more than one hundred thousand Catholics had been exiled from the kingdom to different regions of the world). Therefore, he came

Diversi saeculalres amici & Ecclesiastici serio illum monuerunt ut saluti suae consulere vellet, & sic ad tempus se subducere in aliam aliquam Catholicam regionem, usque dum infernalis haereticorum furor paulatim sedaretur: at in vanum, nam Karneus respondit statui suo non convenire ut timeat corporalis vitae pericula in causa tam justa & occasione tam commoda conservandi in fide tot mille animas, quas in pastorum absentia pestifera Calvinistarum lues facile posset coinquinare; unde ait nullo modo ex patria se velle abire, antequam vi cogeretur aut sancta urgente obedientia compelleretur.

17. Haesit igitur intrepide in patria Pater Karneus, & die noctuque furtive per civitates, oppida & pagos Momoniae Sacramenta administrabat, afflictos consolabatur, vacillantes in fide roborabat, & denique peste laborantes (quorum ingens in Hibernia tunc erat numerus) sine omni timore & horrore pro viribus sustantabat. In his piis exercitiis, durante saeva & a saeculis inaudita persecutione rebellium haereticorum, se dum occupasset per aliquot annos fortis Christi miles Karneus, placuit Altissimo diu desideratum tot laborum praemium illi reddere: anno namque 1652. circa initium Martii, occupante se diligentissimo vineae Domini cultore Karneo Conventus Corkagiensis tunc Guardiano circa frequens charitatis erga proximum ministerium, Casseliae incidit in manus barbari cujusdam militum ductoris Wilmer dicti: qui de capta praeda laetus mitissimum Patrem male mulctatum in vincula conjecit & paulo post, stipatum haereticis militibus leopardis crudelioribus, Clonmeliam viginti circiter Casselia milliaribus misit.

18. Praefuit Clonmelensi Civitati, sicut & toti illi Momoniae tractui, Crumwellista sanguinolentus Hieronymus Sansius, qui< >innocentem

to the firm resolution that he had absolutely no intention to desert his poor fellow countrymen in a condition of subjugation, until his own death. Various friends, secular as well as ecclesiastical, seriously warned him to think judiciously about his own safety, and therefore to temporarily seek refuge in some other Catholic country, until the infernal rage of the heretics would gradually cease. But in vain; for Kearney replied that it would not befit his status to fear the dangers concerning his corporal life in a cause so just and in an occasion so appropriate to saving so many thousands of souls, which in the absence of shepherds the noxious plague of the Calvinists could easily infect. On this basis, he said that by no means was he willing to leave his country, for as long as he was not being constrained to do so by force or bound by the urging of holy obedience.

17. Therefore, Fr Kearney intrepidly held fast to his homeland, and day and night, secretly across the cities, towns and villages of Munster, he used to administer the sacraments, offer comfort to the sufferers, strengthen those who were vacillating in their faith; in a word, he used to give as much support as he could to those who were struggling because of the plague (whose number was great at that time in Ireland), with no fear and no terror. While Kearney, Christ's steadfast soldier, had been engaged with these pious exercises for several years during the heretic rebels' persecution, whose fierceness was unheard-of in centuries, the Almighty decided to reward him for so many toils with the prize for which he had been wishing for a long time. In fact, in the year 1652, around the beginning of March, Kearney, the most diligent cultivator of the Lord's vineyard, who at that time was engaged with fulfilling his regular duties concerning the ministry of Christian love as guardian of the convent of Cork,[579] fell into the hands of a certain commander of soldiers named Wilmer,[580] in Cashel. This barbarous man, glad about the prey he had caught, inflicted an evil punishment upon the truly gentle father and threw him into chains; and shortly afterwards he sent him to Clonmel, around twenty miles from Cashel, with an escort of heretical soldiers more savage than leopards.

18. The man in charge of the town of Clonmel as well as of the entirety of that district of Munster was Jerome Sankey,[581] a bloodthirsty supporter of Cromwell, who made sure that the innocent father be

Patrem in communi ergastulo diversis aliis Ecclesiasticis & Catholicis viris repleto includi fecit. Habita tam commoda Sacerdotum sui Ordinis occasione, Pater Karneus piissime se ad mortem disposuit.

19. Sequenti die Divo Ioachimo sacro, sedente pro tribunali Sansio, educuntur vincti homines omnes ecclesiastici ex carceribus, & ad tribunal trahuntur. Adsunt subito testes iniqui, qui de multis variisque (ut credebant) criminibus contra Parlamenti constitutiones commissis innocentes accusarunt: nominatim vero Patri Karneo pro crimine laesae Majestatis objicitur, "quod in diversis Momoniae locis missas celebraverit, Sacramenta administraverit, & Catholicum populum impediverit quo minus Papismo renunciaret."

20. Karneus animose accusatoribus respondit se Franciscani Ordinis Religiosum & Catholicum esse sacerdotem, cui ex officio incumbebat missas celebrare & sacramenta necessaria Catholico populo administrare, & sic non peccasse in Regem aut rem publicam ullam bene ordinatam, satisfaciendo divinae legi, contra iniquas Parlamenti constitutiones: Tyrannus Sansius hoc audiens Karneum statim morti (proscriptis ex toto Regno aliis omnibus concaptivis illius) adjudicavit. Prolata injusta sententia, trahitur mansuetissimus Pater a lictoribus ad carceres, in quibus, exutis saecularibus vestibus quibus (more aliorum omnium religiosorum per Angliam & Hiberniam) publice utebatur, Sacrum Divi Francisci habitum induit, applicatisque pedibus sandaliis & lateri Rosario, sumptaque in manu Cruce, ad necem, fortem ut decebat Seraphicum pugilem, armatum & paratum se jam esse custodibus carcerum dixit.

21. Audita undecima diei hora neo-candidati Martyris supplicio destinata, educitur ex carceribus & in foro sistitur. Fit subito maximus concursus ex omnibus civitatis angulis, non solum lugentium Catholicorum civium, se etiam ridentium Calvinismi professorum,

shut inside a public jail full of various other clerics and Catholic men. In such a suitable situation for a priest of his order, Fr Kearney prepared for death in the most pious way.

19. On the next day, the feast day sacred to the Divine Joachim,[582] all clerics, tied up, are led out of the prison and are dragged before the tribunal, where Sankey is sitting as a judge. At once, dishonest witnesses are called forth, who accused the innocent men of many and diverse crimes (according to them) committed against the parliament's decrees; in particular, the accusation moved against Fr Kearney as a crime of lese-majesty is "that, in various places of Munster, he celebrated masses, administered the sacraments and hindered the Catholic population from renouncing the acceptance of the pope's authority".

20. To the accusers, Kearney bravely replied that he was a devout and Catholic priest of the Franciscan order, on whom the duties of celebrating masses and administering the necessary sacraments to the Catholic population rested as a consequence of his office; and, therefore, he had committed no sin against the king or his well-governed state[583] by complying with divine law against the unjust decrees of the parliament. Hearing this, the tyrant Sankey immediately sentenced Kearney to death (after proscribing all other fellow prisoners of his from the whole kingdom). The sentence having been pronounced, the truly gentle father is dragged by the guards to the jailhouse. There, he took off the secular clothes he used to wear in public (according to the custom of all other clerics across England and Ireland) and he put on the attire of the divine St Francis; and once he had donned the sandals to his feet and the rosary to his side, having taken up the cross in his hand, he said to the prison's watch-guards that he was already armed and prepared for death, as it was fitting for a strong seraphic pugilist.

21. When the bells sang the eleventh hour of the day, which had been chosen for the execution of the new candidate to martyrdom, he was led out of the jailhouse and placed in the market square. Immediately, a huge crowd quickly gathered around from all corners of the town, consisting not only of grieving Catholic citizens, but also of laughing people who professed Calvinism. These remained stupefied as if they

qui ut rem novam a se antea nunquam visam stupebant aspiciendo religiosum Patrem inusitata illis veste indutum & ad mortem tam intrepide properantem. Ex foro animose pergit cum ductoribus Victima Christi ad patibuli locum; quem cum attigisset, genibus flexis Deo suo gratias egit, quod se tali morte, qua certo acquiritur vita, fecerit dignum; eique lacrymantibus oculis agonem suum brevi ac efficaci oratione commendavit. Finitis precibus scalas ascendit, habitaque a ductore militum loquendi facultate paucis exposuit qualiter captus, incarceratus, accusatus & ad mortem condemnatus non aliam ob causam quam quod missas celebraverit, Sacramenta administraverit & Catholicos in avitae religionis professione ut perseverarent monuerit. "Haec" inquit "omnia in meo examine fassus fui, & defacto non solum confiteor, verum etiam affirmo neminem posse salvari extra Catholicam Romanam fidem, pro qua solatio plenus libenter morior, firmiter sperans in Christi meritis intuitu, quorum hodie expecto mercedem illam magnam quam promisit Deus diligentibus se." Quo dicto a carnifice e scalis turbatur hora undecima die Veneris Anni 1653. & ad caelum, ut credimus, volavit aetatis suae anno 34.

22. Mortuo jam martyre, recurrunt amici ad nequissimum judicem Sansium petuntque defuncti corpus sibi dari; annuit rebellis justae Catholicorum petitioni: qui, deposito ex ligno corpore, Casseliam illud evexerunt ibique honorifice in capituli loco Monasterii Fratrum Minorum Thesaurum suum sepeliverunt.

Refert R. P. Iosephus Saul, sicut & Admodum Reverendus Dominus Galfridus Saulus Metropolitanae Cassiliensis Ecclesiae Provisor & Canonicus (qui Martyris hujus vitam, quam penes me manuscriptam habeo, scripserunt) quod, portantibus amicis corpus Clonmelia Casseliam, in via obviam habuerunt nobilissimam Dominam Mariam

were watching something new they had never seen before, when they laid eyes on the religious father wearing clothes which were unusual amongst them and hurrying to death so undauntedly. From the market square, the victim of Christ bravely proceeded to the location of the gallows together with the guards leading him; and when he reached it, he went on his knees and thanked his God because He had made him worthy of such a death, as the one he had certainly secured with his life; and while shedding tears from his eyes, he entrusted to God's care his struggle by a short but effective prayer to Him. Having finished praying, he went up the ladder; and since the commander of the soldiers who had been leading him forth gave him permission to speak, he explained how he had been arrested, imprisoned, accused and sentenced to death for no other reason but because he had celebrated masses, administered the sacraments and admonished the Catholics to steadfastly continue professing the religion of their forefathers. He said: "I confessed to all these things during my examination; and as a matter of fact, not only do I confess to them now, but I also affirm that nobody can reach salvation outside the faith of Roman Catholicism, in defence of which I willingly die full of comfort, firmly trusting in Christ's consideration of my merits, for which today I expect that great reward which God promised to those who love him." Having thus spoken, he was thrown down from the ladder by the executioner in the eleventh hour of Friday, in the year 1653;[584] and – as we believe – he ascended into heaven at the age of 33.[585]

22. Now that the martyr was dead, his friends hastened to Sankey, the most unfair judge, and asked that the body of the deceased be given to them. The rebel consented to the Catholics' just request; thus, after the taking down of the corpse from the scaffold, they carried it to Cashel and buried their treasure[586] in the chapter hall of the monastery of the Friars Minor there.[587]

Rev. Fr Joseph Sall[588] as well as Adm. Rev. Master Godfrey Sall,[589] provisor and canon of the metropolitan church of Cashel (both of whom wrote a life of this martyr, a manuscript copy of which I personally own) report the following story. While Kearney's friends were carrying the corpse from Clonmel to Cashel, along the way they bumped into Lady Mary Gray, a most honourable woman who

Graiam, Martyris Karnei per complures annos spiritualem filiam ac benefactricem specialem; quae, lacrymantibus oculis ac singulari erga Martyrem affectu, rogavit ut sibi Patris sui spiritualis corpus monstraretur. Aperta tumba, pia Domina, magna animi devotione apprehensa dextera Martyris manu eamque devote oculans, se illius precibus commendavit; quo facto, videntibus tot personis fide dignis, defunctus optimae matronae manum sua compressit manu non aliter quam si vivus existeret. Hoc videntes, Catholici pie crediderunt Catholicae foeminae preces a Martyre fuisse exauditas. Historiam hanc ita contigisse prout narratur ipsa Domina Maria jurejurando coram Ordinario Casseliensi Vicario Generali testata est, & centenis aliis non semel narravit.

23. Anno salutis 1649. occupata vi Wexfordia, maritima in Lagenia civitate, necatisque crudeliter tot centenis sine sexus differentia Catholicis, in manus Crumwellistarum rebellium venerunt Reverendi ac Religiosissimi Patres, Verbi Dei zelosissimi praedicatores, Richardus Synott, Sacrae Theologiae Lector, Ryamundus Staffort, Paulus Synott, Ioannes Esmond & Petrus Staffort, quos omnes in odium Catholicae Religionis in ipso Wexfordensi Conventu gladiis, fustibus & sclopis inhumani rebelles trucidarunt. Horum vita sicut & sequentium aliorum Martyrum fuse scribitur ab uno ex nostris Patribus in Belgio.

24. Reverendus Pater Guilielmus Hicquaeus Tuomoniensis, divini verbi eximius praeco, anno salutis 1651. subjugata jam Tuomonia apprehenditur ab haereticis parlamentariis & examinatur. Hicquaeus intrepide se sacerdotem & Franciscanum esse sine tergiversatione fatetur, quo audito nulla servata juris forma haereticorum militum Capitanei jussu ex proxima suspenditur arbore.

25. Anno salutis 1648. in manus haereticorum incidit sanctissimae vitae religiosus Andreas Hicquaeus Tuomoniensis, Actualis Conventus

had been the spiritual daughter and special benefactress of Martyr Kearney for a great number of years. Thus the woman, shedding tears from her eyes and moved by her individual fondness towards the martyr, asked that the corpse of her spiritual father be shown to her. Once the coffin was opened, the pious lady took the right hand of the martyr with great piety of soul and, looking at it with devotion, she entrusted herself to him by means of prayers; and after she did this, while so many trustworthy people were watching, the dead squeezed the virtuous lady's hand with his own hand, just as if he were still alive. Seeing this, the Catholics devoutly believed that the Catholic woman's prayers had been heard by the martyr. That this story happened precisely as narrated here has been attested by Lady Mary herself, solemnly swearing in the presence of the ordinary general vicar of Cashel, and has also been reported by hundreds of people more than once.[590]

23. In the year of salvation 1649, after the maritime town of Wexford in Leinster had been occupied by force and so many hundreds of Catholics had been cruelly killed without distinction between sexes,[591] the rebellious supporters of Cromwell captured Richard Sinnott, lector of holy theology, Raymond Staffort, Paul Sinnott, John Esmond and Peter Stafford,[592] reverend and most religious fathers. Out of hatred against the Catholic religion, all these incredibly passionate preachers of God's word were slaughtered by the inhumane rebels with swords, clubs and firearms in no less holy a place than the convent of Wexford. Their lives, as well as those of the following other martyrs, are being written down at length by one of our fellow fathers in Belgium.

24. Rev. Fr William Hickey of Thomond,[593] eminent herald of the divine word, was arrested and examined by the heretic parliamentarians in the year 1651, after the subjugation of Thomond. Without hesitation, Hickey fearlessly confessed to be a priest and a Franciscan; these words having being heard, he was hanged on the nearest tree, with no respect for any form of right, by order of the captain of the heretical soldiers.

25. In the year of salvation 1648, a cleric of truly holy life, Andrew Hickey of Thomond,[594] acting preacher of the convent of Adare, fell into the hands of the heretics; out of hatred against the Catholic

Archdarensis Concionator, quem in Sacra qua indutus erat Franciscana veste non procul a suo Conventu in odium Catholicae religionis fune necarunt rebelles.

26. Nominatissimi duo Concionatores Pater Walterus de Wallis et Pater Antonius Musaeus, antiquissimae nobilitatis in Lagenia religiosi, multo nobiliores effecti sunt, fortiter pro Christi Ecclesia certando usque ad mortem, quam 24. Martii anni 1650. quo, ab haereticis comprehensi & cogniti, generose patibuli supplicio penes Mullingare subierunt.

27. R.P. Ioannes Dormer Lagenensis, vineae Domini indefessus cultor, Dublinii anno 1650. captus fuit ab haereticis & ad carceres condemnatus, quorum aerumnis, antequam ad ultimum sibi jam mortis supplicium ob constantiam in fide orthodoxa paratum raperetur, in ipsis carceribus ad meliorem transiit vitam.

28. Pater Nicolaus Uganus, Evangelicae paupertatis imitator exactissimus, anno 1650. ab haereticis Puritanis in Lagenia fuit captus & in odium fidei proprio fune quo cingebatur suspensus.

29. P. Bernardus Gorum<le>us, Seraphici Ordinis sacerdos & Concionator, anno Domini 1649. a parlamentariis haereticis in captivitatem fuit ductus Vadipontum, ibique suspendio martyrii lauream consecutus est.

30. R. P. Hilarius Conreus Momoniensis, Theologus & Concionator insignis, anno salutis 1652. a tyrannis rebellibus Kilkeniae eo quod Sacra fassus sit se celebrasse suspendio vitam finivit.

31. R. P. Ioannes Ferallus eodem anno haereticorum gladiis confossus ad Caelum migravit.

32. P. Philippus Flasberius Lagenensis, Religiosus vita & doctrina clarissimus, anno 1651. ab haereticis prope Dublinum suspensus est.

religion, the rebels killed him with a rope not far from his convent, while he was still wearing his sacred Franciscan habit.

26. Two preachers of great renown, Fr Walter Walsh[595] and Fr Anthony O'Hussey,[596] clerics who came from families of very ancient nobility in Leinster, achieved an even greater degree of nobility by bravely fighting in defence of Christ's Church until their death, which they honourably suffered through the capital death by the gibbet near Mullingar on 24 March 1650, when they were apprehended and judicially examined by the heretics.

27. Rev. Fr John Dormer of Leinster,[597] indefatigable cultivator of the Lord's vineyard, was captured in Dublin in the year 1650 by the heretics, and sentenced to prison. As a consequence of the toils he suffered there, he passed away to a better life in the very same prison, before he could be dragged to the final torture of death, which had been already prepared for him, because of his steadiness in Catholic orthodoxy.

28. Fr Nicolas Ugan, a most accurate imitator of evangelic poverty, was captured in Leinster in the year 1650 by Puritan heretics, and he was hanged with the very same cord which girded him, out of hatred against his faith.

29. Fr Bernard Gormley,[598] a priest and preacher of the seraphic order, was led to Drogheda as a prisoner by the parliamentarian heretics in the year of the Lord 1649, and there he achieved the glory of martyrdom through hanging.

30. Rev. Fr Hilary Conroy of Munster,[599] a distinguished theologian and preacher, reached the end of his life through hanging in the year of salvation 1652, killed by the tyrannical rebels in Kilkenny for having confessed to having celebrated the sacred mysteries.

31. In the same year, the Rev. Fr John O'Farrell[600] ascended into heaven, struck down by the heretics' swords.

32. Fr Philip Flatisbury of Leinster,[601] a cleric most renowned for his life and learning, was hanged by the heretics in the year 1651 near Dublin.

33. P. Franciscus Geraldinus, illustrissima ex familia in Momonia natus, anno 1650. Corcagiae in Hibernia ob Sacramentorum administrationem Missaeque sacrificii celebrationem rebellium jussu suspendio vitam finivit.

34. R. D. Richardus Buthlerus Momoniensis, Theologus & Praedicator ferventissimus, excellentissimaeque suae familiae singulare decus, inter centenos alios Ecclesiasticos & saeculares qui anno salutis 1647. praevalentibus per Momoniam Parlamentariis (occupataque ab eis vi Casseliensi Civitate) in amplissima Cathedrali Ecclesia refugium petierunt, penes ipsum summum altare gladiis fuit confossus, & martiryii corona donatus. Pari mortis genere eadem die & hora Fr Iacobus Saulus laicus vitam consecutus est Caelestem.

35. Fratres Iacobus Chiverus laicus, Iacobus Rocheus laicus, & Joanes Moclous laicus a perfidis Crumwellistis in odium fidei inhumaniter trucidati sunt.

36. Intellexerunt (non sine admiratione) plurimi ecclesiastici & saeculares in Tuomonia nati vel familiariter noti, dolenterque aspexerunt Carrani in patriam, Martyres pro Christo occisos & Bruodinianam familiam calumnias & convicia, sine omni ordinarii facultate, furtive in haeretica Civitate publicata; quare in confirmationem earum quae veridice scripsi de Bruodinis meis plurima testimonia ex diversis Europae Regnis miserunt, ex quibus sequentia subjungere sat erit. Demum nominabo religiosissimos aliquos Franciscanae religionis alumnos, qui in odium Catholicae religionis a rebellibus regicidis Anglis crudeliter occisi sunt & Martyrio affecti, quorum notitiam R. P. Bruodinus habere non poterat quando de Martyribus nostris egit. Cum hac tamen protestatione, quod nolim ea quae refero in hoc toto libello ab ullo accipi <non> tanquam historiam ab Apostolica sede examinatam & approbatam, sed tanquam narrationem, quae a sola virorum fide dignorum authoritate pondus obtinet. Proinde Apostolicum S. Congregationis Decretum Anno 1625. editum, & a Sanctissimo

33. Fr Francis Fitzgerald,[602] born from a family of great renown in Munster, reached the end of his life through hanging by order of the rebels in the year 1650 in Cork, Ireland, because he had administered the sacraments and celebrated the sacrifice of the mass.

34. Rev. Master Richard Butler of Munster, a theologian and most fervent preacher, and a unique honour to his already excellent family of great distinction, was bestowed with the crown of martyrdom in the year 1647, amongst other hundreds of clerics and laity who sought refuge in the large and magnificent cathedral church while the parliamentarians were prevailing across Munster (and after they had occupied the town of Cashel by force). He was struck down with swords near the high altar itself. With a similar kind of death, on the same day and at the same hour, Brother James Sall,[603] a layman, achieved heavenly life.

35. Lay-brothers James Cheevers, James Roche[604] and John Mockler[605] were savagely slaughtered by faithless followers of Cromwell out of hatred against their faith.

36. Very many clerics and secular readers, born in Thomond or family acquaintances of mine, understood (not without surprise) and noticed that Carran's calumnies and insults against his homeland, against martyrs killed for their defence of Christ, and against the family of the Bruodins were clandestinely published in a heretic city without every necessary permission from an ordinary.[606] Therefore, as a confirmation to what I truthfully wrote about my Bruodins, they sent me a great number of written declarations from various kingdoms of Europe, the following selection of which shall be enough to append below. In the appendix above I have named[607] some deeply religious pupils of the Franciscan religion, who were cruelly killed by the regicidal rebels of England out of hatred against the Catholic religion, and who suffered martyrdom; in fact, Rev. Fr Bruodinus could not have knowledge of them when he wrote about our martyrs. However, I also declare that I do not want anybody to take what I have been reporting throughout this whole pamphlet to be a story, to which weight is attributed only by the authority of trustworthy men, but a history which has been examined and approved by the Apostolic See. Therefore, I certify that I am willing to observe the apostolic decree of the holy congregation

Christi Vicario Urbano VIII. anno 1634. confirmatum, integre & inviolate juxta declarationes jam dicti Pontificis me velle servare, ut decet subditum & subjectum S. R. Ecclesiae filium, protestor.

Nos infra scripti Guardianus & Patres qualificati Collegii Neo-Pragensis Beatae Mariae immaculate Conceptae, justas ob causas requisiti ut publico testimonio fateamur quid sentiamus de familia Bruodiniana, omnibus has visuris partim ex certa nostra scientia, partim ex fide dignorum, fidem facimus dictam familiam honestam esse & perantiquae nobilitatis in Hibernia, variisque virtutibus ornatam, maxime hospitalitate, potentem etiam per aliquot saecula dominiis & opibus, denique affinitate & consanguinitate junctam variis illustrissimis & perillustribus respective familiis, nimirum Ô Brienis, de Burgo, Macnamariis, Mathaeis, Clanchiis, Gormanis, Gradiis, Mollonis, & c. In cujus rei firmiorem attestationem ad obviandum calumniis hoc scriptum subscriptione nostra & sigillo munivimus. Datum Pragae in praefato Collegio die 14. Septembris, anno 1671.

Fr Iacobus Coghlanus, Guardianus.

Fr Daniel Bruoder, SS. Theologiae Lector Jubilatus.

Fr. Bernardus Chanchy, Lector Jubilatus.

Fr. Antonius de Burgo, SS. Theologiae Lector Jubilatus.

Fr. Antonius Ferallus, SS. Theologiae Lector Jubilatus.

Fr. Antonius Conorus, SS. Theologiae Lector.

Fr. Antonius Kinraghty, Lector & Vicarius.

Fr. Patritius Vardeus, SS. Theologiae Lector.

Fr. Ioannes Clanchy, SS. Thologiae Lector.

promulgated in the year 1625 and confirmed by the most holy vicar of Christ, Urban VIII, in 1634,[608] in the complete and original form, corresponding to the declarations of the aforementioned pontiff, as is appropriate for a subjected and subdued son of the Holy Roman Church.

We the undersigned, guardian and qualified fathers of the New College of the Blessed and Immaculately Conceived Mary of Prague, have been asked to declare what we think about the family of the Bruodins, for upright reasons. Partly on the basis of sure knowledge we have, and partly on the basis of the knowledge we gathered from trustworthy people, to all readers who shall see the present document we vouch for the fact that the aforementioned family is an honourable one, and of very ancient nobility in Ireland, and splendidly furnished with various virtues, especially hospitality; also, it was powerful for several centuries, with its domains and riches; finally, it was bound by affinity or kindred to various families, in turn very illustrious and of great renown, namely the O'Briens, Burkes, MacNamaras, MacMahons, MacClancys, MacGormans, Gradys, Molonys, etc. To obviate slanders, we have reinforced the present certificate with our signature and seal, as a stronger attestation of the above.

The present document was handed in at Prague, in the aforementioned college, on 14 September 1671.

Friar James Coghlan,[609] guardian.

Friar Daniel Bruoder,[610] lector jubilatus of holy and sacred theology.

Friar Bernardine Clancy,[611] lector jubilatus.

Friar Anthony Burke,[612] lector jubilatus of holy and sacred theology.

Friar Anthony O'Farrell,[613] lector jubilatus of holy and sacred theology.

Friar Anthony O'Connor,[614] lector of holy and sacred theology.

Friar Anthony Kinraghty,[615] lector and vicar.

Friar Patrick Ward,[616] lector of holy and sacred theology.

Friar John Clancy,[617] lector of holy and sacred theology.

Nos infra subscripti Ordinis Sancti Francisci Strictioris Observantiae Provinciae Hiberniae testamur, & fidem omnibus has lecturis certam facimus, Tuomoniae in Hibernia Bruodinianam familiam honoratam, aestimatam, & ab hospitalitate, doctrina ac moribus fuisse merito semper laudatam; ex qua plurimi nobiles viri nobis noti diversa habuerunt haereditario jure bona & subditos ac sequaces multos, usque ad infausta illa tempora, quibus, praevalentibus rebellibus parlamentariis, plerique omnes per Hiberniam magnates & nobiles dominiis & bonis fere omnibus tyrannico ritu sunt spoliati. Veritatem hanc subscriptione manuum & ordinarii Collegii nostri sigilli appositione confirmamus. Actum Romae ad Sanctum Isidorum, 1. Martii, anno 1671.

(L.S.)

Fr. Franciscus ô Molloii, Lector Jubilatus & Collegii Praeses.
Fr. Andreas Vitalis, Lector Jubilatus.
Fr. Franciscus de Burgo, Theologus.

Vera loqui & falsa devitare cum Apostolo volens, tenore praesentium testor ego infrascriptus Ordinis Minorum Strictioris Observantiae mihi a juventute mea Bruodinorum in Tuomonia nominatam familiam notam fuisse, ex qua diversos vidi viros & faeminas nobiles, affinitate & sanguine junctos primariis in Tuomonia nobilibus familiis; quare vilem, pauperem & ignobilem hanc semper fuisse familam non nisi demens aut mentiendi libidine obcaecatus detractor dicere potest. Datum Lovanii in Collegio S. Antonii, die 12. Maii, anno 1671.

(L.S.)

Fr. Franciscus ô Kenedii Ormoniensis, SS. Theologiae Lector Jubilatus.

We the undersigned, members of the Order of St Francis of Strict Observance of the Province of Ireland, to anyone who shall read the present letter attest to, and safely vouch for, the fact that the family of the Bruodins of Thomond, in Ireland, has always been honoured, held in esteem and deservedly praised for its hospitality, learning and customs. A great number of noblemen from this family known to us owned various possessions by hereditary right, and had many subjects and followers, until those unfortunate times in which, while the rebellious parliamentarians were prevailing, the vast majority of all magnates and noblemen across Ireland were robbed of almost all of their dominions and possessions in a tyrannical way. We confirm that this is the truth by signing with our own hands as well as by placing the seal of the ordinary of our college.

The present document was produced in Rome, at the College of St Isidore, on 1 March 1671.

(Place of the seal)

Friar Francis O'Molloy,[618] lector jubilatus and president of the college.
Friar Andrew MacVeigh,[619] lector jubilatus.
Friar Francis Burke,[620] theologian.

As I want to tell the truth and avoid false statements, thus following the apostle's example, by the tenor of the present letter I, the undersigned, member of the Order of the Friars Minor of Strict Observance, attest to the fact that the family of the Bruodins, which enjoys fame in Thomond, has been known to me since my youth. I saw various noble members of this family, both men and women, bound by affinity and blood to first-rank aristocratic families in Thomond; accordingly, nobody but a detractor, out of his mind or blinded by the eagerness of lying, can say that this family was always base-born, poor and not noble.

The present document was handed in at Louvain, in the College of St Anthony, on 12 May 1671.

(Place of the seal)

Friar Francis O'Kennedy of Ormond,[621] lector jubilatus of holy and sacred theology.

Supra assignatas testimoniales litteras Romanorum & Lovaniensium Patrum Ordinis S. Francisci cum suis originalibus verbo ad verbum convenire, ego Balthasar Ignatius Pitz, Protonotarius Apostolicus, Vetero-Boleslaviensis Capituli Canonicus, & Decanus Regiae Trautonoviensis Civitatis, hoc meo manuscripto fidem facio, & appositione ordinarii mei sigilli confirmo.

Actum Trautonovii 8. Septembris, anno 1671.

The sealed testimonial letters above, produced by fathers of the Order of St Francis of Rome and Louvain, correspond to their originals, word by word. I, Balthasar Ignatius Pitz,[622] apostolic protonotary, canon of the old chapter of Bolesławiec,[623] and dean of the royal town of Trutnov,[624] vouch for this by means of the present handwritten document of mine, and confirm it by affixing the seal of my ordinary.

The present document was produced in Trutnov on 8 September 1671.

Notes for Text and Translation

1. Throughout the work, Bruodinus refers to his *Anatomicum Examen* simply as *Anatomia*, a shorter title that will be kept in its Latin form in the English translation, unless otherwise noted.

2. Throughout his work, Bruodinus refers to Carve's *Enchiridion Apologeticum* simply as *Apologia*, a shorter title that will be kept in its Latin form in the English translation, unless otherwise noted.

3. The Latin expression *famosus libellus* has been translated 'infamous pamphlet' (where appropriate) throughout the text, but the reader should bear in mind that the combination of the two words is often sarcastic. Both *famosus* and *libellus* are in fact *voces mediae*, that is words that can have a neutral meaning, a positive one or a negative one, depending on the context: *libellus* can mean 'short book', 'nice little book' or 'slanderous book'; similarly, *famosus* can mean 'famous', 'well-known for good reputation', or 'well-known for bad reputation'. The adjective *famosus* can have an active or a passive meaning: a *famosus liber* is a book that can bring reputation to someone or that can carry reputation itself. Bruodinus, whose sarcasm often emerges from *Anatomicum*, plays with the different meanings of *famosus libellus*. Carve's *Enchiridion Apologeticum* is in fact a handbook (that is, a short book), but also a 'slanderous' one; and it is *famosus* both because it is 'well-known' to the readers, but also because it aims at belittling Bruodinus' reputation, while Bruodinus tries to disgrace Carve.

4. The Sternbergs (Czech: Šternberks) were one of the oldest and most respected noble families of Bohemia. In 1661 three Sternberg brothers, Wenceslas Adalbert (Václav Vojtěch), Johann Norbert (Jan Norbert) and Ignatius Karol (Ignác Karel) were elevated to the rank of counts of the Holy Roman Empire by Leopold I. Following the Thirty Years War, the Sternbergs pursued the policy of re-Catholisation of the Czech lands with considerable vigour. Consequently, the brothers had close associations with the Irish Franciscan community in Prague, and a number of published works of the community were dedicated to them. Antonius Bruodinus' *Propugnaculum Catholicae Veritatis* (1669) was dedicated to the three brothers and it is not surprising that *Anatomicum Examen* (1671), written by Bruodinus but under a pseudonym, also featured a dedication to the aristocratic Sternbergs. The family were generous benefactors of the Irish Franciscans. They donated money for the construction and embellishment of the college chapel, and provided art works and books for the college library. Jan Pařez and Hedvika Kuchařová, *The Irish Franciscans in Prague 1629–1786* (Prague, 2015), pp. 18, 110–11.

5. These are the towns, castles and lands accumulated by the Sternbergs over generations. Bruodinous identifies them by their German or Germanised names. They are better known today by their Czech forms. Unfortunately, not all are now identifiable. Grünberg is the castle of Zelená Hora (Green Mountain), which in the 1680s was transformed by Wenzel Adalbert Sternberg into a baroque-style residence. Wrshchowitz, now called Vršovice, is an upmarket district of Prague. Kanitz is Dolní Kounice, a small town in South Moravia. Durnholtzled is Drnholec, a market town, likewise, in South Moravia. Gischin is Jičín, a town of 16,000 inhabitants in the scenic Hradec Králové region. Plana is Planá nad Lužnicí, a town on the river Lužnice in South Bohemia. Zaluschan is Zalužany, a village located in the district of Příbram in Central Bohemia. Skotzitz is Skočice, a village in South Bohemia; Count Ignatius Karol Sternberg and his wife endowed the village with the church of the Virgin Mary in 1678. Horisedl is Hořesedly, a municipality in Central Bohemia. Libochowitz is Libochovice, a town of almost 4,000 inhabitants, in the Ústí nad Labem region.

6. In keeping with their policy of re-Catholisation, the Sternbergs encouraged the re-opening of former religious houses. The monastery of the Assumption of the Virgin Mary was at Bechin (Bechyně), a town in South Bohemia, where Count Jan Norbert Sternberg resided. Horasciowitz (Horaždovice) is a town in the Plzeň Region of the Czech Republic, where the friars re-established the monastery of Holy Angels. Krupna (Krupka) was an important mining town in north-western Bohemia, where the Friary of All Saints was re-inaurgurated. Zuzana Křenková, *Locus Fratrum – Architecture of Observant Franciscan Monasteries in Bohemia …* (Berlin, 2018), pp. 63, 93, 178.

7. Gaius Maecenas (68–8 BC) was a Roman politician and patron, who became synonymous for his patronage of art and literature.

8. See Antonius Bruodinus, *Propugnaculum Catholicae Veritatis Libris X Constructum, in Duasque Partes Divisum* (Prague, 1669). The title literally translates as follows: 'Bulwark of Catholic Truth, Consisting of Ten Books and Divided in Two Parts'.

9. This is the Protestant city of Nuremberg in southern Germany, where Carve's book was published.

10. Namely slandering. Zoilus was a Greek scholar of the fourth century BC. His bitter criticism of Homer secured him the nickname of 'Homer-scourger', but he harshly attacked other Greek authors of the past as well as living figures too. According to some ancient fictional accounts of his death, he was crucified or stoned as a punishment for his attitude, of which Carve and Bruodinus show awareness.

11. Bruodinus is here making a pun with the short version of the title of his work, *Anatomia*, meaning 'dissection'.

12. The concept of prime mover, first advanced by the Greek philosopher Aristotle and then applied to God in Christian theology, refers to the primary cause of the whole universe. According to Aristotle, the universe is the result of a process of constant change and movement regulated by causality, but the first and earliest item which originated this causality (the prime mover) was not itself caused or put into motion by any prior action. Since an important part of Aristotle's cosmological theory is concerned with the movement of planets, Bruodinus' reference to the concept of prime mover immediately after the astrological imagery and the assimilation of his patrons to stars is particularly fitting.

13. The relationship between patrons and clients was for mutual benefit and characterised the society of ancient Rome. Bruodinus' definition of himself as a client at the end of the introductory letter is consistent with the reference to Maecenas at the beginning, for which see note 7 above.

14. St Clement's College, otherwise called the *Clementinum*, was the first college in Prague where the Jesuits came in 1556. In 1622 the Jesuits transferred the library of Charles University to the *Clementinum*, and the college was merged with the university in 1654. The Jesuits remained until 1773. David H. Stam (ed.), *International Dictionary of Library Histories*, 2 vols (London, 2001), vol. I, p. 583.

15. Matthias Tanner, a native of Pilsen in Bohemia (1630–92), became a Jesuit and spent much of his life in Prague where he was a professor of theology and philosophy and served as rector of the imperial university. He is best known for his publication on the Jesuit martyrs titled *Societas Jesu usque ad sanguinis et vitae profusionem militans* (Prague, 1675). *The Catholic Encyclopedia*, Charles G. Heberman et al. (eds), 15 vols (New York, 1913), vol. XIV, p. 445.

16. Peter Geanor, a native of County Westmeath, was admitted to the Franciscan novitiate at St Anthony's College, Louvain, in 1629. Elected guardian of Ballynasaggat friary, County Longford in 1645, he presided over the chapter of Irish Franciscans that met in Longford, following the death of Oliver Cromwell in 1658. Appointed vicar apostolic of the Irish province by Rome in 1669, he was opposed by some senior Irish Franciscans. Geanor was instrumental in re-establishing conventual life at Multyfarnham and in 1672 issued letters of authorisation to two young friars to proceed to Prague to pursue their studies there. Terence O'Donnell, *Franciscan Abbey of Multyfarnham* (Multyfarnham, 1951).

17. Thomas Pessina (1629–80), of Czechorod, Moravia, a priest and Czech historian, was dean of St Vitus cathedral and vicar general to the archbishop of Prague, Matthew Ferdinand Sobek (1618–75). He is chiefly remembered for his histories of Moravia and his efforts to preserve the Czech language. Howard Louthan, 'Breaking Images and Building Bridges in Early Modern Bohemia', in Will Coster and Andrew Spicer (eds), *Sacred Space in Early Modern Europe* (Cambridge, 2005), p. 288.

18. The title of Thomas Carve's book, published in Nuremberg in 1670, translates as 'Apologetic Handbook against the Medley of Sordid Mendacities of Rev. Fr Antonius Bruodinus'.

19. Although the translation uses the spelling 'Carve', the pronunciation of this word in Latin in fact echoes the Old-English form of the surname 'Carue' (Carew).

20. An ordinary is an officer of the Catholic Church, usually the bishop of a diocese, who by reason of his office has ordinary power to execute Church law.

21. The texts which Bruodinus quotes as sections from the *Annales* are from Thomas Carve's *Lyra seu Anacephalaeosis Hibernica, in qua de exordio, seu origine, nomine, moribus ritibusque gentis Hibernicae succinte tractatur, cui quoque accessere Annales ejusdem Hiberniae necnon rerum gestarum per Europam 1148–1650* (Viennae, 1651; 2nd edn, Sulzbach, 1666). Only the last part of the *Lyra* is entitled *Annales Hiberniae*, but Bruodinus applies the title *Annales* to the entire *Lyra*.

22. This claim is first encountered in Bruodinus' work *Propugnaculum*, p. 985. In that work he claimed that an ancestor of Carve cut off the right hand of *Santus Lactinus Abbas* (Saint Lachtín the abbot) and the arm was enclosed in a silver case and preserved in the church of Kilnamona in Thomond, until it was stolen by a sacristan from Mologhan and brought to County Kerry where it was venerated at Lislaughtin, near Tarbert, until the reformation. The claim of the violent amputation of Lachtín's arm has no historical basis and nothing about the saint's life refers to this violent act. However, Kilnamona appears to have held a reliquary of Lachtín. Nineteenth-century Ordnance Survey maps mark a place nearby called Autkeenlaughteen (*Áit Chinn Lachtín*, head place of Lachtín). This was probably a shrine where a reliquary once stood. The arm-shaped reliquary of Lachtín (*Lámh Laichtín*) was associated with the church of Donaghmore in County Cork, and it is thought to date from the 1120s. Pádraig Ó Riain, *A Dictionary of Irish Saints* (Dublin, 2011), pp. 387–8.

23. The printing industry flourished in Vienna in the seventeenth century. Some forty presses were active. The printer Matthaeus Cosmerovius (1606–74) is credited with 352 books, printed primarily in Latin and German, but also in Italian, Hungarian and Spanish. Marvin J. Heller, *Printing the Talmud* (Boston, 2019), p. 194.

24. The quotation is from a different page than the one indicated by Bruodinus, and contains a mistake that is not in the original text.

25. The Greek speaking name *Pantolabus* (literally: 'the one who grabs everything') is attested in the *Satires* of the Roman poet Horace (65–8 BC), where it is associated with the figure of the social parasite (*Sat.* 1.8.11 and 2.1.22), a stock character in Roman comic and satiric works to whom Bruodinus is here antonomastically referring.

26. This serves as a subtle allusion to the fact that the author's name, Cornelius O'Molony (*Conchobhar Ó Maoldhomhnaigh*), was a pseudonym for Antonius Bruodinus.

27. That is, a sickle.

28. According to Bruodinus, 'Carran' is the real surname of Carve. Bruodinus, reflecting his family's training as Gaelic *literati*, regarded the etymological origin of Carve as a form of the Irish word *corrán*, denoting a sickle or scythe, and that it was an ancestor of Carve's who attained the nickname (which would later become his surname) after infamously amputating the arm of St Lachtín.

29. Bruodinus is here referring to works belonging to the discipline of Christian apologetics (from the Greek word meaning 'defence'), practised since the second century by the early Fathers of the Church in Greek as well as Latin language. Apologetic literature primarily aimed at defending religious principles against objections, but it also had the practical purpose of recommending the Christian faith to outsiders; thus, the authors of Christian apologias showed rigorous logic and great learning not only to refute theological objections, but also to make their works appealing and convincing to readers not directly involved in the debate.

30. Examples of apologias written by St Jerome (*c.* 347–*c.* 420) include his *Against Jovinianus* and *Against Rufinus*; Jerome, a Church Father, is best known for his Latin translation of the Bible. *Catholic Encyclopedia*, vol. VIII, pp. 343, 530.

31. St Augustine (354–430) wrote a great number of apologetic works in response to specific theological objections (refuting the theses of the followers of other religions, such as Manicheanism, as well as Christian heresies, such as Donatism and Pelagianism), but his most important apologia is arguably *The City of God*, where he opposes the pagans' attribution of the fall of Rome to the Christianisation of the Roman Empire. *Catholic Encyclopedia*, vol. II, p. 89.

32. Bernard of Clairvaux (1090–1153) was a French abbot and a major leader in the reform of Benedictine monasticism, which led to the formation of the Cistercian order. Among his many works were his *Book on the Life and Deeds of Saint Malachy, Bishop of Ireland*, as well as his *Apologia to William of St Thierry*. *Catholic Encyclopedia*, vol. II, pp. 498–501.

33. St Thomas Aquinas (*c.* 1225–74) is the author of a comprehensive apologetic work entitled *Book about the Truth of the Catholic Faith against the Errors of the Unbelievers*, generally known as *Summa contra Gentiles*. *Catholic Encyclopedia*, vol. XIV, pp. 666, 670.

34. St Bonaventure (*c.* 1220–74), doctor of the Church and cardinal bishop of Albano, wrote many theological works including commentaries on the Gospels and manuals for the spiritual direction of his fellow Franciscans. Among his most famous smaller works are *Itinerarium mentis in Deum* ('The Mind's Road to God') and *Breviloquium* ('Brief Speech'), which provides an outline of his theology. *Catholic Encyclopedia*, vol. II, pp. 648–54.

35. The reference to pagan gods in this and other idiomatic expressions used throughout *Anatomicum* is yet another piece of evidence of Bruodinus' intention to show his knowledge of, and debt to, classical literature.

36. That is, 'if the *Annales* were truly written by you and not by somebody else'. Bruodinus' comment occurs immediately after the adjective 'your' here and elsewhere, and is consistent with the accusations of plagiarism, which he often makes against Carve (see for example p. 107).

37. That is, a fable. Note the pun with *Apologia*.

38. Ecgfrith (*c.* 645–85), the king of Northumbria (670–85), sent a raiding party to Magh Breagh (a district north of Dublin) and captured many slaves. Adamnán of Iona, best known for his promulgation of *Cáin Adamnáin* (Law of Adamnán), which was a set of laws protecting non-combatants during wartime, travelled to Northumbria and successfully negotiated the release of the captives. *AFM*, vol. I, pp. 291–2.

39. The name of the family that appears in the Latin text is 'O Mohuin' and likely refers to the O'Mahonys (*Uí Mhathghamhna*) for the passage makes mention of other Gaelic families in Desmond including the O'Sullivans and MacCarthys.

40. This appears to be the family from which Thomas Carve claimed descent. In *Lyra seu Anacephalaeosis Hibernica* it is written as *Domini Caruae*, 'Lords Carve'.

41. The O'Dempseys were not English, but an important Gaelic sept of the Laois–Offaly area, who were disposessed in the seventeenth century.

42. This is a reference to the adoption of Gaelic culture and language by the Anglo-Norman settlers in Ireland, who over generations became *Hiberniores Hibernis ipsis* ('more Irish than the Irish themselves'). This was particularly the case with certain Norman families such as the de Burgos (Burkes) who held large estates in Connacht and married into important Irish families over the course of the middle ages.

43. St Malachy (*Máel Máedóc Ua Morgair*, *c.* 1095–1148) was an Irish saint and archbishop of Armagh. He was a leading proponent of reform of the Irish Church. In 1139–40 he travelled to Rome via the Cistercian monastery of Clairvaux, where he met St Bernard. In 1145 he helped establish the first continental religious order in Ireland at Mellifont, County Louth, where the Cistercians founded an abbey. *DIB*, vol. VI, pp. 308–11.

44. This statement is paraphrased, not to say misquoted, from page 105 of Carve's *Lyra*.

45. Known in medieval Europe as *jus primae noctis*, 'law of the first night', in early medieval Ireland an example of this appears in a story in the twelfth-century Book of Leinster (*Lebar na*

Núachongbála). According to the tale *Tochmarc Emire*, Conchobhar mac Nessa, the king of Ulster, had the 'right of the first night' over all marriages of his subjects, known in Irish as *coll cétingen*. R.I. Best and Osborn Bergin, *Lebor na hUidre: Book of the Dun Cow* (Dublin, 1929), p. 317.

46. Probably King Malcolm IV of Scotland (1153–65), called the 'maiden', because he took a vow of chastity and died unmarried and without offspring.

47. *Kystonady*, meaning unclear: *Cís tóna duibhe*, 'tribute of the black buttocks', or perhaps *Cís d'aon oidhche*, 'the one-night tribute'. We are indebted to Prof. Damian McManus for his assistance.

48. Namely *Enchiridion Apologeticum*, where Carve tried to defend what he had said in his *Lyra* from Bruodinus' refutation in *Propugnaculum*.

49. Bruodinus is referring to the *Decretals*, collections of letters from a pope formulating decisions that constitute decrees of the ecclesiastical law of the Catholic Church. In particular, Bruodinus is here referring to the sixth book of the *Decretals* of Pope Boniface VIII (1294–1303).

50. The translation of the ablative *ordine literario* reflects the infelicitous combination of words in Latin, on which Bruodinus remarks at the end of the passage.

51. This is a quotation from the Bible (*Romans* 12:21).

52. St Stephen, stoned to death in Jerusalem *c*. AD 34, was reputed to be the first Christian martyr (*Acts of Apostles* 7:59).

53. The biblical quotation is from King David's *Psalm* 7:4, where, however, the meaning of the sentence is different. In the original context, the verb *retribuo* means 'to repay with something good', the point being that people who behave well should be treated well. Bruodinus turns this meaning upside down, by saying that people who behave badly should not necessarily be treated badly. Though the Latin original is the same, the translation reflects this difference.

54. Namely, criticism by disparagers: see note 10 above on Zoilus.

55. Bruodinus is probably parodying Carve's preface, which is in the form of an epistle to the reader and ends with the word 'farewell'.

56. The Latin adjective *singularis* is generally used to highlight a positive quality, but the reader will soon discover that Carve's case is extraordinary in pejorative terms: his place in an imaginary classroom of *grammatistae* (see note 57) is at the very back, where the worst students deserve to be placed. See further p. 219, and note 392 below.

57. A *grammatista* was a student in a lower-grade class of Latin schools with a focus on traditional humanities courses. The first grades or classes were those of the *rudimentistae* and *grammatistae*, who were taught the rudiments and the grammar of Latin language. After these basic courses, the students proceeded to become *syntaxistae*, *humanistae* and eventually *rhetores*.

58. This appears to be a sarcastic remark by Bruodinus designed to reproach the truthfulness of Carve's *Annales* and perhaps his apparent ability to gather obscure knowledge from times past.

59. Lucius Annaeus Seneca (*c*. 4 BC–AD 65), was a Roman Stoic philosopher who produced a large body of writings. Bruodinus' quotation, however, is spurious, as it combines two statements from works written much later than the first century AD and wrongly attributed to Seneca in the middle ages, namely a book *On Remedies for Accidental Facts* (*De Remediis Fortuitorum*) and a book *On Customs* (*De Moribus*).

60. The work referred to is *Chronicon Generale Ordinis Minimorum* (General Chronicle of the Order of Friars Minor), by Francis Lanovius (Paris, 1635).

61. This biblical misquotation combines various sections of *Daniel* 13:52–6. Susanna had been condemned to death by two old judges, who had conspired against her on false evidence. Once the injustice was uncovered by Daniel and Susanna was exonerated, the crowd of people turned on the old men and, in retribution for their crime, put them to death.

62. On St Lachtín see note 22 above. This reference is notable in that Bruodinus identifies the name of Carve's ancestor whom he credits with violently amputating the arm of Lachtín.

The biblical parallel with Canaan portrays Carve's ancestor as a cursed man, for according to *Genesis* 9:20–7 Canaan had been cursed by Noah, an episode probably constructed to justify the Canaanites' subjection to the people of Israel.

63. This metaphorical use of a mixed animal imagery to describe Carve (here depicted as a 'barking owl' and elsewhere compared to other creatures) anticipates the image of Bruodinus' adversary as a chimera, a monster with a hybrid body, which will be sketched in the poem on p. 275.

64. For the biblical story of Susanna, see note 61 above.

65. The word *cathedra* originally referred to the highest post of a teacher, but it started to be applied to the posts of bishops once Europe and its education system were Christianised. In the context of this sentence it is impossible to establish which of the two meanings the word has, because the list of the clerics' activities includes both teaching duties and religious services.

66. The quotation is from Seneca's spurious *Liber de moribus*. See note 59 above.

67. Bruodinus uses metaphors drawn from the field of sports elsewhere, too: see, for example, 'pugilist' in paragraph 20 of the 'Life of Kearney'.

68. This contrast metaphorically describes the pen as a sword, with reference to battle imagery. The metaphor is quite conventional; it is also used, for instance, in Matthias Tanner's letter of approbation reported by Bruodinus.

69. Moynoe (*Maigh nEo*, plain of the yew trees) is a townland in the parish of Moynoe near Scariff in north-east Clare. Clann Bhruaideadha held church lands at Moynoe in the early seventeenth century, which probably constituted the family's hereditary lands from an earlier period. In 1617 members of both the Meic Cormacáin and Clann Bhruaideadha surrendered their leases of church land at Moynoe. Those surrendering their lands were fflan Mc Broodyn, Charles alias Callogh Mc Broodyn, Donogh O Cormochan and David Mac Cormochan. See NLI, Ms 1777, Rev. James B. Leslie, 'Typescript copy of a survey of lands in the diocese of Killaloe made for Bishop Worth, 1661' (1936), p. 7.

70. Leopold I (1640–1704), Holy Roman emperor, king of Hungary, Croatia and Bohemia.

71. Prince Annibale Gonzaga (1602–68), was commander of the city of Vienna in 1640 and leader of the imperial army in Hungary in 1658; he became president of the imperial war council in 1666.

72. The Cromwellian military campaign in Ireland 1649–52 achieved notoriety for its atrocities against the civilian population and indiscriminate killing of Catholic clerics. The Cromwellians were sympathetic to puritan forms of worship and independent church organisation. They promoted a distinctive Calvinistic theology and regarded themselves as part of a reformed tradition that had its roots in early Protestant reformers such as Zwingli in Zurich and Calvin in Geneva.

73. *Athleta Christi* (or, here and elsewhere in *Anatomicum*, simply *Athleta*) was an honorific title bestowed upon men who had fought in defence of Christianity.

74. Carve turns Bruodinus' title of *lector jubilatus* into *lector frustratus*, making a pun with the two participles.

75. The author is here playing with the word *commentum*. The term generally means 'fabrication, falsehood' or 'contrivance', but in the field of logic it also means 'enthymeme', a technical word to indicate a specific type of demonstration.

76. The quotation comes from a different section than the one indicated by Bruodinus.

77. *Tribus* is translated as 'clan' rather than 'tribe' because the former term is more compatible with the legal and social standing of lineages in Gaelic society.

78. Dermot Nasaffagh (*Diarmuid na sámhthach*, Dermot of the battleaxes). The appellation *na sámhthach* is unusual for a member of a professional learned family.

79. The expression *memoriam facere* is a post-classical one, which entered the Latin language through the translation of the Bible from Greek. The soundness and quality of the translation of this particular expression, as well as of many others, has been questioned by scholars, both in recent and in more ancient times (by Erasmus of Rotterdam, for instance). It is not clear whether *memoriam facere* means 'to commemorate', or simply 'to mention'. In our case, the latter translation is preferable, because of the adverb *obiter*, 'incidentally'.

80. In the Bible, at *Kings* 22:22, these words are spoken by a spirit in support of God's plan to cause a war between Ahab and Ramoth Gilead, by spreading discord between the two. In *Anatomicum*, of course, the 'war' is between Bruodinus (on God's side) and Carve.

81. Grammarian William Lily (1468–1522) was the author of a most widely used Latin grammar. Lily's *Grammar of Latin in English* was published in London by order of Henry VIII between 1540 and 1543. *ODNB*, vol. XXXIII, pp. 801–3.

82. The quotation is untraced. The two lines, a hexameter and a pentameter, form an elegiac distich or couplet. The second line features as part of an anonymous inscription in a note written by a Protestant pastor and mineralogist, Ferenc Benkö (1745–1816), where, however, it is preceded by a different line.

83. As usual, the quotation or paraphrase is imprecise. In particular, Carve refers to Thomond as *Tuamundia* not as *Tuomondia*. In this passage of *Anatomicum*, the original text reads *Tuamundiae*, which needs to be emended to *Tuomondiae* (nominative *Tuomondia*) on the basis of Bruodinus' self-quotation in paragraphs 17 and 22 of this chapter. The translation tries to render Bruodinus' attribution of the wrong toponym to Carve. Bruodinus' objection to Carve's Latinisation, however, is trivial, since the letter 'd' was inconsistently retained in the Latin version of some Irish toponyms.

84. It is reasonable to assume that Carve had personal knowledge of Captain Marcus MacBrody as Carve previously held the position of chaplain to the English, Scotch and Irish forces in Austria and he resided in Vienna until his death, probably in 1672.

85. The author, O'Molony (who was really Bruodinus), states here that he was born in Thomond (County Clare), thereby strengthening his credentials to comment on matters about Thomond. We read elsewhere that Antonius Bruodinus was born at Ballyogan in the parish of Kilraghtis in County Clare. Ballyogan (*Baile Uí Ógáin*, Hogan's homestead) was one of several land holdings of Clann Bhruaideadha, the family lineage of Bruodinus. Bruodinus states that Ballyogan was the place where his parents were domiciled. Bruodinus, *Propugnaculum*, p. 961. Carve was aware of the family's residence at Ballyogan and he criticises it specifically in his book *Enchiridion*. See Carve, *Enchiridion*, pp. 98–9.

86. A misquotation from *Daniel* 13.55: *mentitus es in caput tuum*.

87. This description draws on Bruodinus' own recollections of his family, Clann Bhruaideadha, who are referred to correctly as 'chroniclers' and who maintained and compiled genealogies for the *Principes O Brien*. The passage suggests that the head of the family was denoted 'MacBrody' (in Irish, *Mac Bruaideadha*), on whom was conferred the role of official chronicler or *ollamh*.

88. See Bruodinus, *Propugnaculum*, pp. 767–71, where he explains that the professional chroniclers were of the nobility and traced their genealogical origins to the ancient and noble families of Ireland. He asserts that Clann Bhruaideadha traced their origins from Cas, the progenitor of the Dál Cais and thus they shared kinship with their patrons the Uí Bhriain. The passage also states that the Gaelic learned class were exempt from quartering soldiers and that they enjoyed these and other privileges so that they might be unencumbered in their professional role.

89. Coolcusaun was the principal hamlet of Moynoe parish (*Parliamentary Gazetteer of Ireland*, 1845, vol. II, p.820). In 1618 'Flan McBrody of Moineo, gent.' held one quarter of Aughrim in mortgage from Luke Brady. He is likely to be the Flan McBruodine who was high constable of the barony of Tulla in 1634. See Mark Empey, *Early Stuart Irish Warrants* (Dublin, 2015), p. 228; and PHA, Ms B. 16 B [Tulla barony – Great Office inquisition, 1618].

90. Aughrim (*Eachroim*, horse ridge) is a townland in the parish of Tomgraney, east Clare.

91. He appears to be the same individual recorded elsewhere as Charles, father of Marcus MacBrody, see p. 115. His wife is listed as Onora Minogue the grandaughter of John Burke, master of Pallas in County Galway. See note 325 below.

92. Ballyminoge (*Baile Uí Mhuineog*, Minogue's homeplace) in Tomgraney parish. It may have passed to Charles MacBrody on his marriage to Onora Minogue whose surname indicates a familial connection to the townland.

93. This is probably Shanavogh (*Sean Bhoth*, old cabin) in Kilmurry-Ibrickan parish, west Clare. 'Sheanvoyhe' in Ibrickan was held by Conor McBroady in 1615. See Luke McInerney, 'The Earl of Thomond's 1615 Survey of Ibrickan, Co. Clare', *NMAJ*, vol. 53, 2013, pp. 173–91, at p. 186.

94. Tobercoolan (*Tobar Chúláin*, St Coolan's Well) is a sacred spring, currently protected by an early nineteenth-century well house, situated on the roadside between Tomgraney village and Bodyke in east Clare. It is located in the townland of Callahy, parish of Tomgraney.

95. This placename has not been identified but it is almost certainly in east Clare as Bernard was the brother of Flann MacBrody of Moynoe, and was married to Sláine, daughter of John McNamara. Cuthbert McGrath notes that this is Rosnehealy in the *Fourth Report of the Royal Commission on Historical Manuscripts*, Part 1 (London, 1874), p. 511. However, an inspection of the reference gives no firm evidence that the placename is in County Clare. The name appears in a letter from Austas Comerford to the marquis of Ormond, dated 18 March 1660. Cuthbert McGrath, 'Materials for a History of Clann Bhruaideadha', *Éigse*, vol. 4, no. 4, 1943–4, p. 65.

96. During the uprising of 1641 Maolin MacBrody, father of Bruodinus, was alledged with others to have driven away the horses and cattle of Beatrice Hepditch, Christmas 1641; to have been entrusted with the goods of Anthony Heatcote to the value of £29, January 1642, which were not returned; and according to the deposition of Andrew Chaplin, to have attended at the siege of Ballyallia castle, August 1642. TCD, 1641 Depositions, Ms 829, ff. 73r–74v, 75r–76v, 95r–100v.

97. These are now called Ballyogan (*Baile Uí Ógáin*, Hogan's homeplace) in Kilraghtis parish; Drumbonniv (*Drom Bainbh*, piglet's ridge), Cloonawillin (*Cluain an Mhuilinn*, mill meadow), and Knocknamucky (*Cnoc na Muclaí*, pigs' hill) in Inchicronan parish. In 1641 'Ballyogan alias Gurtnafinch' was held by Moylan Mac Brodin who also held Drumbonniv along with James Oge McBrode. In 1641 Cloonawillin and Knocknamucky were held by James Oge MacBrody and Donogh MacBrody respectively. Robert C. Simington (ed.), *Books of Survey and Distribution 1636–1703, Co. of Clare*, vol. 4 (Dublin, 1967), pp. 107–8, 121.

98. This placename has not been positively identified but it could be Knockatunna (*Cnoc an tSonnaigh*, palisade hill) in Feakle parish.

99. This is Ballyscanlan (*Baile Uí Scanláin*, Scanlan's homeplace) in Inchicronan parish.

100. Giolla Brighde appears to be the same individual mentioned in the *Annals of the Four Masters* for the year 1582. *AFM*, vol. V, p. 1791. See note 329 below.

101. This is Boolyduff (*Buaile Dubh*, dark milking place) on the side of Slievecallan in Inagh parish.

102. Slievecallan (*Sliabh Calláin*, Callan's mountain), otherwise called Mount Callan in the barony of Ibrickan.

103. This is likely Rushaun (*Roiseán*, little wood), which is in Kilnamona parish.

104. In 1618 a Daniel McBrodin held 'Formoil Iaghter' with Dary McBrodin in what is now Inagh parish. He may have been the Danyel MacBrody in a deed concerning lands in Dysert parish along with Boeitus MacBrody in 1637. See PHA, Ms 16 B.E. [Great Office 1618 – Inchiquin]; and NLI Ms 45,682/5.

105. Likely to be Ollamh Maoilín Óg Mac Bruaideadha who died in 1602 and whose son Conchobhar of Kilkee and Lettermoylan gave his approbation to Mícheál Ó Cléirigh's *Annals of the Four Masters* in 1636. See *AFM*, vol. I, p. lxix; vol. VI, p. 2321. It was here that Matthew De Renzy received tutoring in Irish by Conchobhar and Tadhg mac Dáire Mhic Bhruaideadha in *c.* 1606. See Brian Mac Cuarta, 'Conchubhar Mac Bruaideadha and Sir Matthew de Renzy (1577–1634)', *Éigse*, vol. 27, 1993, pp. 122–6.

106. This is Kilkee West (*Cill Chaoi Thiar*) in Ruan parish. In the seventeenth century it was in Dysert parish and was held by Conor mc Moyllin mcBrody, 1641, who was recorded holding 'Kilkie alis Lissinrahahick' followed by John Mc Brodyn of 'Kilkie alias Lissnecreuy'. Simington, *Books of Survey and Distribution*, pp. 553–4. Conor mc Moyllin was Conchobhar Mac Bruaideadha who gave his approbation to the *Annals of the Four Masters*, 1636. Paul Walsh, *Gleanings from Irish MSS* (Dublin, 1933), p. 78.

107. Boetius of 'Rathcahan, gent.' is recorded in marriage articles in 1630 with Finola Fitzpatrick, sister of Dermod Fitzpatrick, a kinsman of the Meic Giolla Phádraig lineage of Lisdoonvarna. In 1641 a Boetius MacBrody held part of Cloonanaha (called Buolliduffe) to the north of Slievecallan. See NLI, Ms 45,666/3 [2 May 1630]; and Simington, *Books of Survey and Distribution*, p. 533.

108. Rathcahaun (*Rath Catháin*, Cahan's fort) in Ruan parish was held in 1618 by 'Teig McBrodin' (that is, Tadhg mac Dáire Mhic Bhruaideadha). See PHA, Ms 16 B.E. [Great Office 1618 – Inchiquin].

109. This is Kilkee East (*Cill Chaoi Thoir*) in Ruan parish. In 1617 a John MacBrody of Kilkee was empanelled as a juror on the *inquisition post mortem* of William O'Nelan. John Ainsworth (ed.), *The Inchiquin Manuscripts* (Dublin, 1961), p. 321. A Constance MacBrody of Ballyogan was recorded on the same inquisition.

110. James was the son of bardic poet Tadhg mac Dáire Mhic Bhruaideadha of Knockanalban (*Cnoc an Albanaigh*, *Mons Scoti*, Mount Scott) in the barony of Ibrickan.

111. Coor (*Cuar*, round hollow) is in Kilmurry-Ibrickan parish. Bernard was probably the brother of bardic poet Tadhg mac Dáire Mhic Bhruaideadha. Coor was held by Teig McBroady (that is, Tadhg mac Dáire) in 1615. In 1618 Bernard McBrodin and Teig McBrodin held 'Lettermollan' on Slievecallan and land at 'Formoil Iaghter'. See McInerney, '1615 Survey', *NMAJ*, vol. 53, 2013, p. 186 and PHA, Ms 16 B.E. [Great Office 1618 – Inchiquin].

112. According to Bruodinus this was Captain Marcus of Ballyminoge in Tomgraney parish.

113. For Carve's wrong use of this toponym, see note 83 above. The term *dominium* is translated here to denote 'lordship' in the sense of a notable landholder, rather than a titled position or peerage.

114. This is Abbas Joannes de Burgo, doctor of theology, a relative of Bruodinus. Later in *Anatomicum*, p. 209, we read that Abbot Burke was the son of Thomas Burke of Poulmore, parish of Doora, and Anna MacBrody, daughter of Giolla Brighde MacBrody. See below note 352.

115. The word *ora* has been emended to *ore*, because of the problems of meaning that the translation of *in ora* would pose: 'he who utters impious words loosens or releases the gods *into the mouths*'. This would make sense only if the gods were devils or pagan gods, which could be let into his speeches by saying impious things. The plural 'gods', which is a literary heritage from the pagan authors, is often used by Bruodinus himself in idiomatic expression such as 'gods granting this'. Assuming that the accusative plural *ora* is a corruption of the ablative singular *ore*, the line refers to the negation of the truth of religion by means of blasphemous speaking, which metaphorically 'dissolves' the gods in the speaker's voice or mouth.

116. Momus, the personified spirit of unfair criticism and biting mockery in Greek culture, soon became unpopular even amongst other Greek gods of mythology, who expelled him from Mount Olympus.

117. Fr Francis O'Mahony (Matthews) appears in the chapter titled *De Martyribus in Hibernia* where Bruodinus outlines the life of a number of Irish clerics killed during the 1640s and 1650s in Ireland. This chapter details the killing of several clerics from Thomond including a kinsman of Bruodinus, Dermot MacBrody, who was burned to death along with six others in a house near Scariff in County Clare. Bruodinus, *Propugnaculum*, p. 717.

118. Francis O'Mahony, author of *Brevis Synopsis*, a short history of the Irish Franciscans, was Irish vicar provincial, 1625–6, minister provincial, 1626–9 and guardian of St Anthony's College, Louvain 1629–32. Dermor F. Gleeson, A *History of the Diocese of Killaloe* (Dublin, 1962), p. 262.

He was put to death, July 1643, in Cork by Inchiquin. O'Mahony had the unenviable distinction of being hanged twice. Benignus Millett, *The Irish Franciscans 1651–1665* (Rome, 1964), p. 538.

119. Or 'at that time'.

120. Dr Nicholas Donnellan OSA (*c.* 1610–79) was Irish vicar general of the Austrian province of the Augustinian order. Residing in Germany in 1664, he had a reputation as a man of sound doctrine and mature judgement. Described as an adviser to the emperor of Hungary and a friend of the English king, he was of the noted ecclesiastical family of Donnellan (*Uí Dhomhnalláin*), County Galway. This family produced a number of notable ecclesiastics including Nehemiah Donnellan (*Fearganainm Ó Domhnalláin*), who translated the New Testament into Irish and became Protestant archbishop of Tuam (1595–1609), and Maurice Donnellan, Catholic bishop of Clonfert (1695–1706). *Collectanea Hibernica*, vol. 36, 1996, p. 79; vol. 41, 1999, p. 16.

121. Fr Edmund Kennedy and Fr Terence O'Flynn (*Ó Floinn*) were two secular priests from Munster and Connacht respectively, who resided in Vienna.

122. This logical fallacy (literally: 'consequently, the stick is in the corner') was used to point out syllogisms and deductions that did not follow logic and therefore had no value. It was typical of the reasoning cultivated by Scotist theologians and deployed in Franciscan theology.

123. The story of Stephen's stoning is found in the fifth book of the New Testament, *Acts* 7:54–60.

124. The *Roman Martyrology*, the official account of saints and martyrs of the Catholic Church, was revised and published by Cesare Baronio, an Italian cardinal and church historian, in 1586.

125. The general visitor's role was to inspect individual Franciscan friaries in terms of their temporal and spiritual affairs and to assess the state of the province in a report which was usually submitted to the vicar provincial.

126. Fr Francis O'Mahony (*Ó Mathghamhna*) used the pseudonym Emundus Ursulanus. In Irish *Mathghamhain* signifies 'bear calf', that is why he used the Latin *Ursulanus*, meaning bear, as a pseudonym. O'Mahony was author of *Examen juridicum censuræ Facultatis Theologicæ Parisiensis* (Frankfurt, 1631), which is a repudiation of eleven propositions falsely attributed to the friars of Ireland in 1629 and condemned by the theological faculty of the University of Paris. Paul Harris, an English priest living in Dublin, replied to O'Mahony in 1633 using the Greek pseudonym *Arktomastix*, meaning 'one who castigates a bear'. *New History of Ireland*, vol. III, p. 580.

127. The word *informatio* must be a technical word indicating a special informative account.

128. The work referred to here is *Threnodia Hiberno-Catholica*, an account of the Catholics of Ireland during the Cromwellian persecution. It was written by Friar Maurice Conry (*Muiris Ó Maolchonaire*) of Thomond, under the pseudonym Morrison, and published at Innsbruck, Austria, in 1659. Maurice was of the learned Uí Mhaoilchonaire family, a branch of which held lands at Ardkyle in County Clare. See Brian Ó Dálaigh, 'The Uí Mhaoilchonaire of Thomond', *Studia Hibernica*, vol. 35, 2009/2010, pp. 45–68.

129. Luke Wadding, O.F.M. (1588–1657), Franciscan, historian and theologian. Born in Waterford; ordained a priest, Lisbon 1613, established Irish College of St Isidore in Rome, 1625. He was Roman agent for Irish Catholics during the Confederate Wars of the 1640s. A prolific author, his best-known work is *Annales Minorum* (1625–54), a history of the Franciscan order. *DIB*, vol. IX, pp. 680–7.

130. *Scriptores Ordinis Minorum*, by Luke Wadding, published in Rome, 1650. It is an alphabetical list of the writers of the Franciscan order with a catalogue of their works.

131. The Irish College at Louvain in Belgium was established by Florence Conry (*Flaithrí Ó Maolchonaire*), archbishop of Tuam in 1607, as a seminary for the training of Irish Franciscan priests. The college is best known for the work of its Gaelic-Irish friars, who were recruited from the Gaelic professional hereditary families and who were instrumental in gathering and compiling lives of saints and historical annals. The best known of these was Mícheál Ó Cléirigh (*c.* 1590–1643), who made several journeys around Ireland to collect and assemble the surviving Irish annals into what became the historical collection known as *Annála Ríoghachta Éireann* (Annals of the Kingdom of Ireland). The Irish College at Louvain operated until 1794

when it was closed by the invading French. Brendan Jennings, *Mícheál Ó Cléirigh, His Associates, and St Anthony's College, Louvain* (Dublin, 1936), pp. 19–25. See also Tomás Ó Cléirigh, *Aodh Mac Aingil agus an Scoil Nua-Ghaeilge i Lobháin* (Baile Átha Cliath, an dara heagrán, 1985).

132. A definitor advised the minister provincial and had charge of disciplinary matters within a province. He also retained voting rights at general chapters and elections exclusive to his office.

133. Differently from elsewhere in the present edition, the Latin titles in this paragraph have been translated into English because of their conspicuous length.

134. The function of this internal note (*nota bene*) is to attract Carve's attention.

135. This is a disguised quotation from the Gospels (*John* 20:27), with Christ inviting St Thomas to put a finger into his side. The reference to the famous episode is reinforced by the similarity between Carve and St Thomas.

136. The word *rudis*, 'uncultivated', is *nudus*, 'naked', in the Latin translation of the *Apocalypse* given in the Vulgate.

137. The term refers to ecclesiastical dress appropriate to the clerical status, except that Carve was not a protonotary but a secular priest. Following the Council of Trent, Pope Sixtus V (1585–90) obliged clergy to wear a black cassock as their distinctive form of dress. In the engraving Carve is depicted in full clerical apparel; he wears a buttoned cassock, a fascia or sash around the waist, a zucchetto or skull cap on his head, and a full-length cape hangs from his shoulders. See image of Carve in ecclesiastical dress, Fig. 1.

138. The portrait illustration of Thomas Carve appears in his second edition of *Lyra seu Anacephalaeosis Hibernica*, reprinted in Sulzbach in 1666. The reprinted version contained maps, plates and the Carve portrait. It was the republishing of this work that compelled Bruodinus to pen his criticisms of Carve (that is, Carran) in his lengthy tome, *Propugnaculum* (1669).

139. The *Bible* has *diligentis* instead of *amantis* (*Prov.* 27, 6), but the two words are synonyms and the latter is sometimes used in quotations by Christian authors.

140. Dermot O'Hurley (*c.* 1530–84), appointed Catholic archbishop of Cashel in 1581, was tortured and put to death for high treason in the reign of Queen Elizabeth I. *DIB*, vol. VII, pp. 579–81.

141. Carve was therefore born in County Tipperary. In his Latin works he refers to himself as *Tipperariensis Mobernans*, indicating that he identified as a Tipperary man from Mobarnan (*Maigh Bearnáin*), a townland around 10 kilometres east of Cashel in Magorban (*Maigh gCorbáin*) parish. In Carve's time a German geographic mile (*geographische Meile*) was equivalent to about 7.4 kilometres. See Thomas Carve, *Responsio veridica ad illotum libellum, cui nomen Anatomicum Examen P. Antonii Bruodini* (Sulzbach, 1672).

142. The verb *inspicere* can mean 'to see' or 'to consider'. It is not clear whether Bruodinus here refers to people who were present at the martyrdom, or to people who wrote about it.

143. Thomas Good (1609–78), also spelled Goud or Guod in *Anatomicum*, was an English academic and clergyman, master of Balliol College, Oxford. He was known as a moderate and an orthodox apologist for the Church of England. His principal published work was *Firmianus and Dubitantius, certain dialogues concerning Atheism, Infidelity, Popery, and other Heresies* (Oxford, 1674).). *ODNB*, vol. XXII, p. 744. Bruodinus appears to have confused him with the Catholic author John Coppinger.

144. The book in question is almost certainly *The Theatre of Catholique and Protestant Religion*, which is now known to have been written by John Coppinger, an Irish cleric with Cork connections. The work was published in 1620, not at Douai, but a hundred kilometres north-west at St Omer, then in the Spanish Netherlands.

145. The word *pectenarius* is attested in a few texts or inscriptions and scholars have debated its meaning. It clearly refers to a profession, but we do not know which one exactly. A *pectenarius* was probably either a 'comber' (that is, a person who prepares wool for manufacture, using a particular kind of comb) or a 'comb-maker' (that is, a person who produces combs).

146. The author is referring to the English language. This is a reference to the fact that Carve's ancestors rarely spoke English but rather Irish. It is suggestive of the fact that Carve's ancestry is Gaelic-Irish not Anglo-Norman, a point repeatedly made by the author.

147. There was an important family of English descent named Carew or Carve in Munster from the fifteenth century. It was from this family that Carve claimed descent, a claim that Bruodinus sought to refute by asserting that Thomas Carve was of a plebeian Gaelic family whose rightful surname was Ó Corráin. See Paul MacCotter, 'The Carews of Cork', *Journal of the Cork Historical and Archaeoloical Society*, vol. 98, 1993, pp. 61–74.

148. Louis I de Lorraine (1527–78), appointed bishop of Troyes in 1545 and of Albi in 1550; he was made cardinal of Guise in 1553 and archbishop of Reims in 1574.

149. Vith is an ancient form of withe or withy. Criminals might be strangled with a willow withe and bog bodies are sometimes found with a willow withy around their necks. The withe or withy was in former times used instead of rope.

150. No doctor of theology called Charles O'Molloy has been traced in Rome before 1671. Perhaps the person intended was the Charles O'Molloy who had been a student of humanities at the Irish College in Lille, Belgium, and was awaiting admittance to the Irish College in Rome. He was admitted to the college in 1674, where he qualified as a doctor of theology in 1681 and returned to Ireland. This Charles O'Molloy (*Calbhach Ó Maolmhuaidh*) of Kiltubbrid, Offaly was likely to be a relative of the Franciscan author Francis O'Molloy (*Froinsias Ó Maolmhuaidh*). *An early manuscript account of the Irish College, Rome 1628–1678* (Rome, 2003), p. 179.

151. The expression *divos tollere* may allude to Cicero, *On Divination* 2.40, where it is applied to the philosopher Epicurus, according to whom the gods had no involvement in the world or in human affairs.

152. Bruodinus is paraphrasing a passage from the Gospels (*Matthew* 5:18).

153. That is, Carran is being blasphemous.

154. Here and elsewhere, Bruodinus makes a pun with the title of the various chapters of his work, all entitled *Anatomia* 'dissection', rather than with the byname he gives to *Anatomicum* as a whole.

155. The Graecism *Pseudolus* is not simply an adjective, but the speaking name of a character of Roman comedy, symbolising a liar.

156. Sir John Burke of Brittas County Limerick was a landowner and Catholic martyr. On the death of Queen Elizabeth in 1603 he tried to restore the open practice of the Catholic faith in Limerick. Having rejected many appeals to conform to the state religion, he was imprisoned and charged with killing a soldier. Found guilty of treason, he was sentenced to death and executed in December 1607. *DIB*, vol. II, pp. 40–1.

157. The Latinised Chrahy is *Mág Craith* in Irish, usually anglicised Magrath or MacGrath. Burke was not married to a Magrath but to Grace Thornton, a daughter of Sir George Thornton, provost marshall of Munster. Patrick J. Ryan, *Archbishop Miler Magrath 1522–1622* (Lisheen, 2014), p. 118.

158. Fr Bernardine Clancy (*Mac Fhlannchadha*, MacClancy) from Thomond (*c.* 1612–84), was a relative and colleague of Bruodinus in Prague. He served as guardian of the college of the Immaculate Conception on six occasions between 1647 and 1675. Fr Clancy enjoyed the support of the archbishop, Cardinal Von Harrach of Vienna, and taught theology at the archiepiscopal seminary in Prague for twenty-seven years. Pařez & Kuchařová, *Irish Franciscans Prague*, pp. 67–72, 180.

159. The syntactical mistakes in the English passage have been deliberately added here because of Bruodinus' comment about Carve's misuse of Latin, but the passage from Carve's work has been misquoted as usual. In fact, the syntax of the original text makes sense in Carve's passage, but Bruodinus here omits the beginning and the end of the sentence.

160. Bruodinus is wrong in naming John Burke's wife as Grace Fitzgerald, her name was Grace Thornton. *DIB*, vol. II, p. 41. Grace Thornton married secondly Terence Magrath, eldest son of

Archbishop Miler Magrath, which is probably what gave rise to the confusion in Prague and Vienna. Ryan, *Archbishop Miler Magrath*, p. 118.

161. The Thomond surname *Ó hAiseadha* is occasionally anglicised O'Hassey but more commonly Hassett.

162. The reference is most likely to the Greek rhetor and sophist Gorgias (*c.* 485–380 BC), here misspelled *Georgias*, by Bruodinus or by the typographer. He is the interlocutor of Socrates in the homonymous dialogue by Plato. Noted for his ability to answer any question, he was author of the thesis '*On Non-Existence*'.

163. Bruodinus' biographical notice on John Burke was published in *Propugnaculum*, p. 473.

164. The Sage here was Shimon ben Yeshua ben Eliezer ben Sira, the author of the *Book of the All-Virtuous Wisdom of Joshua ben Sira* (also known as *Wisdom of Sirach*, or *Book of Ecclesiasticus*), which is part of the Old Testament.

165. The word *fraticellus* (literally, 'little friar'), which applies to a member of the Order of the Friars Minor, is used pejoratively here.

166. Priscian was a grammarian of the sixth century AD whose name here features as a synonym for the correct use of Latin. His *Institutes of Grammar* was the standard textbook for the study of the language during the middle ages. Bruodinus' comment refers to Carve's misuse of Latin syntax, which the English translation tries to reflect.

167. Terence or Turlough Magrath (d. 1619) was the eldest son of Miler Magrath, Protestant archbishop of Cashel. He married Katherine, daughter of Edmund Butler, baron of Dunboyne and secondly Grace Thornton, widow of Sir John Burke. Ryan, *Archbishop Miler Magrath*, p. 118.

168. Miler Magrath (*c.* 1522–1622) of Termon Magrath, County Fermanagh was educated in Rome and entered the Franciscan order. He was appointed Catholic bishop of Down and Connor in 1565, but declaring that he was willing to hold his bishopric of the queen, became Protestant bishop of Clogher in 1570. Translated to the archbishopric of Cashel the following year, he took a Catholic wife by whom he had nine children and who were raised in the religion of their mother. Magrath was notorious for his abuse of church livings almost sixty of which were found to be in the hands of his sons and daughters. He made overtures to Rome for his return to the Catholic Church in 1608 and again in 1612 but there was no formal reconciliation. Dying at the reputed age of 100, he was buried in Cashel cathedral. *DIB*, vol. VI, pp. 261–3.

169. Pope Marcellinus was bishop of Rome 296–304. It is alleged that because of the severity of the persecution of Christians by Emperor Diocletian (244–311), he worshipped idols temporarily but afterwards repented.

170. Diocletian's persecution, named after Emperor Diocletian and also known as 'The Great Persecution', was the last and fiercest persecution of Christians that took place at the beginning of the fourth century AD.

171. Andreas Bodenstein von Karlstadt (1486–1541), German theologian of the Protestant reformation, was excommunicated with Martin Luther in 1521 by Pope Leo X. He was a leading advocate of *Bilderstrum*, the destruction of holy images. Some ninety of his theological works were published during his lifetime. *Neue Deutsche Biographie* 2 (1955), pp. 356–7.

172. The account of Bruodinus is exaggerated. Magrath was recognised and arrested in London when returning to Ireland from Rome. While in the custody of Edmund Grindal, bishop of London, he apostatised and took the oath of supremacy in July 1569. It's possible that he was threatened with torture during his imprisonment. Ryan, *Archbishop Miler Magrath*, pp. 35–9.

173. James O'Nelan (*Séamus Ó Nialáin*) was born in Thomond at the close of the sixteenth century. Entering the Irish College at Louvain in 1610, he was ordained a priest and had returned to Ireland by 1617. A manuscript in the possession of Fr John Colgan contained a collection of his poems. Cuthbert Mhág Craith, *Dán na mBráthar Mionúr* (Baile Átha Cliath, 1967), vol. II, pp. 334–5.

174. The Franciscan friary of Timoleague (*Tigh Molaige*, St Molaga's house) is situated on the south coast of County Cork. Founded in the thirteenth century, it became a chief burial ground

of the Gaelic MacCarthys and the Norman de Barrys. Officially dissolved in the 1540s, the friars retained a presence there until the seventeenth century.

175. The Third Order had a membership of secular people who wanted to live a religious life but were not bound by the rules of a cloistered life.

176. Thomas Lodge (*c*. 1557–1625), English poet, dramatist and prose writer, became a Catholic in 1597 and repented of his former life in his religious tract *Prosopopeia*. *ODNB*, vol. XXXIV, pp. 284–8.

177. Bruodinus is referring to his adversary, Thomas Carve, here in the third person.

178. The syntax of the sentence makes no sense in Latin, partly because of Carve's mistakes and partly because of the way Bruodinus misquotes or paraphrases the passage.

179. The man intended here is Sir Richard Shee (d. 1608), of Upper Court, seneschal and chief servant of Thomas, tenth earl of Ormond. Reconverting to Catholicism late in life, Sir Richard was founder of Shee Alms House, Kilkenny and harboured Catholic clergy in his private residence. David Edwards, *The Ormond Lordship in County Kilkenny 1515–1642* (Dublin, 2003), pp. 241–3, 267–8.

180. Thomas Butler (1531–1614), tenth earl of Ormond, was called Black Tom (*Tomás Dubh*) because of the colour of his hair. As he aged he became incapacitated and blind, which is to what Bruodinus is referring. *DIB*, vol. II, pp. 183–6.

181. Robert Rothe (1550–1622), Kilkenny alderman and Catholic lawyer, for much of his life he acted as legal representative and envoy of the earl of Ormond in London and as manager of his large estates in Ireland. He completed a history of the Butlers of Ormond in 1616. Edwards, *Ormond Lordship, Kilkenny*, pp. 50, 57, 267–8.

182. The translation reflects Carve's misuse of Latin, which Bruodinus stigmatises.

183. Matthew or Mahon Magrath, Catholic vicar general of the diocese of Killaloe (1622), was harboured in the house of Sir John MacNamara of Mountallon. He compiled a book of those who suffered for their faith, during the persecutions of Elizabeth I and James I. The manuscript was brought to Prague in 1660 by Daniel Mulconry and preserved in the Franciscan library. See James Frost, *History of Clare* (Dublin, 1893), p. 553.

184. Martin Becanus (1563–1624), a Flemish Jesuit and acclaimed theologian. Born in the Netherlands, his original surname was Schellekens. He taught theology at the universities of Würzburg, Mainz and Vienna. Author of many books, he engaged in extensive controversy with the theologians of his time. See *Catholic Encyclopedia*, , vol. II, p. 380.

185. There were a number of writers of theology named Sartorius. The man in question here is likely to have been Baltasar Sartorius (1534–1609), a German Lutheran theologian. See *Allgemeine Deutsche Biographie*, vol. 30, 1890, pp. 379–80.

186. Here and in the next sentence, the Latin adverb *charitative* refers to the concept of *charitas* (or *caritas*), one of the three theological virtues of Christianity, consisting of altruistic love for anyone.

187. Bruodinus is here exploiting the double meaning of the Latin word *caput* ('head' or 'chapter'), to insist on the anatomical imagery of his work: Carve's chapter (or head) is without a brain, that is, it has been deprived of any sense.

188. Namely, Carve is unable to respond to critics because he has no solid argument to offer. The image can be found in various classical texts but this is more likely a biblical reference (*Acts* 26, 4).

189. Malachy O'Queely (*Maolsheachlainn Ó Caolaidhe*), archbishop of Tuam (1630–45), was born in Thomond. Educated at the Sorbonne in Paris, he returned to Ireland in 1622 when he was appointed vicar apostolic of Killaloe. A man noted for his preaching and pastoral work, following the 1641 uprising he tried to curb the worst excesses of violence in his diocese. Well regarded, he represented Connacht on the supreme council of the Confederation of Kilkenny. *DIB*, vol. VII, p. 822.

190. In (mis)quoting from Carve's text, Bruodinus has omitted some words, and in particular the subject of the verb *sentit*. In the original passage, in fact, the subject *Lector* (the reader) is outside the parentheses, the use of which deliberately avoids specifying if the title of martyr is given by Bruodinus or assumed by the reader. Bruodinus explicitly refers to the archbishop of Tuam as a martyr (*martyrio afficitur*) in *Propugnaculum*, Book IV, Chapter 3, p. 562. Then, in Chapter 15, p. 724, he speaks about the bishop of Clogher, but he does not explicitly call him a martyr. However, since his name occurs in a chapter entitled 'about the martyrs in Ireland' (*de martyribus in Hibernia*), the reader should assume – Carve says – that Bruodinus regarded him as a martyr.

191. Heber MacMahon (*Éimhear Mac Mathghamha*), bishop of Clogher (1643–50), politician and military commander, led the Irish army of Ulster against English parliamentarian forces at Scarrifhollis, in June 1650, where he was disastrously defeated. MacMahon fled the battle but was captured two days later. *DIB*, vol. VI, pp. 83–4.

192. The translation renders the syntactical mistake in the Latin text reported by Bruodinus, on which he also remarks in this paragraph (by calling Carve a student of elementary grammar) as well as in the next one (by referring to Lily's *Grammar*). The mistake, however, has been deliberately added by Bruodinus when misquoting Carve's words, which are correct.

193. The second sentence of this misquotation or paraphrase is taken from a different passage of Carve's chapter, and it has been shortened.

194. This literally means 'certainly not an eagle'. Although the primary concern of this comparison is to remark on Carve's mental short-sightedness, the parallel with a night-owl also deprives Carve of some positive features traditionally associated with the eagle as a symbol of nobility and power. For Carve as a night-owl, see also p. 105 and the short poem by John Burke quoted on p. 129.

195. Two well-known theologians, whose works were used extensively in Catholic seminaries: Francisco Toledo (1532–96), a Spanish Jesuit, was author of an important commentary on Thomas Aquinas' *Summa Theologiae*, and Paul Laymann (1574–1635), Austrian Jesuit, wrote a compendium of moral theology, *Theologia Moralis in quinque libros partita* (Munich, 1625), that was used in the education of clerics well into the eighteenth century. *Catholic Encyclopedia*, vol. IX, p. 471, vol. XIV, p. 760.

196. Theobald Taffe (1603–77), soldier and royalist of Ballymote, County Sligo, assumed command of the joint royalist-confederate forces of Connacht in 1645 but his army suffered a major reverse at the hands of the English parliamentarians in October of the same year. He had even less success as commander of the Munster army, when Lord Inchiquin scored a stunning victory over him at Knocknanuss in 1647. Taffe joined the royal court in exile at the end of the war. *DIB*, vol. IX, pp. 227–8.

197. Archbishop O'Queely was killed in an encounter with forces loyal to the English parliament near Sligo in October 1645. He never stood trial. See Mícheál Ó Siochrú, *Confederate Ireland 1642–1649* (Dublin, 1999), p. 98.

198. Following his capture in Fermanagh, Bishop MacMahon was imprisoned until his wounds healed. He was executed on the orders of Charles Coote in July 1650 and his head displayed on a spike over the entrance of Enniskillen castle.

199. Namely, *The Irish-Catholic Threnody*, elsewhere referred to as *Threnodia Hibernorum*. See note 128 above.

200. Bruodinus is here exploiting Carve's name to refer to the episode of the incredulity of the apostle Thomas in the Gospels. The words Bruodinus uses are the same as those which Jesus spoke to doubting Thomas (*John* 20:24): *noli esse incredulus sed fidelis*. The adjective *fidelis* has the double meaning of 'faithful' and 'trustful'.

201. As usual, this is not an exact quotation. Bruodinus has also shortened some sentences, making the syntax of the Latin text more difficult to follow here than in the original source.

202. Giovanni Battista Rinuccini (1592–1653), arcbishop of Fermo, papal nuncio to the confederate Catholics of Ireland. His mission was the full restoration of the public exercise of the Catholic religion in Ireland. However, he found Catholics hopelessly divided between those who wished to be loyal to the king of England and those who did not. His mission was a failure and he left for Rome in February 1649. *DIB*, vol. VIII, pp. 502–4.

203. James Butler (1610–88), twelfth earl of Ormond, although born of Catholic parents, was raised a Protestant. Made viceroy of Ireland in 1644, he commanded the royalist forces and staunchly defended the Protestant interest. He conducted extensive negotiations with Rinuccini and the confederate Catholics, all of which proved fruitless. As a military commander he had little success and following his defeat by English parliamentarians at Rathmines near Dublin, he went into exile in December 1650. *DIB*, vol. II, pp. 131–45.

204. The title literally translates as *The Claims of the Catholics of Ireland*.

205. The publication, which was supportive of the Inchiquin truce and Ormond peace, was part of the controversy that erupted in Paris in the 1650s concerning Rinuccini's censure of the supreme council of Kilkenny. The work was ascribed to Richard Bellings, secretary of the confederation, but is now known to have been written by John Callaghan, a Jansenist priest originally of Cork. *DIB*, vol. II, 262.

206. A Spanish stew made of sausage meats and vegetables, here meant to signify an incoherent jumble of ingredients.

207. *Anagyris foetida*, a wild plant of the Mediterranean region also known as stinking bean trefoil, an emetic used in medicine to induce vomiting so as to empty the contents of the stomach.

208. A *nota* was one of the official forms of ecclesiastical censures, inherited from ancient Rome (*nota censoria*), which could be deployed against sinners, especially within the clergy (see the relevant comments to the papal bull, note 210 below). For the technical meaning of the verb *adurere*, which is attested elsewhere, see *Glossar. vet.* ex Cod. reg. 7646: '*Adurit, maculat, notat*'.

209. Antonio Pignatelli (1615–1700), the future Pope Innocent XII, was apostolic nuncio at Vienna 1668–71.

210. The bull of Pope Alexander VII in 1655 revoked the excommunication imposed on all those Catholics both lay and clerical, who had supported the Protestant viceroy, James Butler, earl of Ormond in negotiations with the English parliamentarians against the expressed wishes of Archbishop Rinuccini. See Ian Campbell, 'Truth and Calumny in Baroque Rome: Richard O'Ferrall and the "Commentarius Rinnuccinianus", 1648–1667', *Irish Historical Studies*, vol. 38, 2012, pp. 219–20, 229.

211. *PP.* here stands for the title *Papa Pontifex* (Pope Pontiff), which is part of the official signature of the pope in his letters and documents.

212. Pope Alexander VII (1655–67) succeeded Innocent X to the papacy. The pope was said to have held Luke Wadding in high esteem. He re-established the Franciscan mission to Ireland and granted special faculties to friars working on the Irish mission. See: Franciscan Fathers (eds), *Father Luke Wadding: Commemorative volume* (Killiney, Dublin, 1957), pp. 25, 375.

213. *Charitas* here is not just simply 'love', but one of the three theological virtues of Christianity (faith, hope and charity).

214. A suffrage is a petition to God to make an indulgence available for the souls detained in purgatory, over which the Church has no direct jurisdiction.

215. The 'Piscatory Ring' (or Ring of the Fisherman), part of the pope's *regalia*, was used to endorse documents with his official seal. Only the pope, being the successor of Saint Peter, whom Jesus made 'a fisher of men' (*Mark* 1:17; *Luke* 5:10), may wear it.

216. Giannotto Gualterio succeeded his uncle as archbishop of Fermo in 1668 and was a friend and confidant of Pope Alexander VII.

217. A faculty granted by the papacy allowing a specific deviation from canon law.

218. The Saul or Sall family of Cashel was one of Tipperary's leading mercantile families. Joseph Sall entered the Franciscan order at Kilkenny in 1635. He was guardian of the Carrick-on-Suir friary during the Catholic Confederacy and was forced to flee to Spain to avoid the Cromwellian persecution. Joseph was co-author of an account of the martyrdom of his fellow Franciscan John Kearney, who was hanged at Clonmel in 1652. Returning to Ireland, he was guardian of Cashel friary in 1664, when he was briefly imprisoned by the authorities. He was still alive in 1684. His 'Index of Irish Martyrs' has not been traced and may not have been a printed work. See Paul MacCotter, 'A History of the Sall Family of Cashel', *Irish Genealogist*, vol. 10, 1999, p. 229.

219. The highest-ranking papal envoy appointed by the pope for a specific mission (it literally means: legate from the pope's side).

220. Bruodinus is here referring to the story of Jesus calling the first apostles (Peter, James and John) after the miraculous catch of fish as it is narrated in the *Gospel of Luke*, 5:1–11. The 'apostolic fisherman' is Saint Peter. See note 215 above on the Piscatory Ring.

221. John O'Molony (1617–1702), born in County Clare, was the nephew of John O'Molony, bishop of Killaloe (1630–51). Ordained a priest in 1642, he graduated with a doctorate in theology from the Sorbonne in Paris. O'Molony successfully defended the censures of Rinuccini against the Ormond peace agreement at the university in the late 1640s. Consecrated bishop of Killaloe in 1672, he returned to Ireland, where a bounty of £150 was placed on his head. He became bishop of Limerick in 1688. *DIB*, vol. VII, p. 704.

222. In the Latin, the reference is to a specific form of sacrifice, the holocaust (a Greek term literally meaning 'entirely burnt'), in which the entire animal was destroyed by the fire, and not simply part of the offering (as was more common).

223. The word *corve* (you crow) produces a pun with the name Carve, which is most likely deliberate.

224. For Momus see note 116 above.

225. Adrian IV (1154–9) was the only Englishman to be elected pope. *Laudabiliter*, the papal letter, allegedly issued by him in 1155, authorising Henry II to conquer Ireland so that the Irish Church could be reformed, was the subject of much controversy. No true copy of the letter survives and its authenticity has always been questioned. *ODNB*, vol. I, pp. 357–9. Further down in the current chapter of *Anatomicum* (paragraphs 5 and 6), Bruodinus refers to Pope Adrian as being burnt to ashes upon his death, perhaps as a derogatory remark on the English pope. This, however, was not the case; his corpse was entombed in a costly sarcophagus and placed in the grottoes of St Peter's Basilica, Rome. Wendy J. Reardon, *Deaths of the Popes: Comprehensive accounts* (North Carolina, 2004), pp. 93–4.

226. As usual, the quotation is imprecise. Bruodinus also adds a mistake in the use of Latin (*infert* instead of *inferat*), which is not present in Carve's original passage.

227. Nicholas Sander (*c.* 1530–81), Catholic priest and author, was born in Surrey, England. Appointed papal legate, he accompanied James fitz Maurice Fitzgerald on a crusade to Ireland in 1579. There he called on Irish nobles to support a just war in defence of the Catholic faith. The enterprise ended, however, in 1580 when 600 papal soldiers were massacred at Smerwick (*Dún an Óir*) near Dingle by English troops. Sander remained in Ireland following the catastrophe but died the following year. His principal work, *De origne ac progressu schimatis anglicani*, which recounts the break of the English Church with Rome, was published posthumously in 1585 and went through several editions. *DIB*, vol. VIII, pp. 761–3.

228. Peter Lombard (*c.* 1554–1625), archbishop of Armagh, was born into a prosperous mercantile family in Waterford. Educated at Louvain, he gained a doctorate in theology and became a professor of the university. Proceeding to Rome in 1598 he functioned as Hugh O'Neill's special envoy to the pope. He was elevated to the primacy of Armagh in 1601 but never returned to his native country. His most celebrated work was *De Hibernia insula commentarius*, a commentary on the transfer of the sovereignty of Ireland to the kings of England. The book was published posthumously at Louvain in 1632. *DIB*, vol. V, pp. 553–6.

229. The text quoted by Carve and reported by Bruodinus is in its original form and does not accept the emendation by Giraldus Cambrensis in *Expugnatio Hiberniae*, vol. II, p. 5, where the relative pronoun *quae* was added before the word *documenta*. Giraldus' emendation, however, is absolutely necessary for the text to make sense. Therefore, it has been accepted in the present edition, where the passage has been translated accordingly.

230. The Latin text reads *Corcica*, a toponym which is certainly misspelled. We assume that the reference is to Corsica (*Corsica* in Latin) and not to Corfu (*Corcira* in Latin), given that the former was under the influence of the Catholic Church whereas the latter was under the influence of the Greek Orthodox Church.

231. Dermot MacMurrough (d. 1171), king of Leinster, was deposed and exiled in 1166. He sought the aid of Henry II to recover Leinster. Recruiting forces in Wales, he offered his daughter Aoífe in marriage to Richard de Clare alias 'Strongbow', who became his principal ally. Strongbow landed at Waterford in 1170, captured the city and initiated the English conquest of Ireland. *DIB*, vol. V, pp. 110–13.

232. The first incursion by the Anglo-Normans was in May 1169.

233. Henry II (1133–89), king of England and duke of Normandy, came to Ireland in 1171 to place the conquest firmly under his control.

234. Thomas Becket, archbishop of Canterbury (1162–70), was in dispute with Henry II over Church rights and was consequently murdered by knights of the king. Pope Alexander III humbled Henry and canonised Thomas Becket in 1173. To this day Christians venerate Becket as a saint and martyr. *ODNB*, vol. IV, pp. 701–11.

235. Giraldus Cambrensis (Gerald of Wales) (*c.* 1146–*c.* 1223) produced two works on Ireland, *Expugnatio Hibernica* in 1185, which is a history of the English part-conquest of Ireland, and *Topographia Hibernica*, which circulated from 1187 and contains many fables on the wonders and miracles of Ireland. Cambrensis seized every opportunity to denounce the native people and portrayed them as barbaric and uncivilised. *DIB*, vol. IV, pp. 53–4.

236. John Lynch (*c.* 1599–1677), historian and priest of Galway, fled Ireland in 1652 and resided in France. His principal work, *Cambrensis eversus*, was published at St Malo in 1664. Lynch's book is a comprehensive refutation of Cambrensis' accounts of Ireland. *DIB*, vol. V, pp. 627–9.

237. The use of the words *magister* and *doctor* in opposition aims at suggesting that the authority of Cambrensis is less powerful than the authority of Lynch.

238. There was no rank or dignity of Viscount Cahir in the seventeenth century. What was intended was the title baron of Cahir, which was held by the Butler family of south Tipperary. The Butlers possessed the barony of Iffa and Offa West of which Cahir was the main town and stronghold.

239. A cento was a late-antique poetic form consisting of works composed of verses taken from classical poems and disposed in a new order.

240. St Malachy (1094–1148), archbishop of Armagh, strongly advocated the reform of the Irish Church. While journeying to Rome in 1139 he visited the Cistercian abbey of Clairvaux and befriended the abbot St Bernard. On a second visit to the continent in 1148 Malachy fell ill and died at Clairvaux. Bernard subsequently wrote a 'Life of St Malachy', which emphasised the barbarism and backwardness of Ireland and the urgent need for reform. See Robert T. Meyer (ed.), *The Life and Deeds of Saint Malachy, the Irishman* (Kalamazoo, 1978).

241. Bruodinus is misquoting Carve's words, as he often does, by re-adapting them to the context of the passage so as to make them look like an answer to the question that he is posing. Note, in particular, Bruodinus' addition of the conjunction *quia* ('because').

242. The English translation tries to reflect Carve's misuse of Latin, which Bruodinus stigmatises by means of the reference to Priscian. See note 166 above.

243. An official epithet referring to St Bernard of Clairvaux as one who's teaching 'is as sweet as honey'.

244. St Bernard (1090–1153), abbot of the Cistercian monastery of Clairvaux, Burgundy, in north-eastern France, was noted for his extraordinary zeal and personal magnetism. A primary reformer of the Cistercian order, he is credited with founding sixty-five monasteries. He was the author of many and varied spiritual works and attracted many young men to his order. Bernard was canonised a saint in 1174 and declared a doctor of the Church in 1830. See above notes 32 and 43.

245. The verb *exarare* (literally, 'to plough') is probably used here with a twofold metaphorical meaning. On the one hand, St Bernard 'dug up' information about St Malachy from his sources; on the other hand, he 'wrote down' this information, as if he were 'furrowing' the writing surface.

246. The whole sentence is a metaphor based on a lawsuit.

247. This is Edmund Magranna (*Mac Gráinne*), a man, perhaps of Connacht origin, who was ordained a secular priest in Prague in 1640 and had joined the Franciscan order by 1657. Pařez & Kuchařová, *Irish Franciscans Prague*, pp. 8, 15, 34.

248. In the 1620s and 1630s Carve was chaplain and secretary to the regiment of Count Walter Butler formerly of Tipperary, to whom he was very close. He travelled with Butler through Germany, Bohemia, Hungary and Poland and endured extreme hardship with the Irish troops. Butler was a generous patron of the Irish Franciscans at Prague. When he died in 1634 Butler left 30,000 florins to the Irish Franciscan monastery at Prague. Carew wrote a three-volume history called *Itinerarium* (Mainz, 1639–46) of his experiences with Butler during the Thirty Years War and a particularly detailed account of Butler's assassination of Wallestein, former commander of the imperial armies. It is possible that he wrote this work on the instructions of Butler and perhaps he was owed goods or money from the Butler bequest over which the Franciscans had control. If so, it is in this context we should understand the incident outlined in paragraph 11. The poem is supposed to be an ironic payment to Carve in response to his claims about a supposed debt from the Irish Franciscan friars. *DIB*, vol. II, pp. 188–90, 335–6.

249. The breaking wheel was an instrument of torture used for public execution in Europe from antiquity into the early modern period. Utilised to crush the limbs and bones of the condemned, it caused prolonged pain. In medieval iconography the wheel became a symbol of St Catherine of Alexandria, who was reputedly tortured on a breaking wheel.

250. Or 'you cry out against these words' (that is, the poem's words).

251. The Latin word *bardus* can mean 'fool', but not 'philosopher'. Despite this odd reference to the Latin meaning of the word, Bruodinus is probably referring to the great differences in grades of poets and poetry in Irish culture. A high-grade poet in charge of a bardic school might equate with a philosopher, but a low-grade bard chanting *sráid éigse* (street verse) would be akin to a fool and have little status.

252. In this case, Matthew: see *Gospel of St Matthew* 5:22.

253. Gehenna is a small valley in Jerusalem where some of the kings of Judah sacrificed their children by fire; thereafter it was employed as a synomnyn for hell in Jewish and Christian traditions.

254. Tadhg mac Dáire Mhic Bhruaideadha (*c.* 1550–*c.* 1625), son of Dáire of Knockanalban (*Cnoc an Albanaigh*, *Mons Scoti*, Mount Scott), was employed in the important post of *ollamh* (poet and genealogist) to Donough O'Brien, fourth earl of Thomond. Tadhg farmed extensive lands in the barony of Ibrickan, some of which he held rent-free for his services to O'Brien. Luke McInerney, 'The Earl of Thomond's 1615 Survey of Ibrickan, Co. Clare', *NMAJ*, vol. 53, 2013, pp. 186–9. Approximately thirty of his compositions survive, including one of his earliest, *Mór atá ar theagasc flatha* (Much depends on the tutoring of a prince), a poem of advice to the young earl after his inauguration in 1581. Tadhg also penned O'Brien's official elegy *Eascar Gaoidheal éag aoinfhir* (The undoing of the Gaels is the death of one man) on his demise in 1624. *DIB*, vol. V, pp. 746–7.

255. Tadhg mac Dáire Mhic Bhruaideadha was dead by 1626, when the occupier of Knockanalban was recorded as 'Teig mc Brodies widdowe'. Martin Breen, 'The 1626 Rental of the Thomond Property', *NMAJ*, vol. 54, 2014, p. 25.

256. This sentence, taken from the Bible (*Book of Ecclesiasticus*, Chapter 45, verse 1), was normally used to refer to dead people.

257. According to the *Lebor Gabhála* (Book of Invasions), an eight century composition, *Míl Espáine* (Milesius of Spain) was progenitor of Ireland's peoples. Those of the south (*Leath Mogha*) were descended from his son Éibhear (Eber), and those of the north (*Leath Cuinn*) from his son Éireamhón (Eremon). In *Iomarbhágh na bhFileadh*, the contention that arose in 1617, the nomenclature of *Lebor Gabhála* predominates. *New History of Ireland*, vol. I, p.185.

258. The principal literary legacy of Tadhg mac Dáire Mhic Bhruaideadha is *Iomarbhágh na bhFileadh* (Contention of the Poets). Some fifteen poets made thirty contributions to the contention over a ten-year period. The dispute was concerned with whether Éireamhón's descendants in the north, or Éibhear's in the south, should take precedence in seventeenth century Ireland. Tadhg argued on behalf of his patron O'Brien, who was in the ascent, against O'Neil and O'Donnell of the north, who had been defeated and were in exile. Lambert McKenna (ed.), *Iomarbhágh na bhFileadh: The Contention of the Bards* (London, 1918).

259. Prefect of the court (*praefectus aula*) was the master of ceremonies in the great hall. He decided on the order of the entertainers, and called on players to entertain the lord and his guests. Alan J. Fletcher, *Drama, Performance and Polity in Pre-Cromwellian Ireland* (Cork, 2000), pp. 207–10.

260. Carve writes *Episcopus Ladensis sive Killaloensis*: the latter adjective is based on the Irish toponym, the former on the Latin equivalent, but Bruodinus points out that the Latin toponym used by Carve (*Ladon*, whence *Ladensis*) is wrong. He regards *Laon* and *Laonensis* to be the correct Latin equivalents, but his objection to Carve's Latinisation is trivial: see note 83 above, on the Latinisation of the Thomond toponym.

261. Malachy O'Molony and John O'Molony were Catholic bishops of Killaloe. Malachy's episcopate lasted from 1571 to 1576, when he was translated to the see of Kilmacduagh, where he administered until at least 1603. John's episcopate persisted from 1630 to 1651, during the troubled times of the Catholic confederacy and the opening years of the Cromwellian administration. While these Molony bishops did not immediately succeed each other, their episcopacies of Killaloe lasted for twenty-six years. Their combined episcopacies of Killaloe and Kilmacduagh, on the other hand, continued for more than fifty years. See *New History of Ireland*, vol. IX, pp. 363, 380.

262. John O'Molony (1591–1651), Catholic bishop of Killaloe, was educated in Galway and at the Sorbonne in Paris. He returned to Ireland in 1625 over concern for family lands in Tulla barony. Appointed bishop of Killaloe, 1630, he supported Archbishop Rinuccini during the Catholic confederacy. Raising troops to attack Ormond soldiers, he was captured at Quin in 1650 in possession of a sum of £1,500. Released, he died of the plague during the siege of Limerick the following year. *DIB*, vol. VII, pp. 703–4.

263. This is a quotation taken from the Book of Wisdom, *Wisdom* 1:11.

264. It is clear that Carve confused the holding at Knockanalban with the lands of Lettermoylan. Tadhg mac Dáire Mhic Bhruaideadha did not pay rent to the bishop of Killaloe for Knockanalban, but he did pay an annual fee to the bishop for Lettermoylan on Slievecallan. So although Carve resided in Vienna and had never been to Thomond, he was relatively well informed about the affairs of Clann Bhruaideadha. Luke McInerney, 'Lettermoylan of Clann Bhruaideadha', *NMAJ*, vol. 52, 2012, pp. 97–8.

265. Bruodinus' reference to Priscian (for whom see above note 166) remarks on Carve's misuse of Latin, probably with regard both to the syntax of the sentence and to the use of the word *famulatus* (generally meaning 'servitude' but here, 'entourage') in the plural. The translation tries to reflect these mistakes.

266. An ancient Latin proverb: see for example Quintilian, *Institutio Oratoria*, IV 2, 91; Apuleius, *Apologia*, 69; Jerome, *Adversus Rufinum*, 3, 13.

267. Bruodinus has modified the text when repeating the quotations, but he has kept Carve's mistakes in the use of Latin (see notes 159 and 178 above), so that the reader may notice them once again.

268. This parallel is quite weak as an argument (a member of Carve's family preferred to take an Irish girl as a servant and lover instead of an English one, just as the earl of Ormond had Irish people amongst his entourage), but it offers Bruodinus the opportunity to put Carve's cousin, who had converted to Protestantism, in a bad light.

269. James Carey served as rector of Kilcooly parish (1667–84). The surname Carey was used as synonym for both Carew and *Ó Carráin*. St J.D. Seymour, *Succession of Parochial Clergy in the United Diocese of Cashel and Emly* (Belfast, 2012), p. 69.

270. *Monasterium de Arvi Campo* (monastery of the ploughed field) was the official Latin title of Kilcooly Abbey.

271. Kilcooly (*Cill Cúile*, church haven), a daughter house of Jerpoint Abbey, was founded by Domnall Mór Ó Briain, king of Munster, in 1184. Dissolved in 1540, the property passed to James Butler, earl of Ormond. The Cistercians regained possession of the abbey for a short period in the 1640s. Roger Stally, *The Cistercian Monasteries of Ireland* (London, 1987), p. 247.

272. Domhnall Mór Ó Briain, king of Munster (1168–94), inflicted a heavy defeat on the Anglo-Normans at the battle of Thurles in 1174 and denied them possession of Limerick until after his death. Domnall founded many monasteries, including the Cistercian houses at Corcumroe in Clare and Holy Cross in Tipperary. John O'Donoghue, *Historical Memoir of the O'Briens* (Dublin, 1860), pp. 89–91, 99–100.

273. Educated at the court of Queen Elizabeth, Donough O'Brien, fourth earl of Thomond (1581–1624), became a prime supporter of the English establishment in Ireland. An admirer of English culture, he set about with considerable energy in anglicising his lordship; and while he remained loyal to the families that fostered him, he dismantled much of the Gaelic infrastructure of Thomond, increasing his own wealth considerably. He was appointed president of Munster in 1615. Ivar O'Brien, *O'Brien of Thomond* (Chichester, 1986), pp. 32–8.

274. The Clancys (*Meic Fhlannchadha*) were among the most prominent legal families of Gaelic Ireland. From the fifteenth century they functioned as brehons (judges and arbitrators) to the O'Briens of Thomond. Their principal residences were at Urlanmore near Bunratty and at Knockfin near Doolin in the barony of Corcomroe. They adapted quickly to political change and by the mid-sixteenth century were drawing up deeds using English terminology. Fergus Kelly, *A Guide to Early Irish Law* (Dublin, 1988), p. 256. For a recent study of the family see Luke McInerney, 'The Síol Fhlannchadha of Tradraighe, Co. Clare: Brehon lawyers of the Gaelic tradition', *Eolas*, vol. 9, 2016, pp. 19–54.

275. Thomas Butler (1531–1614), tenth earl of Ormond, was known to his contemporaries as Black Tom (*Tomás Dubh*). Fostered with the O'More's of Laois, he was sent to London to be educated with the future Edward VI. On his coming of age he inherited hundreds of thousands of acres across the provinces of Leinster and Munster. In England he became a favourite of Elizabeth I, who called him her 'black husband'. Butler was a steadying influence on the English of Ireland during the Nine Years War (1594–1603) and prevented the Pale from being overrun following the battle of the Yellow Ford. In old age he became blind and bedridden. *DIB*, vol. II, pp. 183–6.

276. The MacMahons (*Meic Mhathghamhna*) descended from Mahon son of Muircheartach Mór Ó Briain, high king of Ireland, (d. 1119). They occupied the territory of Corca Baiscinn in west Clare and were ranked third in order of importance (after the O'Briens and MacNamaras) in the kingdom of Thomond.

277. In a listing of the sheriffs of County Clare drawn up by T.J. Westropp, 'Notes on the Sheriffs of Co. Clare, 1570-1700', *JRSAI*, vol. 21, 1890, pp. 68–80, the name of Tadhg mac Dáire Mhic Bhruaideadha does not appear. Westropp's list, however, is defective for the early years of the office. Between 1570 and 1624, sheriffs are recorded for only twenty-one of the fifty-four years. While it is possible that Tadhg mac Dáire was sheriff during these years, this was a disturbed period and it is likely that they were years when no sheriff was appointed. It is over a hundred years since Westropp published his list and if Mac Bruaideadha served three times as sheriff of the county, it is strange that no evidence has subsequently emerged. The matter therefore remains uncertain.

278. As one of the principal land holders in the barony, it is likely that Tadhg mac Dáire Mhic Bhruaideadha would have presided as magistrate of the manor court of Ibrickan. Unfortunately, the records of the Ibrickan manor court do not survive for this early period. C.S. O'Mahony, 'Manor Courts of the Earl of Thomond, 1666–1686', *Analecta Hibernica*, vol. 38, 2004, pp. 160–4.

279. For Martin Becanus, see note 184 above. The reference here is probably to his *Examen Plagae Regiae* (Mainz, 1610), 'An examination of the royal blow', written in response to a publication by Konrad Graser in 1610, which had supported the claim of James I of England that the pope was the antichrist. *Neue Deutsche Biographie*, vol. 1, 1953, p. 686.

280. Konrad Graser, or Grasserus (1557–1613), historian and professor of Hebrew at the Reformed Gymnasium in Thorn (modern day Toruń in Poland), published *Historia Antichristi illius magni* (Leiden, 1608) (History of the great antichrist), which was based on passages from the Book of Daniel. He followed up two years later with his *Plaga Regia* to which Becanus responded. Graser, Konrad, Index entry: *Neue Deutsche Biographie*.

281. Namely, (1) that Tadhg mac Dáire Mhic Bhruaideadha was not master of Knockanalban as he had to pay a yearly tribute to the bishop of Killaloe, and (2) that Tadhg mac Dáire was not the prefect of the court of the earl of Thomond as the earl had only Englishmen in his entourage.

282. Dunboyne, a village in County Meath, is located twenty kilometres west of Dublin. In the mid-seventeenth century the settlement consisted of a parish church, 'an English-built stone house' and several common houses and cabins. R.C. Simington (ed.), *Civil Survey of Co. Meath, 1654–56* (Dublin, 1940), p. 129. James Butler, second Baron Dunboyne (1566–1624), occupied Dunboyne house.

283. This is a sarcastic comment on Carve's misuse of Latin. In English no more than in Latin, you would not need 'and notwithstanding' here.

284. Greek, Latin, English and Irish: see p. 187.

285. Carve's claim that Tadhg Mac Dáire travelled everywhere on foot (including to Dublin) is unlikely to be true. Tadhg was a holder of eight quarters of land under O'Brien of Thomond (almost 6,000 statute acres) and could certainly afford a horse. Luke McInerney, 'Earl of Thomond's Survey of Ibrickan, 1615', *NMAJ*, vol. 53, 2013, pp. 177–80.

286. The poem *Rannam le Chéile a Chlann Uilliam* is addressed to the sons of Richard Burke, earl of Clanricard (1544–82), not the sons of his brother John. Neither is the poem written in Latin but in Irish. These inaccuracies indicate that either Bruodinus is exaggerating or that he had not read the composition in some time. Gearóid Mac Eoin, 'Crosántacht Íorónta, a Chúlra agus a hÚdar', Máirtín Ó Briain (eag.), *Téada Dúchais* (Gaillimh, 2002), pp. 113–20.

287. The composition to the Burkes is a mixture of poetry and prose containing under two thousand words. There is, however, just one short Latin quotation ascribed to a subtle poet: *Quidquid in duas partes dividitur altera pars 'semi' dicitur* (whatever is divided in two parts, either part is called half). It can hardly be claimed on the basis of such slight evidence that Tadhg mac Dáire Mhic Bhruaideadha was 'thoroughly instructed' in the Latin language. L. McKenna, 'A Partition of Ireland', *The Irish Monthly*, vol. 57, June 1929, pp. 330–3.

288. Namely, that what Carve wrote about Tadhg mac Dáire Mhic Bhruaideadha and his meeting with him is nothing more than fiction. Aesop (VI century BC) was a Greek author of fables, although his historical existence has been sometimes questioned.

289. The awkward phrasing is to illustrate Carve's misuse of Latin, which the English translation tries to render.

290. The reference to 'Ciceronian eloquence', that is to a perfect use of Latin, is here sarcastic.

291. In actual fact, Bruodinus inverted Carve's references to the last two items. The original text of *Enchiridion* reads *petasique loco cudone*, that is, 'a helmet instead of a hat'.

292. According to Bruodinus the first two meanings refer to the Latin language, the third to Irish: see p. 185.

293. Or, 'as a final flourish of all the insults you have thrown out …' Originally, the *coronis* was a symbol used at the end of manuscripts and papyri for the practical purpose of marking the end of a section, chapter or book. Symbols of this kind, however, were later used simply for ornamental reasons.

294. And therefore unacquainted with the Irish context Bruodinus is describing.

295. This is Maoilín Mac Bruaideadha, who died in 1582. AFM, vol. V, p. 1791. He was father of Maoilín Óg Mac Bruaideadha, who in the 1590s was brought to Dublin to assist with the translation of the bible into Irish. Nicholas Williams, *I bPrionta i Leabhar* (BÁC, 1986), lgh. 29, 41.

296. Tarumun can be identified as 'Tarmon-Igrady', church land (*tearmann*) of Tomgraney and cited in the 1585 Composition of Connacht. Tomgraney was granted to John O'Grady in 1582 on the death of his father. *Fiants, Elizabeth I*, no. 3943; A. M. Freeman, *Compossicion Booke of Conought* (Dublin, 1936), pp. 7, 12.

297. Dáire was the father of bardic poet Tadhg mac Dáire Mhic Bhruaideadha (d. 1625), whose floruit was mid-sixteenth century. Tadhg mac Dáire inherited Knockanalban, a land denomination of around 900 acres, which he held rent-free upon his death and was still held by his widow in the following year. See Breen, 'The 1626 Rental', *NMAJ*, vol. 54, 2014, p. 25.

298. This is Knockanalban in Kilmurry-Ibrickan parish. It was held in 1586 by Teig Mc Brodie of 'Knockinalbie' and recorded again in 1602. See Nicholls and Ó Cannan, *The Irish Fiants*, nos. 4860 [year 1586], 6615 [year 1602].

299. Knockanalban, Ballyscanlan and Ballyogan are situated in Kilmurry-Ibrickan, Inchicronan and Kilraghtis parishes respectively.

300. Ballyankrow (*Baile Chonchró*, MacEnchroe's homeplace) may have been the original 'super denomination' of which the modern Skaghvickincrow (*Sceach Mhic Conchró*, MacEnchroe's bush), in Inagh parish was part. In 1618 it was held by members of the MacEnchroe (Crowe) lineage. See PHA, Ms 16 B.E. [Great Office 1618 – Inchiquin].

301. Conor MacBrody is likely to be the Conoghor McBradine of Moynoe who served as a juror to an inquisition of 1612. See Ainsworth, *Inchiquin Manuscripts*, p. 313.

302. In 1621 a Donogh mcDonnill Merigagh McNemarra, gent, held the castle and lands of Ballynahinch in Kilnoe parish. In 1570 the castle was held by his grandfather Donogh mac Sida. For a genealogy of '*Mic Con [Mara] Fhinn Bhaile na hInnse*' see RIA Ms 23. H. 25, p. 85 printed in Ó hÓgáin, *Conntae an Chláir*, p. 141. Also see PHA, Ms B. 16 B [Great Office 1621, Tulla barony] and Martin Breen, 'A 1570 List of Castles in Co. Clare', *NMAJ*, vol. 36, 1995, pp. 130–8.

303. Tadhg mac Dáire Mhic Bhruaideadha (d. 1625), bardic poet, was a great-uncle of Antonius Bruodinus.

304. This is likely to be 'Tadhcc an Dunaidh' whose death is recorded in the annals for 1589: 'Teige-an-Duna, the son of Donough, son of Murtough, son of Donough, son of Murtough, son of Ballagh, the senior of the MacMahons of Tuath-na-Fearna (that is, of Corca-Bhaiscinn), and of Sliocht-an-Bhallaigh, died. *AFM*, vol. VI, p. 1879.

305. Tuonafarna is an anglicised version of *Tuath na Fearna* or Killadysert parish. See Seán Ó hÓgáin, *Conntae an Chláir: A tríocha agus a tuatha* (Baile Átha Cliath, 1938), p. 106.

306. Domhnall mac Dáire Mhic Bhruaideadha was the brother of Tadhg mac Dáire, some fifteen of his poems are extant. His best-known composition, *Lá dá rábha ós ráith Luimnigh*, is dedicated to Conchobhar Ó Briain, third earl of Thomond. See also Osborn Bergin, 'A Poem by Domhnall mac Dáire', Ériu, vol. 9, 1921/23, pp. 160–74.

307. This is Ballynamona (*Baile na Móna*) in Kiltallagh (*Cill Tulach*) parish in County Kerry where the Fitzgerald family possessed extensive lands.

308. This could be Constance MacBrody who gave evidence during an inquiry into the Church lands of Tulla in 1627. Constance was recorded as eighty years of age and resident of Tirredagh in Tulla for fifty-four years, giving him a birth year of 1547. See RIA Ms 24 D 17, pp. 45–6.

309. Ninduvia corresponds to the modern Irish *Iníon Dubh*, 'black haired daughter', anglicised Ineenduv.

310. Cragbrien (*Craig Bhriain*, Brian's crag) in Clondagad parish was the hereditary land of the Meic Giolla Riabhaigh (Gallerys), who in a deed from 1589 transferred proprietorship of their 'towne, castell and lands of Craigbryen' to the earl of Thomond. See PHA, Ms C.27.A.60 (no. 5 of a bundle C.13.36). See also Luke McInerney, 'A 1589 Deed between McGilleragh and the Earl of Thomond for Cragbrien', *TOC*, vol. 40, 2016, pp. 73–82.

311. Feakle (*Fiadh Choill*, wild wood) names a village and a parish in north-east Clare. In the seventeenth century Feakle was the most forested part of Thomond.

312. Bonaventure MacBrody features in two lists of Irish scholars and students in Prague, where he was recorded as serving as professor of philosophy and theology for fifteen years. He returned to Ireland in 1663 and was appointed guardian of Ennis friary in 1669, but within a year or two had died in a Dublin dungeon. See Alice Stopford Green, *The Making of Ireland and its Undoing* (London, 1913), p. 455; and Millett, *Irish Franciscans*, p. 152.

313. He may have been the same Thomas recorded in 1618 holding 'Caherkenevan' (Cahercannavan) in Kilmihil, the parish adjoining Kilmacduane where Drumellihy is situated. See PHA, Ms 16 D.1. [Great Office 1618 – Clonderalaw and Moyarta baronies].

314. A Daniel macTeig MacBrody held 'Beanormollogh' in 1641, a sub-division of 'Formoylelu-aghteragh' in Inagh parish. See Simington, *Books of Survey and Distribution*, p. 534. Could he also be the Daniel McBrodin, son of Tadhg mac Dáire Mhic Bhruaideadha, who conformed to the Established Church? Ordained in 1624, Daniel served as vicar of Kilfarboy and Killard in 1633. He is described as 'schoolmaster', suggesting a link to the scholastic world of native learning and perhaps ties to the professional learning of Clann Bhruaideadha of Ibrickan. In 1626 the sons of Tadhg mac Dáire were holding land at Kildeema and Finnor More, the former situated within Kilfarboy parish. See Dwyer, *Diocese of Killaloe*, pp. 164–5, p. 171; and Breen 'Thomond 1626 Rental', *NMAJ*, vol. 54, 2014, pp. 24–5.

315. Tadhg Fitzpatrick may have been the Teig McGillipatrick who held 'Glann' and 'Carow-cloghagh' in Clooney parish, Corcomroe, in 1618. He was probably of the Fitzpatrick, or Meic Giolla Phádraig lineage that is recorded in the funerary entry of Derby Fitzpatrick (d. 1637) of Lisdoonvarna. Generations of them were of 'Downsallagh' in Ibrickan. See Genealogical Office Funeral Entries, vol. VII, p. 317. We are grateful to Kenneth Nicholls for this reference. Also see PHA, Ms 16 B.D.2 [Great Office 1618 – Corcomroe].

316. He was the father of Antonius Bruodinus (d. 1680), the author of this work written under the pseudonym Cornelius O'Molony.

317. This could be Constance MacBrody of 'Baleyogan' who was a witness to the *inquisition post mortem* of William Nelyon of Dysert in 1617. Ainsworth, *Inchiquin Manuscripts*, p. 321.

318. Ballyogan the home place of Bruodinus, is in the parish of Kilraghtis, situated on the Galway road, 10 kilometres north-east of Ennis.

319. This is Ballycroum, a sub-division in Gortindune in Feakle parish where a branch of the O'Molonys (*Uí Mhaoldhomhnaigh*) were settled in 1641. See Simington, *Books of Survey and Distribution*, p. 14.

320. A Donogh mcConmea McNemarra held Ballenehensy in 1621. This is Ballynahinch in Kilnoe parish. PHA, Ms B. 16 B [Great Office 1621 – Tulla barony].

321. For O'Molony bishops see notes 261 and 262 above.

322. This is probably Ballymullin recorded in Tulla parish in 1641 where a branch of the MacNamaras held lands. In 1659 it was recorded as 'Ballymoilen'. Séamus Pender (ed.), *A Census of Ireland circa 1659* (Dublin, 1939), p. 170. Simington, *Books of Survey and Distribution*, p. 24.

323. This denomination is difficult to identify. It could be a truncated form of Clonyfernane which was an obsolete denomination in Killinaboy parish. See Ó hÓgáin, *Conntae an Chláir*, pp. 117–18. Alternatively, it could be a misprint for the modern townland of Fortane in Tulla parish.

324. This surname is O'Griffey (*Ó Gríobhtha*), an important lineage in central Clare whose hereditary lands were at Ballygriffy in Dysert parish.

325. This is the same individual, Charles MacBrody, who married Onora Minogue, mentioned at notes 91 and 92 above. He was probably the Charles alias Callogh Mc Broodyn who, together with Flann Mc Broodyn and the MacCormochans, surrendered their leases to the Church land of Moynoe in 1617. See NLI, Ms 1777, p. 7.

326. This lineage of the Burkes erected Pallas Castle near Loughrea in the early sixteenth century.

327. This is the same individual mentioned at note 106 above, John MacBrody of Kilkee, in present day Ruan parish (formerly Dysert). In 1618 he was recorded as Shane McBrodin who occupied half of Kilkee with Conor McBrodin. He may also be the same John who witnessed a lease with Conor's father, Maoilín Óg Mac Bruaideadha, in 1598. See PHA, Ms 16 B.E. [Great Office 1618 – Inchiquin]; and Ainsworth, *Inchiquin Manuscripts*, p. 294.

328. James O'Nelan (Neylon) of Ballyneillan in Kilnamona is untraced. The annals record a Dr James Nelan (Ó Nialláin) dying at Ballyallia in Templemaley parish in 1599 where the family served as hereditary physicians and kept a house of hospitality. See *AFM*, vol. VI, p. 2141. On a genealogy of the Uí Nialláin see McInerney, *Clerical and Learned Lineages*, p. 172. Also see RIA Ms 24 p. 41.

329. Giolla Brighde is the same individual mentioned at note 100 above. Gilbertus or GiollaBrighde succeeded as *ollamh* in 1582 on the death of Maoilín Mac Bruaideadha. *AFM*, vol. V, p. 1791.

330. Killovyeragh (*Coill Ua bhFiachrach*) is situated in the north-west part of the barony of Kiltartan in County Galway and was sometimes known as O'Heyne's country. See John O'Donovan, *The Genealogies, Tribes, and Customs of Hy-Fiachrach, Commonly Called O'Dowda's Country* (Dublin, 1844), p. 4.

331. In 1627 'Daniel O'Shaghnessye' was high sheriff of County Galway. See Ainsworth, *Inchiquin Manuscripts*, p. 335.

332. Flann (Florence) Mac Bruaideadha, who kept a library at Moynoe.

333. He appears to be recorded at Killokennedy townland in Killokennedy parish in 1641 under the name Luke Broadie. In the same parish a number of Cusacks held lands. Simington, *Books of Survey and Distribution*, p. 64.

334. Lismullin is in the parish of Lismullin in County Meath. A branch of the Cusacks was settled there since medieval times.

335. Kilkee is in Ruan parish, but in the seventeenth century it was in Dysert parish.

336. This is likely Drummoyle which was recorded in Dysert parish in 1641. In 1618 'Dromile' was held by 'Mahowne mcMurrogh O Brien of Magowny'. Mahowne may have been 'Matthaeus O Brian', father of Finola. See PHA, Ms 16 B.E. [Great Office 1618 – Inchiquin].

337. The surname Sunigan is listed by Bruodinus as among the 'noble families' of Thomond. See Bruodinus, *Propugnaculum*, p. 971.

338. Philippe Alegambe (1592–1652) of Belgium was a celebrated Jesuit priest and bibliographer.

339. According to Bruodinus, Alegambe was wrong in saying the martyr John Matthews came from Cornwall, claiming instead that his real name was John MacMahon, the son of Conor MacMahon of Killadysert, a close relative of his own from County Clare. John MacMahon at the age of ten was sent to England and lived among the page boys at the earl of Arundal's house. Later he travelled to Rome where he studied for the priesthood and was admitted to the Society of Jesus. He subsequently returned to England and was hanged, drawn and quartered in 1594. (*Propugnaculum*, pp. 458–9). The house of the earl of Arundal belonged to Philip Howard, twentieth earl of Arundal, an ardent Catholic, who refused to renounce his religion and was imprisoned in the tower of London, where he remained until his death in 1595. He was made a saint of the Catholic Church in 1970. It is unlikely that Bruodinus' story has a historical basis. No John MacMahon or Matthews is recorded in the lists of English martyrs and neither is the

name mentioned by Alegambe in his principal work on Jesuit martyrs, *Heroes et victimae caritatis Societatis Jesu* (Rome, 1658). See Frost, *History of Clare*, p. 97.

340. Probably 'Connoghor Maglanchy' who held the tower house of 'Enenshy' in 1574. Enenshy could be Inch in Drumcliff where Boetius MacClancy held the lands there in 1641. See R.W. Twigge, 'Edward White's Description of Thomond in 1574', *NMAJ*, vol. 1, no. 2, 1910, pp. 75–85, at p. 84; Simington, *Books of Survey and Distribution*, p. 274.

341. According to an inquisition taken in 1611 concerning the lands of Termon Tulla, Sir Roland Delahoyde came to Thomond from Leinster and married a daughter of MacClancy of Inch, near Ennis. From this and the previous entry we know that Anna was the daughter of Conor (Conchobhar) MacClancy of Inch and Finola MacBrody, the sister of bardic poet Tadhg mac Dáire Mhic Bhruaideadha. Frost, *History of Clare*, pp. 286–8. Also see RIA Ms 24 D 10.

342. According to R.W. Twigge, Sir Rowland de la Hoyde of Fomerla, knight, married Una, daughter of Conor MacClancy of Inishy, County Clare, and had seven sons. Frost tells us that de la Hoyde was from Leinster and a favourite of the earl of Thomond, from whom he received various lands including the castle of Fomerla. When his son Oliver was brought before Barnabas, the fifth earl of Thomond, in 1642, charged with attacking Protestant settlers, the earl dismissed the charges and conferred upon him the authority to execute martial law. Twigge cites 'Funeral Entry IX, 275', Ulster's Office as his authority. See R.W. Twigge, *Pedigrees of the MacNamara Family* (1908; reprint Martin Breen, Ruan, 2006) p. 39. Also see Frost, *History of Clare*, pp. 287, 295, 341–2.

343. He appears as a witness to an inquisition of 1629 where his residence was recorded as Tyredagh in Tulla parish. See Ainsworth, *Inchiquin Manuscripts*, p. 337.

344. Bruodinus is in error here. In 1585 Honora, daughter of Teige McMurrough O'Brien of Smithstown, son of the first baron of Inchiquin, married Sir Richard Wingfield, not his son Sir Edward Wingfield, who died in 1638. See Edward Kimber, *The Peerage of Ireland: A genealogical and historical account of all the peers of that kingdom; their descents, collateral branches, births, marriages, and issue*, vol. 2 (London, 1768), p. 106. For a deed concerning the lands of Richard and Honora at Smithstown, County Clare and which was witnessed by 'B. McBrody', see Ainsworth, *Inchiquin Manuscripts*, pp. 317–18.

345. The O'Mearas (*Ó Meára*) were an important medical lineage of Toomevara (*Tuaim Uí Mheára*) in north Tipperary.

346. Likely to have been *Tadhg m Domhnaill riabaigh* (Tadhg son of Domhnaill riabaigh) of the important MacNamara Reagh lineage in east Clare and recorded in Cú Choigcríche Ó Cléirigh's *Genelach Meic Con Mara Riabaigh*, compiled in the 1630s. The annals record the death of his grandfather, Domhnaill Riabaich, in 1592. Tadhg was born in *c.* 1603 and made a ward of the earl of Thomond in 1609. He held lands in Tulla and Feakle parishes in 1641 and died in 1678. See Seamus Pender, 'O'Clery Book of Genealogies', *Analecta Hibernica*, vol. 18, Dublin, 1951, §2003. Also see *AFM*, vol. VI, pp. 1909–10; and British Library Add Ms 39270, 'Materials for a History of Clann-Cuilein (the eastern division of Co. Clare)', R.W. Twigge.

347. This is Tullira (*Tulach Aighre*, hill of the heir) in Ardrahan parish, County Galway.

348. Bunnahow (*Bun na hAbha*, river mouth) is in Inchicronan parish.

349. Caher is in Ogonnelloe parish but was recorded as 'Cahir Ballymulrona' in 1659. In 1618 the towerhouse was held by Donogh mcShane neginelagh (MacNamara) and the lands by Maccon McShane, John mcDonogh roe, & Teig mcDonogh roe. See PHA, Ms B. 16 B [Great Office 1621 – Tulla barony]; and Pender, *Census of Ireland, 1659*, p. 171.

350. He was clearly of the Tradraighe branch of the Meic Fhlannchadha. For their pedigree see McInerney, *Clerical and Learned Lineages*, p. 155. See also McInerney, 'The Síol Fhlannchadha', *Eolas*, vol. 9, 2016, pp. 19–54.

351. Ballynacloghy (*Baile na Cloiche*, homeplace of the stone house) now called Stonehall in Kilconry parish. Ballynacloghy towerhouse was held in 1574 by 'Tege Maglanchy'. See Twigge, 'Description of Thomond, 1574', *NMAJ*, vol. 1, no. 2, 1910, p. 79.

352. Abbot John Burke, Poulmore, parish of Doora, in his youth served in the Austrian army. Later he entered the Church and was appointed abbot of the Augustinian Abbey of Clare in Thomond. He acted as vicar-general of Killaloe, 1647–50, but was banished from Ireland by the Cromwellians in 1653. He exercised various clerical functions on the continent until 1671 when he returned to Ireland as vicar-general of Killala. Banished again three years later on a charge of 'bringing Protestants to the Catholic faith', Dr Burke died at Rome in 1683. Myles O'Reilly, *Lives of Irish Martyrs and Confessors* (New York, 1880), pp. 369–71.

353. Crusheen (*Croisín*, little cross) names a small village and townland on the Ennis–Galway road in the parish of Inchicronan.

354. *Bréan Tír* (foul land) is the generic name for lands in the northern and western parts of Ibrickan.

355. The well-known Clare surname Meic an Oirchinnigh (McInerheny). See Luke McInerney, 'Land and lineage: The McEnerhinys of Ballysallagh in the sixteenth century', *NMAJ*, vol. 49, 2009, pp. 7–32.

356. This is possibly Loughvella (*Loch Bhile*, lake of the tree) in Drumcliff parish. MacInerney landholding families are recorded in the adjoining parishes of Templemaley and Kilraghtis in the 1640s and 1650s. See Simington, *Books of Survey and Distribution*, p. 126, and Pender, *Census of* Ireland, 1659, p. 163.

357. Magowna (*Maigh Dhomhnaigh*, church plain) is in Dysert parish. In 1641 'Drummoyle' was recorded in Dysert. In 1618 Mahowne mcMurrogh O Brien held lands at 'Magowny' and 'Dromile', and Therlagh mcMurrough O Breen held lands at 'Magowny' and 'Caherflanchy' (Caherclanchy). Also, 'Donell mcDermot O Brien of Moghowney' was recorded holding land. See PHA, Ms 16 B.E. [Great Office 1618 – Inchiquin].

358. This may be Garraunnatooha (*Garrán na Tuaithe*, country grove) in Kilmacduane parish. Bruodinus recounts details of MacGorman's life where he states that 'Dionysius' was married to his sister Finola and that he was a captain of forces in Thomond but was killed in 1652. Bruodinus, *Propugnaculum*, pp. 712–13.

359. Drumellihy (*Droim Oilche*) is in Kilmacduane parish. It was an important seat of the Meic Gormáin lineage in the seventeenth century. See PHA, Ms 16 D.1. [Great Office 1618 – Clonderalaw & Moyarta baronies].

360. Perhaps Laghvally (*Leath bhaile*, half townland) in Kilmacrehy parish is intended where the Meic Cruitín chroniclers had their chief seat. On the Meic Cruitín see Luke McInerney, 'The Origins of Clann Chruitín: Chronicler-poets of the learned Gaelic tradition', *TOC*, vol. 38, 2014, pp. 19–30.

361. This is now O'Brienscastle in Inchicronan parish. Its former name was Ballaghnafeervarnan (*Bealach na Fir Bhearnán*, way of the men of Bearnan). In 1641 it was called Balnakerevarnagh and according to the 'castle builder's list' (RIA Ms 24 D 10, f. 71) the tower house there was erected by Bishop Toirdhealbhach Ó Briain (1483–1525). It is recorded as Bealnafirberna in Simington, *Books of Survey and Distribution*, pp. 106–7.

362. A Bernard McBrodin held part of Lettermoylan on Slievecallan in 1618. See PHA, Ms 16 B.E. [Great Office 1618 – Inchiquin].

363. Barnaboy (*An Bhearna Bhuí*, yellow gap) is in Ballynakill parish, County Galway.

364. Kinaleghin (*Cineál Fhéichín*, kindred of Féicín) was a former Franciscan friary in the village of Abbey on the Clare–Galway border, known in previous times as Kilnalahan, where many of the Burkes were buried.

365. This is Maoilín Mac Bruaideadha, *ollamh* to O'Brien, who died in 1582. *AFM*, vol. V, p. 1791.

366. Teige O'Higgin of Coolrecuill (*Cúil re Coil*), Kilmacteige parish, County Sligo, was appointed sheriff of Sligo in 1634. His lands at Coolrecuill could 'graze 80 cows and had eight days mowing'. W.G. Wood-Martin, *History of Sligo: County and town* (Dublin, 1889), vol. II, p. 164. Bruodinus makes reference to Teige O'Higgin and his wife Finola MacBrody in an earlier work of his, see Bruodinus, *Corolla Oecodomiae* (Prague, 1664), p. 76. Like Clan Bhruaideadha,

the Uí Uigín was a distinguished Bardic family who produced a remarkable number of poets from Tadhg Mór Ó hUigín (d. 1315) to Tadhg Dall Ó hUigín (d. 1617).

367. The O'Hara (*Ó hEadhra*) and MacDonough (*Mac Donnchadha*) families were extensive landowners in County Sligo. The Jordan (*Mac Siúrtáin*) family was associated more with east Mayo.

368. This is Ballynamona (*Baile na Móna*, townland of the turf) in Finnoe parish, barony of Ormond, in north Tipperary, where the O'Hogan population was concentrated.

369. Barry is a surname of Anglo-Norman origin. Baltynaknock is probably Ballyknock (*Baile an Chamhaicigh*) in the parish Ballynoe, south-east Cork, which once formed part of the de Barry lordship of Olethan. Paul MacCotter, *Medieval Ireland* (Dublin, 2008), p. 161.

370. Fearghal Óg Mac an Bháird (*c.* 1550- *c.* 1620) a celebrated bardic poet and ollamh to Aodh Ruadh Ó Domhnaill of Tyrconnell. Some fifty-nine poems are attributed to him; among them is the poem *Trí Coróna i gCairt Shéamais*, on James VI's ascension to the English throne in 1603. Fearghal's brother, Eoghan Ruadh, trained as a bardic poet in Thomond but was put to death in 1572 by Conchobhar Ó Briain, third earl of Thomond. In later life Fearghal Óg left for the continent and is recorded at the Irish College of Louvain in 1618. Pádraig Ó Macháin, 'Poems by Feargal Óg Mac An Bháird', *Celtica*, vol. 24, 2003, pp. 252–63.

371. The Uí Chléirigh of Donegal and Clann Bhruaideadha were closely connected. For instance Cosnamhach Ó Cléirigh of Tyrconnell kept a house of hospitality in Thomond, 1584 and Macon Ó Cléirigh, '*ollamh* to O'Donnell', died in MacBrody's house at Lettermoylan in 1595. Donough / Donnchadh was a name in use among the Uí Chléirigh: Donnchadh Ó Cléirigh, who married Onóra Ultach, was father of Mícheál Ó Cléirigh, compiler of *AFM*. A Donnchadh Ó Cléirigh authored a poem to Mac Suibhne Fanad (d. 1619), but whether he was married to 'Margaret' sister of Tadhg mac Dáire Mhic Bhruaideadha is unknown. Damian McManus (ed.), *A Bardic Miscellany* (Dublin, 2010), p. 339. On the Uí Chléirigh see Paul Walsh, *The O Cléirigh Family of Tír Conaill, with the O Cléirigh Genealogies* (Dublin, 1938).

372. MacDonleavy (*Mac Duinnshléibhe*) was the name of a professional medical kindred of Ulster. Owen Ultach MacDunleavy, physician to O'Donnell, excelled among the doctors of Ireland. See *AFM*, vol. V, p. 1857. Gabriel Dunleavy is untraced.

373. This is the Irish Franciscan scholar known alternatively as Francis O'Molloy or Froinsias Ó Maolmhuaidh (*c.* 1606–77) whose book *Grammatica Latino-Hibernica nunc compendiata*, printed in Rome in 1677, was the first printed grammar of the Irish language in Latin.

374. It was in the reign of Fionnachta that snow fell on Ireland with the taste of wine (*AFM*, vol. I, p. 55). Red or watermelon snow contains *Chlamydomonas nivalis*, a species of algae with red pigment that thrives in freezing water. The phenomenon was reported from the Scottish Highlands in the nineteenth century and subsequently recorded scientifically from a snow patch in the Cairngorm Mountains in the 1960s.

375. The Latin of this quotation is wrong (in particular, the perfect *resolutae sunt* should be in the subjunctive, *resolutae sint*). The mistakes are tacitly and tendentiously attributed to Carve by Bruodinus, who is in fact deliberately adding them while misquoting from the original text as usual.

376. He is known in Irish as Seathrún Céitinn (*c.* 1569–*c.* 1644), a historian and a priest from County Tipperary, who wrote a number of notable works, including *Foras Feasa ar Éirinn* (Foundation of Knowledge on Ireland).

377. *Foras Feasa ar Éirinn* is often quoted in English as the 'History of Ireland'. The work in translation was published by Dermod O'Connor, *The General History of Ireland* (London, 1726), but the Irish-language text circulated in manuscript form only.

378. Fionnachta son of Ollamh Fodhla held the sovereignty of Ireland twenty years; he was called Fionnachta that is Finshneachta, because it rained showers of wine-snow in his reign. Geoffrey Keating, *Foras Feasa ar Éirinn: The history of Ireland*, D. Comyn and P.S. Dinneen (eds), 4 vols (London, 1902–14), vol. I, p. 135.

379. Dermot MacMurrrough, king of Leinster (d. 1171), see note 231 above. No son of his called Art is recorded although the name was common among the MacMurrough kindred. Dermot's daughter Aoife by his wife Mór Ní Thuathail married the Norman Richard de Clare (Strongbow) shortly after the fall of Waterford in August 1170 in an effort to legitimised Strongbow's succession to the kingship of Leinster.

380. Głogów is a town of 70,000 people now in south-western Poland.

381. Toruń is a city on the river Vistula in northern Poland.

382. This is modern Jičín, a small town 85 kilometres north-east of Prague in the Czech Republic.

383. Blood rain has been recorded in modern times. Scientific examination in the nineteenth century showed that the rain was caused by red dust suspended in the water.

384. The Butlers of Cahir, County Tipperary held the title of baron not of viscount. See note 238 above.

385. This seems to be a reference to biblical stories about idolatry (see *Exodus* 32:1–4; *1 Kings* 12:26–30). In Latin, there is a pun based on the words for 'calves' and 'titles', respectively *vituli* and *tituli*.

386. *Job* 2:9. There are two versions of the same sentence: 'curse the Lord, and die', and 'bless the Lord, and die'. Interestingly, the former appears in the main body of the text, though it is then changed into the latter in the critical apparatus at the end of *Anatomicum*.

387. This statement appears to be completely made up by Bruodinus.

388. Aonghus was the reputed ancestor of the Clann Deaghaidh, rulers of the ancient territory of Cinéal Fhearmhaic in central Clare. Bruodinus believed that his kin group, Clann Bhruaideadha, was descended from the Uí Dheaghaidh (*anglicé* O'Dea), who were of the Dál Cais, the same population group as the O'Briens, the ruling lineage of Thomond. In this he appears mistaken, the Clann Bhruaideadha were descendants of the Corcu Moruadh, a pre Dál Cais population group, largely confined to the Burren and Corcomroe district of north Clare. See Diarmuid Ó Murchadha, 'The Origins of Clann Bhruaideadha', *Éigse*, vol. 31, 1999, pp. 121–30.

389. Cragbrien is in the parish of Clondagad, 14 kilometres south-west of Ennis, County Clare.

390. See p. 185.

391. In this section of *Anatomicum*, the reference to the muses (Greek goddesses of the arts) points at literary authors and men of letters.

392. Within each classroom (in this case, within the classroom of the *grammatistae*: see note 57 above), the best students would sit on the front benches, whereas the worst students would be placed to the back. See p. 101.

393. *Pro Archia poeta* is a famous speech delivered by the Roman orator and politician Marcus Tullius Cicero (106–43 BC), probably in 62 BC in defence of Aulus Licinius Archias, a poet accused of false claims about being a Roman citizen. The opening section of the speech remarks on the important role played by poets in the creation and evolution of Roman culture.

394. Quintus Ennius (239–169 BC), one of the fathers of Roman literature, was author of the famous epic poem *Annales*, the 'national' epic poem at least until the time of Virgil's *Aeneid*. He also wrote works in other genres, such as satires and plays, which are now mostly or completely lost.

395. The first part of this quotation is sound, as it comes from paragraph 18 of Cicero's speech. The second part, however, does not feature anywhere in the *Pro Archia*, but it is attested in some later scholarly works as a remark about Cicero's words concerning Ennius' definition of poets. Thus, it appears that Bruodinus is not quoting directly from Cicero's speech, but from a much later source; and he is mistakenly attributing to Cicero the words which later scholars had written about the passage from the *Pro Archia*. The comment features in a variety of works of different kinds, for example on page 165 of the *Lectiones Antiquae* by the humanist Ludovico Ricchieri (Caelius Rhodiginus), a work of erudition, which included short comments to passages drawn from classical authors (Venice, 1516); on page 663 of *Polyanthea* (Lyon, 1600),

an anthology of memorable quotations from Greek and Roman authors accompanied by short comments by the scholars Domenico Nani Mirabelli, Bartholomeus Amantius and Franciscus Tortius; on page 463 of volume 6 of *Magnum Theatrum Vitae Humanae*, an encyclopaedia by the theologian Lawrence Beyerlink, which was published posthumously (Cologne, Lyon and Venice, 1631–1707). In many of these works, as well as in later ones where the comment on Cicero's *Pro Archia* occurs again, the writers mention the same classical authors as Bruodinus does in this passage of *Anatomicum* (Cicero, Plato, Ovid). This confirms the hypothesis that Bruodinus is relying on one of such sources. It is difficult to establish the 'archetype' for Bruodinus' mistake (Ricchieri is a possible candidate for obvious chronological reasons, though he could be quoting from an earlier scholar in turn).

396. The famous Greek philosopher Plato (*c.* 427–*c.* 347 BC) wrote a number of Socratic dialogues, amongst which the *Republic*, about justice and the features of the ideal city and citizens. The case made in the previous note makes it unlikely that Bruodinus read the original Greek text of Plato's work and translated or paraphrased in Latin a specific passage of it, which is also suggested by the vagueness of the quotation.

397. Publius Ovidius Naso (43 BC–*c.* AD 17), known as Ovid, was a Roman poet whose *Fasti*, an incomplete poem published in AD 8, provided explanations for the origins of the Roman festivals and holidays throughout the year. For the quotation, see 6.5–6.

398. Moses is reputed to have composed the 'Song of the Sea' after the Israelites, fleeing from Phaoraoh's army, crossed the Red Sea to safety. The song in archaic Hebrew is thought to have been written between the twelfth and tenth centuries BC and is much older than the rest of the Exodus text. According to the Jewish writer Flavius Josephus (AD 37–c. 100), Moses penned the song in the metre of the hexameter. It is likely that Bruodinus was familiar with the translation of Josephus by Thomas Lodge (an author he refers to above; see note 176). Lodge's translation, first published in 1602, was reprinted eight times before 1693. Lodge writes, 'Moses likewise composed an Ode in Hexameter verse containing the prayses of God'. *The Famous and Memorable Works of Josephus …*, translated by Tho. Lodge, Doctor of Physicke (London, 1609), p. 52.

399. That is, a variety of metres. It was customary in ancient time to classify poetic genres on the basis of their metre.

400. Jeremiah is one of the major prophets of the Hebrew Bible. According to tradition he authored the *Book of Lamentations*, a collection of five poems mourning the destruction of Jerusalem in 586 BC.

401. The metre is named after Sappho (*c.* 630–*c.* 570 BC), a female poet from the Greek island of Lesbos, known for her lyric poetry.

402. Jews used a great variety of metres when writing poetry, including the trimeter and Sapphic metres but also tetrameters, pentameters, Alcaics, Pindarics and hexameters. It was said 'such was the variety of measures among the Hebrews that it hath beene a great cause why the scansion of their verse is harde to bee found out'. Israel Baroway, 'The Hebrew Hexameter: A study in Renaissance sources and interpretation', ELH (English Literary History), vol. 2, no. 1, April 1935, pp. 70–3.

403. Namely, it was in the form of a dialogue. The Canticle of Canticles or the Song of Songs is a series of love poems attributed to King Solomon. Biblically the composition is unique in its celebration of sexual love. Ein Gedi, a large oasis on the western shore of the Dead Sea, features in Chapter 1, verse 14: 'My lover is like the wild flowers that bloom in the vineyards of Ein Gedi'.

404. Coelius Sedulius was a fifth-century Christian poet of the early Church. Little of his life is known. His fame rests on his *Carmen Paschale*, a long poem based on the four Gospels. He resided in Italy and was almost certainly not Irish: C.P.E. Springer, *Sedulius, the Paschal Song and Hymns* (Atlanta, 2013), p. xvi. Bruodinus, as many other authors did before and after him, may have confused him with Sedulius Scotus, a more famous ninth-century Irish teacher, commentator of the Scriptures and Latin grammarian.

405. The order is respected in the first letter of each stanza.

406. Theodosius II (AD 401–50) ruled as sole eastern Roman emperor from the age of seven in AD 408. He is mostly known for codifying the late Roman law and consolidating Christianity as the official religion of the empire.

407. For this reference to the muses see note 391 above.

408. The Latin words *in tuo sensu* refer both to Carve's alleged opinion on the poets and on the meaning he associates with the Latin noun *bardus*, on which Bruodinus remarks elsewhere (see p. 185).

409. Diodorus of Sicily was a Greek historian of the first century BC who wrote a monumental history of forty books called *Bibliotheca Historica*. The passage to which Bruodinus is referring (directly or indirectly) appears in Book V, Chapter 31.5 in the modern editions of the work.

410. Lese-majesty, 'injured majesty', was the crime of violating the dignity of a reigning monarch, sovereign or state. The concept originated in imperial Rome.

411. The reference may be to trials or other matters of disagreement, for example about religious doctrines or interpretation of the laws.

412. Richard O'Farrell of Longford was a veteran of the Spanish military service in the Low Countries. He returned to Ireland after Owen Roe O'Neill in 1643 and commanded a regiment of foot at the battle of Benburb. Dispatched south, he repulsed Cromwell at the first siege of Waterford in 1649. O'Farrell survived the disaster at Scariffhollis and was in charge of the army of Connacht at the fall of Galway in 1652. He was among the last Irish commanders to surrender and was allowed go to Spain with the remnants of the Ulster army in 1653. His final years were spent in Vienna, so he may have been personally known to Carve and Bruodinus. Stephen Collins, 'Longford Musketeers', *History Ireland*, vol. XI, summer 2003.

413. Jerome Sankey of Shropshire, soldier and politician, graduated from Cambridge in 1644. He followed Cromwell to Ireland where he commanded a regiment of horse. At Waterford, December 1649, Sankey prevented O'Farrell from joining up with the forces of Col. Edward Wogan as they attempted to re-capture the fort of Passage. Inflicting major casualties, Sankey forced O'Farrell back inside the walls of the city. The reverse at Passage discredited O'Farrell and the Ulster army. After the war Sankey was granted confiscated lands in Munster and represented Waterford and Tipperary as MP in the protectorate parliament of 1654. *DIB*, vol. VIII, pp. 771–3.

414. This is the shortened title used in *Anatomicum* as well as by Carve to refer to Bruodinus' first publication, a two-volume work printed in Prague in 1663–4 for the benefit of his students, entitled *Oecodomia minoriticae scholae Salomonis doctoris subtilis ... Hoc est: Vniversae theologiae Scholasticae manualis summa* (The Building of the Minorites' School of Solomon of the Subtle Doctor ... Namely: a summa, to be used as a handbook of the whole scholastic theology). It was among the first published handbooks of Scotist theology to appear in Bohemia. 'Subtle Doctor' was the common epithet of Duns Scotus, Scottish philosopher and theologian of the thirteenth century.

415. The metaphor is based on the meaning of the Latin word *propugnaculum*, that is, a 'bulwark'.

416. *Columna* and *assertio* are technical words to indicate chapters and sections in a work of theology.

417. There are several minor differences between this quotation and the original passage; in particular, Carve refers more than once to the fact that Bruodinus' work is about scholastic theology.

418. Another shortened title for Bruodinus' theological work: see note 414 above.

419. The Latin proverb, which has been translated with its English equivalent, literally reads, 'he is not speaking in favour of his own house'.

420. Literally: 'Shoemaker, not beyond the shoe!' For the history and meaning of the Latin expression, see Pliny, *Naturalis Historia*, 35.85.

421. A semi-quotation from the Gospels: see *Luke* 9:58 and *Matthew* 8:20.

422. Though these quotations are not faithful to the original text, the mistake in misnaming Thomond is indeed Carve's (but see note 83 above, for the triviality of Bruodinus' point about Carve's Latinisation of the toponym).

423. A fine clay suitable for making pottery.

424. Evidently Bruodinus was familiar with the metaphor of the dung beetle, notably used by Seathrún Céitinn in the introduction to his seminal work *Foras Feasa ar Éirinn* (*c.* 1634). Céitinn compares the writers of Elizabethan England, who write insultingly of Ireland, to the dung beetle (*an priompallán*), an insect that passes by the roses, lillies and flowers of the field to roll about in the dung of the horse or cow. Geoffrey Keating, *Foras Feasa ar Éirinn; The history of Ireland*, vol. I, p. 5.

425. Bruodinus includes Carve in a list of 'corrupt' historians who wrote falsely of Ireland (namely Polydore Vergil, George Buchanan and Thomas Dempster) because they knew that the powerful would support them and the gullible believe them. *Propugnaculum*, pp. 763–4.

426. The Gall Burkes of Gaulstown, County Kilkenny were not of Munster but of Connacht origin. A senior line of the Anglo-Norman de Burgos, they were descended from Richard, second earl of Ulster (d. 1326). They appear to have settled in south Kilkenny in the early fifteenth century. The Irish *gall* signifies foreign. Walter Gall Burke was MP for County Kilkenny in 1559. William Carrigan, *History and Antiquities of the Diocese of Ossory* (Dublin, 1905), vol. IV, pp. 141–2.

427. In this passage (which Bruodinus has slightly modified when quoting it) Carve probably refers to what Bruodinus wrote on page 957 of *Propugnaculum*.

428. William Gall Burke of Gaulstown, enlisted in the service of Ferdinand II, emperor of Austria and had a distinguished military career. In reward for his services he was created count of the Holy Roman Empire by Ferdinand III in 1637. He was appointed agent to the emperor by the Confederation of Kilkenny in 1642 but played no part in the wars in Ireland. Count Gall von Bourck died at his castle in Holstein, Jauer, Silesia in 1655. John O'Donovan, 'The Family of Gall Burke of Gallstown, County Kilkenny', *Journal of the Kilkenny and South-East of Ireland Archaeological Society*, vol. 3, 1860, pp. 97–120.

429. Leath Mogha (Mogh's half) refers to a legendary ancient division of the southern half of Ireland.

430. The Bagnall family was founded by Nicholas Bagenal of Staffordshire, who fled to Ireland in 1538 to escape prosecution for a murder. He was eventually appointed marshal of the army in Ireland by Edward VI. His son Dudley Bagenal established himself as a major landowner in Carlow during the 1580s.

431. The Latin words *non bona* ironically allude, and overturn, the common expression *bona senectus* (good old age).

432. MacVeigh (*Mac an Bheatha*), medical kindred predominantly of Ulster, but also found in Connacht, the name takes the form Beaton in Scotland. A Mayo MacVeigh, Hugh, son of James, chirurgeon, received a pardon from the English authorities in 1593, while another of the name, Iolann Mac Beatha, was present at the writing of *Lilium Medicinae* at the medical school of Aghmacart in 1596. John Bannerman, *The Beatons* (Edinbugh, 1998), pp. 53–4, 104.

433. *Protomedici* is a technical term (literally, 'first physicians'). In Roman times they were in charge of the hygiene of a city or region, and of the regulation of medical practices.

434. The Latin syntax adopted by Carve in this passage is wrong, as Bruodinus himself remarks immediately after this semi-quotation; accordingly, our English translation tries to render Carve's misuse of Latin. It must be observed, however, that Bruodinus, when reporting this passage, has added further mistakes originally not present in Carve's text, namely the double negation *non vereatur … minime* ('not afraid … not at all').

435. The metaphor of the skull, which recurs throughout this chapter and fits the anatomical imagery of Bruodinus' work, picks up on the double meaning of the Latin word *caput* ('head' or 'chapter'), for which see note 187 above. Since Carve's *caput* is without a brain (that is, without sense), it is simply a skull (*cranium*). See p. 161.

436. There is a deliberate ambiguity here: *defectus* means 'physical defect, handicap' or 'argumentative defect, nonsense'; similarly, *infirmitas* means 'weakness of the body, illness' or 'weakness of an argument'. The ambiguity fits the metaphor of Carve's work as a body to be dissected.

437. *De gustibus non est disputandum* is an ancient Latin proverb, meaning 'there should be no dispute about taste(s)', namely everyone has their own taste. Bruodinus modifies the motto in a twofold way: he adds the reference to the titles (namely: everyone is free to give their work the title they want), and he builds on the word 'taste' by mentioning wine (the association of Carve with wine is common throughout *Anatomicum*: in this case, he is portrayed not only as a drunkard, but as a drunkard who drinks terrible wine).

438. In Latin, the hendyadis *modice et medice* (literally: 'with the proper measure and in the manner of a surgeon') is reinforced by a word play.

439. The precise reason why Carve left Ireland has never been established.

440. The way in which these words are given in the editions consulted suggests that this may be a quotation or paraphrase, perhaps from a dictionary or the like. César de Rochefort, in his *Dictionaire Général et Curieux* (Lyon, 1685), defines *vanterie* (Engl. 'boasting', Lat. *jactantia*) by using similar Latin words (see p. 76: *inanis et stulta praedicatio*) and mentions the Latin author Varro (1st cent. BC) as a source, but the quotation cannot be traced in Varro. It is quite possible that Bruodinus and Rochefort are relying on an early-modern source, and that Rochefort's attribution of the definition to Varro stems from a process similar to the one described in note 395 above.

441. A poem retracting a statement made in a previous poem.

442. Matthew Roche, educated at the University of Douai, taught school at New Ross, Wexford. He was a brother of John, bishop of Ferns and was appointed vicar apostolic of Leighlin in 1622. Roche had an ingrained hatred of religious orders. He assaulted the abbot of Holy Cross with a wooden bat and instructed his congregations not to receive the sacraments from Cistercian priests. Clashing repeatedly with the Franciscan archbishop of Dublin, his scandalous behaviour gave great offence. Arrested and tried at Waterford, he was executed by the civil power in 1644. Áine Hensey, 'Study of Clergy in the South Eastern Dioceses 1550–1650', unpublished PhD thesis, National University of Ireland, Maynooth, 2012, pp. 263–4.

443. This is now the diocese of Kildare and Leighlin, which is situated within the province of Leinster.

444. A letter of discharge, or dimissorial letter, was given by a bishop or a competent religious superior to certify that a subordinate had the qualifications necessary under canon law for ordination to the priesthood by another bishop.

445. This is a well-attested Latin proverb. Minerva was the goddess of wisdom.

446. Conald O'Carran, schoolmaster of Mobarnan, County Tipperary, was a nephew of Thomas Carve. Carve claimed his nephew could compose in Irish, Latin and English. Conald, however, was not allowed to teach with the Franciscans but under the patronage of the duke of Ormond, he was permitted to open a school where he taught the humanities to Catholic boys, who would otherwise frequent Protestant schools. Thomas Wall, 'Bards and Bruodins', in *Father Luke Wadding: Commemorative volume*, ed. Franciscan Fathers (Dublin, 1957), pp. 456–8.

447. A pun is probably intended: *Lyra – de-Lyrium – delirium*.

448. This paraphrase or false quotation summarises some of Carve's statements at pp. 111–12 of *Enchiridion*.

449. Carve mentions the year 1644, and Bruodinus corrects the mistake in parenthesis (644), although his formulation in doing so is quite ambiguous if translated literally: '… in the year (you have 644 in your *olla podrida*).'

450. There are no contemporary entries in any of the extant annals to indicate that Ireland fell into a state of barbarousness and ignorance in 644.

451. The work referred to here is the *Historia ecclesiastica gentis Anglorum* (Ecclesiastical History of the English People), written by the Venerable Bede in the early eighth century AD, and covering the history of England from the time of Caesar's invasion of the island 55 BC to AD 731. *ODNB*, vol. IV, pp. 758–60.

452. Despite a number of attempts, there were no universities established in Ireland until the setting up of Trinity College Dublin in 1592. In 644 a school could not be described as a university, rather it might have the characteristics of a *scriptorium* overseen by a scribe or monk, the existance of which are well attested in the Irish annals.

453. Vikings, referred to as *geinte* (heathens) in the annals, first appear off the coast of Ireland in 795, when the island of Rechru (Rathlin) was pillaged. In 921 the Viking Ragnall was described as *ri Finnghall is Dubhghall* ('king of the fair-haired and dark-haired foreigners'). It is not until year 987 that the term *Danaraibh* (Danes) first appears in the Irish annals (*Annals of Ulster, sub anno* 987).

454. An *argumentum ad hominem* (argument against the man) is a form of fallacious reasoning, consisting of attacking the person who has put forward a certain argument, instead of the argument itself.

455. This is a quotation from the Latin poet Horace (*Ars Poetica*, line 5).

456. Swedish intervention in Bohemia began in 1630 when the Swedish king, Gustavus Adophus, entered the Thirty Years War in support of the Protestant cause. Marching through Pomerania and Silesia, now in modern Poland, he entered the Czech province of Moravia, before moving onto Saxony, where he defeated the army of the Catholic League at Breitenfeld in 1631. It was the first major Protestant victory. The Swedish army stayed in the field until 1648 when the peace of Westphalia brought the war to a close.

457. The text *quantumvis ama sis et tenebrio* ('although you are a water-bucket and a trickster'), which is printed in the editions of *Anatomicum* consulted, makes little sense. We have therefore emended it, assuming that Bruodinus is here mentioning the name *Amasis*. If so, the reference is probably to the Egyptian Pharaoh Ahmose II (sixth century BC), whose family is mentioned in the Old Testament (*Jeremiah* 44:30). Portraits of this figure can be found in some ancient historiographical works, especially by Herodotus and Diodorus Siculus. Diodorus' description is particularly unfavourable, and refers to Amasis' harshness and unfairness while ruling over the Egyptians (1.60). Given that Bruodinus' parallel between Carve and Amasis aims at criticising the former, it is quite likely that he is referring to Diodorus' description. Diodorus also features as a source for *Anatomicum* elsewhere, see p. 221.

458. The reference in *Enchiridion* is to Speeder's Geography of Ireland (*Geographia Hiberniae*), so the person intended is almost certainly the cartographer John Speed, whose *Theatre of the Empire of Great Britain* (London, 1611) contained several Irish maps.

459. A very old proverb associated with a Greek fable by Aesop (sixth century BC), commonly entitled 'The young man and the swallow'. See B.E. Perry, *Aesopia* (Urbana, IL, 1952), no. 169. The proverb was first recorded in the English form 'It is not one swalowe that bryngeth in somer' by Richard Taverner, London, 1539, in his translation of a collection of proverbs and adages gathered by Erasmus of Rotterdam. Taverner explains the proverb as follows: 'It is not one good qualitie that maketh a man good'.

460. The Fitzgeralds and the Fitzstephens were among the first group of Anglo-Normans to land at Wexford from Wales in the summer of 1169. Robert Fitzstephen was prominent in the early stages of the conquest but died without male offspring *c.* 1185. The Fitzgeralds on the other hand multiplied and carved out large swaths of territory for themselves in Leinster and Munster that would eventually become the earldoms of Kildare and Desmond. *New History of Ireland* (1987), vol. II, pp. 66–85.

461. Pope Adrian IV died in 1159, ten years before the Anglo-Norman invasion.

462. The Latin text has been emended by assuming the misprinting of the word *haut* (*aut* in the original text), a correction which is necessary to restore the relative chronology of the events

mentioned by Bruodinus. As these events are important and well-documented ones, it is hard to believe that Bruodinus' mistake is genuinely his own.

463. Derbfhorgaill (*c.* 1108–93) was the wife of Tigernán Ua Ruairc, king of Breifne. Abducted by Diarmait Mac Murchada in 1152, she was returned to her husband the following year. But great enmity persisted between the two and in 1166 Ua Ruairc drove Mac Murchada out of Ireland. He went to France to seek the assistance of Henry II, thus precipitating the Anglo-Norman invasion of Ireland. *New History of Ireland* (1985), vol. II, pp. 49–50.

464. The kingdom of Bréifne was located north of the Irish midlands; it corresponded roughly with the modern counties of Leitrim and Cavan. The O'Rourkes were the ruling family of West Bréifne (Leitrim) and the O'Reillys the ruling family of East Bréifne (Cavan).

465. Current scholarly opinion is that the papal letter *Laudabiliter* is not a forgery: 'its wording diction and style show it to be a product of the papal chancery of the pontificate of Adrian IV'. Donnchadh Ó Corráin, *The Irish Church, its Reform and the English Invasion* (Dublin, 2017), p. 99.

466. In the usual fashion, this is most likely a paraphrase by Bruodinus, rather than an actual quotation from one of the historians he mentions (despite the way in which the words are introduced in the editions consulted).

467. The editions consulted give this as paragraph 5, but the previous paragraph is also numbered 5. This section, therefore, is either part of the same paragraph, or part of paragraph 6, whose beginnings are marked out further down in the text.

468. The anecdote is reported by various biographers of St Augustine, including Possidius (fourth to fifth century AD), as well as in the biography to be found in the so-called 'Golden Legend' (a collection of hagiographies composed by Jacobus de Voragine in the thirteenth century). In turn, the lines allegedly composed by St Augustine echo and expand on a passage from the Latin poet Horace (*Satires*, 1.4.81).

469. Literally, 'take a bit through the nose'. The expression *accipere parum per nasum* is untraced, but the translation hypothesises that its meaning is connected to the fact that anger was often believed to reside in the nose.

470. Augustine's motto, just quoted by Bruodinus, used to circulate in two forms in late antiquity. In one of them, the Latin text read *hanc mensam vetitam*; in another, *hanc mensam indignam* (this dining table is unworthy [of a disparager]). Bruodinus reports the former, but his reference to the 'worthiness' of Augustine's table seems to point to this latter version of the motto, too.

471. The quotation is from the so-called *Disticha Catonis* (I 30), a collection of proverbs assembled in the third or fourth century AD. This specific proverb, however, was often quoted in later works, on one of which Bruodinus is most likely relying as a source.

472. The grammar and syntax of Carve's words in this quotation are confused and incorrect, insomuch that the meaning of the entire sentence appears unclear. Bruodinus remarks on this both while quoting from Carve's work and, more extensively, in the next paragraph. The translation tries to render the mistakes. The quotation itself is not identical to the original (as usual), though all mistakes are indeed Carve's.

473. The title, invented by Carve, translates as 'The Counties of Ireland'. This is a reference to Book V, the last section of Bruodinus' *Propugnaculum*. Book V treats extensively with the provinces and counties of Ireland. It consists of twenty-four chapters, three appendices and runs to 340 pages.

474. That is, he has gathered various elements from my historiographical work, without a precise order. The Latin word *spicilegium* (literally, a gleaning of ears of wheat) is here used metaphorically.

475. Bruodinus is here playing with the similarity of the Latin words *exarare* ('to write') and *errare* ('to be wrong').

476. Taken from Thomas Aquinas, *Tertiae Partis Summae Theologiae*, Quaest. 132. Art. 4.2. Many textbooks and *compendia* of moral theology repeat this definition. It is likely that Bruodinus memorised the definition from a secondary source, as was the practice in seminaries.

477. The word comes from Thrason, the personification of the spirit of boldness as well as insolence and arrogance in Greek culture. In Roman literature, the playwright Terence (second century BC) famously gave the name Thrason to the character of a braggart warrior in his comedy *Eunuchus*.

478. Edmund Spenser (1552–99), references to Ireland are found in many of his works but principally in *A view of the Present State of Ireland* (written by 1596). *DIB*, vol. VIII, pp. 1092–5.

479. Meredith Hanmer (1543–1604), a Welsh clergyman, came to Ireland in 1591. His book *Chronicle of* Ireland was published by Sir James Ware in 1633. *DIB*, vol. IV, pp. 437–8.

480. William Camden (1551–1623), English antiquarian and historian, is best known as the author of *Britannia*, an in-depth topographical account of the islands of Ireland and Britain. First published in 1587, it went through many editions. Raymond Gillespie et al. (eds), *The Irish Book in English 1550–1800* (Oxford, 2006), pp. 252, 271 n.

481. Fynes Moryson (1566–1630) was secretary to Lord Mountjoy, lord deputy of Ireland and commander of the army. Moryson's *Itinerary* published in 1617 describes his experiences in Ulster during the Nine Years War. *DIB*, vol. VI, pp. 712–14.

482. Sir John Davies, English lawyer and politician, came to Ireland in 1603 and rose to the rank of attorney-general. In 1612 he published the *Discoverie of the True Causes why Ireland was never entirely subdued*, predicting that an Ulster plantation of British and Irish would allow people to grow together as one nation. *DIB*, vol. III, pp. 70–4.

483. Edmund Campion (1540–81), Jesuit and historian, was born in London. His *Two Bokes of the Histories of Ireland* (Dublin, 1633) were written while he was in hiding in Dublin. He was executed at Tyburn, 1581. *DIB*, vol. II, pp. 3024–5.

484. John Barclay (1582–1621), Scottish novelist and Latin poet, his most famous work is the political novel *Argenis* (Paris, 1621). Barclay produced no book on Ireland although the country is mentioned occasionally in his writings. *ODNB*, vol. III, pp. 768–9.

485. No contemporary writer of this name has been traced.

486. William Lindanus (1525–88), Dutch theologian and Catholic bishop, wrote numerous works, among them *De optimo scripturas interpretandi genere* (Cologne, 1558), where he attacked the integrity of the Hebrew Bible as a way of undermining Protestantism. *Catholic Encyclopedia*, vol. IX, pp. 267–8.

487. Laurentius Surius (1523–78), a German Carthusian monk and hagiographer, criticised Sleidanus in his *Commentarius brevis rerum in orbe gestarum* (Cologne, 1566), a short commentary of world events 1500–64. Surius is best known for his *De probatis sanctorum historiis* (Cologne 1570–5), a six-volume collection of saints' lives. *Catholic Encyclopedia*, vol. XIV, pp. 343–4.

488. Johannes Sleidanus (1506–56), born in Luxembourg, became the historian of the reformation. His great work *Commentariorum de statu religionis et reipublicae, Carolo V. Caesare, libri XXVI*, completed in 1555, attracted the opprobrium of many Catholic writers. Donald R. Kelley, 'Johann Sleidan and the Origins of History as a Profession', *The Journal of Modern History*, vol. 52, 1980, pp. 573–98.

489. This paragraph expands on Carve's use of the metaphor of the *spicilegium*, for which see note 474 above.

490. *Tribulus terrestris* is a Mediterranean plant of the caltrop family, which grows in dry climates. Classed as a noxious weed, the fruit bears two or three sharp spikes, thus the name caltrop. It is more commonly known as goat's-head or puncture-vine.

491. This sentence echoes and expands on the famous pun *Beati Hispani, quibus vivere est bibere* ('Lucky the Spaniards, for whom living is drinking'), sometimes wrongly attributed to Julius Caesar. The pun relies on the linguistic phenomenon of the betacismus, which is typical of some populations in Spain, for which *v* is pronounced *b*, and therefore the Latin verb *vivere* (to live) is pronounced in the same way as *bibere* (to drink). In Bruodinus' line, there may be a further word play embedded in the infinitive *esse*, meaning 'to be', 'to exist' (as in the translation given), but also 'to eat'.

492. The office is more commonly termed 'minister provincial' in English.

493. Johannes à Molino, a Spanish Franciscan, was confessor to Margaret Theresa, daughter of the king of Spain. He accompanied the Spanish infanta to Vienna on the occasion of her marriage to Leopold I in 1666. Appointed the minister provincial for the Franciscan province of Upper Germany, he signed the approval for the publication of Bruodin's book *Propugnaculum* in 1668.

494. The Low Countries and Germany were divided into three Franciscan provinces: Cologne, Saxony and Strasburg also known as the province of Upper Germany.

495. Margaret Theresa of Spain (1651–73) was, by marriage, Holy Roman empress. She married Emperor Leopold I in 1666. Several portraits of her as a young child by Velázquez survive.

496. Here and below in the same paragraph, the original text uses the plural to refer to Spain as an empire consisting of different kingdoms.

497. Philip IV (1605–65), king of Spain, Portugal, Naples, Sicily and Sardinia, supported the Holy Roman Empire against the Dutch and the Swedes during the Thirty Years War. He is largely remembered for his patronage of the artist Diego Velázquez (1599–1660).

498. The editions consulted report the following Latin text: *Cum superos Carrane non videris timere, mirum est te non cogitasse quod impune tibi non succederet tantum virum in tali constitutum Viennae authoritate sine causa laedere*, namely 'When you seem to have no fear of those above you, Carran, it is surprising that you did not think that you could not get away safely with damaging without a reason such an important man, who was appointed to hold such a position of authority in Vienna.' As this translation makes little sense, we assume that the text is corrupt, at least in the position of the negations (whereas the mistake in the use of the verb *videris* instead of the subjunctive *videaris* could be genuinely Bruodinus', and therefore has not been emended).

499. The Athenian philosopher Socrates (*c.* 470–399 BC) was and is still often regarded as the founder of the tradition of Western thought. He did not produce any writing, but some of his most famous students, such as Xenophon and Plato, described and expanded on his philosophy in several works.

500. This seems to be a re-elaboration of an episode reported by the Greek historian Diogenes Laertius (second to third century AD) in his *Life of Socrates* (2.21), quoting the philosopher Demetrius of Byzantium (first century BC) as his source. According to him, Socrates had once been kicked by a fellow-citizen of his, who was ill-disposed towards his teaching; to those who asked Socrates why he did not react, he replied that he would not sue a donkey, even if the animal kicked him.

501. Namely, Carran thought that Joannes à Molino would not 'kick back' because of his tolerance and Socratic spirit.

502. A Latin proverb which is attested, for example, in Plautus' play *Captivi*, line 472.

503. Clemens Schram (d. 1678) was a friar of Neulengbach friary (some fifty kilometres west of Vienna). Qualified both in canon and civil law, he often acted as a counsellor for noblemen. Elected definitor of the province of Upper Germany in 1672, he became guardian of Neulengbach in 1677 and died at Vienna on 10 October 1678. *Placidus Herzog, Cosmographia Austriaco-Franciscana* (Cologne, 1740), pp. 130, 134, 504.

504. This expression is first attested in the Roman playwright Plautus (third to second century BC), *Poenulus*, line 332. Both in that context and in this passage of *Anatomicum*, the oil is that of the lamplight, which has been consumed while staying up for writing during the night, but in vain.

505. For this proverb, whose basic meaning is that similar people stick together and do similar things, see Erasmus of Rotterdam, *Adagia* 1.10.71.

506. A quotation from Virgil's *Aeneid* (12.435: Aeneas speaking to his son Ascanius).

507. Formerly a hunting lodge south of Vienna, Kaiser Ebersdorf housed the imperial administration of Leopold I.

508. Maximilian Reichenberger (1613–73), Jesuit and professor of theology at the University of Prague, was the author of a number of theological works, including *Vindiciae cultus Mariani* (Prague, 1677), a book advocating devotion to the Virgin Mary. *Allgemeine Deutsche Biographie*, vol. 27, 1888, p. 674.

509. Samuel Vaclav Hatass (*c.* 1629–85), a diocesan priest, born at Vlasim in Central Bohemia, studied at the Kralovodvorska Theological seminary in Prague. In the years 1660–6 he served as dean at the cathedral of St Lawerence in Vysoke Myto and subsequently as rector of the Kralodvorska seminary. He published both in Czech and Latin, his best-known work is *Scintilla evangelica per evangelia dominicarum totius anni lucens* (Prague, 1668), a commentary on the Sunday Gospels. Josef Jirecek, *Rukovet k Dejinam literatury Ceske do Konce XVIII veku* [Handbook to the history of Czech literature to the end of the eighteenth century] (Prague 1875), p. 232.

510. Fr Wilhelm Anton Brauczek [Vilem Antonin Broucek] (*c.* 1638–90), Czech Franciscan and professor of theology at Prague, entered the order in 1658. He served as Czech minister provincial between 1672 and 1675. His main contribution was to education of monks with his volume *Domus sapientiae, doctoris subtilis Joannis Duns Scoti …* (Prague, 1663), the first printed work of Scotus philosophy published in Bohemia. It served as a basic textbook in Franciscan theological studies for many years. See Matyáš Franciszek Bajger, 'Czech Franciscan Book Culture', unpublished PhD thesis, University of Ostrava, Czech Republic, Ostrava, 2016, pp. 254, 285–6, 303.

511. *Lector jubilatus* was the highest title of distinction that could be conferred on a teacher of theology and was equal to the degree of doctor of divinity.

512. The church of Our Lady of the Snows, Prague was founded in 1347. Given over to the Franciscan order at the beginning of the seventeenth century, Antonius Bruodinus served as guardian of the friary 1668–70.

513. Ernst Schaff (Arnošt Schaff), Franciscan definitor of Bohemia, lectured in theology at Kralodvorska seminary, Prague. In 1663 he co-authored a portion of the volume *Domus sapientiae, doctoris subtilis Joannis Duns Scoti* with his colleague Wilhelm Anton Brauczek. Schaff, a former pupil of Bruodinus, was guardian of Olomouc, 1665–6 and Kroměříž, 1672. Pařez and Kuchařová, *Irish Franciscans Prague*, p. 80.

514. That is during the week after the feast of Pentecoste; at the time the feast of Pentecoste was celebrated for seven days, which was known as the Octave of Pentecoste.

515. The Basilica of St Mary of the Altar of Heaven (*Basilica Sanctae Mariae in Ara coeli*) is among the oldest churches of Rome. Situated on top of the Capitoline hill, in the seventeenth century it was the centre of religious and civil life of the city.

516. Leopold I (1640–1705) was Holy Roman emperor, king of Hungary, Croatia and Bohemia. The second son of Ferdinand III, he succeeded as emperor in 1658. He fought successive wars against the Turks in the east and the French on his western boundary. Internally he was obliged to suppress Protestant unrest in Hungary. Originally intended for the Church, he was influenced more by the Jesuits than Franciscans and was a strong proponent of the counter-reformation.

517. Girolamo Colonna (1604–66), an Italian cardinal, was a member of the noble Colonna family of Rome. The family supplied one pope and many Church and political leaders to Renaissance Italy. *Catholic Encyclopedia*, vol. IV, pp. 125–7.

518. The Holy Roman emperors were drawn exclusively from the house of Habsburg from 1438 to 1740. The Habsburgs, named after a castle in Switzerland, were one of the most powerful and influential lineages of the early modern period; daughters of the family married into almost all the royal houses of Europe.

519. Count Jan Hartvik Nostitz-Rieneck (1610–83), supreme chamberlain to the emperor and builder of the Nostitz palace of Prague 1662–75. The Nostitz family, named after Nostitz in Saxony, had a history dating back to 1280. The family contributed significantly to the cultural life in Prague. *Neue Deutsche Biographie*, vol. 19, 1999, p. 354.

520. Bernard Sannig (1637–1704) of Silesia entered the Franciscan order in 1665 and studied Scotus theology under Bruodinus at the monastery of the Virgin Mary, Prague. A brilliant student, he is considered one of the most important Czech theologians of the baroque period. Teaching philosophy at the University of Prague, he was elected minister provincial of Bohemia and later served as vicar general of the order. He wrote many works on theology, history and Franciscan spirituality. *Allgemeine Deutsche Biographie*, vol. 30, 1890, p. 363. See also John Hennig, 'St Nicholas' Bread', *Béaloideas*, vol. 13, 1943, pp. 268–9.

521. Frederick Landgrave of Hesse-Darmstadt (1616–82), a German Protestant and soldier, who converted to Catholicism as a young man, entered the Order of the Knights Hospitalers and was eventually elevated to crown-cardinal of Austria. *Catholic Encyclopedia*, vol. VII, p. 299.

522. Fr Bernardine Clancy, see note 158 above.

523. Although this is clearer in Carve's original text than in Bruodinus' misquotation (or, better, paraphrase) of it, this final statement is taken from the Bible (*Wisdom* 11:17) and applied to Clancy's and Bruodinus' case.

524. Fr Clancy was of the Thomond family, the Meic Fhlannchadha, who historically were brehons (judges and arbitrators), attached to the ruling O'Brien family. On the family see McInerney, 'The Síol Fhlannchadha', *Eolas*, vol. 9, 2016, pp. 19–54.

525. See the short poem reported above, p. 255. The presence of ryegrass in the corn spoils the quality of the harvest.

526. The Irish College of St Anthony in Louvain, Belgium was founded in 1607 for the training of Irish Franciscan priests. Among the college's many accomplishments was the initiation of a project in the 1630s undertaken by Mícheál Ó Cléirigh (*c.* 1590–1643), who travelled throughout Ireland collecting the ancient annals and histories of the country for a compilation that became known as the *Annals of the Four Masters*. On completion of the project Ó Cléirigh visited Thomond to secure the approbation of Conchobhar Mac Bruaideadha of Kilkee and Lettermoylan, a member of Bruodinus' extended family. Another notable friar of the college was Anthony Hickey (1586–1641), who was also of Thomond and descended from a learned family of hereditary physicians. The Irish College was closed in 1794 by the forces of the French Revolution.

527. Graz is a large city in south-eastern Austria famous for its universities. The oldest, the Karl-Franzens University, was founded in 1585 and remained under the authority of the Catholic Church until 1782, when the state took control of educational establishments.

528. Cardinal Ernst Adalbert von Harrach (1598–1667) was an Austrian priest, who was appointed archbishop of Prague in 1624 and made primate of Bohemia in 1626. With Fr Malachy Fallon he was instrumental in founding the Irish College at Prague in 1629. Cardinal Harrach also established the Kralodvorska seminary for the education of priests in the Old Royal Court in 1631 and opposed the influence of the Jesuits on the education of young clergy in Prague. When the Swedes attacked the city in 1648, he was captured but released on payment of a ransom. It was Cardinal Harrach who first appointed Fr Bernardine Clancy to the chair of theology at Kralodvorska seminary in 1650. *Catholic Encyclopedia*, vol. XII, p. 343; see also note 158 above.

529. The O'Loughlins were the former lords of the Burren in northern Thomond. Maurice studied both laws, meaning that he was qualified in canon and civil law.

530. The University of Prague was established by the Holy Roman emperor Charles IV in 1348. Its faculty of arts became a centre of the Hussite movement in the 1420s. The Jesuits were invited to Prague in 1562 where they established an academy of theology called the Clementinum. In 1654 the emperor Ferdinand III merged the oldest college of the university, the Carolinum, with the Clementinum and the new institution was renamed the Charles Ferdinand University. The Charles University of Prague, currently (2021), accommodates 49,236 students.

531. A monstrous creature of Greek mythology, whose hybrid body was composed of the parts of a goat, a snake and a lion.

532. In the *Aeneid*, Achates was Aeneas' most faithful companion. His name soon became a byword for intimate friendship.

533. Iros was the beggar who, in Homer's *Odyssey* (Book XVIII), insulted Odysseus when the hero came back to Ithaca under disguise.

534. Croesus was the powerful king of Lydia in the sixth century BC who, secure in his own great wealth and pleasure, regarded himself as the happiest man who ever lived, until struck by a sudden and devastating reversal of fortune. His name became a synonym for a self-satisfied man before a fall. In Carve's original passage, which Bruodinus has modified and abridged as usual, the opposition between King Croesus and the arrogant beggar Iros is enhanced by a quotation from Ovid, *Tristia* 3.7.42, where these two figures feature as a pair.

535. For Thrason, a figure associated with arrogance, see note 477 above.

536. The earliest Fathers of the Church in whose works this saying is attested, albeit in a different form, are St John Chrysostom (*Ad Theodorum lapsum*, Epistle 1.15: *nam peccare quidem humanum est; at in peccatis perseverare, id non humanum est, sed omnino satanicum*) and St Augustine (*Sermo* 164.14: *humanum fuit errare, diabolicum est per animositatem in errore manere*). The two were contemporaries (fourth to fifth century AD), but the text by Chrysostom (written before 381) is at least thirty years earlier than the one by Augustine (written after 410). Modern sources generally credit Augustine with this saying, though they are almost certainly wrong.

537. Literally, this translates as 'three-city Prague'. This epithet refers to the three divisions characterising the city: the Old Town, the New Town, and the area around the castle. These were once separated one from another by a wall, and each of them was a town in itself.

538. The *conventus discretorium* was the convent's governing council. Originally the *discretus discretorum* was an official, who had charge over certain Franciscan houses. He could also accompany his minister provincial to the general chapter for the election of the minister general of the order. *Catholic Encyclopedia*, vol. IV, p. 578.

539. Ludwig Kauka is untraced.

540. From Nysa in Silesia, Archangel Mascula was a Franciscan of German origin. Becoming involved in the management of the Czech Franciscan province, he was appointed provincial secretary in 1669, provincial definitor in 1671 and eventually minister provincial 1681–4. Mascula sought with others to promote greater autonomy for German-speaking brethren in the Czech province. He died at Prague in 1699. F. Bajger, 'Czech Franciscan Book Culture', unpublished PhD thesis, Ostrava, 2016, p. 402.

541. Humprecht Jan Černín of Chudenic (1628–82), diplomat and art collector, was a descendant of one of the oldest noble families of Bohemia. Appointed imperial ambassador to Vencie in 1659, he amassed a large collection of paintings. His major architectural contribution to Prague was the monumental Czernin Palace, which housed his extensive art collection. Bruodinus dedicated his synopsis of the life of St Peter of Alcantara (Prague, 1669) to Černín. Pařez and Kuchařová, *Irish Franciscans Prague*, p. 85.

542. Many monasteries kept apothecary stores where botanical or herbal medicines for the use of the monks were preserved. Occasionally these products were made available to the public. In the 1680s the pharmacy of the Capuchin monastery of Hradčany dispensed medicines to the citizens of Prague. In Dubrovnik the pharmacy of the Franciscan friars, dating from 1317, continues to operate. See also T. Strocchia, 'The Nun Apothecaries of Renaissance Florence: Marketing medicines in the convent', *Renaissance Studies*, vol. 25, no. 5, 2011, pp. 627–47.

543. An enclosure set aside for the raising of plants or animals.

544. This translation adds a comma between the words *granarium* and *tectum*, which does not feature in the editions consulted. Without it, the translation would read as follows: 'the renovation of quite a large part of the church and convent's roofed-over granary' – which makes less sense, considering that churches are generally not provided with granaries, and all granaries have a roof.

545. Olomouc is the historical capital of Moravia in the eastern Czech Republic. The Franciscan convent was founded by Saint John of Capistrano in 1454. Following the Thirty Years War, Olomouc University was re-established and the city became a centre for the revival of

Catholicism in central Europe. Bruodinus became guardian of Olomouc convent, 1662–3 and guardian of Our Lady of the Snows in Prague, 1668–70. However, the Jesuits rather than the Franciscans predominated in Olomouc and the friars' presence ended prior to 1780. The old monastery currently belongs to the Dominican order.

546. The *custos* was an official of the Franciscan order, who presided over a number of covents collectively called a *custodia*. A *custos* was subject to his provincial but had the right to participate in the election of the order's minister general. *Catholic Encyclopedia*, vol. IV, p. 578.

547. Hostinné is a town in the north of the Czech Republic near the Polish border. The first Franciscans arrived in 1666 but the building of a monastery proper did not begin until 1677. Clearly Bruodinus is speaking of Hostinné when the monks were still in temporary accommodation there.

548. That is, these priests are far more knowledgeable than Bruodinus in Irish matters. In Latin, the contrast between the unreliability of Bruodinus' information and the potential knowledge of other priests (according to Carve) is stressed by a clever use of words. The term *caput*, 'head', can also mean 'chapter' (see notes 187 and 435 above), while *auricularis* may hint at private confession (*confessio auricularis*). If so, Carve may be suggesting that the confessions that the priests hear are a better source of information about Irish affairs for them, than Bruodinus' entire chapter.

549. Rather than a real quotation, this is a reference to the opening passage of Chapter VII of Carve's *Enchiridion* (p. 104). Carve then puts forward his testimonial letters in Chapters VIII and IX, so as to disprove Bruodinus' statement.

550. This is not a quotation – and certainly not from page 115 of Carve's *Enchiridion*. Bruodinus is simply referring to the fact that Carve intended to use Roche's letter to defend himself from his antagonist's claims. This letter features on pp. 125–6 of *Enchiridion*, and is preceded by a short introduction to the figure of Roche, which Bruodinus' paraphrase or false quotation echoes.

551. This appears to echo and re-adapt a passage from Geoffrey of Clairvaux's 'Declamationes de colloquio Simonis cum Iesu' (*Bene, Petre, et optime, et non ad insipientiam tibi*). In turn, the sentence *ad insipientiam tibi* echoes *Psalms* 21.3, a passage also recalled and re-adapted by St Augustine (*Confessions* 1.9.14).

552. This individual has proved difficult to trace. He seems to have been a Protestant teacher in the south Munster area, who tutored young students both Catholic and Protestant in Latin. He is probably the same person as *Magistro Brok, haeretico* (Master Brok, heretic), who taught grammar to the young clerical student Ross MacGeoghegan in the area around Clonmel in 1601, before he entered the Irish College at Salamanca, Spain. See Denis J. O'Doherty, 'Students of the Irish College, Salamanca (1595–1619)', *Archivium Hibernicum*, vol. 2 (1913), p. 11.

553. This saying (of which various slightly different forms are attested) implies that the wickedness of Roche, which Bruodinus has just described and on which he will expand in this paragraph, characterises Carve's soul as well.

554. Thomas Fleming, archbishop of Dublin (1623–51), was a son of William, baron of Slane. He entered the Franciscan order at Louvain in 1610. When archbishop he was accused of partiality towards his own order and a bitter onslaught was launched upon him by author and priest Paul Harris. In the wars of the 1640s he aligned with the papal nuncio Rinuccini but also supported an accommodation with the royalist James, duke of Ormond. A year before his death he witnessed the devastation wrought by Cromwell's soldiers on the people of Dublin. A fresco of Fleming survives at St Isidore's College, Rome. *DIB*, vol. III, p. 1017.

555. The juxtaposition of the nominative of the sender with the dative of the addressee is the standard opening of letters written in Latin, but this formula does not feature in Carve's testimonial letter in *Enchiridion*. Bruodinus is making it up, relying on what Roche says about Carve at the beginning of the letter.

556. In the editions consulted, the closing parenthesis is placed between *fui* and *in Hibernia*. If so, however, Bruodinus would be both contradicting himself and repeating the words 'in Ireland'

twice: "neither you nor anyone of your family (...) ever called himself 'Carve' in Ireland in Ireland (*sic*) before you". Assuming that the text is not sound, we have moved the parenthesis to a different position, between *ante te* and *unquam*.

557. A *schola trivialis* was the school where the three 'trivial arts' were taught: grammar, rhetoric and philosophy.

558. From what is known of Bruodinus' early life it is unlikely that he was educated in Tipperary under Conald O'Carran. It is more probable that he is speaking here in the persona of the fictional author Cornelius O'Molony. For Conald O'Carran, see note 446 above.

559. James Butler is one of several of the name who served with the imperial armies, thus making identification difficult. He was probably the Colonel James Butler, known to be a relative of Colonel Walter Butler (d. 1634) of the Paulstown branch, with whom Thomas Carve also served (see note 248 above). James held the command of a regiment during the 1640s, which is sometimes referred to as the 'Younger Butler' regiment. *DIB*, vol. II, p. 131.

560. Two more paragraphs follow, but the actual dissection ends in paragraph 6.

561. The closest traceable parallel is a comment to *Apocalypse* 3:3 by Joachim of Flora, an Italian theologian of the twelfth century, author of an exposition of the Book of Revelation (*Expositio in Apocalypsim*): 'generally, he who starts by behaving wickedly ends by behaving wickedly, and not only does he neglect to feel sorrow about his sins, but he also commits worse ones day by day' (*Plerumque qui male incipit male consummat, & non solum peccata deflere negligit, sed etiam de die in diem deteriora committit*). Not all Christian authors, however, would agree with this. In particular, in the treatise *De tribus habitaculis animae* (On the three dwelling-places of the soul), we read that 'he who starts life well sometimes finishes badly, and he who starts out badly often finishes well' (*qui bene incipit vivere aliquando male finit, et qui male incipit saepe bene finit*). The authorship and date of this treatise are still debated, but it has been often attributed to St Patrick, most likely incorrectly: see E. Boyle, 'The Authoriship and Transmission of *De tribus habitaculis animae*', *The Journal of Medieval Latin*, vol. 22, 2012, pp. 49–65.

562. Domitian, emperor of Rome (AD 81–96), is depicted by Christian sources as a cruel ruler and a persecutor of Christians: see for example Eusebius of Caesarea, *Historia Ecclesiastica*, 3.17 and Orosius, *Hist. adversus paganos*, 7.10. Particularly relevant to Bruodinus' mention of Domitian in this paragraph is the association of the emperor with the practice of slandering Christian doctrine, according to Melito, bishop of Sardis in the third century, quoted by Eusebius (*ibidem* 4.26.9). Classical sources distinguish between an earlier phase of Domitian's reign, during which the emperor proved himself to be a righteous and wise ruler, and a later phase, characterised by cruelty. Describing this latter phase, the Roman biographer Suetonius (*c*. AD 70–*c*. 140) says that Domitian used to confiscate properties of living as well as dead citizens on any charge brought by any accuser, apparently regardless of their truthfulness and reliability: see Suetonius, *Life of Domitian* 12.1. This account may have contributed to the picture of Domitian which we find in Bruodinus' *Anatomicum*.

563. Vitellius was Roman emperor for eight months in AD 69. Ancient as well as Christian sources depict him as a depraved man. In Suetonius, we read that he resorted to false accusations to get rid of his creditors: see *Life of Vitellius*, 7.2. Bruodinus may be referring to this move, through which Vitellius paved the way for his election as emperor by the Roman troops.

564. Although Antoninus Pius was a pagan ruler, Christian sources agree with classical ones in describing him as one of the best and most righteous Roman emperors. During his reign (AD 138–61), the empire enjoyed a period of peace and growth. In this passage, Bruodinus may be referring (directly or indirectly) to an alleged decree by Antoninus, reported by the Christian historian Eusebius of Caesarea in his *Historia Ecclesiastica*, 4.13 (quoting Melito, bishop of Sardis), according to which the Christians should not be persecuted unless they attempted something affecting the Roman government: accusers who persisted in bringing accusations against the Christians simply because of their religion should be punished. The decree probably played a role in the martyrdom of Apollonius, recounted by *Eusebius* at 5.21: both Apollonius and his accuser were punished.

565. This is a readapted quotation from *Acts* 9:1 (where the subject is Paul, to whom Bruodinus compares Carran in the next sentence). Two different readings are attested for that passage in Latin: *spirans minarum et caedis* (two genitives) or *spirans minas et caedes* (two accusatives). If the text in the editions of *Anatomicum* consulted is sound, Bruodinus is using a mixed reading, with a genitive (*minarum*) and an accusative (*caedes*).

566. That is, God.

567. The most complete account of the life and death of John Kearney is in Benigus Millett, 'John Kearney OFM', in Patrick Corish and Benignus Millett (eds), *Irish Martyrs* (Dublin, 2005), pp. 165–75.

568. The cathedral Church of St Patrick on the Rock of Cashel was attacked by English parliamentarian troops under Murrough O'Brien, Lord Inchiquin, in September 1647. Between 800 and 1,000 townspeople, who had sought refuge in the church, were massacred in the storming of the cathedral. Conleth Manning, *Rock of Cashel* (Dublin, 2000), p. 10.

569. Loreto is a hill town in Ancona province, central Italy. The shrine of the Holy House of Loreto is believed by the faithful to be the house where the Blessed Virgin Mary lived. The Litany of Loreto is a prayer to the Virgin, composed in the middle ages, and approved by Pope Sixtus V in 1587.

570. Joseph Everard, a native of Cashel, was Franciscan minister provincial 1635–8. It was on his authority that Friar Mícheál Ó Cléirigh sought out Flann Mac Aodhgáin and Conchobhar Mac Bruaideadha as scholars qualified to vouch for the authenticity of the *Annals of the Four Masters*. Fr Everard was recommended for the see of Ferns in 1644. He was reappointed guardian of Cashel in 1650 but news reached Rome in 1653 that he had been found dead in a cave, where he had been hiding from priest-hunters. Millett, *Irish Franciscans*, p. 525.

571. The surname Sall (*Saulus* in Latin) clearly derives from Saul, the Jewish name of St Paul, so that the comparison with the apostle Paul's conversion is apt.

572. Fr Dominic Dempsey was guardian of Kilkenny friary in 1629 and was still at Kilkenny in 1637 when Kearney and Sall entered as novices. He functioned as guardian of Kildare, 1642 and of Wexford, 1645. Fleeing to the continent during the Cromwellian prosecution, he was appointed definitor of the order by a brief of Pope Alexander VII in 1656. He served briefly as guardian of St Anthony's College, Louvain, 1659, before returning to Ireland in 1661 where he served again as guardian of Kildare. Millett, *Irish Franciscans*, pp. 15, 21, 115–16

573. This episode clearly echoes the miracle of Jesus calming the storm, narrated in the Gospels.

574. *Salus infirmorum* ('health for sick people') is a common epithet for the Virgin Mary.

575. This episode probably serves as a parallel to the miracle of Jesus healing a leper in the Gospels.

576. This was not the case, because Kearney publicly defended a series of theses on Scotist theology in Louvain on 15 June 1644 before his professor, Raymond Caron. Corish and Millett, *Irish Martyrs*, p. 167.

577. The *eculeus* or spike was an instrument of torture commonly used in ancient Rome to extract evidence from slaves. The sufferer was made to sit upon a sharp point with weights attached to his arms and legs. Harry Thurston Peck, *Harpers Dictionary of Classical Antiquities* (New York, 1898).

578. This episode offers a parallel to the story of Jesus tempted in the wilderness in the Gospels.

579. Kearney was guardian of Carrick-on-Suir not Cork friary. The mistake may have arisen from a misreading of *Corkagiensis* for *Carrigiensis* or alternatively from a scribal error made during transcription. Corish and Millett, *Irish Martyrs*, p. 165.

580. No officer of this name has been traced. A William Willer was among the signatories of the articles of agreement with the citizens of Limerick in April 1652. Corish and Millett, *Irish Martyrs*, p. 170.

581. Col. Jerome Sankey followed Cromwell's army to Dublin in 1649. A man imbued with religion, he was re-baptised an Anabaptist in Ireland. He led the attack on Clonmel in 1650 and after its submission was appointed governor. Notably anti-Catholic, Sankey proved ruthless. He reported his men had killed 400 Irish by April 1652. The receiver of large tracts of confiscated lands, he retired to his estate at Coolmore, Tipperary, following the restoration of the English monarchy. *DIB*, vol. VIII, pp. 771–3.

582. In 1653 the feast of St Joachim, the father of the Blessed Virgin Mary, was celebrated on 20 March. The current liturgical calendar celebrates the saint's feast day on 26 July.

583. That is, against God and Heaven. In Kearney's speech, the ambiguity between the divine world and the crown of England is deliberate. A similar ambiguity is the core of St Augustine's work entitled *The City of God*, a cornerstone of Christian doctrine.

584. John Kearney departed this life on Friday, 21 March 1653, the day directly following his trial.

585. Literally, this translates as 'while he was in his thirty-fourth year of life'. Note that Bruodinus refers to the month of Kearney's death by mentioning the feast of St Joachim (see note 582 above), but he had not specified his date of birth in the year 1619. The reference to Kearney's age at the time of his death provides a parallel with the life of Jesus Christ, who also died at the age of thirty-three according to the tradition.

586. That is, Kearney's body, here referred to as a relic.

587. This scene parallels that of the deposition of Christ in the Gospels, following Joseph of Arimathea's request to Pilate. Bruodinus himself suggests this by using the Latin words *deposito ex ligno corpore*, where *lignum* is an allusion to the Cross.

588. According to Bruodinus, Joseph Sall was the author of an 'Index of Irish Martyrs' (see note 218 above). It is likely that the substance of Sall's index appears in the listing below of Franciscans killed in the provinces of Leinster and Munster during the Cromwellian campaign (22 individuals). If this is the case it means that Sall's Index was not available to Bruodinus when he published *Propugnaculum* in 1669 but came into his possession subsequently, which is why he published it as an appendix to *Anatomicum Examen* in 1671.

589. It is likely that Canon Godfrey Sall of Cashel was present at the removal of the body as he afterwards sent a little piece of Kearney's habit and a few of his hairs to his cousin Peter Creagh, SJ, in France. Godfrey Sall also compiled an account of Kearney's later life, whereas Joseph Sall, who was then exiled in Spain, supplied the details of Fr Kearney's early years. Corish and Millett, *Irish Martyrs*, pp. 165, 174.

590. As suggested by the name of the Christian lady, this episode serves as a parallel to, though not an equivalent of, the story of Mary Magdalene discovering and announcing Christ's resurrection in the Gospels, together with another Mary (generally identified either with Mary of Clopas or with the mother of James, also called Mary). The parallel is further stressed by the reference to Kearney's coffin as sepulchre (*tumba*) in the Latin text.

591. English parliamentarian troops broke through the defences of Wexford, 11 October 1649, while negotiations were still in progress, and proceeded to massacre the inhabitants of the town, combatants and non-combatants alike. Some 1,500 people lost their lives. The sacking of Wexford is counted as one of the worst atrocities of the Cromwellian conquest.

592. Seven Franciscans, five priests and two brothers, lost their lives in the carnage. Fr Peter Stafford, who had functioned as parish priest of Wexford for the previous fifteen years, was killed in the church of the friary along with three of his confrères: Fr Richard Sinnott, Fr John Esmond and Fr Paul Sinnott. Fr Raymond Stafford was killed in the market place, while addressing the people. Denis Murphy, *Cromwell in Ireland* (Dublin, 1897), p. 165.

593. In July of 1651 a substantial parliamentarian military force under Cromwell's son-in-law, Henry Ireton, entered County Clare. Perhaps it was at this time that Fr Hickey lost his life. William Hickey's name first appeared on a list of martyrs compiled by the minister provincial, Anthony Doherty, 1663. Millett, *Irish Franciscans*, pp. 251, 541.

594. Fr Andrew Hickey, not of Thomond but of Anhid, County Limerick, whose name was William before he entered religious life, was almost certainly one of four friars killed by parliamentarian troops at Adare in 1647. A contemporary poem addressed to *An Bráthar Bocht Uilliam Ó h-Íceadha* praises the amiable disposition of the man. Cuthbert Mhág Craith, *Dán na mBráthar Mionúr* (Baile Átha Cliath, 1967), vol. I, lch. 240, vol. II, lgh. 233–5.

595. Fr Walter Walsh was a former guardian of Wicklow friary. Although recorded above, p. 323, as expiring on the gallows near Mullingar in 1650, according to the Harold manuscript at St Isidore's in Rome he died while imprisoned in Dublin in 1652. Millett, *Irish Franciscans*, p. 254.

596. This Franciscan has not been identified. The Latinised Musaeus is aimed, we suggest, at casting this friar as a well-educated man, since Musaeus was a legendary Greek polymath, seer and poet. Even so, the reason why Musaeus should be anglicised O'Hussey (*Ó hEódhusa*) is unclear. See Millett, *Irish Franciscans*, p. 254.

597. Educated at Lovain, Fr Dormer was ordained sub-deacon in March 1639 and on his return to Ireland served as guardian of Castledermot and of New Ross friaries. In his politics he supported James marquess of Ormond and opposed Papal Nuncio Rinuccini. The Doherty martyrology agrees with Bruodinus that Dormer died in a Dublin prison but neither gives his date of death. Millett, *Irish Franciscans*, p. 254.

598. The surname reads *Horumleus* in the main body of the text, which is corrected to *Gorumbaeus* in Bruodinus' 'Errata'. We assume a mistake also in the 'Errata', and read *Gorumleus*, which is likely to be the north Leinster name Gormley. Fr Bernard Gormley is probably to be identified with Friar Brian O'Gormooley (*Ó Gormshúiligh*), who served under Guardian Dominic Dempsey at Kildare at the outbreak of the Catholic uprising in 1642. Friar Brian with his guardian is reported saying, 'the King had long usurped the tithes and rights belonging to the Catholic Church, but now God was pleased to bring it to them to whom it did belong'. TCD, 1641 Depositions, Ms 813, f. 261.

599. There is much confusion concerning Fr Conroy. Bruodinus previously recorded that a Hilary Conroy of County Roscommon entered the order in Elphin and was hanged at Castlecoote, Roscommon, 1642. *Propugnaculum*, pp. 727–8. The above account, based on Joseph Sall's Index, claims that Fr Conroy was of Munster origin and was killed in 1652. Another contemporary report says that a Franciscan of this name was hanged in 1650 and that the killing took place in Leinster. Denis Murphy, *Our Martyrs* (Dublin, 1896), p. 287. Perhaps here we are dealing with different individuals with similar names.

600. John O'Farrell was such a common name that this Franciscan cannot be identified with certainty; a John O'Farrell entered the order at Louvain before 1622. He may be the same John O'Farrell who attended Louvain at about that time and was noted for his preaching and poetry. He authored *De Stigmatibus Sancti Francisci*, among other poems. See *The Whole Works of Sir John Ware Concerning Ireland* (Dublin, 1746), vol. III, p. 105. A Fr John O'Farrell was appointed confessor of lay people in 1647 but whether any of these men were related to the friar struck down by the Puritans in 1652 is unknown. Millett, *Irish Franciscans*, p. 264.

601. Philipp Flatsbury, clerk of Kildare, is recorded on the List of Outlaws (1641–7). *Analecta Hibernica*, vol. 23, 1966, p. 349. Philippus Flasburg, confessor, is appended to a document signed in support of Raymond Caron, canonical visitor to Ireland, Kilkenny, July 1649. John Callaghan, *Vindiciae Catholicorum Hiberniae* (Paris, 1650), p. 181. He was put to death for being a priest and because for the purpose of disguise he had changed his name. Millett, *Irish Franciscans*, p. 253.

602. The Harold manuscript, 1654–8, is the earliest to record the death of Fr Fitzgerald, indicating that he died in 1652. The Doherty martyrology, compiled in 1663, says simply that Fitzgerald died in prison, while the account above, published in 1671, maintains he died by hanging in 1650. Millett, *Irish Franciscans*, pp. 254–5.

603. Fr Richard Butler and Br. James Sall were killed during the storming of Cashel cathedral in 1647. Their inclusion here adds further weight to the suggestion that the martyr list originated with Rev. Joseph Sall. Both killings are also mentioned by John Lynch in *De Praesulibus Hiberniae*, ed. J.F. O'Doherty (Dublin, 1944), vol. II, p. 51.

604. Brothers James Cheevers and James Roche were killed during the massacre at Wexford in 1649. Br. Cheevers was over seventy years of age and blind when he was struck down. Murphy, *Cromwell in Ireland*, p. 165.

605. Mocleus is taken to be a Latinised form of Mockler, a surname of Anglo-Norman origin recorded in Tipperary from the thirteenth century. Mocklershill, a townland in Magorban parish, is a short distance east of Cashel. Br. John Mockler is untraced.

606. *Enchiridion Apologeticum*, although written in Vienna, was printed 500 kilometres to the north-west at Nuremberg. Nuremberg, an early centre of mechanical innovation and printing, embraced the Protestant reformation. Carve's book was published without any ecclesiastical authorisation or approbation as was normal for works written by Catholic clergymen.

607. The translation of the Latin text is 'finally, I will name …', but in his *corrigenda* Bruodinus writes as follows: 'The clerics whose biography is promised here are precisely those about whom the author has already written from page 233 onwards' (*Religiosi quorum vita hic promittitur sunt illi ipsi de quibus jam a folio 233. scriptor egit*). Shortly after the publication of the volume, he must have realised that this paragraph had been mistakenly printed after his list of names, instead of before. Our translation takes this into account.

608. During the pontificate of Pope Urban VIII (1623–44), the papacy sought to gain control over the declaration of saints. In his papal bull *Sanctissimus Dominus Noster*, 1625, Urban instructed Catholics not to venerate the dead as saints without papal authority. The bull became a foundational document in the process of sainthood. In 1634 Pope Urban VIII issued two decrees centralising the entire procedure of canonisation in Rome. By reforming the process, the pope rendered sainthood more difficult to achieve. *Catholic Encyclopedia*, vol. II, p. 366, vol. XV, p. 219.

609. James Coghlan of Leinster, a student of theology at the College of the Immaculate Conception, 1650–1, promoted to lecturer of philosophy, 1653–4. Having lectured a number of years at the Benedictine monastery, Kladruby, he was made guardian of Prague, 1670. Pařez and Kuchařová, *Irish Franciscans Prague*, p. 180.

610. Daniel Bruoder (*c.* 160–87) of the *Ó Bruadair* family of Connacht, whose family turns up in several deeds in Irish in the sixteenth century and who, according to Bruodinus, had hereditary lands in south-east Galway near Lough Derg. He was a lecturer of philosophy at the archiepiscopal seminary, 1642, and lecturer of theology at the College of the Immaculate Conception, 1651. He left for Vienna in 1652 to recover from illness. Wadding proposed him as guardian of St Isidore's, Rome, 1655, but he remained at Prague. He died September 1687. *Propugnaculum*, p. 72; Millett, *Irish Franciscans*, pp. 121, 162–3; Pařez and Kuchařová, *Irish Franciscans Prague*, p. 75.

611. Although the name is here given as Bernard (*Bernardus*), this is Bernardine Clancy (*c.* 1612–84) of Thomond, a man of keen intellect and erudition, who taught theology and philosophy at the archiepiscopal seminary for many years. During a dispute at the College of the Immaculate Conception in 1652, he was obliged to leave the college and live at St Mary's of the Snows for three years. He served as guardian in 1660 and again in 1673. A volume of his lectures survives at University Library, Prague. Millett, *Irish Franciscans*, pp, 152, 161, 494.

612. Anthony Burke of Connacht lectured in philosophy at Prague, 1650, and served as guardian of the college in 1664. He returned to Ireland by 1672 where he functioned as guardian of Rosserrilly. Serving as Irish minister provincial, 1684–7, he held the title *Pater Provinciae* in 1690. Pařez and Kuchařová, *Irish Franciscans Prague*, p. 182.

613. Anthony Farrell (*c.* 1618–81) of Leinster, sent to Prague, 1641, lectured in philosophy, 1651, and theology, 1653. He served as guardian of the College of the Immaculate Conception, 1657–60, and replaced Bernardine Clancy as lecturer of theology at the archiepiscopal seminary, a post he held for twenty years. He died 12 Jan. 1681. Pařez and Kuchařová, *Irish Franciscans Prague*, p. 183.

614. Anthony O'Connor of Connacht was a student of philosophy, 1651, vicar, 1653 and guardian of the College of the Immaculate Conception, 1656–7. A student at the archiepiscopal seminary, he subsequently returned to Ireland. Described as confessor, preacher and guardian of Elphin,

1672, he was *lector generalis*, 1676. Pařez and Kuchařová, *Irish Franciscans Prague*, p. 181. While in Prague Fr O'Connor compiled a Gaelic manuscript, which included the text *Déorchaóineadh na hEírionn* (Ireland's lamentation); his manuscript survives at Gottingen Univesity in central Germany. Pádraig Ó Macháin, 'Imirce agus Filleadh Lámhscríbhinní na nGael', in Ríona Nic Chongáil et al. (eds), *Litríocht na Gaeilge ar fud an Domhain* (Baile Átha Cliath, 2015), vol. I, p. 125.

615. Anthony Kinraghty (*Mac Ionnrachtaigh*), a Thomond surname today more commonly anglicised Enright. He came to Prague in 1650, a student of philosophy, 1653. Returned to Ireland and became confessor and preacher at Quin, 1678; reappointed guardian 1680, 1684, 1689 and guardian of Ennis, 1681. In 1697 he celebrated fifty years in religion. Pařez and Kuchařová, *Irish Franciscans Prague*, p. 187.

616. Patrick Ward (*c.* 1622–78) was lecturer of philosophy, 1665, lecturer of theology at the archiepiscopal seminary, 1672, and *lector jubilatus* 1677. He spent fourteen years teaching at the archiepiscopal seminary. Pařez and Kuchařová, *Irish Franciscans Prague*, p. 194.

617. John Clancy, *lector jubilatus*, who taught theology and philosophy at the archiepiscopal seminary, died 19 Oct. 1680. Pařez and Kuchařová, *Irish Franciscans Prague*, p. 180.

618. Froinsias Ó Maoilmhuaidh (Francis O'Molloy), of Meath diocese, entered St Isidore's, Rome, 1632 and taught philosophy in Vienna, 1642. He returned to St Isidore's, 1647, where he spent the remainder of his career. He was author of three Latin and two Irish works: *Lucerna Fidelium* (Rome, 1676), an Irish-language catechism, and *Gramatica Latino-Hibernica* (Rome, 1677), the first published Irish grammar. He died in France, while returning to Ireland, 1677. Diarmuid Breathnach, *Beathaisnéis, 1560–1781* (Baile Átha Cliath, 2001), lgh. 157–9.

619. Andrew MacVeigh, probably of Connacht origin, was a teacher of philosophy at St Isidore's, Rome, 1663. He also taught at the archiepiscopal seminary in Prague. Approved *lector jubilatus*, by 1674 he was in Louvain where he was permitted to preach and hear confessions in Malines diocese. He returned to Ireland, 1677 and was guardian of Claregalway, 1680, of Galway, 1682 and of Rosserilly, 1686. Millett, *Irish Franciscans*, p. 366.

620. Francis Burke was completing his studies for the priesthood at St Isidore's, Rome, 1660. Millett, *Irish Franciscans*, p. 125.

621. Francis O'Kennedy, lecturer of theology at St Anthony's, Louvain, presided over defences of his students' theses, two of which were published, one in 1663 and the other in 1667. *Analectes pour servir à l'histoire ecclésiastique de la Belgique*, vol. 22 (Louvain, 1890), p. 437; *Collectanea Hibernica*, vol. 48, 2006, p. 27. He was made *lector jubilatus*, 1667 and definitor, 1675. Returned to Ireland and appointed guardian of Limerick, 1676.

622. A church official of the diocese of Wrocław (German: Breslau), in Silesia, who served under Cardinal Friedrich von Hessen-Darmstadt (see endnote 520). Why Bruodinus should seek authentication of documents in a neighbouring diocese rather than at Prague is unclear. Balthasar Ignatius Pitz is untraced.

623. Bolesławiec (German: Bunzlau) is a city of Lower Silesia and an administrative capital of its region. It became an important centre of the reformation but was pillaged by Swedish forces in 1642 and reduced to ruin. In the seventeenth century the town was in the Habsburg Empire, in the eighteenth century it was part of Prussia and is now located in south-western Poland.

624. Trutnov (German: Trautenau) is a large town in the Hradec Králové region of the Czech Republic, situated 160 kilometres north-east of Prague. Denoted a royal city in 1399, it meant Trutnov could not be sold or pledged by the king and the citizens enjoyed a higher legal and social status than other subjects. Conquered by the Hussite army in 1421, the town suffered much in the Thirty Years War and experienced a re-introduction of Catholicism after the peace of Westphalia, 1648.

APPENDIX 1

Chronology

c. 1590	Birth of Thomas Carew (Carve), Mobarnan, County Tipperary.
c. 1615	Carve is ordained priest for diocese of Leighlin.
1618	'Defenestration of Prague', start of Thirty Years War.
c. 1618	Birth of Anthony MacBrody (Bruodinus), Ballyogan, County Clare.
1624	Carve travels from Ireland to Bohemia.
1624	Donough O'Brien, earl of Thomond, patron of Clann Bhruaideadha (MacBrodys), dies.
1625–6	Tadhg mac Dáire Mhic Bhruaideadha, bardic poet, dies.
1629	Opening of the Irish Franciscan College in Prague.
c. 1630	Carve serves as chaplain to Irish regiment of Col. Walter Butler.
1634	Albrecht Wallenstein, Bohemian military leader, killed by Butler's men (25 February). Walter Butler dies (25 December).
1635	Carve continues as military chaplain under Walter Devereux.
1639	Carve publishes first volume of *Itinerarium* (3 vols).
1641	Uprising in Ireland, start of Catholic Confederate Wars.

1643	Carve appointed vicar choral in Cathedral of St Stephen, Vienna.
1644	Bruodinus, attending the Franciscan *studium* of Quin, is sent to study at St Isidore's, Rome.
1646	Bruodinus is ordained priest in Rome (31 March).
1648	Peace of Westphalia, end of Thirty Years War.
1649	English conquest of Ireland under Oliver Cromwell begins.
1650	Bruodinus, lecturer in theology, joins Prague Franciscans.
1651	Cromwellian army begin assault on Thomond.
1651	Publication of Carve's *Lyra* (History of Ireland, 1148–1650).
1652	Upsurge in Irish diaspora to Prague.
1666	Revised edition of *Lyra* with Carve self-portrait.
1669	Bruodinus publishes *Propugnaculum Catholicae Veritatis*.
1670	Carve responds with *Enchiridion Apologeticum*.
1671	Bruodinus refutes Carve with *Anatomicum Examen*.
1672	Carve's *Responsio Veridica* is last book of the contention.
c. 1672	Death of Carve (circumstances unknown).
1680	Bruodinus dies of plague in Prague (7 May).
1721	Publication of Bruodinus' posthumous work *Descriptio Regni Hiberniae Sanctorum Insulae*, Rome.

APPENDIX 2

Irish Surnames

Bruodinus displays little consistency in his use of surnames. For some names he employs up to five different spelling variations. With Gaelic surnames he uses the traditional prefixes of O and Mac only sparingly, preferring in many cases to omit them. He does, however, observe certain conventions. Following Gaelic practice he uses separate feminine forms of names. For example, the surname MacNamara, which he spells variously, in the feminine form is rendered de Mara. Similarly, O'Molony is rendered de Mollonii and O'Brien simply Brien. Bruodinus follows an unusual convention in the spelling of the anglicised form of *Mac Conmara*. During the anglicisation of surnames in the seventeenth century the ruling branches of the family spelled their name MacNamara to distinguish themselves from their common kinsmen who spelled it MacNemara.[1] Bruodinus observes this convention, using the form MacNamara only once, when referring to the ruling MacNamara Reagh, otherwise he uses MacNemara, the common form of the name in the seventeenth century. The Latinised names, which appear in the following table, are shown in their nominative case, singular. The list is not definitive, only the more significant variations of surname forms, found in *Anatomicum Examen*, are included.

1. 'Origin of the Family of MacNemara in Thomond', *c.* 1700, National Library of Ireland, Ms 1500, f. 45.

Anatomicum Forms	Anglicised Forms	Gaelic Forms
Bahius, Vitalis	MacVeigh	Mac Beatha, Mac an Bheatha
Bary	Barry	de Barra
Bruodinus, Mac Bruodin	MacBrody	Mac Bruaideadha
Butlerus, Butlerianus	Butler	de Buitléir
Carovallus	O'Carroll	Ó Cearbhaill
Chiverus	Cheevers	
Chracheus, Crachius, Ghrahis	MacGrath, Magrath	Mag Craith
Chlanchy, Clanchy	MacClancy, Clancy	Mac Fhlannchadha
Clery	O'Cleary	Ó Cléirigh
Coghlanus	Coughlan	Ó Cochláin
Conreus	Conroy	Ó Maolchonaire
Creagh	Creagh	Craobhach
Cruttin	MacCurtin	Mac Cruitín
de Burgo	Burke	de Búrca
de Wallis	Walsh	Breathnach
Dela Haid	Delahoyd	
Demsii	Dempsey	Ó Díomsaigh
Donlevi	Dunleavy	Mac Duinnshléibhe
Donnelanus	Donnellan	Ó Domhnalláin
Dormer	Dormer	
Esmond	Esmonde	Easmonn
Everardus	Everard	
Ferallus, ô Feralli	O'Farrell	Ó Fearghail
Fitzpatrick	Fitzpatrick	Mac Giolla Phádraig
Flemengus	Fleming	Pléamonn
Geraldinus, Geraldiny	Fitzgerald	Mac Gearailt
Geanor	Gaynor	Mag Fhionnbhairr
Gilriegh	Gallery	Mac Giolla Riabhaigh
Gormanus	MacGorman, Gorman	Mac Gormáin
Gorumleus	Gormley, O'Gormooley	Ó Gormghaile, Ó Gormshúiligh
Grady, Gradii	O'Grady	Ó Grádaigh
Graius	Gray	de Grae
Gripha	Griffey	Ó Gríobhtha
Hara	O'Hara	Ó hEaghra
Hicquaeus	Hickey	Ó hÍceadha
Hurlaeus, Hurleus, ô Hurley	O'Hurley	Ó hUrthuile
Karneus, Kerneus	Kearney	Ó Cearnaigh
Ketten, Kettengus	Keating	Céitinn
Kinraghty	Enright	Mac Ionnrachtaigh
Kusag	Cusack	Cíosóg

Anatomicum Forms	Anglicised Forms	Gaelic Forms
Linceus	Lynch	Ó Loinsigh
Loghlen	O'Loughlin	Ó Lochlainn
Mac Iordan	MacJordan, Jordan	Mac Siúrtáin
Mac Nemara, Mac Namara	MacNamara	Mac Conmara
Mac Nerinhy	MacInerney	Mac an Airchinnigh
Mag Donoghu	MacDonagh	Mac Donnchadha
Magranna	Greaney	Mac Gráinne
Maguivir	Maguire	Mag Uidhir
Matthaeus, ô Mohuin, Ursulanus	O'Mahony	Ó Mathghamhna
Minogh	Minogue	Ó Muineóg
Moclus	Mockler	Móicléir
Mohuny, Mohunii, Mac Mohony	MacMahon	Mac Mathghamhna
Nelanus	Nelan, Neylon	Ó Nialláin
ô Brien, ô Brienus	O'Brien	Ó Briain
ô Carran	Carran, Carew	Ó Corráin
ô Conorus	O'Connor	Ó Conchubhair
ô Dea	O'Dea	Ó Deághaidh
ô Donel	O'Donnell	Ó Domhnaill
ô Fluing, Fluin	O'Flynn	Ó Floinn
ô Hassie	O'Hassett	Ó hAiseadh
ô Hein	O'Hynes	Ó hEidhin
ô Higen	O'Higgins	Ó hUiginn
ô Hogan	O'Hogan	Ó hÓgáin
ô Kenedii, Kenedy	O'Kennedy	Ó Cinnéide
ô Mary	O'Meara	Ó Meadhra
ô Mollonii, ô Mollony, Mollonii	O'Molony	Ó Maoldhomhnaigh
ô Molloy, ô Molloii	O'Molloy	Ó Maolmhuaidh
ô Morphei	Murphy	Ó Murchadha
Quaeleus	O'Queely	Ó Caollaidhe
Rocheus	Roche	de Róiste
Route	Rothe	
Saghnassii	O'Shaughnessy	Ó Seachnasaigh
Saulus	Sall, Saul	de Sál
Schea	Shee	Ó Seaghdha
Staffort	Stafford	de Stafort
Synott	Sinnott	Sionóid
Taffe	Taffe	Táth
Waddingus	Wadding	Uaidín
Wardaeus, Vardeus	Ward	Mac an Bháird

APPENDIX 3

List of Authors and Texts

The following are mentioned or quoted in *Anatomicum*:

Ancient authors/texts

- Aesop (as a symbol for fables and fabrications)
- Cicero: *Pro Archia* (quoting Ennius in turn)
- Diodorus Siculus: *Bibliotheca*
- Diogenes Laertius (?): *Life of Socrates*
- *Disticha Catonis*
- Horace: *Ars Poetica*
- Ovid: *Fasti*
- Plato: *Republic*
- Priscian (as the personification of perfect knowledge of Latin)
- Seneca: *De remediis fortuitorum* and *De moribus* (both spurious)
- Various proverbs attested in ancient texts
- Virgil: *Aeneid*

Postclassical, Early-Christian and Ecclesiastical authors/texts

- Caelius Sedulius: *Work of Marvels* (or *Carmen Paschale*); *Hymn to Christ*; songs in praise of Theodosius the Younger
- Pope Adrian IV: bull (authorship debated between Carve and Bruodinus)
- Pope Alexander VII: bull
- Pope Boniface VIII: decretals
- St Augustine: apologetic writings; couplet attributed to him by later biographers, reported by Carve and quoted by Bruodinus
- St Bede: *Historia Gentis Anglorum* (as source debated between Carve and Bruodinus)
- St Bernard: apologetic writings; 'Life of St Malachy' (authorship debated between Carve and Bruodinus)

- St Bonaventure: apologetic writings
- St Jerome: apologetic writings
- St Thomas Aquinas: apologetic writings
- various proverbs attested in Christian texts

Bible

- Acts of the Apostles
- Book of Daniel
- Book of Ecclesiasticus
- Book of Exodus
- Book of Job
- Book of Kings
- Book of Proverbs
- Book of the Apocalypse
- Gospels: Matthew and John
- Isaiah's Prophecies (Book of Isaiah)
- Jeremiah's Lamentations (Book of Lamentations)
- King David's Psalms
- Solomon's Canticle of Canticles

Early modern and contemporary authors/texts

- Barclay (as a source used by Carran)
- Becanus (addressing Sartorius, and addressing Graserus)
- Bruodinus: *Propugnaculum Catholicae Veritatis*; *Theologia Scholastica*
- Cambrensis (as a source debated between Carran and Bruodinus)
- Camden (as a source used by Carran)
- Campion (as a source used by Carran)
- Carve: *Enchiridion Apologeticum*; *Annales* (or *Lyra*)
- Cesare Baronio: *Martyrologium Romanum*
- Davies (as a source used by Carran)
- Documents in the archive of the province of Ireland

- Ernst Schaff: *Domus Sapientiae* (co-author)
- Francis Lanovius: *Chronicon Fratrum Minorum* (reference to Carran quoting from it)
- Francis O'Mahony (Edmund Ursulan): *Juridical examination of the censorship of the Faculty of Theology of Paris and of the Archbishop of the same city …; Treatise on Saint Francis' Stigmata; In defence of the privileges conceded to the same Saint Francis and to his religion; Brief History of the Province of Ireland* (all mentioned in Luke Wadding's *Scriptores Ordinis Minorum*)
- Franciscan friars in Belgium: biographies of martyrs being written down
- Franciscan friars in Toledo: 'Life of Fr O'Mahony'
- Geoffrey Keating: *History of Ireland*
- Godfrey Sall: 'Life of Kearney'
- Hanmer (as a source used by Carran)
- John Lynch: *Cambrensis Eversus*
- Joseph Sall: 'Index of Irish Martyrs'; 'Life of Kearney'
- Lindanus (as a source used by Carran)
- Lombard (as a source used by Carran and refuted by Bruodinus)
- Ludwig Kauka, Ernst Schaff, Archangel Mascul, Bernard Sannig: informative account on the condition of the Convent of the Snows
- Luke Wadding: *Scriptores Ordinis Minorum*
- Matthew Roche: letters to Carve (reported by Carve and quoted by Bruodinus to prove they are false)
- Maurice Conry: *Threnodia Hibernorum* (or *Threnodia Hiberno-Catholica*)
- Moryson (as a source used by Carran)
- Philopatrus Ireneus: *Vindiciae Catholicorum Hiberniae* (as a source used by Carran)
- Samuel Hatass: two volumes of orations
- Sander (as a source used by Carran and refuted by Bruodinus)
- Speeder (as a source used by Carran and refuted by Bruodinus)
- Spender (as a source used by Carran)

- Spenser (as a source used by Carran)
- Surius (as a source; accompanied by a reference to Sleidanus)
- Tadhg MacBrody: Irish-Latin rhymes
- Thomas Good: *Theatrum Catholicae et Protestanticae Religionis*
- Thomas Lodge
- Wilhelm Anton Brauczek: theses of theology; *Domus Sapientiae* (co-author)
- William Lily: *Grammar of Latin in English*

Authors of the short poems about Carve or Bruodinus (when not anonymous)

- Charles O'Molloy
- Francis O'Molloy
- John Burke
- John O'Molony
- Master Magranna
- Maurice O'Loughlin

Index